THE SOCIALIST PYRAMID:
ELITES AND POWER IN YUGOSLAVIA

Lenard J. Cohen

THE SOCIALIST PYRAMID:
ELITES AND POWER IN YUGOSLAVIA

Mosaic Press
Oakville - New York - London

CANADIAN CATALOGUING IN PUBLICATION DATA

Cohen, Lenard J.
　The socialist pyramid

ISBN 0-88962-386-4 (bound)　ISBN 0-88962-385-6 (pbk.)

1. Elite (Social sciences) – Yugoslavia.
2. Power (Social sciences). 3. Social
structure – Yugoslavia. I. Title.

HN635.2.E4C6　1989　　　305.5'2'09497　　　C89-093935-7

No part of this book may be reproduced or transmitted in any form, by any means, electronic or mechanical, including photo-copying and recording information storage and retrieval systems, without permission in writing from the publisher, except by a reviewer who may quote brief passages in a review.

Published by MOSAIC PRESS, P.O. Box 1032, Oakville, Ontario, L6J 5E9, Canada. Offices and warehouse at 1252 Speers Road, Units# 1&2, Oakville, Ontario, L6L 5N9, Canada.

Mosaic Press acknowledges the assistance of the Canada Council and the Ontario Arts Council in support of its publishing pro-gramme.

Copyright © Lenard J. Cohen, 1989
Design by Rita Vogel
Typeset by Aztext　Electronics Publishing Ltd.
Printed and bound in Canada.

ISBN 0-88962-385-6　PAPER　　ISBN 0-88962-386-4　CLOTH

MOSAIC PRESS:
In Canada:
　　MOSAIC PRESS, 1252 Speers Road, Units# 1&2, Oakville, Ontario L6J 5N9, Canada. P.O. Box 1032, Oakville, Ontario L6J 5E9

Distributed to the trade in the United States by:
　　Kampmann National Book Network, Inc
　　4720 Boston Way Lanham, M.D.,
　　20706　USA

*FOR
STOJAN AND ŽIVKO,
DRAGI I DOBRI PRIJATELJI*

TABLE OF CONTENTS

                                                                                            Page

Preface 9
List of Tables 11
List of Figures 17

PART ONE
INTRODUCTION

Chapter 1   Elites and Socialism: Yugoslavia in Comparative Perspective 21

PART TWO
ELITE TRANSFORMATION: REVOLUTIONARY AND EVOLUTIONARY DIMENSIONS

Chapter 2   From Monarchy to Marxism: A Comparison of Elite Social Backgrounds 97

Chapter 3   Partisans, Professionals and Proletarians: Elite Change in Modernizing Yugoslavia 147

PART THREE
STATE ELITES AND SELF-MANAGERS: THE BATTLE AGAINST BUREAUCRACY

Chapter 4   Politics as an Avocation: Legislative Professionalism and Participation in Yugoslavia 187

Chapter 5   Self-Management's Civil Servants: The Political Role of the Administrative Elite 225

Chapter 6   Judicial Elites in Yugoslavia: The Professionalization of Political Justice 257

PART FOUR
ELITES AND ETHNONATIONALISM: REGIONAL AND CULTURAL CONFLICTS

Chapter 7   Balkan Consociationalism: Ethnic Representation and Ethnic Distance in the Yugoslav Elite Structure 297

Chapter 8   Elites in Yugoslavia's Third World: The Case of Kosovo 335

PART FIVE
CHOOSING TITO'S COMRADES AND HEIRS: YUGOSLAV ELITES IN FLUX

Chapter 9   Elite Recruitment and Elite Composition: The Past and the Future 395

Epilogue   The Pyramid Imperiled 439
Bibliography   449
Index   495

PREFACE

This book represents research on Yugoslav elites carried out over the past twenty years. The focus of that research has been the empirical analysis of power and political rule under Yugoslav socialism, and particularly the efforts of Belgrade's unusual Marxist regime to surmount the challenging problems of bureaucracy and socio-political inequality. In contrast to the myriad academic studies which assess the Yugoslav experiment through observation of its unique institutions for local citizen participation and enterprise self-management, this book is concerned primarily with the strategic political actors in the upper tiers of a still decidedly hierarchical and stratified society.

Part One of the book explores the major theoretical issues concerning elites and socialism that have attracted attention both within and outside Yugoslavia. A survey of the spirited debate concerning the role of political leadership in the creation of a socialist state provides the historical and comparative context for subsequent sections of the study. The second part of the book presents an empirical analysis of elite transformation during the first six decades of Yugoslavia's existence as a state, both in terms of the revolutionary changes in the elite structure which occurred at the end of World War II, and the evolutionary development of the political elite during the socialist modernization of the society. Aspects of the Yugoslav regime's novel methods to curtail bureaucratic power and to limit political professionalization are examined in Part Three of the book, which contains separate chapters on the legislative, administrative, and judicial spheres of the country's political system. The salient role of ethnic and regional cleavages in contemporary Yugoslavia is the backdrop of the elite research reported in Part Four, which devotes special attention to the role played by the intelligentsia and other elite sectors in the emergence of political nationalism. A detailed assessment is also made of changing ethnic relations in the volatile province of Kosovo, where Albanian nationalism continues to threaten the political stability of the Yugoslav regime. Finally, the last section of the book offers an analytical review of elite recruitment during successive stages of Yugoslav socialist development, and also explores the changing composition and internal differentiation of the country's political elite structure during the crisis-ridden post-Tito period (1980-1988).

I would like to express my appreciation to Professor Peter Potichnyj for suggesting the preparation of this book, and, who along with Howard Aster and Michael J. Walsh of Mosaic Press, patiently encouraged its completion. Appreciation is also extended to Professors Seweryn Bialer and Jerry Hough for stimulating my initial interest in elite studies, and to Professor Henry Mayer for inspiring my concern with Yugoslav communism. Considerable gratitude is also owed to the many citizens and officials of Yugoslavia who provided hospitality, as well as the information and answers which are essential to any research endeavour: *mnogo hvala*. Terri Sussel, Wendy Knight, Olga Stankovic, and Natalie Minunzie all provided valuable research assistance at various stages in the preparation of this book, and Margaret Sharon of Simon Fraser University's Computing Services division offered very useful advice regarding the intricacies of word processing. Lastly, I wish to express special thanks to all those friends, colleagues, and students whose courage in the face of malfeasant bureaucracy and the iniquitous cries of the crowd made this book possible.

Lenard J. Cohen
October, 1988

LIST OF TABLES

Table	Page
Table 1.1 Inequalities in Yugoslav Society	53
Table 1.2 The Attitudes of Yugoslav Occupational Groups Concerning the Stratification of Their Society	56
Table 2.1 The Distribution of Yugoslavia's Economically Active Population by Social Class and National Income, 1938	102
Table 2.2 Yugoslav Student Enrollments at Various Educational Levels for Selected Years as a Percentage of the School-Age Population at Each Level	107
Table 2.3 Educational Level of the Yugoslav Political Elite, 1918-1941, 1948	109
Table 2.4 Higher Education of the Political Elite by Location	111
Table 2.5 Type of Education of the Higher-Educated Members of the Political Elite and the Structure of Enrollment	113
Table 2.6 Occupational Background of Interwar Parliamentary Deputies and Cabinet Ministers	117
Table 2.7 The Occupational Background of the Partisan Movement's Army; Officer Corps and the 'Heroes' Compared to the Communist Party's Central Committee Members (1940-1952)	119
Table 2.8 The Class Background of the Interwar Political Elite	121

Table 2.9
　　Elite Birthplaces by Size and Centrality 125

Table 2.10
　　Women in the Yugoslav Political Elite (1948) 127

Table 2.11
　　Ethnic Composition of the Yugoslav Military
　　Establishment Before and After World War II 128

Table 3.1
　　The Occupational Background of the Yugoslav Party Elite,
　　1952-1974/78 163

Table 3.2
　　The Educational Background of the Yugoslav Party Elite,
　　1948-1974/78 164

Table 3.3
　　The Educational Background of New Members of the Central
　　Committee by Period of Political Recruitment 165

Table 3.4
　　The Age Composition of the Party Elite, 1948-1974 ... 166

Table 3.5
　　The Yugoslav Party Elite by Political Generation,
　　1952-1974/78 167

Table 3.6
　　The New Members of the 1974 Party Elite by Political
　　Generation and Occupational Group 168

Table 3.7
　　The Pattern of Ethnic Representation in Yugoslavia's
　　Party Elite, 1948-1974/78 169

Table 4.1
　　Occupational Composition of the Yugoslav Federal
　　Assembly, by Chambers, 1963-1978 191

Table 4.2
    Participation and Political Influence in the Yugoslav
    Federal Legislature: 1968-1969 198

Table 4.3
    Participation of Professional and Amateur Delegates in
    the Yugoslav Federal Legislature: 1975-1976 202

Table 4.4
    Participation in the Debates of the Yugoslav Federal
    Legislatures, May 15, 1974 - May 15, 1978 205

Table 5.1
    The Sample of Federal Administrative Functionaries and
    Legislators 230

Table 5.2
    The Role Orientations of Higher Administrative
    Functionaries in Yugoslavia 232

Table 5.3
    The Pattern of Interaction between Federal
    Administrative and Legislative Elites in Yugoslavia 234

Table 5.4
    The Pattern of Influence Between Federal Administrative
    and Legislative Elites in Yugoslavia 239

Table 5.5
    Persons Mentioned by Yugoslav Federal Administrators and
    Legislators as Having An Influence on Their Opinions
    Concerning Matters in Their Own Field 245

Table 5.6
    The Distribution of University-Trained Employees in
    Federal Political and Administrative Institutions by
    Type of Higher Education Received 246

Table 6.1
    The Ethnic Composition of Judges and Prosecutors in
    Yugoslavia, 1937 263

Table 6.2
    Political Crime by Religion, (1929-1938) 264

Table 6.3
    The Age Composition of Yugoslav Judicial Staff 277

Table 6.4
    The Yugoslav Judicial Elite by Ethnicity and Region, (1979-1980) 279

Table 6.5
    Opinions of Yugoslav Judges Concerning the Five Major Factors for the Advancement in a Judicial Career 286

Table 7.1
    The Ethnic Composition of Elites in Yugoslavia: A Country-Wide Profile (1971) 301

Table 7.2
    The Ethnic Composition of Elite Sectors in Croatia.................... 303

Table 7.3
    The Ethnic Composition of Elite Sectors in Bosnia-Hercegovina 304

Table 7.4
    The Ethnic Composition of Elite Sectors in Vojvodina 306

Table 7.5
    The Ethnic Composition of Elite Sectors in Kosovo 308

Table 7.6
    Graduates from 'Higher Schools of Political Science' by Ethnicity and Region 309

Table 7.7
    Graduates from Faculties of Economics by Ethnicity and Region 310

Table 7.8
    The Ethnic Composition of the Survey Sample by Elite Sector and Respondents to Questions on Interaction 316

Table 7.9
Internationality Contact in the Yugoslav Elite 317

Table 7.10
Ethnic Interaction in the Yugoslav Elite, by Elite Sector
and Selected Ethnic Groups 318

Table 8.1
Ethnic Composition of Kosovo, 1921 339

Table 8.2
Occupational and Ethnic Background of Parliamentary
Deputies for the Kosovo Region, 1918-1939 341

Table 8.3
The Ethnic Origins of Partisans Who Fought in World War II
As of December 31, 1977 346

Table 8.4
Albanians in Yugoslavia, 1948-1981 349

Table 8.5
Kosovo Residents With Higher Education Degrees in 1948,
By Age and Specialization 351

Table 8.6
Higher Education, Generational Change and Ethenticity in
Kosovo, 1961-1971 358

Table 8.7
Elite Sectors in Kosovo: Selected Ethnic Groups, 1971 362

Table 8.8
Higher Education and Ethnicity in Kosovo, 1966-1979 363

Table 9.1
Size of the Yugoslav League of Communists and the Party
Apparatus, 1950-1981 400

Table 9.2
Organizational Background and Circulation of Regional
Political Elites, 1972-1980 411

Table 9.3
  Age Structure of Yugoslav Regional Political Elites,
  1980 414

Table 9.4
  Yugoslav Regional Elites By Political Generation 415

Table 9.5
  Yugoslav Regional Elites by Level and Type of Education 417

Table 9.6
  Ethnic Composition of Selected Yugoslav Regional Elites 419

Table 9.7
  Perceptions of Communal Legislators in Croatia Concerning
  the Main Criterion Which Determined Their Own
  Nomination 424

LIST OF FIGURES

Figure   **Page**

Figure 4.1
The Structure of the Yugoslav Assembly System
(1974-1988) 188

Figure 4.2
Legislative Specialization/Professionalization, Percent
of Federal Deputies Who Previously Served in the
Assembly System 193

Figure 5.1
Percentage of Different Persons Mentioned by Yugoslav
Federal Administrators and Legislators as Interaction
Partners on Matters in Their Own Field 235

Figure 5.2
Percent of Different Persons Mentioned by Yugoslav
Federal Administrators and Legislators as Having an
Influence on Their Opinions Concerning Matters in
Their Own Field 240

Figure 8.1
Political Crime Convictions as a Percent of All Crime
Convictions for Selected Ethnic Groups in
Yugoslavia 355

Figure 8.2
Newspaper Readership in Kosovo by Language 360

Figure 8.3
Changes in the Ethnic Composition of Kosovo's Population
and Party Organization, 1953-1981 365

PART ONE

INTRODUCTION

... the working class having come to power ... must, in order not to lose its newly won supremacy, on the one hand, eliminate the old machine of oppression previously used against it, and on the other hand, protect itself against its own deputies and functionaries ...
          Frederick Engels

Emotional revolutionism is followed by the traditionalist routine of everyday life; the crusading leader and the faith itself fade away, or what is even more effective, the faith becomes part of the conventional phraseology of political Philistines and banausic technicians .... After coming to power the following of a crusader usually degenerates very easily in a quite common stratum of spoilsmen.
          Max Weber

CHAPTER 1

SOCIALIST ELITES: COMPARATIVE AND YUGOSLAV PERSPECTIVES

Issues concerning political leadership and bureaucracy have been the source of extensive controversy thoughout the history of political thought and the social sciences. Debates regarding those subjects have been particularly contentious with respect to the contemporary communist party-states which proclaim, in varying degrees, an ideological commitment to the elimination of political inequalities and bureaucratic patterns of administration. Discrepancies between the inflated claims and the very limited achievements of communist regimes with respect to such goals have naturally generated considerable attention, including many polemical attacks upon Marxism's utility as an ideology for socio-economic and political transformation. How to explain and characterize the existence in communist states of powerful and privileged leadership groups which routinely influence the formation of public policy - groups that will be referred to here as political elites - have been especially compelling topics for political analysts.[1]

This book focuses upon political elites in Yugoslavia during and after the establishment of that country as a communist party-state. As subsequent chapters of the book will explore, communist Yugoslavia has functioned as a fundamentally *elite-managed regime*, although endowed with some rather unique and well known mechanisms for citizen participation. Throughout their very unorthodox course of communist development, however, Yugoslav political leaders have affirmed their commitment to Marxist ideological principles. It is therefore useful to briefly consider Marx's principal ideas regarding political elites, as well as the major theoretical responses to those ideas, both before and after their reception in the Yugoslav context. Explicitly or implicitly, it is the protracted debate about the fate of political and bureaucratic leadership groups in Marxian socialist regimes which motivated the empirical research studies of Yugoslav elites included in this book.

Elitist Socialism: 'Illusion' or 'Iron Law'?

Some of the most troublesome issues for Marxist revolutionary theory and practice have centered around the displacement and necessity of political elites. Although Marxist revolutionaries are programmatically committed to the ultimate elimination of pre-socialist forms of state and party rule, once ensconced in positions of public power they typically find it exigent to maintain conventional modes (if not the traditional nomenclature) of political officeholding. Such occupational continuity includes not only the extension of the revolutionaries' own tenure as professional politicians and the retention of many administrative officials from the former regime, but also the nurturing of a new "formation" or "corps" of public office-holders. Unfortunately, neither Marx and Engels, nor their principle ideological heirs, provided very much guidance regarding the way party and state officials would be held accountable by the broader working class that is purported to hold power after a Marxist revolution, or how to prevent the long term dominance and acquisition of extensive privileges by the new regime's governing functionaries. "Marxist political theory," Thomas Bottomore points out, "still needs to develop a more precise concept of elites, and to examine in a more comprehensive way the relation between elites and classes, particularly in relation to socialist regimes and to the distinction between leaders and followers, not only in social life as a whole, but in socialist parties themselves."[2]

Marx had, of course, shown a keen interest in the power and resilience of capitalist political elites. For example, in his famous remarks made in the *Civil War in France*, Marx inveighed against "salaried state functionaries," "state priests," "state parasites," "the directing hierarchy," "the haughteous masters of the people," "centralized state power," "hierarchic division of labour," "the organized public force," "the political engine," and the "usurpatory dictatorship of the governing body over society," to mention only a selection of his epithets regarding ruling minorities.[3] As an alternative to conventional political leadership Marx endorsed the Paris Commune's "organized means of action" whereby power, he believed, could be "shifted from the few upon the many." In his opinion, the Commune if not genuinely socialist, was at least a "rational medium" that might do away with the "delusion as if administration and political governing were mysteries, transcendent functions only to be trusted to the hands of a trained caste." Marx was impressed by the fact that the Commune's executive bodies were composed, not of traditional state officials, but of "responsible agents of society itself" who were paid "like skilled workmen" and were "always removable servants." Such a group of "workmen or acknowledged representatives of the working class" would not,

The Socialist Pyramid: Elites and Power in Yugoslavia

Marx argued, become a new "state power apparently soaring high over society." Previously those charged with the execution of public functions had succumbed to the "irresistible allurements of place, pelf and patronage." The "central functions" or "public functions" of governance would still exist after a working class revolution, but Marx claimed that:

> ... the functionaries themselves could not, as in the old governmental machinery, raise themselves over real society, because the functions were to be executed by communal agents, and therefore always under real control. The public functions would cease to be a private property bestowed by a central government upon its tools.[4]

Although apparently devoted to the revolutionary "emancipation of labour" from capitalism, Marx seemed quite untroubled about the possibility that the peasant sector of society might find itself under the control of a new elite located in urban centers. "After rural producers," Marx observed, came "under the intellectual lead of the central towns," the urban working men would become the "natural trustees" of peasant interests. In an earlier formulation on the same theme, Marx expressed confidence that the "peasants would soon acclaim the townish proletariat as their own leaders and seniors."[5]

The possibility of political elitism in a workers' state also appears in sharp perspective during the caustic dialogue between Marx and the anarchist Bakunin. For Marx, the existence of leading or managing personnel in a working class movement such as his own, or in a future working class state, did not imply domination by state or party officials in the conventional sense. He chided Bakunin for suggesting that once the "whole people" become the "rulers of the state" and private property is replaced by state property "there lurks the despotism of a ruling minority" or a "privileged minority." "If Mr. Bakunin were in the know," wrote Marx, "he would send all his illusions about domination to the devil." As for Bakunin's suggestion that the Marxist program implied the eventual rule by "learned socialists" or a "government of savants," Marx glibly rejoined: "What ravings."[6]

Marx, as well as his associate Frederick Engels, regarded Bakunin's views as malicious distortions, all the more so because the Russian anarchist's own political movement and mentality were so blatantly authoritarian and elitist.[7] The problem of potential elitism in a state ostensibly to be governed by the working class could not, however, be entirely ignored. For example, although Engels claimed that following the end of class rule the state "withers away of itself," he also observed in 1891 that, in the short run at least, the proletarian revolution must "safeguard itself against its own deputies and officials, by declaring them all, without exception, subject to recall at any moment."[8] Like Marx, however, Engels was not particularly troubled about the use of centralized political authority during the revolutionary struggle of the working class, or after the establishment of a workers' state. Perhaps there was a danger, Engels observed, that an elitist regime might emerge from a movement "organized under the dictatorship of one or a few individuals" which advocated the "*coup de main* of a small revolutionary minority" (a conception associated with Louis Blanqui). This was not the case, Engels argued, in the broad-based movement to which he and Marx belonged.[9] As an outgrowth of the "whole revolutionary class" the admittedly "authoritarian political state" established by a proletarian dictatorship, Engels claimed, need not be "abolished at one stroke," as the anarchists advocated, but only after "the social conditions that gave birth to it have been destroyed."[10] The expectation that a workers' state would continue to be troubled by class stratification, as well as resistance from reactionary elements, necessitated, in this view, political functionaries temporarily wielding authority. Whether the opposite tendency might also prevail, i.e., proletarian state authorities exploiting and actually perpetuating residual class divisions, was an eventuality that Marx and Engels considered, but did not seriously fear.

Interestingly, Bakunin relied partially on evidence from the Balkans to make his case that class rule and exploitation by state office-holders have no particular connection to either the appearance or disappearance of capitalism. In the same 1873 study in which he attacked the potential elitism of Marx's proposed proletarian state, Bakunin also pointed to the dangerous "statist path" which had befallen the "microscopic Kingdom of Serbia." As soon as Serbia completed its liberation from the Turks and established its own state institutions, Bakunin argued, the population became "victims of bureaucratic plunder and despotism."

> There are no nobles, no big landowners, no industrialists, and no very wealthy merchants in Turkish Serbia. Yet in spite of this there emerged a new bureaucratic aristocracy composed of young men educated, partly at state expense ... no sooner did they enter the state's service than the iron logic of their situation, inherent in the exercise of certain hierarchical and politically advantageous prerogatives, took its toll and the young men became cynical bureaucratic martinets while still mouthing partriotic and liberal slogans .... Since there is no other employment for educated young men, they become state functionaries, and become members of the only aristocracy in the country, the bureaucratic class. Once integrated into this class, they inevitably become enemies of the people .... The one and only function of the State therefore, is to exploit the Serbian people in order to provide the bureaucrats with all the comforts of life.[11]

Bakunin's information about Serbian elite development was provided to him by Nikola Pašić, a fellow non-Marxist member of the international socialist movement, who was studying in Western Europe. Ironically, Pašić later served as prime minister of Serbia, and was the architect and prime minister of the royalist Yugoslav state after 1918. Marx also had potentially prominent supporters among the Serbian radicals, including Svetozar Marković, the most influential socialist from the Yugoslav region during the pre-Communist period, and Peter Karageorgević who later became King of Serbia, and the founder of the dynasty which ruled Yugoslavia until the Second World War.[12] Pašić and Karageorgević quickly moved from revolutionary politics to more conservative styles of public service (Marković died a revoltuionary at age 29) but, as will be discussed below, the troubling issues of state power and political elitism continued to interest political activists in Southeastern Europe.

Lenin would also address themes first raised during the Marxist-anarchist debate. The contribution of the future architect of the Soviet state would, however, have very significant and immediate consequences for elitist socialism. For Lenin, any working class movement seeking to carry out a revolution - particularly in an authoritarian state like Tsarist Russia - required a highly disciplined and centralized party organization guided by a specialized "corps of professional revolutionists." It was essential, he believed, to discard the "amateurish methods" which had previously hobbled the revolutionary movement and "raise the amateurs to the level of revolutionaries." The linkage between the leadership of the "vanguard" party and the working class, Lenin optimistically maintained, would be preserved by operational principles for reconciling centralized control with democratic expression.[13] In *State and Revolution* written just before he took power, Lenin evinced faith in Marx's basic methodology for preserving the accountability of leaders in a movement devoted to the working class: recall from office, rotation of personnel, and wage equalization between functionaries and proletarians. Using such methods, Lenin argued, the dictatorship of the proletariat (the working class state) and the vanguard of the proletariat (the working class party) could "cut bureaucracy down to the roots" and also ensure that "under socialism functionaries will cease to be 'bureaucrats,' to be 'officials.'"[14] Lenin would belittle as an "infantile disorder" of "left-wing communism" any objections suggesting that the proletarian vanguard had become a "dictatorship of leaders" or an "oligarchy." After all, he claimed in 1921, while classes still existed it was elementary for a political party to be "run by more or less stable groups composed of the most authoritative, influential and experienced members, who are elected to the most responsible positions, and are called leaders."[15]

Although he vigorously endorsed centralized party and state control, Lenin was by no means naive about the problem of bureaucratic rule. Bureaucracy, he also argued in 1921, cannot be quickly swept away especially in a peasant country with deeply embedded bureaucratic traditions: "one can only *reduce* it, by slow stubborn effort.... It can only be *cured*. In this matter surgery is an absurdity, an *impossibility*, only *slow cure* - all else is charlatanism or naiveté .... Bureaucrats are tricky types; there are many rascals among them, arch-opportunists. You will not catch them with bare hands." Moreover, even if one did "sweep away" what one of Lenin's younger comrades referred to as the "carbuncle called bureaucratic chief administrations and centers," Lenin wondered, "what are you going to put *in their place*?" The answer he offered was "not to *sweep away*, but to cleanse, cure, cure and cleanse ten times and a hundred times."[16] Here Lenin was essentially restating views about the longevity of bureaucratic domination which he had expressed from the very first days of the revolution, and which were considerably more realistic than his pre-revolutionary formulations on the future proletarian party and state. He also saw the need to closely monitor and if necessary challenge the activities of the state bureaucracy. For example, Lenin disagreed with suggestions that trade union organizations were no longer necessary in a worker's state. After all, he pointed out, the Soviet state is a "worker's state with bureaucratic distortions," and therefore "we must utilize these workers' organizations for the purpose of protecting the workers from their own state." Such protection would be necessary, Lenin felt, for at least 15 to 20 years, if not longer. In the meantime, the central and local leaderships of organizations such as the trade unions, and most importantly the party, were necessary as "reservoirs of state power" which would both guide and oversee the activities of state bureaucrats belonging to the "sphere of coercion."[17]

Lenin's solution to the problem of bureaucracy, it should be emphasized, did not imply any reduction in the political power held by the party leadership, or the elimination of the state apparatus. The bureaucratic apparatus, he wrote soon after the Revolution, "must not, and should not be smashed .... It must be subordinated to the proletarian Soviet; it must be expanded, made more comprehensive, and nation wide ..." Such an apparatus could not immediately be staffed with direct producers: "We are not utopians. We know that an unskilled labourer or cook cannot immediately get on with the job of state administration."[18] Indeed, as Lenin put it elsewhere, the proletarian state would have to suffer from the presence of leaders who were not proletarians by profession, but had become "professional proletarians."[19] Moreover, when debating with his colleagues during 1920 and 1921, Lenin stressed that the proletariat, as the "ruling, dominant, governing class" or the class "which is exercising state coercion," still needs a "complicated system of cogwheels and transmission belts" to effect a linkage between the vanguard and the masses. "It would be madness," Lenin wrote, "to renounce coercion particularly in the epoch of the dictatorship of the proletariat. Here administering and the administrator's approach are essential." But he hastened to add: "The Party is the direct vanguard of the proletariat, it is the leader."[20]

Lenin's belief that the hegemony of the ruling party and its state apparatus could be reconciled with the elimination of bureaucracy reflected a view that would frequently reappear in discussions of socialist elites, even by those writers highly critical of the Leninist model and its later Stalinist corruption. Very near the end of his political life, however, Lenin became more troubled by the attitude and behaviour of higher party public officials. He continued to criticize the "bureaucratic deformity of the state apparatus," but also warned against the "enormous undivided prestige enjoyed by the thin stratum which may be called the old guard of the party." As earlier, however, Lenin's main concern was not with hierarchical political control, but with the poor skills and errors of the party vanguard. A threat even existed that the vanguard might be overwhelmed by the "huge bureaucratic machine" presided over by those he termed the "top drawer," "literati," and "grandees," many of whom had been inherited from the old regime. The issue he posed was "who is leading whom?"[21] Lenin's complaint was that the state elite was directing the party elite, ignoring the danger that sustained elite domination might be inherent in his vanguard model of socialist rule.

Potential political elitism deriving from the Marxist and Leninist brands of revolutionary socialism stimulated extensive commentary during the first half of the twentieth century. The most influential non-Marxist critique was offered by Max Weber. Although he accepted Marx's basic thesis regarding the significance of class conflict in historical development, Weber argued that political rule in every state involves the domination of some individuals over others. Such domination can be justified or legitimated in a variety of ways, and therefore the motivations for citizen acquiescence to authority are quite diverse. It is characteristic of all states, however, that the rulers have final recourse to methods of force in order to extract obedience. Forms of state power and domination may vary, but they will not, he suggested, "wither away" after a working class revolution. Moreover, for Weber, both political inequalities and competitive political struggles are inherent features of all societies. Such inequalities and struggles are not derived solely from an individual's or group's position in the system of economic stratification, property ownership, or division of labour, but can also be traced to distinct conflicts based on power, prestige, and other social differences (including ethnic and racial affiliations). Whatever the basis of conflict and inequality, however, Weber believed that political action is always determined by the "principle of small numbers," and this gives superior "political manoeuvrability" to "small leading groups."[22]

Weber provides a number of additional observations that are important to consider when evaluating the development of contemporary communist party states. For example, he viewed as naive the Marxist expectation that a proletarian dictatorship would, in Lenin's words, "cut bureaucracy down to the roots." Indeed socialism, Weber observed, would "require a still higher degree of formal bureaucratization than capitalism," a situation which would very likely accentuate "the dictatorship of the official" and not that of the worker.[23] State ownership of the means of production, he felt, would actually diminish the freedom of the working class:

> ... since every power struggle with a state bureaucracy is hopeless and since there is no appeal to an agency which as a matter of principle would be interested in limiting the employee's power such as there is in the case of private enterprise ... state bureaucracy would rule alone if private capitalism were eliminated. The private and public bureaucracies which now work next to, and potentially against, each other and hence check one another to a degree, would be similar to the situation in ancient Egypt, but it would occur in a much more rational - and hence unbreakable - form.[24]

According to Weber's analysis, the most critical problem which resulted from the general process of increasing bureaucratization was the diminished ability of political leaders in all societies to control the power of the bureaucratic apparatus. "Under normal conditions," he wrote, "the power position of a fully developed bureaucracy is always overtowering. The `political master' always finds himself in the position of a dilettante who stands opposite the `expert,' facing the trained official who stands within the management of administration."[25] For Weber, the solution to increasing bureaucratic power was not to dismantle the established machinery of the state, or to eliminate bureaucratic tasks. Such a course, he felt, would only result in "chaos" and was an idea which "becomes more and more utopian" as the process of bureaucratization proceeds. Society, he believed, "cannot dispense with or replace the bureaucratic apparatus once it exists ... anymore than it can avoid the political rule of small leading groups."[26] What is essential, therefore, is the democratic selection of political leaders who will, in turn, effectively control and ensure the accountability of bureaucratic officials. In the Weberian perspective, there is less emphasis on which classes are ruling, represented, or repressed by the state, and more on whether the individuals and small groups who actually govern the state and society (whether capitalist or socialist) can control the enormous power of the bureaucracy. "It is not a question," he wrote, "of the *economic* position of the *ruled*, but rather the political qualification of the *ruling* and *ascending* classes which is the ultimate issue in the social-political problem."[27] Only well-trained professional politicians affiliated with modern party organizations and working through strong parliamentary institutions would effectively restrain the power of professional bureaucrats.

Lenin had viewed bureaucracy as a relatively short term difficulty that could be contained and eventually eliminated by the skilled leadership of a revolutionary party during the construction of socialism. Weber, in contrast, saw bureaucracy as a permanent phenomenon and he was extremely doubtful that social democratic parties - whether revolutionary or reformist - could obstruct the trend toward bureaucratic domination, either within their own organizations or within society as a whole.[28] The German Social Democratic

The Socialist Pyramid: Elites and Power in Yugoslavia

Party, he suggested, was unlikely to "become anything else but ... a party which exists for its own sake and that of its office holders" and in which the party members are supposed to "knuckle under" to the "ruling bosses." In order to better understand such issues, Weber suggested the empirical study of party leadership including:

> (1) the relationship between the organized elite of the labour movement and the masses of followers (2) the impact of non-proletarian groups within the party versus the necessity to appeal to non-proletarian groups outside the party ... (3) the character and the background of the elements controlling the local organizations and ... (4) the professional politicians who live 'off' or for the party ... (5) [the] difference between academically trained members and those who, due to class barriers, could not acquire higher education .... [29]

In contrast to Marx and Lenin, Weber was not impressed with the potential of either local citizen assemblies or amateur political activists (whether workers or other social elements) to manage a large and complex modern state, or to successfully control the power of professional bureaucrats.

> Both immediate democracy and government by amateurs are technically inadequate, on the one hand in organizations beyond a certain limit of size, constituting more than a few thousand full fledged members, or on the other hand, where functions are involved which require technical training or continuity of policy. If, in such a case, permanent technical officials are appointed alongside of shifting heads, actual power will normally tend to fall into the hands of the former, who do the real work, while the latter remain essentially dilettantes.[30]

Weber recognized that historical efforts to achieve "anti-authoritarian" forms of government had employed various "procedures appropriate to immediate democracy," such as short terms of office, liability to recall, the principle of rotation, or selection by lot in filling offices, etc. Although such techniques might be utilized to limit the power of technical experts and bureaucratic officials, he believed that their usefulness is essentially limited to small groups or small territorial units, that is, in the absence of "qualitative functions which can only be adequately handled by professional specialists." Forms of direct democracy and rule by amateurs become quickly outmoded or overwhelmed, Weber also stressed, in the presence of highly bureaucratized political parties which contain their own professional leaders and administrative staffs.[31]

Another highly influential perspective advanced at about the same time as Weber's views, and also in reaction to the Marxist paradigm, can be termed the "classical elitist argument." The ideas of the major elitists - Pareto, Mosca, and Michels - do not constitute a tidy or neatly unified school of thought, but their arguments concerning socialism and elites have much in common. Going well beyond Weber's skepticism about the promises of socialism, the elitists maintained that members of powerful political minorities - the "governing elites," the "political class," the "oligarchy" - *had* always ruled societies, *would* always rule, and *should* always rule. The elitists' belief in the persistence and necessity of political control by a small minority was grounded upon two common assumptions: first, that Marxist claims about the inevitable end of class stratification and the ascendency of a proletarian majority are scientifically unsound; and second, that efforts (such as Weber's) to perfect or strengthen *mechanisms* for democratic participation and accountability would not essentially alter the subordination of the masses to political minorities.

Recasting Marx's dictum that the "history of hitherto existing society was the history of class struggle," Pareto concluded that "the history of man is the history of the continuous replacement of certain elites: as one ascends, another declines." Pareto identified different elite types based upon contrasting sets of psychological characteristics evident in particular leadership groups, and he believed that "due to an important physiological law elites do not last." In his view, the changing talents for societal management manifest by one elite type or another, and the biologically diminished capacity which afflicts all aging elite groups determine whether the "circulation of elites" is either evolutionary or revolutionary. He emphasized, however, that "except during short intervals, people are always governed by an elite."[32] In his book *Socialist Systems*, published in 1902 (the same year Lenin suggested the need for a professional corps of revolutionaries), Pareto argued that a potential proletarian victory would actually result in the victory of those who speak on behalf of the proletariat, in short, another privileged minority which would resemble preceding elites.[33] Mosca placed less stress on the psychological bases of elite rule, emphasizing instead the political and organizational control of minorities. Like Pareto, however, Mosca concluded that "communist and collectivist societies would beyond any doubt be managed by officials" and that the majority of citizens in any state can exercise little more than "spasmodic, limited, and often ineffective control" over "organized minorities." In the 1923 edition of his book, *The Ruling Class: Elements of the Science of Politics*, first published in 1896, Mosca offered a trenchant assessment of the Marxist perspective in general, and the implications of the Soviet experiment in particular.

> The heads of a communist or collectivist republic would control the will of others more tyrannically than ever; and since they would be able to distribute privations or favours as they chose, they would have the means to enjoy, perhaps more hypocritically but in no less abundance, all the material pleasures, all the triumphs of vanity, which are now prerequisites of the powerful and the wealthy .... It is inevitable that a new

The Socialist Pyramid: Elites and Power in Yugoslavia

bourgeoisie should emerge in Russia from the ranks of the very men who carried the revolution through, and that private property should be reestablished in substance if not in form .... Nor can we believe that if communism were to triumph in other parts of Europe it would be possible to avoid a similar experiment, which would inevitably yield the same results, and perhaps worse ones.[34]

The most academically rigorous and influential expression of the classical elitist perspective was offered by Robert Michels. As a friend of Max Weber, a disciple of Mosca, and an active revolutionary Marxist during the first part of his political life, Michels enjoyed an unusually eclectic theoretical background and practical basis for making his own analysis of political elites. After conducting systematic empirical research on the European social democratic parties,[35] Michels concluded that socialist parties were essentially elitist in terms of their own organizational dynamics. Even before abandoning his commitment to revolutionary syndicalism and Marxism, Michels adopted the view that all revolutions, including a socialist one, amounted to a "rotation of elites" in which an ascendant political minority or party vanguard mobilizes a passive majority to unseat an established, albeit decaying, governing elite. As early as 1909, Michels advanced the idea of "an iron law of elites,"[36] the anticipation of his more famous "iron law of oligarchy" which maintains that all political conflict involves organization, and that all organization necessarily breeds elitist or oligarchic tendencies.

Perhaps Michels' most original contribution was his emphasis on factors which foster conservatism in all organizational leaderships. He was especially intrigued with how a revolutionary socialist movement can become deradicalized as the proletarian leaders become detached from their class of origin and then, together with their intellectual comrades in the socialist elite, become assimilated to the values of the incumbent or former bourgeois elite.[37] Another interesting facet of Michels' analysis was that the oligarchic bureaucratization and embourgeoisment of the socialist movement and its elite were accompanied by increasing stress on nationalist values at the expense of proletairian internationalism. In his lecture on patriotism, published in 1927, he remarked that it is usually during times of international tension that "socialist parties which represent the class struggle, turn into socio-patriotic parties," a development which derives from the commitment by party leaders to their own state, and also from the stake of the working class in its own "native industry" and economic well-being.[38] Thus, Michels envisioned socialism as a bureaucratized system, dominated by an essentially conservative and nationalistic elite vanguard.[39]

In contrast to Michels who fashioned his disillusionment with Marxism into a particularly incisive variant of elite theory, and eventually into outright association with fascism, other revolutionaries chose to express dissent from within the socialist movement. In 1898 for example, Waclaw Machajski, a

Lenard J. Cohen

revolutionary from Russian Poland concluded that Russian socialism was essentially the ideology of an ascendant middle class of intellectuals and white collar professionals. Despite all of their strident revolutionary rhetoric about the proletariat, Machajski argued that such "intellectual workers," together with their self-educated ex-worker comrades, wished to become privileged members of a "neo-bourgeois class," or a dictatorship of the "knows" over the "know nots."[40] After ten years in exile Machajski returned to Russia during the first years of the Soviet regime, but he did not alter his earlier beliefs. "The workers," he wrote, "will not have their 'workers' government' even after the capitalists have disappeared ... the workers will not be in possession of power, they will not have an obedient governmental apparatus in their hands." Machajski believed that the political domination of the "intellectual workers" in the revolutionary socialist state would only be eliminated if the working class rank and file "dictate the law to the government."[41] Such views were very similar to those advanced by Bakunin in the 1870's, namely, that the only way to guard socialism against rule by a "new privileged scientific class" was to to rely on a direct struggle by the members of the working class themselves. Unfortunately, neither Bakunin nor Machajski ever fully explained how trade unions could prevent the problem of rule by a political minority, nor did they ever really abandon their own less publicized ideas of a "revolutionary dictatorship" by a conspiratorial organization of manual workers. Machajski had very limited influence on the Russian revolutionary movement, but as another prophet of revolutionary socialism's elitist potential his views were naturally treated as heretical by the Soviet regime.[42]

Other Russian revolutionaries better known that Machajski also raised troublesome questions concerning the Marxist-Leninist brand of socialism. Rosa Luxembourg, for example, suggested in 1904 that a highly disciplined party organization would distance the "real active nucleus" of the party from the "surrounding revolutionary milieu," and thereby force the movement into a "straightjacket of bureaucratic centralism." Luxembourg worried about the abuses which might be committed by an "ambitious intelligentsia," preferring, she claimed, a socialist movement that occasionally made mistakes to the conservative "guardianship of an omniscient and omnipresent central committee."[43] In a later pamphlet written just after the Bolshevik victory, she expressed continued apprehension about socialist development in terms quite similar to the arguments put forward by Michels, Mosca, and Machajeski.

> Without a free struggle of opinions, life dies out in every public institution, becomes a mere semblance of life, in which only the bureaucracy remains as the active element. Public life gradually falls asleep, a few dozen party leaders of inexhaustible energy and boundless idealism direct and rule. Among them in reality only a dozen outstanding heads do the leading, and an elite of the working class is invited from time

to time to meetings where they are to applaud the speeches of the leaders ...; at bottom then, a clique affair - a dictatorship, to be sure; not the dictatorship of the proletariat, however, but only the dictatorship of a handful of politicians, that is dictatorship in the bourgeois sense.[44]

In 1904, Leon Trotsky also worried that the Leninist design for a revolutionary movement might create a situation whereby the interests of a group of "politicos," or a "central general staff," and eventually even a dictator, might be substituted for the interests of the working class. At the time, however, Trotsky expressed confidence that "a proletariat capable of dictatorship over society will not tolerate a dictatorship over itself."[45] Even after witnessing and then experiencing the dictatorial abuses of the Stalinist period, however, Trotsky was unwilling to accept Machajeski's view that the Soviet bureaucracy and party leadership was becoming a new bourgeois class.[46] For Trotsky, the Marxist designation "ruling class" was only appropriate when a leadership group technically owned the means of production i.e., in a juridical sense. Writing in exile, Trotsky maintained that the USSR had been betrayed and was being victimized by an "uncontrolled caste alien to socialism." In his view, Stalin, although a powerful dictator was essentially "the personification of bureaucracy" or the "sum total of the collective pressure of a caste which will stop at nothing in defense of its positions." Trotsky's hope was that power would be wrested from the hands of Stalin's "commanding caste" or "stratum" of state bureaucrats and returned to the party vanguard. He was not worried by the temporary rule of a workers' state by a political elite, but by the rule of *Stalin's elite*. With regard to the broader issue of elitist socialism, Trotsky believed such development "derives primarily from the iron necessity to give birth to and support a privileged minority so long as it is impossible to guarantee equality."[47] Trotsky thus shared Michel's belief that the tendency toward *elites* was a law wrought in iron, but the Russian revolutionary never abandoned his belief that it was a law which could eventually be rescinded.

Trotsky's hesitancy to describe Soviet political and bureaucratic elites as the nucleus of a new ruling class was not characteristic of other dissident Bolsheviks, or for that matter other Trotskyists. For example A.A. Bogdanov, who had criticized Lenin's organizational model in 1910, gradually concluded that the basic source of class exploitation was not the ownership of property, but the relationship between the organizers of production and those who were organized. In 1919, after breaking with the Bolsheviks, Bogdanov described the Soviet system not as a working class regime, but as a dictatorship of the political and industrial "organizers" representing a new bureaucratic class.[48] In the late 1920's, Christian Rakovsky, an exiled Russian Trotskyist, reached a similar conclusion.

> From the workers' state with bureaucratic perversions - as Lenin defined our form of government - we have developed into a bureaucratic state with proletarian communist - survivals. Before our eyes, a great class of rulers has been taking shape and is continuing to develop .... The unifying factor of this unique class is that unique form of private property, governmental power.[49]

During the late 1930's and early 1940's, Trotskyists such as Max Shachtman and James Burnham in the United States, as well as Bruno Rizzi in Italy, were also to conclude that Soviet governing elites had become a new ruling class.[50]

In the early 1920's, Nikolai Bukharin also made some very interesting observations regarding the Soviet bureaucracy's consolidation of power on a class basis. Like Lenin, Bukharin recognized the serious obstacles to establishing the "power of a new class, the proletariat, upon the ruins of the old bourgeois power." Russia's "low level of general culture" and its "imperfect development," Bukharin suggested, temporarily resulted in rule by a "vanguard" or a "comparatively thin stratum" which consisted of "the bold spirits, of those who are active in body and mind, of those who are well informed."[51] In his book, *Historical Materialism* published in 1921, Bukharin offered an explanation of why *in the long run* his "thin stratum" of fellow Bolshevik leaders would not confirm the elitist prophecy and become a permanent ruling minority. At the same time, however, he conceded that the chances of the Soviet regime avoiding an oligarchical outcome, as mentioned in Michels' "very interesting book," still remained very much an open question.

> [What] constitutes an eternal category in Michels' presentation, namely the "incompetence of the masses" will disappear, for this incompetence is by no means a necessary attribute of every system .... We may state that in a society of the future there will be a colossal overproduction of organizers, which will nullify the *stability* of the ruling groups .... But the question of the *transition* period from capitalism to socialism, i.e., the period of the proletarian dictatorship, is far more difficult .... There will inevitably result a *tendency* to 'degeneration,' i.e., the excretion of a leading stratum in the form of a class-germ. This tendency will be retarded by two opposing tendencies; first by the *growth of the productive forces*; second, by the *abolition of the educational monopoly*. The increasing reproduction of technologists and of organizers in general, out of the working class itself, will undermine this possible new class alignment. The outcome of the struggle will depend on which tendencies turn out to be stronger.[52]

In 1923, Bukharin went even further and suggested that "if we imagine conditions in which a break is produced between the mass of the workers and a section

The Socialist Pyramid: Elites and Power in Yugoslavia

which has arisen from them we will find that a new class made up of ex-proletarians will be created."[53] Unfortunately, political and personal factors constrained Bukharin from ever fully developing his important insights about the "excretion of a leading stratum" or "new class" under socialism. He was continuously troubled by the revolution's potential for "bureaucratic degeneration" and "organized mismanagement," but such views were accompanied by an ambiguous optimism that socialism can establish such a thing as a "non-bureaucratic bureaucracy."[54] Bukharin's approach - much like Trotsky's contrasting faith that the working class could "debureaucratize the bureaucracy" - proved highly inadequate for a life and death struggle with the Stalinist elite.

The Italian communist, Antonio Gramsci, also grappled with the issue of revolutionary socialist elites. Gramsci drew special attention to the "division between rulers and ruled" as a "primordial" and "irreducible fact" in any society containing social classes, and he also maintained that "one could and should study how to minimize the fact and eliminate it, by altering certain conditions."[55] For Gramsci, concepts such as Mosca's political class and Pareto's elite referred to "nothing other than the intellectual section of the dominant social group" in a society, or to put it in Marxist terms, a section of the ruling class. "Mosca's book," Gramsci observed, "is an enormous hotch-potch of a sociological and positivistic character." He also suggested that it is necessary "to confront a whole series of problems of a much less simple kind than Robert Michels, for example, believes - though he is considered an expert on the subject."[56] The concept of an elite, however, was central to Gramsci's own discussion of social classes. It is possible, he points out in essays written between 1929 and 1935, for coercion to be "exercised by the *elite* of a class over the rest of the same class," and also such party coercion is sometimes accomplished (and here he attacks Trotsky's view on industrialization and the militarization of labour) by the creation of "*elites* necessary for the historical task." The development of "critical self-consciousness" in society, he also argued, "means historically and politically the creation of an *elite* of intellectuals." Indeed, because "there is no organization without intellectuals, that is without organizers and leaders ... innovation cannot come from the mass, at least in the beginning, except through the mediation of an *elite*."[57]

Gramsci was particularly concerned with a group he identified as "the organic intellectuals," i.e., persons who act somewhat like "functionaries," or spokesmen of their class in various political, social, and economic spheres. The relationship of such intellectuals to the "world of production is not as direct as it is with other members of social groups," but he felt that it was necessary and possible to measure the linkage between those intellectuals and the broader social class whose consciousness they allegedly represented.[58] A major task for the proletariat in Gramsci's view, was to create their own "category of organic intellectuals directly in the political and philosophical field," i.e., "*elites* of intellectuals of a new type which arise directly out of the masses, but remain in contact with them." The creation of such intellectuals would be a difficult task which required the creation of a proletarian party organization, and which might not be fully accomplished until after the seizure of state power.[59] The "realistic" analysis of all states included, he also maintained, an examination of "the function of elites or a vanguard, i.e., parties in relation to the class which they represent."[60] Gramsci's emphasis on the significance of "organic intellectuals" working within a vanguard party bears a certain resemblance to Lenin's concern with the relationship between "professional revolutionists," and the intelligentsia. The Italian Marxist, however, presents a broader treatment of intellectuals within and outside politics, as well as the "organic" linkages between the intellectual leaders and their proletarian followers.[61]

As the preceding discussion illustrates, issues concerning the place of political elites in socialist movements and regimes were of major concern to the founders of Marxism, as well as to many of their most prominent supporters and critics. Sharp differences are apparent among the representative selection of writers surveyed above, especially with regard to the inevitability, proper description, and acceptability of socialist elites. The diverse viewpoints all focus, however, upon a common problem: who actually governs in revolutionary movements and regimes devoted to the interests of the working class? Although the role of social classes and class struggle, rather than the issue of elitism was the leitmotiv in the writing of Marx, Engels, and Lenin, all of those theorists were keenly aware that specialized groups of political and administrative officials would be needed to manage the affairs of a post-capitalist state. Indeed one of the major problems for early Western and Eastern European Marxists was how to imbue socialist intellectuals with the leadership skills necessary to capture and retain political power, a process which Alvin Gouldner succinctly describes as the "eerie transformation of elites into elite-devouring revolutionaries."[62] The danger that the leaders of a working class movement might succumb to elitist temptations and practices in the post-revolutionary period was certainly recognized by the early Marxists, but in the natural preoccupation with the task of achieving and holding state authority, they seriously neglected the problem of controlling the political office-holders of a socialist regime. Not surprisingly, it was the expression of such tendencies toward elite domination, first by the revolutionary socialist movements in the nineteenth and early twentieth centuries, and then in the Bolshevik revolution and Soviet state, which stimulated widespread controversy among both the friends and foes of Marxism. With the formation of several new Marxist states in the wake of World War II, the debate concerning elites and socialism became even more pertinent and intense.[63] Considerable attention would be focused on Communist Yugoslavia, first the most militant, and then the leading maverick among the East European Marxist states.

The Socialist Pyramid: Elites and Power in Yugoslavia

Political Elites In Yugoslav Theory and Practice

Prior to the Second World War, relatively little attention was devoted to the issue of revolutionary socialist elites within the Yugoslav context. Combining aspects of a traditional monarchy and unstable parliamentarism with an overwhelming agrarian socio-economic structure, the Yugoslav Kingdom from 1918 to 1941 could accurately be described as a European "developing area" undergoing the initial stages of the state-building process. Critical commentary regarding political leadership and methods of political control in the new state focused upon a governing elite of party politicians, senior administrators, and royal retainers. That elite, for the most part, was recruited from the Serbian middle and upper classes which dominated Yugoslavia in the period between the two World Wars. The faction-ridden Communist Party of Yugoslavia, forced to operate underground in the two decades after 1920, was primarily concerned with organizational survival rather than any potential difficulties which might arise from its vanguard model of political leadership.[64] It was only during and after their wartime conquest of state power in the 1940's that Yugoslav Marxists would begin to systematically reflect upon the problems of elitist socialism within and outside their own country.

Problems of elite development and even elitist socialism were not, however, entirely ignored by Yugoslav writers during the pre-communist period. For example, a small group of interwar "bourgeois" sociologists had begun to investigate their country's pattern of class stratification and elite formation. Indeed, several members of Yugoslavia's emergent sociological community who were educated in Western Europe before the First World War, had been strongly influenced by the ideas and political values of the classical elitists.[65] Mirko Kosić, Yugoslavia's most well-known sociologist before World War II, had a particularly high regard for the elite studies of Pareto, Mosca, and Michels, and considered Pareto the "very best" sociologist of the time. Kosić carefully examined the features of different social strata in Yugoslav society including the peasantry, proletariat, employees, businessmen, intelligentsia, and the "political classes." In his opinion, the process of industrialization in Yugoslavia, together with the continual agrarian crisis, had resulted in a situation whereby the weak lower-agricultural strata were increasingly proletarianized, while a new petty bourgeois elite group was elevated into the capitalist higher class. Kosić felt that the process of class stratification had also created "political classes," or those strata of the population whose political power was dependent - either through direct participation or indirect association - on the authority of public-legal institutions.

Kosić also examined the impact of different regional and ethnic groups on the process of social stratification. For example, according to Kosić, Yugoslavia's different levels of economic development and different traditions accounted for the diverse social origins of bureaucratic personnel in different regions of the country. Thus in Serbia, the social backgrounds of state bureaucrats could generally be found in the peasantry; in Croatia, from the administrative classes, and in Slovenia, from among the petty bourgeoisie and craftsmen. In Serbia, the state bureaucracy seemed to be a "political organ" of the people, while in Slovenia, administrative employees were more of a distinct stratum with a specific class consciousness. Basically conservative in his political outlook, Kosić believed that the unity and success of the state depended upon the selection of the most "qualified and creative people," as well as upon the role played by the monarchy and its bureaucratic apparatus. While unsympathetic to communism and admiring the theoretical perspectives of the classical elitists, Kosić and most other interwar Yugoslav sociologists also remained highly critical of the non-democratic and racist aspects of national socialism. Subscribing to a kind of "democratic elitism" they equally condemned the authoritarian features common to both Nazism and Bolshevism during the interwar period.

A minority of interwar Yugoslav scholars went beyond simple esteem for professional sociologists such as Pareto, and embraced a combination of elitist sociological analysis and fascist politics. For example, Mirko Kus-Nikolayev, perhaps the most controversial representative of this extreme right-wing group, gravitated from support of Marxist historical materialism to strong advocacy of a "new elite" which could liberate Europe from what he saw as the twin dangers of bolshevism and bourgeois democracy. At the other end of the political spectrum, most Yugoslav Marxist writers in this period accepted the standard Soviet view of classes, the state, and elites. Based on prevailing Marxist-Leninist theory, this view dogmatically contrasted the negative features of ruling elites in the class-stratified bourgeois states, with the proletarian vanguard in the allegedly more egalitarian Soviet state. Filip Filipović, a leading theoretican of the interwar Yugoslav Communist Party, expressed this doctrinaire view of his country's class structure in his 1920 book, *For a Soviet State*.

> In the present state in which we live, factories, workshops, mines, banks, steamships belong to the rich, to the capitalists, to the great property spahijas, largeowners, agas, begs, all of the wealth and the tools of labour are the property of one small mob of the wealthy, united in different institutions. And all those different institutions of wealth, speculators, factory owners, bankers, agas, and begs comprise one large league of entrepreneurs, of capitalists, which is called the bourgeois state.[66]

Filipović disappeared in the USSR during the Stalinist purges, which also claimed the lives of many other Yugoslav communists. While most Yugoslav Marxists chose, or were compelled to ignore the defects that could befall a revolutionary socialist state, there were exceptions. For example, Ante Ciliga, a member of the Yugoslav Communist Politburo who belonged to the Trotskyist

The Socialist Pyramid: Elites and Power in Yugoslavia

"Left Opposition," arrived at a rather different conclusion from his comrades concerning the evolution of the USSR. Ciliga lived in the Soviet Union from 1926 to 1936, during which time he spent five and one-half years in prisons and labour camps. Fortunately able to return to Western Europe (born in Istria he was able to obtain an Italian passport), he wrote *In the Country of the Great Lie*, published in 1940 in Paris. Writing at almost exactly the same time as other Trotskyists such as Bruno Rizzi, James Burnham, and Max Shachtman, Ciliga concluded that Soviet society was ruled by bureaucratic officials who had become a Communist "elite," or what he also termed a "new privileged class." The "bureaucratic elite," in Ciliga's analysis - which reads like a combination of Bakunin and Trotsky - formed an "aristocracy of the new rich."

> I knew of course that they belonged to the new privileged class, but what was new to me was that they were fully conscious of it and were permeated with the spirit of hierarchy and caste .... The new privileged class was subdivided into strata that were invisible to the outsider, but that were carefully distinguished. It was not merely strict hierarchy. People belonging to the same hierarchic stratum were still differentiated in accordance with all sorts of criteria: their seniority, the way in which they had formed their career, their social and political biography. The solidarity that linked the members of each stratum was directed only toward the lower strata; within the privileged class, the groups waged an insidious and malevolent strife.[67]

Ciliga's shift from a critical Marxist to an openly pro-fascist position during World War II (he apparently worked for the Independent State of Croatia), considerably reduced sympathy in the West for his interpretation of communist regimes. He deserves distinction, however, for being the first former high-ranking Yugoslav communist official to apply a "new class analysis" to both the Soviet Union and Yugoslavia. Thus in 1951, a decade after writing his minor classic on the USSR, Ciliga utilized a very similar perspective to characterize the leadership of the Yugoslav communist regime.

> This system has nothing that is truly socialist, the workers do not play any role in the direction of production and public life, and equality and social liberty do not exist. The new class dominates - the communists over the political and social echelon, and the engineers and directors over the technical echelon - it has completely substituted for the bourgeoisie in the role of the exploiter of the workers.[68]

Ciliga's critique of the early Yugoslav communist regime has generally been ignored, most likely because it expresses the views of an extremely anti-Marxist emigré writer (albeit a former top communist official). Moreover, the

Lenard J. Cohen

Yugoslav swing toward a more reformist brand of communism at the beginning of the 1950's, appeared to contradict Ciliga's pessimistic analysis. What proved more fascinating and consequential not long after Ciligia's polemic against Tito's "new class," however, was the emergence of very similar views at the very summit of Belgrade's political leadership.

The details of the wartime struggle to power by the Yugoslav revolutionaries (1941-1944), their dramatic break with the Soviet Union in 1948, and their decision to embark on a new road of communist development in the early 1950's are all relatively well-known stories. More interesting for the present analyis, however, is that so much of the Yugoslav communists' ideological readjustment during their turbulent first decade in power focused upon the issue of elitist socialism. The centrality and difficulty posed by that issue for the early Yugoslav communist regime is well illustrated by the views of two major political associates at that time - Edward Kardelj and Milovan Djilas. Confronted with problems of bureaucracy and elitism in a socialist regime, Kardelj and Djilas underwent a roughly similar process of ideological reflection and evolution, yet eventually reached fundamentally different conclusions. As a result, Kardelj would go on to become the principal theoretician and architect of "Titoism," while Djilas would be banished to the political wilderness.

Kardelj directed attention to the elitist tendencies of Yugoslav communism several years before Djilas. In 1942, during the wartime struggle for power, Kardelj warned his fellow communist leaders about a certain "dizzyness with power" which was infecting the higher echelons of the Partisan movement. "People who were previously good fighters are becoming bureaucrats and dukes when they take leading positions."[69] In another wartime communique he was even more emphatic about the problem which had arisen in the military command structure:

> When I speak about "dukes," don't get the idea that it is a question of some foreign elements. On the contrary, I believe that 80 percent of our commanders are members of the Party, as are all of the political commissars. Moreover, the majority of our commanders are workers. Such a "dukedom" and similar phenomena isn't something that we can't liquidate by the minimal effort of our Party. All that results from a dizzyness with success. Some of those commanders and commissars will simply be talking to themselves after we rout the enemy occupiers. And so I think we will liquidate those dangerous phenomena very quickly.[70]

The use of a standard Stalinist slogan - "dizzyness with success" - to attack bureaucratic abuses below the summit of the political leadership, was not unusual for a communist with Kardelj's Comintern background and devotion to the Soviet Union. Once in power, Kardelj would continue to criticize bureaucratic tendencies in the new state apparatus. In May 1945, for example, he

The Socialist Pyramid: Elites and Power in Yugoslavia

warned that "bureaucratic rot had already started to cover up the image of the national warrior fighting for a better future for the people." Many bureaucrats, he added, "crave for the days of 'peace' when the common people did not interfere in the affairs of state, when there was no control "from the street, etc." Kardelj argued, however, that such negative tendencies could be overcome, and that the power of the "popular masses" could break through the "bureaucratic layer (where it exists)."[71]

In the years after the break with the Soviet Union, Kardelj would expand his critique of socialism to factors other than simply the leftover habits of bourgeois public administration or the arrogance of certain deviant officials. He explained, for example, that as a result of the Cominform indictment of Yugoslavia he had undergone a painful personal crisis with respect to his political outlook. After reflecting upon the causes of the quarrel with Stalin, Kardelj identified three major reasons for the behaviour of the Soviet Union. First, because the communist party in the USSR had become intermeshed with the state apparatus, and particularly the police, an unbridled personal dictatorship had risen in the USSR. Secondly, the working masses had been "isolated from the execution of power" and "the worker became some sort of hired hand of the state." Finally, the backwardness and pre-socialist mentalities of Old Russia had contributed to a bureaucratic degeneration. "It became clear to me," Kardelj remarked in retrospect, "that we had to concentrate on solving those issues in Yugoslav society which were associated with the first two causes."[72] Speaking to the Yugoslav Parliament in May 1949, Kardelj emphasized that one of the essential ingredients of socialism is to "safeguard the revolution" - as Marx said - "from its own bureaucrats."

> We must never forget that, however brilliant its leaders, no bureaucratic apparatus can build socialism. Socialism can grow only out of the initiative of the millions of common people with the proletarian party in its leading role .... Therefore the development of socialism can take no other path but that of the constant strengthening of socialist democracy, in the sense of the increasing self-management of the common people, of their greater participation in the machinery of the state from the lowest forms to the highest ....[73]

Kardelj's explication of the Stalinist system and his estimation of what needed to be done in order to escape its pernicious influence, was carefully formulated in a manner that did not undermine the legitimacy or authority of Yugoslavia's one-party Marxist regime and its political leadership. Thus, while Kardelj suggested that those who controlled state property in the USSR had become a despotic "bureaucratic caste" isolated from the working class, he did not suggest, as had so many earlier Marxist dissidents, that the Soviet political leadership constituted a new "ruling class."[74] Kardelj also avoided Trotsky's more critical description of the Stalinist state as a system which combined "social property" with "bourgeois norms of distribution" (or what Lenin had called a "bourgeois state without the bourgeoisie"). "Bureaucratic despotism" resulting from the fetishization and overcentralization of the state was the main enemy for Kardelj, and not features of post-capitalist society such as socialist property, socialist bureaucracy, or the overall guidance of society by the top leadership of the party vanguard. The model for constructing a socialist society could no longer be the aberrant Stalinist state, but Kardelj's endeavour to elucidate a new theoretical framework did not include jettisoning the basic ingredients of Leninism. Looking back at the early post-revolutionary period, Kardelj would admit "that a rather too bureaucratic rule had been gradually taking place within Yugoslavia," but he also pointed out that Belgrade's position in the conflict with Stalin "was not a demand to 'free' state power and economic administrative functions from the influence of the Communist Party."[75] During his thirty years of political activity which followed the break with the Soviet Union, Kardelj strove to develop methods and theoretical arguments which would *combine* the continued rule of a socialist political elite - or what he preferred to term "the advance guard" of the working class - with expanded citizen participation in public policy formation. The well-known novelties and limitations of Yugoslavia's system of self-management, as well as its alternating periods of liberalization and internal repression resulted largely from the inherent tension of that endeavour.[76]

Milovan Djilas' interpretation of the Stalinist system was initially very similar to the views expressed by Kardelj. From the 1948 Yugoslav break with the Cominform to approximately the middle of 1950, Djilas attributed the defects of Soviet socialism to the monopolistic practices of a "privileged bureaucratic stratum" and "bureaucratic centralism" which "temporarily transformed the state into a force above society."[77] Djilas still had faith that current "revolutionary practice" could overcome bureaucratic flaws in a communist system. After all, he observed in March 1950, "Marx and Lenin foresaw two dangers threatening the triumphant working class in socialism: from the overthrown bourgeoisie on the one hand, and its own bureaucracy on the other."[78] In many respects these early criticisms of the USSR were an expansion on comments that Djilas had previously made regarding various forms of "bureaucratism" within Yugoslavia. For example, as early as 1946 he had warned against "separating authorities from the masses" as a result of bureaucratic tendencies and "callous" attitudes on the part of local officials.[79] During the first years after the Yugoslav revolution, Djilas later claimed he was still unaware that the "sudden distancing of those in power from the common people stemmed less from negligence and preoccupation than from the transformation of communists themselves into a special category, alien and privileged." It was the dispute between the Soviet Union and Yugoslavia which impelled Djilas to abandon his role as simply another one of the regime's "agile critics of 'inequalities,'"[80] and adopt a more radical critique of communist bureaucracy and elitism.

By the Autumn of 1950, Djilas had reached the conclusion that the Soviet Union was a new kind of class society which he labelled state capitalism.[81] According to this view, state ownership in the USSR had created a stratified society in which wage labourers were exploited by a "bureaucratic caste" (not simply a bureaucratic stratum). Djilas now charged the "Soviet 'socialist' bureaucracy" with practicing "untold brutality in all aspects of contemporary life," and having a "glutonous, parasitic spirit," "ravenous and insatiable like the bourgeoisie, but without the spirit of enterprise and thrift."[82] Although Djilas indicted the "mental and spiritual poverty of the Soviet bureaucratic leadership, he was still unwilling to describe that leadership as a ruling class. In an article entitled "Class or Caste?" he gave two reasons for his position: first, the Soviet leadership "did not own the means of production," and second, "the bureaucracy does not reproduce itself as a set of individuals, or as a set of positions." Djilas revealed a deeply ingrained political sensitivity in describing the Soviet leadership as a "caste" (a use of the term he differentiated from the "bureaucratic adventurist" Trotsky).

> It is very important, both for us in Yugoslavia and for socialism in general to be sure of the answer .... Thus if we were dealing here with a class, a new class, and not a caste, the struggle against the bureaucracy would be futile and utopian, and we who fought would be comical reactionary figures. But since the bureaucracy is not a class, but a reactionary anti-socialist tendency that appears in the transition from capitalism to communism, the struggle against it is revolutionary and progressive and can succeed.[83]

Perhaps more interesting than Djilas' concern with correct sociological and political terminology was the fact that his own ideological introspection was leading him closer to a crucial and extremely difficult problem, namely, the futility and fradulence of incessant campaigns against bureaucracy by socialist political leaders who themselves - whether as a caste or a new bureaucratic class - have a vested interest in the preservation of their power.

Djilas' reluctance to use the label "new class" was not shared by all Yugoslav communists. For example, in mid-1952 Žvonomir Kristl and Janez Stanovnik, in a published debate with Djilas, argued not only that the Soviet bureaucracy had become a new class due to its economic privileges based on *de facto* ownership of state property, but also that the same situation had existed in Yugoslav before 1948. As a Yugoslav communist leader, Djilas could not accept a view which negated both the 1917 October revolution and the Yugoslav revolution.[84] If it was possible, Djilas asked almost plaintively, for a new class to arise after the expropriation of the capitalists "then why was the expropriation of the bourgeoisie an historical inevitability?"[85] Still unable to accept that a socialist revolution could result in the formation of a new class, Djilas concluded that the main problem of socialism in the USSR and Yugoslavia up to 1948, was that the "the decision-making power of the proletariat had been transferred not just to the party, but to the party elite."[86] Although in 1952 Djilas still refrained from using the concept of a "new class," his arguments had already become rather discomforting to most of the Yugoslav party leadership. Expressing the party's more mainstream view, Kardlj argued for example, that the Stalinist system had not degenerated into "state capitalism" as Djilas maintained, but rather had deteriorated into "deformed socialism" (that is, what Lenin had warned against in 1921). The Soviet Union, Kardelj claimed, was a type of "bureaucratic despotism" that was neither really socialist, nor capitalist.[87] The ideological distance between Djilas and Kardelj still appeared to be a matter of nuance and semantics, but matters would soon reveal that Tito's two closest comrades had completely different visions of both their country's and their own future.

The next and more radical stage in Djilas' intellectual metamorphosis occurred when he turned his attention directly to various aspects of Stalinism within Yugoslavia. No longer able to justify the flagrant privileges and hierarchical practices of the communist regime - a personal dilemma he later described as a "split between being an emotional malcontent" and a "prisoner" of an "ideological future" - Djilas began to openly describe the reality he and his colleagues had created.[88] In a series of articles published in *Borba* between October 1953 and January 1954, Djilas chose to ignore the reform measures adopted by his own regime - a theme Tito and his comrades would have enjoyed reading about - and decided to emphasize the residual aspects of the Stalinist model still present in Yugoslavia. Djilas demanded that the decentralization of the Yugoslav political system begun around 1950 be carried forward, even if that meant virtually eliminating the political hegemony of the League of Communists. He had become particularly disillusioned during the summer of 1953 by the Party leadership's decision to curtail the drive for liberalization and downgrade the campaign against bureaucratism. Such a policy demonstrated, in his opinion, that "bureaucrats cannot fight bureaucratism" but are mainly interested in a "sterile search" for the few large powerless remnants of the former "class enemy," i.e., the bourgeoisie.[89] Djilas had become obsessed with new enemies: communist bureaucracy and elitism. When the more conservative wing of the party leadership criticized Djilas for being unrealistic, writing for a foreign audience, breaking with Marxism-Leninism, and aiding the "forces of reaction," his explanation only further angered his comrades.

> Like most of the leadership I, too, have been living in seclusion in my office and at home .... It is precisely this way of life and this kind of reaction which must be eliminated. It is unnatural. It is unnatural in

present conditions, it is inhuman, it is not even socialist. My purpose in writing these critical articles is to cause myself, and others to emerge from the unreal, abstract world of the 'elite' and the chosen and enter as profoundly as possible into the real world of the simple working people and ordinary human relations.[90]

Djilas' most heretical analysis of the Yugoslav political elite, however, appeared in a bitter and more derisive essay, "Anatomy of a Moral," published in the journal *Nova Misao* on January 1, 1954. Although essentially not a theoretical study, and filled with certain melodramatic flourishes, the essay, nevertheless, provided a fascinating sketch of life in the higher echelons of the Yugoslav party leadership. Djilas describes the privileges and social behaviour of a group he alternatively refers to as a "sham aristocracy," the "upper caste," "caste people," a "hallowed and secluded class," and a "self-animated circle with craved preeminence and exclusiveness." The pretext for Djilas' vivid diatribe against the lifestyle of his comrades was rather bizarre. It involved his strong personal revulsion with the way some wives of leading communist officials had treated "a beautiful young actress," who had married the army chief of staff. Djilas' reaction, however, went beyond a simple outburst regarding social airs and the arrogant mentality of a "higher social circle." He had begun to probe the basis of that mentality:

> It grew, somewhat unawares, from a quite natural logic: namely, that favorable conditions should be afforded leaders so they can work and live. This attitude and the system it fostered, proliferated in all directions, from top to bottom, everywhere. Thus people were classified into categories and strata, new strata, divided categories or professions, etc., each neatly placed in a secluded pigeonhole, but bound together by a common solidarity that was not so much the product of ideological or moral unity as the product of the same way of life, of similar interests arising from the nature of the official authority they wielded and the manner in which they had acquired that authority.[91]

Djilas' analysis of the Yugoslav political elite was remarkably similar to Ante Ciliga's description of the Soviet elite written a dozen years earlier. Whether at the time this was obvious to anyone, including Djilas, is unknown. In any case, he had finally gone beyond the point where he could avoid the wrath of his comrades. Not only had his earlier articles achieved a certain popularity among the general population, but a few party leaders had even begun to voice similar views. Sixteen days after the publication of "Anatomy of a Moral" the Third Plenum of the Yugoslav League of Communist's Central Committee met and considered the sensitive "case" of Milovan Djilas. Kardelj, who played the most prominent role in the attack against Djilas, made it clear that the Yugoslav regime's fight against bureaucratic tendencies in its ranks did not permit the kind of elite self-criticism that might unleash "uncontrollable anarchist forces." Djilas' conception of democracy, Kardelj observed, "is not ours, it is not socialist, but a mixture of anarchism and bourgeois-liberalistic forms."[92] Kardelj also divulged remarks which Djilas had made to him in a conversation in which he had suggested that Tito was the "standard-bearer of bureaucracy" (years later Djilas would attribute Kardelj's public citation of those remarks to political opportunism, and the fact that the conversation was probably bugged; that is, Tito knew about it, and Kardelj wanted to clear his own record)[93] Kardelj, who a decade before had criticized the elitist behaviour of certain "dukes" in the socialist revolution, had now become Tito's crown-prince and henchman in the political annihilation of a potentially dangerous pretender to communist orthodoxy. Sharply rebuked by all of his closest comrades in a well-orchestrated offensive, Djilas at first wavered, admitted certain errors, and finally agreed to follow party discipline. But his remarks at the Plenum indicated little repentance concerning his fundamental dissatisfaction with Yugoslav communist development. Although he was stripped of all his party and government posts, the matter of his party membership prompted a personal intervention by Tito: "He should not be expelled, or the foreign press will write that we are behaving like Stalinists." Two months after the Plenum, Djilas resigned from the party on his own initiative.[94]

Outcast and politically "dead" (a phrase Tito applied to him) Djilas reflected on the ideas that had caused him to be driven from power. In 1956 he completed *The New Class* (originally entitled *Freedom and Ownership*, but at the suggestion of a friend later changed to the title of one of its chapters) which was smuggled abroad and published in 1957.[95] Abandoning his earlier conception of the Soviet bureaucratic leadership as "state capitalist" or a "caste," Djilas now fully embraced the idea he had tried so hard to resist: "In contrast to earlier revolutions, the Communist revolution, conducted in the name of doing away with classes, had resulted in the most complete authority of any single new class. Everything else is sham and an illusion." In Djilas' scheme, the communist party and the new class are not identical: "the core and the basis of the new class is created in the party and at its top, as well as in the state political organs." He also differentiated between routine administrative officials in the bureaucracy, and a "special stratum" of bureaucrats who comprise the "governing bureaucracy," or the "political bureaucrats," i.e., the new class. Greater or lesser privileges are distributed along the hierarchical ladder of "every socialist society," with the most benefits reserved for "the highest bureaucracy, for the elite of the new class."[96] Djilas had also given up any illusions about the antibureaucratic campaign in his own country. His analysis although focusing on the USSR, applied to all communist countries, including Yugoslavia.

In order to arrive at such a sweeping and cohesive analysis of communist systems, Djilas had found it necessary to overcome what he later called the

The Socialist Pyramid: Elites and Power in Yugoslavia

"greatest obstacle"[97] in the way of his thinking, namely, the idea that a communist political bureaucracy did not technically or formally own state property. In *The New Class* Djilas recognized that in a purely juridical sense state property in communist regimes is collectively owned, but he went on to emphasize that "it is the bureaucracy which formally uses, administers, and controls both nationalized and socialized property, as well as the entire life of society." Moreover, the political bureaucrats "enjoy" immense privileges of their economic well-being.[98] As Djilas would point out in an interview much later, "property is less important that Socialist theoreticians, including Marx taught - that with the liquidation of capitalist property the problem would be solved. Really the problems start *after* this."[99]

In *The New Class* Djilas credits Trotsky with having discerned the origin of the Stalinist type bureaucracy in the "narrow stratum" of pre-revolutionary professional politicians established by Lenin. But Trotsky, Djilas claims, failed to detect "the beginning of a new class of owners and exploiters." By attacking the degeneration of the party bureaucracy and the "cult of the party" in the USSR, Djilas argued, Trotsky, although not conscious of it, had actually been attacking the new class.[100] Although he deserves credit for going beyond Trotsky's analysis (as had many of Trotsky's own followers before World War II), Djilas was certainly not original in labelling the party bureaucracy's privileged social stratum as "the new class." His early assertions of such originality written in a "jail diary" during the late 1950's,[101] were correctly abandoned in his later studies. Undoubtedly he rethought the issue of originality after reading more widely and putting his own work into a broader context. Djilas maintains, however, that when he wrote *The New Class* during 1955 and 1956, he was unaware that such writers as Bukharin, Bertrand Russell and N.A. Berdiaev had used the same terminology (he does not mention the more important, but ideologically tainted work of Michels, Machajski, Ciliga and others), and he suggests that, in any case, their work was "more predictive about it than analytical."[102] Clearly as has been shown above, Djilas was building upon ideas from a long established tradition of Marxist and anti-Marxist thought. It was not his use of the term "new class" which gave Djilas' study such prominence (although the title may have helped), but rather that it was a searching and eloquent indictment of that class by one of its previously high ranking members. The authenticity of earlier new class analyses seemed to be confirmed by the revelations of an authentic communist leader who had forsaken his top elite position. The fact that *The New Class* was published in the West shortly after the death of Stalin, during the first stages of de-Stalinization in the USSR, and in the wake of the Hungarian revolution, also help to explain the enthusiastic reception of Djilas' ideas. The most accurate statement about his contribution is probably the one he made himself in 1981: "my ideas were really not all that original, not even for Yugoslavia. I felt I was giving voice to something that emanated from everywhere."[103]

Lenard J. Cohen

In the thirty years since writing *The New Class*, Djilas has remained the leading "renegade" of Yugoslav political life. His book and conclusions have consistently been treated as heresies by the regime in Belgrade - even after Tito's death - and Djilas himself typically pillored as a "pawn who dances obediently to the time of an anti-communist orchestra."[104] Although suffering through several prison terms and other privations, Djilas has been steadfast in his views. "Time has proved me right," he claimed in February 1984, "my thesis that communism would spawn a new class, for example, has been proved .... We see that new class in Yugoslavia now."[105] Djilas is equally critical of the Yugoslav regime's novel mechanisms to expand citizen participation both at the work place and in the political system: "self-management legalized criticism of the bureaucracy. It also supressed bureaucratic wilfullness .... But it did not substantially influence the character of power, or of political circumstance."[106] Djilas' conclusions and behaviour will undoubtedly continue to arouse controversy, but what is perhaps even more interesting is that many of his basic concerns have become conventional topics of discussion within Yugoslav political and intellectual circles. Thus especially since the mid-1960's, Yugoslav writers have openly recognized and analyzed aspects of class stratification and political elitism in their country, although in almost all cases taking pains to avoid the direct use or citation of Djilas' specific formulations. As Djilas wryly noted in his 1969 book, *The Unperfect Society: Beyond the New Class*: "in Yugoslavia today hardly anyone can be found, even in the ruling circles, who is so unreasonable as to maintain that antagonisms and various social groups, including privileged ones, do not exist in socialist systems."[107]

Yugoslav discussions of social classes and political elites written after the publication of *The New Class* can be divided into two broad clusters: first, those by members of the academic social science "establishment," mainly comprised of political scientists and sociologists, and; second, those by the radical intellectuals, mainly philosophers, but also including some social scientists. The first group is centered in Yugoslav universities and research institutes. Its members are typically in close contact with professional politicians in the governing circles of the country, and indeed many members of this group combine public service with their academic work, or move in and out of political positions on a regular basis. The radical intellectuals, while also mainly working in academic and research settings, are generally in a state of confrontation with the political authorities. This tendency has been equally true of the so-called "Praxis group," whose members have been among the most articulate and nonconformist of the intellectuals, and who, since 1964, have constituted almost a permanent noninstitutionalized opposition to the regime. Not all of the radical intellectuals, however, can be identified with a particular journal or school of thought. Many are "free-floating" individuals and members of ad-hoc groups who take a highly critical and unorthodox stance on the major issues of Yugoslav society. Whether or not specific members or segments of the social

The Socialist Pyramid: Elites and Power in Yugoslavia

science establishment and radical intellectual community can be accurately labelled as "dissidents," depends largely on changing phases in the cycle of liberalization and internal political repression which has been so characteristic of Yugoslav political life.

The Djilas affair cast a lingering shadow over Yugoslav discussions of social and political stratification. Condemnation and avoidance of "bureaucratism" in a socialist society remained the hallmark of regime policy, and indeed the moving force behind the entire structure of self-managing institutions. It became a high risk enterprise, however, for political officials or academics to suggest that Yugoslavia's own bureaucratic defects had already resulted in the creation of a "new class" or a privileged and isolated political elite. Moreover, while Yugoslavs might criticize the USSR and other Soviet-type regimes for having encouraged a "cult of personality" around their top leaders, it was not permissible to apply the same concept to Tito, who was officially alleged to be playing a special "historic role" (both the 1963 and 1974 Constitutions formally exempted Tito from rules limiting an individual's tenure in political office). This situation would not completely dissuade Yugoslav writers from discussing domestic political elitism, but it considerably limited the scope of their research and discussions. This was well illustrated as early as 1959 when Radomir Lukić, one of Belgrade's leading sociologists, opened discussion about "the role of elites in socialist societies, the role of specialists in the management of society, and also the problem of bureaucracy."[108]

Lukić observed that during socialism's very early stages of development certain people unfortunately have greater capability and talent to decide upon matters which affect the entire society. Such a minority of individuals, i.e., an elite, must play a creative role in solving political conflicts among society's different interests, but must never give the "working masses" the "impression" that the socialist system is not theirs, or allow them to lose confidence in that system. "Only complete democracy makes possible a stable system, and the role of the elite as a real active force." It is when the political elite begins to use "the state's force against the will of the majority that the majority gradually loses confidence in the elite, a gap develops between the elite and the masses, and finally the elite and state which it holds become bureaucratized." The bureaucratic elite thereby abandons its role as a representative of society and begins to defend its own interests. At this crucial point in his analysis Lukić paused to remark that it is a very "serious question" whether the privileges secured by such a bureaucracy become a new form of "exploitation," transforming the bureaucracy into a "new class." The charge which the heretic Djilas had made only two years earlier in *The New Class*, created an awkward situation for Lukić:

> It is difficult to give an answer to this question. Theoretically we can avoid the danger of such development.... A series of negative phenomena

> in this sense can be seen in the practice of constituting socialism, but unfortunately they are insufficiently researched to draw any certain conclusions about their character .... By all means, one shouldn't be an excessive pessimist. With the raising of the consciousness of the working masses which continuously progresses, the danger from bureaucratism and new forms of exploitation certainly is only temporary. Socialism must be able to overcome this difficulty, so that bureaucratization to that extent can only be a temporary deformation of socialism, and it is difficult to believe that it can become a permanent social system.[109]

The emergence of a more "reformist" or liberal phase of political development during the 1960's considerably broadened the opportunities for Yugoslav political and sociological research. Official limitations and assaults on intellectual inquiry continued during the next two decades and were particularly visible in the early 1970's as a result of Tito's aggressive campaign against liberalism and nationalism. Nevertheless, professional social scientists enjoyed considerable latitude in probing their country's political and social structure. Elite studies were a major beneficiary of this trend. Serbo-Croatian translations of C. Wright Mills', *The Power Elite* in 1964, and of Thomas Bottomore's, *Elites and Society* in 1967, both reflected and stimulated the growing acceptance of the elite concept and elite research on the part of Yugoslav scholars.[110] It was particularly appealing to these academics that Bottomore encouraged research on political and bureaucratic elites in socialist regimes, but still rejected Djilas' notion that such elites had become a new class. In the introduction to the Yugoslav edition of Bottomore's book, Najdan Pašić, one of Belgrade's most prominent political scientists, expressed what became the mainstream academic and official view regarding the issue of socialist elitism.

> There is no doubt that in the first phase after the revolution, in the phase of "revolutionary statism" when changes in basic social relations are being created, primarily with the help of the state power, there exists a strong tendency to the bureaucratization of state-political mechanisms and the relative independence of the direct carriers of centralized political authority. But that doesn't mean either the formation of a new bureaucratic class, nor a ruling political elite which lacks any kind of class basis. It is only a question of a particular historically new form expressing the contradiction between the ruling class (in a historical and socio-economic sense) and the "political elite," that is, the social stratum which in the name of the working class exercises the functions of political authority.[111]

The Socialist Pyramid: Elites and Power in Yugoslavia

Embracing the concept of elites, Pašić and other Yugoslav social scientists carefully distinguished their approach from both the "vulgar pragmatic-political" Marxist interpretation which had allegedly neglected the role of those wielding proletarian state power, and also the "one-sidedness" of arguments made by the classical elitists who had attacked Marxism. As one social scientist from Zagreb put it:

> The concept of an "elite" can be separated from elite theory and can be accepted in the Marxist analysis of a social structure .... The problem of an elite is in fact the problem of a class society. The Marxist concept makes it possible to speak of an elite (or elites) as a structure which in a specific manner is connected to its class.[112]

Having accepted a "dialectical synthesis" between Marxism and selected aspects of elite analysis, Yugoslav scholars proceeded to carry out empirical research on various aspects of political power and class stratification in their society. Conflicts between elites and masses - or what most Yugoslav scholars still preferred to term "relations" between the working class "vanguard" and the working class "base" - as well as other societal cleavages (class, ethnic, ideological, etc.) were recognized as long term features of a socialist society.[113] The gap between the theory and practice of the self-management system became a legitimate area for Yugoslav researchers, as long as they accepted the underlying legitimacy of that system and its rulers.[114] For example, studies were undertaken of power and control in the structure of workers' councils, the extent and effect of citizen political participation, as well as the operation of political and governmental institutions such as legislative assemblies, the state administration and the League of Communists. Other studies concerning the values and attitudes of Yugoslav citizens, and periodic samplings of public opinion trends also shed light on questions of political and social stratification. The regime's experiment with new electoral mechanisms, and the effort to deprofessionalize political activity through the rotation of political office-holders became a particularly popular area of investigation for political scientists. Meanwhile, Yugoslav sociologists devoted close attention to aspects of social mobility and the features of the country's different social groups.

The various weaknesses in the self-management system identified by Yugoslav social science researchers - oligarchic tendencies, obstacles to citizen participation, inter-group conflict, etc. - were generally blamed on the residual impact of "statism," i.e., the centralized and monopolistic tendencies of the bureaucracy. In this perspective the bureaucracy was viewed not as a class (as Djilas came to see it), but as a "relatively independent social stratum" whose domination of political decision-making derives from rights delegated to it by the working class.[115] Beginning in the 1950's, "bureaucratic-étatistic" forces

Lenard J. Cohen

supplanted the prewar bourgeoisie as the main target of criticism by Yugoslav political officals and academic writers. Criticism of statism was almost always balanced, however, by an attack upon traces of "bourgeois liberalism" and also "anarchistic" ideas. Evidence of statism and the tendency of some socialist bureaucrats to abuse their rights should not be extended, according to this view, into a wholesale indictment of the socialist state and its leading officials. Privileged groups and even powerful elites may exist but, it is alleged, they are atomized and unable to assert themselves as a ruling class:

> ... the coefficient of class differences and inequality is great. However the social forces which arise on the wave of this tendency *is not a unified 'new class.'* It is an unusually fragmented formation of different shades and interests, *a conglomerate of different privileged strata* in relation to the basic body of producers, particularly the industrial workers. Individual social groups have begun to segmentally differentiate themselves by their way of life, by their position in income differentation and consumption, psychologies, and values .... The privileged groups cannot transform themselves into a unified separate class, they cannot assume a legitimate social status. On the contrary they must continually conceal their shape.[116]

One of the most interesting and ambitious studies of social groups in Yugoslavia was conducted by a group of Belgrade sociologists in the late 1970's. Confirming the findings of several other research projects, the Belgrade study revealed extensive inequalities of opportunity, ownership, income, and influence among different Yugoslav occupational groups.[117] For example, (see Table 1.1) while only about ten percent of agriculture workers and unskilled industrial workers owned automobiles - a very important badge of social "recognition" in Yugoslavia - 70 to 80 percent of the intelligentsia and leading personnel surveyed could afford a car. Similar differences emerged with respect to patterns of leisure activity, educational opportunity, and consumption of consumer goods. The study also empirically confirmed the distinct "life styles" which characterize different occupational sectors in Yugoslav society. Intellectuals and elite economic and political personnel exhibited a life style stressing the "norm of social status," i.e., "prestige and social distinction" relative to other groups in society. This status orientation is expressed in various forms of behaviour.

> A permanent invention of new status symbols, purchasing of consumers goods and household appliances abroad, purchasing of the entire household equipment in a relatively short period after marriage. Purchasing expensive articles, buying of land and the building of weekend houses ... avoiding some forms of mass culuture ... summer holidays are spent in

Table 1.1
Inequalities in Yugoslav Society (%)

	Agriculturalists		Workers		Middle Stratum		Leading Personnel (Directors, Political Functionaries)	Total
	"Pure" Farmers	Agriculture Proletariat	Unskilled Workers	Skilled Workers	Employees	Intellectuals		
A. Automobile Ownership by Social Strata								
Type of Automobile*								
Lower Category	5	9	7	20	28	24	16	17
Middle Category	2	2	2	10	9	38	53	18
Higher Category	0	1	0	1	2	6	13	3
No Automobile	93	88	91	69	61	32	18	62
Total	100	100	100	100	100	100	100	100
(Number)	(100)	(100)	(100)	(200)	(100)	(200)	(100)	(900)
B. Location of Annual Holidays by Social Strata								
Location of Annual Holidays								
At Home	95	92	73	41	30	7	12	36
At a Tourist Resort	1	3	6	41	62	78	80	43
Another location (e.g. at a friend's home)	2	1	18	18	3	3	6	8
No Annual Holiday	2	4	1	1	5	2	2	13
Total	100	100	100	100	100	100	100	100
(Number)	(100)	(100)	(100)	(200)	(100)	(200)	(100)	(900)

* The lowest category includes automobiles which in the period from 1972 to 1974 cost up to 50,000 dinars. The middle category autos cost between 50,000 and 75,000 dinars, and the higher category cars cost more than 75,000 dinars.

Source: Vesna Pešić, "Društvena Slojevitost i Stil Života," in *Društveni Slojevi i Društvena Svest*, eds. Mihailo Popović, *et al.* (Belgrade: Centar za sociološka istraživanja, Institut društvenih nauka, 1977), pp. 159 and 166.

> well known tourist spots that secure a definite amount of prestige, going to well known cafes and restaurants, etc.[118]

The preceding life style characterized what the group of Belgrade researchers called the "new middle class." According to the same research study, the highest position in Yugoslav society is occupied by a top "stratum" of "state-political leaders" who enjoy a life style which can be termed "exclusive-high status":

> ... this social grouping, exercising management and leading functions in society, has a *tendency* to concentrate social and economic power in its hands, and also the possibility of taking decisions about all essential social questions. This kind of social position, opens the possibility for the *control of surplus labour* and the division of income, securing a series of material and social advantages which essentially establish their style of life ... they are essentially guaranteed a high personal income, high living standard, job security, allocation of living space, etc. They are as a rule protected from all the economic "storms" which can strike at the existence of other social strata, which not only frees them from any worries about maintaining the established standard of living, but also makes it possible for them to possess and buy the kind of goods which are not "on a mass scale," conventionally accessible to everyone.[119]

Most respondents in the Belgrade study expressed the view that Yugoslavia was socially stratified (Table 1.2), although attitudes differed about whether that meant the existence of "particular social classes."[120] For example, 37 percent of the sample claimed that Yugoslav society is composed of social classes while another 26 percent viewed the social structure as being made up of different "strata." Approximately 10 percent claimed that their society has neither classes nor strata, while a slight one percent thought that only one class - the working class - exists. Another 26 percent of the respondents, either out of genuine ignorance or perhaps prudence, said they simply did not know. The most pronounced perception of social differentiation was expressed by the members of the intelligentsia, some three-quarters of whom recognized the existence of either classes (42 percent) or strata (32 percent). The attitudes of political and economic leaders contrasted sharply with the general pattern of responses. Only 26 percent of such elite level respondents recognized the division of their society into classes, the lowest percentage of any occupational group surveyed. Although another 27 percent of the leaders claimed that different strata exist, 30 percent viewed Yugoslavia as having neither classes nor strata, and 7 percent that one class exists in society (10 percent of the leaders did not answer the question). Thus, 37 percent of the leaders believed the country had an essentially homogeneous, although not completely egalitarian, social structure:

The Socialist Pyramid: Elites and Power in Yugoslavia

> ... the category of economic and political leaders is relatively more attached to a 'classless' vision of this society, not so much because they belong to the grouping of objectively higher social strata (with regard to material standards, education, degree of social power and prestige), but because they are decisively in favour of the evaluation of the existing relations in society. Namely ... the idea of creating a classless society ... is of first-class importance.[121]

The image of the country's social structure expressed by the leaders also had a bearing on how they viewed their own position in Yugoslav society. Most leaders who acknowledged the existence of "classes" in Yugoslavia, saw themselves as members of the working class. Those who believed that different "strata" exist in a society held varying ideas of their own group's position in the social structure. Some considered themselves in a "stratum of leaders," while others identified with the intelligentsia, the "higher class," or the "working people."[122]

When describing the highest ranking social groups in Yugoslav society respondents in the Belgrade study rarely used conventional labels such as "bourgeoise," "capitalists," or "the rich." Most often the highest "class" or "stratum" of society was perceived to be composed of those individuals whose positions depended upon non-manual skills connected with higher education, expertise, and political influence (e.g., "the others," "non-producers," "directors," "leaders," bureaucrats," "those who live from somebody else's labour," etc.). Working class respondents generally attributed their social group's low social ranking to economic and educational factors. Members of the intelligentsia and middle strata, however, tended to view social differentiation as a component of several different factors (type of occupation, degree of education, amount of income, degree of social power, social prestige) which resulted in a division between the "rulers" and the "ruled."[123] The authors of the Belgrade study concluded that Yugoslav society is not divided by "relations of exploitation and class stratification," but rather by relations of "strata inequality" with "some transitory class characteristics." A "strata hierarchy" allegedly exists in which different social strata - that become more like professional groups than classes - are divided by an "uneven distribution of economic and political powers." The elitist propensities in Yugoslav socialism are carefully documented and explained, but Djilas' conception of a "new class" is both rejected and ignored. Moreover, although the top "stratum" of "state-political leaders" under the system of self-management may enjoy an "exclusive" life style and relatively high degree of political and economic power, it is argued, nevertheless, that those leaders function within a state which strives to "satisfy the interests of the working class and other working people."[124] As within the state socialist regimes there is a *socialist elite*, but the Yugoslav variant is portrayed

Table 1.2
The Attitudes of Yugoslav Occupational Groups Concerning the Stratification of their Society

Occupational Groups	Attitudes Concerning Social Structure*					Total	
	There Are Classes	There Are Strata	There Are No Classes Or Strata	There Is Only One Class	Don't Know	(%)	(Number)
Agriculturalists (farmers)	33	21	6	–	40	100	(100)
Agricultural Proletariat	43	21	5	1	30	100	(100)
Craftsmen and Private Entrepreneurs	29	30	5	–	36	100	(100)
Total Private Sector	35	24	5	1	35	100	(300)
Unskilled and Semi-skilled Workers	38	16	9	2	35	100	(100)
Skilled and Highly Skilled Workers-Industry	43	29	11	1	16	100	(100)
Skilled and Highly Skilled Workers- Service Activities	34	22	11	–	33	100	(100)
Total Workers in Socialist Sector	38	22	10	1	28	100	(300)
Employees with Secondary School Training	42	35	5	–	18	100	(100)
Technical Intelligentsia	46	26	5	–	23	100	(100)
Humanistic Intelligentsia	37	36	10	–	17	100	(100)
Total Intelligentsia	42	32	7	–	19	100	(300)
"Leading Personnel" (managerial cadre and political-administrative functionaries)	26	27	30	7	10	100	(100)
TOTAL: All Occupational Groups in Sample (Number)	37 (371)	26 (263)	10 (97)	1 (11)	26 (258)	100	(1.000)

* This table combines data from two tables in the original source with slight modifications in the labelling of categories to aid the non-Yugoslav reader.
Source: Miloslav Janićijević, "Klasna svest i društvena struktura," in *Društveni slojevi i društvena svest*, eds. Mihailo V. Popović, *et al.* (Belgrade: Centar za sociološka istraživanja, Institut društvenih nauka, 1977), pp. 215 and 220.

as considerably more open, closer, and accountable to the non-elite sectors of society.[125]

Not all Yugoslav scholars have been content to empirically analyze and describe social divisions and political inequalities in their country. Thus, the "liberalization" of the political climate beginning in the early 1960's, which benefited the development of professional social science, also spawned a more 'radical' perspective concerning the flaws of the self-management system and the regime's political leadership. Such a radical Marxist critique was advanced by a relatively small number of intellectuals - perhaps a few hundred - the most vocal of whom were associated with the journal *Praxis*, published in Zagreb from 1964 to 1975.[126] Although the radical intellectuals can be distinguished from the mainstream scholars in a number of ways, both groups tend to view Yugoslavia as a highly stratified society governed by a powerful political elite. For example, Svetozar Stojanović, one of the most prolific members of the Praxis group, suggested early in his career that a principal legacy of the Yugoslav socialist revolution was society's "sharp division between an administrative power elite and common powerless man." When criticized by party conservatives for basing his analysis on the idea of an elite-mass dichotomy, instead of the officially more acceptable vanguard-working class model, Stojanović defended his underlying assumption:

> One of the motives of our revolution was the effort to create conditions which could begin to overcome the gap between those who administer and those who are administered. That for me is a process of de-elitization. I think that a really long process of further de-elitization remains before us.[127]

Elsewhere, Stojanović has suggested that the notion of power elites is an important "theoretical-critical tool" often neglected in Marxist theory:

> ... the concept of an elite has proven to be fruitful in sociological, historical, economic and political studies ... social thought was already sufficiently advanced when the Bolsheviks became unlimited avantgardists. Indeed nothing was changed by renaming this form of elitism, for avantgardism *is* elitism, no matter how revolutionary it purports to be. The danger, of course, becomes even greater when the competition among elites is replaced by the monopoly of one of them.[128]

The consequences which flow from elitism in a socialist regime, and the best means to combat those consequences are the issues which most sharply divide the radical intellectuals from other Yugoslav writers. The radicals, for example, view the statist or bureaucratic features of Yugoslav socialism not simply as residual features of the Stalinist or "administrative" phase of political development, but as far more integral components of the present single-party communist state. Although conceding that the establishment of *self-management in the economic sphere* has been an important contribution to "destatization," the radicals perceive this development as a rather limited achievement. They argue that outside the workplace a kind of "liberalized statism" prevails that is based on the hegemony of state and party officials at different territorial levels of the Yugoslav federation. Moreover, while the role of the political-state apparatus may be smaller than in other communist party regimes, it is still larger than in most other countries. Thus, they maintain, "the state is not withering away, but becoming stronger."[129] Proclamations about the need to expand democracy, deprofessionalize political work, and eliminate the privileges of party leaders, are seen by the radicals as having done little to curtail the domination of professional politicians in the "self-managing system." Collectively the political officials are viewed as constituting a "professional politocracy" or "oligarchial elite" which has a vested interest in its self-perpetuation, and whose policies are usually at odds with the interests of other social groups, particularly the working class. "The Yugoslav politocracy has never *in practice*," Stojanovic claims, "abandoned the Stalinist model of the political system of socialism ... the myth that the working class is the ruling class is, nevertheless, very influential, although the working class as a *class* is not present on the political scene."[130] Marx and most Marxists, it is further alleged, underestimated the political basis for class formation within the bureaucratic apparatus of a socialist regime - an incipient "politico-economic class" - while exaggerating the capacity of the working class to successfully wield state power. The working class may be the "non-ruling dominant class" after a socialist revolution but it is not the "ruling class." The "ruling class" is only that class which directly, be it totally or partially, runs the state and through its rule completely excludes one or the other classes from the political process:

> ... being an economic and not a politico-economic class the working class has not only not become, but could not have become the new ruling class. Since the working class is not a class of owners of the means of production, its domination over the new state apparatus would have to base itself on special organizational-institutional arrangements. Within this class paradigm, however, such issues did not arise. Having started with an inadequate conceptualization of the new society ... Marxists, as a rule, did not seriously search for the institutional guarantees and remedies against all embracing statization, or the foundations of a new class.[131]

The Yugoslav radicals' condemnation of socialist political elites and aspects of class rule in their country includes sharp criticism of the social group variously referred to as the "petty bourgeois stratum," "middle stratum," or "middle class." The creation of this middle sector in the social structure was allegedly hastened by the influence of "bourgeois liberalism" in Yugoslav economic thought and particularly the introduction of market mechanisms in the economy. The expanded opportunities for private ownership and the accumulation of wealth increased the level of social differentiation and opened the door to what is termed "vulgar consumerist hedonism" and "group-particularistic forms of self-management."[132] It is political power rather than economic power, however, which is usually claimed to have been the major impetus to the rise of "bourgeois socialism" in Yugoslavia.

> The power of the petty bourgeoisie derives from the fact that it revives social forces that had not been completely finished off and from the fact that it finds powerful allies not only in the still vital bourgeois world around us (to which we somewhat thoughtlessly opened wide our borders) but also in the bureaucracy itself, which had quickly begun to enrich itself .... The triumphant revolutionary advance guard, as in France in the era of the restoration, adapted many elements of the life style of the deposed class, including lavish interior decorations, inessential splendor and luxury, typical bourgeois status symbols and rituals, the accumulation of expensive objects, and isolation from the plebs in exclusive clubs, resorts, and hunting preserves. To justify such a life, its material base had to be expanded: others had to be allowed to enrich themselves.[133]

According to the radical critique, the "new middle class is closely linked with the administrative apparatus and partially with the political elite."[134] Moreover, the fact that many members of the middle class have a "bad conscience" about their wealth and influence may explain their tendency to downplay or disagree with the notion - by now quite firmly established by sociological studies - that Yugoslav society is stratified into classes. Faced with its incongruous position in a Marxist regime officially committed to the working class, the middle class seeks legitimacy by identifying itself with symbols of ethnic solidarity and by supporting the "homogenization of all inhabitants on a national basis" within the territorial units of the Yugoslav federation. Indeed, noting the political leverage enjoyed by middle class elements in the republican and provincial organizations of the Yugoslav League of Communists, one radical critic has suggested that it might be accurate to speak of "six or eight (middle bourgeois) classes and their parties."[135] The nationalistic "glorification of the past" and support for other "romantic notions" allegedly provide the middle class with an "ideological platform" in contrast to the official "proletarian platform." In the radical view, the middle class constantly refers to the tenets of Marxism and socialism while really wanting to rid itself and society from such beliefs. Enthusiasm for traditional ethnic appeals exemplified in concepts such as "pride," "honour," and "national inheritance" is said to be more popular among the humanistic intellectuals than within the technocratic segment of the middle class, or the so-called "techno-bureaucracy," although the latter group may be susceptible to nationalism "in a more modern attire." The technocratic strata is primarily devoted, however, to the economic aspects of bourgeois liberalism because, it is observed, "they sensed the prospects for oligarchic groups would be very bright in self-management so conceived."[136]

According to the radicals, neither elite rule, nor the embourgeoisment of Yugoslav socialism can be eliminated simply through "bureaucratic activism" which results in the periodic and piece-meal institutional reforms that have typically been made to the self-management system. The "endless reorganizations" of the governmental party and economic structures have actually created, it is argued, more "distance between the elite and masses," and produced an "esoteric institutional reality" that is only really understood and experienced by members of the elite.[137] The radicals advocate a fundamental transformation of the regime, including greatly expanded opportunities for citizen participation in decision-making at the middle and upper echelons of the political system (the partial effectiveness of enterprise self-management is generally conceded), a more extensive reduction and eventual elimination of conventional state administration, the replacement of the single party system by either a non-party arrangement or a multi-party system, and genuine protection of free expression and human rights. There is no "'iron law' or revolutionary degeneration" in the radical view, if the "revolutionary forces" are willing to wage a "persistent struggle" against statism.[138] The liberalizing efforts made by the Yugoslav regime up to now, such as the decentralization of the state, and the rotation of political activists and citizens through powerful state and party positions are seen as having a very limited impact:

> ... every criticism of bureaucracy ends on the ground of *the very bureaucracy* and by the very nature of things, remains illusor and impotent. In the final analysis there is no radical solution for in the best of cases it is possible to achieve only 'correction' of the work of the bureaucratic apparatus and 'greasing' of the state mechanism, a true *surpassing* of this historic category cannot be achieved. Even the thesis that in socialism 'all are bureaucrats, so that no one will be a bureaucrat' is precisely in this line .... The possibility that every citizen can become a state official shows that the official class is far from being a 'general class,' the class of the general interest. On the contrary, both before and after that the bureaucracy remains 'alien power,' the 'other sphere' and not the citizens' own sphere.[139]

In the radical vision of a socialist society the tasks of societal management must be performed by citizens serving in office for very short periods of time on a

The Socialist Pyramid: Elites and Power in Yugoslavia

strictly non-professional basis. "Self-governing institutions," writes Belgrade philosopher Mihajlo Marković, "presuppose the elimination of all ruling classes and elites." "Supreme" authority will exist in self-governing bodies, but their temporary representatives must not be allowed to enjoy any material privileges which would allow them to become an "alienated social elite."[140] Marković admits, however, that modern development has created new elites (political, managerial, military, etc.) which may not disappear even when all classes have been abolished.

> Any theory that tried to understand social inequalities only in terms of class differences fails to understand this phenomenon. This is part of the reason why many Marxists fail to give adequate accounts of social stratification in socialist countries .... The elite of political power is not the same as the ruling class. Political power is not always and simply the emanation of economic power.[141]

Although Yugoslavia's radical Marxist intellectuals have tended to focus on many of the same themes that were raised earlier by Milovan Djilas, they have generally avoided direct association with Tito's former associate or any reference to his publications.[142] Many regime officials have found it politically useful, however, to associate Djilas and the radical critics as part of a common threat to Yugoslav socialism. In 1967, for example, Vladimir Bakaric, a relatively moderate member of the party elite, sought to counteract intellectual attacks on what he called "our own bureaucracy," i.e., "the bureaucracy which arises in the class structure of our own society."

> State authorities must exist, their organizations must exist. The social stratum not employed in direct production must exist, i.e., that stratum which we may conditionally call bureaucracy. If, however, we proclaim this stratum to be a new class, then the consequence would be! Beat bureaucrats wherever you find them! Destroy them! .... This thesis which does not support Djilas fully, is nevertheless, reminiscent of his views, it is very prevelant, and leads, or proposes to lead, our development in the wrong direction.[143]

Yugoslav politicians and mainstream academics were especially sensitive to the assertion by *Praxis* group member, Svetozar Stojanović, that statist degeneration in systems like the USSR and even reformist Yugoslavia results not in aberrant forms of socialism, but in the formation of a new class, namely, the statist class. For example, the Belgrade sociologist, Miroslav Pečujlić, claimed that Stojanović's argument was nothing but a repetition of views advanced earlier by the one time American Trotskyist, James Burnham. Pečujlić also intimated that the radical version of a future self-governing society amounted to a new intellectual elitism which, he asserted, is actually the "twin" of bureaucracy in obstructing the rule of the working class.[144] Other party leaders took exception to the radicals' suggestion that the state in Yugoslavia needed to wither away at a faster pace. Thus in February 1973, Edward Kardelj, who had designed the regime's alternative to Djilas' heretical brand of debureaucratization, suggested that the state appartatus must protect the self-management system and help it to function. This continued role for the state administrative organs did not mean, Kardelj claimed, the existence of a "strong hand regime" by the authoritative bureaucracy, "but rather the cooperation of the state and self-managing organs in a system of mutual democratic responsibility." While a gradual reduction in the role of thestate may benefit the working class, Kardelj and like-minded party theorists argued, the same process also works to the advantage of the "techno-bureaucracy," or "technocratic class" made up of specialists concentrated in individual enterprises and institutions. An alliance between the workers and the technocrats would, it was feared, not only threaten the future of self-management but also the party itself. Moreover, Kardelj maintained, if Yugoslavia wished to avoid a return to a "state ownership and a state-capitalistic mode of economy," it must tolerate the existence of a market and the problem of social inequalities for some time to come.[145]

The endorsement by Kardelj and other regime spokesmen of a hybrid political system combining a state apparatus, a single party organization, a semi-market economy, and self-governing institutions, contrasted strongly with the type of socialist society envisioned by the radical Marxist intellectuals. In 1973, after years of sniping at the radicals, party conservatives finally succeeded in banning the journal *Praxis* and punishing several dissident radical theorists. Such repression, however, only exacerbated the ideological debate about the elitist and class features of Yugoslav socialism. Indeed, Kardelj himself in the last major theoretical statement of his career prepared in 1977, still seemed to be troubled by the problems which had been at the heart of his longstanding disagreement with Djilas and other Yugoslav "opportunists":

> ... although conflicts on the basis of social differences do not have the character of class conflicts, they nervertheless express differences in the direct interest of different parts of the working class .... There always exist conflicts which have a character of a class conflict, or potentially could assume such a character, namely the conflict between the working class and that part of it which, as Karl Marx put it, constitutes its own bureaucracy unsurping a monopoly of the dispostion of social capital: that conflict by itself does not make the bureaucracy a 'new class' but is expresses in productive relations elements of wage labour, or class relations. In fact, that is the most serious contradiction of contemporary socialist societies.[146]

The Socialist Pyramid: Elites and Power in Yugoslavia

The advent of the post-Tito era in May 1980, together with the serious deterioration of economic conditions which followed shortly in its wake, stimulated Yugoslav discussions concerning the character and problems of the self-management socialist system. While various differences still remained between radical and moderate critics of the regime, almost all Yugoslav political and sociological analysts entertained doubts about the capability of those individuals to rule the country. Strong policy divisions within the political leadership about the best way to deal with economic problems and to react to political dissent only intensified the criticism levelled at the regime. Tito's absence, together with the deaths of other major leaders from the older generation, such as Kardelj (1910-1979) and Bakarić (1912-1983), also seemed to increase the indecisiveness and vulnerability of the political elite. "In the past," observed the Zagreb historian Dušan Bilandžić, "it was Tito, Kardelj, and other leading personalities who made changes, but also halted them if things took the wrong direction. We do not have this sort of leading center now, something that is of enormous significance."[147] The rapid proliferation of studies which both criticized the country's economic and political situation, and suggested the adoption of possible solutions, spawned an entire new genre of analysis, which one observer referred to facetiously as "crisisology."[148]

During the post-Tito debate concerning Yugoslavia's internal "crisis," many of the country's prominent social scientists have adopted a somewhat less optimistic and sympathetic tone than in their earlier writings. A good deal of the blame for the regime's present difficulties is attributed to aspects of political elitism, privilege, and social inequality which have flourished within the framework of self-managing socialism. For example, the sociologist Radomir Lukić, who had argued in 1959 that bureaucratization and exploitation were only "temporary features" of Yugoslav socialism, concluded twenty-five years later that the incomplete implementation of self-management has created a "socialist bourgeoisie."

> Our organizations of associated labour [working enterprises] are in large measure privatized and social property within them transformed into petty ownership, of course not as individual ownership, but as collective ownership. But each of these collective petty owners exhibit all the basic characteristics of an individual "bourgeois," of a smallholder, only as a rule daubed in a socialist color ... the major portion of the socialist elite, or the leaders, the intelligentsia, are bureaucratized and either formally become petty owners, or if that isn't possible, they remain as such in a practical sense, securing different privileges for themselves, some justified, but some especially unjustified for socialism. As a general law those down below imitate what they see up above and therefore, according to the possibilities, they also join the bourgeoisie ... embour-

geoisment will be our fellow traveller for a long time to come.[149]

The political scientist, Najdan Pašić, reached similar conclusions about the configuration of power and wealth in Yugoslavia during the 1980's. While still rejecting the idea that the political leadership group is a new ruling class, Pašić nevertheless, maintains that a "stratum of political professionals and carriers of administrative functions in the economy and political system" display a "high level of internal coherence and cohesion of interests in relation to all other social groups including the working class."

> The legitimate influence and authority which draws its roots from the revolution and which renews itself on the basis of the unified, officially accepted ideology and the recognized status of representatives of the working class, secured for the administrative stratum a very stong total social position in contemporary Yugoslav society ... the power and influence of the professional political-administrative stratum also has its powerful material underpinning, that is the quasi-property relations toward the holding of the means of production, toward social capital. Those who administer all those means de facto possess enormous social power - the power of ruling the material conditions of existence.[150]

Many Yugoslav analysts have concluded that decentralization and the operation of the federal system have failed to obstruct bureaucratization and the concentration of political power, as previously had been hoped, and instead have resulted in a simply more enlightened or diffused form of statism than exists in other communist regimes. Under what is variously termed "polycentric statism," "republican-provincial statism," or "decentralized statism," it is alleged that political and economic power has gravitated into the hands of regional and local elites whose "delegated" representatives constitute the different contingents of the political elite on the federal level. The Zagreb sociologist Josip Županov, for example, takes issue with Kardelj's 1977 assertion that Yugoslav socialism has transcended "classical political pluralism" by establishing a "truly *self-managing political pluralism*."

> Speaking completely openly, we have only implemented a pluralism of self-managing interests as a pluralism of republican and communal elites and their enterprises. That is what pluralism is in our country. We simply don't recognize any kind of vertical expression of self-management ....
> We have created a decentralization of elites, a decentralization of the politocracy, and that isn't a problem of federalism or confederalism, nor even of national economics, but rather it is a class problem. The basic cause of the crisis is in the monopoly of elites who don't for one moment

have a serious intention to develop the path of self-management. Fundamentally the politocracy doesn't wish to give up its monopoly over surplus labour, over ideology, and over decision-making.[151]

Other Yugoslav social scientists, and especially members of the radical intellectual community, have been even more scathing in their assessments of the regime's weaknesses. Miroslav Živković, for example, argues that the crisis faced by Yugoslavia in the 1980's (including an enormous foreign debt, the return of a million "guestworkers" from Germany, a million unemployed young people, and deep social and regional inequalities) cannot be solved by the further development of self-management. The claim that "underdeveloped self-management" and statism are responsible for the country's problems is, according to Živković, a "myth" or some kind of "bugaboo." "It is not possible to build self-managing socialism through a combination of party monism and economic pluralism." Moreover, he maintains, the party's claim to be the vanguard of the working class is premised on a number of false assumptions, namely, that the League of Communists is infallible, that it has "distanced itself from power," and that it functions along the principles of democratic centralism. With regard to the last claim, Živković points out that according to present party procedures, the members of the Central Committee are elected by the party Congress, but their manadate can be terminated by the Central Committee itself. "In this way the core of the party leadership ensures obedience of all members of the Central Committee, and its control over the whole party." Such procedures allow "metropolitan" party leaders at different levels of the federation, rather than the working class, to dominate the decision-making process.[152] Professor Slobodan Inić of Belgrade University, has suggested that Yugoslavia's communist rulers, or a group he describes as the "politocrats" and "socialist private owners," have enriched themselves at the expense of the people they govern. In a special kind of "class struggle" against the party bureaucracy, the working class has reduced its productivity and along with the elite seeks opportunities to engage in various forms of illegal economic behaviour. Not only is this non-violent "struggle" destroying the economy, but also "theoretically," Inić facetiously observes, "one day a purely 'non-exploitative state of affairs' might emerge in which politocrats could no longer have anything left to take away from the people."[153] Members of the former *Praxis* group have also joined in the recent outpouring of commentaries on the Yugoslav economic and political crisis. For example, at a national meeting of over 250 sociologists held in November 1983, Rudi Supek, the former editor-in chief of *Praxis*, claimed that Yugoslavia exhibited the "total bureaucratization of a socialist society" and that "the worst and most incapable" individuals are being chosen for the most responsible positions. Professor Ivan Kuvacić told the audience that the Yugoslav "state is indeed dying, but in the wrong way. The state is losing its coordinating and planning function, while its repressive functions are growing, particularly at the republican level." Svetozar Stojanović proposed a comprehensive program of political reforms for the country and observed that "without radical democratization, the Communist party would only be able to retain its role by naked force."[154] Elsewhere Stojanović was even more emphatic about the weaknesses of the regime.

> If things continue to develop in Yugoslavia as they have done up to now, the last ground for legitimizing party rule will disappear .... It is inadmissible to attribute past successes to the country's leading politicians while blaming the people for the present crisis .... The political system as such is the main root of the Yugoslav crisis. The main contradiction of the system is the fact that the competition required by the market economy has been advanced, but at the same time the monopoly of the nomenklatura has been retained.[155]

The regime's conservative officials and their supporters have reacted sharply to the recent chorus of criticism directed against the party and the self-management system. For example, in 1985, Branko Mikulić, a party leader from Bosnia (who was elected Prime Minister in 1986 for a two year term) attacked those oppositional forces who advocate a "third Yugoslavia" without the Communists, or who want to carry out "de-Titoization and de-Kardeljization" through the introduction of a multi-party system.[156] Many top party leaders have called for more discipline in the political system through a full fledged implementation of democratic centralism which makes leadership decisions binding upon the membership. In a rather revealing illustration of elite insecurity one party leader suggested that in view of recent attacks on the party's legitimacy "as the vanguard of the revolution ... we see how farsighted it was to build the role of the League of Communists into our Constitution."[157] Some conservative leaders often deflect responsibility for the current economic crisis onto the republican-provincial "technocracy" and other "autarkic forces" connected with nationalistic and local interests. Other party officials have also charged that the country's economic crisis is being exploited and exacerbated by various "rightist elements," and that a close connection exists between the ideas of the dissident Marxist intellectuals and various "anti-socialist forces." In May 1984, the Croatian party official and political sociologist, Stipe Šuvar, himself a frequent critic of social and political inequalities, castigated those who had demeaned Tito's memory and questioned the hegemony of the League of Communists. Speaking in Zagreb, Šuvar provided members of the Croatian Central Committee with a long inventory of epithets which dissidents have used to deride communist "activists." The terms in his list reveal the depth of strong feeling against the regime, and are reminiscent of the inflamatory language used by Marx against political and state officials over a century earlier.

The Socialist Pyramid: Elites and Power in Yugoslavia

> The new class; a group of inciters; the jailers; hooded crows; censors; the idiots; monsters; microphone powerholders; old men; the mandarins of conservatism; dustcloths in the form of human beings; professional ideological governors and commissars; people who chew documents prepared by political leaders; spiritual janissaries; ideological pagan priests; commissars for the sciences, literature and the arts; vulgar materialists; feeble followers of empty apologists and dogmatists; leaders of Zhdanovite ideas, the Cerberuses of spritual life, modern sycophants; self-appointed ideological and solicitious spirits; the careerist swindlers, etc.[158]

Šuvar called for an ideological struggle against such defamatory ideas, but proudly emphasized that their existence demonstrated the freedom of expression which currently exists in Yugoslavia.

Faced with a serious crisis atmosphere, as well as by a constant stream of attacks on their legitimacy and abilities, some party leaders adopted a quite candid and self-critical tone. A member of the party's Central Committee Presidium on the federal level, for example, pointed out that the League of Communists has a "political monopoly" and all the characteristics of "a party in power, a leading party in a one-party system." The "main force the party relies upon," he added, "is not the working class and the workers, but on the state, or to be more precise the administrative apparatus - from management organs in associated labour to executive organs in communes, republics, and the Federation."[159] At a July 1985 Central Committee meeting held in Belgrade, another top official conceded that although the same individuals no longer jointly held posts in both the party and state structures - the so-called "personal accumulation of functions" - there was, nevertheless, a "powerful" tendency toward the "horizontal rotation of cadres from the party into the state and visa-versa" which perpetuated the statist character of the political system.[160] In the mid-1980's, Yugoslav politicians not only admitted to serious problems with their efforts to transcend traditional models of state and party control, but suggested that such difficulties would not be likely to diminish in importance. For example, in a fascinating interview about his political career, Mitija Ribičič, a member of the liberal wing in the Central Committee who previously served as both Party President (1982-1983) and Prime Minister (1969-1971), pointed out that the political system not only suffered from a linkage between the party and the state, but also from the pressure to maintain consensus in all political organizations. Kardelj's pluralism of self-managing interests would never be achieved, according to Ribičič, until both majority and minority opinions were officially permitted in the party (a point frequently advanced by the radical theorists). He also explained that most of his political life had been spent in a "circle of comrades" and that his contact with the "masses" had actually been limited to "contacts with the leading aktivs of a certain locality or economic organization" during prearranged visits in which everything was put in the best possible light. "I believe," Ribičič added, "that all this ... is too little for a link between politics and the people, too little to feel the pulse and take the temperature of our people's mind, will and interests." Moreover, he expressed doubt about the constant official claims that self-management would eventually eliminate traditional forms of state power or the practice of politics as a profession.

> I believe we will be satisfied if we can prevent an increase in the number of professional politicans. For at least 25 years or more we have written obituaries to the state, yet the state is still very much alive and is even increasing its influence on all levels ranging from the commune to the federation. Modern society also needs a modern capable administration.[161]

As socialist Yugoslavia approaches the last decade of the 20th century, the issues of political elitism and bureaucratization remain highly pertinent and troublesome. Whether sympathetic or opposed to the present regime, almost all Yugoslav analysts have come to recognize and raise "open questions" about the social and political inequalities which obstruct the development of their socialist system.[162] Together with serious economic difficulties and enduring ethnic conflicts, the reality of rule by a Marxist political "class" or "elite" continues to cloud the theory and practice of Yugoslav self-management.[163] The views and concepts of Milovan Djilas, while still anathema in official circles and intellectually unpopular have, nevertheless, been largely confirmed by the research findings and observations of his own countrymen. Djilas, certainly the most famous living Yugoslav in the post-Tito era, is only a small thorn in the side of the regime, but his ideas about a socialist new class have become the guilty conscience of his former comrades and their heirs.[164] Distinguished among the communist party-states for its highly innovative arrangements to combat elitism and bureaucracy, the Yugoslav regime and its many internal critics continue to struggle with their respective "illusions about domination."

NOTES: CHAPTER ONE

1. The conceptualization of "the political elite" in this book follows Harold Lasswell's view that "a term like 'leaders' or leadership carries the connotation of persons who are affirmatively engaged in politics; and the connotation is convenient. The political elite, on the contrary, are not necessarily active participants at a given moment. We think of the power elite as the collectivity from which active decision-makers are drawn during particular periods in the life of a body politic. Not all members of a 'ruling family' try to rule; nor do they necessarily rule all the time." See Harold Lasswell, "Introduction: The Study of Political Elites,"*World Revolutionary Elites*, eds. Harold Lasswell and Daniel Lerner (Cambridge: MIT Press, 1965), 12. A related definition of "national elites" also parallels the usage in this book: "persons with power individually, regularly, and seriously to affect political outcomes at the macro-level of organized societies ... persons capable, if they wish of making substantial trouble for high officials (i.e., other elite persons who happen to be the incumbents of authoritative positions) without being promptly repressed. In this sense the elite consists not only of prestigious, relatively 'established leaders' - such as recognized politicians - but also in various degrees in different societies of relatively transitory and less individually known leaders of mass organizations such as trade union leaders, some intellectuals, and other persons leading various organized interest categories." John Highly, *et. al., Elite Structure and Ideology* (New York: Columbia University Press, 1976), 17-18. For a survey of the conceptual electicism and ambiguity in elite research see Paolo Zannoni, "The Concept of Elites," *European Journal of Political Research*, VI, No. 1 (March, 1978), 1-30.

2. Lawrence Harris, V.G. Kiernin, and Ralph Milibrand (eds.), *A Dictionary of Marxist Thought* (Cambridge: Harvard University Press, 1983), 145-146. Donald MacRae has put the problem more starkly: "Marxists are hostile to elite analysis. Their thought would on the one hand repudiate as needless an account of minority rule in a society which is not based on a theory of economic class .... On the other hand their utopianism rejects any suggestion that elites are or can be permanent features of social relations and politics in complex societies .... By putting the future majority on the side of communism, communist eschatology is the fig leaf of elitism now." "Notes on Elites," *Comparative Government and Politics*, eds.

Dennis Kavanagh and Gillian Peele (Boulder: Westview Press, 1984), 151-152, 154.

3. Karl Marx and Frederick Engels, *Writings on the Paris Commune*, ed. Hal Draper (New York: Monthly Review Press, 1971), *passim*, as for the following quotes in this paragraph.

4. *Ibid.*, 200.

5. *Ibid.*, 75, 157.

6. Marx, Engels, Lenin, *Anarchism and Anarcho-Syndicalism* (New York: International Publishers, 1972), 150-151. See also Marx's, "Conspectus of Bakunin's State and Anarchy," published in *Marx-Engels Werke*, Volume XVIII (Berlin: Dietz Verlag, 1964), 636.

7. For the argument that Marx and Engels opposed the development of any kind of "revolutionary elitism" and the "evident hypocrisy" in Bakunin's "public anti-authoritatianism," see Richard N. Hunt, *The Political Ideas of Marx and Engels* (Pittsburgh: University of Pittsburgh Press, 1984), 316-324.

8. Karl Marx and Frederick Engels, *Writings on the Paris Commune*, 32.

9. On this point see Monty Johnstone, "Marx, Blanqui and Majority Rule," *The Socialist Register 1983*, eds. Ralph Milibrand and Jack Saville (London: The Merlin Press, 1983), 304-305.

10. Marx, Engels, Lenin, *Anarchism and Anarcho-Syndicalism*, 103.

11. Sam Dolgoff (ed.), *Bakunin On Anarchy* (New York: Alfred A. Knopf, 1972), 343-344.

12. Max Nomad, *Apostles of Revolution* (New York: Collier Books, 1961), 202, note 12. See also, Woodford D. McClellan, *Svetozar Markovic and the Origins of Balkan Socialism* (Princeton: Princeton University Press, 1964), 187-191.

13. James E. Conner (ed.), *Lenin on Politics and Revolution: Selected Writings* (New York: Pegasus, 1968), 31-78, and *passim*.

14. V.I. Lenin. *The State and Revolution* (Moscow: The Foreign Languages Publishing House, n.d.), 188, 198.

15. Robert C. Tucker (ed.), *The Lenin Anthology* (New York: Norton and Company, 1975), 566-572.

16. *Ibid.*, 716-717.

17. V.I. Lenin, *Selected Works, Volume IX* (New York: International Publishers, 1937), 9-10, 70.

18. Robert C. Tucker (ed.), *The Lenin Anthology*, 401, 404.

19. V.I. Lenin, *Collected Works, Volume XLV* (Moscow: The Foreign Languages Publishing House, 1960), 64-165.

20. V.I. Lenin, *Selected Works*, 4, 6, 70.

21. *Ibid.*, 322, 328, and V.I. Lenin, *On the Intelligentsia* (Moscow: Progress Publishers, 1983), 157, 278-279. On November 13, 1922, in one of his last reports, Lenin observed: "we took over the old machinery of state and that was our misfortune ... we now have a vast army of government employees, but lack sufficiently educated forces to exercise real control over them."

22. Guenther Roth and Claus Wittich (eds.), *Max Weber, Economy and Society* (New York: Bedminster Press, 1968), 1414.

23. Walter Garrison Runciman, *Max Weber, Selections in Translation* (London: Cambridge University Press, 1978), 260, and Talcott Parsons (ed.), *Max Weber: The Theory of Social and Economic Organization* (New York: The Free Press, 1964), 339. Weber observes (337) that should a socialist economy achieve a level of technical efficiency comparable to a capitalist system "it would mean a tremendous increase in the importance of specialized bureaucracy."

24. Guenther Roth and Claus Wittich (eds.), *Max Weber, Economy and Society*, 1402. Wolfgang J. Mommsen has observed that "a modern theory of socialism must, above all, be able to handle the problem of how economic decision-making can be effectively controlled by the people at large instead of falling into the hands of indecisive bureaucrats or new authoritarian elites. In this respect, Weber's analyses deserve even the attention of those who do not share his

Lenard J. Cohen

convictions." "Capitalism and Socialism: Weber's Dialogue with Marx," *A Weber-Marx Dialogue*, eds. Robert J. Antonio and Ronald M. Glassman (Lawrence: University Press of Kansas, 1985), 256. For a similar view see Frank Parkin, *Max Weber* (London: Tavistock Publications, 1982), 104.

25. Hans Gerth and C. Wright Mills, *From Max Weber: Essays in Sociology* (New York: Oxford University Press, 1958), 232.

26. Guenther Roth and Claus Wittich (eds.), *Max Weber, Economy and Society*, 988.

27. Cited in Anthony Giddens, *Politics and Sociology in the Thought of Max Weber* (New York: Macmillan, 1972), 17-18.

28. See Eric Olin Wright, "To Control or To Smash Bureaucracy: Weber and Lenin on Politics, The State, and Bureaucracy," *Berkeley Journal of Sociology*, XIX (1974-1975), 69-108, and by the same author, *Class, Crisis and the State* (London: NLB, 1978), 194-225.

29. Reinhard Bendix and Guether Roth, *Scholarship and Partisanship: Essays on Max Weber* (Berkeley: University of California Press, 1971), 248-249.

30. Talcott Parsons (ed.) *Max Weber: The Theory of Social and Economic Organization*, 415.

31. *Ibid.*, 413, 415.

32. Vilfredo Pareto, *The Rise and Fall of Elites: An Application of Theoretical Sociology*, ed. Hans L. Zetterberg (Totowa, N.J.: The Bedminster Press, 1968), 8, 36.

33. *Les systèmes socialistes* (Paris, 1902), summarized in Raymond Aron, *Main Currents in Sociological Thought*, Volume II (Garden City: Doubleday, 1970), 182. See also, James Hans Meisel, *Pareto and Mosca* (Englewood Cliffs, N.J.: Prentice Hall, 1965), 8-14.

34. Gaetano Mosca, *The Ruling Class: Elementi Di Scienza Politica*, ed. Arthur Livingston (New York: McGraw Hill, 1939), 280, 485. Mosca also observed (486-487) that: "An experiment in so-called 'moderate socialism,' which would allow private property to exist

provisionally and nominally but would subject it to such burdens and limitations as to deprive it of significance ... would either degenerate into pure communism, or merely lead to a development of the present political and economic system into a bureaucratic and military dictatorship." See also, James Hans Meisel, *The Myth of the Ruling Class: Gaetano Mosca and the 'Elite'* (Ann Arbor: The University of Michigan Press, 1958).

35. Robert Michels, *Political Parties* (New York: Dover Publications, 1959). Michels saw no "essential contradiction" between elite theory and Marxist class theory: "The principle that one dominant class inevitably succeeds another, and that oligarchy is, as it were, a preordained form of the common life of great social aggregates, far from conflicting or replacing the materialist conception of history, completes that conception and reinforces it" (390).

36. The ideas Michels formulated in 1908-1909 are discussed and documented in A. James Gregor, *Italian Fascism and Developmental Dictatorship* (Princeton: Princeton University Press, 1979), 50-51. In 1908, Max Weber had written Michels that "every idea of eliminating the domination of man by man through any form of social system (however socialistic) or through ever so meticulously devised forms of 'democracy' is utopian." Wolfgang J. Mommson, "Capitalism and Socialism: Weber's Dialogue with Marx," 260, note 53. Michels dedicated his 1911 classic, *Political Parties*, to Max Weber.

37. Robert Michels, *Political Parties*, 365-376. Michels' earlier ideas on this theme are discussed in David Beetham, "From Socialism to Fascism: The Relation Between Theory and Practice in the Work of Robert Michels," *Political Studies*, XXV, No. 1 (1977), 3-24 and in No. 2 of the same Volume, 161-181. R.J. Bennett has criticized Beetham for overemphasizing Michels' role as a "fascist ideologue" and the connection of elite theory with fascism. According to Bennett, elite theory usefully raises the question of whether "modern industrial societies and parties are compatible, or can be made compatible, with the goals of democracy and socialism." "The Elite Theory as Fascist Ideology - A Reply to Beetham's Critique of Robert Michels," *Political Studies*, XXVI, No. 4 (1977), 474-488.

38. Robert Michels, *First Lectures in Political Sociology*, trans., Alfred de Grazia (New York: Harper and Row, 1965), 163.

39. A very eclectic and creative mixture of the ideas explored by Marx, Weber, and the classical elitists is relfected in the elite research of C. Wright Mills. Variously referred to as a "post-Weberian," a "radical Weberian," a "post-Marxian," and a "non-dogmatic Marxist," Mills argued that "merely to study elite groups is not automatically to accept some one definite theory of elites.... Pareto's theory of the circulation of the elite? I don't accept that. Michels' iron law of oligarchy? I think it's a fairly good description of what has in fact happened in most mass organizations.... The study of elites does not rule out an acceptance of the kind of structural view one finds for example in Marx. In fact one must pay attention to both." "Comment on Criticism," G. William Domhoff and Hoyt B. Ballard, *C. Wright Mills and the Power Elite* (Boston: Beacon Press, 1968), 247-248. Near the end of his life Mills sketched plans for a study of the Soviet elite. During a visit to the USSR, he asked a Soviet newspaper editor "the Marxist questions, are there any since Lenin ... give me an example?" Unsatisfied with his respondent's abstract answers regarding peace, war, and co-existence, Mills commented: "these are policies, not theories .... Anything on the theory of state power?" Irving Louis Horowitz, *C. Wright Mills: An American Utopian* (New York: The Free Press, 1983), 309-310.

40. Machajski's ideas are explored in Max Nomad, *Aspects of Revolt* (New York: The Noonday Press, 1959), 96-117.

41. *Ibid*, 115.

42. *Ibid*. See Paul Avrich, "What is Macheavism?" *Soviet Studies*, No. 17 (1965), 66-75, and Marshall Shatz, "Jan Waclaw Machajski: The Conspiracy of Intellectuals," *Survey*, No. 62 (January, 1967), 45-57.

For a less flattering portrait of Machajski's opposition to a "new class" of intellectuals detaling his support for the proto-facist Black Hundreds, and his contempt for "all democratic intitutions, see Ernst Haberkern, "Machajsky: A Rightfully Forgotten Prophet," *Telos*, No. 71 (Spring, 1987), 111-128.

43. Dick Howard (ed.) *Selected Political Writings of Rosa Luxembourg* (New York: Monthly Review Press, 1971), *passim*.

44. Rosa Luxembourg, *The Russian Revolution and Leninism or Marxism?* (Ann Arbor: University of Michigan Press, 1961), 71-72.

45. Leon Trotsky, *Our Political Tasks* (London: New Park Publications, n.d.), 76-77, 87, and Robert V. Daniels (ed.), *A Documentary History of Communism, Volume I* (New York: Vintage, 1962), 32-33.

46. In his autobiography written in exile, Trotsky mentions his own and Lenin's exposure to the ideas of Waclaw Machajski at the turn of the century. Trotsky claims ironically, that Machajski had arrived at "the amazing conclusion that socialism is a social order based on the exploitation of the workers by a professional intelligentsia." *My Life* (New York: Universal Library, 1930), 129, 143.

47. Leon Trotsky, *The Revolution Betrayed* (New York: Merit Publishers, 1965), 55, 265-279, and *passim*. See also, David Lovell, *Trotsky's Analysis of Soviet Bureaucratization* (London: Croom Helm, 1985), 36-57, and Martin Krygler, "Bureaucracy in Trotsky's Analysis of Stalinism," *Socialism and the New Class: Towards the Analysis of Structural Equality within Socialist Societies*, ed. Martin Sawer (Adelaide: Australian Political Studies Association, 1978), Monograph No. 19, 46-67.

48. See Max Nomad, *Aspects of Revolt*, 116, and Stephen Cohen, *Bukharian and the Bolshevik Revolution* (Oxford: Oxford University Press, 1980), 143-144.

49. Christian Rakovsky, "Bureaucracy and the Soviet State," *Essential Works of Socialism*, ed. Irving Howe (New York: Bantam Books, 1971), 371. Rakovsky's views on the Soviet system were drawn on extensively by Trotsky in *The Revolution Betrayed*, 100-103.

50. For an excellent analysis of these ideas in Trotskyist circles see Adam Westoby's "Introduction" in Bruno Rizzi, *The Bureaucratization of the World, The USSR: Bureaucratic Collectivism* (London: Tavistock Publications, 1985), 1-33. It is ironic that Ramon Mercader, the NKVD agent who assassinated Trotsky in August 1940, gained access to his victim by proposing to discuss with him the dispute among American Trotskyists about whether or not the Soviet Union could accurately be described as a workers' state. Paolo Spriano, *Stalin and the European Communists*, (London: Verso, 1985), 146.

51. Nikolai Bukharin and E. Preobrazhensky, *The ABC of Communism* (London: Penguin Books, 1970), 237.

52. Nikolai Bukharin, *Historical Materialism: A System of Sociology* (Ann Arbor: University of Michigan Press, 1969), 310-311.

53. Cited in Michael Haynes, *Nikolai Bukharin and the Transition from Capitalism to Socialism* (London: Croon Helm, 1985), 124, note 10.

54. N.I. Bukharin, *Selected Writings on the State and the Transition to Socialism*, ed. Richard B. Day (Armonk, New York: M.E. Sharpe, 1982), 338-339, 346-347.

55. *Selections from the Prison Notebooks of Antonio Gramsci*, (eds. and trans.) Quentin Hoare and Geoffrey Nowell Smith (New York: International Publisher, 1971), 144.

56. *Ibid.*, 6, 150.

57. *Ibid.*, 300-301, 334-335.

58. *Ibid.*, 12.

59. *Ibid.*, 10, 15-16, 340.

60. *Ibid.*, 269.

61. *Ibid.*, 3-23. For the influence of elite theory on Gramsci see Giorgio Galli, "Gramsci e le teorie delle 'elites'," *Gramsci e la Cultura Contemporanea, Volume II* (Rome: Ediotori Riuniti-Instituto), 1975, 201-217. I would like to thank Annamarie Oliverio for her translation of the preceding article.

62. *Against Fragmentation: The Origins of Marxism and the Sociology of Intellectuals* (New York: Oxford University Press, 1985), 6. According to Gouldner: "Marxism is only about but not by the proletariat." Historically Marxism has been an ideology of "an elite without power ... subordinated to other elites ... an elite without riches .... Yet for all that an elite with great expectations" (32-35).

63. There is a voluminous post-World War II literature on class power and elite rule in socialist regimes. In addition to works already cited the most important theoretical issues are discussed in David Lane, "The End of Inequality," *Class Status and Power Under State Socialism* (London: George Allen and Unwin, 1982), and Lane's "The Structure of Soviet Socialism: Recent Western Theoretical Approaches," *The Insurgent Sociologist* (Winter-Spring, 1984), 101-112, Donald C. Hodges, *The Bureaucratization of Socialism* (Amherst: The University of Massachusetts Press, 1981), Archie Brown, "Political Power and the Soviet State: Western and Soviet Perspective," ed. Neil Harding, *The State in Socialist Society* (London: Macmillan Press, 1984), 51-103, Maria Hirszowicz, *The Bureaucratic Leviathan: A Study in the Sociology of Communism* (Oxford: Martin Robertson, 1980), Anthony Giddens and David Held (eds.), *Classes, Power, and Conflict: Classical and Contemporary Debates* (Berkeley: University of California Press), 1982, and Giddens', *A Contemporary Critique of Historical Materialism* (London: Macmillan, 1981), Frank Parkin, *Marxism and Class Theory: A Bourgeois Critique* (New York: Columbia University Press, 1979), Ralph Milibrand, *Marxism and Politics* (London: Oxford University Press, 1977), and Milibrand's *Class Power and State Power* (London: Verso, 1983), Alvin Gouldner, *The Future of Intellectuals and the Rise of the New Class* (New York: Oxford University Press, 1979), and Frederic L. Pryor, "The 'New Class': Analysis of the Concept, the Hypothesis, and the Idea as a Research Tool," *American Journal of Economics and Sociology*, XL, No. 4 (October, 1981), 366-379.

East European Marxists (outside Yugoslavia, which will be discussed in the next section) have also made an important contribution to this debate. See, for example, Wladyslaw Bienkowski, *Theory and Reality* (London: Allison and Busby, 1981), Marx Rakovski, *Toward an East European Marxism* (London: Allison and Busby, 1978), Gyorgy Konrad and Ivan Szelenyi, *The Intellectuals on the Road to Class Power* (New York: Harcourt Brace Jovanovich, 1979), Rudo Bahro, *The Alternative in Eastern Europe* (London: New Left Books, 1978), and Ferrenc Feher, Agnes Heller, and Gyorgy Markus, *Dictatorship Over Needs* (Oxford: Basil Blackwell, 1983). The Polish sociologist Wodzimierz Wesolowski, has drawn attention to the "theoretical and practical gains" to be achieved from research on elites while still taking account of "the full Marxist heritage." The argument that capitalist systems are ruled by a power elite, while in socialist systems it is the working class that governs, creates, in his opinion, "intellectual confusion" among Marxists and facilitates "the theoretical victory of their opponents." Under both capitalism and socialism, Wesolowski argues, "the direct government of a country is a task carried out by a specialized group of people ... the existence of such a group can be seen as a functional necessity of contemporary societies ... in both systems there exists power elites or political elites." *Classes, Strata, and Power* (London: Routledge and Kegan Paul, 1979), 119-120. See also Jerzy Wiatr, "Political Elites and Political Leadership: Conceptual Problems and Selected Hypotheses for Comparative Research," *Indian Journal of Politics*, No. 7 (1973), 137-149.

64. Yugoslavia's interwar history and elite structure are discussed more fully in Chapter 2.

65. The quotations in the following discussion of interwar Yugoslav sociology are drawn from Milovan Mitrović, *Jugoslovenska predratna sociologija* (Belgrade: SSO Srbije, 1982), 98-112, 164-180, 206-222.

66. *Ibid.*, 209.

67. Ante Ciliga, *The Russian Enigma* (London: George Routledge and Sons, 1940), 117-118.

68. *La Yugoslavie sous la menace intérieure et extérieure* (Paris: Les Iles D'or, 1951), 30.

69. Cited in Gojko Miljanić, *Rukovodjenje komandovanje u oslobodilačkom ratu, 1941-1945* (Belgrade: Vojnoistorijski institut, 1980), 228. Miljanović's study provides a well-documented portrait of the growth of elite privileges and bureaucracy in the Partisan movement. Elsewhere he points out that although the senior officers "emerged from the ranks of the fighters and were of the same social origins, many officers managed to quickly forget that." *Kadrovi revolucije, 1941-1945* (Cetinje: Obod, 1975), 350.

70. Vladimir Dedijer, Momčilo Stefanović, Mirjana Stojanović and Rudolf Rizman (eds.), *Svedočanstva o drugom svetskom ratu* (Belgrade: Narodna knjiga/Partizanska knjiga, 1980), 351. The statute of the Partisan movement's "Proletarian National Liberation Shock Brigades" called for "iron discipline" and "the strict unconditional execution of the orders of military superiors and political

leaders," adding, however, that "between the commanders and fighters, there should be a real comradely relationship." The "command sector" of each brigade was composed of a commander, a political commissar, and their deputies. "The commanders," the statute emphasized, "are independent in directing operations after the passing of decisions and drawing up plans. The political commissars are the souls of the units. They are representatives of the people and guardians of the people's interests ...." "Selected Documents on the National Liberation War," *Yugoslav Survey*, XXVI, No. 2 (May, 1985), 16-17.

71. Edward Kardelj, *Reminiscences* (London: Blond and Briggs, 1982), 228-229.

72. *Ibid.*, 122.

73. *Ibid.*, 233.

74. A. Ross Johnson, *The Transformation of Communist Ideology: The Yugoslav Case, 1945-1953* (Cambridge, Mass.: MIT Press, 1972), 114.

75. Edward Kardelj, *Reminiscences*, 123, 242-243.

76. A collection of essays devoted to different facets of Kardelj's political legacy and a bibliography of his writings from 1928 to 1978 are found in a special issue of *Arhiv za pravne i društvene nauke*, LXV, Nos. 1-2 (January-June, 1979).

77. Cited in A. Ross Johnson, *The Transformation of Communist Ideology*, 100-103.

78. Cited in John McDonald, Jr. *Political Themes in the Thought of Milovan Djilas* (Ph.D. Dissertation, Columbia University, 1971), 165-166.

79. *Ibid.*, 159.

80. Milovan Djilas, *Rise and Fall* (New York: Harcourt Brace Jovanovich, 1985), 17, 73.

81. A. Ross Johnson, *The Transformation of Communist Ideology*, 103-104.

82. Michael and Deborah Milenkovitch (eds.), *Milovan Djilas: Parts of a Lifetime* (New York: Harcourt Brace Jovanovich, 1975), 172-173.

83. *Ibid.*, 174-177.

84. A. Ross Johnson, *The Transformation of Communist Ideology*, 107-112.

85. *Ibid.*, 109.

86. Michael and Deborah Milenkovitch, *Milovan Djilas: Parts of a Lifetime*, 182.

87. A. Ross Johnson, *The Transformation of Communist Ideology*, 106-107.

88. Milovan Djilas, *Rise and Fall*, 71.

89. Abraham Rothberg, *Anatomy of a Moral: The Political Essays of Milovan Djilas* (London: Thames and Hudson, 1959), 107. "Once," Djilas claims (109), "men gave everything, even life itself, to become professional revolutionaries. They were indispensable to social progress. Today they are obstacles to it."

90. *Ibid.*, 99. "I was," Djilas observed recently, "a believer in Communism when it was not a form of manipulation. But when I saw it was not realistic and a mere struggle for power among a small elite I became disenchanted." *Foreign Broadcast Information Service Daily Bulletin, Eastern Europe*, (July 1, 1986), I10.

91. Abraham Rothberg, *Anatomy of a Moral*, 165, 145-176, and passim.

92. Michael and Deborah Milenkovitch, *Milovan Djilas: Parts of a Lifetime*, 228.

93. Milovan Djilas, *Tito* (New York: Harcourt Brace Jovanovich, 1980), 109, 158-159. Djilas argues that his own range and freshness as a theoretician threatened Kardelj: "he knew that in a monopolistic hierarchy a weakening of his role would automatically mean a weakening of his authority .... Kardelj practiced the theory of truth, that without organization and without power, ideas are little

The Socialist Pyramid: Elites and Power in Yugoslavia

more than a pipe dream. He was posed between dictatorial power and dreams of freedom."

94. Milovan Djilas, *Rise and Fall*, 363.

95. *Ibid.*, 386.

96. Milovan Djilas, *The New Class* (New York: Praeger, 1957), 36, 38, 40, 57.

97. Milovan Djilas, *The Unperfect Society: Beyond the New Class* (New York: Harcourt, Brace and World, 1969), 176.

98. Milovan Djilas, *The New Class*, 35, 44.

99. Michael Charlton (ed.), *The Eagle and the Small Birds* (Chicago: The University of Chicago Press, 1984), 113. The higher echelons of communist regimes, Djilas has also argued, see to it that "the appearance of social property is preserved; but the granting of rewards and privileges to one's own Party cadres is also preserved. Disregard of the market in the appointing and rewarding of officials is the reason for the horrendously unsuccessful management found in socialist countries. In 'self-managing', 'market economy' Yugoslavia, this policy has gone so far that even cleaning women are required to have 'moral/political suitability'. Graft and cliquishness, protectionism, and 'connections' are built into the system, arising as they do, from the privileges accruing to ideological Party membership." Milovan Djilas, *Of Prisons and Ideas* (San Diego: Harcourt Brace Jovanovich, 1986), 143.

100. Milovan Djilas, *The New Class*, 39, 50.

101. Michael and Deborah Milenkovitch, *Milovan Djilas: Parts of a Lifetime*, 333.

102. Milovan Djilas, *The Unperfect Society*, 9-10.

103. Milovan Djilas, *Tito*, 167. Djilas is usually credited with popularizing the concept of a "new class" in the English language, although Daniel Moynihan has facetiously also taken credit: "it could be I was the first to use the 'The New Class' in the sense which appears to have found acceptance over here. It seemed to me that Djilas was simply discovering the bourgeoisie - nothing new save perhaps in

Serbia." B. Bruce-Briggs, "An Introduction to the Ideas of the New Class," *The New Class?* (New Brunswick, N.J.: Transaction Books, 1979), 17, note 1. A useful and brief survey of the new class concept is in Martin Sawer, "Theories of the New Class from Bakunin to Kuron and Modzelewski: The Morphology of Permanent Protest," *Socialism and the New Class: Toward the Analysis of Structural Inequality Within Socialist States*, 3-14. See also Frederic L. Pryor, "The 'New Class': Analysis of the Concept, the Hypothesis and the Ideas as a Research Tool."

104. *Večernije novosti*, (April 14, 1983), cited in Slobodan Stankovic, "Detention of Djilas Seen as a Warning to the Opposition," *Radio Free Europe RAD Background, Yugoslavia, No. 176* (May 11, 1984), 3. "It isn't accidental," wrote one leading Yugoslav politician, "that in the centers of world reaction Djilas' 'New Class' was quickly translated into many languages as an anti-communist bible, and distributed throughout the world, but particularly in countries engaged in the anti-colonial revolution." Dušan Dragosavac, *Aktualni aspekti nacionalnog pitanja i Jugoslavija* (Zagreb: Globus, 1985), 31.

105. *Reuter*, (February 20, 1984), cited in Stankovic, *ibid.*, 3.

106. Milovan Djilas, *Tito*, 74-75. "Tito's pragmatic Leninism," Djilas claims, "together with Kardelj's blend of social and democratic verbalism, and the notion of Leninistic party monopoly are merging gradually into a Yugoslav variant of Marxist authoritarianism." *Ibid.*, 44. The Yugoslav model of self-management is mainly valuable, Djilas argues, as a negative illustration of "two of the most senseless fallacies ... that self-management, in itself, can solve the problems of democratizing socialism, and operating a thriving socialist economy .... Both the problem of the economy and the problem of socialism can be solved only by the free play of a political democracy - of social forces working within a given framework of law and institutions .... The second senseless fallacy is that self-management is the 'finally found' form of transition to a classless society ..." Self-management, Djilas claims, is simply a new ideology "to secure the monopoly of the Party and the proparty bureaucracies ... an ideology that lacks the will to shake loose from its obsession with power." *Milovan Djilas, Of Prisons and Ideas* (San Diego: Harcourt Brace Jovanovich, 1986), 157.

107. Milovan Djilas, *The Unperfect Society*, 13.

108. Radomir Lukić, "O sukobima interesa u socijalističkom društvu," *Arhiv za pravne i društvene nauke*, XLVI, No. 1 (January-March, 1959), 20, 21-23.

109. *Ibid.*, 22. Lukić had begun to explore the issues of caste and class raised by Djilas as early as 1955. "O pojmu kaste i klase," *Pregled*, No. 9 (1955), 101-108. In 1961, Lukić re-emphasized that under workers' self-management "the managerial, predominantly intellectual bureaucratic stratum remains subordinate to the workers' authority ... it is a servant, and not the master. There is no doubt that elements of authority have not completely disappeared from this managerial function, and that they have disappeared more in a formal-legal sense than in a real sense .... Because of that, such phenomenon need sociological research ... remnants of class consciousness exist among our working people, but they are insufficient to be considered as a particular class consciousness and to project class differences among their different strata." "Uticaj radničkog samoupravljanja na klasni sastav Jugoslovenskog društva," *Sociologija*, (1961), 18, 26.

110. C. Wright Mills, *Elita vlasti* (Belgrade: Kultura, 1964), and Thomas Bottomore, *Elite i drustvu* (Belgrade: Sedma Sila, 1967). In 1965, a workbook prepared for the training of political activists and political analysts at the Higher School of Political Science in Belgrade, one instructor drew attention to "the relations of classes and the political representatives of class ('political elites') .... By political elites in this sense we understand a narrow circle of representatives, *representatives of class interests*, of classes, which occupy leading positions in basic institutions of state power, and its organizations. They are furthermore those of its representatives who exercise command in the important centers, in the organizations of decision-making .... As used here, this concept (which is useful in the absence of a better one) is essentially differentiated from the conception of the political elite as used by Pareto, Mosca, etc. It is identical and related only to the *representatives of classes*. Miroslav Pečujlić, *Studija za političke sociologije* (Belgrade: Visoka škola političkih nauka, 1965), 38-39. See also, Radomir Lukić, "Teorije elite u Pareta i Marksa," *Sociologija*, VII, No. 1 (1965), 19-28, Milan Matić, *Politička misao Rajta Milsa* (Belgrade: Institut društvenih nauka, 1966), Svetozar Stojanović, "Rajt Mils o Marksizmu," *Gledišta*, No. 2 (1966), 301-307, and Vladimir Stambuk, "Teorijski model socijalne stratifikacije C.W. Milsa," *Sociologija*, Nos. 1-2 (1968), 32-43.

Lenard J. Cohen

111. Najdan Pašić, "Pregovor," *Elite i društvo*, 10.

112. Dušan Zubrinić, *Marksizam i teorije elite* (Zagreb: Skolska knjiga, 1975), 23-24. Another Yugoslav author suggested that although Marxist theory is "in opposition" to theories of the elite, the introduction of the idea of an organized minority in the establishment of a socialist state creates the need for "a simple leading select stratum .... In recent time this question which Marxist theory has neglected and evaded, has become all the more pertinent." Vojislav Stanovćić, "Elita," *Mala politička enciklopedija* (Belgrade: Savremena administracija, 1966), 286.

113. A distinction between the positive features of a vanguard, and the negative features of an elite is often made by Yugoslav political scientists. "Each class (or class alliance) which struggles for influence in society (or has and holds it) creates its leading stratum, its 'elite'. But a vanguard isn't an elite .... While an elite rests upon a class, taking advantage of it, a vanguard leads a class, and itself is used for the work of a class .... A vanguard is a class organization and lasts during the class struggle and the political-ideological heterogeneity of society (including socialism). An elite is a temporary, alienated and alienating class group which eagerly strives to blunt the class struggle and maintain a social and political hierarchy." Jovan Djordjević, "Prilog teoriji avangarde," *Pregled*, No. 4 (1975), 409. See also Vladimir Sultanović, "Elita i avangarda," *Zbornik radova, Ekonomski Fakultet-Univerzitet Sarajevo*, VI, No. 6 (1971), 35-46, and Stojan Tomić, *Profesionalizam u politici* (Belgrade: Radnička stampa, 1975), 181-193. Branko Horvat has argued, in contrast, that bourgeois and socialist systems although "clearly very different ... have one important feature in common: they are elitist. Western theory refers to it as an elite; Eastern theory, as the vanguard party. What the socialist polity will have to do is to overcome the basic contradiction between elites and the masses; the elitist democracy must give way to one based on participation." *The Political Economy of Socialism* (Armonk, New York: M.E. Sharpe, 1982), 319-320.

114. For a survey and bibliography of such research see Lenard J. Cohen, "Political Science in Socialist Yugoslavia: The Regime-Management and Self-Management of a Discipline," *The Soviet Union and East Europe Into the 1980's: Multi-disciplinary Perspectives*, eds. Simon McInnes, William McGrath, and Peter Potichnyj (Oakville, Ontario: Mosaic Press, 1978.)

115. Miroslav Pečujlić, *Studija za političke sociologije*, 56-61, and also by the same author, *Klase i savremeno društvo* (Belgrade: Savremena administracija, 1967), 85-88. See also Jovan Djordjević, *Ogled o birokratiji i birokratizmu* (Belgrade: Kultura, 1962).

116. Miroslav Pečujlić, "Promene u socijalnom sastavu Jugoslovenskog socjalističkog društva," *Društveno-politički sistem, SFRJ* (Belgrade: Radnička stampa, 1979), 155.

117. Mihailo Popović et. al., *Društveni slojevi i drustvena svest* (Belgrade: Centar za sociološka istraživanja, Institut društvenih nauka, 1977). For earlier Yugoslav studies of class and social stratification see *ibid.*, 7-23, and Zagorka Golubović, Djordjije Usković, Miša Stojanović, Aljoša Mimica, "Analiza studija u strukturi Jugoslovenskog društva," *Klase i slojevi*, ed. Rudi Supek (Zagreb: "Čovjek i sistem," 1977), 7-52. The sociological basis and consequences of the Yugoslav elite structure are also illustrated in Miroslav Živković, "Jedan primer segregacije u razvoju naših gradova," *Sociologija*, X, No. 3 (1968), 37-58, and Stevan Vujović, "Socijalna diferencijacija i socijalne segregacija u našim gradovima, " *Lica,* No.5 (May, 1972), 52-67.

118. Mihailo Popović, *ibid.*, 452.

119. *Ibid.*, 152.

120. *Ibid.*, 213-227.

121. *Ibid.*, 455-456. The Belgrade research team repeated their survey in 1986 and found a similar level of belief in a class society among high officials. There was a significant decrease, however, in the number of workers who view Yugoslavia as classless (from 34 percent in 1974 to eight percent in 1986). *Nedeljne Informativne Novine*, (November 9, 1986), 28-29.

122. *Ibid.*, 246-258.

123. *Ibid.*, 456-458.

124. *Ibid.*, 429-430, 32-37.

125. According to the authors of the Belgrade study, state socialism has significantly reduced private property but "simultaneously condi-

tioned the further growth of a political and economic elite, this time a *socialist elite*. Their political and economic power is proportionately greater than the power of managers and professional politicians under capitalism, but at the same time there is a change in their social role. They are historically called upon to primarily defend the interest of the working class and other strata in socialist society. To the extent they actually do so, they deserve the title of a *socialist elite."* Ibid., 35. Mihajlo Popović, the senior sociologist in the pathbreaking 1977 Belgrade study, has argued that the sharp fall in Yugoslavia's living standard after 1980, especially for those with lower incomes, exacerbated "class-strata" inequalities in the country. By 1987 this trend not only resulted in serious economic and political malaise in the working class, according to Popovic, but also generated a disturbing backlash: "Although there has been a significant increase in social inequalities between strata and within them, social levelling [*uravnilovka*] remains the strongest varient of socialist ideology. Moreover, as a reaction to the growth of social differentiation there has been an increase in the number of supporters of the philosophy of 'equal stomachs.' The 'old socialism' offers a very tenacious resistance to the 'new socialism'." *Nedeljne Informativne Novine*, No. 1912 (August 23, 1987), 15-16.

126. For the background of radical dissent and the "Praxis group" see Gerson S. Sher, *Praxis: Marxist Criticism and Dissent in Socialist Yugoslavia* (Bloomington, Indiana: Indiana University Press, 1977), David A. Crocker, *Praxis and Democratic Socialism* (Atlantic Highlands, N.J.: Humanistic Press, Inc.), 1983, and Oskar Gruenwald, *The Yugoslav Search for Man: Marxist Humanism in Contemporary Yugoslavia* (South Hadley, Mass.: J.F. Bergin, 1983), and Mihajlo Marković, "Praxis: Critical Social Philosophy in Yugoslavia," *Praxis Yugoslav Essays in the Philosophy and Methodology of the Social Sciences,* eds. Mihajlo Marković and Gajo Petrović (Dordrecht, Holland: D. Reidel Publishing Co., 1979), xi-xxxvi. Mihajlo Marković has explained that it was the "mere economic liberalization" of Yugoslavia rather than a real "political deomcratization" which radicalized him and his colleagues. "In order to resist this trend we had to pass from our purely philosophical studies toward a more concrete social research, from a general criticism of Stalinism and Bourgeois liberalism to a specific critique of our own Yugoslav bureaucracy and the capitalist tendencies in our own economy." "The Purpose of Social Research," *Social Science — For What?* eds. Hans Henrik Holm and Erik Rudeng (Oslo: Universtetsforlaget, 1980), 47. Predrag

Vranicki, another one of the leading members of the original Praxis group, recalled in 1987 that the radical's creed was premised on the assumption that "nothing can be excluded from criticism. That simply meant that we struggled against taboo-themes, which later avenged themselves in social development, and that the best intentions can have their limits, stages, etc., and that we must illustrate all that." *Nedeljne Informativne Novine*, No. 1902 (June 14, 1987), 35.

127. "Socijalistička demokratija i SKJ," *Marks i savremenost*, eds. Dragutin Leković, et. al. (Belgrade: Institut za izučavanje radničkog pokreta i Institut društvenih nauka, 1964), 27-28, 138, 165 and 158.

128. "Marxism and Democracy: The Ruling Class or the Dominant Class," *Praxis, International Edition*, I, No. 2 (July, 1981), 164. While Praxis Marxists disappointingly acknowledge the applicability of the concepts of "elites" and "mass" to contemporary socialism, including Yugoslavia, they also condemn the assumption of classical elite theory that the role and temporary rule of minorities must inevitably lead to elite domination. "Elite rule is certainly the hegemony of a minority, but that doesn't mean that every politically relevant influence of a minority unconditionally also means the power of an elite, although under specific historical conditions that can happen. It can become the power of an elite only under such social conditions that democracy disappears ... where a privileged and popularly uncontrolled minority seize the public functions in their hands ...." Ljubomir Tadić, "Moć, elite, i demokratija," *Praxis*, VII, Nos. 1-2 (January-April, 1970), 74.

129. Svetozar Stojanović, *In Search of Democracy in Socialism* (Buffalo: Prometheus Books, 1981), 80-81 and Mihajlo Marković, "Struktura moći u Jugoslovenskom društvu i dilema revolucionarne inteligencije," *Praxis*, VIII, No. 6 (1971), 819. Marković emphasizes (816) that "there are considerable differences in the utilization of social power in our country and that in societies of the Soviet type. Our bureaucracy governs in a much more elastic and liberal way, it avoids the use of brute force and the most primitive forms of ideological indoctrination, it applies a far more refined method of rewards and punishment in the most varied forms. In this way one acquires the impression that those who are being governed are free."

130. "From Post-revolutionary Dictatorship to Socialist Democracy," *Praxis, International Edition*, IX, No. 4 (1973), 319-320, 333.

131. Svetozar Stojanović, "The Social Theory and Ideology of Marxism," *Alternatives*, IX, No. 3 (Winter, 1983-1984), 405-406.

132. Svetozar Stojanović, *In Search of Democracy in Socialism*, 84-86.

133. Mihajlo Marković, "The Power Structure in Yugoslav Society," *Student* (November 2, 1971), *Joint Publications Research Service, Eastern Europe, Political, Sociological, and Military Affairs*, No. 475 (Belgrade: February 4, 1972),71.

134. Ivan Kuvačić, "Middle Class Ideology," *Praxis, International Edition*, IX, No. 4 (1973), 353-355.

135. Milan Kangrga, "Fenomenologija ideološko-političkog nastupanja Jugoslavenske srednje klase," *Praxis*, VIII, Nos. 3-4 (May-August, 1971), 440, note 11.

136. Svetozar Stojanović, *In Search of Democracy in Socialism*, 85.

137. Veljko Rus, "Institutionalization of the Revolutionary Movement," *Praxis, International Edition*, III, No. 2 (1967), 206.

138. Svetozar Stojanović, *Between Ideals and Reality* (New York: Oxford University Press, 1973), 40-41. See also, Mihajlo Marković, *Democratic Socialism, Theory and Practice* (New York: St. Martin's Press, 1982), 201-210.

139. Ljubomir Tadić, "Order and Freedom," *Self-Managing Socialism*, eds. Branko Horvat, Mihajlo Marković, and Rudi Supek (White Plains, New York: International Arts and Science Press, 1975), 410.

140. "Decentralization: A Precondition for More Rational Societies," *The Future of Politics: Governance Movements and World Order*, ed. William Page (London: Frances Pinter, 1983), 122. The "critical question" for a revolutionary elite in a Marxist state, Marković points out, is "will this elite ... find the moral strength and consistency to voluntarily pass to the basic element of the socialist revolution, i.e., the realization of self-management and consequently the gradual setting aside of itself as a power elite (this does not mean that it cannot permanently remain as an elite of the mind

- if it has a powerful mind)?" "Socialism and Self-Management," *Praxis, International Edition*, I, Nos. 2-3 (1965), 178-179.

141. Marković concedes, moreover, that it is theoretically less difficult to prevent the emergence of class differences and a hierarchy of power than it is to prevent individuals from acquiring high status and prestige in the performance of "certain social roles." "High status may lead to great influence and eventually to political power. Society can fight this danger only by developing a critical awareness of it and by jealously prescribing its democratic norms. In that case the only elite in society would be the elite of spirit, or moral authority, of taste. Nevertheless this form of inequality does not jeopardize human relations, does not degrade anybody, it is beneficial rather than dangerous for the society." *The Contemporary Marx: Essays on Humanist Communism* (Nottingham: Spokesman Books, 1974), 132-133.

142. Djilas' support for a multi-party system is particularly objectionable to most of the radical intellectuals, who generally feel that any type of party system facilitates elite rule. For other similarities and differences between Djilas and the radical intellectuals see Dennis Reinhartz, *Milovan Djilas: A Revolutionary as a Writer* (Boulder: East European Monographs, 1981), 75-76, and Gerson Sher, *Praxis: Marxist Criticism and Dissent in Yugoslavia,* 142. In the mid-1980's, Djilas and the radical intellectuals began to co-operate more closely as part of the so-called "democratic movement" for reform.

143. Quoted in Slobodan Stankovic, "Top Yugoslav Leader Polemicizes with Djilas' 'New Class' Theories," *Radio Free Europe, Yugoslavia: International Affairs*, (November 7, 1967), 2.

144. *Horizonti revolucije* (Belgrade: Institut za političke studije Fakultet političkih nauka, 1970), 76-81, and *Društvene grupe i politički život* (Belgrade: Komunist, 1969), 31-32. Stojanović's response to Pecujlić is in *Between Ideals and Reality*, 37-40. Stojanović associates his own idea about statism as a new form of class society with the earlier views of Machajski, Rakovsky, Ciliga, and Rizzi. Conservative regime spokesmen typically referred to the radical perspective as the "anarcholiberalistic view of Stalinism." For example in 1968, Veljko Vlahović suggested that Yugoslavia's intellectual "extremists have replaced Marx's theses with the theses of C. Wright Mills who proclaimed that the 'proletariat is no longer

the historical force of the future'. In place of the working class, the humanistic intelligentsia projects itself. This thesis among others, is accepted by the journal *Praxis*. The solutions which are offered constitute a new elitism." "Samo u akciji mogu se prepoznati i ljudi i odnosi," *Klasa i avangarda: Jugoslovensko iskustvo* (Prvi svezak), eds. Jovan Mirić, *et. al.* (Zagreb: Globus, 1983), 585.

145. Quoted in "Kardelj Changes his Mind on the Role of the State," *Radio Free Europe Research, Yugoslavia*, (February 26, 1973), 4-6, and Slobodan Stankovic, "Yugoslav Communists Struggle over 'Social Inequalities'," *Radio Free Europe Research, Yugoslavia*, (December 22, 1971).

146. *Pravci razvoja političkog sistema socijalističkog samoupravljanja* (Belgrade: Komunist, 1978), 114.

147. *Danas* (November 6, 1983) quoted in Slobodan Stankovic, "Threat of a 'Big Stick' Regime in Yugoslavia," *Radio Free Europe Research, RAD Background Report, Yugoslavia*, (November 25, 1983), 3.

148. *Nedeljne Informativne Novine*, No. 1778 (January 27, 1985), 28. For important examples of the new literature see Josip Županov, *Marginalije o društvenoj krizi* (Zagreb: Globus, 1983), Silvan Bolčić, *Razvoj i kriza Jugoslovenskog društva u sociološkoj perspektivi* (Belgrade: Studentski izdavački centar Univerzitetske Konferencije SSO Beograda, 1983), and Jovan Mirić, *Sistema i kriza* (Zagreb: Cekade, 1984).

149. *Nedeljne Informativne Novine*, No. 1734 (February 26, 1984), 9.

150. *Komunist*, (January 7, 1983), 15. In 1987, sociologists at Belgrade's Institute of Social Sciences empirically supported such conclusions about the distribution of power in Yugoslav society: "The condition that a stratum of leading personnel have a dominant position in education, in their material situation, in social positions, and in political power confirms the possibility that our country has gradually formed its own kind of power elite, which has a key role in all social processes .... So the three hierarchical dimensions which scholars in our country recognized back as far as twenty years ago - a hierarchy which depends on roles in occupations, one which depends on roles occupied in politics, and a hierarchy in consumption - are increasingly replaced by a unified social hierarchy which

The Socialist Pyramid: Elites and Power in Yugoslavia

as a rule is simply a copy of the political [hierarchy]. *Danas*, (April 4, 1987), 8-9.

151. *Nedeljne Informativne Novine*, No. 1786 (March 24, 1985), 23. See also Neca Jovanov, *Dijagnoza samoupravljanja 1974-1981* (Zagreb: Sveučilista naklada liber, 1983), 92-98. For the burgeoning post-Tito discussion of social and political stratification and its effect on continued political elitism in Yugoslavia see Ivan Bernik, "Klasna i slojevna struktura Jugoslovenskog društva i pluralizam samopravnih interesa," *Sociologija*, XXIV, Nos. 2-3 (1983), 358-352, Mihailo Popović, "Administracija, birokratija, birokratizam," *Sociologija*, XXV, No. 4 (1983), 383-395, Duško Sekulić, "O pristupima izučavanju stratifikancione strukture Jugoslovenskog društva," *Sociologija*, XXV, No. 2-3 (1983), 221-245, Vjeran Katunarić, "Kriza i revizija društvene strukture," *Naše teme*, VII, No. 9 (1983), 1378-1392, Ivan Šiber, "Empirijski pristupi istraživanju socijalne strukture," *Naše teme*, XXVIII, No. 11 (1984), 2248-2254, Pero Nasakanda, "'Središnji slojevi' u Jugoslovenskom društvu," *Naše teme*, XXVIII, Nos. 4-5 (1984), 633-652 and Eva Berković, *Socijalne Nejednakosti u Jugoslaviji* (Belgrade: Ekonomika, 1986). An interesting Yugoslav article has also recently appeared contrasting Bruno Rizzi's ideas about the ruling class under socialism with the views of James Burnham, Ante Ciliga and the "intellectually inferior" book by Milovan Djilas. *Milan Mesić*, "'Nova klasa' ili novo društvo i nova klasa," *Naša teme*, XXVIII, No. 9 (1984), 1670-1682.

152. "Mit i dogma u Jugoslovenskoj ideologiji," *Sociologija*, XXVIII, Nos. 1-2 (1985), 167-171. Dr. Mladen Lazić of Zagreb University maintains that Yugoslavia is ruled by a "class of collective owners" composed of professional politicians and mangers who monopolize planning and control production at each level of the country's political structure. Although essentially hierarchical in organization, Lazic argues that the segmentation of the political structure into different territorial components together with various other aspects of dentralization have allowed for the development of "real" - albeit not self-managing - forms of democracy. "Through the establishment of a series of parallel hierarchies on the republican and provincial levels [total] control is impossible and an open space exists for democratization. It is an empty space which arises from the mutual competition of different structures. Thus, to a certain degree it is wrested from the system, and simultaneously also is a means for the reciprocal settling of accounts inside of the

elite. It results in the disintegration of the hierarchy, so that one no longer knows who is controlling whom." Ljuba Stojić, "Tatini sinovi," *Nedeljne Informativne Novine*, (September 14, 1986), 21.

153. Quoted in Slobodan Stankovic, "The Social Effects of Communist Rulers Becoming Rich," *Radio Free Europe Research, Yugoslavia*, (August 12, 1985), 30.

154. Supek, Kuvačić, and Stojanović as quoted in Zdenko Antic, "Yugoslav Sociologists Urge Democratic Reform," *Radio Free Europe Research, RAD Background Report, Yugoslavia*, No. 283 (December 29, 1983), 1-5.

155. Quoted in Slobodan Stankovic, "Communist System Blamed for Crisis," *Radio Free Europe Research, Yugoslavia* (November 14, 1985), 4.

156. *Borba*, (July 5, 1984), 6. Although considered a hardliner, Mikulić conceded in 1979 that many people in Yugoslavia still suffered from a bureaucratic mentality: "This behaviour is based on humility toward superiors, the establishment of hierarchical relations among people, insistence on protocol ... which often leads to a tasteless ranking of people not according to what they have done ... but according to what office one occupies at a given moment and so forth. There is something in this which quite frequently isolates us from the people and the masses." *Borba*, (December 29, 1985), 3.

157. *Foreign Broadcast Information Service Daily Bulletin, Eastern Europe*, (November 26, 1985), I3.

158. Quoted in Slobodan Stankovic, "Yugoslav Dissidents Accused of Demeaning Tito's Memory," *Radio Free Europe Research RAD Background Report, Eastern Europe*, No. 112 (June 22, 1984), 2. Šuvar's candid appraisals of developments in his society and elite political culture have made him the frequent target of attacks by the conservative wing of the party. See "Croat Party Ideologist Publicly Attacked" and "Professor Šuvar's Counterattack." *Radio Free Europe*, (March 29, 1977 and April 5, 1977). Despite his controversial views on elite privileges, Šuvar has consistently defended the legitimacy of the party's vanguard, joining that very g r o u p through his June 1986 election as a member of the Presidency of the League of Communists in. See also note 2 in Chapter 3.

159. *Borba*, (February 14, 1984), 2. In 1986, an officially sponsored analysis concluded that the Yugoslav political system was afflicted with excessive political professionalization and other problems such as "the privatization of social functions, the monopoly of individuals and narrow groups ..., subjectivism, a tendency toward leadership domination [*liderstvo*], careerist ambitions, sectarianism, group alliances, etc." Commenting on the analysis, a deputy in the federal legislature inquired how it was possible to have such problems in a "self-managing socialist society, where the working class and the working people have great constitutional and formal-legal authority and self-managing rights. Some commentators try to prove that such informal groups or centres of power are a product of the system, which is partially accurate, but there are more arguments which demonstrate that they are the product of ideological-political deformations, where master-subject relations are created, that is the dependence of a large number of people on the power of individuals and groups in high positions, and also the fact that such powerful leaders are exempted from legal responsibility for failures, incompetence and the abuse of positions .... The political and moral crisis in our society represents a greater danger than the economic crisis, because the latter is a product of the former." *Skupština SFRJ, Stenografske Bilješke*, XLV, No. 52 (March 12 and 13, 1986), 48. Forty years after the creation of communist Yugoslavia, an official history of the League of Communists briefly explained that "the process of establishing associated labour as the ruling economic and political force of society proceeded more slowly than was expected." Janko Pleterski *et.al., Istorija Saveza Komunista Jugoslavije* (Belgrade: Komunist, 1985), 475.

160. *Foreign Broadcast Information Service, Eastern Europe*, (July 22, 1985), I10.

161. *Foreign Broadcast Information Service, Eastern Europe*, (September 7, 1983), I10.

162. Recently one of Belgrade's oldest publishers, "Naucna Knjiga," began a new series of publications on "Contemporary Yugoslav Society." The first titles announced for 1986 offer a good illustration of the wide scope of issues treated in Yugoslavia's current debate on power, social conflicts, and the country's crisis: Jovan Djordjević, "Ten Perspectives Covering Open Questions," Zoran Pjanić, "The Depth of the Economic Crisis," Alexander Grličkov,

"Contradictions in Contemporary Yugoslav Society," Milan Vucinić, "The Role of the Army in the Yugoslav Political System," Radoslav Ratković, "The State, Socialism, and Self-Management," Smiljan Jurin, "The Market in the Economic System of Yugoslavia," Predrag Radenović, "Who Rules in Self-Management," Miroslav Pečujlić, "Sociological Research of Crises," Dragoje Žarković, "Economic Crisis and Political Voluntarism," Miroljub Labus, "The Controversy Around Social Ownership," Marjan Korošić, "Inflation and Its Results," Živko Surčilija, "Nationalism and Social Contradictions," and Smilja Avramov, "The Control of Yugoslvia's Foreign Policy."

163. Between January 1, 1980 and the end of 1986, retail prices in Yugoslavia rose by 1,653 percent, the price of industrial products by 1,470 percent and the cost of living by 1,636 percent. In the first part of 1987, the country suffered its highest upsurge of labour unrest (roughly 400 strikes in three months) as a result of deteriorating economic conditions and government measures to freeze wages. Party Presidency member, Stipe Šuvar, commented that not more than 20 percent of Yugoslav workers are able to live on their personal income or retirement pay. The rest live, he claimed, on income from the "parallel economy." As a result, he added, the material basis for the implementation of a self-managing system has been significantly reduced. *Foreign Broadcast Information Service* (May 5, 1987), I1.

164. In May 1987, the Slovenian student periodical, *Katedra*, published the first interview with Djilas to appear in Yugoslavia in 34 years. Although the editors' note accompanying the interview remarks that the editorial board does not wish to judge Djilas' work, the note also acknowledges that Djilas has provided "a crucial description of our modern history from the viewpoint of a revolutionary and a thinker" and that "certainly Djilas is one of the most important figures in our modern history." *Radio Free Europe Report*, (May 4, 1987), 21-23.

PART TWO

ELITE TRANSFORMATION: REVOLUTIONARY AND EVOLUTIONARY DIMENSIONS

(A peasant soldier, Mališa, comforting his wounded commanding officer, a village schoolmaster, in a small Yugoslav Partisan detachment surrounded by enemies in occupied Serbia, 1943.)

"If your arm hurts, then think about something else. If ever I have a pain anywhere, I think about something else ... think about what it will be like after the war. You'll be a big boss then .... You'll have a fine time."
"Mališa, old chap ... even then I don't want to be a gentleman."
"But why not? You deserve it. You and comrade Paul" (the political commisar of the detachment).
"Mališa, I'm fighting so that you and your generation, and all my pupils, can live like gentlemen - that you shall be gentlemen."
"And who will work if we're all to be gentlemen."
"Well, we'll all work, but we'll all live like gentlemen."
"Oh, but my god that's impossible ...."

Dobrica Ćosić

The Revolution can be ruined only by those who participate in it.

Antonije Isaković

CHAPTER TWO

FROM MONARCHY TO MARXISM: A COMPARISON OF ELITE SOCIAL BACKGROUNDS

Revolution, by definition, involves the rapid and extensive transformation of a country's political elite. A useful method for understanding the nature and extent of such transformation is to systematically examine the social background characteristics of the major winners and losers in the revolutionary struggle. As a complex phenomenon involving both long-festering societal problems and more short-term precipitants (e.g., war, invasion, breakdown of authority, etc.), revolution cannot, of course, be explained solely by the social characteristics of successful revolutionary leaders and the political decision-makers who they displace. A careful political and sociological comparison of pre-revolutionary and post-revolutionary elites can, however, offer significant insights about the underlying causes and immediate repercussions of revolutions, and also identify some of the important problems which may confront a society and its elites during less turbulent times. Revolutions result from prior failures in elite management, but the elite victors are soon tested by problems of both their own and their predecessors' making.[1]

This chapter provides a comparative analysis of Yugoslavia's interwar political elite with the communist elite that assumed power after World War II. The study of the two elite groups will explore several major social background characteristics for which data was available: educational backgrounds, occupations, class origins, urban and rural birthplaces, age, gender, and ethnic affiliations. The period covered by the analysis begins with the establishment of the Yugoslav state in 1918 (initially designated as the Kingdom of Serbs,

Lenard J. Cohen

Croats, and Slovenes, and from 1929 to 1941 as the Kingdom of Yugoslavia), and ends in mid-1948 just after the Tito-Stalin rift and the Cominform denunciation of the Yugoslav Communist Party. In order to understand the causes for revolutionary elite circulation, it is essential to first briefly survey the political development and socio-political structure of Yugoslavia during its first three decades of existence.

Elite Structure and Political Power: The Historical Context

The South Slav (in Serbo-Croat, "Yugoslav") state established in 1918, was the outcome of negotiations among political leaders from three of the largest ethnic groups in the Balkans: the Serbs, Croats, and Slovenes.[2] The major catalyst for the creation of the new state was the defeat and disintegration of the Hapsburg monarchy, which had consistently stifled the nationalist aspirations of the emergent Slavic elites in Southeastern Europe. Serbia, which was among the victorious Allied powers in 1918 and had used its position as an autonomous state (beginning in the mid-19th century after 500 years of Turkish rule) to spearhead the drive for South Slav unification, naturally viewed itself as the core unit in an independent Yugoslavia. Thus, much to the chagrin of the Croats and Slovenes, as well as the small but constitutionally unrecognized or unrepresented nationalities (Montenegrins, Macedonians, Hungarians, Albanians, etc.), it was the Serbian royal dynasty, the Serbian capital of Belgrade, and Serbian central elites, which acquired a dominant position in the new country. Despite strong opposition, especially from the Croats, the Constitution of June, 1921 established a unitary and highly centralized regime which denied the provinces and regions any voice in the governance of the country. During the three weeks which followed the adoption of the Constitution, members of the small but active Communist Party of Yugoslavia engineered an abortive attempt on the life of the Prince Regent Alexander, and then the successful assassination of the Minister of the Interior. Quickly suppressed by the regime, the Communist Party (whose 58 deputies were expelled from the Parliament) was forced to go underground where its members spent the next twenty years working for a political revolution.[3]

The challenge of Yugoslav unification - namely, how to achieve it and once realized how to structure and sustain it - was not a new problem in the years after World War I, and in fact, different positions on the issue had accounted for much of the volatility in Balkan political history. In a broad sense, most of the citizens in the new Kingdom shared a common ancestral and tribal background, and most also spoke rather similar languages. Unfortunately, such similarities were far less politically salient than the host of ethnic, religious, linguistic, and economic cleavages also present in the new state. Moreover, most of the

The Socialist Pyramid: Elites and Power in Yugoslavia

cleavages tended to reinforce one another, creating a kind of fault line which ran roughly through the middle of the country. On one side, in the northwestern areas (Slovenia, Croatia-Slavonia, Dalmatia and Vojvodina), the population was predominantly Roman Catholic, more culturally-oriented to Central Europe, used the Latin alphabet, and enjoyed a relatively high standard of living for a basically agrarian country. In the southeastern regions (Montenegro, Serbia, Kosovo-Metohija, and Macedonia - the latter two referred to at that time as "South Serbia"), the inhabitants were adherents of the Eastern Orthodox branch of Christianity, bore the imprint of Ottoman rule, mainly used the Cyrillic script, and outside of the few large towns, lived in a situation of striking economic backwardness. The highly diverse region of Bosnia-Hercegovina, containing elements of both the northwestern and southeastern patterns (including a large Moslem population which in 1918 was still labouring under vestiges of the Ottoman serf system) was situated along this unstable fault line, and frequently became the epicenter of political unrest.

As a result of the different traditions and customs rooted in such north-south divisions, the inhabitants of Yugoslavia's different regions (indeed of different towns and villages in the case of the many multi-ethnic regions) were often divided from their fellow citizens by a "wall of prejudice" which seemed to have survived as if in an "historical deep freeze."[4] Beyond the new country's many cultural and historical divisions there were also many practical difficulties to overcome, such as distinct railway lines, currencies, legal systems, and even calendars. Thus, although the idea of Yugoslav unification enjoyed considerable popular support in many areas, the leaders who had "invented" the new state were faced with tremendous challenges. Ethno-regional conflicts proved to be the most salient cleavages in the new state, however, and were especially pronounced in the constant difficulties between the Serbs and the Croats, who respectively constituted approximately 39 percent and 23 percent of the population in 1921. The Serbian-Croatian conflict dominated the political process throughout the interwar period, resulting in recurring periods of political stalemate and instability which greatly impeded the country's overall efforts at state-building and modernization.[5]

In operation, the parliamentary system established by the Constitution of 1921 was a classic example of party fragmentation and cabinet instability. For example, during its first decade of existence, as one political crisis followed another in rapid succession, the country experienced 25 governments and 130 changes of cabinet ministers.[6] Despite the disruption and cynicism caused by such "hair trigger government," substantial continuity of personnel existed from one cabinet to another. New faces did appear, but the individuals chosen for the most important cabinet posts were usually drawn from a pool of 50 to 60 prominent parliamentary deputies. In retrospect, the 1920's can be viewed as a relatively democratic phase in the country's political history, but the well-known financial corruption and electoral manipulation practiced by many elite actors significantly undermined the regime's effectiveness and legitimacy. As one incisive study of the country's public service noted:

> Most politicians do not always maintain the dignity and honesty requisite with their functions and appear unworthy of the confidence which the people have shown in them. Many endeavor to fish in troubled waters and to profit from the situation. Their own interests and that of their friends always comes before that of the State and the people .... The public administration is completely at the mercy of the political parties. The functionaries become their serfs .... Politics has completely devoured the public service. The administration is considered as the patrimony of the majority in the Chamber of Deputies. The supporters of the government parties are rewarded at the expense of functionaries from the opposition .... Functionaries appointed under these conditions neglect their functions and do not dedicate themselves to policies. Useless positions are created non-stop. Some perfectly vital and competent functionaries go into early retirement. Favouritism and nepotism triumph. Waste reigns everywhere.[7]

In early 1929, thoroughly frustrated with the inability of the volatile and fragmented party system to address the country's serious ethnic and economic problems, the King abrogated the constitution, suspended the National Assembly, and sharply curtailed political liberties in the country.

In an effort to legitimate a more authoritarian and cohesive regime a new constitutional structure was enacted in 1931, including a politically weakened parliamentary system. The reality of a centralized royal dictatorship remained in place, however, until the assassination of the King by ethnic extremists in 1934. During the next seven years, an unpopular regency controlled the country through its agents in the cabinet and government-sponsored parties in Parliament. In 1939, limited progress was achieved in reaching an accommodation between Serbian and Croatian elites, including the adoption of consociational-type political arrangements which might have led to the gradual federalization and democratization of the country, but such belated political experimentation was side-tracked by growing external threats to the regime's survival. In March, 1941 a group of military officers successfully carried out a coup d'état in protest over the government's tilt toward the Axis powers. This was quickly followed by the conquest, occupation and territorial dismemberment of Yugoslavia by Germany, Italy and their pro-Axis allies.

Throughout the interwar period under discussion, Yugoslavia's political elite was largely a composite of three subgroups: 1) the cabinet ministers, or what will be referred to as the governmental elite; 2) the high ranking civil servants in the public bureaucracy, or the administrative elite; and 3) the major

The Socialist Pyramid: Elites and Power in Yugoslavia

industrialists, entrepreneurs, and financiers, or the economic elite. Three other groups - the royal family, high ranking members of the military bureaucracy, and the clergy - were also integral elements of the interwar power structure (especially in the second decade of the state's history), but they are rather special components of the regime which go beyond the focus of this analysis.[8]

Most analysts of interwar Yugoslavia have described the process of political decision-making during that period as a lively pattern of interaction among members of the governmental, administrative, and economic elites. The state's dominant role in the economy made control over the governmental apparatus the primary object of political activity and inter-elite coalitions:

> The biggest capitalist in the Balkans was the state. In Jugoslavia, the state owned many forests, railroads, mines, lumber mills, banks, spas, sugar refineries, and armaments factories. It owned and operated all radio stations and PTT (Post Office, Telephone, and Telegraph) lines and offices. It also owned some textile manufacturers and most river boats and harbor facilities. The state industrial monopolies were reinforced by state sales and trading monopolies ... the industrial, commercial, and financial community, known in the Balkans as the *čaršija*, was closely associated with the state administration. Far from being an autonomous force, capitalism was dependent upon the largess of government bureaus and ministries, and government officials were rarely "large" unless business was kind in turn.[9]

Although those individuals at the top of the governmental, administrative, and economic hierarchies collectively comprised a political or governing elite, that elite group constituted a relatively small core of top decision-makers who cannot be sharply distinguished from the more numerous and diffuse "middle sectors" of interwar Yugoslav society. The members of the middle sectors - a broad social configuration sometimes referred to as the "bourgeoisie" or the "intelligentsia" - enjoyed both the greatest access to the political elites and the highest eligibility for achieving elite standing. Thus, the political elite in the interwar period was closely connected to the middle sectors in terms of social characteristics, broad political beliefs, and socio-political behaviour.[10] The most characteristic features of the middle sectors during the interwar period were their relatively high educational attainments and concentration in urban and semi-urban localities. Membership in the middle sectors, however, did not automatically bestow membership in the political elite. As one author put it: "the middle sectors comprised the social strata that had mastered the techniques or routines which facilitate the duties of the policy making or political class. They were the policy conforming elements, the elements that after the policy makers, had benefitted the most from the process of social, cultural, political and economic rationalization."[11]

Lenard J. Cohen

Table 2.1
The Distribution of Yugoslavia's Economically Active Population by Social Class and National Income, 1938

Social Classes and Groups	Economically Active Population		Wages, Salaries, and Entreprenurial Income*	
	(In thousands)	(%)	(Millions of dinars, 1938 value)	(%)
Proletariet and Peasantry				
Non-agricultural wage earners	453	6.5	3,488	5.6
Peasants and agricultural workers	2,113	30.5	8,003	12.8
Peasants, holding 2.01-5 hectares	1,631	23.5	9,185	14.7
Peasants, holding 5-20 hectares	1,560	22.5	13,346	21.4
Others	263	3.8	499	0.8
Agricultural Middle Class				
Peasants, holding over 20 hectares	124	1.8	2,671	4.2
Non-Agricultural Middle Class				
Salaried employees and public servants	357	5.1	6,858	11.1
Artisans and minor entrepreneurs	296	4.3	5,726	9.1
Higher Bourgeoise				
Senior government officials (including high clergy and Royal Court)	19	0.3	1,120	1.8
Higher managerial staff	12	0.2	760	1.2
Professions	20	0.3	980	1.6
Major entrepreneurs	79	1.1	9,645	15.4
Total	6,927	100.0	62,281	100.0

* Excludes income originating from the ownership of dwellings.
Source: Ivo Vinski, *Klasna Podjela Stanovnistva i Naciaonalnog Dohotka Jugoslavije, u 1938* (Zagreb: Ekonomski Institut, 1970), pp. 142, 150.

Closer examination of Yugoslavia's interwar class structure provides a better understanding of the relative size and social position of the middle sectors. Table 2.1 offers a statistical breakdown of Yugoslavia's economically active population in 1938 by social class and income. Approximately 87 percent of the work force was comprised of peasants, agricultural workers, and non-agricultural wage earners. Another 11 percent of the population fell into the middle class, a mainly non-agricultural category composed of state and commercial employees, small entrepreneurs and artisans, but also including some wealthier peasants. The remaining two percent of the active population constituted a higher and urbanized bourgeoisie made up of higher governmental officials, managerial personnel, businessmen, and professionals. These last two class groupings - the middle class and higher bourgeoisie - comprised interwar Yugoslavia's middle sectors, i.e., social groups situated directly below the monarchy and top political personalities, and generally enjoying life styles and opportunities quite distinct from the "toiling masses." The peasant and proletarian sectors of Yugoslavia, which together made up well over four-fifths of the economically active population, received only a little more than half of the total national income distribution, while the top two percent of the work force, in terms of property, specialized skills, and political power, absorbed 20 percent of the national income.

It is important to note that neither the middle sectors of Yugoslav society, nor the political elite derived from this group, can be considered as highly cohesive elements of the social structure manifesting uniform political attitudes

The Socialist Pyramid: Elites and Power in Yugoslavia

and patterns of political behaviour. Thus, along with the high degree of interaction and collusion among members of the middle sectors, there were significant generational, ideological, and ethnic cleavages which tended to work in the opposite direction. Moreover, within the political elite itself the rapid turnover of cabinets and parliamentary coalitions resulted in constant shifts of influence among various patron-client networks and different party leadership cliques, making all political alliances a highly temporary and risky affair. Even during the more democratic parliamentary period from 1918 to 1929, this fluid situation resulted in a limited and essentially oligarchic form of political pluralism, characterized by frequent alternations of political "ins" and "outs" among the members of a rather small elite pool.

Situated at the bottom of the social structure and hierarchy of power was the peasantry, a social group which constituted far more of an object than a subject in the country's political life. For example, although the peasant parties established in interwar Yugoslavia did have some success in politically mobilizing the agricultural sector of the population (especially in Croatia), such populist movements had relatively little influence on the formation of public policy. As one study pointed out, if the record of these peasant movements in any area "is measured by the standard of attaining and holding power, by organizing the state and conducting the state policies in the interests of the peasants, or if the achievements are compared with the program, this record was one of failure."[12] The real and clearly perceived political impotence of the large peasant population generated the one cleavage in Yugoslav society which affected all ethnic groups and regions, namely, the conflict between town and village (see below).

The Axis occupation of Yugoslavia, together with the violent resistance struggle and civil war which raged for nearly five years in the country, completely shattered the interwar power structure. By the end of the war, under circumstances well known and frequently related, the previously isolated and politically frustrated Communist Party emerged as the dominant political force in the country.[13] Besides the political opportunities for radical change wrought by the foreign occupation and the wartime holocaust, the communists owed their success to a combination of organizational skill, genuine military effectiveness, some external support (mainly from the Western Allies rather than the beleagured USSR), and the appeal of their political program which stressed both ethnic and social equality. A Yugoslav historian has described the wartime relationship of the Communist Party (CPY) to the new state authorities - the "national-liberation committees" - which the victorious Partisan forces established in the liberated regions of the country.

> Although the [CPY] did not appear as the highest power, nor had declared itself as such, it had in essence a decisive role in the creation of the national-liberation committees .... The highest organ of the Communist

> Party, the Central Committee of the CPY working in practice as a Politburo, or even more narrowly, as a group of leading members of the central leadership, insured ... the integrative connection of the parts and the whole, connecting the centers of the revolution, creating a unified political line .... Already in the course of the war the CPY insured its leading role in the socio-political system, holding the government, the military, the security organs and the mass organizations, as levers of its power and influence .... The CPY was in principle opposed to party pluralism, having in mind the experience of the Yugoslav Kingdom ....[14]

By 1946, Tito and his colleagues were able to jettison their shortlived and largely symbolic coalition with "bourgeois" politicians from the prewar parties, and to consolidate the political control of the Communist Party. The communists' wartime victory had not only resulted in the displacement of the interwar elite, but also greatly reduced the actual size of Yugoslavia's middle class and higher bourgeoisie. Thus, in the wake of the revolution, most members of the interwar political elite and middle sectors who had left the country at the outset of the war chose not to return. Still later in 1944 and 1945, as the communists consolidated their power, another large portion of the prewar ruling class also chose to emigrate (either because they had collaborated or sympathized with the foreign occupiers and domestic fascists or, in most cases, because of their opposition to the new regime). Yet a bigger blow was delivered to the former bourgeoisie by the nationalization of property and the implementation of a land reform program by the communist regime soon after the war. For example, one Yugoslav sociologist estimates that by 1947, as a result of the new economic policies, the "urban bourgeoisie" declined to about one-fifth of its size in 1938, while the "rural bourgeoisie" shrank to about one-tenth of its prewar size.[15] The members of the former middle sectors and political elite still residing in the country thus became a kind of "class relic," while at the same time elements of new middle sectors and also an elite sector - Djilas' "new class" - began to take shape.

Employment opportunities proliferated not only in the rapidly expanding Communist Party and mass organizations (the trade unions, the People's Front, organizations for women and youth, etc.), but also at the managerial levels of both the state administration and economic system. The elaboration of a federal political structure to replace the former unitary system also created a large number of new positions for "leading cadre" in the public bureaucracy at the communal, district, republican-provincial, and central levels.[16] If precise data were available with regard to the total number of persons occupying such roles during the early post-revolutionary period, the size of the new communist officialdom or political class would most likely correspond closely to the politically active members of the higher bourgeoisie during the prewar period. At the summit of the new political system, presiding over the party and state bureaucracies as well as all other organizational hierarchies, were the "higher party organs": the Politburo, the Central Committee, and the Central Control Commission. Between 1945 and 1948 the Yugoslav political elite could be equated with membership in these three top party bodies.

The Sample and Elite Similarities

Social background data was gathered from a variety of different sources for as many members of the Communist and interwar political elites as possible.[17] Information was collected for all 120 individuals who comprised the early postwar communist elite, i.e., the members of the Politburo, Central Committee, and Central Control Commission elected at the Fifth Congress of the Yugoslav Communist Party in July 1948. As membership in the interwar political elite was highly diffuse, however, it was impossible to obtain a complete "universe" of data for this analysis. Social background data was acquired, nevertheless, for 170 of the 220 cabinet ministers who served between 1918 and 1941, or 75 percent of that sub-elite group. Moreover, these 170 ministers were distributed among the different parties, cabinets, and political sub-phases during the interwar period, and thus constitute a fairly representative sample of the pre-communist elite. Data was also gathered for 94 higher civil servants and 46 members of the interwar economic sub-elite, but information was only available for individuals listed as holding such positions between 1932 and 1936. The relatively high continuity of membership in the higher state bureaucracy and the economic elite during the interwar period, compared to the more rapid turnover of cabinet ministers, compensates to some extent for such limitations in the data. A more difficult problem - and this is true in all positionally defined elite samples - is differentiating among administrators and economic leaders with respect to the extent of their actual influence on public policy. Of course, information on the differential political influence of the cabinet ministers is also absent, but it can be surmised that nearly all members of the governmental elite had at least some impact on the formation and implementation of state policies. The social background data obtained for the interwar economic and administrative sub-elites is offered, therefore, primarily to explore (systematically, if not definitively) the social characteristics of leadership in those special areas, and also to compare those sub-elite groups with both the interwar governmental elite and the political elite after 1945.

It should be mentioned at the outset of the analysis that despite rather striking and anticipated differences between the interwar and communist elites, the two leadership groups also possessed certain common characteristics. Both elites, for example, assumed power after wars of "national liberation": the interwar elite after the Serbian-led confrontation with the Austro-Hungarian Empire over the question of South Slavic self-determination which had precipitated World War I; the communist elite after bitter warfare with foreign invaders and domestic internal opponents during World War II. Just as most members of the new communist elite had struggled for many years in underground activity, many members of the interwar elite had spent portions of their youth and early careers in the South Slav nationalist movement.[18] Thus, the members of both elites looked upon themselves as state-builders, with the task of establishing a new political system for the region. Taking power after devastating wars which had demolished the country's economy, the members of both elites also shared a common desire to reconstruct and modernize Yugoslav society. While industrialization was far more of an ideologically-conditioned goal for the communists than for their predecessors, the interwar elite also wished to overcome their country's economic backwardness and achieve a more "European" standard of development. Each elite also achieved power at a time when significant popular and multi-ethnic support existed for new experiments in state-building. Both the communists and their predecessors were to be deeply frustrated, however, by the highly volatile and intractable character of ethnic relations in the Yugoslav context. Moreover, for both elites the solution of the "national problem" was closely connected to the issue of economic development. In the interwar years, constant quarreling over ethnic and regional matters precluded any real economic progress. In contrast, the communist elite after enjoying some initial success in the area of internationality relations, found the specter of ethnic conflicts haunting them again precisely because of their extremely successful, but highly unbalanced economic achievements.[19] While the two elites experienced many of the same basic problems, it is worth examining the factors which also divided them in their bitter struggle for control of contemporary Yugoslavia.

Elite Social Backgrounds

Educational Levels and Experience

Two important features characterize the educational background of the interwar Yugoslav elites: first, the extremely limited opportunities for educational training at the time when the members of the elite were of school age, and second, the close connection between educational achievement and sociopolitical stratification. The small percentage of students enrolled at the secondary and higher levels, even in the relatively more developed sections of the Yugoslav lands (i.e., Slovenia, Croatia-Slavonia, Dalmatia, and Serbia) before World War I, reflects the backward stage of post-primary education throughout the region. Thus, between 1885 and 1919, annual school enrollments in these regions for the secondary and higher levels combined ranged from

0.4 to 0.7 percent of the population over 15 years of age.[20] The extreme underdevelopment of educational facilities in the Balkan region emerges even more clearly when the almost complete absence of educational facilities and students in Bosnia-Hercegovina, Montenegro, and Macedonia is considered. Thus while there was some student attendance in foreign schools and universities, for the overwhelming majority of the population educational opportunities were extremely inadequate. Moreover, although the population was predominantly peasant and rural, most secondary and university students had urban origins.[21] The educational system did undergo some expansion during the interwar period, and increasing numbers of peasant youth were able to obtain post-primary school training (see Table 2.2), but by the eve of World War II higher school enrollments were nowhere near the educational needs of the population and society.[22]

Table 2.2
Yugoslav Student Enrollments at Various Educational Levels for Selected Years as a Percentage of the School-Age Population at Each Level (%)

Educational Level	Year					
	1918/19[a]	1926/27	1938/39	1945/46	1952/53	1960/61
Higher	0.2	1.1	1.2	1.5	2.7	5.0
Secondary	3.3	6.3	17.2	13.1[b]	13.8	22.9
Elementary	22.6	27.6	51.5	39.6	57.7	68.8
Total Enrollment (5-24 age group)	13.4	17.1	37.8	24.4	38.6	48.4

[a] Listed as estimates in sources.
[b] 1946/47.
Sources: see footnote 22.

During the interwar period, the political elite used the educational system primarily as an instrument to systematically propogate their beliefs and preserve their positions at the top of the socio-political hierarchy. The two major aims of interwar educational policy were the creation of "Yugoslav" patriotism and solidarity, and the training of qualified public employees for an expanding state bureaucracy. These aims seem rather practical considerations for an underdeveloped society, since political cohesion and qualified personnel both contribute to the achievement of modernization. The regime's policy did not, however, stimulate mass educational improvement for the general population. Indeed, one observer described the secondary gymnasiums as "factories for producing bureaucrats, never intended to be schools for ordinary citizens."[23]

Educational backwardness was a central factor in the social and political stratification of interwar Yugoslavia. The paucity of indigenous educational facilities, together with the poverty of the peasant population made formal education, and particularly higher education, almost unattainable, except for a small number of individuals. Along with the country's many other divisions, differential educational attainment was clearly a major source of socio-political tension (although strong attitudinal differences certainly existed among individuals of the same educational level). Thus, while educational achievement was difficult to obtain, it was viewed very positively by the peasant population. Education not only had intrinsic value and was a symbol of achievement, but it also offered the most effective means for obtaining a position in government service - the sure path to upward mobility. The small size of the educational system in the "Yugoslav lands" both before and after 1918 had a predictable impact on literacy rates. For example, the average rate of illiteracy for the country was 51 percent in 1931, and 44.6 percent in 1931. As a result of the regional diversity in school enrollments, illiteracy varied considerably from one area of the country to another. For example, in 1921 illiteracy for the total population above ten years of age was only 8.8 percent in Slovenia, while for Serbia the percentage was 65.4, and in Macedonia, 83.8 percent.[24]

The government's limited enthusiasm for broadening the educational system was illustrated in part by the legal treatment of adult illiteracy. For example, certain laws forbade private societies and institutions from holding courses for illiterate adults on the grounds that such courses were provided for by elementary schools. Moreover, individuals who were illiterate and under twenty-five years of age were nominally obliged to attend classes, but these classes were only organized at the request of a designated number of illiterate adults. Under these conditions, not more than four or five thousand illiterates per year throughout the country learned to read. Not much improvement existed at the upper end of the educational ladder. Although higher educational credentials were the prerequisite for attaining elite status, the individuals directing the regime appeared to favour maintaining traditional limitations to higher educational growth. Thus, the total appropriations for higher and university education formed only 0.6 percent of the national budget in 1920-1921, and 0.7 percent in 1927-1928.[25]

The importance of having received an education was reflected in the social backgrounds of those who achived positions of power and influence in interwar Yugoslavia. The data in Table 2.3 reveal that in a country, where on average approximately 50 percent of the population could not read or write, close to 100 percent of the political elite had received a higher education. Complete statistics on the proportion of the entire interwar Yugoslav population that had completed university level education are not available, but if the region's historically underdeveloped educational situation (Table 2.2) is considered together with the elite's educational composition (Table 2.3), higher schooling certainly stands out as the "hallmark" of the pre-communist political elite. The extremely high percentage of those receiving higher education among

Table 2.3
Educational Level of the Yugoslav Political Elite, 1918-41, 1948

Level of Educational Attainment	Governmental Elite		Interwar Political Elites, 1918-41				1948 Communist Political Elite	
			Administrative Elite		Economic Elite			
	Number	(%)[b]	Number	(%)	Number	(%)	Number	(%)
Higher education[a]								
Higher finished	162	95	47	100	76	89	54	45
Higher unfinished	2	1	-	-	-	-	13	11
Total higher	164	96	47	100	76	89	67	56
Secondary education								
Secondary general schools finished	1	1	-	-	4	5	2	2
Secondary general schools unfinished	1	1	-	-	1	1	5	4
Secondary vocational-technical schools	1	1	-	-	-	-	10	8
Total secondary	3	3	-	-	5	6	17	14
Elementary eduation								
One to eight grades of elementary school or no elementary education	-	-	-	-	-	-	36	30
Total elementary	-	-	-	-	-	-	36	30
Unknown	3	2	-	-	4	5	1	1
Total	170	100	47	100	85	100	121	100

[a] University facilities and postsecondary education including teachers' colleges and military education.
[b] Figures are rounded and may not add to 100 percent.

the interwar administrative elite was primarily the result of a bureaucratic system that recruited its members on the basis of educational qualifications.[26] The very high level of educational achievement among the economic elite is somewhat surprising for an entreprenurial group in a developing society, although the small sample makes it rather difficult to reach any definitive conclusions. Finally, the high educational attainments of the governmental elite can be explained by the prevailing recruitment of so many lawyers, administrators, and professional men as cabinet ministers.

The revolutionary events which occurred during World War II brought about a fundamental change in both the educational backgrounds of the elite, and the regime's educational policies. The ascendancy of political activists from the under-privileged social strata (in alliance with young people from more traditionally influential groups) was reflected in the 44 percent of the 1948 communist elite lacking higher education. Moreover, 19 percent of the more educated communist leadership had not finished their higher studies, and 88 percent of those receiving some secondary education either had not completed that level, or had only graduated from a vocational-technical school (which did not meet the admission requirements for entrance into Yugoslavia's higher educational institutions). Although more representative of the general educational makeup of Yugoslavia's population, the new communist elite clearly lacked many of the special skills necessary for the modernization of a developing society.

It is not only the extent of higher educational training which distinguished the interwar elite from their communist successors, but also the location where such training occurred (Table 2.4a). The foreign higher education enjoyed by a select minority of Balkan students before 1918, appears to be a defining characteristic of the political elite between the wars. For example, three-fifths of the interwar governmental and administrative elite who received higher education attended foreign universities, with the figures nearly as high in the case of the administrative and economic elites. The educational background of the communist decision-makers reflects a complete reversal in this pattern. Thus, more than 70 percent of the highly educated Central Committee members received their education in local universities, and 60 percent of those individuals (mainly Serbs) attended the University of Belgrade - a hotbed of revolutionary dissent in the interwar period. Only 13 percent of the communists with higher education studied outside Yugoslavia, although these figures do not include the 11 communist leaders who received higher *political* education in the Soviet Union or served in the Comintern's Moscow headquarters (seven of whom also had indigenous higher education).[27] Calculated with these additions, the total foreign educational contact for the communist elite rises to 30 percent of the entire 1948 group who received a higher education. It should also be noted that the above figures on the interwar elite only apply to foreign contact through formal education. Given the high status and special

Table 2.4
Higher Education of the Political Elite by Location

	Governmental Elite (%)	Interwar Political Elite		Economic Elite (%)	Communist Political Elite, 1948 (%)
		Administrative Elite (%)			
A. Location of Higher Schooling					
Indigenous only	34.8	38.3		10.5	70.2
Foreign	59.8	57.4		55.3	13.4
Unknown	5.4	4.3		34.2	16.4
Total	100.0	100.0		100.0	100.0
(Number)	(164)	(47)		(76)	(67)

Interwar Governmental Elite by Major Nationalities

	Serbs and Montenegrins (%)	Croats and Slovenes (%)
B. Location of Foreign Education		
Western Europe only[a]	33	—
Tsarist Russia	7	3
Germany	17	3
Austria	20	55
Austro-German[b] and East European	4	13
Austro-German and other	13	10
East European only	6	16
Total	100	100
(Number)	(54)	(31)
C. Location of Indigenous Education		
Belgrade	88	—
Zagreb	9	83
Other	3	17
Total	100	100
(Number)	(34)	(12)

[a] Other than Austria and Germany.
[b] Austro-German signifies Austrian or German.

opportunities available to this group, there would probably be a significant increase in the total percentage of elite members having foreign contacts if travel connected with leisure time and occupational duties were also taken into consideration. This situation would further widen the gap in foreign experience already existing between the communist and interwar elite groups.

As distinct political "styles" and "tempermants" associated with different nationalities and regions are often alleged to have been important sources of intra-elite cleavage during the interwar period, it was also tempting to examine whether different domestic and foreign educational experiences may have contributed to such cleavages. In general, the analysis reveals that the members of the interwar elites received their educational training in quite varied environments, a factor which may have (and such findings can only suggest this tendency) fostered or exacerbated other culturally based elite conflicts. As Table 2.4b indicates, the members of the governmental elite gravitated to many different university centers in their foreign higher educational experiences. The enrollment of Croats and Slovenes in Austrian, German, and East European universities, was substantially greater than the percentage of Serbs and Montenegrins who attended schools in those regions. Paris was particularly favoured by the Serbs and Montenegrins, and in the late 1800's the law faculty of the University of Paris was already referred to in Serbia as "the school for ministers."[28] The nearby Austrian and German schools appeared to have attracted students from all the South Slav groups, with Berlin and Munich preferred by the Serbs and Montenegrins and Vienna and Graz by the Croat and Slovene members of the interwar elite. The pattern of domestic experience is even more fragmented, with the Serbs heavily concentrated at Belgrade, and the Croats at Zagreb.

These patterns of foreign educational attendance may be explained by various factors such as the 1878 Austrian occupation of Bosnia-Hercegovina, the escalation of Austro-Serbian emnity, and the formal requirements of Serbian state scholarships for study abroad. Other more universal factors, such as academic specialization and differentiation of faculty offerings by various national universities were also at work. The Serbs, as members of a sovereign political entity, also had opportunities for choice that the Croats and Slovenes, as subjects of the Austro-Hungarian monarchy, lacked. Many of the Croats and Slovenes naturally gravitated to Vienna, which before 1918 was their "national capital" in fact, if not in spirit.[29] Finally, those who did not leave their country for educational purposes, did not stray far from their homes for their schooling. Politics, borders, and the high cost of education probably all played a role in such choices.

Another interesting aspect of educational background to consider is the type of education which elite members received. Analysis of which academic fields facilitated the attainment of elite status sheds some light on the kinds of concerns which may have shaped elite values and behaviour, and also the extent

Table 2.5
Type of Elite Education, Higher Educated Members of the Political Elite, and the Structure of Enrollment

Faculty or School	Interwar Political Elite			Communist Political Elite, 1948 (%)	Structure of Enrollments	
	Governmental Elite (%)	Administrative Elite (%)	Economic Elite (%)		1919-1940 (%)	1945-1957 (%)
Engineering-polytechnical [a]	7	6	14	5	14	22
Agricultural [b]	1	-	3	9	9	15
Medical [c]	8	3	-	11	9	21
Law	60	79[e]	32[f]	40	44	12
Economics	4	3	46	9	3	10
Arts and Natural Sciences	11	9	5	16	23	20
Military	9	-	2	-	-[g]	-[g]
Other	-	-	-	10[h]	-	-[i]
Total All Faculties	100	100	100	100	100	100
(Number)	(164)	(47)	(76)	(67)	(30,334)	(49,278)

[a] Including architecture and high technical schools; [b] including veterinary medicine and forestry; [c] including pharmacy and dentistry; [d] including higher commercial schools; [e] including political science and social science; [f] three individuals have a combined law and economics education, and two had law and philosophy; [g] no information; [h] pedagogical education; [i] less than 1%.

Source: For structure of enrollments, Rade Aleksić, "Inteligencija u Jugoslavenskom društvu," *Sociologija*, VI, No. 1-2 (1964), p. 124.

of elite capability for managing and modernizing the state. The figures in Table 2.5 reveal that more than 80 percent of the interwar elite receiving higher education attended faculties other than science, technology, and medicine. The trend toward the more "traditional vocations," notably law, was particularly pronounced among state administrators (79 percent of the administrative elite and 60 percent of the governmental elite having received a legal education). Philosophy was the next most popular field of training for both elite groups, if the military officers in the cabinet are excluded. In contrast, 46 percent of the economic elite obtained degrees in commercial-business faculties, although even among the entrepreneurs, 32 percent had been trained as lawyers.[30] It is particularly interesting that in a country in which approximately 80 percent of the total population was involved in agricultural pursuits, only one percent of the governmental elite had formal training in the field of agriculture, and no such educational background was evident among the members of the administrative elite. This situation becomes more comprehensible, however, when it is considered that the intention of most students who actually did enroll in agricultural schools was to get out of the agricultural milieu and become government employees.[31]

A comparison of elite educations and interwar university enrollment figures indicates that the percentage of interwar leaders completing a legal education was exceedingly high, even in view of the universities' strong emphasis on legal studies. From a practical standpoint, law was a good choice for the aspiring young man in the Balkans, particularly because legal studies were an essential requirement for admission into the public service. In a country in which the state was the biggest employer, a government job and pension accorded both status and security. Secondly, Yugoslavia was a society of small land owners where traditional property rights were acquiring legal status. This involved constant peasant disputes over land ownership, and the costly legal proceedings which resulted made law a good way to earn a living.[32] Another incentive for undertaking a legal education was that this course of study did not require frequent attendance at the university, and was therefore less expensive for those students who could not afford to live in an urban setting for the entire year. Finally, legal studies were a sensible choice for those who wanted to enjoy some flexibility in choosing their career pattern. This factor is well illustrated by the remarks of Vladko Maček who led the Croatian Peasant Party from 1928 to 1941.

> I was ready to choose a career. I had already made up my mind to devote my life to the struggle for the liberation of Croatia and the Croatian people, but to do this without restriction one had to have an independent existence. The best course to take, therefore, was to enter a university and continue my studies. Should it be theology, philosophy or law? One

had little choice, for those three faculties were the only ones taught at the time at the University of Zagreb .... I became convinced that I would never make a model priest. The other two faculties led me one way or another to official service, which meant to serve the regime blindly. Agronomy, forestry or science would have been more to my taste, but these were out of the question - first because the requisite schools did not exist in Croatia, and second because, even assuming I could complete my studies abroad, such an education would have again led ultimately to civil service .... After careful deliberation, I decided to become a lawyer, although that profession did not hold much attraction for me. Nevertheless, law was practically the only profession in which one had some freedom to act politically and even to oppose the government - providing, of course, one was not primarily interested in making money.[33]

The tendency toward law and other non-technical faculties by the interwar Yugoslav intelligentsia led to the overcrowding of the so-called "talking professions," fields which were well suited to disputation about political trends, but less relevant for the modernization of the country. Moreover, many intellectuals who declined to serve the bureaucratic system and were unable to find suitable employment for their legal and philosophical training outside the state framework, naturally were attracted to radical socio-political activity as a viable career alternative.[34]

Only 56 percent of the 1948 communist elite received a higher education, but of those who did 40 percent were trained in law and 16 percent studied philosophy, a distribution which corresponds closely to the interwar pattern of higher university enrollments. The proportion of highly educated communist elite members with training in technical fields was about 8 percent higher than for the interwar governmental elite, although communist leaders with such technical education constituted only 12 percent of the entire 120 members in the 1948 elite group. The 10 percent of highly educated communists who received pedagogical training reflects the important role which a career in teaching can have on the upward mobility and political mobilization of individuals in developing societies. Most of those who had attended faculties of education actually had no formal teaching experience in Yugoslavia, while some used their pedagogical skills for political indoctrination, as in the case of Edward Kardelj, who taught in a Moscow political school. This situation is quite different from the experiences of the interwar elite members having academic or teaching careers, most of whom were highly trained university professors. The absence of military training among the communist elite, which is revealed in Table 2.5, refers only to formal education in military academies and not to the valuable experience of the revolutionaries in the "school of life" (e.g., the Spanish Civil War, World War II, etc.).

The wartime victory of the communist intelligentsia and their more

Lenard J. Cohen

modestly trained worker and peasant allies not only resulted in a political and social revolution, but also in an educational revolution. Indeed, an emphasis on educational training was an important facet of the communists' program both before and during the wartime period, and was a contributing factor to the Party's appeal among the peasantry. Once in power, the imperatives of the new regime's modernizing ideology and industrialization policies demanded that mass education receive priority attention. By 1948, for example, as a consequence of strenuous efforts to stimulate educational development, the illiteracy rate had been reduced to 25 percent, compared to 45 percent in 1931. The communists' modernization program also necessitated the acquisition of new types of skills by both the elite and the general population. Thus, the modestly educated professional revolutionaries and those leaders with traditional educations, were obliged to provide training and opportunities for a new generation of managerial and technically-oriented specialists - a gradual process sometimes involving difficult adjustments for the communist political elite (see Chapter 3). The growing importance of technical skills is reflected in the university enrollment figures for 1945-1957 (Table 2.5). The course of industrialization now required that emphasis be placed on engineering, medicine, agriculture, and economics, while the number of students recruited for legal studies was allowed to drop off sharply. As in the case of economic growth, however, the communists' success in rapidly accelerating and restructuring educational development would eventually result in certain unintended political consequences (see Chapter 8).

Occupation and Class

The occupational backgrounds of the interwar political leaders closely resembles their distribution in different fields of higher education. The major occupations of the governmental elite members prior to entering the cabinet were law, politics, and state administration (Table 2.6). Over half of the cabinet ministers between the wars were recruited from these occupations, and most had received education in either law or philosophy. The boundaries between occupations such as law, professional politics, and journalism ("publicists") are far from precise, however, because of the constant individual career movement between these fields of work. Individuals in these occupational categories make up 44 percent of the governmental elite sample and can broadly be considered as "politicians" or "men of public affairs."[35] The large number of professors attaining cabinet positions suggests the existence of an "educator-politician" elite type in interwar Yugoslavia.[36] Closer examination of this subgroup reveals that most of the professors, and also a smaller group of engineers and doctors, occupied positions in the cabinet requiring a certain degree of "expert" knowledge such as the portfolios of education, health, agrarian reform, transpor-

Table 2.6
The Occupational Background of Interwar Parliamentary Deputies and Cabinet Ministers (%)

Occupational Sector	Parliamentary Deputies							Cabinet Ministers 1919-1941	Yugoslavia's Economically Active Population 1938
	Multi-Party System				Authoritarian System				
	1920	1923	1925	1927	1931	1935		
Agriculture	20.2	29.1	24.7	15.8	14.7	19.7	1.0	78.3
Labour (Private Employees, Workers and Craftsmen)	7.8	1.6	1.3	1.9	1.0	4.8	-	14.6
Business (Merchants and Entrepreneurs)	2.8	8.0	8.2	11.4	16.7	15.4	5.0	2.9
Medicine, Engineering	4.4	4.7	3.8	8.6	5.6	5.4	12.0	0.3
Education, Culture	10.2	13.1	12.0	7.0	5.6	10.0	16.0	
Journalism	4.8	3.2	2.5	3.4	2.6	3.5	6.0	
Law	12.6	14.7	15.5	14.6	19.7	18.6	22.0	
State (Public) Administration, and Party Officialdom	28.6	15.7	24.1	27.3	21.0	13.5	28.0	3.8
Military	-	-	-	-	-	1.6	9.0	
Religion	4.2	6.0	3.1	3.4	7.5	4.8	2.0	
Other	4.2	3.5	4.4	6.3	3.9	0.3	-	
Total	100.0	100.0	100.0	100.0	100.0	100.0	100.0	100.0
(Number)	(419)	(312)	(315)	(315)	(305)	(370)	(165)	(6,927,000)

Source: see footnote 38.

The Socialist Pyramid: Elites and Power in Yugoslavia

tation, and commerce. These specialists, who constituted almost one-third of the governmental elite, served mainly in a bureaucratic and technical capacity, exerting a limited influence on the formation of public policy. In contrast, the underrepresentation of the commercial, landowning, military, and ecclesiastical occupations in successive cabinets does not correspond to the considerable influence of these groups on public policy. In view of what is known about interwar Yugoslavia, the absence of these groups from cabinet positions tends to confirm the important caveat that ease of entry into an elite, and the ability to exert influence on an elite are not the same thing and may not even vary together.[37]

Additional insights regarding the occupational composition of the political elite in interwar Yugoslavia are offered in the analysis of data on parliamentary deputies (Table 2.6).[38] When data for all the legislatures elected between 1918 and 1936 is combined (no official information is available for 1938) it appears that occupational groups which composed roughly four percent of the population provided three-quarters of all the parliamentary deputies. As in the case of the cabinet elite, party politicians, state officials, and lawyers together composed the largest proportion of individuals serving in the interwar legislatures. The presence of spokesmen from the agricultural, commercial, and religious sectors is much greater in the legislatures than on the cabinet level, however, with the reverse situation prevailing in the case of technical specialists such as doctors, engineers, and professors. The cabinets were, of course, chosen from the pool of parliamentary deputies, but not all of the members of the legislature were considered suitable for service in the highest government body. The almost total absence of proletarian representation in the legislature is especially striking, particularly when considered in relation to the postwar communist elite (see below). The information on the occupational composition of interwar legislatures also highlights the difference between the multiparty system of the 1920's and the authoritarian regime in the 1930's. Thus, in the two Parliaments (1931 and 1935) elected after the proclamation of royal dictatorship in 1929, there is a marked decline in the representation of politicians from the traditional parties including the spokesmen of the peasant movements and various supporters (professors and journalists) of a more liberal political order, while at the same time the authoritarian regime's supporters in the clergy, the military, and in entreprenurial circles are clearly more visible.

The occupational composition of the 1948 communist elite again illustrates the nature of the revolutionary changes brought about by the war. Although the available biographical data is extremely limited with respect to information concerning the early occupational backgrounds of the communist leadership, it can reasonably be determined that nearly all the individuals in the 1948 elite had been members of the intelligentsia (including students) or the industrial proletariat who, either before or during the war, had become professionally engaged in revolutionary political activity.[39] In contrast, the peasantry

The Socialist Pyramid: Elites and Power in Yugoslavia

Table 2.7
Occupational Background of the Partisan Movement's Army, Officer Corps and "Heroes," compared to the Communist Party's Central Committee Members, 1940-1952 (%)

Occupational Background	Partisan Movement			Communist Party Central Committee Members		
	Participants[a]	Senior Officer Corps 1945[b]	"Peoples Heroes"[c]	Oct. 1940[d]	1948[e]	1952
Workers	30.8	30.0	37.5	47.4	39.0	37.6
Peasants	61.1	42.0	17.3	2.6	4.8	2.8
Employees	8.1	28.0	45.2	7.9	2.9	1.8
Intelligentsia	-	-	-	42.1	53.3	57.8
Total	100.0	100.0	100.0	100.0	100.0	100.0
(Number)	(907,949)	(c. 9,300)	(1,307)	(38)	(105)	(109)

[a] Based on records for Partisan veterans living in 1960. At the end of World War II the Partisan Movement included roughly 1.4 million members. Approximately 305,000 Partisan soldiers and officers died in the war (along with 1.4 million civilians or about 10.8% of Yugoslavia's population). The social composition of the Partisans varied according to the year of the war and the region of the country. Many of the first Partisan brigades were mainly comprised of workers and members of the intelligentsia, but as the war progressed peasants clearly predominated in the ranks.

[b] Approximately 92.3% of all officers were members of the Communist Party or its youth organization.

[c] 1,307 Partisan fighters and leaders were awarded the "Order of National Hero," 807 posthumously.

[d] 14 members of the entire Central Committee died in the war.

[e] The data on the Central Committee members refers to their "primary occupation," rather than the social origin (father's occupation) or the major adult career sector of the individuals included. Thus professional party workers are not listed as a distinct occupational category. For example, professsional revolutionaries such as Tito and Alexander Rankovic are described as "workers" while Moshe Pijade and Edward Kardelj are listed as "publicists." Approximately 24 of the 68 full members of the 1948 Central Committee were "professional revolutionaries" and roughly 23% of the entire Central Committee were Partisan military officers.

Sources: see footnote 40.

which provided the bulk of the fighting manpower in the Partisan movement, were almost completely absent in the Party elite. The figures provided in Table 2.7 on the "social positions" (i.e., primary occupations) of those serving in the Partisan military forces and officer corps, as well as those recognized as "heroes" of the Partisan movment, also illustrate the disproportionately high representation of intellectuals and workers in the party elite relative to the movement they were leading.[40] Just as the interwar governmental elite had overrepresented the bureaucratic and legal professions in a predominantly agricultural country, so too the early postwar communist elite overrrepresented the industrial labour force and the intelligentsia.

The early occupational experiences of the communists had a direct impact on their commitment to a revolutionary movement, and their recruitment to top political roles (i.e., the ideological imperative of including workers in the leadership). The actual attainment of elite status by the communist members, however, occurred primarily as a result of success in the National Liberation War and the displacement of the interwar elite. In the course of the war, "ideologically advanced" but administratively inexperienced individuals were transformed into a new military and political leadership group under the direction of a small core of seasoned professional revolutionaries. Thus, very few members of the 1948 communist elite had any prewar experience in actual leadership positions outside the underground opposition. Two major factors facilitated the communists' attainment of the occupational skills necessary to acquire and retain state authority: first, the participation of several hundred Yugoslav communists in the Spanish Civil War, and second, the organizational demands of armed resistance and the political management of territory liberated during the war. For example, information on the prewar and wartime activity of the 1948 political elite reveal that approximately one-third of the group had been members of the Communist youth movement (SKOJ), 95 percent joined the Party before the outbreak of World War II, 15 percent participated in the Spanish Civil War, and 85 percent took a direct part in the Partisan struggle.[41] Alexander Ranković, in his report to the first postwar Party Congress, paid tribute to the importance of wartime experience of the Partisans as a basis for leadership in the new regime:

> What were the sources of cadres for the state apparatus ...? First, the Party organizations and organs of the people's authority that existed and functioned on liberated territory, and partly on unliberated territory, during the course of the war. Many people from these party organizations, and especially from those in the regions of the uprising, were transferred and appointed to responsible leading positions in the federal and republican state institutions .... Second, the Army. Without weakening its militance, a large number of fighters and officers were demobilized and assigned to leading positions in the state apparatus. This cadre was on a high political level and has been tested through the National Liberation Struggle. *It was only necessary to work patiently on the reorientation of the man who had been a fighter, military or political leader during the war, so that he would become a good leader in economy, administration, and cultural-educational work, etc., as soon as possible. The workers, peasants and a large number of intellectuals found themselves doing work which they had never done before.* [Author's emphasis.][42]

Thus far the analysis has shown that the interwar elite constituted a highly

Table 2.8
The Class Background of the Interwar Political Elite (%)

A. Father's Occupational Sector	Governmental Elite	Adminstrative Elite	Economic Elite
Commerce	34.7	23.3	58.5
Civil Service	26.5	26.7	18.5
Agricultural	18.4	20.0	7.7
Professional	6.1	16.7	9.2
Military	4.1	6.7	1.5
Clergy	10.2	-	4.6
Industrial Labor	-	6.7	-
Total	100.0	100.0	100.0
(Number)	(49)	(30)	(65)
B. Father's Social Class[a]			
Higher Bourgeoise[b]	20.4	10.0	23.1
Middle Class	69.4	66.7	73.8
Proletariat and Peasantry	10.2	23.3	3.1
Total	100.0	100.0	100.0
(Number)	(49)	(30)	(65)

[a] Estimated from the occupational position of the fathers of the elite.
[b] Includes industrialists, financiers, landowners, and the higher ranks of the civil service and military.

educated group in the midst of educational backwardness, but also a group which was more suited to the game of party politics than to the tasks of rapid socio-economic modernization. A large portion of the communist elite lacked higher educational training, but on the whole the Partisan political leadership was more representative of the previously excluded sectors of the population. Comparison of the class backgrounds of the communist and interwar elites can shed further light on Yugoslavia's changing "opportunity structure" and also, at least to some extent, the basis and consequences of revolutionary change. Because an individual's occupation is an important determinant of his social ranking, the occupations of the fathers of the elite members provide a good index of an elite member's class background. The material gathered on class background in most complete for the administrative and economic sub-elites, although the more partial date for the governmental sub-elite is representative of that group as well.

The class composition of the fathers of the interwar elite shown in Table 2.8b highlights the predominant role of society's "middle sectors" as a basis for leadership recruitment in the "Yugoslav lands." More than two-thirds of all the individuals in the elite sub-groups had fathers who were situated in the middle class occupational strata. Only ten percent of the governmental elite, and three percent of the economic elite had origins below the middle social sectors. The more modest social origins of the administrative elite confirms the importance of public employment as an avenue for upward social mobility, although three-quarters of the higher civil servants also came from the middle and upper sectors of society. The breakdown of the occupational sectors of the fathers in Table 2.8a reveals that even though the commercial, landowning, and ecclesiastical backgrounds were rare among the actual incumbents of top governmental positions (see Table 2.6), a substantial basis existed for elite identification with those social sectors. Mercantile occupations were quite common in the class backgrounds of all three interwar elite sub-groups, but particularly among the fathers of the economic elite, the group which exhibited the highest level of occupational similarity between fathers and sons (58 percent). The high proportion of elite members whose fathers were state officials, again demonstrates the importance of the state bureaucracy as a basis for upward social mobility. Although the advantages of middle class social origins in interwar Yugoslavia did not serve as a substitute for the educational prerequisites of elite status (attendance at university, bureaucratic examinations, etc.), such a class background was a considerable aid in obtaining higher and particularly foreign education. Many sons of peasants and workers were able to attend university in the 1920's and 1930's, but their limited numbers and very slow upward mobility had no appreciable affect on the regime's strong oligarchical features.[43] Almost all the members of the interwar governmental elite were drawn from a very restricted pool of eligible persons who enjoyed life styles, incomes, and interests which closely resembled the top ranks of the middle class.

Viewed in Balkan historical perspective, it might be argued that the movement of individuals with middle class origins into top government, economic, and administrative positions provides evidence of considerable upward mobility. Thus, information on the grandfathers of the interwar elites would probably indicate that those elite incumbents were only one or two generations removed from either the more prosperous ranks of the peasantry or a very small and only modestly endowed professional and bureaucratic strata. In this regard it must be remembered that the grandfathers of the interwar elite were individuals who reached adulthood in the first half and middle of the 19th century. As Serbian society (the ethnic group from which most of the interwar elite derived) was largley composed of peasants at that time (approximately 90 percent) and was just beginning to develop a ruling professional and bureaucratic class, it can be surmised that a process of considerable social mobility had occurred over three generations.[44] A satisfactory analysis of this hypothesis, however, requires a more systematic examination of the social mobility patterns of the fathers and grandfathers of the elite than the available data will support.

Limitations in the available data also create certain difficulties for comparing the class backgrounds of the communist elite with their predecessors. Even with incomplete information, however, some conclusions can be reached. For example, it is reasonable to assume that the 44 percent of the 1948 elite who were peasants and workers in terms of their primary occupations (see Table 2.7) came from peasant, and to a lesser extent, working class families. Thus, it is extremely unlikely that the individuals in these two occupational categories were downwardly mobile from upper-bourgeoisie and middle class families.[45] As for the remaining 56 percent of the 1948 elite group, it is often pointed out that many of the intelligentsia in the communist elite came from upper middle class families, some of whom were actually part of or closely connected with the ruling elite. For example, among Tito's wartime associates were Koča Popović, the son of a wealthy Belgrade industrialist, Boris Kidrič, the son of a well-known university professor, and Vladimir Bakarić, the son of a supreme court judge. By combining various biographical sources, it is possible to obtain a more precise class breakdown of the 1948 elite. Considering only those members of the communist elite who were neither peasants nor workers in terms of their own occupational backgrounds before the war, approximately 59 percent had social origins in the middle sectors while the remainder were either the children of peasants (35 percent) or workers (6 percent). When the first generation members of the intelligentsia are added to the worker and peasant contingent in the elite itself (again in terms of primary occupations), it appears that roughly two-thirds of the entire 1948 elite had either peasant or proletarian origins.[46] Thus, while a large number of the communist elite were themselves members of the intelligentsia with middle class and upper class social origins, it nevertheless remains that the outstanding feature of social mobility in Yugoslavia after 1941 was the collective revolutionary ascent of former peasant and workers, or the children of peasants and workers, into elite positions. In Yugoslavia, as in many other continental European countries, the substantial rise of working class leaders to elite status has been almost exclusively associated with the success of the working class party.

Town and Village

As previously mentioned, the conflict between town and village was the one major social cleavage in interwar Yugoslavia that cross-cut ethnic, regional, and religious lines. The peasantry in every section of the country appeared to have a common distrust and dislike of their fellow citizens in the towns and cities. Such negative attitudes were historically directed against the non-Slavic merchant element in the developing Balkan towns and markets, but were later directed toward the urban members of the indigenous middle class.[47] Although the anti-urban orientation of the Yugoslav peasantry rarely created any strong bonds of solidarity among peasants from different nationality and religious groups, the special conditions of foreign conquest and guerrilla struggle during World War II provided an unusual opportunity for cross-ethnic contact in the rural areas. Whether such wartime peasant interaction resulted in violent conflict or a new comradeship, however, depended on a host of local circumstances and factors, and only partially involved the deeper convictions of the rural masses themselves.

The rural-urban distribution of elite birthplaces indicated in Table 2.9 reveals that less than one-third of the communist elite came from communities with populations of over 5,000 people, although one-half of the interwar elite were born in towns of that size.[48] Moreover, whereas 24 percent of the interwar elite were born in the national capital or in regional centers, only six percent of the communists came from those birthplaces. Twenty-five of the interwar cabinet ministers (17 percent) were born in Belgrade, compared with only one member of the 1948 communist group. The small number of communist leaders with urban childhood backgrounds becomes even more significant when it is remembered that only five percent of the post-World War II leadership were peasants by primary occupation. The predominance of village backgrounds among the communists, again illustrates the modest social origins of the 1948 elite and the presence of a large number of first generation intellectuals.[49] Although belonging to the vanguard of a party which sought to establish the "dictatorship of the proletariat," the social origins and primary occupations of the communist leadership linked them closely to the peasantry, as did the requirement of making a revolution in an essentially agrarian society. Describing the wartime migration of the communist intelligentsia and urban proletarians from the capital city and industrial centers to the villages, and the successful recruitment of rural leaders and young people into the Partisan movement by such outsiders, one Yugoslav analyst has remarked:

> ... during the course of executing the armed part of the revolution (1941-1945) the brightest intellectual forces of the working class lived, worked and directed activities in the village - metal workers, printers, intellectuals, communists, and communist leaders .... In many villages famous doctors, philosophers, poets, authors, historians, actors, agronomists, teachers, soldiers and generals, lived for four years and above all were exceptionally good comrades who in a very impressive way established direct, and close human and political relationships with the people from the villages. After the conclusion of the war in 1945 all of that avantgarde quickly left for the cities, taking with them a large number of politically and intellectually capable rural people cultivated by the Party and thereby denuding the village of cadre ....[50]

The Socialist Pyramid: Elites and Power in Yugoslavia

Table 2.9
Elite Birthplaces by Size and Centrality

	Governmental Elite 1918-1941	Communist Elite 1948	Total Population 1931
	(%)	(%)	(%)
A. Size of Elite Birthplace[a]			
Rural (under 5,000)	50	69	81
Urban (over 5,000)	50	31	19
Total	100	100	100
(Number)	(139)	(92)	
B. Centrality of Elite Birthplace			
Belgrade	17	1	1
Regional centers[b]	7	5	2
Other	76	94	97
Total	100	100	100
(Number)	(139)	(92)	(14.5 M)

[a] The rural-urban dichotomy used here is based upon the official definition used in the 1921 and 1931 censuses. It focuses on the number of persons in a locality rather than on the population's functional composition. Thus, many towns of over 5,000 people had a substantial portion of their population employed in agriculture.
[b] Zagreb, Sarajevo, Ljubljana, Cetinje and Skopje.
Sources: see footnote 48.

There is, of course, a certain tendency by Yugoslav communist writers to romanticize the behaviour and appeal of the "good comrades" from the cities. During the war, nevertheless, an only recently urbanized Marxist counter-elite, (or indeed intially an anti-elite) managed to catapult itself, and many newly won allies from the rural sector, directly into positions of power and influence, thereby displacing the former state authorities and achieving a truly revolutionary circulation of elites. Once ensconced at or near the top of the new social and political structure, only a few of those newly urbanized village revolutionaries and their only slightly more urbanized recruiters would again return to the countryside, except for short business and holiday trips.

Generational and Genderic Backgrounds

A comparison of the age structure of the interwar and communist elites reveals that together with the differences in education, social class, and occupation, the two elites were also divided by a sharp generation gap. For example, two-thirds of the senior cadre in the Partisan movement were under 28 years of age, and nearly all of the commanders of the Partisan armies, corps, and divisions were between 22 and 32 years old.[51] At the end of the war in 1945, the average age of the communist elite (i.e., the group formally elected in 1948) was 35, 17 years younger than the last interwar cabinet appointed in 1939 (excluding the short-lived government set up by the coup de'état of March 1941). The average age at which the members of the interwar leadership achieved elite status was 47 years of age, 12 years older than the average age of the communist leadership group when they assumed power. In 1948, the members of the new Central Committee on average had been members of the Communist Party for 14 years, and their average age of enlistment in the party was 26. The youthful appeal of communism in interwar Yugoslavia is further underlined by the 38 percent of the 1948 communist leadership who joined the party before they had reached 22 years of age.

Age also reveals the different recruitment patterns of the two elites. For example, the average age of the total interwar governmental elite group from 1918 to 1940 increased by only five years, that is, when the cabinet's average age is measured at the beginning and end of that 22 year period. Moreover, the average age of almost every cabinet between the wars was 47 to 49 years. This rather constant age level of succeeding cabinets reflects the continual recruitment of younger men into the interwar elite, although not necessarily the assimilation of new perspectives and attitudes. On the other hand, the average age of the communist elite group as a whole increased about 10 years in the two decades after World War II, a time in which Tito and his colleagues underwent a good deal of ideological readjustment. By the mid-1960's, the average age of the communist elite group appeared to be levelling off at almost exactly the same level as their interwar predecessors in 1940.[52] This change reflected the general aging of the Party membership. In 1950, for example, 40 percent of the Party's members were below 25 years of age, but by 1966 the equivalent figure had dropped to 13 percent.[53] The potential seriousness of a new generation gap between the political leadership and the younger intelligentsia - a pattern reminiscent of the interwar period - was frequently mentioned by the communist leaders in the 1960's. Measures designed to improve the situation, such as new rules for the "rotation of cadre" were not, however, always entirely successful and sometimes had quite unexpected repercussions (see Chapters 4 and 5).

Perhaps the most striking contrast between the communist and the interwar elites was the postwar appearance of women in political leadership positions. Between 1918 and 1941, women were completely unrepresented in the higher political elite (excluding influential female members of the royal family). Some women from middle class and even peasant backgrounds did attend university or served in the "free professions,"[54] but their numbers were very small and they exerted no real influence on political decision-making. The emancipation and mobilization of women was a major component of the Communist Party's wartime program and was implemented through an auxillary organization for women (The Women's Anti-Fascist Front). It was the involvement of approximately 100,000 women in the wartime Partisan forces (or about 12 percent of the total movement) which completely altered the role of women in Yugoslav public life. Over 2,000 women served as officers in the

Table 2.10
Women in the Yugoslav Political Elite, 1948 (%)

Location or Level	Federal and Republican Party Central Committees (full and candidate members)			District Party Committees	Percentage of Women in Communist Party
	Total Number	Number of Women	Percentage of Women	Percentage of Women	
Yugoslavia	105	6	5.7	-	16.7
Republican Level					
Slovenia	65	6	9.2	6.6	28.1
Croatia	84	9	10.7	12.5	23.3
Serbia	103	6	5.8	7.1	20.1
Macedonia	61	6	9.8	15.0	14.1*
Montenegro	48	3	6.3	15.2	28.1*
Bosnia and Herzegovina	67	4	6.0	n.a.	17.4

* Figures are for 1949.
Sources: see footnote 55.

Partisan armies, and women composed seven percent of those awarded the status of "People's Hero." The figures in Table 2.10 demonstrate the postwar participation of women in the leading bodies of the Communist Party.[55] In 1948, women constituted approximately six percent of the Central Committee and 17 percent of the entire Communist Party membership. The figures on the representation of women in the republican party elites and organizations display considerable regional variation. The more economically developed areas of Croatia and Slovenia stand out in terms of the high percentage of women in both the party membership and leadership. The relatively high percentage of women in the party membership of Montenegro, and in the party leadership of Macedonia - two very economically depressed and traditionally patriarchical areas - suggests, however, that the environments of most pronounced male domination also engendered strong revolutionary commitments among women.[56]

Lenard J. Cohen

Table 2.11
The Ethnic Composition of the Yugoslav Military Establishment
Before and After World War II (%)

	Total Population	Officer Corps		Generals	
		Interwar	Partisan	Interwar	Communist
	(1948)	(1941)	(1946)	(1941)	(1970)
Ethnic Groups					
Serbs	41.5	⎫	51.0	⎫	46.7
Montenegrins	2.7	⎬ 70.2*	9.2	⎬ 86.5	19.3
Macedonians	5.1	⎭	3.6	⎭	3.9
Croats	24.0	16.2	22.7	9.1	19.3
Slovenes	9.0	11.5	9.7	4.4	6.3
Bosnian Moslems	5.1	2.1	1.9	-	3.2
Other	12.6	-	-	-	-
Total	100.0	100.0	100.0	100.0	100.0
(Number)	(15.8 M)	(191)	(n.a.)	(230)	(n.a.)

* Interwar data on the Serbs includes the Montenegrin and the Macedonian nationalities.
Source: see footnote 59.

Ethnic Origins

The historical importance of the "national question" in Yugoslav political life has made the ethnic representativeness of elites an important gauge of regime success and stability, both before and after World War II. Thus, any ethnic discrimination in the assignment of important political positions has usually been seized upon by group spokesmen to illustrate the failures or illegitimacy of the ruling elite and the existing political institutions. The symbolic importance of the elite's ethnic composition is well illustrated by remarks made by the Croatian Peasant Party leader, Stjepan Radić, concerning the composition of the government in 1926:

> ... at the time of the fourth partial revision of the Government I succeeded in introducing a Slovene into the actual coalition Government to represent the entire Slovene people, so that there are now thirteen Serbian Ministers, four Croats and one Slovene. *The time is approaching when there will be nine Serbs and nine Croats and Slovenes, which will be a visible sign and an irrefutable proof of the real and practical equality between the Croats and Slovenes and our brother Serbs.* [Author's emphasis.][57]

The Socialist Pyramid: Elites and Power in Yugoslavia

The political opposition of Radić, his party, and the majority of the Croatian people to the Yugoslav state was a major cause of the interwar regime's continual crises, and its failure to develop any real cross-ethnic legitimacy. There is little doubt that the gross inequities in the ethnic makeup of the top political elites intensified the Croatian opposition. For example, between December 1918 and March 1941, a period of 268 months, Serbs held the office of prime minister for 264 months, the Ministry of the Army and Navy for 268 months, the Ministry of the Interior (controlling the police) for 240 months, the Ministry of Foreign Affairs for 247 months, the Ministry of Finance for 216 months, the Ministry of Education for 236 months, and the Ministry of Justice for 237 months.[58] The underrepresentation of the non-Serbian ethnic groups was also highly visible in the diplomatic corps and in the military establishment (Table 2.12).[59] Non-Serbians composed approximately 59 percent of the total interwar population, but in 1941 they accounted for only 14 percent of the active generals, and for only about 30 percent of the officers in the military. The situation in the upper echelons of the state bureaucracy was somewhat better for non-Serbs, and recent evidence reveals that by the eve of World War II the striking ethnic disproportions in the military were decreasing, but there was no real progress toward equitable representation for interwar Yugoslavia's many nationalities.[60]

By the late 1930's the Communist Party had begun to make good tactical use of the grievances generated by the interwar elite's discriminatory nationality policies. During the war an emphasis on ethnic equality and the promise to establish a new federal system permeated communist propaganda, and party leaders made a genuine effort to ensure that their movement's multi-national strategy was supported by the behaviour of the rank and file party members. Although, as frequently related in studies of the Partisan movment, Serbs made up a disproportionately high share of the Partisan membership, the ethnic representativeness of the top party organs was, nevertheless, an important feature of the communists' nationality program.[61] The communists' effort in this regard was certainly reflected in the ethnic composition of the 1948 elite (considering the full and candidate members of the Central Committee together): Serbs, 33.3 percent; Croats, 20.1 percent; Slovenes, 15 percent; Montenegrins, 13 percent; Macedonians, 11.4 percent; Albanians one percent; Hungarians, one percent; and "Yugoslavs" (mainly Bosnian Moslems), two percent.[62] The ethnic composition of the new elite reflected a radical improvement from the prewar situation, although it was by no means perfectly representative of the total population's ethnic makeup. Indeed, some of the smaller nationalities received a greater number of elite posts than their strength in the population would seem to justify. This was especially noticeable in the case of the Montenegrins, whose allotment of the leading political and military positions was several times greater than their percentage of the population

129

(roughly 2.7 percent in 1948). This situation reflects both the very active participation of Montenegrins in the Partisan movement and the Communist Party, and also illustrates the use of criteria in elite recruitment which went beyond proportional ethnic representation.

The more equitable pattern of ethnic group representation introduced by the communists is often acknowledged as an important factor in their wartime success and postwar consolidation. The presentation of statistical information on the representiveness of political elites in itself, however, tends to beg a number of important questions concerning the relationship between a leadership's ethnic composition and the overall management of cultural diversity. First, what are the particular functions performed by leaders from different ethnic groups, and how much political influence actually derives from such positions? For example, a balance of "nine Serbs" to "nine Croats and Slovenes" means little, even symbolically, in terms of ethnic accommodation or political cohesion if the Croats in the elite are considered traitors by the majority of the Croatian people (as was sometimes the case in interwar Yugoslavia). Politically significant representation results from the articulation and attainment of specific group interests perceived as such by the members of the ethnic group. Finally, do fixed ethnic quotas in the elite actually perpetuate cleavages by creating focal points for sub-cultural loyalties, or do they operate as a vehicle for political incorporation by giving culturally distinct groups a common stake in the political institutions of their society? Some of these important and analytically very difficult questions will be given further attention in later sections of this book (see Part 4).

Conclusion: Revolutionary Leadership in Transition

This chapter has examined the circulation of Yugoslav political elites brought about by revolutionary war. Significant differences have been observed between the social background of the interwar and communist elites in terms of their education, occupation, class origin, age, gender, and ethnic affiliation. The differences between the two elite groups both reflected and affected the socio-economic development and changing political dynamics of Yugoslav society during the period discussed. Because ruling elites stand at the strategic center of a country's development, the analysis has focused on the impact which particular social-background characteristics may have had for the process of modernization and political stability. Elite recruitment patterns and social characteristics have also been utilized to illustrate general features of societal change such as the level and focus of educational development, the structure of occupational talents, and the state of ethnic relations. Caution must be exercised, however, in directly relating social-background characteristics to

The Socialist Pyramid: Elites and Power in Yugoslavia

elite attitudes and behaviour, or attributing the advent of a particular revolutionary elite group to weaknesses or inequities in the social composition of their predecessors. Although the question of elite values and behaviour requires a more extensive examination than biographical data can offer, the data analyzed here does, nevertheless, provide strong evidence that the unrepresentative and essentially oligarchial structure of the interwar elite was an important factor in the development of a "revolutionary impulse" among the more disaffected sectors of Yugoslav society.[63] That impulse, and the special circumstances occasioned by World War II, ultimately contributed to a radical change in both the elite structure and the political regime.

Between 1941 and 1948 (as well as during the twenty previous years of underground activity), revolutionary intellectuals and some workers held almost all the top Communist Party positions in a society that was overwhelmingly peasant in composition. It was only the disruption brought about by World War II, and the now very familiar linkage of peasant nationalism and communist mobilization, which allowed the Party to overcome its political isolation from the masses and make a successful bid for power. As late as October 1940, Tito complained that the absence of peasant cadres was the "weakest organizational point" in the communist movement.[64] Even after the war, however, when peasants comprised 73 percent of the economically active population, and 49 percent of the entire Communist Party membership, peasant representation in the political elite did not noticeably increase relative to the position of other social groups. Under the "dictatorship of the proletariat," members of the intelligentsia and former industrial labourers provided the political elite for a predominantly peasant society. As one Yugoslav scholar has aptly remarked: "One of the basic antinomies of socialism up to now has been that the revolutionary avant-garde is the interpreter of the interest of the class for whose development it is only creating the condition."[65] Although the data presented in this chapter does reveal the predominance of intellectuals and workers in the communist elite, the findings also indicate that the revolutionary leadership was far more representative than the preceding elite with regard to Yugoslavia's overall social composition and demographic features. Thus, the revolutionaries may have been alienated from the society's traditionally dominant norms and preferences, as well as quite modest in their skills and experience for political management, but they were hardly marginal to the social diversity of the Yugoslav population.

The social composition of the elite winners and losers in a revolutionary struggle does not by itself, of course, reveal very much about the broader sociopolitical basis and character of the actual struggle, and even less about the consequences of the revolution. As C. Wright Mills and Hans Gerth have reminded us "modern revolutions are not watched by masses as they occur within the palace of elites .... In modern history always behind the elites and parties there are revolutionary masses. Without such masses, parties may shout revolution, but no matter how expert they may be they cannot make it."[66] Equally important is the extent to which the goals of the revolutionary movement are realized after the seizure of power. In the Yugoslav case, it is clear that the communist leaders who took power in 1945, irrespective of their particular social characteristics and how their backgrounds may have differed from the former elite, were dedicated to the radical transformation of their society. The members of the new elite had a clear awareness of their country's underdevelopment, and they were convinced that rapid industrialization and modernization would provide a brighter future. The significant socio-economic progress of Yugoslav society during the next forty years resulted mainly from policies initiated by the young communist revolutionaries described in this chapter. The same revolutionary elite group must, however, also bear the responsibility for the costs and failures which have accompanied "the construction of socialism" in Yugoslavia. The analysis in the following chapters of this book will focus on some of the important factors associated with the transformation of Yugoslavia's revolutionary leaders in the years since 1948, and also on the emergence of a new generation of political decision-makers and activists - Tito's younger comrades and heirs - who reached elite status during the last several decades.

NOTES: CHAPTER TWO

1. See for example, Thomas Greene, *Comparative Revolutionary Movements, 2nd Edition* (Englewood Cliffs: Prentice-Hall, 1984), Mostafa Rejai, *Leaders of Revolution* (Beverly Hills: Sage Publications, 1979), Harold D. Lasswell and Daniel Lerner, *World Revolutionary Elites: Studies in Coercive Ideological Movements* (Cambridge: MIT Press, 1965).

2. For further information concerning the formation of the interwar Yugoslav state see Dimitrije Djordjevic, (ed.), *The Creation of Yugoslavia 1914-1918* (Santa Barbara: CLIO Books, 1983), Ivo J. Lederer, *Yugoslavia at the Paris Peace Conference* (New Haven: Yale University Press, 1963), Barbara Jelavich, *History of the Balkans 2 Volumes* (Cambridge Mass: Cambridge University Press, 1983), John Lampe and Marvin Jackson, *Balkan Economic History 1550-1950: From Imperial Borderlands to Developing Nations* (Bloomington, Indiana: Indiana University Press, 1982).

3. For the formation and early activity of the Yugoslav Communist Party see Ivo Banac, "The Communist Party of Yugoslavia during the Period of Legality, 1919-1921," *War and Society in Central Europe*, ed. Bela K. Kiraly (New York: Atlantic Research and Publications, 1983), 188-230.

4. Vladimir Dedijer, *The Beloved Land* (New York: Simon and Schuster, 1960), 97-99, 188-189.

5. See Marvin Jackson and John R. Lampe, "The Evidence of Industrial Growth in Southeastern Europe Before the Second World War," *East European Quarterly*, XVI, No. 4 (January, 1983), 385-415.

6. See Joseph S. Roucek, "The Social Character of Yugoslav Politics," *Social Science*, IX (1934), 300, and Charles A. Beard and George Radin, *The Balkan Pivot: Yugoslavia, A Study in Government and Administration* (New York: Macmillan, 1929), 172. See also, Vladimir Dedijer, *et. al.* (eds.) *History of Yugoslavia* (New York: McGraw Hill, 1974), 534-539.

7. Bogomir Raikovitch, *L'Avancement et le traitment des fonctionaires publics du Royaume des Serbes, Croates et Slovenes* (Paris: Labour, n.d.), 148. R.W. Seton-Watson observed in 1925 that: "the gang in power have justly earned the name of *Korupcionasi* the [corrupt ones] and stand for a lowering of standards, favouritism and administrative chaos which the people from the old Austria-Hungary feel to be intolerable and which is intensely resented by a large section of public opinion." R.W. Seton-Watson, *R.W. Seton-Watson i Jugoslaveni: Korespondencija 1906-1941, Volume II* (Zagreb, London: Sveučilište u Zagrebu/British Academy, 1976), 126. Zvonimir Kulundzic, *Politika korupcija u Kraljevskoj Jugoslaviji* (Zagreb: Stvarnost, 1968).

8. On the royal family's political role see Stephen Graham, *Alexander of Yugoslavia* (New Haven: Yale University Press, 1936), and by the same author, *Peter II King of Yugoslavia, A King's Heritage* (London: Cassell, 1955). See also Neil Balfour and Salley MacKay, *Paul of Yugoslavia* (London: Hamish Hamilton, 1982). A study of the Yugoslav military between the wars remains to be written, but useful discussions of the armed forces in politics can be found in Jacob B. Hoptner, Yugoslavia in Crisis 1934-1941 (New York: Columbia University Press, 1962), 246-259, and Dragisa Ristic, *Yugoslavia's Revolution of 1941* (University Park: Pennsylvania State University Press, 1966). See also note 60.

9. Traian Stoianovich, "The Social Foundations of Balkan Politics, 1750-1941," *Balkans in Transition*, eds. Charles Jelavich and Barbara Jelavich (Berkeley: University of California Press, 1963), 336. Although the state was one of the biggest capitalist elements, it is important to note that both the public and private sectors of the Yugoslav economy were very dependent on foreign capital. See Jozo Tomasevich, "Foreign Economic Relations, 1918-1941," *Yugoslavia*, ed. Robert J. Lerner (Berkeley: University of California Press, 1949), 185-197.

10. See for example, Jozo Tomasevich, *Peasant, Politics, and Economic Change in Yugoslavia* (Stanford: Stanford University Press, 1955), Dragoljub Yovanovitch, "Les Classes Moyennes Chez les Slaves du Sud," *Inventaires III. Classes Moyennes* (Paris: Felix Alcan, 1939), 244, and Dinko Tomasic, *Personality and Culture in Eastern European Politics* (New York: George W. Stewart, 1948), 223.

11. Traian Stoianovich, "The Social Foundations of Balkan Politics, 1750-1941," 335. The most exhaustive study of Yugoslavia's interwar intelligentsia is Milosav Janićijević, *Stvaralačka inteligencija medjuratne Jugoslavije* (Belgrade: Institut društvenih nauka, 1984). The routine of political life in interwar Yugoslavia was aptly described by an Englishwoman who had lived in Yugoslavia. "Democracy in a poor country consists largely of 'intervention.' One citizen seeks to a permit to open a business, another claims a pension, a teacher wants a transfer. The applications lie for weeks neglected in the desks of underpaid officials. The applicants write to members of parliament, or prospective candidates, or anyone who may one day be in a position to grant a favour - or not grant it - to the said struggling official ... a 'friend's' application is mentioned by the way of hints of services to come." Louisa Rayner, *Women in a Village* (London: William Heinemann, Ltd., 1957), 6.

12. Jozo Tomasovich, *Peasants, Politics, and Economic Change*, 251.

13. A good summary is found in Paul Shoup, "The Yugoslav Revolution: The First of a New Type," *The Anatomy of Communist Takeovers*, ed. Thomas T. Hammond (New Haven: Yale University Press, 1975), 244-272.

14. Branko Petranović, *AVNOJ-Revolucionarna smena vlasti: 1942-1945* (Belgrade: Nolit, 1976), 356, 368. See also, Petranović's, *Revolucija i kontrarevolucija u Jugoslaviji (1941-1945), Tom II* (Belgrade: Rad, 1983), 230, and also, *Politička i ekonomska osnova narodne vlasti u Jugoslaviji za vreme obnove* (Belgrade: Institut za savremenu istoriju, 1969), 52-53, 261-262.

15. Vladimir Milić, *Revolucija i socijalna struktura* (Belgrade: Mladost, 1978), 66-70. Edward Kardelj claimed on December 5, 1946 that the nationalization of private economic enterprises was a complex process prepared in great secrecy: "When on the morning of the day chosen to implement this policy the commissions for nationalization arrived at the various enterprises concerned, the owners did not even have time to remove the typewriters. Of course the whole operation had to be controlled from the center ... in the conditions then prevailing, it was simply not possible to pay out sums that corresponded to the real economic value of the property being nationalized ... we tried hard to find work for the former

owners in jobs which they had appropriate qualifications." *Reminiscences* (London: Blond and Briggs, 1982), 74, 178-182.

16. For example, before the war Yugoslavia was composed of nine provinces (banovinas), 378 districts and 4,645 communes. In 1948 there were six republics, one autonomous province, one autonomous region, 50 subprovinces (two oblasts and 48 okrugi), 407 districts and 11,566 communes or people's committees.

17. Data on the interwar elite was obtained from: *Who's Who in Central and East Europe* (Zurich: Central European Times, Ltd., 1935-1937), *Ko je ko* (Zagreb, 1928), Stanoje Stanojević (ed.) *Narodna enciklopedija srpsko-hrvatsko-slovenačka* (Zagreb: Bibliografski zavod, 1925-1929), *Almanah Kraljevine Jugoslavije: IV. Jubilarni svezak 1929-1931* (Zagreb 1932), 144-160. See also different issues of *L'Echo de Belgrade: Journal Yugoslave Hebdomadaire* and *La Yugoslavie: Hebdomadaire Parassant a Belgrade*. Data on the communist elite was drawn from the following sources: *Ko je ko u Jugoslaviji: Biografski podaci o Jugoslovenskim savremenicima* (Belgrade: Sedma Sila, 1957), *Osmi Kongres SKJ: Stenografska beleška* (Belgrade: Kultura, 1965), 2180-2209, "Biographies of the Members of the Central Committee of the League of Communists or Yugoslavia," *Joint Publications Research Service, Eastern Europe, Political, Sociological, and Military Affairs* (Belgrade: February 1, 1967), and *V. Kongres Komunistične Partije Jugoslavije* (Ljubljana: Cankarjeva založba, 1948), 584-589.

18. See Wayne Vucinich, "The Yugoslav Revolutionary Movement 1908-1914," *Slavia*, XVI, No. 4 (August, 1941), 103-117, Uroš Nedimović, "A Comparison of the Actions of Young Bosnia (1914) and Red Justice (1921)," *Survey*, II, No. 1 (1975). See also, Dubravka Skarica, "The Attitude of Progressive Youth of Bosnia-Hercegovina Between The Two World Wars Toward the Young Bosnian Movement," *Survey*, II, No. 1 (1975), 27-32, 44-46. Young Yugoslav communist revolutionaries during World War II liked to point out that although certain similarities existed between themselves and the most "progressive" young people of the pre-World War I period, the communist youth had a broader social base. Franc Cengle, "Toward a Marxist Interpretation of Political History," *Survey*, II, No. 1 (1975), 56-57.

19. Lenard J. Cohen and Paul Warwick, *Political Cohesion in a Fragile Mosaic: The Yugoslav Experience* (Boulder: Westview Press, 1983).

20. The figures are based on data drawn from the statistical research files of the *Balkan National Development Project* compiled by Elinor Despalatovic (unpublished, 1964-1965).

21. In 1839 the Serbian government began to finance the education of select students in foreign schools. By 1859 the number of Serbians educated in Russian, German, French, Austrian and Italian schools numbered over 200. The South Slavs living under Hapsburg control had direct access to the more developed Austrian educational system. For example, during the winter term of 1884-1885, 189 students from Dalmatia alone attended higher schools in the Austrian provinces or Crown lands. The data is derived from the statistical research files of the *Balkan National Development Project*. For an interesting account of the foreign education of a member of the Serbian elite see Gale Stokes, *Legitimacy Through Liberalism, Vladimir Jovanovic and the Transformation of Serbian Politics* (Seattle: University of Washington Press, 1975), 6-13.

22. Table 2.2 is calculated on the basis of data in Charles A. Beard and George Radin, *The Balkan Pivot: Yugoslavia, A Study in Government and Administration* (New York: Macmillan, 1929), 256-257, Ruth Trouton, *Peasant Renaissance in Yugoslavia, 1900-1950* (London: Routledge and Kegan Paul Ltd., 1952), 161-171 and 267-280, and *Yugoslavia: The Mediterranean Regional Project, Country Reports, Education and Development* (Paris: OECD, 1965), 52.

23. Ruth Trouton, *Peasant Renaissance in Yugoslavia*, 1900-1950, 107.

24. Milan Babić, "Statistika pismenosti u Jugoslaviji," *Statistička revija*, Nos. 1-2 (July, 1959), 209-229. Vera St. Erlich in her study of 300 Yugoslav villages found that illiteracy reinforced the cleavage between peasants and non-peasants, but was an insignificant factor in intra-peasant relationships. *Family in Transition* (Princeton: Princeton University Press, 1966), 355.

25. John Lampe and Marvin Jackson, *Balkan Economic History, 1500-1950*, 502-504.

26. Charles A. Beard and George Radin, *The Balkan Pivot*, 182.

27. In 1940 the Party organized a number of short (7-45 days) political schools for "leading cadre," and such training was expanded during the wartime struggle. Gojko Miljanić, *Kadrovi revolucije 1941-1945* (Cetinje: Obod, 1975), 17-18, 389-391. The schools organized by imprisoned communists between the wars also served as a supplementary form of education for many members of the postwar elite. Milovan Djilas, *Memoir of a Revolutionary* (New York: Harcourt Brace Jovanovich, 1973), 226-229.

28. Traian Stoianovich, "The Pattern of Serbian Intellectual Evolution: 1830-1880," *Comparative Studies in Society and History*, I, No. 3 (March, 1959), 254.

29. Although a large portion of the late 19th century and early 20th century Croatian intelligentsia was educated in Austria-Hungary, or in the case of Dalmatians, in Italy, most university students attended local schools. Zorica Stipetić, *Komunistički pokret i inteligencija* (Zagreb: Centar za kulturnu djelatnost, 1980), 81. A university did not exist in Croatia until 1874, in Serbia until 1905 and in Slovenia until 1919, although many forms of higher education did go on in all those areas well before formal universities were founded. Joseph Roucek, "Yugoslavia's History of Education Before 1918," *Paedagocica Historica*, XIII (1973), 66-84.

30. Legal studies also composed a large proportion of the studies in interwar Yugoslavia's higher schools of commerce and economics. The remaining emphasis mainly focused on commercial policy, finance and bookkeeping. See Severin K. Turoslenski, *Education in Yugoslavia* (Washington: Government Printing Office, 1939), 91.

31. Jozo Tomasevich, *Peasants, Politics and Economic Change*, 463.

32. In 1870 a Russian observer commented that in Serbia "in all affairs, even the most minor details among simple people, all had to be on paper, with lawyers handling everything," while in Russia, "innumerable commercial transactions take place without any kind of written documents." Cited in Woodford D. McClellan, *Svetozar Markovic and the Origins of Balkan Socialism* (Princeton: Princeton University Press, 1964), 206, note 92. See also Ruth Trouton, *Peasant Renaissance in Yugoslavia, 1900-1950*, 70-74, 176.

33. Vladko Maček, *In the Struggle to Freedom* (New York: Robert Spellner and Sons, 1957), 36-37.

34. It is very difficult to discern any propensity by students in one or another faculty or discipline to join a Communist rather than a Fascist political organization. Ivan Avakumovic found that at Zagreb University the Ustasha Fascist movement was the largest student group in 1940 and derived its main strength from the faculties of law, agriculture and veterinary medicine. In other faculties at the University the followers of Maček's Peasant Party and Tito's Communists also were quite numerous. At Belgrade University, however, the Communists were strongest in the law faculty, while in the 1930's the student council in the engineering faculty was dominated for a time by Ljotić's Serbian Fascist group. Thus, there does not appear to be a strong correlation between type of faculty attended and political persuasion. Ivan Avakumovic, "Yugoslavia's Fascist Movements," *Native Fascism in the Successor State, 1918-1945*, ed. Peter Sugar (36. On the special prestige which scholars enjoyed among the Balkan public see Dimitrije Djordjevic, "Historians in Politics: Slobodan Jovanović," *Journal of Contemporary History*, VIII, No. 1 (1973), 21-40.

37. William Kornhauser, *The Politics of Mass Society* (Glencoe: Free Press, 1959), 53.

38. The information on the background of parliamentary deputies in Table 2.6 is obtained from official reports of each interwar legislative election: *Statistički (pregled) izbora narodnih poslanika za Ustavotvornu Skupštinu Kraljevine Srba, Hrvata i Slovenaca* (Belgrade: Narodna Skupština, 1921), *Statistika izbora narodnih poslanika Kraljevine Srba, Hrvata, i Slovenaca* (Belgrade: Narodna Skupština, 1924, 1926, 1928). *Statistika izbora narodnih poslanika za Narodnu Skupštinu Kraljevine Jugoslavije* (Belgrade: Narodna Skupština, 1932, 1938).

39. Milovan Djilas has claimed that after 1937 most of the principal communist leaders could be classified as professional revolutionaries. "After Tito returned from a trip to Moscow in the spring of 1940 the salaries of the Politburo members were regulated. At first each was never more than 2,000 dinars a month. As times went on this was increased, and just before the invasion of Yugoslavia it was high - 3,000 dinars. Tito's salary was still higher, 6,000 dinars, if I am not mistaken. He proposed his salary and we proposed ours

	.... We began giving salaries to comrades in hiding .... The pay was not high, but it was regular." Milovan Djilas, *Memoir of a Revolutionary*, 338-339.
40.	The data in Table 2.7 is from *Zbornik narodnih heroja Jugoslavije* (Belgrade: Omladina, 1957), 907, Gojko Miljanović, *Kadrovi revolucije, 1941-1945*, (Cetinje: Obod, 1975), 20 and 320, and Igor Graovac, "O proučavanju struktura sudionika NOB-A i socijalističke revolucije u Hrvatskoj 1941-1945," *Časopis za suvremenu povijest*, VI, No. 2 (1974), 59.
41.	Over 1,800 Yugoslav volunteers fought in the Spanish Civil War. Among the Yugoslav fighters in Spain were two lieutenant colonels, eight majors, 35 captains, 105 lieutenants, three brigade commanders, and 47 political commisars. During the war in Yugoslavia, 29 veterans from the Spanish war were promoted to the ranks of general and a total of 61 of the veterans became commanders and political commisars at various levels of the Partisan Army (54 veterans were also declared national heroes). "Association of Yugoslav Volunteers in the Spanish Republican Army," *Yugoslav Survey* (October-December, 1961), 959. See also, Vlajko Begović, "The Communist Party of Yugoslavia and the Spanish Civil War (1930 to 1939)," *Socialist Thought and Practice*, No. 4 (April, 1975), 71-86.
42.	Alexander Ranković, *Report on the Organizational Work of the CPY* (Belgrade, 1948), 52-53. Of approximately 12,000 prewar Party members, 9,000 were killed between 1941 and 1945. By 1946, the Party had 141,066 members, about 50,000 of whom had joined the communists after 1943.
43.	The number of students at Belgrade University with working class and peasant social backgrounds doubled between the 1928-1929 and 1938-1939 school years. Even by the end of that decade, however, such students constituted only 28 percent of the total university enrollment. Milica Damjanović, *Napredni studentski pokret na Beogradskom Univerzitetu, 1929-1941*, Volume II (Belgrade: Nolit, 1974), 58. A Yugoslav study of secondary school students in 1935-1936 revealed that students from more well-to-do families were considerably more successful in school than their classmates. Ivan Leko, *Velike revolucije i obrazovanje* (Belgrade: Zavod za izdavanje udžbenika Socijalističke Republike Srbije, 1968), 271-272.

44. Prior to the 1830's and the development of an autonomous Serbian principality, most town inhabitants were non-Serbs including Turks, Tsintsars, Greeks, Germans and Jews. The waning of Turkish control led to the rather rapid growth, differentiation, and urbanization of the Serbian professional intelligentsia and middle class. By the second part of the 19th century the highest ranks in Serbia's emergent middle class elements comprised a small elite core, but this elite's relatively newly urbanized members often served as tribunes for the representation of rural interests in what was essentially an agrarian nation-state. Indeed, one Yugoslav sociologist points out that the founders of the modern Serbian state were illiterate peasants, but "yet the elite." Moreover, in the 19th century most Serbian "cabinet ministers and high military men were not only the sons of peasants but often thought of themselves as peasants." Vera St. Erlich, "Historical Awareness and the Peasant," *The Peasant and the City in Eastern Europe*, eds. Irene Portis Winner and Thomas G. Winner (Cambridge: Schenkman, 1984), 101. See also Ružica Guzina, *Opština u Kneževini i Kraljevini Srbiji 1804-1839* (Belgrade: Institut za pravnu istoriju, 1966), and *Opština u Srbiji 1839-1918* (Belgrade: Rad, 1976), Traian Stoianovich, "The Conquering Balkan Orthodox Merchant," *The Journal of Economic History*, XX, No. 2. (1960), 312, and Georges Castellan, "Les villes serbs au milieu du XIX siecle: Structures sociales et modèles cultures," *Southeastern Europe/L'Europe de Sud-Est, Part II*, (1979), 121-133. For contrasting insights on the development of an upper middle class in the other South Slav lands see Mirijana Gross, "The Position of the Nobility in the Organization of the Elite in Northern Croatia at the End of the Nineteenth Century and the Beginning of the Twentieth Century," *The Nobility in Russia and Eastern Europe*, eds., Ivo Banac and Paul Bushkovitch (New Haven: The Concilium on International and Area Studies, 1983), 137-176, and by the same author, "Social Structure and National Movements among the Yugoslav Peoples on the Eve of the First World War," *Slavic Review*, XXXVI, No. 4 (December, 1977), 628-643, and Igor Karaman, "The Socio-Economic Structure of the Urban Population in Northern Croatia During the Early Industrial Period (Before World War I)," *Southeastern Europe/L'Europe du Sud-Est, Part II* (1979), 134-147.

45. Eugene Hammel has demonstrated that in times of economic contraction before 1920 and during the depression, some members of the Yugoslav work force took lower status jobs than those held

by their fathers, Eugene Hammel, *The Pink Yo-Yo: Occupational Mobility in Belgrade, 1915-1965* (Berkeley: Institute of International Studies, 1969), 46-48. It is doubtful, however, that more than a few of the communist leaders who began their job histories as workers or peasants had social origins in the middle sectors. Of course, in the years preceding 1941, the deliberate decision by many offspring of the intelligentsia and middle class to join an underground political movement with rather dim employment prospects, and where they often led rather disciplined, indigent and harassed lives as "revolutionary workers," might be viewed as a kind of ideologically motivated downward mobility of a temporary, or calculated, nature. See Milovan Djilas, *Memoir of a Revolutionary*.

46. For similar findings on the background of the regional and local communist leaderships see Bette S. Denich, "Sources of Leadership in the Yugoslav Revolution: A Local-Level Study," *Comparative Studies in Society and History*, XVIII, No. 1 (January, 1976), 64-84, and Pero Nasakanda, "Razvoj promjena klase strukture KP Hrvatske u NOB-u i socijalističkoj revoluciji," *Časopis za suvremenu povijest*, Volume II (1982), 117-123, and Stojan Tomić, *Politički profesionalizam* (Sarajevo: Fakultet političkih nauka, 1972), 218.

47. Ruth Trouton, *Peasant Renaissance in Yugoslavia*, 52-54, 79-82, 245-248.

48. Sources for elite birthplaces include: *Statistički godisnjak Kraljevina Hrvatske Slavonije*, Volume I (1905) (Zagreb, 1913), Statistika Kraljevine Srbije, XIII (Belgrade, 1899), Sava Obradović, *et. al.*, *Stanovništva Narodne Republika Srbije od 1834-1953* (Belgrade: Zavod za statistiku i evidencija, 1953).

49. Tito attributed the communists' close link with the masses during the war to the large number of communist youth from Belgrade University who came from peasant families. Vladimir Dedijer, *Tito* (New York: Simon and Schuster, 1953), 48. See also Žarko Jovanović, *KPJ prema seljastvu 1919-1941* (Belgrade: Narodna knjiga, 1984).

50. Stojan Tomić, "Sociološke dijagnoze i prognoze savremenog sela," *Sociologija*, XXI, No. 3 (1979), 317-318.

51. Gojko Miljanić, *Kadrovi revolucije 1941-1945*, 324. A 1960 survey of over one million veterans of the National Liberation Movement revealed that approximately 60 percent of them were less than 25 years old when they joined the movement. Igor Graovac, "O proučavanju struktura sudionika NOB-e i socijalisticke revolucije u Hrvatskoj 1941-1945," 38.

52. The average age of the new Exectuve Committee (formerly the Politburo) selected in 1964 was 54, and in 1969 the top state leadership had an average age of 48. Zdenko Antic, "Yugoslavia's New State Leadership - A Sociological Breakdown," *Radio Free Europe Research Report*, (July 3, 1967), 2.

53. Slavko Filipi, "On the Admission of the Young in the LYC," Komunist, (May 19, 1966), 4. *Joint Publication Research Service, Eastern Europe, Political, Sociological, and Military Affairs* (Belgrade: May 20, 1966), 46.

54. For example, from 1930 to 1940 women made up approximately one-fifth of the students at Belgrade University. Milica Damjanović, *Napredni studentski pokret na Beogradskom Univerzitetu, 1929-1941, Volume II*, 57.

55. The data in Table 2.10 is from Alexander Ranković, *Report on the Central Committee of the Communist Party of Yugoslavia on the Organizational Work of the CPY* (Belgrade, 1948), 72.

56. Sociological research with respect to the family in interwar Yugoslavia revealed that Macedonian women were the least liberated in the country. Vera St. Erlich, *The Family in Transition*, 249. In his report to the Fifth Party Congress in 1940, Tito commented that "the greatest attention to and greatest understanding of the women's question, on the part of comrades, is to be noted precisely in that province where one would have least expected it, i.e., in the Montenegrin Party Organization, than in that of any other province, although the conditions for work among women are even more favourable in other provinces." Josip Broz Tito, "Report of Comrade Tito on the Previous Work and the Tasks of the Party," *Komunist*, No. 1 (October, 1946), 73.

57. Stephen Radich, "The Autobiography of Stephen Radich," *Current History* (October, 1928), 106.

58. Jozo Tomasevich, *Peasants, Politics and Economic Change*, 241-242.

59. The data in Table 2.11 is from A. Ross Johnson, *The Role of the Military in Communist Yugoslavia: An Historical Sketch*, (Santa Monica: The Rand Paper Series, January, 1978), P-6070, and Stevan K. Pavlowitch, "How Many Non-Serbian Generals in 1941," *East European Quarterly*, XVI, No. 4 (January, 1983), 447-452.

60. Joseph Rothschild and several other authors have claimed that on the eve of World War II, there were 165 generals in Yugoslavia's military forces of whom 161 were Serbs, two Croats and two Slovenes. These figures are derived from Rudolf Bićanić's 1938 book concerning the "Croatian question." Stevan Pavlowitch has shown that the ethnic breakdown for the 165 generals can be traced back to 1933 and the Yugoslav historian, Vladimir Dedijer and his associates claim that the figure of 165 refers to 1926. In view of the data in Table 2.11, based on Pavlowitch's research for 1941, it would appear that there was at least some improvement in the military's ethnic balance by World War II. See Joseph Rothschild, *East Central Europe Between the Wars* (Seattle: University of Washington Press, 1974), 278-279, Rudolf Bićanić, *Ekonomska podloga Hrvatskog pitanja* (Zagreb: Stjepan Vidović, 1938), 120, Stevan Pavlowitch, "How many Non-Serbian Generals in 1941?" *East European Quarterly*, XVI, No. 4 (January, 1983), 447-452, and Vladimir Dedijer et. al. (eds.), *History of Yugoslavia*, 538. See also Ivan Babić, "Military History," *Croatia: Land, People, Culture Volume I*, eds. Francis Eterovich and Christopher Apalatin (Toronto: University of Toronto Press, 1964), 163 and R.V. Burks, *The Dynamics of Communism in Eastern Europe* (Princeton University Press, 1961), 125-126. The view that the Royal Military's ethnic composition showed a trend "running against the Serbs" is argued in M. Deroc, "The Former Yugoslav Army," *East European Quarterly*, XIX, No. 3 (September, 1985), 364-365.

61. One Yugoslav historian reports that at the end of the war the "leading cadre" in the armed forces had the following ethnic composition: Serbs 51 percent, Croats 23 percent, Montenegrins nine percent, Slovenes eight percent, Macedonians six percent, Moslems three percent, and all others nine percent. Gojko Miljanić, *Kadrovi Revolucije 1941-1946*, 320.

62. Othmar Haberl, *Parteiorganisation and Nationale Frage in Jugoslavien* (Berlin: Otto Harrassowitz, 1976), 204.

63. On emotional and intellectual motivations for enlistment in the Communist Party see Milovan Djilas, *Memoir of a Revolutionary*, 92-96. Revolutionary elites are usually, of course, only intervening variables which express deeper and broader socio-economic problems in a society. A more complete study of the rise of communism would also have to take into consideration the impact of external economic factors on Yugoslavia during the interwar period. This general point has been emphasized in Andrew Janos, *Politics and Paradigms: Changing Theories of Change in Social Science* (Stanford: Stanford University Press, 1986), 120.

64. Josip Broz Tito, "Report of Comrade Tito on the Previous Work and the Tasks of the Party," 79.

65. Svetozar Stojanović, "The Morality of the Revolutionary Avant-Garde as the Historical Presupposition of Socialism," *Praxis*, Nos. 1-2 (1966), 163. A complex love-hate relationship existed between the intellectual and proletarian members of the communist leadership. Rodoljub Čolaković, one of the leading members of the Yugoslav Communist Party between the wars (an intellectual with an unfinished higher education from a well-to-do family), describes a prewar exchange with another party functionary entrusted with the organizational affairs of the Central Committee: "Hudomalj directed my attention to the fact that the ideological level of our activists was very low and that one could not converse 'intellectually' with them, but only on a 'much lower level.' It was amusing for me to hear instructions regarding 'levels' from a man whose level, god knows, was not that high. He related to the intellectuals with a sense of superiority considering them some sort of ballast in the party which must be dragged along, but whom one should not believe in very much. Such a relationship toward intellectuals existed among certain workers who had only recently assumed party functions and had raised themselves to a certain extent, a conceited view that only physical workers alone can be real proletarians, but that all other types were questionable. The role which intellectuals had in our movement, particularly in factional struggles, contributed to that view. Many of them were abnormally ambitious, inclined to cliquish behaviour, scheming, sophistry, and empty conversations 'about the revolution,' but less inclined to undertake those small unseen jobs, usually anonymous, 66.

Lenard J. Cohen

> Joseph Bensman, Arthur Vidich, and Nobuko Gerth (eds.), *Politics, Character, and Culture: Perspectives from Hans Gerth* (Westport, Conn.: Greenwood Press, 1983), 163.

CHAPTER 3

PARTISANS, PROFESSIONALS AND PROLETARIANS: ELITE CHANGE IN MODERNIZING YUGOSLAVIA

Who would replace Tito as Yugoslavia's top political leader? What impact would Tito's departure from political authority have on the subsequent development of Yugoslavia's unique brand of socialism? For thirty-five years following World War II, those important questions were routinely posed by both specialists and interested observers of the Yugoslav scene. Answers to such questions typically involved either speculation concerning various highly visible individuals viewed as likely candidates to succeed Tito, or discussion about the many internal and external factors which have influenced Yugoslavia's potential to survive as a "non-aligned," multi-national, one-party state.[1] Serious reflection about the probable course of Yugoslav political development, however, devoted relatively little systematic attention to the somewhat broader group of individuals who, together with Tito and the very top political leadership, played a central role in shaping public policy. For analytical purposes this broader group can be termed the political elite, i.e., an aggregate of politically influential individuals occupying various positions at or near the summit of the political power hierarchy.

As conceived in this book, the Yugoslav elite occupies an intermediate position between a small group of leaders at the summit of the political structure and an extremely large number of amateur political activists and participants at the "base" of the system (for example, the nearly one million members of enterprise and organizational "delegations" who comprise the theoretically powerful foundation of Yugoslavia's multi-tiered "Assembly System").[2] To a large extent, an exaggerated foreign concern with Yugoslavia's most outstanding, or visible political leaders, as well as the natural interest generated by the regime's elaboration of some very novel and potentially important structures for citizen participation (workers' councils, communal self-government, the "delegational" electoral system, etc.), have obscured the persistent hegemony of central and regional political elites in the Yugoslav policy-making process. As pointed out in Chapter 1, the imperatives of consolidating and managing political authority in socialist Yugoslavia, engendered the formation and perpetuation of a well crystallized elite structure not unlike the type found in most other states. Thus, despite the regime's very admirable efforts to combat "statism" and vestiges of the Stalinist political model, contemporary Yugoslavia has been, and is likely to remain an elite-managed rather than a self-managed society. Indeed, the avowedly anti-elitist goals and participatory institutional mechanisms of the Yugoslav regime, which certainly go far beyond the theory and practice of the other communist party-states, make the formation and persistent influence of a political elite in that country an especially interesting and important subject for political inquiry.

The existence and political importance of elites in Yugoslavia raises several interesting questions. What kinds of changes are evident in the composition of the political elite during the course of the country's socialist political development, and what impact have such changes had on the political process? What is the extent of uniformity and diversity in the composition of the political elite? Do various aspects of elite characteristics (e.g., age, sex, occupation, career, education, ethnicity, etc.) help explain elite attitudes and behaviour? How representative is the political elite when compared to the highly variegated structure of Yugoslav society? Is the political elite sufficiently qualified to deal with current and anticipated societal problems? How does Yugoslav elite development compare with patterns of elite change in other regimes? Despite the frequently noted limitations of elite social background analysis as a tool in political inquiry, information which provides even tentative answers to the preceding questions can aid the understanding of Yugoslav and communist political development. "The link between elite transformation and broader social trends is complex," notes the author of a synthesis of the voluminous literature on the subject, "but most scholars agree that changes in the composition of the political elite can provide a crucial diagnostic of the basic tides of history."[3]

This chapter focuses on one organizationally definable *segment* of the Yugoslav political elite, namely, the members of the Central Committee of the League of Yugoslav Communists (before 1952, the Yugoslav Communist Party) on the national level of the political system between 1948 and 1978.[4] Although the relative influence of the party organization underwent several changes during that period, membership in the Central Committee at the federal level, nevertheless, can be regarded as a rough positional indicator of an individual's political eliteness, or the high likelihood of belonging to the elite. Clearly, not all members of the political elite are in the Central Committee, and not every member of the Central Committee is in the political elite. The Central Committee's position within the League structure and within the political system as a strategic site for leadership representation and interaction, however, makes membership in the body a departure point for any analysis of the political elite. An examination of the Committee's membership can reveal the characteristics of the politically most powerful individuals and groups in Yugoslav society, and also indicates which elements and interests in society the regime feels obliged to politically accommodate. As in most other communist states, the party's top-level Central Committee has been politically significant, not as a result of its formal authority or activity, but because "the pattern of composition of the Central Committee ... reveals the concentration of leading figures in various fields of social life."[5]

Elite Consolidation, 1948-1962: Partisans in Power

He was a soldier of a hundred battles,
a revolutionary. That was his form, his
character. For it had been the battles
which he fought that had shaped him, not
biological forces ... one or two generations would
have to be like that. Making of themselves a
boxer's fist .... Ah, but what ... afterwards,
tomorrow? What of the revolutionary after the
revolution ...?

Oskar Davičo

The individuals elected to the party's Central Committee at the Fifth (1948), Sixth (1952), and Seventh (1958) Congresses consisted primarily of revolutionary leaders who had successfully consolidated their collective position as the governing elite. For this new political elite, which had survived the first major challenge to its rule (the Tito-Stalin split), it was a period of difficult readjustment, of tenatative self-confidence in their audaciously independent posture, and of anxiety regarding the long-term viability of their non-Soviet path to "socialist construction." Under formidable external and internal pressures, the regime was literally scrambling to establish a new Marxist formula for legitimation which differed from that of their former allies in Eastern Europe. It was a dynamic, but contradictory period, in which intense theoretical reflection and practical experimentation were conducted in a climate of rigid elite control and elite entrenchment.

An examination of the data on the Central Committee's occupational composition (Table 3.1)[6] reveals a highly stable and homogeneous membership throughout the 1950's, composed almost exclusively of professional sociopolitical functionaries, most of whom were formerly "professional revolutionaries."[7] Although important differences existed in their social origins, early occupational experiences, and specialized tasks in the party leadership, those factors were less significant than the common "professional" political bonds forged during the days of prewar underground activity, by the wartime struggle, and by the exigencies of postwar political survival.[8] The occupational differentiation which was beginning to take place in the broader social structure was not yet reflected in the composition of the political elite.[9] By the early 1950's most of the leading political figures who were opposed to Tito's new interpretation of "socialist democracy," or what came to be termed by foreign observers as "national communism," had already been purged or had defected from the political elite.[10] Those individuals still voicing reservations, such as Milovan Djilas, were about to be removed.

As was the case at the Fifth Party "Congress of Victors" in 1948, the Central Committees elected in 1952 and 1958 were largely comprised of party members whose initial political activity pre-dated the wartime civil war and liberation struggle. Even the few newly recruited members of the Central Committee had for the most part joined the party either before or during the first stages of the war (Table 3.5). It was still a young elite group (Table 3.4) by comparative standards and nearly half of its members (46.6 percent) had no higher educational training or skills (Table 3.2). Newly recruited members of the Central Committee who did have some higher educational credentials were trained predominantly in non-technical and non-scientific areas of study (Table 3.3). In fact, relatively few new members were added to the Central Committee ranks during this period: only 18 (or 16.5 percent) in 1952, and 27 (20 percent) in 1958. Moreover, the number of new members in 1958 was roughly equal to the increased size of the committee, suggesting that the new members represented more of an addition than an integral change in the structure of the committee, which continued to be dominated by the revolutionary elite generation.

Ethnically (Table 3.7), the Central Committee membership reflected the multi-national character of the Partisan movement and leadership. In terms of "ethnic arithmetic," the committee's membership was considerably more representative of the country's nationality structure than the central elite of the pre-communist regime. The striking overrepresentation of Montenegrins in the Central Committee (11 percent in 1953 when they made up 2.7 percent of the general population), and the miniscule presence of smaller nationality groups (2.7 percent in 1953 when, for example, Albanians were 4.4 percent and Hungarians 3.0 percent of the general population) were noticeable exceptions in an otherwise proportionately well-balanced elite structure.[11]

The Socialist Pyramid: Elites and Power in Yugoslavia

Overall, the party elite in the period from 1948 to 1962 was a relatively closed group, compared to both the preceding wartime party leadership and the political elite during the next period. It is clear in retrospect, however, that during the 1950's members of the political leadership underwent an important process of political resocialization. This process involved the adoption of a bureaucratic mentality by most members of the political elite and the party. Political conformity and political careerism replaced the revolutionary outlook or Partisan political culture which had predominated during the war years. The purging, defection, or death of various leading members of the prewar party intelligentsia (e.g., Milovan Djilas, Vladimir Dedijer, Boris Nešković, Boris Kidrić, and Moša Pijade), and the upward mobility of younger and less broadly educated individuals recruited during the turbulent war years, also contributed to the elimination of the prewar revolutionary leadership type.[12] Indeed, to some extent the "Djilas affair" (see Chapter 1) symbolized in personal terms the general, but less visible, transformation or resocialization of the Yugoslav elite during the 1950's. Many idealists who had become professional revolutionaries before and during the war were forced to decide whether they should serve as loyal bureaucratic functionaries or remain wedded to their original political motives and goals. The pressures connected with the Soviet-Yugoslav rift and Tito's consequent need for strict internal solidarity, contributed to this process of elite bureaucratization, although the regime's break with Moscow also provided loyal political activists with opportunities for limited theoretical and institutional innovation. Not surprisingly, it was Belgrade's anti-Soviet innovations and not the Yugoslav elite's increasing attitudinal and behavioural bureaucratization[13] which received most attention abroad. Thus, Djilas' book about a communist "new class" was initially regarded by most Western observers as an analysis of political developments in Soviet society and the Soviet "bloc," and therefore not applicable to the increasingly "self-managed" Yugoslavia.

Elite Succession, 1962-1971: The Cooptation of the New Professionals

The period encompassing the Eighth (1964) and Ninth (1969) Congresses of the League of Communists witnessed an acceleration of the decentralizing and modernizing policies which had been initiated during the 1950's. The Yugoslav elite's commitment to these policies was expressed through measures enacted roughly parallel to the two congresses. Most noteworthy were the establishment of a new constitutional structure in 1962-1963, including such innovations as multi-cameral legislative bodies, a Constitutional Court, the mandatory rotation of state officials, and the increasing use of plural-candidate contests in legislative elections. The "liberal" effect of these constitutional changes was enhanced by the economic reforms of 1965 (including greater emphasis on enterprise autonomy) and, perhaps most significantly, by the removal of Alexander Ranković and the purge of the secret police at the Fourth Plenum of the Central Committee in July 1966. It was the impact of the latter event - breaking two decades of overt (1945-1950) and covert (1951-1966) police control - which provided the necessary momentum for the 1967 reorganization of the League of Communists on a less centralized basis, and the emergence of the legislative system as an important site for the resolution of political conflicts.

The general process of "liberalization" and change was both complemented and expedited by the transformation of the Central Committee membership. One of the most significant features of elite development in this period was the high rate of turnover in the membership of the Central Committees and other leading party organs. Whereas the membership of earlier Central Committees had been "renewed" almost exclusively through the admission of new members and the *enlargement* in the size of the Committee, personnel policy in the 1960's stressed the *replacement* of the old members by new ones. Thus, while the formal size of the 1964 Central Committee was 15 percent larger than in 1958, the rate of membership renewal was 47.2 percent.[14] The extent of elite circulation which followed the purge of the secret police and the reorganization of the League was even more striking. At the Ninth Congress in 1969, 56 percent of the members elected to the "leading" party organs (the "Presidency" and "Standing Part of the Conference" were functionally equivalent to the earlier and now nominally defunct Central Committee) were newly recruited to central party positions, although the size of these higher organs had actually been reduced in size (122 members, or 21 percent smaller than the 1964 Central Committee).

The composition and political beneficiaries of elite circulation during the 1960's emerge from an examination of the data on social background. The data relating to political generation (Table 3.5) clearly point to 1964 as the first year in which individuals who had not taken part in the prewar movement or the revolution, at least not as party members, were recruited into elite positions (although still not into the very top political leadership). This trend, which was also expressed in the more youthful composition of the Central Committee, was even more apparent at the 1969 congress. The number of incumbent members with prewar party experience dropped from the 88.1 percent re-elected in 1964, to 55.6 percent in 1969. Such experience was clearly avoided as a criterion for the selection of new members (only one of 68 new members had joined the party before 1940).

A very noticeable increase (Table 3.2) also occurred in the number of Central Committee members who had received a higher education (from 58.5 percent in 1958, to 76.1 percent in 1964, and reaching its peak at 86.9 percent in 1969). The new members elected in this period also exhibited (Table 3.3) a much broader range of educational skills, with law declining sharply as the "hallmark" of elite higher education. Educational training in established educational disciplines (including professional "political science" training and formal military education) had replaced the earlier and quite natural emphasis on practical experience in the "school of life."[15] The number of new members having a higher educational background in technical and economic faculties more than doubled.[16]

The trends in the educational background and political experience of the party elite are closely related to the older leadership's need for new forms of expertise capable of dealing with the requirements of political management in a modernizing society. Skills in revolutionary struggle, societal mobilization, and traditional ideological issues were no longer a sufficient basis for political decision-making. The new criteria for elite selection were noted by Mijalko Todorović, the Secretary of the League's Executive Committee, in an interview concerning preparation for the Ninth Congress. His comments reveal the dilemma of an aging and somewhat obsolete revolutionary elite seeking to maintain control and continuity, but also aware of the changing demands of a new environment:

> ... we have abandoned the former methods of our cadres policy, but have not yet found the proper criteria and methods of selection corresponding to the new conditions and requirements .... During the past 25 years new generations have stepped on the scene, generations who have been raised under the conditions of a developing socialist democracy, who have been steeled in the fires of the country's construction, in the struggle for its economic development and for the establishment of the system of direct democracy, who possess a considerable experience in technical know-how, production and self-management and have a much broader education. Consequently, we are faced with the general historical responsibility and need of finding ways and means for a smooth and purposeful replacement of people holding various functions, while ensuring at the same time, the indispensable continuity of the revolutionary transformation which provides a guarantee that we shall advance painlessly and with the least perturbation ....[17]

The 1964 and 1969 data concerning occupational composition (Table 3.1) illustrate the new recruitment priorities of the party leadership. The earlier numerical hegemony of the socio-political functionaries continued, but the well-known *professional politicians* (albeit, some of whom were now more highly educated) were now joined by a new political elite type - the *politicized professionals*. This new elite group included individuals whose working life had largely been spent in various specialized occupations *outside* the party, mass organizations and the state administration, and for whom politics is an avocation.[18] The majority of the *new professionals* were managers (i.e., not the earlier "red managers" or "socio-political workers in production," but persons with higher educations and careers in management positions), technical specialists (mainly engineers), and members of the cultural intelligentsia (especially a new group of scholar-political-activist social scientists).[19] The combined representation of these occupational sectors on the Central Committee level increased from a mere two percent in 1958 to 21 percent in 1969.[20] Moreover, the influence of this new elite group on policy formulation during this period went well beyond their presence or relative number in the composition of the party elite.[21] Despite the regime's campaign to "deprofessionalize" politics and its more tacit policy of "anti-professionalism" with respect to new fields of work, Yugoslav society's occupational structure was undergoing a steady process of differentiation, specialization, and professionalization.[22]

As if to compensate for the influx and influence of the new professional specialists, a token contingent of skilled workers (5.7 percent) were coopted into the central organs of the League in 1969. These skilled workers represented the first "real" proletarians (who practiced what Lenin called the "proletarian profession" and have not yet become "professional proletarians"[23]) at this level of party leadership since before the war. Another change, having more than symbolic importance given the resurgence of the "national question" in this period, was an increase in the representation of smaller ethnic groups within the party elite (Table 3.7). The nationality structure of this elite reflected the regime's general effort at this time to allocate all leadership positions among the country's nationalities and regions on a more equitable basis - the so-called ethnic "key" (for the major nationality groups, the principle of parity representation rather than proportionality was increasingly employed; see Chapter 7). The decreasing number of Serbs in the party elite and the diminished overrepresentation of Montenegrins also resulted from this new policy, as well as from the previous concentration of those groups in the declining contingent of professional politicians. The "reference groups" to whom Central Committee members oriented themselves were, however, more important than their ethnic affiliations. Increasingly, members of the Central Committee behaved as *delegates* of the regional party organizations which elected them rather than as agents of the central party establishment. In fact, beginning in 1969, the republican and provincial units of the League chose the central representatives at congresses held prior to the central congress of the League, instead of after the higher level meeting, as is traditional in other communist regimes.

In 1969, twenty-five years after coming to power, the members of the revolutionary generation who had joined the party in the 1930's and early 1940's appeared to be moving into elite retirement, or into equally comfortable but less influential positions outside the party apparatus.[24] As one observer remarked, "the center of power in the party was shifted from a small group, united by old associations, to a broader base of elected regional representatives .... Partisan heroes were praised and honoured, but many Partisans were retired. The Ninth Congress was forward-looking, professional and mature."[25]

The Socialist Pyramid: Elites and Power in Yugoslavia

Elite Retrenchment, 1971-1978: The Return of the "Heroes"

We have been very liberal up to now. I have never been in favour of this liberalism.

Josip Broz Tito (April 15, 1971)

The political "crisis" which emerged in Yugoslavia between the Ninth and Tenth Congresses had a significant impact on both elite composition and the pattern of elite development. The "crisis" reached its climax during late 1971 and early 1972 following Tito's decision that the unity and survival of the regime would be seriously endangered unless drastic steps were taken to alter the course of political development. The danger, as Tito saw it, was reflected in a number of interrelated factors, the most important of which was the resurgence of intense and highly divisive forms of "national chauvinism" on the part of Yugoslavia's principal ethnic groups. In Tito's view, the reappearance of nationalism and the "national question," particularly in Croatia, threatened nothing less than "civil war." The growth of nationalism both outside and within party ranks, together with such other negative phenomena as "rotten liberalism," "bureaucratism," and "technocratism," had fostered, it was argued, the development of "monopolistic groups" or "elites" opposed to the system of self-managed socialism. The "unprincipled jockeying for power" by these elites, and especially by the so-called "techno-managerial centers of power," was alleged to have eroded the unity and central authority of the party, paralyzed the decision-making process in the government and state administration, and brought the country to the brink of political and economic disaster.

The deeper source of the "crisis," however, could be traced to the organization and role of the League of Communists. In what amounted to a sweeping indictment of political changes over the preceding two decades, Tito revealed his earlier reservations and dissatisfaction with the transformation of the party's role initiated in 1952. As he expressed it during an interview in October 1972:

> After the Sixth Congress the Party began losing its prestige because attempts were made simply to eliminate it as the most important factor in the process of the development of socialism .... There was a sudden democratization of everything so much so that the Party's role in all the important domains in social life was relegated into the background. Its job was only to serve as ideological guide. The Party indeed, has that role, but it is not sufficient.[26]

Lenard J. Cohen

The antidote to the political passivity of the party organization, and thereby to the centrifugal forces created by nationalism and the quasi-market economy, was a campaign initiated in late 1971 to re-establish "discipline" and "unity" by means of a "strengthened party center." The neglected concepts of "democratic centralism" and the "dictatorship of the proletariat" were now resurrected as the proper terminology and operational principles for a "revolutionary and unified organization."[27] The preference for the pre-1952 term "Party" rather than "League" in speeches made by Tito and his supporters was a cue to political activists of the new change in policy.

Having diagnosed the source and nature of the problems facing the country, Tito, with the support of the military, acted boldly to correct the situation. In early 1972 an extensive purge of the League of Communists in Croatia removed party leaders and rank-and-file members accused of "nationalist" and "techno-managerial" sentiments. Targeted offenders comprised a diverse group including both seasoned professional politicians and members of the new generation of "politicized professionals" which had emerged so prominently in the 1960's. A large number of individuals working in the media and educational institutions, as well in as other sensitive areas, were also removed from their positions and expelled from the party. Arrest and criminal prosecution were employed on a selective basis primarily with respect to individuals accused of internal or foreign subversion. By late 1972 similar purges and measures to reassert central party control had also been carried out in Serbia and the other republics. Although Tito and his supporters vigorously denied foreign and domestic accusations that they had returned to the repressive "administrative methods" or to the "statist-bureaucratic" model of socialism which had existed before the early 1950's, it was clear that the political dynamics and development of the regime had been altered, at least temporarily.

The Tenth Congress of the League of Communists, which took place in May 1974, formally institutionalized the changes which had been occurring during the preceding years. Although some changes had already taken place in the composition of the top leadership, the impact of the regime's new direction in terms of both philosophy and personnel was not fully apparent until 1974. The label "Central Committee," abandoned in 1966-1967 following the reorganization of the party, was readopted to describe "the highest organ of the League of Communists of Yugoslavia between two congresses." The new committee was enlarged to 166 members, 44 more than the combined Presidency and "Standing Part of the Conference" elected in 1969, and slightly larger than the 155-member Central Committee of 1964. The regime's commitment to fundamental change was more apparent, however, as indicated by the high rate of renewal: 75.3 percent of the total membership elected in 1974 had not served in the equivalent organs of the League elected at the preceding congress in 1969.[28] This greatly exceeded the 1969 renewal rate of 55.7 percent, and the 1964 rate of an 47.2 percent.

The Socialist Pyramid: Elites and Power in Yugoslavia

The regime's new course is illustrated by the 1974 Central Committee membership. The nature of changes in the elite and the relationship of these changes to earlier patterns of elite development are more complex, however, than a superficial glimpse at the data might indicate. A thorough examination of the occupational profile of the 1974 Central Committee reveals, for example, important elements of both continuity and change. One of the most obvious changes, and a feature of elite composition to which the regime naturally devoted a great deal of publicity, was the substantial increase in the proletarian contingent (Table 3.1). Workers made up 19 percent of the total membership, and 25 percent of the new members. In fact, all of the workers elected in 1974 were "new" members and thus completely inexperienced in policy-making at the central level of the political system. That lack of experience, together with the fact that the 13 percent increase in the number of workers in the Central Committee (compared to 1969) was larger than that encompassed by the 27 percent increase in the committee membership size, suggests the regime's intention to symbolically provide for proletarian representation without diminishing the representation or influence of other occupational groups. Workers and employees did, however, achieve "token" elite representation much closer to their relative number in the economically active population. This tokenism contrasts dramatically with representation from the agricultural portion of the population. The peasantry, which had formed the bulwark of the party during the Partisan resistance struggle and whose membership in the party had been steadily dwindling since the war, was "represented" by one lone member of the Central Committee, the first "genuine" peasant member in the entire postwar period.

Despite the regime's campaign against "technocratic-managerial centers of power" and "intellectual elites" at the Tenth Congress, the proportional representation of managerial personnel and the technical intelligentsia actually increased from 13 to 17 percent. The percentage position of the cultural intelligentsia declined slightly, although its numerical representation increased. It is worth noting, however, that nearly all of the managerial cadre and members of the intelligentsia were newly recruited to the Central Committee; many (except for the technical specialists) had joined the party in the wartime or immediate postwar period, that is, before the temporarily discredited 1952 party reforms. Moreover, in contrast with 1969, the selection process for the Central Committee in 1974 appeared to place greater emphasis on the ideological conformity of "politicized professionals" than on their expertise and professional credentials. To use the conventional but oversimplified analytical dichotomy of elite studies on communist regimes, it was not a question of selecting either "reds" or "experts," but rather of recruiting the proper *red experts*. This new emphasis on the political reliability of specialists is illustrated by the lower educational level of most managers joining the Central Committee in 1974, i.e., recruitment of the so-called *red-manager* type as opposed to the professionalized manager.[29]

The occupational composition of the 1974 Central Committee also reveals a continued decrease in the category of professional politicians, i.e., the group of "socio-political functionaries." Dominating the party elite in 1952 with 92 percent of the total Central Committee membership, the relative size of this occupational group had been more than halved to 45 percent during the thirty-year period covered by this chapter. More significant than the decline in the percentage representation of this group, however, is the fact that half of the socio-political officials were incumbents re-elected from the 1969 Committee (the lowest turnover rate of any occupational category), and that the remaining half, although new to the 1974 Committee, was largely composed of veteran professional politicians from the pre-revolutionary political generation (see Table 3.6). Moreover, some members of the latter group had actually served in Central Committees prior to 1969, and were now being "recalled" to elite service. Whereas "red-experts" composed the new contingent of managers and technical intelligentsia in the Central Committee, the "new" politicians for the most part were not expert-reds (such as the more highly educated type of professional politicans recruited in 1969), but rather revolutionary Partisan "heroes." This particular aspect of elite recruitment was signalled on the very first day of the Tenth Congress in a report presented by Tito:

> I should like to say a word or two about the cadres of the revolution, of the period of pre-war revolutionary work and the National Liberation Struggle. These comrades have sometimes suffered injustices or been the victims of mistaken policies. The need for renewal of cadres and for bringing younger persons to executive posts was frequently understood too rigidly, so that many capable older men were removed from office. And even more serious, the cadres of the revolution were often kept out of political life .... These things must be rectified. Everyone who is fit to do so should continue to be active in every way, for communists must work in the interest of the revolution to the very end.[30]

The re-election of a small core group of veteran professional politicians who had served continuously in the elite from at least 1945, together with the recall of loyal members of the same generation dropped from high office during the 1960's (people who often had shared Tito's reservations about the post-1952 reforms and supported his move against the forces of "counter-revolution" in 1971-1972), provided a source of "revolutionary" continuity and signalled a return to the "old politics." Of the three major occupational groups elected to the Central Committee in 1974 - Partisans, professionals and proletarians - the first group was clearly in command.[31]

The Socialist Pyramid: Elites and Power in Yugoslavia

Among the most significant changes in elite occupational composition, and a change closely related to the reascendance of the party and of professional politicians from the Partisan generation, was the increase of military representation in the Central Committee. The percentage of military officers elected to leading party organizations had remained relatively unchanged at each successive congress, dropping only slightly in 1969. In 1974, the proportion of military officers in the Central Committee doubled to form 10.8 percent of the total membership. Moreover, the "new" military contingent (16 of the 18 officers) was made up almost entirely of members of the prewar and wartime political generation (Table 3.6), many of whom (as was the case with the large contingent of newly elected professional politicians) had served in higher party offices in the 1950's and had been retired during the "liberal" 1960's. The increase of military representation in the Central Committee, and particularly of older more conservative military personnel, was clearly related to the support that Tito and the "party center" received from the armed forces during the political crisis of 1971-1972. The re-emergence of what has been described as the "virtually symbiotic" relationship of the party and the military during the Partisan resistance, reflected conservative disenchantment with the constellation of reformist political forces that had achieved elite office during the 1960's.[32]

The above trends in occupational composition and political seniority are reflected in an age and educational profile of the 1974 party elite (Tables 3.2, 3.3, 3.4). The age structure of the 1974 Central Committee clearly illustrates the return to central authority of old party loyalists with tested reliability and more conservative attitudes. As would be expected from the earlier discussion, the recruitment of old guard politicians and military officers contributed to the aging of both contingents in the Central Committee. This was most striking in the "new" military, with 72.2 percent of that group being over fifty years of age. The same trend, although not quite as extreme, was also apparent in the newly elected group of "loyal" intelligentsia and managers. The youngest Central Committee members were found among the largely symbolic contingent of newly elected workers, but even this group was older than their proletarian predecessors in the 1969 committee (86 percent were under 39 years of age in 1969, while in 1974 only 42 percent were in that age bracket).

The drop in the average educational level of the party elite derived from the same trends: an influx of workers lacking post-secondary education and a return of older politicians and military officers whose "professional" skills were acquired during years of practical experience rather than through formal higher education. As in earlier Central Committees, the intelligentsia and managerial group exhibited the highest average level of education, although even the educational credentials of these groups showed a small decline compared with the high level of training recorded in 1969. The party clearly remained able, however, to coopt ideologically acceptable members of the much criticized "technocratic-managerial" stratum without sacrificing educational competence to a great degree.

In terms of its ethnic composition, the Central Committee elected in 1974 continued the trend toward relatively balanced "parity" representation of the principal ethnic groups begun in the 1960's, as well as a proportional increase in the number of members from the smaller nations and nationalities. The percentage of Serbs in the Central Committee was lower than at any time in the postwar period (Table 3.7). The large number of Montenegrins among the "new" contingent of military officers and professional politicians coopted in 1974, accounts for the overrepresentation of that nationality group in the Central Committee. In contrast with 1969, however, the members of the 1974 party elite were selected primarily for their loyal support of a unified "party center," rather than their responsiveness to ethnic and regional constituencies.

Transformation or Petrification?

When an elite declines ... on the one hand it makes the yoke heavier, and on the other, it has less strength to maintain it.

Vilfredo Pareto

When one generation succeeds another, the dead cling to the living.

Leon Trotsky

The obsolescence and displacement of revolutionary political elites in the wake of rapid societal modernization has frequently been noted by social scientists. John Kautsky, for example, has suggested that the modernization of societies both requires and produces a process of "elite succession," in which "revolutionary intellectuals" are gradually replaced by an emerging "managerial intelligentsia." For Kautsky, the growing attitudinal cleavages and policy conflicts between the aging revolutionary elite and the new stratum of managers and technicians comprise the core of the political struggle in modernizing regimes.[33] Numerous case studies of communist regimes in particular, have also pointed to a relationship between modernization, elite transformation, and the drift of political change. Richard Lowenthal, among others, argues that the "dualism of elites" in communist regimes is one of the basic factors influencing their political development: "the elite of revolutionary veterans identified with the utopian orientation and the new technocratic elite aspiring to influence in the name of rational economic development."[34]

The foregoing discussion of elite transformation in Yugoslavia over a span of three decades lends support to the general argument regarding the rise and decline of elite "types" in modernizing societies. It also suggests, however, that this process is not unilinear or irreversible when serious political contingencies come into play. Thus, the rather striking trend toward "elite succession" illustrated by the high turnover and changed membership (e.g., the cooptation of "politicized professionals" and younger more highly educated professional politicians) of the leading party bodies elected during the period between 1962 and 1972, was followed by a process of elite retrenchment characterized by the resuscitation of older "elite types" (e.g., the veteran professional revolutionary, the "red-manager," the military) and the token proletarianization of the Central Committee in the next phase of political development. The nature of elite recruitment and composition did not, however, turn full circle to the relatively closed political elite structure of the post-revolutionary period of elite consolidation (1948-1962), when almost all higher party positions were held by professional socio-political functionaries.

After 1971, the cooptation of the intelligentsia into political roles continued, albeit with more emphasis placed on ideological criteria. While the effort to "deprofessionalize" political activity continued, there was also a limited rehabilitation of professional politics as a legitimate vocation in a "self-managed" regime. The number of older professional socio-political functionaries in the top party ranks continued to decline owing to death, retirement, or their "horizontal rotation" into symbolically important but less powerful political positions. The replacement of the old guard, however, was considerably slower in comparison with the replacement pattern of the mid-1950's. After years in which the study of politics as an academic subject seemed to have been completely overshadowed by a more traditional ideological approach to education, the 1970's witnessed a renewed emphasis on training in Marxist political theory and party management, modified this time by the principles of Yugoslav self-management. A new network of "Marxist centers" and political schools, capped by the "Josip Broz Tito Political School" in Croatia, were established to train a new generation of professional "socio-political workers." Instead of attempting to rekindle a concern with Marxism through some kind of anti-bureaucratic or anti-elitist Red Guard, the regime launched a campaign for younger political activists to emulate the values of the old guard. As one young functionary from a student organization remarked in 1977: "I consider the attitude 'paid functionaries are no longer necessary to us' to be super-demagogic: somebody in this country must really involve themselves in these affairs the whole of the livelong day."[35]

Viewing themselves as the guardians of the revolution and self-managed socialism, many members of the older generation of politicians and their new apprentices exhibited a fundamental distrust of the non-political professionals and intelligentsia. Such distrust had always been a latent aspect of tension within elite ranks. As Edward Kardelj remarked in 1969, during the halcyon days of socialist pluralism and the "new professional" in politics:

> If we could conduct a referendum among the technical intelligentsia today, 'for' or 'against' self-management, they would in principle declare themselves for self-management. But if society would entrust that same technical intelligentsia with the regulation of self-management in the way they choose, they would quickly liquidate it. That results from the present attitude of the technical intelligentsia. That is a fact with which our society must take account.[36]

How long the older members of the party elite would be able to guide the course of political life and also to withstand what has been termed the "permanent revolution of modernizing intellectuals" remained an open question at the end of the Tito era.[37] Both the natural attrition of the older revolutionary generation of professional politicians, and the steadily increasing complexity of the tasks facing Yugoslav decision-makers had increased the urgency of greater accommodation between the party leadership and Yugoslav society's emergent professional elites. The problems surrounding Yugoslav political elite development involved more than a confrontation between an aged group of party leaders and a younger generation of non-political technical specialists, or a simple dichotomy between reds and experts. Career politicians in Yugoslavia at the beginning of the 1980's were significantly better educated and more experienced than they were in the 1950's at the outset of the experiment in self-management.[38] Many older political leaders had acquired (often through on-the-job experience or continuing education) considerable specialization and familiarity with technical issues. Moreover, although the emphasis in elite recruitment during the mid-1970's was primarily on tested individuals with the correct type of political experience and ideological outlook, any policy ignoring technical and professional skills could not be sustained for very long.[39] Thus, the late 1970's and early 1980's (see Chapter 9) would witness a return to a pattern of political elite recruitment which favoured individuals exhibiting a combination of political activism and highly specialized non-political skills, that is, the politicized professionals or technically professionalized politicians who were so prominent in the 1960's.[40] As elsewhere in Eastern Europe, the Yugoslav political elite has also selectively coopted individuals whose specialized training and careers have been developed outside political life. Tito's holding action against the "techno-managerial," "intellectual," and "nationalist" elites proved temporarily successful during the 1970's, but it could not eliminate the inexorable forces which foster the emergence (or re-emergence in the case of

The Socialist Pyramid: Elites and Power in Yugoslavia

nationalist and traditional elite types) of such political sub-elites in all modernizing societies.

Table 3.1
The Occupational Background of the Yugoslav Party Elite, 1952-74/78 (%)

Occupational Sector	Central Committees by Number of Party Congress				
	VI (1952)	VII (1958)	VIII (1964)	IX (1969)	X (1974)
Socio-Political Functionaries	91.7	92.6	84.3	68.0	45.1
Military Officers	5.5	5.2	5.7	4.9	10.8
Managerial Personnel	-	-	3.1	8.2	9.6
Technical Intelligentsia	1.0	0.7	1.9	4.9	7.8
Cultural Intelligentsia	1.8	1.5	5.0	8.2	7.2
Workers	-	-	-	5.7	18.7
Peasants	-	-	-	-	0.6
Unknown	-	-	-	-	-
Total %	100.0	100.0	100.0	100.0	100.0[c]
(Number)	(109)[a]	(135)	(159)[b]	(122)	(166)

[a] The "primary occupations" of the 109 members of the Central Committee elected in 1952 were as follows: 41 workers, 3 peasants, 63 "intellectuals" and 2 employees.

[b] Includes 4 members who entered between 1964 and 1969.

[c] Percentages on this Table and the others in this chapter have been rounded and therefore may not add to exactly 100.0%.

Source: see footnote 4.

Table 3.2
The Educational Background of the Yugoslav Party Elite, 1948-74/78

Year Committee Selected	Central Committee Members by Level of Education							Newly Recruited Members		
	Total Membership				Higher Education			No Higher Education		Total
	Higher Education	No Higher Education	Total		N (%)			N (%)		N (%)
	N (%)	N (%)	N (%)							
1948[a]	56 (53.3)	49 (46.6)	105 (100.0)		13 (72.2)			[see total membership[b]]		18 (100.0)
1952	63 (57.8)	46 (42.2)	109 (100.0)		18 (66.7)			9 (33.3)		27 (100.0)
1958	79 (58.5)	56 (41.5)	135 (100.0)		65 (86.7)			10 (13.3)		75 (100.0)[c]
1964	121 (76.1)	38 (23.9)	159 (100.0)[c]		58 (85.3)			10 (14.7)		68 (100.0)
1969	106 (86.9)	16 (13.1)	122 (100.0)		77 (61.6)			48 (38.4)		125 (100.0)
1974	112 (67.5)	54 (32.5)	166 (100.0)							

[a] Full and candidate members.
[b] The Central Committee elected in 1948 was almost entirely composed of new members. Out of the 38 full and candidate members of the Central Committee elected at the Fifth National Conference of the Communist Party in October 1940, 14 died in the war.
[c] Includes four members added between 1964 and 1969.

Lenard J. Cohen

The Socialist Pyramid: Elites and Power in Yugoslavia

Table 3.3
The Educational Background of New Members of the Central Committee By Period of Political Recruitment (%)

Level and Field of Education	Period of Recruitment to Central Committee		
	1952-58	1964-69	1972-78
Higher Education	68.9	86.0	61.6
Higher Education by field:			
Political (Higher Party Schools)	9.7	21.1	14.3
Journalism	-	2.4	-
Philosophy, Social Science, History	12.9	13.8	7.8
Pedagogy	-	4.1	2.6
Law	51.6	19.5	15.6
Economics	6.6	15.4	11.7
Technical	6.6	14.6	16.9
Medical-Pharmacy	12.9	1.0	2.6
Military	-	8.1	7.8
Higher Other or Field Unknown	-	-	20.8*
Total Higher Education	100.0	100.0	100.0
(Number)	(31)	(123)	(77)
No Higher Education	31.1	14.0	38.4
Unknown	-	-	-
	100.0	100.0	100.0
Total New Members (Number)	(45)	(143)	(125)

* The sixteen individuals who claimed to have a higher education but did not indicate their specific field of study were mainly military officers (6) and older managers (7). Most of such "unknown higher education" was probably at political schools.

Table 3.4
The Age Composition of the Party Elite, 1948-74 (%)

	V (1948)	VI (1952)		VII (1958)		VIII (1964)		IX (1969)[c]		X (1974)	
Age Structure	Total	Total	New	Total	New	Total	New	Total	New	Total	New
-39	69.5	47.7	44.5	17.0	37.0	17.0	34.6	18.0	30.8	21.7	21.6
40-49	22.9	39.4	50.0	60.7	63.0	47.9	57.3	49.1	55.8	44.6	44.8
50-59	6.7	8.3	5.5	16.3	-	31.4	8.0	30.3	13.2	28.3	28.0
60 +	0.9	4.6	-	5.9	-	3.0	-	2.5	-	4.8	4.8
No Data	-	-	-	-	-	0.6	-	-	-	0.6	-
Total	100.0	100.0	100.0	100.0	100.0	100.0	100.0	100.0	100.0	100.0	100.0
(Number)	(105)	(109)[a]	(18)	(135)	(27)	(159)[b]	(75)	(122)	(68)	(166)	(125)

[a] Full and candidate members.
[b] Includes four members coopted between 1964 and 1969.
[c] The Presidency and "Standing Part of the Conference."

Table 3.5

The Yugoslav Party Elite by Political Generation 1952-74/78 (%)

Period in which members joined the Party/League	New Members				Central Committee Members				Incumbent Members			
	1952	1958	1964	1969	1974	1952	1958	1964	1969	1974
Pre-war (-1940)	55.6	44.4	21.3	1.5	13.6	94.5	90.7	88.1	55.6	39.0
Wartime (1941-45)	27.8	44.4	60.0	50.0	27.2	5.5	7.4	11.9	40.7	51.2
Post-war (1946+)	-	-	18.7	42.6	58.4	-	-	-	3.7	9.8
Unknown	16.7	11.1	-	5.9	0.8	-	1.9	-	-	-
Total (%)	100.0	100.0	100.0	100.0	100.0	100.0	100.0	100.0	100.0	100.0
(Number)	(18)	(27)	(75)*	(68)	(125)	(91)	(108)	(84)	(54)	(41)

* Includes four members who entered between 1964 and 1969.

Table 3.6
The New Members of the 1974 Party Elite by Political Generation and Occupational Group

Occupational Group	Period in which New Members Joined the Party/League					Total	
	Pre-war (-1940)	War time (1941-45)	Post-war (1946-49)	Post-war (1950+)	Unknown	N	(%)
Socio-political functionaries	11	12	4	11	-	38	(30.4)
Military	5	10	-	1	-	16	(12.8)
Managerial Personnel	-	7	2	6	-	15	(12.0)
Technical Intelligentsia	-	1	3	8	-	12	(9.6)
Cultural Intelligentsia	1	4	2	5	-	12	(9.6)
Workers	-	-	4	26	1	31	(24.8)
Peasants	-	-	-	1	-	1	(0.8)
Total Number	17	34	15	58	1	125	(100.0)
(%)	(13.6)	(27.2)	(12.0)	(46.4)	(0.8)		

The Socialist Pyramid: Elites and Power in Yugoslavia

Table 3.7
The Pattern of Ethnic Representation In Yugoslavia's Party Elite, 1948-74/78 (%)

Ethnic Group	Central Committees by Year					
	1948[a]	1952	1958	1964	1969	1974
Serbs	39.7	34.9	31.9	36.8	31.1	27.7
Montenegrins	15.9	11.0	10.4	11.6	10.7	13.3
Croats	19.1	21.0	22.2	18.1	14.8	15.1
Slovenes	12.7	15.6	15.6	15.5	15.6	13.3
Macedonians	7.9	9.2	10.3	10.3	11.5	10.8
Moslems[b]	-	-	-	-	4.1	6.6
"Yugoslavs"[b]	1.6	2.8	3.7	0.6	1.6	1.2
Albanians	-	0.9 ⎫	1.5 ⎫	2.6 ⎫	7.4 ⎫	7.8 ⎫
Hungarians	-	0.9 ⎬ 2.7	0.7 ⎬ 2.9	1.3 ⎬ 4.5	1.6 ⎬ 9.8	2.4 ⎬ 12.2
Other Minorities	-	0.9 ⎭	0.7 ⎭	0.6 ⎭	0.8 ⎭	1.8 ⎭
Unknown	3.2	2.8	3.0	2.6	0.8	-
Total (%)	100.0	100.0	100.0	100.0	100.0	100.0
(Number)	(63)	(109)	(135)	(155)	(122)	(166)

[a] The data for 1948 only include "full members" of the Central Committee.

[b] The category "Moslem" was not considered as an ethnic identity in statistics on leadership until 1969. Until that time most Moslems opted for ethnic designation as Serbs, Croats, or "Yugoslavs." Ethnic self-identification as a "Yugoslav" was very popular after the war, but has been officially frowned upon since the mid-1960s as allegedly indicating a "centralist" or "unitarian" political orientation.

NOTES: CHAPTER THREE

1. An interesting example of how conclusions are drawn about Yugoslav political development on the basis of inferences concerning the political leadership surfaced during the U.S. presidential debates betweed Gerald Ford and Jimmy Carter. When asked about his apparent commitment to aid Yugoslavia in the face of a hypothetical Soviet attack after Tito's death, Carter responded that his personal envoy, Averell Harriman, had "talked to the leaders in Yugoslavia, and I think it is accurate to say that there is no prospect in their opinion, of the Soviet Union invading Yugoslavia should Mr. Tito pass away. *The present leadership there is fairly uniform in its purpose. I think it is a close knit group* and I think it would be unwise for us to say that we will go to war in Yugoslavia if the Soviets should invade - which I think would be an extremely unlikely thing." *New York Times*, October 23, 1976, 10, (emphasis added). For two excellent studies concerning succession contingencies see William Zimmerman, "The Tito Succession and the Evolution of Yugoslav Politics," *Studies in Comparative Communism*, IX, Nos. 1-2 (Spring-Summer, 1976), 62-79, and Ross Johnson, *Yugoslavia in the Twilight of Tito* (Beverly Hills: Sage Publications, 1974).

2. In 1971 Stipe Šuvar provided an interesting sketch of Yugoslavia's elite structure. "Today in our country there are around 7,000 political professionals in socio-political organizations, and around 5,000 elected individuals in representative assemblies. That is the group which still adopts all major decisions in the communes, provinces, republics and the federation, which revolves in its own circles, which is connected hierarchically by an identity of interests and views, notwithstanding struggles which go on between cliques, and despite the fact that it is no longer one monolith, but is formed of relative independent centers of political power. Within this professional core a broad political elite is gathered in the communes and on higher levels. One can observe the privileged position of this stratum of the political-administrative bureaucracy through its material 'allowances.' It has the right to a higher personal income, to earn more outside their place of work, connections for influence and representation, honours, awards, etc. Its standard of living is guaranteed at the top and never falls to the bottom; its members are protected from unemployment, lack of a place to reside etc. One enters this group according to criteria of loyalty and conformism,

and falls only in the case of a rough blow as the result of some 'case' and excommunication in the settling of accounts between cliques." In a footnote to this paragraph, Šuvar provides the following example: "Let us take the example of one high state or social functionary today in our country, let's say one of the members of the newly formed Presidency of the SFRJ. I don't know how much the monthly income of such a member is but probably it isn't less than 6,000 new dinars [about $500, or $6,000 annually, when the per capita annual income was approximately $700] not calculating extra income for travel. But outside his personal income, such a member has many indirect privileges; he has an office and staff in Belgrade and in his own republic; at both places a chauffeur and automobile which stands waiting for him each moment; a small plane is available for travel longer distances; at his destination the best automobile in the locality is available to him, the best accommodation, the best local food; he is shown the main local attractions, etc ...; his speeches are carried in their entirety by the media at least in his own republic, but I don't know whether he is paid an honourarium for this. Indeed, it isn't pleasant to constantly travel, but it also becomes difficult in that way to have to lay out one's regular personal income." See "Sredniji slojevi ili sredna klasa u Jugoslovenskom društvu," *Marksističke sveske*, Nos. 1-2, (1972), 92. In an earlier work, Šuvar points out that the "real division of social power in Yugoslav society is still such that an elite structure clustered at the summit of social institutions has a decisive role in the guidance of society." See *Sociološki presjek Jugoslovenskog društva* (Zagreb: Školska knjiga, 1970), 173.

3. Robert D. Putnam, *The Comparative Study of Political Elites* (Englewood Cliffs, N.J.: Prentice Hall, 1976), 166. For the utility and limitations of elite research for the study of political development see also John Nagle, *System and Succession: The Social Basis of Elite Recruitment* (Austin: University of Texas Press, 1977), William B. Quandt, *The Comparative Study of Political Elites* (Beverly Hills: Sage Publications, 1970), Heinz Eulau and Moshe M. Czudnowski (eds.), *Elite Recruitment in Democratic Politics: Comparative Studies Across Nations* (New York: Halstead Press, 1976), Moshe M. Czudnowski (ed.), *Does Who Governs Matter?: Elite Circulation in Contemporary Societies* (Dekalb, Illinois: Northern Illinois University Press, 1982), and Gwen Moore (ed.), *Research in Politics and Society, A Research Annual: Studies of the Structure of National Elite Groups* (Greenwich, Conn.: JAI Press, 1985).

Lenard J. Cohen

4. The terms *Party* and *League* are used interchangeably. Biographical data was collected from a variety of sources on members of the Central Committee (The "Presidency" and "Standing Part of the Conference" from 1969 to 1974) elected at the Sixth (1952), Seventh (1958), Eighth (1964), Ninth (1969) and Tenth (1974) Congresses of the League of Communists. In addition to biographical material available in the stenographic reports of each congress, the major sources of social background data on the party elite were: *Zbornik Narodnih Heroja Jugoslavije* (Belgrade: Omladina, 1957), *Ko je ko u Jugoslaviji: Biografski podaci o Jugoslovenski savremenici* (Belgrade: Sedma Sila, 1957), "Biographies of the Members of the Central Committee of the League of Communists of Yugoslavia," *Joint Publications Research Service, Eastern Europe, Political, Sociological, and Military Affairs* (Belgrade: 1967), *Jugoslovenski savremenici, Ko je ko u Jugoslaviji* (Belgrade: Hronometer, 1969), *Konferencija Saveza Komunista Jugoslavije održana od 29 do 31, oktobra 1970* (Belgrade: Komunist, 1971), 299-319, "Central Komitet SKJ," *Komunist* (June 3, 1974), 5-9. Data on Central Committee members were also obtained in some cases from a number of biographical handbooks covering the membership of federal republican and provincial legislative assemblies from 1952 to 1977.

5. *Report on the Work of the Central Committee and the Central Auditing Commission of the League of Communists of Yugoslavia from the Seventh Congress to the Eighth Congress of the League of Communists of Yugoslavia* (Belgrade, 1964), 35. One of the alleged purposes of the 1966-1967 party reorganization was to reverse a trend which had resulted in "the concentration of competence and responsibility within the Executive Committee and in a passive attitude on the part of the Central Committee," Mijalko Todorović, "Reorganization of the Leading Bodies of the League of Communists of Yugoslavia," *Socialist Thought and Practice*, No. 24 (October-December, 1966), 53. Two good treatments of Yugoslav politics during the period covered by this study are Dennison Rusinow, *The Yugoslav Experiment, 1948-74* (Berkeley: University of California Press, 1977), and Fred Singleton, *Twentieth-Century Yugoslavia* (New York: Columbia University Press, 1976). For the role of the party throughout the period, see Paul Shoup, "The Limits of Party Control: The Yugoslav Case," *Authoritarian Politics in Communist Europe: Uniformity and Diversity in One-Party States*, ed. Andrew Janos (Berkeley: University of California Press, 1976), 176-196.

The Socialist Pyramid: Elites and Power in Yugoslavia

6. "Occupational background" represents a composite category which takes into consideration both an individual's "current occupation" at the point of entry into the Central Committee and a person's occupational history, i.e., the occupation in which a person spent most of his working life. A member of the Central Committee was classified as having a particular occuaptional background depending on which of the following seven sectors occupied the greatest number of years during his adult working life: (1) *socio-political functionaries*, composed of professional party (League), mass organization, government (executive and legislative personnel) and adminstrative officials; (2) *managerial personnel*, made up of directors and management staff in various economic enterprises and non-economic institutions; (3) the *technical intelligentsia*, composed of engineers, technical experts in industry, scientific researchers, medical personnel, etc; (4) the *cultural intelligentsia*, working in fields such as education, literature, the arts, etc.; (5) *workers,* the skilled and unskilled proletariat working "in direct production"; (6) *peasants*, or more commonly referred to in recent Yugoslav usage - agriculturalists; and (7) professional *military personnel*.

7. One of the best statements on the formation of the Yugoslav professional revolutionary is Milovan Djilas, *Memoir of a Revolutionary* (New York: Harcourt Brace Jovanovich, 1973). For the occupational background of the Communist elite between 1940 and 1948 see Chapter Two.

8. Djilas has argued that the formation of a "new class" among the leaders of the Partisan movment permitted Tito's regime to withstand Soviet pressure. See Milovan Djilas, "The Storm in Eastern Europe," The New Leader, (November 19, 1956), 4. In 1956, a leading Yugoslav diplomat noted in his diary that relations between the members of the Yugoslav elite still had some elements of "mutual trust" forged during the war. "Although we have already been in power in Yugoslavia for ten years and although power spoils people more quickly than anything, attacks their morale, and ruins relations between them, personal relationships between us have not yet become rigidly hierarchical in every field. The long years of conflict with Stalin after the war probably helped us more than anything else to preserve some human qualities from the war period and our youth and to slow down the process of deterioration, with the result, as you see, that there can still be sudden spontaneous outbursts of those qualities which were the best in us but which are

steadily fading into the past." Veljko Mićunović, *Moscow Diary* (Garden City, N.Y.: Doubleday, 1980), 15.

9. "In the early post-war period," observed two Yugoslav political sociologists, "the open character of the group of leading cadres was undeniably predominant.... A considerable number of professional leaders and representatives of the new class-authority [*nove klasne vlasti*] were, in effect, the top of the tree growing from the skilled and highly-skilled traditional (in the best sense of the word) part of the working class. They were its direct political superstructure, in the same manner as its other important source was the radical revolutionary intelligentsia, transformed into professional revolutionaries .... Although the first seeds of a privileged way of life appeared among them already at the time, internal differentiation and partial interests were to emerge more clearly at a later date." Miroslav Pečujlić and Dušan Ničić, "Skica strukture društvene svesti," *Gledišta*, No. 12 (December, 1966), 1421-1422. For a rough translation of the Serbo-Croatian see "Early Stage of Socialist Reconstruction and Awareness of It," *Socialist Thought and Practice*, No. 29 (January-March, 1968), 68-89.

10. Between 1948 and 1963, 55,663 Yugoslavs were accused of supporting the Cominform resolution against Yugoslavia including: a) *in the party organization*, two members of the Politburo, eight members of the top Central Committee, 16 members of republican Central Committees, 50 members of regional committees, 773 members of district committees, 318 members of communal committees, and b) *in the state bureaucracy*, six federal ministers, 14 assistant federal ministers, 17 republican ministers, 85 assistant republican ministers, 30 federal and 33 republican legislative deputies, 43 colonels, and six generals. *Nedeljne Informativne Novine*, (January 9, 1987), 55.

11. The ethnic composition of the party elite reflected the high level of Montenegrin and Serbian involvement in the Partisan movement, especially during the initial stage of the war. An official sociological analysis of the Partisan forces points out that "the historical conditions in which the First Proletarian Brigade was formed [December 1941] conditioned that it was composed mainly of the members of the two nationalities: Serbians 61.7 percent and Montenegrins 31.4 percent [i.e., 1,118 out of 1,199 individuals in six battalions]. In addition to them, the Brigade had 20 Croatian communists, a Slovene detachment [of] 27, 17 Jews and others.

Owing to its socio-political and military-strategic role in the National Liberation War, the Brigade later filled itself out with recruits from all the regions of Yugoslavia." Milos Prelevic, "Neki podaci o oruzanim formacijama NOR-a 1941-1944 godine," *Zbornik radova: politicka skola JNA, Volume III* (Belgrade: Politicka skola JNA, 1970), 127-129. By the spring of 1944 Tito reported that the national composition of the Partisan movement was 44 percent Serbs, 30 percent Croats, 10 percent Slovenes, four percent Montenegrins, two and one-half percent Muslims and six percent others. *Borba za oslobodjenje Jugoslavije 1941-1944* (Belgrade: Drzavni izdavacki zavod Jugoslavije, 1945), 180. The ethnic derivation of a sample of 438 Partisan military officers was as follows: 31.8 percent Serbian, 17.1 percent Montenegrin, 27.9 percent Croatian, 12.3 percent Slovenes, 0.9 percent Macedonians, 10.0 percent Muslims, but no minority group members. R.V. Burks, *The Dynamics of Communism in Eastern Europe* (Princeton: Princeton University Press, 1961), 126. See also Table 2.11.

12. Djilas' vocal anti-bureaucratic protest was the exception rather than the rule. A 1970 diary entry by Serbian party leader, Dragoslav Marković, expresses a more typical example of how elite level purges beginning in 1948 eroded the political ideals of party activists. "I was educated and became a believer, 'believing' in the Communist Party of Yugoslavia. I remained a believer, only I changed my political beliefs: in place of the Communist Party of the Soviet Union and Stalin I believed in the Communist Party of Yugoslavia and Tito, Ranković, Kardelj, Djilas, Kidrić.... And then they began to leave - Hebrang, Žujović, Nešković, Djilas.... With the [departure] of the 'gods' the beliefs disappeared. I survived the Fourth Plenum and the departure of Rankovic as an athiest, already a non-believer.... This has lasted a long time. Perhaps it is difficult, but it's better to live without a faith. They can't sell you a 'horn for a candle' ['bill of goods' or 'pig in a poke']." *Nedeljne Informativne Novine*, No. 1914, (September 6, 1987), 51.

Alvin Gouldner has observed that "one of the latent functions of the vanguard structure is, by habituating them to discipline and hierarchy, to resocialize intellectuals into (administrative and communication) intelligentsia, and accommodate them to bureaucratic styles. In other words to 'discipline' them." "Prologue to a Theory of Revolutionary Intellectuals," *Telos*, No. 20 (Winter, 1975-1976), 17. For the failure of resocialization to a bureaucratic orientation see Dennis Reinhartz, "Milovan Djilas: The Transcendence of a Revolutionary," *The Walter Prescott Webb Memorial*

Essays on Modern Revolutionary History, eds. Bede K. Lackner and Kenneth Roy Philip (Austin: University of Texas Press, 1977), 69-88.

13. As opposed to numerical or structural bureaucratization, as the bureaucracy was reduced in size and was decentralized.

14. The rate of membership renewal in the Central Committees of the republican and provincial party organizations was even greater (e.g., 59 percent in Montenegro and 58 percent in Serbia). See *1965 Kongresi Saveza Komunista Republika* (Belgrade: Sedma Sila, 1965), 8, 70, 131, 201, 272, and 332.

15. On professional political science and professional politicians in the 1960's, see Lenard J. Cohen, "Political Science in Socialist Yugoslavia: The Regime-Management and the Self-Management of a Discipline," *The Soviet Union and East Europe into the 1980's: Multi-disciplinary Perspectives*, eds. Simon McInnes, William McGrath, and Peter Potichnyj (Oakville, Ontario: Mosaic Press, 1978), 59-98. A military sociologist in the Yugoslav army has argued that "the military organization of self-managed society, as a contemporary technically and technologically organized military force, demands a special skilled staff of experts whose profession will be an exclusively military one," but that "measures of socialization of the people's defense have eliminated the objective basis of the development of the elitist social status" which developed in the Yugoslav military's "commanding cadre" during the postwar period. Mensor Ibrahimpashich, "The Military Profession in a Self-Managed Society." Paper presented at the Seventh World Congress of Sociology, Varna, Bulgaria, 1970, 8, 19.

16. The number of university graduates in the fields of law and philosophy dropped from 75.3 percent of the total graduates in the years 1919-1940, to 27.4 percent in those fields during the years 1945-1961. Graduates in the technical (engineering), economics, and natural science faculties increased from 16.8 percent in the interwar period to 39.6 percent in the 1945-1961 period. "Diplomirani studenti: 1970," *Statistički Bilten*, No. 714 (Belgrade: Savezni zavod za statistiku, 1972), Rade Aleksić, "Inteligencija u Jugoslovenskom društvu," *Sociologija*, VI, Nos. 1-2 (1964), 115-133.

17. "An Interview with Mijalko Todorović," *Komunist* (October 26, 1967), reprinted in *Socialist Thought and Practice* No. 28 (October-December, 1967), 121.

18. The *politicized professional* as an *elite type* falls somewhere between the amateur political activist and the *career* politician, although the degree to which any single member of the party elite approximates the ideal type suggested by the concept varies considerably. Many Western scholars have distinguished *recruited* party functionaries, lacking broad technical background and little prior occupational experience outside the political sector, from *coopted* officials who have spent a significant portion of their careers in specialized non-party and non-political positions. *Intermediate, hybrid, dual* elite career types, who have both specialized in non-political backgrounds and fulltime political experience in roughly equal proportions, also are frequently discussed in the literature. The concept of the politicized professional used here approximates the coopted and intermediate types often used in other studies. See Frederick J. Fleron, Jr., "System Attributes and Career Attributes: The Soviet Political Leadership, 1952 to 1965," *Comparative Communist Political Leadership*, ed. Carl Beck, et. al. (New York: David McKay Co., 1975), 43-85, Carl Beck, "The Career Characteristics of East European Leadership," *Political Leadership in Eastern Europe and the Soviet Union*, ed. Barry Farrell (Chicago: Aldine Publishing Co., 1970), 157-194, Joel Moses, *Regional Party Leadership and Policy-Making in the USSR* (New York: Praeger Publishers 1974), 137-141, 234-240, John D. Nagel, "A New Look at the Soviet Elite: A Generational Model of the Soviet System," *Journal of Political and Military Sociology*, III, No. 1 (Spring, 1975), 1-13, Robert A. Scalapino, "The Transition in Chinese Party Leadership: A Comparison of the Eighth and Ninth Central Committees," *Elites in the People's Republic of China*, ed. Robert A. Scalapino (Seattle: University of Washington Press, 1972), 67-148, Dae-Sook Suh, "Communist Party Leadership," *Political Leadership in Korea*, eds. Dae-Sook Suh and Chae-Jin Lee (Seattle: University of Washington Press, 1977), 159-191, Robert H. Donaldson and Derek J. Waller, *Stasis and Change in Revolutionary Elites: A Comparative Analysis of the 1956 Party Central Committees in China and the USSR*, Sage Professional Papers: Comparative Political Series I, II (Beverly Hills: Sage Publications, 1970), Donaldson and Waller's, "A Comparison of the Current Chinese and Soviet Central Committees," *Studies in Comparative Communism*, VI, Nos. 1-2

Lenard J. Cohen

(Spring-Summer), 1973, 51-65, Peter C. Ludz, *The Changing Party Elite in East Germany* (Cambridge: MIT Press, 1972), especially section 3, and Thomas A. Baylis, *The Technical Intelligentsia and The East German Elite* (Berkeley: University of California Press, 1974), 185-218.

19. For trends in the Yugoslav managerial elite during this period, see Josip Županov, "Da li se rukovodjenje preduzćem profesionalizira?" *Moderna Organizacija*, No. 10 (1968), 803-823, translated as "Is Enterprise Management Becoming Professionalized?" in *International Studies of Management and Organization*, III, No. 3 (Fall, 1973), 42-83, Predrag Radenović, "Sve veći broj pravih direktora," *Direktor*, No. 2 (1969), 54-56, Solomon Rawin, "Social Values and the Managerial Structure: The Case of Yugoslavia and Poland," *Journal of Comparative Administration*, II, No. 2 (August, 1970), 131-159. The Slovene sociologist, Zdravko Mlinar, described the profile of the new Yugoslav "organization man" in the 1960's: "a middle-aged male in good physical condition, he holds a managerial position in his place of work, is a functionary in an organization or a member of a self-managing organ (workers' council, etc.), has a relatively high living-standard (good apartment, a car, all the modern trappings, etc.), probably lives in the city, travels extensively in other regions and countries (by the most comfortable means, automobile, sleeping car, plane), stays overnight in the best hotels, eats in the best and most expensive restaurants, subscribes to several journals, is generally serious, isn't religious, goes to the theatre, concerts and the opera ... is precisely informed about specific socio-economic and political problems, has a well-developed viewpoint on affairs, has a big obituary in the newspaper when he dies" (cited in Stipe Šuvar, *Sociološki presek*, 173). A large number of such "new" Yugoslav managers emerged as part of the poltical elite in the 1960's but they could be differentiated from the professional politicans in that elite. The new managerial type contrasted with the earlier manager-director who "belonged to the top echelons of the political structure, and was primarily, although not exclusively, recruited from that section of society." Pečujlić and Ničić, "Skica Strukture Društvene Svesti," 1422.

20. The cooptation of politicized professionals in 1969 was even more striking at the next tier of the central party elite. In the "Temporary Part of the Conference" made up of 210 members, 25 percent were directors and managerial personnel, 16 percent were members of

the non-technical intelligentsia and 9 percent were from the technical intelligentsia.

21. On the rapid growth in the size and influence of the Yugoslav intelligentsia during this period see Miroslav Pečujlić, *Promene u socijalnoj strukturi Jugoslavije* (Belgrade: Visoka škola političkih nauka, 1963), Rade Aleksić, "Inteligencija u Jugoslovenskom društvu," *Sociologija*, VI, Nos. 1-2 (1964), 115-133, Živan Tanić, "Direktori i predstavnici samoupravnih tela," *Naše teme*, XIII, No. 2 (February, 1969), 186-206, Ivan Perić, "Nosioci stručno-rukovodenih funkcija i društveno političke organizacije i poduzećima," *Direktor u samoupravnim odnosima*, eds. Drago Goropić and Jovo Brekić (Zagreb: Informator, 1967), 103-109, and Rudi Supek, *Humanistička inteligencija i politika* (Zagreb: Razlog, 1971), Mihajlo Marković and Robert S. Cohen, *The Rise and Fall of Socialist Humanism: A History of the Praxis Group* (Nottingham: Spokesman Books, 1975). The growing political involvement of many members of the intelligentsia in the 1960's - such as technical specialists and managers, philosophers, social scientists - contrasts with the political disengagement and "privatization" of many writers. See Gertrude Robinson, "The New Yugoslav Writer: A Socio-Political Portrait," *Mosaic*, VI, No. 4 (Summer, 1973), 185-198. See also Rudi Supek and Maja Minček, *Likovni Stvaraoci i kultura sredina* (Zagreb: Institut za društvena iztraživanja sveučilišta u Zagrebu, 1970).

22. Another factor contributing to the declining number of professional politicians in the party elite in this period was the reduced number of individuals simultaneously holding positions in different political and governmental organizations (the so-called "de-accumulation of functions"). Actually this also contributed to the growing professionalization of distinct types of political tasks (e.g., legislative, administrative, party, etc.) within the broad socio-political occupational sector. For different interpretations of the regime's policy intentions and achievements, see Krsto Kilibarda, "Changes in Public Office," *Socialist Thought and Practice*, No. 9 (January, 1963), 105-115, and Josip Županov, "Egalitarizam i industrializam," *Naše teme*, XIV, No. 2 (February, 1970), 271-276.

23. V.I. Lenin, *Collected Works, Volume XLV* (Moscow: The Foreign Languages Publishers, 1960), 164-165.

24. On the "horizontal migration" of professional politicians among party, state administrative, and legislative positions, see Radomir Lukic, "Rotation Among Top Government Officials in Yugoslavia," *The Mandarins of Western Europe: The Political Role of Top Civil Servants*, ed. Mattei Dogan (New York: John Wiley and Sons Inc., 1975), 293-304.

25. Phyllis Auty, "The Ninth Congress of the League of Communists," *The World Today*, XXV, No. 6 (June, 1969), 265, 275.

26. Interview in *Vjesnik* (October 8, 1972), reprinted in *Socialist Thought and Practice*, No. 49 (August-December, 1972), 7.

27. Interviewed by the Sarajevo daily *Oslobodjenje* on November 1, 1971, Vladimir Bakarić, Croatia's top party leader on the federal level remarked, "Until the society becomes classless, a kind of dictatorship must exist. Do I believe a dictatorship of the proletariat is ruling now? It rules, but it is a little slack, however. This slackness has been used by those who want to use the present situation in society." *Foreign Broadcast Information Service*, (November 4, 1971), I15.

28. According to the Statute of the League of Communists adopted at the Ninth Congress, the composition of all leading "bodies and organs ... must be renewed by at least one third ... in regular election" (Part II, Section 18) and "modifications between two congresses may not involve more than one-third of the total composition" (Part VII (b), Section 56). The same provisions were readopted at the Tenth Congress (Part II, Section 20 and Part VII (b), Section 60).

29. The type of managers coopted into the Central Committee reflected a basic change in general recruitment of the managerial elite in this period. "From 1945 to around 1962," writes a prominent Slovene sociologist, "the highest managers were recruited primarily from the administrative-political sphere, and less from the `technostructure' .... They were not elected only from the political-administrative sphere, but they were dependent on it (and wished more independence from it). After 1972, again the recruitment of higher directors - and particularly chief directors - was expressly from the political-administrative sphere." Janez Jerovšek, "O stručnim kadrovima," *Gledišta*, XV, No. 10 (October, 1974), 985.

30. "The Tenth Congress of the League of Communists of Yugoslavia," *Socialist Thought and Practice*, XIV, Nos. 6-7 (June-July, 1974), 79.

31. An analysis of data on persons elected to the Central Committee of the League of Communists at the Eleventh Congress in 1978 and Twelfth Congress in 1982 reveals the continued importance of the Partisan generation in the top party elite. For example, in 1978, 37 percent of the Central Committee was 56 years of age or older, a figure which rose to 53.4 percent in 1982.

32. Robin Alison Remington, "Armed Forces and Society," *Political Systems: Comparative Perspectives*, ed. C. Kelleher (Beverly Hills: Sage Publications, 1974), 167. Party membership in the officers corps, which has always been very high (96 percent of officers, 76 percent of non-commissioned officers in 1964), rose to an all-time high in 1977 (98.5 percent of officers and over 90 percent of NCO's). *Foreign Broadcast Information Service*, (March 31, 1977), I9.

33. John Kautsky, "Patterns of Elite Succession in the Process of Development," *Journal of Politics*, XXXI, No. 2 (May, 1969), 59-396, John Kautsky, *Communism and the Politics of Development* (New York: John Wiley and Sons Inc., 1968), 165, and John Kautsky, *The Political Consequences of Modernization* (New York: John Wiley and Sons Inc., 1972), 149-151. In one discussion Kautsky seems rather pessimistic about the possibilities of systematically establishing any association between modernization and elite change, or even the value of doing so: "we cannot test, much less validate the hypothesis that industrialization and the replacement of revolutionary managerial modernizers accompany each other if we cannot clearly distinguish between the two types of modernizers. Since this is precisely our position now, the hypothesis will have to remain no more than a hypothesis for some time to come .... It may or may not be true that it takes one type of man to build a political movement and another to build a factory. But there is, in any case, reason to believe that it is not so much attitudes and values that shape policies ... as it is the prevailing system characteristics and, especially, the availability of wealth." John Kautsky, "Revolutionary and Managerial Elites in Modernizing Regimes," *Comparative Politics*, I, No. 4 (July, 1969), 466. See also David Apter, *The Politics of Modernization* (Chicago: University of Chicago, 1966), 172-178, Robert A. Scalapino, "Political Moderni-

zation and the Intellectual," *Comparative/International Series* (Berkeley: University of California Press, n.d.), Reprint No. 218, 502-508, and Clark Kerr, *et. al.*, "Postscript to 'Industrialism and Industrial Man,'" *International Labour Review*, CIII, No. 6 (June, 1971), 519-540.

34. Richard Lowenthal, "Development vs. Utopia in Communist Policy," *Change in Communist Systems*, ed. Chalmers Johnson (Stanford: Stanford University Press, 1970), 51-52. Alfred Meyer has distinguished between the elite traits relevant to the "system-building" and "system management stages" of communist political development in Alfred Meyer, "Authority in Communist Political Systems," *Political Leadership in Industrialized Societies*, ed. Lewis Edinger (New York: John Wiley and Sons Inc., 1967), 84-107. On the question of elite transformation in communist regimes see also Paul Wong, *China's Higher Leadership in the Socialist Transition* (New York: The Free Press, 1976), especially pages 173-180, Seweryn Bialer, "The Soviet Political Elite and Internal Developments in the USSR," *The Soviet Empire: Expansion and Detente*, ed. William Griffith (Lexington: Lexington Press, 1976), 25-55, Carl Beck, et. al., "Political Succession in Eastern Europe," Studies in Comparative Communism, IX, Nos. 1-2 (Spring-Summer, 1976), 35-61, and Martin McCauley and Stephen Carter (eds.), *Leadership and Succession in the Soviet Union, Eastern Europe, and China*, (Basingstoke: Macmillan, 1986).

35. Teodor Anbelić, "Trnje političke ruže," *Nedeljne Informativne Novine*, No. 1374 (May 8, 1977), 8. The resolutions on "cadre policy" adopted by the Presidium of the Central Committee on December 12, 1975 stress that "it is necessary to strengthen even more the interconnection and unity of the moral-political, working and vocational qualities .... In practicing the principle of the interchangeability and mobility of cadres for a decrease in the number of offices, it is necessary to thoroughly analyze all practical experience gained in every environment. Any stereotyped application of these principles and tasks could weaken the united front of the socialist forces." *Foreign Broadcast Information Service*, (December 15, 1975), I7.

36. "Da li je samoupravljanje u Jugoslaviji gradilište ili fasada jednog empirijskog socijalizma," *Socijalizam*, Nos. 7-8 (1969), 900.

37. Harold Lasswell, "The World Revolution of Our Time: A Framework for Basic Policy Research," *World Revolutionary Elites*, eds. Harold Lasswell and Daniel Lerner (Cambridge: MIT Press, 1965), 68. For the factors which may foster or constrain the political influence of technocratic elites, see Robert D. Putnam, "Elite Transformation in Advanced Industrial Societies: An Empirical Assessment of the Theory of Technocracy," *Comparative Political Studies*, X, No. 3 (October, 1977), 383-411.

38. The higher educational level of professional politicians in the top elite is also apparent in census data on occupational groups. For example, the number of career "socio-political workers" who had no higher educational training of some type dropped from 88 percent in 1953 to 71.5 percent in 1961, to 49 percent in 1971.

39. Jack Bielasiak has argued that generalist political managers have retained a commanding position in the other East European communist elites by devising strategies to recruit specialists but restricting their authority. "Lateral and Vertical Elite Differentiation In European Communist States," *Studies in Comparative Communism*, XI, Nos. 1-2 (Spring-Summer, 1978), 121-141.

40. In a related trend, the number of workers in the Central Committee dropped from 19 percent in 1974 to 9 percent in 1978, and 5 percent in 1982. See Chapter 9 for elite development in the period right before and after the conclusion of the Tito era.

PART THREE

STATE ELITES AND SELF-MANAGERS: THE BATTLE AGAINST BUREAUCRACY

...officials are as necessary to every ruler and government as wings to an eagle, or hands to a man.

Vuk Karadžić (1832)

There is only one type of apparatus in our country for which you don't have to import extra parts — the state apparatus.

Yugoslav joke (1982)

CHAPTER 4

POLITICS AS AN AVOCATION: LEGISLATIVE PROFESSIONALIZATION AND PARTICIPATION

Developing legislative institutions and processes which can facilitate citizen participation in the formulation of public policy has been an explicit objective of the Yugoslav effort to construct a "self-managing socialist community." Beginning in 1953, the Yugoslav regime has endeavoured to devise an "assembly system" which avoids the alleged defects of representative institutions found in both liberal democracies and "statist" regimes. The present constitution, adopted in 1974, is the latest incarnation of Yugoslavia's quest for a more participatory and truly Marxist legislative system. The 1974 constitution replaced a novel structure of governmental institutions that had been adopted just a decade earlier.

The current arrangement of legislative institutions (see Figure 4.1) consists of a complex multi-tiered structure of "delegations" and assembly chambers. The system extends from its base of delegations elected in approximately 21,000 neighbourhood, enterprise, and organizational units (Basic Organizations of Associated Labour), through local (communal and inter-municipal) and regional (provincial and republic) assemblies, to the apex of the system, the Assembly of the Socialist Federal Republic of Yugoslavia (previously called the Federal Assembly). The base of the legislative structure is connected to the federal legislature by a process of indirect elections and various provisions for accountability whereby each tier of the assembly system emanates from, and is theoretically accountable to, each lower level.

Lenard J. Cohen

Figure 4.1
The Structure of the Yugoslav Assembly System (1974-1986)

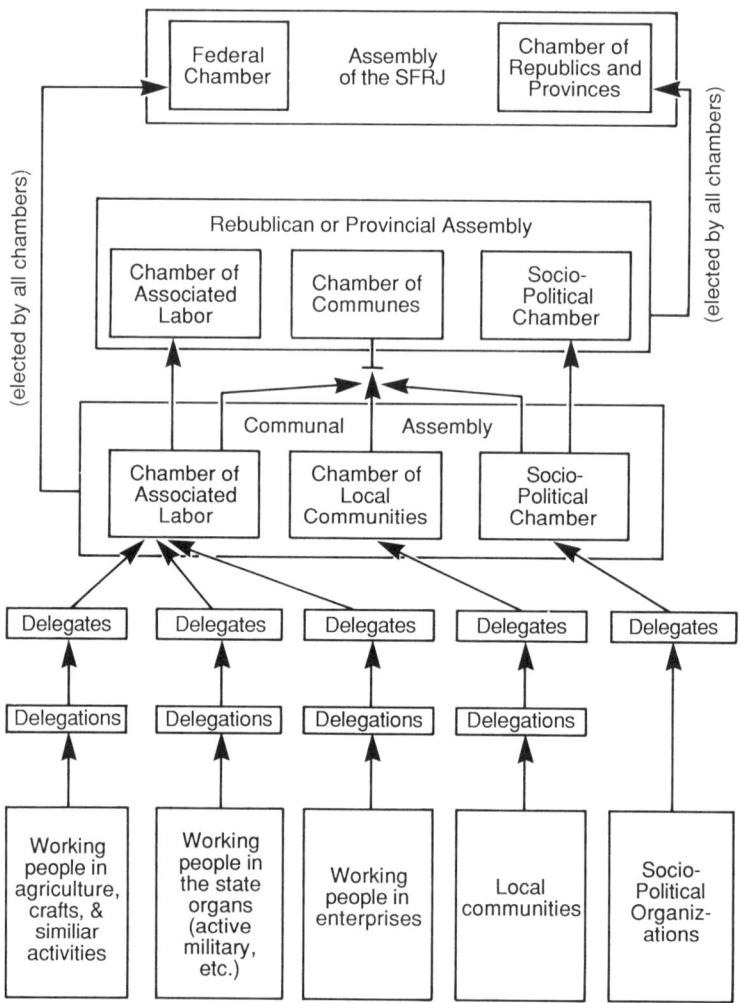

Source: Adapted from Najdan Pašić and Balša Spadijer, *Društveno-Politički Sistem SFRJ* (Belgrade: Radnička Stampa, 1975), p. 462.

The Socialist Pyramid: Elites and Power in Yugoslavia

As was the case with earlier Yugoslav legislative models, the system established in 1974 is more often a source of fascination and philosophic enthusiasm by Western scholars than the subject of serious political analysis. The frequent changes in Yugoslavia's government structure also contribute to the usual difficulties of probing the labyrinth of a complex legislative process. Moreover, because officials tend to emphasize the defects of each abandoned set of institutional arrangements when reorganization occurs, observers have generally been either reluctant or unable to subject important facets of the Yugoslav experiment to analysis over time. Such institutional flux and research problems have obscured significant continuities of behaviour and persistent problems germane to the study of socialism, democracy, and legislative development.

A central component of the 1974 assembly system that built upon and expanded earlier theoretical and practical measures adopted during the 1950's and 1960's, is the principle of "deprofessionalizing" the job of legislative representation. According to this principle, the majority of elected delegates in representative assemblies should perform their tasks as an "honourary function" on a part-time or amateur basis. Most delegates are expected to return to their regular pre-election occupations and areas of specialization after serving for a limited period of time as legislative decision-makers. In addition to being an essential part of legislative recruitment policy, deprofessionalization is encouraged by provisions for personnel "rotation" which place mandatory limits on the amount of time an individual can serve in any one legislative assembly (presently two consecutive terms or eight years). It is also understood, however, that a portion of the delegates who are professional "socio-political workers," and thus elected from delegations in the basic organization of the party (League of Communists) and other mass organizations, are likely to serve more frequently as legislative delegates (subject, of course, to the same rotation provisions) and to perform their legislative tasks in a more politically professionalized manner.

Yugoslavia's unique effort to transform elected legislative office-holding into an avocation, together with official claims regarding the success of that venture, makes the actual involvement of Yugoslav delegates in legislative decision-making an important subject for inquiry. How do amateur delegates who serve for a short term in assemblies compare with delegates who are more professionalized in their political and legislative work? What are their comparative rates of participation and influence in the legislative process? What trends and problems have emerged, and what consequences does this experience suggest for Yugoslavia and other models of socialist development? This chapter addresses such questions, utilizing empirical data gathered by the author, as well as Yugoslav analytical studies. The analysis specifically focuses on the role of delegates serving in the federal legislature before and after the adoption of the 1974 constitutional system.

Lenard J. Cohen

The Pattern Before 1974: Professionalization and Institutionalization

Trends in Legislative Recruitment

One striking anomaly of Yugoslav legislative development prior to 1974 was the *de facto* professionalization of elected legislators. This process occurred despite a vocal campaign by official spokesmen to encourage exactly the opposite trend. The regime's commitment to the deprofessionalization of work in assemblies and other political organizations was expressed in a number of ways: the creation of special chambers in assemblies for the representation of socio-economic groups and interests in areas other than the state administration and professional political activity (first in 1953 and then expanded in 1963); mandatory provisions for the rotation of legislative personnel, encouraging elected representatives to return to their original occupations after serving in assemblies; and a legislative recruitment policy emphasizing the importance of electing women, young persons, and working people who are not professional politicians.

Rotation and deprofessionalization were conceived as major devices to diminish the scope and influence of bureaucratic management in society and to encourage broad citizen participation in the formulation of public policy, leading eventually to an essentially nonpartisan and depoliticized process of self-management.[1] According to the official Yugoslav view during the 1960's, professional office-holding, although not necessarily identical with bureaucracy, nevertheless contained the seeds of bureaucratization. It was, therefore, important for a democratizing socialist regime to deprofessionalize public service as much as possible. This goal had a long tradition in Marxist ideology (see Chapter 1), but had never been operationalized to the extent which the Yugoslavs proposed.

Despite the vocal disparagement of professional political activity, the first two decades of self-management witnessed a steady increase in the number of elected deputies who could be classified as professional legislators in terms of either their occupational self-identification, their source of income, or their extended tenure and frequent re-election to assemblies at different levels of the Yugoslav federation. For example, although there was a relative decrease in the number of "socio-political workers" (functionaries in the party and mass organizations, legislators, and civil servants) elected to the Federal Assembly as a whole between 1953 and 1974 - most dramatically from 73 percent in 1953 to 32.8 percent in 1969 - there was actually a parallel growth in the number of individuals drawing their salaries exclusively from the legislature and involved full time in the activity of the legislature's most politically influential chambers (see Table 4.1).[2]

Table 4.1
Occupational Composition of the Yugoslav Federal Assembly, by Chambers, 1963-1978 (%)

Occupation	Political Chambers(s)[a]						Functionally Specialized Chamber(s)[b]					
	1963	1965	1967	1969	1974	1978	1963	1965	1967	1969	1974	1978
Party and mass organization functionaries	31.6	28.4	24.7	21.5	18.2		17.1	21.4	16.3	2.5	11.8	
Professional legislators in representative bodies	15.3	46.8	38.4	41.9	56.8	95.3	7.5	6.5	6.5	2.2	21.3[c]	68.7
State administrative functionaries	27.4	11.6	17.4	5.8			5.0	6.7	5.2	1.7		
Managerial personnel in noneconomic institutions	12.1	3.7	4.7	4.6	12.5		22.0	20.0	15.8	31.9	17.7	
Managers of economic enterprises	0.5	5.8	6.3	13.5			15.0	20.4	16.5	26.1		
Specialized-professional personnel	9.0	1.1	2.1	6.9	5.7	2.3	25.2	25.6	27.2	31.3	20.8	18.9
Workers, peasants, and employees	2.1	1.1	1.0	–	5.7	2.4	6.9	2.4	5.0	1.1	28.3	11.5
Others and unknown	2.1	1.6	5.8	5.8	–	–	1.3	2.1	2.7	3.1	–	0.9
Total	100.0	100.0	100.0	100.0	100.0	100.0	100.0	100.0	100.0	100.0	100.0	100.0
(Number)	(190)	(190)	(190)	(260)	(88)	(88)	(480)	(480)	(480)	(360)	(220)	(220)

[a] Political Chambers: 1963-1967, The Federal Chamber including The Chamber of Nationalities; 1969-1974, The Chamber of Nationalities and the Socio-Political Chamber; 1974-1978, The Chamber of Republics and Provinces.
[b] Functionally Specialized Chambers: 1963-1974, The Economic Chamber, Educational-Cultural Chamber, Social-Health Chamber, and until 1969 the Organizational-Political Chamber; 1974-1978, The Federal Chamber.
[c] Includes six military officers.
Source: see footnote 2.

Lenard J. Cohen

While the number of individuals without previous regional or federal legislative experience elected to the functionally specialized chambers of the Federal Assembly tended to be quite substantial, the number of such deputies in the political chambers markedly decreased from 1959 to 1969. By 1969, 83.3 percent of the deputies in the Chamber of Nationalities (at that point the politically most influential chamber of the legislature) had previously served in the Assembly System either at the federal or republican-provincial levels (see Figure 4.2). Even after the cooptation of a large group of more youthful industrial workers and employees into the Assembly in 1974, the proportion of delegates with earlier legislative experience remained very high in the Chamber of Republics and Provinces (72 percent), which is the main "political chamber" in the federal legislative structure (the post-1974 situation will be treated more fully in the next section).

The failure to deprofessionalize legislative activity in the period from 1953 to 1974 can be traced to a number of factors. One such factor was the shrinking number of political offices available to professional socio-political workers in other organizational sectors such as the League of Communists and the federal civil service. Fewer jobs in the central party apparatus resulted from the policy of deprofessionalization itself. Devolution of authority to regional and local party organizations, as well as the decreasing number of administrative positions filled on the basis of political criteria, promoted a visible "migration" of professional politicians into full-time legislative work at all levels of the federation.[3] The growing political influence of the assembly system both encouraged and was itself fostered by such migration of politicians and their personal commitments to legislative tasks.[4] One Yugoslav political scientist has even suggested that the frequent conflicts which arose between different groups and individuals during legislative elections resulted partially from a scramble for the few political positions which were available.[5]

A policy to "de-accumulate" the number of offices held by any one individual, and particularly the former "personal union" by which top level party and state posts were held by the same people, also contributed to the growing distinctiveness of legislative service as an occupational category. Moreover, the ambiguous and less privileged role of the party after 1952 provided more incentive for politically ambitious persons to direct their energies toward other political institutions and organizations such as legislatures, administration, and mass organizations. The increase in the number of federal deputies classified as professional legislators can also be attributed to the genuine occupational transformation or specialization deriving from the long-term involvement of socio-political workers in legislative assemblies.[6]

Another facet of emerging legislative professionalization in the 1960's was the growing number of professional managers and technical cadre who were actively and continuously engaged in assemblies at different levels of the federation. Although the members of this "techno-managerial stratum" retained

The Socialist Pyramid: Elites and Power in Yugoslavia

Figure 4.2
Legislative Specialization/Professionalization
Percent of Federal Deputies Who Previously Served in the Assembly System
(In Federal, Republican, and Provincial Assemblies) By Chamber

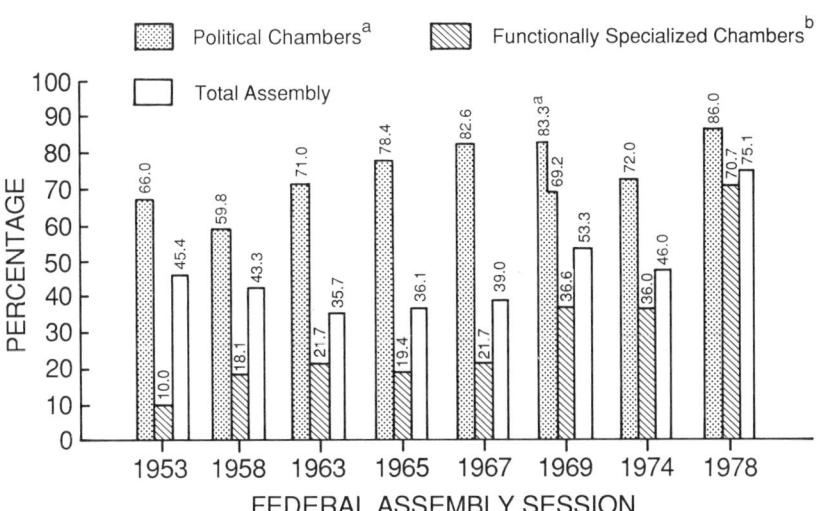

[a] Political Chambers: form 1953 through 1968 this designation refers to the Federal Chamber which included a Chamber of Nationalities. In 1969, the Chamber of Nationalities became a separate branch of the Assembly and together with the Socio-Political Chamber constituted the "Political Chambers." In 1974/78, this category refers to the Chamber of Republics and Provinces. Data for each of the two political chambers is offered for 1969 (83.3% for the Chamber of Nationalities, and 69.2% for the Socio-Political Chamber).

[b] Functionally Specialized Chambers: in 1953 and 1958, the Chamber of Producers. From 1963 through 1969, the Economic Chamber, Educational-Cultural Chamber, Social-Health Chamber, and (except for 1969 when it was discontinued) the Organizational-Political Chamber. In 1974/78, the Federal Chamber.

Source: See note 2.

their occupational and organizational affiliations while serving as legislative deputies, their ability to take extended leaves of absence from their enterprises and organizations and to move easily between managerial and legislative positions enabled them to become highly adept at legislative work. The need for more technical expertise in day to day decision-making, and the desire of economic firms to influence legislative decisions, also were trends which naturally led to greater managerial involvement in the assemblies.

The legislators recruited from the managerial and specialist sectors were most pervasive in the various functionally specialized chambers of Yugoslav assemblies, originally devised for the representation of the "producer population" and as an extension of the workers' self-management structure. In fact, "direct producers," i.e., genuine proletarians and peasants, disappeared almost entirely from the regional and federal assemblies between 1963 and 1973. The persistent and politically influential role of managers and specialists in assemblies throughout the 1960's constituted what one Yugoslav critic called a kind of "veiled professionalization" of legislative tasks which, along with the "pure professionalization" in the political chambers of the assemblies, distorted the aims of self-management.[7] Public opinion surveys conducted during this period reveal that the recruitment of technical and managerial specialists was favoured by most citizens and also by functionaries involved in the legislative recruitment process.[8]

Formal constitutional and statutory restrictions with regard to the length of legislative service proved a futile barrier to the legislative professionalization described above. For example, the 1963 Constitution (Articles 81 and 82) specified that members of assemblies would be elected for four-year terms and that no deputy might be a member of the same chamber of the same assembly for more than two terms. Yet rotation among various legislative chambers and political positions at different levels, or on the same level ("horizontal rotation") of the federation, provided considerable latitude for the maintenance of a professional legislative or political career.[9]

Professionalization and Participation

Legislative professionalization and active participation in the work of Yugoslav assemblies were closely related during the 1960's. For example, the more professionalized deputies tended to frequently intervene in the floor debates of the chambers and committees of the legislature, and they also played a more active role than their less experienced colleagues in submitting questions to the executive and administrative branches of the assembly system, offering amendments to legislation, and taking other initiatives in the legislative process. Indeed, one of the most interesting features of legislative behaviour in Yugoslavia during the 1960's, was the appearance of a small number of deputies who devoted an extremely large portion of their time and activity to persistent and highly visible participation in the work of assemblies. The most active deputies in the assembly system during the most vital period of development from 1967 to 1971 were concentrated in the "political chambers" of the assemblies composed largely of "professional socio-political workers," the largest segment of whom were self-classified professional legislators with considerable experience as elected legislators (Table 4.1 and Figure 4.2).

The level of legislative activity, and the impact of professionalization is well-illustrated by an analysis of deputies who took the floor to speak in plenary sessions of the Federal Chamber of the Federal Assembly. The analysis is based on the official stenographic records of that chamber. The table of contents of each stenographic report of a chamber session includes a list of participants in the proceedings, and it is possible to determine whether those listed are elected deputies, executive and administrative officials, or invited participants and specialists from outside the assembly system. If a deputy's name appeared on the list of participants in the record of the session, this analysis included the session on the individual's record of participation. This research method was intended to provide a rough indicator of the relative degree of individual legislative participation.

An analysis of the records for 10 out of 14 sessions of the Federal Chamber held between June 1968 and March 1969 revealed that 41 percent of the deputies did not participate in any sessions of the chamber, 46 percent of the deputies spoke in either one or two sessions, and 13 percent or 25 individuals spoke at three or more sessions.[10] Systematic examination of each participant's record indicates that, unlike the 1940's and 1950's when the most visible deputies were professional politicians holding important posts in the party outside the assembly system, the most active deputies in the 1960's were less well-known professional socio-political workers experienced in the work of legislative assemblies.

The most prominent example of a professional activist-deputy in the 1960's was Zdenko Has, a representative in the Federal Chamber of the Federal Assembly (and after 1969 in the Socio-Political Chamber) elected from the constituency of Našice in Croatia. In the analysis of legislative participation in the Federal Chamber, Has emerged as the deputy who intervened in the most sessions (nine out of the ten examined). Moreover, he generally spoke a number of times at each session, usually engaging in lively debates with his fellow deputies, and also with members of the executive and administrative branches. Although relatively unknown in Yugoslavia outside political circles, and not a subject of foreign commentary, Has is a classic example of what one student of legislative behaviour refers to as a "legislative workhorse," that is, a representative who devotes most of his time during his electoral mandate to the activities of the legislative assembly. Such an individual attracts considerable attention from his colleagues and constituents, as well as the government, but has a relatively low profile outside of the legislative system.[11] As in the case of other activist-deputies in the Federal Chamber, Has possessed considerable experience in legislative work, having served several terms in the Yugoslav assembly system (the deputy having the next highest level of participation - eight out of ten sessions - had been elected four times to the Federal Assembly and three times to the Republican Assembly). Has also displayed particular expertise in the special area of social health and policy (particularly health insurance), having spent part of his career as a civil servant in that field. Thus, Has exhibited both legislative experience and expertise in a specialized sector, features which are often the hallmark of the activist-deputy in legislative assemblies.

The level of legislative professionalization exhibited by Has and other activist-deputies deserves serious consideration in the light of the effort by the Yugoslav regime to achieve effective and influential legislative assemblies composed largely of deprofessionalized political participants. The study's findings do not indicate that all deputies with legislative experience were activists, or that all short-term avocational politicians were passive, but only that both professional political and legislative experience were very prominent characteristics among the most active deputies in Assembly sessions. In January, 1971 the Assembly correspondent of the Belgrade weekly *Nedeljne Informativne Novine*, featured a story on Has entitled "The Balance of a Deputy" in which the following observations were made:

> Zdenko Has, deputy of the Socio-Political Chamber of the Federal Assembly, is one of those personalities of Yugoslav political life who has no reason to be dissatisified at the end of the year just concluded. Unlike some deputies who fulfill their representative role by attendance at meetings and in a disciplined raising of hands for or against, he has attracted the attention of the broad political public by his numerous critical remarks, interesting questions, and proposals during the last year.[12]

Participation and Influence

The importance of legislative and political professionalization also emerges from an examination of the relationship between participation and the structure of political influence within the Assembly. What difference does such participation make? Do federal deputies who routinely speak in the chambers have more political influence within the Assembly than deputies who do not? Does greater frequency of participation lead to greater influence? In order to probe these questions, this section will go beyond a simple analysis of the number of times a deputy spoke at plenary sessions, and will examine data on the structure of influence within the Assembly.

Data relating to the structure of influence in the Federal Chamber is

The Socialist Pyramid: Elites and Power in Yugoslavia

revealed in survey interviews conducted during 1968 and 1969 in Yugoslavia by the *International Study of Opinion Makers' Project*. The study was supervised by a team of researchers from Columbia University and the Institute of Social Sciences in Belgrade.[13] Six subgroups of "opinion makers" were interviewed, including a random sample of 65 federal legislators, most of whom (54 or 83 percent) were members of the Assembly's then politically dominant Federal Chamber (including 16 deputies who were members of the Chamber of Nationalities, at that time a semi-autonomous chamber within the Federal Chamber).

One question asked of federal legislators was: "In your opinion which three deputies are most prominent in the work of your chamber?" For purposes of this analysis, persons nominated as being the most prominent in the work of a chamber are regarded as having reputed influence on the routine legislative affairs of that chamber. Defined in this manner, the degree of influence can be measured, albeit somewhat roughly, by the number of times a person is nominated as being "prominent" in the work of a chamber.[14] Forty-eight deputies responded to the question, 39 of whom were members of the Federal Chamber and its Chamber of Nationalities (or 21 percent of the 190 members who comprised the membership of this dual chamber). Those 39 deputies nominated a total of 35 fellow legislators (out of 109 responses) as being the most prominent in the work of their chambers. The breakdown of the nominations is as follows:

Number of nominations received from respondents	Number of individuals nominated as being "prominent"
more than 10	1
5-10	3
3-5	8
1-2	23

The findings suggest that, as in most legislative bodies and task-oriented groups in general, a relatively small group of individuals either influences or appears to influence the process of decision-making. The single federal deputy receiving more than ten nominations was Zdenko Has, who actually was nominated by 30 respondents. Has, as reported above, emerged as the most active participant in floor speaking at plenary sessions of the chamber (based on this author's analysis of stenographic reports of the proceedings in the Federal Chamber during the same period that the reputational survey analysis was conducted). Moreover, an examination of the dozen deputies nominated three or more times by respondents as prominent, that is, the "top influentials," reveals

Lenard J. Cohen

that nine of them spoke at three or more sessions of the Assembly during 1968 and 1969.

Table 4.2 cross-tabulates data from the analysis of floor speaking participation in the Assembly and the survey interview data on the structure of influence. A close connection appears to exist between participation in Assembly debate by a deputy, and his or her level of reputed prominence or influence in the work of the chamber. In brief, the deputies who do not participate in the assembly rarely have influence, while most of those deputies with some reputed influence engage in more active participation. Significantly, none of the deputies who are in the category of "very influential" are non-participants.

Table 4.2
Participation and Political Influence in the Yugoslav Federal Legislature, 1968-1969 (%)

Reputed Level of Influence[a]	Frequency of Debate Participation[b]			
	None	1-2 sessions	3 or more sessions	Total
Noninfluential	91.0	86.2	36.0	81.6
Influential	9.0	10.3	28.0	12.1
Very influential	-	3.5	36.0	6.3
Total	100.0	100.0	100.0	100.0
(Number)	(78)	(87)	(25)	(190)

[a] The variable "reputed level of influence" is based on survey interview answers to the following question which was put to one-fifth of the deputies in the Yugoslav Federal Assembly during the Fall and Winter, 1968-1969: "In your opinion which three members are the most prominent in the work of your chamber?" The respondents named 35 fellow deputies as being prominent in the work of the chamber; twelve MPs who received three or more nominations are treated as "very influential" in the above table, and the remaining 23 who were nominated one or two times are labeled as "influential." For more information on the survey methodology see Allen H. Barton *et al.* (eds.), *Opinion-Making Elites in Yugoslavia* (New York: Praeger Publishers, 1973).

[b] The variable "participation" is based on speaking in legislative debates at the plenary sessions of the Federal Chamber of the Federal Assembly. The data in the table are from a sample of ten sessions (out of 14) held between June 19, 1968 and March 6, 1969 for which stenographic reports were available. The table of contents of each report of a session includes a list of participants in the proceedings. If a deputy's name appears on the list the session was counted once on the individual's record of participation.

A closer examination of the data summarized in Table 4.2 reveals some other noteworthy factors associated with participation and influence in the federal legislature. For example, the dozen deputies emerging as very influential and who also participate in the chamber are, in all except one case, professional politicians who either hold higher elected jobs in the Assembly (a chamber president, a president and a deputy-president of committees, etc.) or are members of "leading organs" of the League of Communists on the federal and regional level.[15] All twelve of the top influentials joined the Communist Party before the end of World War II, and three of the four most prominent (i.e., having received five or more nominations), joined before the war.

An examination of the seven deputies who were designated as non-participants yet regarded as "influential" reveals a group of very highly placed and experienced professional politicians, all of whom were members of the leading organs of the League of Communists during the period being discussed, and some of whom were also simultaneously holding leadership positions in the Assembly. The legislative influence wielded by such individuals would appear to derive from their political stature or power bases outside the Assembly and not from direct participation in the chambers of the Federal Assembly. Their parallel political activity outside the legislature also suggests the continued role and the significant level of influence exercised by the League of Communists in the legislative process, although perhaps less obtrusively than in earlier years. Such political activity would also tend to support other research findings which indicate, for example, that multiple organizational membership is an important source of political influence.[16]

In contrast to the influential non-participants, another subgroup, the non-influential participants, were generally indivduals with far less professional political experience, and except in one case, no parallel membership in a higher organ of the League of Communists. It appears that this latter group was composed primarily of actively participating legislators who lacked a power base either outside or within the legislature (with the exception of one of the nine non-influential participants who was a vice-president of the Federal Assembly), and thus were not attributed much prominence or influence by their fellow deputies. A contrasting interpretation might suggest, of course, that the active participants who emerged as non-influentials in terms of the survey results were in fact a part of the legislative elite, but they were insufficiently recognized by their colleagues responding to the reputational survey interviews. This intepretation is doubtful, however, in view of the rather convincing correlation of findings with respect to Zdenko Has and other deputies who were ranked high in terms of all three factors, i.e., prominence (or influence), participation, and political professionalization (legislative and party experience).[17]

The growth of legislative professionalization during the 1960's, a trend directly in contrast to the regime's policy, cannot be attributed simply to problems in policy implementation (in Yugoslav terms "anti-self-management forces" and pre-socialist "vestiges"), or to the efforts of an aging elite of professional politicians to maintain their power - although these factors were both at work to some extent. The failure of deprofessionalization can also be explained by the process of legislative development itself. That is, having been endowed with greater formal responsibilities and a more liberal political climate in which to develop, the assembly system rapidly engendered "professional" legislative behaviour and commitments among at least a portion of its elected members. The growing scope, volume, and complexity of legislative decision-making encouraged deputies to become more professionally involved in the assemblies in order to effectively conduct routine business and to fulfill their formal responsibilities.

Ironically, the process of legislative professionalization during the 1960's, which was regarded as a deformation of the regime's policy, tended to produce elected deputies with considerable understanding of legislative affairs and more commitment than their predecessors to the expansion of the assembly system as an autonomous sector of Yugoslav political life. Taking advantage of ambiguities in the official conception of the duties connected with the legislative mandate, many professional deputies developed their own interpretation of the representational role. In addition to fulfilling their vague constitutional mandate to represent both the interests of diverse constituencies and the country as a whole, these deputies became committed to the political institutionalization of the assembly system as a "valued" and influential component in the political system. Such institutionalization enabled deputies to enhance their own professional role and political influence, and thereby also more readily achieve their personal goals and specific interests.[18]

The moderate growth of legislative institutionalization in the 1960's, fostered in part by professionalization, contributed to the development of a more organizationally pluralized socialist regime. Such a landscape of competing political institutions and political sub-elites (party, mass organization, legislative, administrative, managerial, etc.) within a one-party framework did not, however, contribute to the exercise of political control by Yugoslav citizens located at the "base" of the self-managing system over the decisions and decision-makers at the higher levels of the system. This last and very obvious defect - namely, the problem of combining vertical or participatory pluralism, together with horizontal, organizational pluralism - led to a fundamental restructuring of the legislative system in the post-1974 period.

The Period After 1974: The Rise and Decline of the Amateur Delegate

Symbolic Amateurization and Resurgent Party Control

During the early 1970's, Yugoslav leaders frequently alleged that the persistence of professional legislative representation had frustrated the ability of the average citizens "to govern themselves." This problem was cited as a prime reason motivating the creation of a new constitutional system in 1974. Beginning in 1972, and coinciding with Tito's vigorous campaign against other "rotten forms of liberalism," sharp criticism was levelled against the long debates, obstructionist tactics, inter-regional conflict, and persistent criticism of the central government which had often characterized legislative politics. Ironically, these were the same characteristics regarded by many foreign and

Yugoslav observers as indicators of a more open and democratic political system. Legislative deputies, some political leaders and experts argued, had become too isolated and independent of their producer constituents, too willing to represent the territorial and cultural interests of nationalist bureaucratic cliques in the regional party organizations, and (especially in the case of managers and specialists) too infected with the mentality of "techno-managerial elitism." The inherent weakness of the earlier assembly system was pointed out by its architect, Edward Kardelj, who also designed the 1974 legislative model:

> Our assemblies used to be elected in a classical way, namely, deputies were elected on the basis of general political elections and not on the basis of elections in self-management communities. This led to a situation in which these self-management communities could present their interests in assemblies only via intermediaries, i.e., via that 'general' political deputy. Naturally, this weakened the direct influence of self-management communities or assemblies, which was not to the satisfaction of self-managers in these communities. They sought direct participation in the work of the assemblies and not just participation through so-called 'political deputies' .... What we are doing today has nothing in common with the liberalism of the sixties. The aim of the liberalism then was to abolish or to substantially restrict self-management and to impose a centralistic state behind the mask of apparent parliamentarism.[19]

To eliminate defects caused by the "general political deputy," the legislative system introduced in 1974 provided for the election of "delegates" to assemblies at each level of the federation. Although serving as temporary decision-makers or representatives, these delegates were theoretically closer to the self-managing "base" of society in terms of their mode of election, personal characteristics, and responsiveness to constituents (i.e., the "delegational base"). Inspired by Marx's endorsement in *The Civil War in France* of political structures and principles adopted by the short-lived Paris Commune of 1871, the Yugoslav assembly system introduced in 1974 was designed to eliminate the remaining "vestiges" of "classical bourgeois parliamentary democracy," which allegedly had impeded the preceding legislative system. As described above, the entire system emanates from delegations elected by citizens in the "self-managed" enterprises, organizations, and communities that comprise the basic electoral constituencies for the delegational system. There no longer exists, as there did prior to 1974, a chamber of the Federal Assembly, or of the regional assemblies, composed of "general" political deputies directly elected in the single-member constituencies apportioned on the basis of population.[20]

The assembly system established in 1974 initially resulted in the election of more "direct producers" to the federal legislature, reversing a trend which had developed over the preceding twenty years (see Table 4.1). New channels and

Lenard J. Cohen

procedures were also introduced to link federal delegates more closely to the base of the system. The assembly system retains, however, features of political representation and hierarchy. For example, certain individuals stand in the place of other individuals, and federal legislative delegates are elected only through an indirect process, accountable to the delegational foundation of the system through intermediate delegates on the local and regional level (Figure 4.1). Moreover, information on the operation of the assembly system after 1974 reveals that many problems of representation, such as the disproportionately high activity and influence of professional politicians and civil servants in the state administration, have continued to characterize the legislative process. These difficulties are illustrated by an examination of deputies participating in the Federal Assembly during 1975 and 1976.

Table 4.3
Participation of Professional and Amateur Delegates
in the Yugoslav Federal Legislature, 1975-1976

Type of Delegates	Frequency of Participation			
	None	1-2 sessions	3 or more sessions	Total
Professional "Socio-Political Workers" (n=69)	39.1	36.2	24.6	100.0
Amateurs:				
Technical specialists (n=51)	68.6	27.5	3.9	100.0
Non-technical specialists (n=33)	66.7	30.3	3.0	100.0
Industrial Workers, agricultural workers, and employees (n=61)	78.7	19.7	1.6	100.0
Military (n=6)	100.0	-	-	100.0

Note: "Participation in sessions" refers to speaking in legislative debates at plenary sessions of the Federal Chamber. This table is based on 14 sessions held between May 22, 1975 and May 28, 1976. The table of contents of each stenographic report of a session includes a list of participants in the proceedings. If a delegate's name appears on the list, the session was counted once on the individual's record of participation. This analysis does not measure the duration of speaking, the number of times an individual delegate spoke at each session, or discriminate among different issues on the legislative calendar. Remarks made at sessions by the Chamber's presiding officer and by nondelegates such as the members of the Federal Executive Council or the Federal Administration, etc., are not included.

of 14 sessions of the Federal Chamber of the Federal Assembly, held between May 1975 and May 1976.[21] The Federal Chamber is one of the two chambers in the Federal Assembly established by the 1974 Constitution. This chamber is composed mainly of non-political professionals and skilled workers "delegated" from the various economic and organizational sectors of society and is made up partially (31.4 percent) of professional politicians (the other chamber, the Chamber of Republics and Provinces, is composed almost entirely of professional politicians). The occupational diversity of delegates elected to the Federal Chamber after 1974, and particularly the clear distinction between delegates who are professional politicians and those who are avocational or amateur politicians, facilitates research concerning the impact of professional political experience on the level of participation.

Analysis of the data in Table 4.3 reveals that despite claims by the Yugoslav regime regarding the importance of the Federal Chamber as a forum where a self-managing "depoliticized" working class can decide on public policy, *politically professionalized* delegates tend to participate most frequently in debates of the chamber. For example, approximately 60 percent of the 69 professional politicians in the Federal Chamber participated in at least one session of the Federal Assembly, and 25 percent of the total group took part in three or more sessions, making up over 80 percent of all the delegates in that category. Moreover, unlike the situation existing before 1974 when many of the professional politicians who were active deputies were highly experienced and committed to legislative tasks, Assembly activists in the succeeding period are primarily individuals whose power base and reputation derive from political work outside the Assembly. Technical and non-technical specialists with professional training in areas other than politics have the next highest level of participation, although over two-thirds of that group did not speak in any of the 14 sessions examined. The lowest level of participation was exhibited by the 61 "direct producers" in the chamber (mainly industrial workers), over three-fourths of whom failed to intervene in any of the sessions. Only one worker took part in three or more sessions of the chamber in the period under study. Ironically, one of the few occasions when a number of direct producers spoke at a plenary session of the Federal Chamber was during a debate on a proposed federal law limiting remuneration for legislative service to those delegates having leadership positions in the chamber (94 percent of whom were political professionals in 1976, and the remainder non-political professionals). The remarks of one worker from Montenegro are extremely revealing of the difficulties and issues surrounding the policy of deprofessionalizing political activity:

> I think that delegates who come from associated labour are in an unequal material position with delegates who are so to speak on the payroll of the Assembly. I agree with what Comrade Rakovac said - that all of the delegates are elected in the same way. I think that we need to find some kind of solution in order to bring all the delegates into the same material position. I just want to say this: carrying out affairs at their work place,

for the personal income which they earn at their work place, these delegates in their free time must involve themselves in other activities, they must perform the same socially useful job which delegates who don't have obligations towards their work perform. We have examples of delegates from associated labour, miners for example, who have a personal income no more than 250,000 dinars. It would be no exaggeration to say that such a delegate coming to the Assembly, must be, if nothing else, properly dressed. How will he ensure that he is decently attired if he has a personal income of 250,000 dinars?[22]

In response to the remarks of the above worker-deputy, the Vice-President of the Federal Assembly pointed out that "it is impossible for all delegates in the Federal Chamber to receive personal income from the Assembly. According to our agreements, and principles, and also constitutionally, one part of the delegates are from direct production. They perform this function explicitly as an honourary function."[23]

Additional insights concerning the pattern of delegate participation in the Yugoslav legislative decision-making process is also provided by some very rare official statistical information on the assembly system.[24] The data summarized in Table 4.4 include a description of all the participants in the debates of different branches and areas of the Federal Assembly structure, and their frequency of participation during the entire first "mandate period" of the legislative system from May 1974 through May 1978. It appears, not surprisingly, that a broad cross-section of political and governmental actors and also various specialists take part in the debates and discussions of federal legislative bodies, together with elected delegates. The level of non-delegate involvement is greatest in the work of legislative committees, commissions, and other "working bodies" of the Federal Assembly and its branches. For example, although elected delegates comprise over 80 percent of the participants in plenary sessions of the Assembly (the sessions which were analyzed above in terms of participation and influence), delegate participation is much lower in the legislature's committee system (including working bodies, permanent and ad hoc commissions, etc.) which is, as in most active legislative bodies, the major site of policy discussion and modification. Even more importantly, with regard to the character of participation and the opportunity for influence in the period beginning in 1974, the proportion of non-delegate interventions in committee debate is most pronounced in the less politically professionalized branch of the federal legislature (i.e., the Federal Chamber). Thus, from 1974 to 1978, elected delegates made up just a bare majority of the speakers in the committee debates of the Federal Chamber. The rate of delegate participation in the equivalent bodies of the more politically professionalized Chamber of Republics and Provinces was, however, 62 percent. Non-delegate participation reaches its highest level in the permanent and ad hoc "joint committees" and also in the

Table 4.4
Participation in the Debates of the Yugoslav Federal Legislature
May 15, 1974 - May 15, 1978 (%)

Participants in Debates	Plenary Sessions of Chambers			Committees, Commissions & Working Bodies of the Chambers				
	Federal Chamber	Chamber of Republics & Provinces	Joint Sessions	Federal Chamber	Chamber of Republics & Provinces	Commissions of the Federal Legislature	Joint Working Bodies of the Legislature	Total
Members of Federal Legislative Bodies								
Elected delegates	81.0	88.0	53.3	51.0	61.5	50.8	45.2	57.0
Political functionaries from mass political organizations and federal organs	-	-	-	0.3	-	6.7	-	0.8
Specialists/public and scientific workers	-	-	-	5.8	2.7	10.8	31.0	5.7
Elected Delegates from Other Legislative Bodies	1.8	-	-	3.8	2.2	6.0	4.8	3.2
Representatives of Those Proposing Legislation[a]	6.8	3.3	-	12.4	17.1	2.6	0.8	12.6
Participants Representing the:								
Federal executive organs[b]	0.5	5.0	6.6	0.5	0.6	2.2	1.5	0.8
Organs of the federal administration[c]	7.1	-	6.6	13.4	4.9	2.8	7.2	8.1
Republican and provincial legislatures	-	-	-	0.5	0.4	1.0	-	0.1
Mass sociopolitical organizations	1.3	3.3	33.3	1.4	0.4	1.5	1.1	1.1
Self-managing enterprises and communities	0.2	0.4	-	2.2	3.2	1.2	2.4	2.4
Scientific experts and specialists	1.4	-	-	1.8	1.3	2.4	0.2	1.5
The specialized administrative staff of the federal legislature	-	-	-	6.5	5.7	12.2	6.0	6.5
Total Participants[d]	100.0	100.0	100.0	100.0	100.0	100.0	100.0	100.0
(Number of Participants)	(562)	(242)	(15)	(6301)	(6892)	(1759)	(630)	(16,401)

[a] Includes mainly members of the Federal Executive Council and Federal Administration.
[b] Includes members of the Federal Executive Council, and a small number of participants from the State Presidency and Council of the Federation.
[c] Includes a small number of participants from Federal Judicial Organs.
[d] Totals may not add up to precisely 100.0 percent because of rounding.
Source: See footnote 24.

working bodies of the Assembly which focus on special legislative tasks and issues. The formal membership of these latter bodies includes a large number of specialists, political functionaries, and administrative personnel.

The above situation acquires even more significance when recalling that amateur and proletarian delegates have a very low rate of participation in the Federal Chamber's plenary sessions (it seems highly probable that a very similar pattern of low amateur participation also occurs in the committee system of the Federal Chamber). Consequently, legislative debates, with few exceptions, consist of elected political professionals, administrators, and technical specialists. The extensive participation and influential role of administrative functionaries and specialists in the committees of the Federal Assembly is not a new development; this situation was evident to observers even before the latest constitutional system was adopted, that is, at a time when "professional deputies" were assuming more "prominence" in the legislative process. The above data clearly indicate, however, that the very active participation of bureaucratic and expert personnel in political decision-making has not been altered by the new and allegedly more deprofessionalized delegate system.[25]

The very active participation of professional politicians serving as elected delegates in Yugoslavia, as well as the important role played by civil servants and technical specialists in the legislative process, is not unlike the situation in other regimes with vital representative assemblies. Such participation also contrasts markedly with the ubiquitous dominance of professional party leaders and the more restricted role of legislative institutions in most other communist systems. The persistent limitations on the political influence of amateur politicians in Yugoslavia, and of "direct producers" in particular, however, challenges the assault on bureaucracy and technocracy which is an integral feature of the regime's socialist model. Moreover, the course of Yugoslav political development throughout the period after 1971 suggests that the impediments to amateur citizen participation, and more generally to the political influence of the legislative system, have actually intensified rather than diminished.[26]

The post-1971 expansion in the influence of the central and regional party organizations considerably reduced the vitality and autonomy of the legislative system as a distinct decision-making site.[27] From the viewpoint of the party leadership, the benefits accruing to the stability and survival of the existing political system - through the reduction of the disruptive regional and ethnic conflicts in the federal legislature - far outweighed any damage to the previous, and often suspect, course of legislative development.[28] The novelty of the "delegational" assembly structure adopted in 1974 (Figure 4.1) and its promise of enhanced citizen participation, did not alter the reality of increased party control over legislative decision-making. Renewed party hegemony in the political process after 1971, and within the legislative assemblies in particular, has been expressed in a number of measures. For example, the earlier

The Socialist Pyramid: Elites and Power in Yugoslavia

prohibition against the simultaneous holding of elected functions in both state and party organs (the so-called personal de-accumulation of functions established in order to deconcentrate power) was considerably relaxed in the mid-1970's. This measure partially restored the interlock between the parallel party and state hierarchies so typical of most communist regimes. As part of the post-1971 emphasis on the role of the party "within the system" (rather than the earlier slogan of "divorcing the party from power"), party functionaries and members serving in legislative assemblies either as elected delegates or in an advisory capacity (e.g., on personnel commissions) are required to take responsibility for the implementation of decisions made by their party organizations. This climate requires party members who are delegates to become more accountable to parallel party bodies, thereby creating a horizontal line of authority in addition to the formal (i.e., vertical) responsibility of delegates to their constituencies on lower tiers of the legislative system (now under greater control by lower level party organizations as well). These trends have also been facilitated by the lower number of non-party member delegates elected in recent years.[29]

Yugoslav political research concerning the operation of the 1974 delegate system confirms the decisive political influence of party leaders and professional politicians, as well as the serious obstacles to amateur citizen participation which still are in place. Moreover, these studies suggest that such influence and obstacles are not limited to the federal and regional levels of the political system. For example, respondents to a survey interview study of communal assemblies and local participation carried out in 1976 by political scientists in Serbia, Croatia and Slovenia revealed that a combination of administrative and executive functionaries, officials of the party and other mass organizations, and technical experts are perceived as having the greatest influence on the initiation and final adoption of decisions in the delegate system.[30] Empirical studies in other Yugoslav regions have also reached similar conclusions concerning the structure of influence.[31] In Croatia, for example, answers from over 2,500 respondents active in the delegate system indicated that representatives of socio-political organizations including the party, did not regularly attend meetings of local assemblies, and also that elected delegates did not mechanically discuss and adopt the instructions of socio-political organizations. These organizations, nevertheless, were perceived to have the most decisive influence on overall decision-making in the system (followed by professional politicians, and specialized staff services). In contrast, elected delegates in assemblies, members of delegations (see Figure 4.1), and the "delegate base" (working people and citizens) were perceived as having only a medium or small amount of influence.[32]

It is important to stress that Yugoslav studies of these issues do not indicate the direct or overt dominance of the party organization, qua organization, but rather the strong influence of a political *aktiv* including party leaders, governmental and administrative executives, and officials from various socio-political organizations. This *aktiv* is made up of an organizationally heterogeneous grouping of professional politicians who can "manipulate" the self-management system according to their own goals. The behaviour of such political circles is informal and ad hoc rather than direct and "programmed activity." Inexperienced amateur delegates are at a great disadvantage when confronted by such professional politicians with their special resources and leverage.[33] As one Yugoslav political scientist studying the delegate system concluded:

> ... the delegate remains rather powerless, located in an undefined social space, and opposite to him there appears a rather sizeable and powerful grouping of political professionals, who also have under their control a powerful specialized apparatus, having information relevant for decision-making, and also a great influence on the means of mass communication and specialized institutions whose activity is significant for the decision-making process, and especially for perceiving the articulation of interests. One of the sources of the political bureaucracy's power is its stability in relation to the posiiton of the delegates. It is true that the political professionals are rotated, but that rotation mainly turns in a circular fashion on the same level. That continuity permits them in practice to form themselves into a social-interest group. Remaining for long periods in the same communities in different functions they become, as individuals and as a group, connected and create a zone of their influence in spheres of life, so that their real influence in the process of decision-making, as a rule, is always broader and greater than it should be according to the letter of the law. All of these groups [of professional political functionaries] act as stage managers of this process.[34]

The major concern expressed by Yugoslav observers is not that the party organization and membership play an important role in the delegate system - a role now firmly established in constitutional design[35] and political theory - but rather that informal activity of professional politicians in the delegate structure, and especially in the state and party bureaucracies, detracts from citizen self-management.[36] In fact, the obstacles to self-management identified in studies of the 1974 delegate system[37] are very similar to those noted in studies of decision-making and legislative development in the earlier period.[38]

Serious difficulties associated with the accountability of elected delegates also weaken the control which citizen and amateur delegates (who are more numerous in the lower tiers of the legislative structure) can exercise over political professionals. Studies by Yugoslav political analysts and practitioners reveal that numerous problems, including deliberate distortion, apathy, pressures of time, and difficulties of inadequate, faulty or overly technical information have impeded the ability of citizens to perform the complex task of controlling their elected delegates.[39] As a result, professional politicians serving in legislative bodies under the 1974 delegational system appear to have have considerable latitude for independent action vis-à-vis their citizen constituents,[40] but are more closely accountable than in the preceding period to lateral and higher level officials (in the case of communal and regional assemblies) outside the legislative system.[41]

Accelerated Rotation and the Return of the Professionals: Trends in Recent Elections (1978-1988)

Data on the characteristics of delegates elected to Yugoslavia's Federal Assembly in 1978, 1982, and 1986 sheds further light on trends and problems in the country's recent legislative development. For example, while only 20 percent of all the delegates elected to the Federal Assembly in 1978 had served in that body during the immediately preceding "mandate period" (1974-1978), a closer look at the composition of the legislature reveals some striking changes. The contingent of workers, peasants, and employees elected in 1978 was less than half as large as the same occupational sector elected in the previous session. A decline in the number of non-political specialists and expert personnel also occurred (Table 4.1). In the Federal Chamber alone, i.e., the branch of the legislature which previously was touted as the strategic site of working class influence in the society, the proportional representation of "direct producers" declined by nearly two-thirds. Moreover, none of the 21 industrial and agricultural workers elected to the Federal Chamber in 1978 served in the previous session of that body. This situation, as the preceding analysis would suggest, undoubtedly has a negative impact on the potential of blue collar delegates to participate and wield influence in the legislative process.

In 1978, the combined group of elected political leaders, administrative functionaries, and managerial personnel rose by 15 percent, to constitute three-quarters of the entire Assembly membership (and 95 percent of the Chamber of Republics and Provinces). The proportion of federal delegates over the age of 50 also rose from 32 percent in 1974 to a postwar high of 52 percent in 1978, a trend clearly enhanced by the influx of "new" delegates who are seasoned politicians. The same influx, together with the sharp decline in the number of "direct producers" elected in 1978 (the occupational group which had the lowest level of formal education in the previous session), also contributed to a 14 percent increase in the number of delegates with a faculty level higher education. In brief, skilled workers tended to be replaced by skilled politicians at the top level of the citizen self-management system.

The trend toward a pattern of legislative recruitment combining increased political professionalization with accelerated rotation was also evident in the large number of delegates elected in 1978 who possessed at least some prior service in post-1945 representative bodies. This is particularly true with respect to the previously more youthful, proletarian, and amateurized Federal Chamber of the Federal Assembly. Only 14 percent of the delegates elected to the Federal Chamber in 1978 had served in that body in the preceding mandate period, but 71 percent had previous postwar experience as legislators (44 percent had served two or more terms). In the Chamber of Republics and Provinces, the number of delegates with previous legislative experience rose significantly from 72 percent in 1974 to 86 percent in 1978, the highest such percentage during the entire postwar period (73 percent of the delegates in that chamber had been elected two or more times, 35 percent four or more times).[42]

The above-mentioned trends, also found in regional and communal assemblies but at lower rates, indicate the prominent role of professional politicians among Yugoslav self-managing delegates. The changes that occurred in 1978 were in some ways similar to those that were experienced in the 1958 to 1973 period, when the representation of workers in the federal legislature declined. Unlike the earlier period, however, in 1978, professional politicians in the party and mass organizations, rather than the managerial group, technical specialists, and previously important "political deputies," exhibited the largest increase in group representation.

The prominence of older professional politicians in the federal legislature continued after the election of 1982, although at a slightly reduced level compared with 1978. Moreover, while there was a modest increase in the number of workers elected to the federal legislature, and also to the republican and provincial assemblies, the number of genuine "proletarians" actually decreased in the communal assemblies. It was only in 1986, as economic conditions in Yugoslavia continued to seriously deteriorate, that the numerical and operational hegemony of professional politicians in the legislative system began to noticeably wane. Again, as in the 1960's, it was not the "direct producers" that emerged as the main beneficiaries of new imperatives and changes in elite recruitment, but rather the much villified "techno-managerial stratum." Thus as a result of the 1986 election, members of the technical and cultural intelligentsia - or the group referred to as "specialists" in Yugoslav legislative statistics - constituted 47 percent of the 220-member Federal Chamber, compared to 29 percent in 1982, and roughly 20 percent in 1974 and 1978 (the 88-member Chamber of Republics and Provinces remained the domain of professional politicians). The proportional representation of specialists in the Federal Assembly after the election of 1986 was higher than at any other point in the history of the communist regime, even surpassing the halcyon days of techno-managerial influence at the end of the 1960's. The importance of this trend acquires even more significance when it is noted that nearly three-quarters of the specialist intelligentsia elected to the Federal Chamber in 1986 were below 50 years of age, compared to only 20 percent of the professional politicians and administrative functionaries of that age group who were elected that year. At the end of the 1980's, legislative service in Yugoslavia appeared to be primarily a short-term avocational activity engaged in by competing and generationally divided professionals from the political and non-political sectors, i.e., the two groups who jointly control the "self-managing" system.[43]

Conclusion

The above findings significantly qualify official Yugoslav claims regarding the activity of the politically "deprofessionalized" delegate in Yugoslav legislative assemblies. For example, research indicates that the "direct producers" and other delegates who engage in legislative decision-making as an avocation are far less active than professional politicians. Amateur delegates are also perceived as being less "prominent," in legislative affairs, a rough measure of reputed influence. The weak position of amateur delegates, together with the political changes after 1971 requiring that professional politicians serving as delegates in the federal legislature be responsive to the central and regional party organizations rather than acting as independently oriented "professional legislators," has done little to enhance legislative institutionalization or the influence of average Yugoslav citizens over "higher self-management formations." Indeed, it appears that the professional deputies specializing in legislative affairs, who emerged so "prominently" in the late 1960's, actually provided the most effective linkage between the base and summit of the political system as a result of their efforts to balance or satisfy a variety of different interests, including constituency pressures, the party organization, and personal preferences.

The trend toward legislative professionalization and institutionalization, although philosophically unacceptable to many party leaders, did increase the political autonomy and influence of the Yugoslav assembly system as a distinct organizational sector. The symbolic amateurization of the legislative assemblies after 1974 - combined with the greater political influence of central and regional party bodies, and also executive and administrative agencies - considerably reduced the potential for either a return to the horizontal organizational ("liberal") pluralism of the 1960's, or the creation of a self-management form of pluralism advocated by many Yugoslav politicians and theorists.[44]

The findings in this chapter also bring into question the regime's official assault on the role of political professionalization in the goverance of an industrialized society. Even if a regime succeeded in offering large numbers of amateur or avocational political activists both a quantitative share of policy-making positions and also real decision-making influence (which the Yugoslav regime has only minimally accomplished above the enterprise and local levels), other serious difficulties exist which negatively impact upon the achievement of democratic goals. For example, in view of the continued need for some form of political representation in modern society, a system of self-management must ensure that part-time political delegates - no matter how temporary their tenure in office, or how much their personal characteristics resemble those of their constituents - will be responsible and responsive to those constituencies.

Advocates and observers of liberal democratic systems often suggest that one of the major factors "linking" political leaders to their constituents is the personal ambition of the individual leader or representative to survive in political office, which in turn enhances a professional political career.[45] Faced with periodic re-election and competition from other candidates in their own and other parties, politicians in liberal democracies must, at least to a certain extent, respond to the preferences of the electorate and cultivate the support of their constituents.[46] Amateur politicians by definition are not motivated by the same long-term concerns.[47] In a legislative system such as the Yugoslav model, where most terms of legislative office-holding are constitutionally limited to two four-year terms in any one office and where delegates are elected in conditions of very limited competition, the individual delegates are not subject to the same personal pressures or constraints with regard to either their constituents or their performance as political decision-makers. One Yugoslav political observer recently drew attention to similar problems which can result from an expansion in the tempo of rotation both for amateurs and professional politicians:

> In the system of 'rotation' the psychological element has a great influence. Namely if individuals perform their functions for a short period of time, they usually have a feeling of impermanence as a result of which they wish to preserve the status quo, i.e., to prevent anything great or negative taking place during the time of their mandate. This is the presupposition for a successful new 'rotation circle.' For this reason one must ask what are the psychological consequences for the people performing their functions for a short term: will they have enough motivation and time to turn their creative power into daily practice?[48]

Other findings discussed in this chapter relating to the deprofessionalization of legislative activity also have a bearing on the potential for creating a participatory form of socialist democracy in Yugoslavia and elsewhere. For example, the analysis indicates that during the 1953 to 1973 period, professional politicians with long-time experience and specialization in the assembly system were the legislative decision-makers who demonstrated the greatest interest and success in scrutinizing the activities of state administrators. Such findings suggest that transient amateur political decision-makers, no matter how highly educated or specialized they are in their own non-political professions, are confronted with great difficulties when attempting to control the public bureaucracy of a modern society.

The Socialist Pyramid: Elites and Power in Yugoslavia

The ability to exercise supervision over policies routinely prepared and implemented by executive and administrative agencies, not only requires the capacity to grapple with complex technical issues (an ability which many amateur legislators exhibited in the 1960's and again in the late 1980's), but also calls for an inclination and sustained opportunity to seriously deal with such issues. This is particularly true when, as in the case of the Yugoslav Federal Assembly, the administrative staff services of the legislature tend to work closely and identify with the state administrative agencies formally accountable to the legislature. Although the Yugoslav regime has attempted to reduce the political influence of the state bureaucracy through a number of novel organizational measures (separation of "political" and "administrative-technical" executive functions, the mandatory rotation of state officials, etc.), the internal logic of administrative growth fostered by the demands of government in an industrialized society has tended to increase the size, resources, and also the political weight of the Yugoslav public bureaucracy.[49] Thus, while the Yugoslav state bureaucracy was considerably more decentralized after 1953, its weight and power in the horizontal pluralism of political organizations at each level of the federal structure has actually expanded. Indeed, the political participation and influence of the state bureaucracy gradually *increased* with the decline in the level of partisanship (e.g., degree of experience in the party apparatus, simultaneous holding of party functions, etc.) among its functionaries, and the reduction of its subordination to the external control of the party's bureaucratic apparatus.[50]

Moreover, as indicated by the Yugoslav research discussed above, citizen participants have not fared much better in challenging the influence of party and state bureaucrats in the myriad local units of the structurally decentralized governmental system, than at the regional and federal levels. Bureaucratic accountability can, of course, be accomplished by other mechanisms than legislative oversight by elected representatives.[51] However, such mechanisms (e.g., the court system, the press, the social composition and norms of civil servants, etc.) have not contributed very significantly to the systematic control of bureaucratic officials, and currently contribute little to the influence of the amateur citizen in the delegate system, that is, the officially touted centerpiece of the Yugoslav self-management model.

It has become almost an axiom of political thought that elected politicians are at a considerable disadvantage when confronting the technically specialized appointed officials found in the administrative sector of modern states. As illustrated by the Yugoslav case, the disadvantages of the avocational politician in this regard, are even more acute than those of the professional politician. The persistence of a single-party organization exerting, at least for the present, a dominant influence and very close guidance over the internal dynamics of representative assemblies, introduces yet another obstacle to amateur citizen participation in political decision-making. The need to stimulate both the quantitative and qualitative levels of avocational political participation necessary to achieve the goals of a self-managing political system, remains a major unresolved problem of socialism in Yugoslavia and elsewhere. The problem, as Leszek Kolakowski has pointed out, "is not how to get rid of bureaucracy, which means destroying modern industrial civilization, but how to control its activity by means of representative bodies."[52] Although the Yugoslav regime still faces considerable difficulties in resolving the problems which have obstructed the establishment of a truly participatory democracy, the Yugoslavs have, nevertheless, engaged in one of the most imaginative and instructive efforts to seriously solve those difficulties.

NOTES: CHAPTER FOUR

1. Stojan Tomić, *Politički profesionalizam* (Sarajevo: Institut za društvena istraživanja Fakulteta političkih nauka, 1972), and also by the same author, *Profesionalizam u politici* (Belgrade: Radnička stampa, 1975), K. Kilibarda, "Changes in Public Office," *Socialist Thought and Practice*, IX (January, 1963), 105-115.

2. Data concerning the social composition of the federal legislature between 1953 and 1980 were obtained from a number of sources: *Savezna Narodna Skupština izabrana 22 i 23 Novembra 1953 godine* (Belgrade: Sedma Sila, 1955), D. Tozi and D. Petrović, "Politicki odnosi i sastav skupština društveno-političkih zajednica," *Socijalizam*, XI (1969), 1581-1599, Miroslav Pečujlić, "Sastav predstavničkih tela i izborni sistem," *Izborni sistem u uslovima samoupravljanja*, ed. F. Džinić (Belgrade: Institut društvenih nauka, 1967), 100-105, *Statistički bilten*, Nos. 266, 372, 491, 590, 888 (Belgrade, 1964, 1965, 1967, 1969, 1974), Pero Divjak, "Sastav delegacija osnovnih samoupravnih organizacijia i zajednica i delegata u skupštinama društveno-političkih zajednica u 1978," *Jugoslovenski pregled* (March, 1979), 91-100. Data on the 1978 election were supplied by the Department of Self-Management and Judiciary Statistics of the Federal Institute of Statistics.

3. Milica Damjanović, "Rezultati izbora u 1967 godini: Načelo smenjivosti i promene u sastavu skupština," *Skupštinski izbori 1967*, eds. Milan Matić *et. al.* (Belgrade: Institut društvenih nauka, 1968), Radomir Lukić, "Rotation Among Top Government Officials in Yugoslavia," *The Mandarins of Western Europe*, ed. Mattei Dogan (New York: Halstead Press, 1975), 293-304.

4. Milan Matić, "Skupštinski izbori 1967: Dalja evolucija društveno-političkog sistema," *Skupštinski izbori 1967*, eds. Milan Matić *et. al.* (Belgrade: Institut društvenih nauka, 1968).

5. Najdan Pašić, "How the Manner of Nominating Candidates Affects the Character and Role of the Assembly, II," *Review of International Affairs*, XII (September, 1966), 26-27.

6. The decrease in the number of party and mass organization functionaries in the legislature, and the increase in the number of "professional legislators" partially represent the same group of

individuals undergoing a process of occupational reclassification. Since the occupational designation used in the official statistics is based on self-definition of one's occupation by individual legislators, this process of reclassification partially reflects the changing locus of influence in the political system in the mid-1960's, i.e., from the party and state organs to the assemblies.

7. Čedo Crbić, "Udruženi rad i skupštinski sistem," *Skupštinski sistem u ustavnim promjenama* (Zagreb: Centar za aktualni politički studij, 1972).

8. Sergije Pegan, *Skupštinski izbori, 1965* (Belgrade: Institut društvenih nauka, 1966).

9. Milica Damjanović, "Rezultati izbora u 1967 godini: Načelo smenjivosti i promene u sastavu skupština," *Skupštinski izbori 1967*, Stojan Tomić, Politički *profesionalizam*.

10. The stenographic reports of the Federal Chamber (*Savezna Skupština, Stenografska beleške, Savezno veće*, Belgrade) analyzed were for sessions 69, 72-79, and 84.

11. Ralph Huitt, "The Outsider in the Senate: An Alternative Role," *American Political Science Review*, LX (September, 1961), 566-575.

12. Milan Mišović, "Bilanc poslanika," *Nedeljne Informativne Novine*, (January 10, 1971), 13.

13. A discussion of the methodological procedures and techniques employed by the International Study of Opinion-Makers' can be found in Dragomir Pantic, "Some Practical Problems of Compiling the Universe and Its Characteristics," *Working Papers of the International Study of Opinion-Makers', Volume 1*, ed. Bogdan Denitch (New York: Columbia University, 1968), and Bogdan Denitch, "Elite Interviewing and Social Structure: An Example from Yugoslavia," *Opinion-Making Elites in Yugoslavia*, eds. Allen Barton, *et. al.* (New York: Praeger, 1973), 3-23.

14. The question in Serbo-Croatian was: "Po našoj oceni, koja se tri poslanika najvise istiću u radu vašeg veća?" ("In your opinion which three deputies are the most prominent in the work of your chamber?") The verb *istaci se* conveys the idea of being prominent,

excelling, distinguishing oneself, or standing out. The question thus elicits perceptions about those deputies who "distinguished themselves in the work of the chamber" and therefore probably had an influence on the legislative process, although not necessarily on their fellow representatives.

15. The importance of formal leadership positions as a basis of influence in legislative bodies has been discussed in other studies. See Heinz Eulau, *Micro-Macro Political Analysis* (Chicago: Aldine, 1969), 259-270, Allan Kornberg and William Mishler, *Influence in Parliament: Canada* (Durham, N.C.: Duke University Press, 1976), 102-126.

16. Robert Perucci and Marc Pilisuk, "Leaders and Ruling Elites," *American Sociological Review*, XXXV, No. 6 (December, 1970), 1040-1056.

17. These findings are similar to research findings concerning workers' councils in enterprises which reported a relationship between professional status, participation and influence. See Josip Obradović, "Participation in Enterprise Decision-Making," *Workers' Self-Management and Organizational Power in Yugoslavia*, eds. Josip Obradovic and W.N. Dunn (Pittsburgh: University Center for International Studies, 1978), 232-261.

18. Lenard J. Cohen, *Devolutionary Socialism: The Politicial Institutionalization of the Yugoslav Assembly System, 1963-1973* (Ph.D Dissertation, Columbia University, 1978), 307-317.

19. *Foreign Broadcast Information Service*, (September 29, 1971), 13.

20. "The System of Election for the Delegation of Basic Self-Managing Organizations and Communities and of Delegates of the Assemblies of the Self-Managing Communities," *Yugoslav Survey*, XVI (February, 1977), 21-53.

21. The stenographic reports of the Federal Chamber (*Skupština SFRJ, Stenografske bilješke, Savezno vijeće*, Belgrade) analyzed for 1975 and 1976 included sessions 10-23.

22. *Skupština SFRJ, Stenografske bilješke, Savezno vijeće* (Belgrade, 1975), 35.

23. *Ibid.*, 37.

24. *Kumulativni statistički pregled rada skupstinških tela u periodu od 15.05. 1974 do 15.05. 1978 godine* (Belgrade: Skupština SFRJ, Služba za informativno-dokumentalističke poslove, 1978).

25. See Chapter 5 for a more detailed examination of the administrative elite's role in the political process.

26. For the origin of these changes see Dennison Rusinow, *The Yugoslav Experiment 1948-1974* (Berkeley: University of California Press, 1977), Paul Shoup, "The Limits of Party Control," *Authoritarian Politics in Communist Europe*, ed. Andrew Janos (Berkeley: Institute of International Studies, University of California, 1976).

27. The practice of federal legislators of putting oral and written questions to members of the federal government and administration dropped off significantly after 1974 compared with the situation in the period 1967-1972. See *Kumulativni statistički pregled rada skupstinških tela u periodu od 15.05. 1974 do 15.05. 1978 godine*, 1978, Lenard J. Cohen, "Conflict Management and Institution-Building in Socialist Yugoslavia: The Role of the Parliamentary System," *Legislatures in Plural Societies*, ed. A.F. Eldridge (Durham, North Carolina: Duke University Press, 1977). In addition to changes in the political climate, the decrease in the number of federal delegates has affected the total number of questions asked. During 1978-1979 there was a greater frequency of questions asked. This increase was almost entirely due to questions asked by professional politicians, whose numbers have increased in the federal legislature. See below and S. Spasojević, "Tridset i tri pitanja SIV-u," *Nedeljne Informativne Novine*, (July 1, 1979), 6-8.

28. Milun Perović, *Process političkog odlučivanja u skupštini SFRJ* (Ph.D. Dissertation, Faculty of Political Science, Belgrade University, 1979).

29. A top party official reported that close to 50 percent of the citizens in delegations for the election of delegates to assemblies (Figure 4.1) are not members in the League of Communists; 74 percent of the total number of delegates in communal assemblies are members of the League, as are 93.5 percent in the regional assemblies, and 99.3 percent in the federal legislature. See *Borba*, (October 19, 1979), 5. Only one of the 308 delegates in the federal legislature (a

Slovenian member of the Federal Chamber) is not a party member. See Milun Perović, *Proces političkog odlučivanja u Skupstina SFRJ*, 302. Since 1974, regional and communal legislative assemblies each have a "socio-political chamber" (Figure 4.1) comprised of representatives of the party or mass political organizations. These chambers, which also participate in the selection of federal delegates, are key sites for party influence in the delegate system. See *ibid.*, 294-312.

30. Radovoje Marinković, *Delegatski sistem: Funkcionisanje i ostvarivanje* (Belgrade: Institut za političke studje Fakulteta političkih nauka, 1979), Ivan Šiber and Zdravko Tomac, *Teorija i praksa delegatskog sistema* (Zagreb: Fakultet političkih nauka, 1979). France Vreg, *Delegatski sistem v SR Sloveniji* (Ljubljana: Centar za samoupravno normativno dejavnost, 1979).

31. Ljubisa Simovska et. al., *Funkcioniranjeto i ostvarivanjeto delegatskiot sistem vo opstinite vo SRM* (Skopje: Institut za sociološki i političko-pravni istrauvania, Fakultet za pravni i politicki nauki, 1979), Mladen Stojanov, "Nekoliko podatka o uticaju u praksi delegatskog odlučivanja," *Savremenost*, I-II (January-February, 1978), 99-111.

32. B. Caratan, "Društveno-Političke organzacije u Delegatskom Sistemu," *Teorija i Praksa Delegatskog Sistema*, eds. Ivan Šiber and Zdravko Tomac (Zagreb: Fakultet političkih nauka, 1979), 238-242, S. Ivanišević, "Isvršno vječe u delegatskom sistemu općine," 250-254, Josip Županov, "Struktura utjecaja u delegatskom sistemu, 295-312.

33. B. Caratan, *ibid.*, 239. Jovan Marjanović, "Delegacije i delegati društveno-političkih organizacija," *Funkcionisanije delegatskog sistema: Iskustva i aktuelni problemi*, ed. Radovoje Marinković (Belgrade: Institut za političke studije Falkuteta političkih nauke 1976), 172-173, Radovoje Marinković, "Ostvarivanje delegatskog sistema-postojeći i moguci obici etatizma, birokratizma i manipulicije," 70, Stipe Šuvar, *Samoupravljanje i alternative* (Zagreb: Centar za kulturnu djelatnost Saveza Socijalističke Omladine Zagreba, 1978), 87-91.

34. Radovoje Marinković, "Polozaj, moć i uticaj osnovnih subjekata delegatskog sistem," *Delegatski sistem: funkionsanje i ostvari-*

vanje, ed. Radovoje Marinković (Belgrade: Institut za političke studije Fakulteta političkih nauka, 1979), 306.

35. Borislav Blagojević, *Položaj i uloga društveno političkih organizacija u ustavnim i političkim sistemu SFRJ* (Belgrade: Savremena administracjia, 1977).

36. Edward Kardelj, *Pravci i razvoja političkog sistema socijalističkog samoupravljanja* (Belgrade: Komunist, 1978).

37. Ivan Šiber, "Nekoliko napomena o istraživanju delegatskog sistema," *Politička Misao*, III (1978), 325-330, Zoran Polić, "Učvršćivanje i razvijanje skupštinskog sistema", *Socijalizam*, XXII (1979), 15-31, Milun Perović, *Proces političkog odlučivanja u Skupštini SFRJ*.

38. Janez Jerovšek, "Struktura uticaja u opstini," *Sociologija*, II (1969), 257-578, Radovoje Marinković, *Ko odlučuje u komuni* (Belgrade, 1971), Najdan Pašić, "Self-Management as as Integral Political System," *Yugoslav Workers' Self-Management*, ed. J.J. Broekmeyer (Dordrecht, Holland: D. Reidel Publishing Co., 1970), 1-29. A number of Yugoslav studies have examined legislative development over the entire socialist period. The usual assumption is that each succeeding reorganization corrected earlier problems, not that obstacles to self-management may be unsolvable. See Pavle Nikolić, *Skupstinški sistem* (Belgrade: Savremena administracija, 1973), Milan Matić, *Skupstinški i delegatski sistem* (Belgrade: Delta Press, 1975), Jovan Marjanović, *Delegatski sistem i političke studije*, (Fakultet političkih nauka, 1978), Ciril Ribičič, *Razvoj skupščinskega sistema v Jugoslaviji* (Ljubljana: Pravna Fakulteta v Ljubjani, 1978).

39. France Vreg, *Komuniciranje odločanje v delegatskem sistemu* (Ljubljana: Centar za samoupravno normativno dejavnost, 1978), Pavle Novosel, *Delegatsko informiranje* (Zagreb: Centar za informicije i publicitet, 1977), Mahmut Mujačić, "Značaj informisanja delegatski baze za proces dogovaranja republika i pokrajina," *Novinarstvo*, I-II (1978), 129-135.

40. Slobodan Vucetić, "Delegatski sistem u organizacijama udruženog rada," *Gledišta*, XVI (January, 1975), 36.

41. An internal report on the work of the Federal Chamber of the Federal Assembly (i.e., the chamber made up of predominantly "direct producers" and amateur politicians) made during 1974 and 1975 remarks that "delegates ... and the working bodies of the chamber do not have time to attentively analyze or consider matters in preparation for sessions of the Chamber." As a result, the Federal Chamber has not been able to become "a place for agreements or a place where, in the framework of the rights and duties of the Assembly, policies are created and adopted." See *Neka iskustava iz dosadašnjeg rada saveznog vijeća i njegovih radnih tijela* (Belgrade: Skupština SFRJ, Savezno Vijeće, 1975), 11. The 1975-1976 reports on the work of the Federal Chamber and the other branch of the federal legislature - the Chamber of Republics and Provinces - indicate that the "real influence" of central and regional party organs and leaders on the legislative process (which is acknowledged to differ from the "normative position of the federal legislature as the highest organ of self-management") is of "exceptional significance" for the solution of ethno-regional conflicts. See *Neka zapažanja iz dosadašnjeg rada veća Republika i Pokrajina, Period Od 15. Maja 1974. do Kraja 1975 Godine* (Belgrade: Skupština SFRJ vece Republika i Pokrajina, 1976), 22-31, 9.

42. Zlatija Dukić-Veljović, "The Assembly of the Socialist Federal Republic of Yugoslavia," *Yugoslav Survey*, XVIII (February, 1977), 3-34, Radovoje Marinković, "The Organization and Work of the Commune Assemblies," *Survey*, XVIII (May, 1977), 3-21.

43. During 1986 and 1987 there was increased discussion about the creation of a new "Chamber of Associated Labour" as a third chamber in the Federal Legislature, in order to enhance working class reprensentation and to function as a "central workers' council." One observer suggested, however, that such a reorganization would make little sense while similar existing chambers at lower levels of the federation remained on the "margins of political life." *Nedeljne Informativne Novine*, No. 1851 (June 22, 1986), 34-35.

44. Edward Kardelj, *Pravci i razvoja političkog sistema socijalističkog samoupravljanja*, 1978, Najdan Pašić, "Pluralism of Interests Within the Political System of Socialist Self-Management." Paper presented at the Canadian Association of Slavists, 1979.

45. Joseph Schlesinger, *Ambition and Politics: Political Careers in the United States* (Chicago: Rand Mcnally, 1966), Gordon Black, "A

Lenard J. Cohen

Theory of Professionalization in Politics," *American Political Science Review*, LXIV, No. 3 (September, 1970), 865-878.

46. Kenneth Prewitt, *The Recruitment of Political Leaders: A Study of Citizen Politicians* (Indianapolis: Bobbs-Merrill Co., 1970), 189-203, Heinz Eulau and Kenneth Prewitt, *Labyrinths of Democracy: Adaptations, Linkages, Representation and Policies in Urban Politics* (New York: Bobbs-Merrill Co., 1973), 444-456.

47. A 1977 survey of nearly one thousand Zagreb workers from different skill levels, revealed extreme skepticism about the ability of amateur activists to remain politically deprofessionalized. Asked if one of their comrades who had been elected to some well-paid political function would return to his earlier working place upon the expiration of his term of office, 36 percent of the respondents felt that such a person wouldn't return, but would remain in a similar function, and 21 percent said the comrade should return but doubted that he or she would. See Milan Mesić, "Politička kultura samoupravljanja radnicke klase Zagreba," *Naše teme*, II (February, 1978), 372.

48. This remark was made by Professor Franjo Kozul of Sarajevo who was reacting to a party Central Committee resolution (June 19, 1979). Growing out of a personal initiative by Tito, the resolution proposed, among other things, that Presidents and Vice-Presidents of legislative assemblies would perform their duties for a one-year period (as opposed to the previous four years). A constitutional amendment to incorporate these proposals was recommended to the federal legislature by Yugoslavia's state presidency and was adopted in 1981.

49. Yugoslav observers of self-management frequently draw attention to the persistent growth in size and influence of the federal bureaucracy. See *Borba*, (February 21, 1978), 5, and *Borba*, (September 13, 1979), 4. Such specific criticisms differ from the even more constant and very abstract official incantations about the evils of bureaucracy. For example, one university professor observed that while the 1974 Constitution anticipated a transfer of federal functions to the regions, in fact, over a two-year period the federal administrative apparatus grew by 24 percent, and the number of appointed functionaries increased by 43 percent. See N. Jovanov, "Kako raste moć administracije," *Politika*, (January 21, 1979), 8. The same data were used as the basis for a question in the

Federal Chamber by one of the delegates - a professional politician - who wanted the federal government to explain the growth in the civil service. The government's answer revealed that from 1974 to 1978 the federal bureaucracy had increased by 3,999 people. *Politika*, (March 29, 1979), 10. The fact that such questions can be asked, answered, and publicized demonstrates, nevertheless, the unique course of Yugoslav legislative development in Eastern Europe.

50. See Chapter 5 in this book.

51. Mark Nadel and Frances Rourke, "Bureaucracies," *Governmental Institutions and Processes Handbook of Political Science, Volume 5*, eds. Fred I. Greenstein and Nelson Poslby (Menlo Park, Calif.: Addison-Wesley Publishing Co., 1975), 411-429.

52. Leszek Kolakowski, *Main Currents of Marxism, Volume I* (Oxford: Clarendon Press, 1978), 160.

CHAPTER 5

SELF-MANAGEMENT'S CIVIL SERVANTS: THE POLITICAL ROLE OF THE ADMINISTRATIVE ELITE

The political power of administrative officials holding high-level positions in the public or state bureaucracy has been a subject of vital concern to contemporary social scientists. As a result of their location in the governmental structure of most political systems, and particularly their involvement in key stages of formulating and executing public policy, professional civil servants have the potential ability to initiate, modify and even completely sabotage the decisions made by those individuals exercising political authority. Although the pivotal role that top administrative functionaries may play in shaping the outcome of political decisions is frequently acknowledged, students of communist political systems have devoted relatively little attention to the attitudes and behaviour of administrative officials in the state bureaucracy. Beyond the difficulty of conducting systematic research in communist systems, many scholars have believed that the political control exercised by the party organization over government agencies and the state administration, reduced the importance of communist civil servants as a distinct or significant factor influencing political development. Studies of "bureaucracy" in communist systems have therefore tended to either focus almost exclusively on the party bureaucracy, or to treat party leaders and government functionaries as indistinguishable parts of a single "bureaucratic" elite or stratum. For example, Carl Beck, in one of the few studies of communist administrative development, observed that:

> ... it is impossible to pinpoint a formal state bureaucracy in Eastern Europe in the sense one can do so in describing politics in Great Britain

or France. The course of administration is not determined by a bureaucracy in the sense of a formal state administrative system that is independent and instrumental, but is determined instead by the interplay between the leaders, the movement, and a series of administrative organizations. The latter because of the power of the party to intrude at any time displays few of the functional and behavioural characteristics that are ascribed to classical bureaucracy.[1]

While the primacy of the party apparatus over the top echelons of the governmental structure remains an essential feature of all of the East European communist states, the political importance of the state bureaucracy in many of these countries has tended to expand over the last two or three decades.[2] The most explicit case of such development, as in so many other areas of communist political innovation, has occurred in Yugoslavia. The increased importance of the state administration in the Yugoslav political process stems in large part from the convergence of two closely related changes which began in the early 1930's: (1) the growing autonomy of governmental institutions from *direct* party control, and (2) the *development* of Yugoslav legislative institutions as important arenas for political decision-making.

The transformation of the Yugoslav Communist Party from a command-oriented instrument of revolutionary change into an "ideological-guiding force" (reflected in its designation after 1952 as the League of Yugoslav Communists) provided the major impetus to the appearance of the state administration as a meaningful "political" institution. Beginning in the early 1950's, as part of the institutional reorganization that followed in the wake of the rift with the Soviet Union, the Yugoslav leadership embarked on a policy of gradually upgrading the political status and influence of the formal structure of state institutions. In an effort to combat the "bureaucratization" of society, the Yugoslav regime acted to sever the close relationship between the party apparatus and the state administration that is characteristic of other communist political systems. After 1953, the party (League) apparatus no longer maintained special organizational units for the control of administrative agencies. Party cells within governmental organizations were also disbanded and the practice of political leaders simultaneously holding high-level positions in both the party organs and the state administration (the so-called personal accumulation of functions) was strongly discouraged, although not totally eliminated. As early as 1956 one Yugoslav political analyst noted the growing division between professional party workers and administrative personnel in the state bureaucracy: "many politically educated administrative cadre left the administrative service only because they were in some allegedly political functions, and others would feel that there isn't a place for them in the state administration. The idea began to create differences in everyday social relations between personnel in our state organs."[3]

The emancipation of the state administration from direct party tutelage,

The Socialist Pyramid: Elites and Power in Yugoslavia

together with other measures such as the sharp reduction of administrative personnel and the decentralization of federal agencies to the regional and local level, succeeded in eliminating many of the cumbersome and dysfunctional aspects of bureaucratic control over the economy and society. At the same time, however, these changes also provided the remaining administrative agencies and personnel with considerably more latitude for independent action than they had previously enjoyed. Characterizing this development in conceptual terms, it may be said that as the *partisanship* of Yugoslav state administrators diminished during this period, their level of *politicization* markedly increased:

> ... *politicization involves a heightening of the influence of officials*, both military and civil, in the making of policies for a whole polity. Such officials may not also be active in a political party or take part in electoral and legislative politics. *To the extent that public officials are associated with a political party, they may be called "partisan."* [The] degree of partisanship provides no measure of bureaucratic power. Some spoilsmen in a bureaucracy, having been rewarded for party work, may hold unimportant positions and exercise no significant influence, either inside or outside the bureaucracy. However, other political appointees, holding high office, may exercise significant power. Thus bureaucratic partisanship may be high while degree of bureaucratism varies from high to low. Conversely, we can find systems in which a low degree of partisanship is associated with a wide range of variation in degree of politicization.[4]

Thus, during the height of the so-called bureaucratic or administrative period of Yugoslav socialism from 1945 to 1951, it was the party bureaucracy that dominated political life. During the subsequent phase of Yugoslav development the state bureaucracy would become a more important political force.[5]

In addition to the changes made with respect to the control of the administration, the withdrawal of the League of Communists from operational management over broad areas of social and economic activity stimulated the development of parliamentary assemblies as focal points for the adoption of political decisions. After 1963 and the establishment of a new constitutional system, many key issues which had been exclusively in the domain of top party bodies were transferred to the jurisdiction of legislative representatives serving in the structure of parliamentary assemblies on the federal, republican-provincial, and local levels.[6]

One result of this development was that Yugoslav representative bodies which had formerly enjoyed only nominal authority over the state bureaucracy, gradually assumed practical responsibility for the political control of administrative functionaries. In operation, this change meant that the tasks of recruiting senior civil servants, monitoring their activities, and holding them "accountable" for the performance of their duties, fell largely into the domain of elected parliamentary deputies. The organs of the League of Communists continued to exert an influence on the selection and behaviour of administrative officials in Yugoslavia, but did so far less directly and extensively than in the other communist states. As a consequence of these changes, the relationship between elected legislative representatives and appointed officials in the state administration, which has drawn so much attention in studies of non-communist regimes, became an interesting area for political inquiry with respect to the Yugoslav political system.

The major aim of this chapter is to explore the political influence of senior civil servants in Yugoslavia on the process of legislative decision-making. Three factors affecting the extent of administrative involvement in the legislative process at the top (federal) level of government have been selected for consideration: (1) the attitudes of higher civil servants regarding their own activities in the policy-making process, that is, their role orientations; (2) the pattern of interaction between senior state administrators and elected parliamentary deputies; and (3) the pattern of influence between administrative officials and parliamentary deputies. It is an underlying assumption of the study that the attitudes and activities of higher administrative functionaries can have a significant influence in determining what kinds of legislative decisions are formulated, and how, or if, such decisions are implemented. Therefore, the way in which administrative officials view their own responsibilities, and the nature of their relationship with elected political officials, is an important factor in understanding the overall process of political development in Yugoslavia. Moreover, an examination of the role played by administrative officials in the legislative process can shed additional light on the capacity of Yugoslav representative institutions to control and delimit activities of the state bureaucracy (see Chapter 4).

The data used in this chapter derive primarily from survey interviews with Yugoslav federal administrators and federal legislators conducted from March 1968 to January 1969 by the *International Study of Opinion-Makers' Project*,[7] as well as the results of field research conducted by the author on parliamentary and administrative development in Yugoslavia. The survey carried out by the *International Study of Opinion-Makers' Project* included interviews with Yugoslav leaders in six functional sectors: federal legislators, federal administrators, party and mass organization leaders, economic managers, communications experts, and intellectuals. As the major focus of this study concerns the involvement and political influence of senior civil servants in the legislative process - a subject that primarily includes the relationship between administrative officials and elected parliamentary representatives - only the first two subgroups, namely, federal legislators and federal administrators, are discussed in this chapter. Table 5.1 includes a breakdown of the types of positions included in the two subgroups and the composition of the sample.

The Socialist Pyramid: Elites and Power in Yugoslavia

The Role of Higher Administrative Officials

One of the few opinions that appears to be shared by elites and citizens alike in most political systems is that administrative officials should be subject to the control of political authorities. "With few exceptions," writes one student of comparative administration, "there is common agreement, transcending differences in political ideology, culture, and style, that bureaucracy should be basically instrumental in its operation, that it should serve as an agent and not as a master."[8] Regardless of the institution or group in which political authority may happen to be vested at a particular time (e.g., legislature, party, military, etc.), "administrators" are expected to develop a self-image or conception of their role in accordance with this norm and to behave accordingly.[9]

The Yugoslav case is no exception in this respect. According to constitutional theory and administrative law, the administrative function consists of two basic activities: (1) the implementation and enforcement of the laws, regulations, and policies adopted by representative institutions; and (2) the provision of specialized assistance to elected decision-makers in carrying out their duties, such as the detailed preparation of legislation, drawing up of reports, providing information, and various other forms of "technical consultation." A handbook for employees in the state administration emphasized that the legislative process is guided by a combination of rules which are designed to:

> ... secure the complete and absolutely decisive role of the competent legislative organs in the adoption of laws and other regulations, and in that way their responsibility for the laws which are adopted. In addition, it is the aim of these rules to achieve the full consideration and evaluation of all possible solutions and alternatives, the participation of political and other legislative factors, the confrontation of various interests in the solution of special social problems, as well as consultation with representatives of different interests and opinions, etc. ... However, the particular aim of the rules of legislative procedure is to ensure the complete freedom and all other conditions for the realization of the rights of members of representative bodies, to express their will, and unhindered participation in this procedure.[10]

An examination of the attitudes expressed by higher administrators in Yugoslavia regarding the duties they consider most important in carrying out their work reveals a close correspondence between their own role orientations and the official conception of the administrative function (Table 5.2). Of 81 federal administrators interviewed in 1968 and 1969, the largest number (38 percent) indicated that professional assistance in policy-making was the most important aspect of their responsibility. About 25 percent of the administrators

Lenard J. Cohen

Table 5.1
The Sample of Federal Administrative Functionaries and Legislators

	Total in the State Structure on the Federal Level, 1968-69		Sample of Respondents		Sample as a Percent of Total in State Structure
	Number	Percent	Number	Percent	Percent
I. Federal administrative functionaries.					
A. Senior civil servants in the federal assembly (secretaries of the chambers, committees, commissions, advisors, assistants, etc.)	37	24.5	26	32.1	70.3
B. Senior civil servants in the federal administration					
1. in the Federal Executive Council[a] (secretaries, undersecretaries, assistants, advisors, etc.)	23	15.2	15	18.5	65.2
2. in the state secretariats, federal secretariats, councils, commissions, administrations, etc. (secretaries, undersecretaries, deputy-secretaries, directors, advisors, assistants, etc.)	91	60.3	40	49.4	44.0
Total federal administrators	151	100.0	81	100.0	53.6
II. Deputies in the Federal Assembly					
A. Deputies in the "political chambers"					
1. Chamber of the Nationalities	70	28.6	16	24.6	22.9
2. Federal Chamber	120	49.0	38	58.5	31.7
B. Top-ranking deputies in the functionally specialized chambers[b]	55	22.5	11	16.9	20.0
Total deputies	245	100.0	65	100.0	26.5

[a] The 17 members of the Federal Executive Council (FEC) during 1968-69 are not treated as "administrative functionaries" in this study. The president and members of the Council were elected by the deputies of the Federal Assembly from among their own ranks, that is, elected legislators, and functioned very similarly to a cabinet or ministerial council in parliamentary systems.

[b] This subgroup includes deputies in the Social-Health Chamber, Educational-Cultural Chamber, and Organizational-Political Chamber of the Federal Assembly who served as members of Assembly commissions, the presidents of committees in these chambers, and the presidents and vice-presidents of these chambers. Top ranking deputies in the Economic Chamber of the federal Assembly were treated as part of the "economic" rather than the "legislative" elite, and are therefore not included in the total number of deputies from the functionally specialized chambers included in this table.

regarded the implementation of policies adopted by the Federal Assembly and the members of the Federal Executive Council as the chief features of their work. A smaller, although not insignificant number of the respondents expressed a more participatory definition of their roles (14.8 percent), indicating their most important task to be participation in the formulation of the long-term goals and policies for society, or the presentation of new ideas (8.6 percent) that contribute to the efficiency and modernization of society. Only five (6.2 percent) of the higher administrators regarded responsiveness to the public as the most important aspect of their duties. These responses clearly indicate that most Yugoslav administrators emphasize those facets of their work that are officially prescribed and frequently stressed. Indeed, the answers closely resemble those offered by administrators in other countries in response to similar work-related questions.[11]

The tendency of Yugoslav civil servants to give "correct" responses concerning their role in the political process is undoubtedly affected by the politically sensitive environment in which they work and their undoubtedly defensive attitude to survey interviews administered by social scientists. One interesting pattern does, however, emerge from the above responses. Thus, the administrators interviewed tended to place a much greater emphasis on the professional-advisory or consultative aspects of the administrative function than on the implementation of policy. Although policy counsel is an officially acceptable administrative function, it is the execution of laws or policy implementation that is usually given priority in Yugoslav constitutional theory. The strong orientation toward policy counsel among administrative functionaries working in the Federal Assembly is probably due to the fact that they are required to assist elected officials in the preparation of legislation. The professional-advisory or policy-counsel orientation of federal administrative officials working outside the legislature, however, is also very high. One factor that may explain this pattern of responses is the changing functions of the federal administration during the second half of the 1960's. Briefly, the decentralization of numerous governmental functions to the republican and communal levels considerably diminished the responsibilities of the federal administration for the direct implementation and enforcement of laws. Moreover, many federal administrative tasks were transferred to various "self-managing institutions" that have quasi-independent positions (e.g., federal institutions for banking, insurance, employment, etc.), and are therefore no longer directly within the jurisdiction of senior civil servants. As a result of these changes, federal administrators became preoccupied with providing professional staff assistance to legislators rather than executing laws and regulations. This development is particularly significant considering that one of the principle avenues through which administrative officials influence the content and outcome of political decisions in any regime is "professional," "technical," or "specialized assistance" in the formulation of policy.[12] While it is impossible to determine the extent and nature of this influence simply from the survey interview responses

Table 5.2
The Role-Orientations of Higher Administrative Functionaries in Yugoslavia
Question: Which of the following duties do you consider most important in your work? Choose three and rank them.

Role-Orientation[a]	First Choice of Administrative Functionaries in the							
	Federal Administration		Federal Assembly		Total			
	Number	Percent	Number	Percent	Number	Percent		
Policy counsel (professional assistance in the formulation of decisions of federal legislative and executive organs)	18	32.7	13	50.0	31	38.3		
Policy implementation (the precise implementation of the decisions and policies of federal legislative and executive organs)	14	25.1	6	23.0	20	24.7		
Program formulation (participation in the formulation of the long-term goals and policies of society)	9	16.4	3	11.5	12	14.8		
Innovation (the presentation of new ideas that contribute to the efficiency and modernization of society	5	9.1	2	7.7	7	8.6		
Administrative efficiency[b] (ensure effective and rational administration, check waste, and avoid unnecessary expenditures)	5	9.1	1	3.9	6	7.4		
Responsiveness to the public (ensure the influence of citizens and the publicity of administrative work)	4	7.2	1	3.9	5	6.2		
Total responses	55	100.0	26	100.0	81	100.0		

[a] The description of each role-orientation in parentheses is a translation of the choices offered to the respondents in the questionnaire.
[b] This orientation combines two choices on the questionnaire.

of administrative officials concerning their most important duties, the importance and prospect of some type of administrative involvement in legislative decision-making is clearly evident in the outlook of Yugoslav civil servants. Consequently, nearly two-thirds of all the administrators interviewed emphasized either the consultative aspect of their duties, direct participation in policy formulation, or the presentation of new ideas. The responses tend to confirm the observation made by many Yugoslav authors that higher state functionaries devote a major portion of their time providing assistance to elected officials, and give relatively little attention to the implementation or enforcement of laws. As one administrator observed when responding to such criticism:

> Although the primary task of the administrative organs is to implement laws and regulations, these organs, according to some analyses, spend 60 to 80 percent of their effective working capacity, especially the leading personnel, in the preparation of analyses and proposals for representative bodies and their organs ... one only needs to stroll through the halls, for example, of the Federal Assembly and see how many professional employees and functionaries of the administration are engaged in the work of different committees, commissions, and chambers at the request of these organs of the Assembly, *and not on the initiative of the organs of the administration.*[13] [Author's emphasis]

The Pattern of Interaction

The frequency and character of interaction between legislators is an important factor affecting the extent of administrative influence in the legislative process. A high rate of communication and contact between the two groups may facilitate the ability of the legislature to control the administration by allowing elected deputies to oversee the work of civil servants and question them concerning their activity. Interaction with elected officials may also provide an opportunity for administrators to advance their own beliefs in the framing of policy. Whatever the outcome may be, a close working relationship between administrators and legislators promotes a mutual awareness of each others' problems, strengths, and weaknesses.[14] How extensively do Yugoslav legislators and administrators interact with one another? An analysis of the responses offered by Yugoslav federal administrators and members of the Federal Assembly when asked about their work-related pattern of interaction illustrates the network of such contacts between the two functional groups. The specific question put to federal civil servants and legislative deputies during 1968-1969 was: "During the past month, who are the three people with whom you have most often had discussions about problems in your own field?" The responses are presented in Table 5.3, and again schematically in Figure 5.1, in order to indicate the pattern of interaction between different institutional sectors of the political system on the federal level.

Table 5.3
The Pattern of Interaction between Federal Administrative and Legislative Elites in Yugoslavia (%)
Question: During the past month, who are the three people with whom you have most often had discussions about problems in your own field?

	Sector of Elite Respondents		
	Administrative Functionaries in the		
Persons Names by Institutional Sector	Federal Administration (N-46)	Federal Assembly (N-22)	Federal Legislators (N-57)
Administrative functionaries in the Federal Administration	34.4	10.9	2.2
Administrative functionaries in the Federal Assembly	-	20.0	1.0
Members of the Federal Executive Council (the cabinet)	13.8	1.8	4.5
Federal legislators	16.2	41.9	33.1
Party and mass organization leaders[a]	9.2	5.5	10.5
Other/nonpolitical or nonadministrative individuals	4.6	7.3	8.2
Outside universe List[b]	21.8	12.7	41.3
Total persons named as interaction partners	100.0 (N-87)	100.0 (N-55)	100.0 (N-133)

[a] The "party" refers to the central organs (federal) of the Yugoslav League of Communists. Mass organizations include the Socialist Alliance of the Working People of Yugoslavia, the Trade Union federation, the veterans' association, and the organizations for women and youth on the federal level.
[b] See footnote 15.

The Socialist Pyramid: Elites and Power in Yugoslavia

Figure 5.1
Percent of Different Persons Mentioned by Yugoslav Federal Administrators and Legislators as Interaction Partners on Matters in Their Own Field (according to the institutional sector of the persons mentioned)

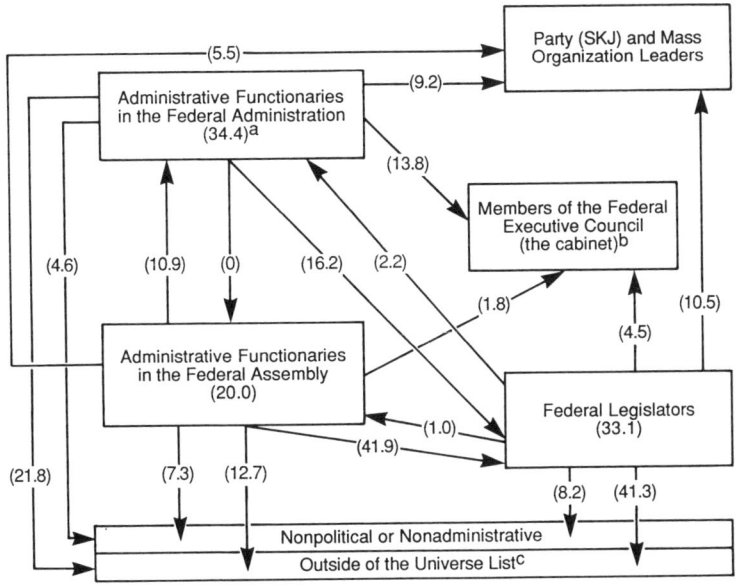

[a] Percent of individuals mentioned by respondents from within their own sector appears on each box.
[b] See note [a] in Table 5.1.
[c] See footnote 15.

Lenard J. Cohen

The responses given by administrators indicate their close working relationship with deputies in the Federal Assembly; a confirmation of the analysis of administrative role orientations. Of the 55 persons named by administrative officials in the Federal Assembly as "discussion partners" on matters in their own field, the majority (41.9 percent) were deputies in the Federal Assembly. The fact that 15 out of 23 legislators named by administrators in the Federal Assembly as discussion partners were elected officials in the Assembly (e.g., presidents of the chambers, presidents of various committees and commissions, etc.), illustrates the point at which administrative involvement in the legislative process takes place. Direct contacts between administrative functionaries and deputies serving in the Federal Assembly appear to be much more extensive than the degree of interaction among the various parliamentary administrators themselves (20 percent of the responses). Administrative functionaries working for a particular committee or commission are more likely to develop a close working relationship with those legislators who either preside over, or are intimately involved, in the work of these bodies than with fellow administrative officials who perform tasks on other matters in the legislative process. This situation is a natural consequence of the functional and topical division of labour among various committees and commissions in the Federal Assembly, and certainly undermines the solidarity and cohesiveness of the parliamentary administrators as a group.

Administrative functionaries working outside the legislature tended to choose a higher level of interaction partners from within their own ranks (34.4 percent). The fact that federal administrative agencies fall either directly within the organizational framework of the Federal Executive Council (the rough equivalent of the cabinet or "government" in other parliamentary systems) or under its direct supervision, explains the high rate of interaction between senior civil servants and members of the Council (13.8 percent of the nominations). Federal administrators also indicated some interaction with deputies in the Federal Assembly (16.2 percent), usually with legislators holding key parliamentary functions such as the presidents of various committees. The data on interaction does not, however, reveal a very high rate of contact between federal administrators and higher party officials. While a general affinity of views undoubtedly persists between top administrative officials and some high-ranking members of the League of Communists (due to common experiences, social affiliations, ideological outlook, etc.), the frequency of direct professional contacts between individuals holding positions in these two institutional sectors is not very extensive. In contrast to earlier years when the League exercised close supervision over the state administration, these findings suggest a growing occupational and organizational differentiation between the party and state apparatuses.

While Yugoslav administrators, particularly those serving in the Federal Assembly, claim to have a major portion of their working discussions with federal legislators, this pattern of interaction is not indicated by the deputies themselves. When questioned about the most important discussion partner in their "own field," federal legislators typically chose other members of the Assembly (33.1 percent) or, in most cases (41.3 percent), individuals completely outside the "universe list" of federal leaders.[15] One effect of the decentralization of governmental authority in the Yugoslav system has been to "territorialize" political power and therefore make both the members of the Federal Assembly and the federal administration more responsive to interest groups and elites on the regional and local level. The high level of persons named outside the "universe list" reflects the close ties that leigslators maintain with various individuals and groups on the republican-provincial and communal levels of the federation. The large number of interaction partners chosen by legislators from among their own colleagues in the Federal Assembly (33.1 percent), rather than from among party leaders, may reflect the increasing organizational vitality of the parliamentary system as an independent component of the political system during the period analyzed (see Chapter 4). The line separating legislators serving in the "political chambers" of the Federal Assembly from functionaries working in the party and in mass organizations remains a rather thin one, however, since most individuals in both subgroups share a common background in professional "socio-political activity" (Party-League, mass organization, and government).[16]

The most important finding with respect to this discussion is the fact that federal deputies report very little interaction with administrative officials. This situation is partially explained by the fact that only a small portion of the legislators interviewed held those positions in the Federal Assembly where they would be most likely to have frequent contact with administrators (i.e., heads of committees and commissions who constantly deal with administrative officials during the preparation of legislation and various other aspects of legislative activity). As mentioned above, the responses of administrators regarding their contacts in the Federal Assembly seem to illustrate that their pattern of interaction with deputies, while very frequent, was limited to particular legislators holding key positions in the Assembly. It is not entirely surprising, therefore, that when asked to name the people with whom they most frequently discussed matters in their "own field," federal legislators named only a small number of administrative officials. Although the data on interaction cannot help to specify the precise nature and extent of administrative involvement in the formulation of policy, it does suggest that such activity occurs with respect to specific issue areas and phases of the legislative process rather than a diffuse pattern of frequent contacts between administrators and parliamentary deputies.

Lenard J. Cohen

The Pattern of Influence

While socio-metric data on interaction patterns sheds some light on the frequency of contacts between legislators and administrators, there is no way of knowing from the available data how such behaviour affects the distribution of influence between these two groups. Knowing that communication exists between certain individuals suggests the extent to which potential for the development of influence exists, in one way or another, but offers little insight into how that influence is structured, or if any influence relationship actually exists. A second socio-metric question from the *International Opinion-Makers' Study* of the Yugoslav elite offers additional information concerning the pattern of influence between federal administrative officials and elected deputies. The question asks: "Could you tell us the names of the three people who have had the greatest influence on your opinions, concerning the most essential problems in your field?" The responses by both federal administrators and legislators (Table 5.4 and Figure 5.2) reveal a significantly different pattern than the data on interaction.

To begin with, while the rate of response to this question was only slightly lower than for the question on interaction, the number of individuals nominated as being "influential" was considerably smaller than the number of persons identified as interaction partners. On the question of interaction, the responses were widely diffused among a variety of individuals, with most respondents naming different people as discussion partners. The responses to the question of influence, however, centered on a more limited number of individuals, most of whom were named by several of the respondents. This result may derive from the general tendency of elite studies using a reputational approach (of which the above question on influence is one variant) to reveal a narrower spread of leadership than studies that focus on the involvement or interaction of elites regarding specific issues and decisions.[17]

More important than the number of persons nominated as influentials for the purpose of this discussion, however, is the source of that influence. This also differs considerably from the responses on interaction. What emerges most clearly with regard to those individuals nominated as influential is the importance accorded to high-ranking members of the League of Communists and other mass organizations. Among the persons named by administrative functionaries in the Federal Assembly as having the most influence on opinions in their field, the largest number (27 percent) were party and mass organization leaders. This group also made up a large proportion (20.8 percent) of the individuals named as influential by functionaries in the federal administration, although the close association between senior civil servants and officials on the republican-provincial level accounted for a greater number of responses (26.4 percent)

Table 5.4
The Pattern of Influence between Federal Administrative and Legislative Elites in Yugoslavia (%)
Question: Could you tell us the name of the three people who have had the greatest influence on your opinions, concerning the most essential problems in your field?

Persons Named by Institutional Sector	Sector of Elite Respondents Administrative Functionaries in the		
	Federal Administration (N-43)	Federal Assemby (N-18)	Federal Legislators (N-52)
Administrative functionaries in the federal administration	15.1	11.5	3.4
Administrative functionaries in the Federal Assembly	-	-	-
Members of the Federal Executive Council (the cabinet)	13.2	7.7	6.8
Federal legislators	20.8	23.1	18.6
Party and mass organization leaders	20.8	27.0	25.4
Other/nonpolitical or nonadministrative individuals	3.7	11.5	10.2
Outside universe list*	26.4	19.2	35.6
Total persons named as influentials	100.0	100.0	100.0
	(N-53)	(N-26)	(N-59)

* See footnote 15.

falling outside the "universe list." In addition, both subgroups of administrators also nominated a large number of legislators as influential on opinions in their field.

It is surprising that the number of legislators named was not greater, given the formal accountability of the administration to members of the Assembly, and the growing activity of the parliamentary system after 1963. Moreover, the fact that a large proportion of the legislators named are professional politicians by occupation and are members of the Central Committee of the League of Communists makes it difficult to determine whether their influence derives mainly from their positions as elected members of the parliament, or because they are generally influential "socio-political workers" who happen to be in the legislature. It seems likely that a combination of both institutional affiliations - League and Federal Assembly - provides a basis for their influence over the opinions of administrative officials.

Lenard J. Cohen

Figure 5.2
Percent of Different Persons Mentioned by Yugoslav Federal Administrators and Legislators as Having an Influence on Their Opinions Concerning Matters in Their Own Field
(according to the institutional sector of the persons mentioned)

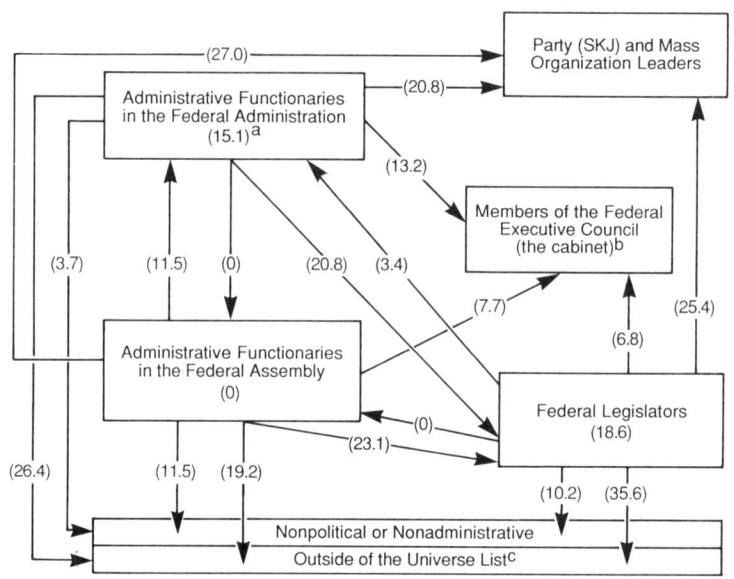

[a] The percent of individuals mentioned by respondents from within their own sector appears in each box.
[b] See note [a] in Table 5.1
[c] See footnote 15.

The Socialist Pyramid: Elites and Power in Yugoslavia

The continued significance of the League and other mass socio-political organizations as the locus of political power in the Yugoslav political system emerges even more clearly from the responses of legislators themselves. Leaving aside the large number of persons nominated as influential by deputies in the Federal Assembly who are outside the universe list of the federal elite (i.e., regional and local leaders), the greatest percentage of their choices are leaders in the League of Communists and the mass organizations (25.4 percent). This finding reflects the fact that although Yugoslav parliamentary deputies displayed increasing independence beginning in the mid-1960's, the overall "guidance" of the League of Communists remained an essential feature of the legislative process.[18] When it came to choosing influentials in their own "field," the legislators quite naturally also named a large portion of their fellow deputies in the Federal Assembly (18.6 percent). It is necessary to emphasize again, however, that Yugoslav legislators who are professional politicians by occupation (as most deputies in the survey are) make very little distinction between political leaders serving in party organizations, mass organizations, and the parliamentary system. Legislators consider activity in each of those institutional sectors as closely related and largely interchangeable facets of "socio-political work." To distinguish, therefore, between persons nominated by legislators who are involved in one or another sphere of "political" activity may be more of an analytical than a real distinction. What appears more clearly is that only a fraction of all the persons named by legislators as having an influence in their own field were civil servants in the state administration (3.4 percent). If high administrative officials have any influence in the policy-making process, as other evidence certainly indicates, it certainly is not apparent from the responses of the federal legislators.

The reputed influence of a small number of party and mass organization leaders on both legislative and administrative matters emerges even more noticeably by comparing the number of nominations received by individuals in various organizational sectors (Table 5.5). If those persons who received five or more nominations (that is, who were named by five or more respondents as having an influence on opinion in their field) are considered as highly influential, then - according to the perceptions of both federal legislators and federal administrators - a relatively small number of party and mass organization leaders at the summit of the Yugoslav political system appear to have the most influence. It should be emphasized that this finding in no way suggests that the *direct* intervention of the party leaders in the activities of state institutions is of the same magnitude or has the same consequences as in earlier years, particularly before 1966. In the case of *routine* decisions, which constitute the overwhelming portion of decision-making, both federal civil servants and legislators enjoy significant latitude for independent action.

Lenard J. Cohen

Technical Expertise and Political Influence

The major aim of the preceding discussion has been to examine the evidence from survy interview data gathered by the *International Study of Opinion-Making Project* concerning the influence of Yugoslav administrative officials on political decision-making. The findings from the analysis are highly suggestive, but must be regarded with caution. They reveal that the way in which administrators perceive their roles corresponds closely to the official-legal conception of their duties. The senior civil servants who were interviewed tend to place primary emphasis on the consultative aspects of their work, that is, specialized assistance in the formulation of policy, rather than on the implementation of policy. While the attitudinal data on role orientations suggests the evaluation that administrators place on their past behaviour, as well as their expectations of future behaviour, it does not indicate whether their activities have actually conformed to these perceptions, or are likely to do so in the future.

The analysis of the socio-metric data on interaction between administrators and legislators reveals the frequency and general pattern of contact between members of the two groups. Administrators claim to have frequent contact with elected deputies in carrying out their duties. In contrast, federal legislators appear to maintain a broad variety of contacts in their work, most of which are either with individuals and groups holding positions below the federal level or with top leaders in the party and other mass organizations. It is not known, however, *how* this pattern of interaction affects the relationship between administrators and legislators. Do such contacts, for example, enhance administrative influence on the formulation of policy, or perhaps provide an opportunity for legislative control over the state bureaucracy? The data on influence offer a somewhat more conclusive picture. When federal administrators and legislators were asked to name the people most influential in their field, they tended to choose a relatively small number of professional political activists in the League of Communists and the Federal Assembly. Again, the data does not reveal if, or in what way, this reputed influence affects the day-to-day tasks carried out by both administrative officials and parliamentary deputies.

The analysis of the survey interview data leads to the conclusion that administrative functionaries are primarily professional staff consultants who, although interacting frequently with legislators in the Assembly, exercise very minimal influence in the formulation of political decisions. Indeed, Allen Barton's analysis of data specifically dealing with the attitudes and values of the same administrative officials treated in this study, concludes that "federal administrators tend to be the servants of those in power, rather than interest groups in their own rights, and do not express distinctive interests or values related to their position."[19] To what extent is this an accurate description of the political role of Yugoslav federal administrators? While the findings from the analysis in this chapter generally seem to support Barton's view, such a conclusion differs substantially from the view frequently encountered among direct participants in the Yugoslav legislative process, namely, that professional civil servants exercise a strong influence on both the shape and substance of decisions made in the Federal Assembly. The following statement by the President of the Committee for the Federal Budget in the Chamber of Nationalities is typical in this respect:

> It is difficult to overlook the reality that a single appartus such as the Federal Administration of over 8,000 workers is a social force which generates a tendency to preserve its position in the creation of legislative and economic policy. This was evident from its program of work during debates in committees in the Federal Assembly concerning the federal budget last year. Namely, one saw that the administrative organs established a program of work which the Assembly later adopted, as its program of work, rather than the opposite situation .... The fact is that the administration which is primarily authorized to execute laws and other regulations, formulates and also initiates the majority of laws and proposals. It is true that they formulate them according to directions, and within the boundaries of their authority. However, by their nature, they cannot fail to use their professional supremacy for the promotion of their views and solutions.[20]

The preceding view, in contrast to the survey interview data analyzed in this chapter suggests that Yugoslav civil servants have a very substantial political influence in the policy-making process. Moreover, unlike many official pronouncements and routine criticisms regarding the dangers and evils of "bureaucracy" and "technocracy," this view is highly representative of remarks frequently made by political functionaries, legal and constitutional specialists, and political scientists concerning the influence of the state administration in the federal legislative process.[21] In order to obtain a more complete picture of the state bureaucracy's political role, it is useful to go beyond the analysis of the survey data and briefly examine some additional evidence concerning administrative involvement in the policy-making process.

As suggested above, federal administrators devote a significant amount of their time providing "professional assistance" to the members of the Federal Assembly. This involves a variety of tasks including drafting proposals of laws, preparing the Assembly's "Program of Work," submitting reports and information to committees of the Assembly, and consultation about various aspects of administrative and legislative affairs. Some of this assistance is provided by the appointed functionaries and staff services of the federal Assembly. The major portion of such activity, however, is carried out by senior officials in the federal administration and the administrative agencies of the Federal Executive Council. One of the most important bodies involved in this work is the Secretariat for Legislation and Organization (the Secretariat for Legislation and Legal Affairs after 1971), which is the administrative arm of the Federal Executive Council for the preparation of legislative proposals.

Despite efforts to upgrade the Federal Assembly and make it the "highest organ of state authority," the executive and administrative agencies have continued to exercise almost exclusive control over the initiation of federal legislation. For example, out of 1,015 legislative proposals submitted to the Federal Assembly between 1963 and 1968, 84 percent were initiated by the Federal Executive Council and the Federal Administration, 15 percent by chambers and committees of the Assembly, and approximately one percent by individual deputies.[22] This situation, not unlike the role of executive and administrative agencies in other political systems, provides senior civil servants with an important source of leverage for advancing their own political values and opinions. As one leading Yugoslav specialist on public administration, who also served as head of the important Legislative Legal Commission of the Federal Assembly, observed in 1967:

> It is impossible to construct a new parliamentary system alongside the continuing domination of the administration. And its domination is still evident. It imposes and pushes its attitudes, and it creates policies. Of course, not on the biggest questions, but certainly on everday ones. The administration needs to implement policy and not to create it. Its role of policy making is only in the implementation of the laws. But that doesn't seem to be the case. We, in fact, don't have a real administration, *but rather a professional service for creating and influencing policies, in the federation, republics, and communes.*[23] [Author's emphasis]

The dominant role played by executive and administrative agencies in the initiation of federal legislation stems primarily from its pivotal position as a source of expertise and information. As Table 5.6 illustrates, the federal administration enjoys an overwhelming advantage with respect to the amount of technical expertise at its disposal. More important than the absolute number of technically trained personnel in the federal administration, is the fact that only a small percentage of the administrative functionaries in other political institutions possess the technical skills necessary to deal with the complex issues they increasingly must confront. An important factor contributing to the monopoly of the federal administration as a source of technical expertise in the policy-making process has been the failure or disinclination of the Federal Assembly to sufficiently utilize the services of various experts and specialized groups outside the administration. Although such "free-floating" and politically independent specialized resources are available in Yugoslavia, they have not

Table 5.5

Persons Mentioned by Yugoslav Federal Administrators and Legislators as Having an Influence on their Opinions Concerning Matters in Their Own Field (according to the number of nominations received by persons in each institutional sector)

	Institutional Sector of Respondents								
	Administrative Functionaries in the							Federal Legislators	
	Federal Administration			Federal Assembly					
Sector of Persons Nominated	High[a]	Medium[b]	Low[c]	High	Medium	Low	High	Medium	Low
Administrative functionaries in the federal administration	-	1	-	-	-	3	-	-	1
Administrative functionaries in the Federal Assembly	-	-	7	-	-	-	-	-	-
Members of the Federal Executive Council (cabinet)	1	3	3	-	1	1	1	-	3
Federal Legislators	-	2	9	-	2	4	1	2	8
Party and mass organization leaders	3	3	5	3	1	3	4	4	7
Other/nonpolitical and nonadministrative individuals	-	-	2	-	-	3	-	1	5
Outside universe list[d]	-	2	12	-	-	5	-	2	19
Total persons mentioned as influentials	4	11	38	3	4	19	6	9	44

[a] High=persons who received 5 or more nominations.
[b] Medium=persons who received from 2 to 4 nominations.
[c] Low=persons who received 1 nomination.
[d] See footnote 15.

Table 5.6

The Distribution of University-Trained Employees in Federal Political and Administrative Institutions by Type of Higher Education Received (%)

Type of Higher Education	Institutional Sector				Party and Mass Socio-political Organizations[a]	Total by Field of Education	
	Federal Administration	Federal Executive Council (Cabinet)	Federal Assembly				
Agriculture	4.9	1.6	1.7	2.5	1.2	100.0	(N-79)
Technical (engineering)	7.1	1.0	1.0	0.1	1.6	100.0	(N-110)
Economics	24.7	16.6	26.7	6.9	17.7	100.0	(N-449)
Law	39.1	78.3	51.7	7.6	32.3	100.0	(N-792)
Philosophy	11.8	1.6	12.1	5.8	29.0	100.0	(N-242)
Other[b]	10.9	-	4.3	2.6	16.7[b]	100.0	(N-197)
Two or more	1.5	1.0	2.6	10.7	1.6	100.0	(N-28)
Total university-trained employees	100.0 (N-1475)	100.0 (N-120)	100.0 (N-116)	100.0	100.0 (N-186)	100.0 (N-1897)	

[a] The *professional apparatus* of the Central Committee of the Yugoslav League of Communists, Central Council and Central Committee of the Yugoslav League of Trade Unions, Federal Conference of the Socialist Alliance (SSRNJ), Central Committee of the Yugoslav Youth League, the Central Committee of the Yugoslav League of War Veterans, and the Conference for the Social Activity of Yugoslav Women.

[b] Degrees received from Higher Party and Political Schools are probably represented in this category.

Source: *Pregled broja i strukture kadrova u saveznim organima, organizacijama, i ustanovama* (Belgrade: Savezno Izvršno Veće, Uprava za personalne poslove, 1967), pp. 43-44, 55-56.

played a significant role in the policy-making process.[24] The need for tapping such alternative sources of expertise has been particularly acute considering the rapid turnover of legislators in Yugoslav representative assemblies. Serving primarily as short-term amateur politicians who face mandatory rotation out of their elected positions after two terms, the majority of Yugoslav legislators, even more than their counterparts in foreign representative bodies, generally have neither the time nor the motivation to become well acquainted with the complex technical issues presented to them by executive and administrative agencies.[25] This situation naturally leads most deputies to solicit, and rely heavily upon specialized advice from professional civil servants. Moreover, those legislators most technically competent to comprehend, scrutinize, or challenge the provisions of programs initiated by the state bureaucracy generally have had the least "political weight" in the legislative process.[26] Despite the overall improvement in the educational qualification of federal deputies, and the effort by the Assembly to develop its own specialized staff as an alternative source of expertise and information, almost all technical information used as a basis for legislative decisions has continued to emanate directly from officials in administrative agencies. The influence of administrative officials is most apparent in the various committees and commissions of the Federal Assembly which have assumed an important role in legislative affairs. One Yugoslav political scientist has even suggested that independent specialists from outside the administration be invited to meetings of those committees specifically in order to counter the influence of civil servants in policy making:

> This method would ensure that the influence of the administration on the decision of deputies would occur within tolerable proportions. The administration would use its specialized knowledge and offer the legislators its opinions and attitudes. Specialists from outside the administration, from working organizations and institutions, would then be in a position to show the legislators when the administration attempts to chart its own course. *From personal experience I have seen that the administration often uses its great competence so that the legislators very often, although personally not agreeing, accept the judgments and suggestions of the administration, because they don't have sufficient counterarguments against the views which the administration explains are necessary.*[27] [Author's emphasis]

Politicized Bureaucrats or Servants of Power?

As might be anticipated from a study of the bureaucratic "grey eminences" in a one-party communist regime, the research findings concerning the political role of Yugoslav federal administrators are somewhat contradictory. Although claiming to have a close working relationship with political decision-makers, the survey data reveals that administrative officials regard themselves as playing an essentially instrumental role in the legislative process and that they are similarly perceived by elected deputies serving in the Federal Assembly. There is also considerable alternative evidence, however, that administrators are deeply involved in the formulation of political decisions, precisely as a consequence of their "instrumental" role.

The fact that both administrators and legislators present a considerably more idealized picture of bureaucratic activity in the political system than other evidence indicates is, of course, neither unusual nor difficult to understand. It is also important to remember that the interview data discussed in this chapter was collected in connection with a project prepared by an international team of social scientists, a fact which must certainly have intensified the normal proclivity of administrators to provide officially "correct" answers. This is not to suggest, however, that the attitudes expressed by higher administrative officials concerning their activities should be disregarded, but only that different avenues of research must be utilized when probing the issue of bureaucratic influence in the decision-making process. As Wallace Sayre aptly observed:

> What is the role of the bureaucracy? The formal and official answer in most countries is that the bureaucracy is an agent of the decision-makers, not in itself one of the decision-makers but rather their instrument, not an autonomous brain in their own right but rather the neutral executor of plans made by others. This formal theory of the bureaucracy is of course a myth. It is a myth which serves several purposes, but it does not help in a realistic description of the decision-making process. The fact is that in all countries the bureaucracy is one of the important actors in the making of governmental decisions; in some systems the bureaucrats are the leading actors, and in most systems their power as decision-makers would seem to be increasing.[28]

A major question not raised in this chapter concerns the extent to which senior Yugoslav civil servants possess a clearly defined "mentality" or "ideology" and in what ways, if any, their attitudes differ from those of elected legislative representatives. It will remain impossible to adequately understand the political influence of administrators as a group unless it can be determined whether such officials share a distinctive outlook regarding specific issues, in what ways they have actually sought to advance their interests, and how successful such methods have been in attaining desired goals.

NOTES: CHAPTER FIVE

1. See Carl Beck, "Bureaucracy and Political Development in Eastern Europe," *Bureaucracy and Political Development,* ed. Joseph La Palombara (Princeton: Princeton University Press, 1963), 281-282, and in the same volume, Merle Fainsod, "Bureaucracy and Modernization: The Russian and Soviet Case," *Bureaucracy and Political Development,* 233-267. On the political role and influence of the state bureaucracy in various communist systems, see also the articles by A. Barnett, Carol Beck, Ezra Vogel, and Joseph Berliner, *Frontiers of Development Administration,* ed. Fred Riggs (Durham, N.C.: Duke University Press, 1970), 415-436, 437-455, 556-568, 569-600, Paul Hollander, "Politicized Bureaucracy: The Soviet Case," *Newsletter on Comparative Studies of Communism,* IV, No. 3 (May, 1971), 12-22.

2. Carl Beck has argued that the role of the state bureaucracy in the political process of East European countries is likely to increase, and "that members of the state bureaucracy will tend toward advocacy roles in regard to innovative proposals." In Beck's view, however, "the available evidence suggests that the state bureaucracy has not played a very significant or innovative part in Eastern European political developments. When members of the state bureaucracy were involved and took an innovative position they did so as advocates rather than as initiators." "Unfortunately," he adds, "we do not have available to us any surveys of the perspectives of state bureaucrats. A body of case studies identifying and categorizing participants in the decision-making process is also not available. Almost all studies of politics in Eastern Europe focus on policy *outputs* rather than on policy-making processes." See Carl Beck, "Bureaucratic Conservatism and Innovation in Eastern Europe," *Comparative Political Studies,* I, No. 2 (July, 1968), 282, 291, and note 7. For the utility of the "Western model of modern bureaucracy" in the study of administrative behaviour in a community policy see Jerry Hough, "The Bureaucratic Model and the Nature of the Soviet System," *Journal of Comparative Administration,* V, No. 2 (August, 1973), 134-167.

3. Leon Gerškovič, *Državna uprava* (Belgrade: Savez udruženja pravnika Jugoslavije, 1956), 15. For a discussion of the change in the relationship between the party and governmental institutions in Yugoslavia, see Paul Shoup, "Problems of Party Reform in

Lenard J. Cohen

Yugoslavia," *American Slavic and Eastern European Review*, XVIII, No. 3 (October, 1959), 334-350, George Zaninovich, "Yugoslav Party Evolution: Moving Beyond Institutionalization," *Politics in Modern Society: The Dynamics of Established One-Party Systems*, eds. Samuel Huntingdon and Clement Moore (New York: Basic Books, 1970), 484-508, Winston Fisk, "The Constitutional Movement in Yugoslavia: A Preliminary Survey," *Slavic Review*, XXX, No. 2 (June, 1971), 277-298. A good summary of the Yugoslav view of these developments is found in Najdan Pašić, "Self-Management as an Integral Political System," *Yugoslav Workers' Self-Management*, ed. M. Broekmeyer (Dordrecht, Holland: D. Reidel Publishing Co., 1970), 1-29.

4. Fred Riggs, "Bureaucratic Politics in Comparative Perspective," *Journal of Comparative Administration I*, No. 1 (May, 1969), 31.

5. See Alexander Stojanović, *Uloga funkcionera i upravnih stručnjaka u razovju javne uprave* (Belgrade: Savez udruženja pravnika Jugoslavija, 1965). An excellent analysis of pre-1952 party control over the state administration based on official sources is Branko Petranović, *Politička i ekonomska osnova narodna vlasti u Jugoslaviji za vreme obnove* (Belgrade: Institut za savremenu istoriju, 1969), 256-278.

6. For a more detailed analysis of Yugoslav parliamentary development see Chapter 4 and Lenard J. Cohen, "Conflict Management and Institution-Building in Socialist Yugoslavia: The Role of the Parliamentary System," *Legislatures in Plural Societies: The Search for Cohesion in National Development*, ed. Albert Eldridge (Durham, N.C.: Duke University Press, 1977).

7. See note 13 in Chapter 4.

8. Ferrel Heady, *Public Administration: A Comparative Perspective* (Englewood Cliffs, N.J.: Prentice-Hall, 1966), 98.

9. The concept of "role" or "role-orientation" as used in this chapter refers to "that organized sector of an actor's orientation which constitutes and defines his participation in an interactive process. It involves a set of complementary expectations concerning his own actions and those of others with whom he interacts. Both the actor and those with whom he interacts possess these expectations." Talcott Parsons and Edward Shils (eds.), *Toward a General Theory*

of Action (New York: Harper and Row, 1962), 23. This chapter is concerned with the role-orientation of Yugoslav federal administrators as it relates to their responsibilities in the legislative process.

10. *Normativna delatnost društveno-političkih zajednica: priručnik za kadrove u državnim organima i stručnim službama posebno opštinskim* (Belgrade: Republički zavod za javnu upravu, 1967), 148-149.

11. See, for example, Raymond Hopkins, *Political Roles in a New State: Tanzania's First Decade* (New Haven: Yale University Press, 1971), especially Chapter 4, "The Role of the Administrator," 108-139, Richard Harris, "The Effects of Political Change on the Role Set of the Senior Bureaucrats in Ghana and Nigeria," *Administrative Science Quarterly, XIII*, No. 3 (December, 1968), 386-401, Robert Putnam, "The Political Attitudes of Senior Civil Servants in Western Europe: A Preliminary Report," *British Journal of Political Science*, III, Part 3 (July, 1973), 257-290, Jerry Weaver, "Role Expectations of Latin American Bureaucrats," *Journal of Comparative Administration*, IV, No. 2 (August, 1972), 133-166.

12. For a discussion of the difference between "policy counsel" and "program formulation" as alternative bases for administrative influence in the policy-making process see Fritz Moorstein-Marx, "The Higher Civil Service as an Action Group in Western Political Development," *Bureaucracy and Political Development*, ed. Joseph La Palombara (Princeton: Princeton University Press, 1963), 77-85. See also Hahn Been-Lee, "The Role of the Higher Civil Service Under Rapid Social and Political Change," *Development Administration in Asia*, ed. Edward Weidner (Durham, N.C.: Duke University Press, 1970).

13. Ljubomir Mijatovic, "Predstavinicki organi i uprava," *Nedeljne Informativne Novine*, (December 24, 1967), 4. See also Chapter 4.

14. For the use of data on interaction to explain administrative-legislative relations, see Victor A. Olorunsola, "Patterns of Interaction Between Bureaucratic and Political Leaders: A Case Study," *Journal of Developing Areas*, III (October, 1968), 51-68, Norman Thomas, "Bureaucratic-Congressional Interaction and the Politics of Education," *Journal of Comparative Administration*, II, No. 1 (1970), 52-80.

15. The "universe list" of Yugoslav opinion makers was initially defined in terms of a set of positions in six institutional sectors: federal legislators, federal administrators, federal party and mass organization leaders, economic leaders, mass communicators, and intellectuals. It comprised a total of 1,413 positions occupied by 1,290 individuals. A sample of 517 individuals occupying 569 of these positions was interviewed in the period from March 1968 to January 1969, and included the two subgroups analyzed in this chapter. The choices made outside the "universe list" generally refer to individuals nominated by the respondents who hold positions on the republican-provincial and communal levels of authority. As this chapter is concerned primarily with administrative-legislative relations on the federal level, a detailed analysis of these "out of universe" responses is not included.

16. During the period in which the survey was carried out (1968-1969), the term "political chambers" refers to the Federal Chamber and the Chamber of Nationalities. Of the 65 deputies interviewed, 83 percent were members of those chambers, (which were composed almost entirely of professional politicians).

17. Charles Kadushin and Peter Abrams, "Social Structure of Yugoslavia Opinion-Makers'," *Opinion-Making Elites in Yugoslavia*, eds. Allen Barton *et. al.* (New York: Praeger, 1973), 164.

18. In reporting to the Federal Assembly on parliamentary development between 1963 and 1967, its president, Edward Kardelj, emphasized that: "deputies increasingly developed into independent and responsible factors in Assembly work at all stages .... But I must again repeat: this role of deputies would be unthinkable if they did not at the same time rely on the social role of the League of Communists as the most important factor at the present level of the development of socialist social relations .... Naturally the Federal Assembly reached its decisions independently, but these decisions would not have been arrived at in a democratic way, would not have relected the real needs of society and have been successfully implemented had it not been for the mobilizing and integrating activity of the Leage of Communists, the Socialist Alliance, trade unions, and other factors of socialist consciousness. For the entire structure and method of work of the Assembly has been devised so that is successful action necessarily required maximum reliance on these factors." Edward Kardelj, *Neka pitanja daljeg razvoja skupštinskog i političkog sistem* (Belgrade: Sekretarijat za

informativnu službu Savezne Skupština, 1967), Sveska 4, Kolo IV, 22-23.

19. Allen Barton, "Determinants of Leadership Attitudes in a Socialist Society," *Opinion-Making Elites in Yugoslavia*, eds. Allen Barton, *et. al.* (New York: Praegar, 1973), 237.

20. Marin Cetinić, "Uvid i kontrola koristenja i raspolaganja društvenim sredstvima," *Simpozijum Savezne Skupštine: Sistem finansiranja i poreski sistem, Referati*, (Belgrade: Kultura, 1970), 92.

21. See for example, Slavko Miloslavevski and Milan Nedkov, *Uloga i položaj državne uprave u našem samoupravnom društvu* (Belgrade: Jugoslavenski savez udruženja za upravne nauke i praksu, 1970), Veljko Mratović, "Uloga organa državne uprave u ostvarivanju funkcija skupstina društveno-političkih zajednica," *Naša zakonitost*, XXV, No. 1 (January, 1971), 7-15, and Branislav Marković, "Uprava i zakonodavni proces federacija," *Karakter i funkcije federacije u procesu konstituisanja samoupravnog društva*, ed. Ljubiša Stankov (Belgrade: Institut za političke studije, VŠPN, 1968), Političke sveske IV/I, 323-330.

22. *Dokumentacija Savezne Skupštine Prilog 4*, (Belgrade, February, 1969).

23. *Borba*, December 17, 1967, 4. Yugoslav studies of political decision-making at the republican and local levels have also revealed the dominant position of administrative agencies in initiating laws and policies. For example, in the entire six-year period from 1963 to 1969 only one deputy in the Serbian Assembly initiated a legislative proposal. See Miodrag Zečević, *Skupština SR Srbije u periodu 1963-1969 godine* (Belgrade: Institut za političke studije Fakulteta političkih nauka, 1972), 301-309. See also Angel Klisinski, *Uloga organa uprave, odnoso stručnih služba radnih organizacija u normativnoj delatnosti skupštine društveno-političkih zajednica odnoso organa upravljanja radnih organizacija* (Belgrade: Jugoslovenski savez udruzenja za upravne nauke i praksu, 1969), *Žena: odbornika i zastupnika* (Zagreb: Konferencija za društvena aktivnost žena Hrvatska, 1969), Niko Toš, *Pregled skupnih podatkov iz raziskave poslanska aktivnost* (Ljubljana: Visoka šola za sociologijo politične vede in novinarstvo-Centar za raziskovanje javnog mneja, 1968), 36.

24. The prominent Yugoslav economist and former government advisor on planning, Branko Horvat, observed: "As things presently stand, the federal government, the Federal Assembly, the trade unions, the Central Committee, and the Economic Chamber do not have a single long-term arrangement with any scientific organization in the country for the investigation of fundamental problems within the jurisdiction of these leading bodies and social organizations. Moreover, up to now all suggestions and initiatives of scientific organizations in this sense have been unsuccessful." Branko Horvat, "Integriranost Jugoslovenski privrede i samoupravne dogovoranje," *Ekonomist*, XXII, No. 2 (1969), 389-390. While admitting that many leading economic specialists have been awarded posts in the Federal Administration, Horvat has argued nevertheless that these men "are in positions which require from them a specific conduct and discipline, and second when somebody is an official, he has no possibility for dealing with research ... *scientific workers engaged in administration are not the same as science in administration.*" [Author's emphasis]. *Privredni Pregled*, April 21, 1969, 3.

25. There are, of course, important exceptions as was pointed out in Chapter 4. Thus, in each session of the Federal Assembly there have been a few so-called freelance federal legislators who have subjected executive and administrative officials to extensive criticism and interrogation. The general difficulties of legislative control over administration described above have continued through the 1980's. As one analysis put it: "the small influence exercised by delegates and delegations on decision-making in assemblies relative to other actors is most likely the result of the excessive complexity of the delegate system which prevents electors from exercising any major influence ... intervention by administrative and executive organs appears to be objectively indispensable and in some cases this can even lead to the monopolization of decision-making." Milan Jovanović, "Elections for the Assemblies of Socio-Political Communities Held in 1982," *Yugoslav Survey*, XXIV (November, 1983), 46. The federal administration continued to grow in size during the 1970's and 1980's, increasing from 10,286 employees in June 1974 to 15,460 in June 1982. As one observer remarked: "the state withers, but the administration also grows and is strengthened." Milan Miljević, "Jedinstvo vlasti i samoupravljanje," *Arhiv za pravne i društvene nauka*, No. 1 (January-March, 1985), 33.

26. Professor Eugun Pusić has also pointed to the weak position of deputies who are members of the functionally specialized Chamber of Producers when they are dealing on the communal level with officials from the "administrative apparatus." See Eugun Pusić, *Samoupravljanje: Prilozi teoriji i praktični problemi* (Zagreb, "Narodne Novine," 1968), 218 and 224. During the early 1970's, parliamentary deputies in the functionally specialized chambers of the Federal Assembly (at the time the so-called Chambers of the Working Communities, the Economic Chambers, the Social-Health Chamber, etc.), were best qualified to deal competently with administrative officials concerning complex policy issues. These chambers, however, had the least amount of formal authority to exercise political control over the state administration. Moreover, the highest rate of membership turnover occurred in the functionally specialized chambers thereby preventing technically qualified legislators from developing an intimate familiarity with various policy questions. In contrast, the "political chambers" of the Federal Assembly (the Federal Chamber and Chamber of Nationalities), which had primary responsibility for the control of federal administrative officials (e.g., the power of appointment and dismissal), were composed almost entirely of older career politicians. Although considerably experienced in legislative assemblies at different levels of the federal system, these older members possessed neither technical education backgrounds, nor in many cases any form of higher education.

27. Hamdija Čemerlić, *Mesto i uloga odbora i komisija predstavnickih tela*, ed. Borislav Blagojević (Belgrade: Saveza udruženja pravnika Jugoslavija, 1969), 237.

28. Wallace Sayre, "Bureaucracies: Some Contrasts in Systems," *Readings in Comparative Public Administration*, ed. Nimrod Raphaeli (Boston: Allyn and Bacon, 1967), 347-348.

CHAPTER 6

JUDICIAL ELITES IN YUGOSLAVIA: THE PROFESSIONALIZATION OF POLITICAL JUSTICE

The judicial sector of the state bureaucracy, and the elite bureaucrats who function in that sector, are among the most neglected topics of political research on Yugoslavia and Eastern Europe. The absence of research on the judicial bureaucracy can be traced to a number of factors. First, most Western studies of communist party-states have treated the legal process in general and judicial behaviour in particular, as auxiliary and highly manipulated aspects of overall party control unworthy of systematic analysis. The basically accurate perception of judicial institutions as "transmission belts" and "guardians" of regime policy during the "mobilization phase" of communist party rule has tended to direct scholarly attention away from the areas of legal and judicial development. A small and growing body of valuable research has focused on communist legal development in the post-totalitarian or post-mobilization period, but most such work concentrates on the explication of laws, Marxist jurisprudence, and constitutional change, rather than on the political dimension of legal systems.[1] The few political research studies which do touch upon communist legal systems, tend to be concerned with quasi-judicial or extra-judicial themes such as political dissent (and especially prominent dissenters), the secret police, and various forms of political arbitrariness and corruption. Thus, despite communist Yugoslavia's very early departure from conventional Marxist-Leninist models of development, the role of the legal system and judicial institutions in that reorientation have received very little attention.

Lenard J. Cohen

Yugoslavia's cultural and territorial diversity has also impeded foreign research on the country's legal development. Thus, during much of the country's history, scholars have been faced with a complex and analytically formidable mosaic of legal traditions, institutions and practices. For example, throughout the life of the interwar Yugoslav state (1918-1941) several quite distinct "legal regimes" existed alongside one another in the area of civil law: in Serbia and Macedonia (then known as "South Serbia") civil law followed the Serbian Civil Code enacted in 1844 (based on the French Code Civil) along with an admixture of German and Austrian law; in Montenegro the General Property Code of 1888 was utilized together with a rationalized form of various customary (i.e., tribal) laws; in Slovenia and Dalmatia the Austrian Civil Code of 1811 as amended during the course of the First World War was adopted; in Croatia the same code without the wartime amendments was followed; in Vojvodina, Hungarian law (customary law) was utilized; and in Bosnia-Hercegovina, both Austro-Hungarian and Moslem law were practiced. Attempts at legal unification were only partially realized by 1941 and even the important area of criminal law was not standardized until 1929. Such traditions and diversity, although considerably diminished by trends since the Second World War, continue to exercise an influence on legal subcultures and legal behaviour in Yugoslavia.[2]

Finally, since 1945 Yugoslavia's fluid and highly innovative political evolution has itself inhibited research on legal and judicial development. Thus, not only has the occurrence of frequent changes in the country's political climate resulted in several distinct stages of Yugoslav communist development, but also the political leadership's penchant for institutional experimentation and reorganization has made it difficult to conduct longitudinal research on various aspects of legal and judicial development. Moreover, the same pattern of experimentation has tended to direct foreign attention away from legal development and toward other interesting features of the Yugoslav scene such as self-management, nonalignment, federalism, and mechanisms for popular political participation. For all these reasons, legal and judicial development remain very underdeveloped areas of foreign scholarship on Yugoslavia. This situation has also prevented many valuable scholarly Yugoslav contributions concerning legal development from receiving adequate attention.

In an effort to redress the research gap described above, this chapter will examine the characteristics and role of judicial elites in Yugoslavia during successive phases in that country's political development. While the chapter follows a basically chronological pattern, three major dimensions of judicial development are examined during each period surveyed: 1) the social composition and recruitment of judicial personnel; 2) the role of judicial elites as actors in the political system; and 3) the relationship of the judiciary to other major political actors, with special attention devoted to the judiciary's political autonomy and political influence. The primary focus of this analysis is the Yugoslav judicial elite over the last 40 years of socialist development. It is

The Socialist Pyramid: Elites and Power in Yugoslavia

useful, however, to begin this discussion with an examination of judicial development in the pre-communist period.[3]

The Precommunist Period: Legal Anthropology and Legal Federalism

At its inception in 1918, the Yugoslav state contained a variety of different legal systems. Consequently, the role and recruitment of the judiciary and also the relationship of judges to the political order varied significantly from one section of the country to another. Two Amercian students of public law and civil administration who surveyed the Yugoslav regional situation in 1928 observed that although the interwar Yugoslav Kingdom may have been a unitary state, its judicial system exhibited *a de facto* "legal federalism," and functioned as a "marvelous chaos." The same authors also observed that "the laws, both material and formal, substantive and objective, the organization of the courts and the methods for the execution of judgements, and the status of judges reveal extensive differences .... As if to reinforce the tenacity of local law, the law schools of the several sections, naturally concerned with practice rather than with theories and hopes, teach the law of their respective jurisdictions."[4] In areas of northwestern Yugoslavia such as Croatia and Slovenia, which were under Hapsburg rule until 1918, judicial reforms reflected the bureaucratic formalism, basic efficiency, and "vigorous legality" typical of the Austro-Hungarian legal pattern.[5] In the most ethnically diverse sections of the new country, it was possible to come across two or more varieties of law courts in the same administrative district. For example, in Bosnia-Hercegovina, an area with interspersed Moslem and Christian populations, residual Ottoman legal institutions coexisted after 1918 with more recent practices imposed during Austro-Hungarian rule.[6] In the economically underdeveloped areas of Southeastern Yugoslavia such as Montenegro and Kosovo, a dual legal order also usually prevailed with parallel courts based on either modernized Slavic tribal customs (with selected West European legal additions) or Moslem judicial practices inherited from the Ottoman period.

Montenegrin legal traditions provide an interesting illustration of the "tribal" pattern of justice inherited by the new Yugoslav state.[7] The dominant influence on the 19th century Montenegrin legal system was the *bratstvo* (literally brotherhood), a village settlement composed of individual households. Each *bratstvo* was headed by a civil leader who presided over a group of elected leading men from the village. Juridical functions for each Montenegrin *bratstvo* were based on oral traditions as interpreted by judges elected on a yearly basis at an assembly of all *bratstvo* members. The reputation of a judicial candidate was closely scrutinized, and as one visitor to a Montenegrin *bratstvo* pointed out, the criteria utilized in judicial recruitment were quite diverse: "As judge a man is chosen who is strong, has many friends, and is a good shot."⁸ Judges in each *bratstvo* had the final say in adjudicating the transgressions of its members, although (in the 1870's) the *bratstvo* was obliged to ratify its choice of judges with Montenegro's ruling prince at the capital city of Cetinje. Judges also travelled to the capital for general meetings which served to bring together all of Montenegro's judges, and established a communication link between the central government and the citizens of what was essentially a tribal principality. Tribal self-rule and traditional legal practices in Monetengro were slowly eroded by more secularized and centralizing methods introduced in the latter half of the 19th century, but on the eve of the first World War the region's ruler, Prince Nikola (1841-1921), still dispensed his own brand of personal justice under an ancient elm tree in Cetinje.

Among the various regional legal traditions that existed in interwar Yugoslavia, the customs and legal processes practiced in Serbia were the most important and influential. Having extracted themselves from the grip of Ottoman political control by force of arms and diplomacy in the mid-19th century, the Serbs had acquired considerable experience in self-rule by 1918, and could also take the most credit for the unification of the South Slav peoples into a single state. As was shown in Chapter Two, such political experience together with their position as the largest demographic group in the new Kingdom contributed to the political hegemony of the Serbian elite and Serbian institutions throughout the interwar period. Although early Serbian legal development bore a close similarity to simultaneous trends in Montenegro, the Serbian case quickly assumed a more complex and significant role. Thus, Serbian judicial evolution before 1918 was characterized by constant fluctuation between tendencies toward the development of an independent judiciary, and counter-pressures - usually from more aggressive and dictatorial rulers - to impose political control over the legal sector. As early as 1830 the President of Belgrade's Magistrate Court, Vuk Karadžić (a man later to emerge as one of Serbia's most prominent literary figures), found himself at odds with Prince Miloš Obrenović over the question of judicial autonomy. Miloš, with a disdain for due process, empowered the Chief of the Belgrade Police to attend the meetings of the court, personally sign the court minutes, and take measures without consulting the magistrates against "persons suspicious from a political point of view." The police chief was also authorized to monitor the conversations and movements of political suspects, as well as to use contacts to "find out people's secret thoughts and see that they did not disturb the public peace."⁹ These and other arbitrary measures essentially reduced Serbian judges to powerless figureheads. Although at one point Miloš asked Vuk to help draft a new legal code for Serbia based on the Code Napoleon, the project was soon shelved in favour of less democratic Austrian models. Two months after becoming Chief Magistrate in 1830, Vuk decided that the job was not sufficiently lucrative and asked to be pensioned off. Under the circumstances, Vuk claimed, one could find someone in practically every village to perform the role of President of the Court.[10]

When a more democratic constitution was forced upon him in 1838 - requiring among other things that state officials not meddle in the work of the courts and that judges could not be dismissed except by due process - Miloš chose to abdicate (twenty years later he was called back for two more years of service). While the role of the judiciary considerably improved after the new constitutionalist regime revised its civil codes in 1844 and 1853, the matter of judicial independence was by no means fully resolved.[11] In 1864, for example, an interesting challenge to judicial independence arose when the Supreme Court acquitted a group of individuals charged with plotting to assassinate the ruler. The members of the Court ruled that while a conspiracy was punishable, mere talk of a conspiracy was not an offense. Deciding that the acquittal was unjustified, the government of Prince Michael responded by putting five members of the Court on trial for malfeasance. Four of the accused judges were sentenced to three years imprisonment, and the fifth received a two-year sentence. The affair of the "Destruction of the Supreme Court" again illustrated the fragility of judicial independence as a norm in Serbian political life.[12] It was not until 1881 that a Law on Judges, following French and Belgian models, established a judiciary that was independent of the executive branch, a provision which was further institutionalized through the Constitutions of 1888, 1901, and 1903. Serbian political life continued to be volatile, but when the Kingdom entered the broader union of South Slav peoples in 1918, the idea of judicial independence from political control enjoyed broad support in both general public opinion and professional legal circles.

Upon its establishment in 1918, the Kingdom of the Serbs, Croats and Slovenes fashioned its own "national" juridical institutions above and around the mosaic of traditional legal processes found in the new state. The Constitution of 1921, for example, provided for a Court of Cassation residing in Zagreb, Courts of Appeal, courts of first instance, and *Sheriat* courts for family and inheritance affairs of the Moslem population. Judges were appointed by the King and enjoyed permanent tenure (Article 112). Despite this new structure, however, regional legal arrangements continued to predominate throughout the interwar period. A Ministry of the Unification of Laws was established, but it was abolished in 1925 due to its inactivity. The more centralized royal dictatorship established by King Alexander in 1929 made some progress in the matter of codification and consolidation of the legal system (after a decade of lethargy a unified criminal law was established and adopted in two months), but the country's *de facto* legal federalism remained largely intact. Under the authoritarian Constitution of 1931, judicial authority technically remained vested in independent courts and judges were deemed irremovable, the article on irremovability, however, not coming into effect for five years. Thus, until

1938 judges were to be appointed and retired by the King, who under special emergency powers could impose measures independently of "constitutional or legal norms." Despite such formal acknowledgement of judicial autonomy, under King Alexander's "police dictatorship," the position of the judiciary was more akin to that found during the absolutist periods of Serbian political history.

In August 1939, on the eve of World War II and under pressure to reach a compromise for the long-festering "Croatian question," the Yugoslav regime adopted new constitutional provisions granting Croatia (and potentially other major regions) increased control over its own regional affairs. From the point of view of judicial development, the most interesting aspect of such belated reform was the provision for a new Constitutional Court to be established in Zagreb. The Court was intended to adjudicate conflict of competence between the central government and the new regional administration of Croatia. The war and dismemberment of Royal Yugoslavia intervened, however, before this constitutional court was even established. It would be a quarter century before a similar judicial body with a mandate to resolve conflicts between the central and regional jurisdictions was created.

Ironically, the legal fragmentation and inertia of the interwar state contributed to some degree of ethnic representativeness in the judicial bureaucracy, at least with respect to the largest nationalities. An examination of 1937 data on the ethnic composition of over 2,000 Yugoslav judges in the regular court system (Table 6.1) reveals that the three principle "peoples of the state," i.e., Serbs, Croats, and Slovenes, were proportionally well represented in the legal system. As in most sectors of the bureaucracy and political life, the Serbs (a group which at that time statistically included Montenegrins and Macedonians) were overrepresented, but at least in the regular court structure not to a very great extent.[13] A more serious flaw in the ethnic composition of the interwar judiciary was the underrepresentation of the country's smaller nationalities. Especially striking in this regard was the virtual exclusion of the Moslem population, a group which included Albanians, Turks, and a large part of the population in Bosnia-Hercegovina.

Serbian overrepresentation and minority underrepresentation in the legal system were most excessive in the prosecutorial organs of the state, and in the ethnically unbalanced structure of the military courts. Approximately 84 percent of the judges in military courts were Serbian, a figure which corresponds closely to the very dominant Serbian presence in the officer corps. Serbian judges also dominated the State Court for the Defence of the State, a special tribunal created to control political criminality. Not coincidentally, non-Serbs were the major source of anti-regime dissidence and also the major target of regime repression. This conclusion is supported by data on the religious composition of individuals sentenced for crimes against the state between 1929 and 1938 (Table 6.2). Croats and other Roman Catholics made up between roughly half to three-quarters of those sentenced for political crimes, although

The Socialist Pyramid: Elites and Power in Yugoslavia

Table 6.1
The Ethnic Composition of Judges and Prosecutors in Yugoslavia, 1937 (%)

Ethnic Groups	Yugoslav Population (1921)	Judges and Judicial Officers of Regular District and Regional Courts	Judges of the State Court for Defense of the State	Judges of the Military Courts	State Prosecutors	Judges and Judicial Personnel in Training (Pripravnici)
Serbs	48.0[a]	55.7	68.8	83.7	67.4	78.9
Croats	23.0	31.4	25.0	9.5	21.7	12.5
Slovenes	8.5	9.3	6.2	4.1	7.2	5.2
Moslems[b]	11.2	2.6	-	-	1.0	1.7
Others	9.3	10.0	-	2.7	2.7	1.6
Total	100.0	100.0	100.0	100.0	100.0	100.0
(Number)	(13.9 M)	(2061)	(16)	(147)	(221)	(1214)

[a] The data for "Serbs" includes all members of the Orthodox religious community in Yugoslavia during 1921, i.e., Serbs, Montenegrins, and Macedonians.
[b] "Moslems" as used here is based on religious affiliation and includes members of the Turkish, Albanian, and Bošnjak ethnic groups.
Source: R. Bićanić, *Ekonomska podloga hrvatskog pitanja* (Zagreb: Stjepan Vidović, 1938), pp. 73-74.

Table 6.2
Political Crime by Religion, 1929-1938 (%)

Religion	Total Population (1921 Census)	Total Crime 1929	Total Crime 1938	Political Criminals by Year 1929	1930	1931	1932	1933	1934	1935	1936	1937	1938
Orthodox	48.6	55.5	48.9	11.6	36.2	24.8	30.8	20.1	19.2	23.7	38.9	36.5	22.1
Roman Catholic	37.5	31.4	42.3	81.8	52.9	67.1	60.7	73.2	75.7	65.6	45.9	52.3	65.0
Greek Catholic	0.3	0.2	0.3	-	0.2	-	0.3	0.2	-	0.2	0.5	0.7	-
Protestant	1.7	0.5	0.9	0.4	1.7	1.9	1.3	0.3	0.6	2.4	1.1	0.9	0.6
Moslem	11.2	10.2	7.2	3.7	5.7	3.8	5.2	4.1	3.3	6.7	6.5	6.3	5.2
Jewish	0.5	0.2	0.4	0.8	2.8	1.0	1.8	0.8	1.9	1.4	7.1	1.4	1.0
Others	0.2	0.2	0.0	1.7	0.6	1.0	-	0.9	-	-	-	-	0.2
Unknown	-	1.8	0.0	-	-	0.5	0.3	0.5	-	-	-	1.9	-
Total	100	100	100	100	100	100	100	100	100	100	100	100	100
(Number)	(13,934,038)	(23,363)	(19,587)	(242)	(473)	(420)	(387)	(661)	(667)	(506)	(368)	(575)	(515)

Source: L. Cohen, "Political Criminality in Yugoslavia: 1918-1985" (unpublished paper).

that religious group only constituted about 38 percent of the country's population. Political criminality for those of the Orthodox religious group (including Serbs, Montenegrins, and Macedonians) was far below the group's representation in the general population (or among those sentenced for all forms of crime). One interwar Croatian political criminal proved especially defiant and would ultimately lead a wartime movement to destroy the royal political system. Refusing to justify his actions before a Zagreb court in November 1928, Josip Broz Tito explained to the presiding judge that the advent of communism would eliminate the need for laws to repress political crime:

> *The Presiding Judge*: Have you ever heard of the Law for the Protection of the State?
>
> *The Accused, Josip Broz (Tito)*: I have heard of it, but I have not read it. It did not interest me.
>
> *The Presiding Judge:* Do you know that it forbids all communist propoganda?
>
> *Broz*: I do. But it is only a temporary law, a law brought in by one class against another, a law that will be swept away.[14]

The Early Communist Period (1945-1950): People's Judges and Revolutionary Justice

Formerly the victims of repression by the interwar judicial elite, Yugoslavia's postwar communist leaders soon found themselves in need of mechanisms for the protection of their new state. Faced with legal chaos and a legal vacuum left by the war, the communist regime quickly moved to establish its own legal structure and methods. At the local governmental level, People's Courts were established to administer post-revolutionary communist justice. Composed mainly of party members and their wartime Partisan allies, these courts relied upon the "achievements of the National Liberation War" rather than the principles of natural law as the basis for legal interpretation. As one of Tito's comrades later remarked, the laws or the "achievements" of the communist-led Partisan struggle were interpreted by judges "according to common sense and their conception of justice, which is incomparably higher than the conception of the former representatives of authority, though they [the new judges] are only half-literate peasants."[15] When dealing with the political opponents of the new communist state the people's judges were expected to render a quick verdict that would correspond to the regime's immediate goals, namely, "an assault on the main capitalist positions" in the economy through trials of "felonious reactionaries." During this period, as one Yugoslav professor later wrote, "laws and lawyers were an obstacle to direct revolutionary action. Law with its criteria for equality and long procedures hinder the revolutionary élan."[16] The same cases were sometimes tried several times before the same people's court until the proper verdict was obtained. Another Yugoslav specialist put the regime's conception of justice in succinct terms: "the law is that which is useful to the National Liberation Struggle, and crime is that which is opposed to it."[17]

Judges in the People's Courts were either permanent personnel (a still very inexperienced and poorly educated "professional" group), or so-called "judge-jurors." This latter group (sometimes classed "provisional" or "lay" judges) was made up of citizens from the general community, but had no similarity to a Western style jury. Lower level courts since 1945 usually consist of one judge and two judge-jurors. Under a 1945 law all citizens who had the right to vote might be elected as judges or judge-jurors. The right to vote was given to all Yugoslavs over 18 years of age, *or* participants in the Partisan struggle regardless of their age.[18]

The judicial structure above the people's courts consisted of a simple hierarchy of criminal and civil courts with each succeeding higher court having supervisory functions over the courts below. The structure was as follows: the Federal Supreme Court, the supreme courts of the six republics and the autonomous region of Vojvodina (the highest court in the autonomous region of Kosovo-Metohija at this time was the Serbian Supreme Court), the regional courts, and the district courts. At each tier of the federal structure judges were chosen by the legislative assemblies at the corresponding level. This process ensured strict party control over judicial recruitment since at the time Yugoslav parliamentary bodies were composed largely of professional party and state officials directly responsible and monitored by the central party apparatus.

In the first years after attaining power, the central party appartus took a special interest in the working and staffing of the judicial organs. As one official party historian put it:

> The organizational and personnel improvement of the judicial network and composition was located under the influence of the Party through the Commission for the Construction of the People's Authority attached to the CK KPJ [Central Committee of the Yugoslav Communist Party]. The concrete work of the Party and Judicial Administration from 1945 to 1947 involved the attainment of greater functional efficacy in their various tasks: the establishment of a network of courts, the correct proportion of specialized judges, raising the judges' level of competence, and cleansing the courts of judges who had unfriendly orientations toward the new order, or who were incompetent.[19]

Although the Yugoslav judicial system in the immediate postwar period was largely inspired by the Soviet (Stalinist) model, some interesting differences existed between the two communist systems. Yugoslav judges, for example, were appointed for an indefinite period of service rather than for a fixed term and they remained in office until removed. Moreover, while the lowest Soviet courts were directly elected, in Yugoslavia all courts were elected indirectly, i.e., by representative assemblies. The significance of such technical differences was reduced, however, by the similiarities existing between the Office of the Public Prosecutor in Yugoslavia, and the Soviet Procuracy.

Unlike judges who were chosen at each government level by legislative bodies, the prosecutorial branch of the Yugoslav judicial system was composed of a corps of officials structured in a strictly hierarchical manner. The Public Prosecutor at the federal level was appointed by the federal legislature, *but* appointments of all lower ranking public prosecutors throughout the country were made by the federal prosecutor's office (as in the USSR). Courts at each tier of the Yugoslav judiciary acted upon charges laid by the office of the public prosecutor which functioned as the "executive organ of the government for the liquidation of its adversaries."[20] Prosecuting attorneys were closely connected with, and often recruited from the Intelligence Services, the Military, and the Secret Police. As early as May 1944, Tito had established a "Department for the Protection of the People" attached to the Provisional Ministry of Defence. It was this Department (better know by its abbreviation OZN-a, and later renamed the Administration of State Security or UDB-a) together with the Office of the Public Prosecutor and the courts which were the pillars of the post-revolutionary Yugoslav judicial system. Alleged opponents of the regime - many quite innocent it was later revealed - were routinely identified by the secret police, indicted by the public prosecutors, and convicted by the pliant judges and judge-jurors in the courts. The party leadership relied on the centralized prosecutorial service to ensure that the lay judge-jurors were not overshadowed by more experienced and, perhaps, more politically neutral judges:

> ... the competence of the lower courts was relatively weak, because it was a question of having judges on the side of the revolution, who were often without judicial experience; the development of the district prosecutorial network was needed to prevent judges from the people (judge-jurors) as a lay element finding themselves under the influence of professional judges.[21]

It was only in the wake of the Yugoslav conflict with the Soviet Union that a structural reorganization and more democratic reorientation of the Yugoslav judicial system was initiated. Ironically, this reorganization did not occur until after the Soviet-style judicial system which had been used to prosecute so many anti-communist "political criminals" was itself turned against thousands of Yugoslav communists charged with sympathizing with the Soviet Union.[22] A full account of the arrests, and often the brutalization of those former loyal communists would not be fully revealed, however, until after Tito's death.

Socialist Experimentation (1950-1966): Judicial Reforms and Illiberal Remnants

Changes in the administration of justice were an important facet of the distinctly Yugoslav road to socialism improvised by Tito and his colleagues in the early 1950's. Endeavouring to abandon Soviet-inspired "revolutionary étatism" as a mode of governance, the Yugoslav communists focused their energy on measures to prevent abuses of "socialist legality," and wherever possible to also reduce the influence of the centralized bureaucratic apparatus.

The regime touted the adoption of a new criminal code (1951) and new code of criminal procedure (1954) as steps to overcome the earlier arbitrariness by the courts and the police. The federal level Ministry of Justice was dissolved and its functions absorbed by a new Federal Supreme Court. This latter body was entrusted with the functioning of all other regular courts in the judicial system (which included in 1954, for example, the Supreme Courts of the six republics and the Province of Vojvodina, 63 county courts, and 354 district courts). The Federal Supreme Court was empowered to review issues being adjudicated in the lower courts, but it (and any other higher court) was prohibited from directly interfering in the judgments rendered by the lower courts. Judges at each tier of the reformed court system were elected by legislative assemblies at the parallel level of the federal system, but could only be recalled under unusual circumstances specified by law. Legislative election and recall allowed for continued, if more indirect, party supervision over the judicial selection process, but the normal permanence and independence of judges after their inital selection was strongly emphasized in statutes, regime pronouncements, and scholarly commentaries. Indeed, the 1954 Law on the Courts made it a punishable offence to subject judges or judge-jurors to any extra-judicial pressure.

Upgrading the professional qualifications of personnel in the judicial system was another important aspect of the Yugoslav reform undertaken in the 1950's. The wide latitude accorded to so many highly politicized judges, judge-jurors and public prosecutors during the immediate postwar years was considered responsible for much of the lawlessness and arbitrariness in the administration of justice. Official figues compiled in 1951 revealed striking deficiencies in the training of judges.[23] For example, in Bosnia-Hercegovina 110 out of 184 judges had received no legal training and three district court judges had only received elementary education. In Serbia two judges of a district court had only finished elementary school, and in the heavily Albanian Kosovo region of the Serbian Republic 65 judges (almost the entire judiciary), had only completed elementary school. In the more developed areas of the country such as Croatia, there was some improvement in the situation. The 1954 Law on Courts sought a remedy to the problem of unqualified judges by prescribing (Article 46) that future judges should be professional jurists with an academic degree from a law faculty. This provision was implemented gradually, as a new generation of lawyers viewed by the regime as more trustworthy began to emerge from Yugoslav universities.

The low educational level of judge-jurors (that is, lay judges), was a factor complicating the effort to enhance professionalism in judicial decision-making. Judge-jurors in this period were only required to be citizens over 27 years of age, without a criminal record, and with a general apptitude to perform "a judge's duties." Judge-jurors enjoyed equal voting rights with regular (professional) judges, and far outnumbered the latter officials in the judicial system. As a rule, professional judges wielded more influence in resolving legal issues and disputes before the court, but the judge-jurors nonetheless were often resented by those regular judges and specialists seeking higher professional and legal standards in the justice system. As one Yugoslav lawyer put it in 1958:

> ... [the judge-jurors] are undisciplined, do not regularly attend their judicial business, arrive late, are quickly tired and become disinterested after a few cases, lack professional knowledge, do not understand special terminology, be it legal or technological, industrial, commercial, etc., and yet they are equal to professional judges.[24]

At the beginning of 1962, 50,871 Yugoslav citizens were engaged as judge-jurors in the regular courts. Occupationally, the majority of judge-jurors were white collar employees (34 percent in district courts and 55 percent in regional courts), most of whom likely had some form of elementary or secondary education, followed in order of representation by smaller contingents of peasants, workers, and craftsmen. Women comprised approximately 12 percent of the judge-jurors. From the regime's perspective, the judge-jurors constituted an element of direct democracy in the legal process, bringing "everyday social life and its needs and interests closer to the professional judicial apparatus as part of the state apparatus in general."[25] It was also maintained that the role of judge-jurors had an educative function by allowing thousand of citizens to increase their knowledge through participation in the administration of justice. Even an official commentator had to concede, however, that "sometimes court presidents do not even brief the juror-judges" on the cases before them, and that the skills, attention span, and interests of the judge-jurors were frequently below standard.[26]

The judicial reform of the early 1950's also included a number of measures designed to somewhat depoliticize and curb the broad powers of Yugoslav public prosecutors. For example, prosecutors were no longer allowed to make arrests or conduct criminal investigations unless authorized to do so by the courts. The regular courts also assumed the task of pre-trial investigation which had previously been within the jurisdiction of the public prosecutor. The 1954 Law on the Public Prosecutor's Office also required future prosecutors to undergo legal training, and special courts were established to try cases of legal violations made by the prosecutors themselves. The statutory restriction of the public prosecutor to just another contending party in the legal process instead of the initiator, major agent, and preordained victor in that process (as he had been previously) provided an impetus to the resuscitation of the legal profession in Yugoslavia. The number of lawyers, which had dropped from 2,905 in 1939 to 1,908 in 1953, slowly increased to 2,348 in 1958, and 3,044 by 1970. The 1957 Law on Advocateship defined the lawyer's functions as a "public service," and most advocates were attached to various economic organizations and state institutions. A portion of the legal profession was able to practice as private counsel and had a reasonable chance - especially in non-political cases - to protect their clients' rights and interests. Those lawyers who had received their training in the pre-communist period naturally were most suspect by the regime and experienced the greatest difficulty working within the new legal framework.

The changes introduced in the Yugoslav judicial system described above resulted primarily from a new political climate initiated by the top leadership of the communist regime. Once the party organization decided to play a less direct and coercive role in the political system, an opportunity existed for a basic change in the country's legal system. The regime's commitment to a more consensual and evolutionary model of communist rule after 1950, for example, considerably narrowed the definition of what constituted an act of political criminality, and reduced the incidence of arbitrariness in the administration of justice. Such innovations did not, as some observers thought at the time, herald the disappearance of political intervention in the judicial system or the imminent withering away of state-sponsored political coercion and repression.[27] As Mose Pijade, one of the new regime's major institutional architects remarked in 1953: "we are letting power descend, but are not letting it go."[28]

Instead of eliminating the involvement of higher party and state officials in the judicial system, such activity simply became more indirect, selective, and focused upon certain areas of political opposition. The political "enemy" was no longer the entire "bourgeoisie," or the regime's wartime opponents, but rather certain types of anti-state dissidence as defined by those in top positions of political control. The regime's weapons for controlling and repressing such dissidence remained quite impressive, even after the judicial reforms of the 1950's and the adoption of other well-known facets of Yugoslav "national communism" (worker's self-management, nonalignment, etc.). For example, although considerably reformed, the Office of the Public Prosecutor remained one of the few hierarchically organized institutions in Yugoslavia until 1967. A further impetus to socialist legality and anti-hierarchical measures was generated by a new Constitution in 1963, but the Federal Public Prosecutor was still authorized to appoint his own deputies and in agreement with the republican executive councils, to appoint republic prosecutors. The police apparatus, UDB-a, under the control of top party and state functionary Alexander Ranković, also continued as a "sword" of the communist revolution, although its operation became more subtle, scientific, and secretive. Internment of pro-Soviet Yugoslavs and other regime opponents continued throughout the 1950's, often at the notorious Goli Otok (Naked Island) concentration camp in the Northern Adriatic. Approximately 12,000 political prisoners were sent to Goli Otok where they were subjected to brutal treatment as a means of "political rehabilitation." One top-ranking former communist who allegedly recommended that the camp be shut down claims that his initiative was opposed because allegedly there were too many pro-Soviet opportunists to process through the courts, and also that Tito "still had no confidence in the country's judiciary."[29]

The continued politicization of justice during the 1950's and early 1960's, as well as the very limited boundaries for political dissent, are clearly illustrated by the prominent cases of Milovan Djilas and Vladimir Dedijer. Djilas, as was shown in Chapter 1, incurred the wrath of his fellow comrades in the Politbureau by writing articles bluntly critical of the regime's foibles, and calling for more extensive democratization of the political system. One sector which Djilas believed was badly in need of reform was the judiciary. As he wrote in *Borba*:

> In my opinion the judiciary ... should be freed from the present interference of the Party in their work. Otherwise they will not be able to avoid (however good their intentions) the destruction of democracy, if they go on making their activities conform to political and ideological criteria or even local views. They must become representatives of the state and of the law - which means the people - and not of political interests and opinions inside the Party .... How much longer will we make use of ideological instead of legal arguments? How long will verdicts continue to be based on dialectical and historical materialism, and not the law?[30]

Unwilling to tone down his criticisms, even after being warned by the party leadership, Djilas was called before a plenary session of the Central Committee in early 1954, chastised, stripped of his party and state functions, and subsequently expelled from the party. Dedijer, who supported Djilas at the time, suffered the same fate.

Lenard J. Cohen

Almost one year after having been subjected to *party justice*, criminal charges were laid against Djilas for engaging in "hostile propaganda" against the regime. Dedijer, with intentional irony, hired the same lawyer who had defended Tito in 1928 against charges of violating the "Law for the Protection of the State." Djilas hired a lawyer from the prewar socialist party, an essentially "liberal" organization that had not condoned the communists' commitment to revolution. At an *in camera* trial lasting one day Djilas and Dedijer were both found guilty and given short suspended sentences as a further warning. Djilas' continued criticisms of Soviet and East European communism - even after Tito's rapprochment with the USSR in 1956 - became especially embarrassing to the Yugoslav regime. In November 1956, after publishing an article condemning Yugoslavia's support of Soviet intervention in Hungary, Djilas was sentenced to a three year jail term which he would serve in the same prison that he had been detained in before the war. "You are not the state," the trial judge reminded Djilas. "You seem unaware of the damage you've done to the Party."[31] Djilas was now on the receiving end of the very political justice he had earlier complained about from his position at the summit of the party.

Djilas was conditionally released from prison in January 1961, after signing a regime-drafted petition in which he promised to refrain from publishing hostile propaganda. Less than a year and a half later, Djilas was re-arrested, and in another secret trial, sentenced to five more years in prison. This time he was alleged to have revealed state secrets in a book which discussed early postwar conversations between Yugoslav officials and Stalin. According to a new paragraph that had been added to the Criminal Code - what one observer called the "lex Djilas" - it was an offence for former officials to reveal secrets dating from their earlier employment. Djilas was released at the end of 1966 and would continue to play an important, albeit indirect and unofficial, role in Yugoslav political life. Looking back at the period under discussion here, Djilas recently observed:

> I used to think that after 1950 Security and the party committees had stopped collaborating in handing down sentences for criminal offences. But while in prison I became convinced, both from conversations and from reading verdicts, that plenty of this kind of meddling continued. For the same deed, the compliant and the non-compliant got very different sentences.[32]

To a certain extent the Djilas-Dedijer affair was somewhat idiosyncratic, the institutionalized or bureaucratized revolution devouring its most gifted and obstreperous children. Aside from hard-core political opponents of the regime (such as supporters of the USSR) and more flagrant acts of dissent, the number of convictions for political criminality actually decreased significantly after 1950. Moreover, both restraints on prosecutors and opportunities for defense

The Socialist Pyramid: Elites and Power in Yugoslavia

lawyers noticeably increased in non-political cases. It was only after the fall of Alexander Ranković in July 1966, and the purge of the secret police (factors both contributing to the release of Djilas), that the full extent of past clandestine illegality became known. Briefly, it was revealed that Ranković and his subordinates in the Secret Service had not only "bugged" conversations of Tito and other major Yugoslav leaders, but also had engaged in various other illegal activities directed at those Yugoslav citizens considered "enemies" of the regime. In some cases this involved the use of arbitrary measures against entire ethnic groups such as the Albanians, who had been targeted by Ranković as politically unreliable. Tito, in summarizing the charges against Ranković and his protegés, put the entire decade and a half of police practices after 1950 into perspective: "while entire social development moved rapidly forward, the State Security not only stagnated, but actually went backwards."[33]

The details of the Djilas case and the revelations concerning Ranković did not confirm all of the many criticisms levelled against the Yugoslav regime. They did indicate, however, the continued use of the judicial system for political ends, as well as serious violations of legality and constitutional protections. Although Ranković was expelled from the Party and a new era in Yugoslav judicial development began, Tito was unwilling to dispense with political justice or the punitive practices of the Security Service. In spite of all the incriminating evidence against Ranković, legal investigation of his case was halted and criminal proceedings were discontinued. As for the Security Service, Tito emphasized that is should never again over-ride the Party: "if it is used, it should be turned against the class enemy within and without, and not against our own comrades, communists and officials."[34] Thus, those dissident intellectuals who tried to exercise constitutional protections and the right to freedom of expression - even on the eve and during the midst of the Ranković affair - were brought before the courts and publically condemned by Tito himself.

It is interesting and not coincidental that the last few years of illegality perpetrated by Ranković and his faction coincided with the introduction of a new and more democratic constitutional framework. The new 1963 Constitution designed by Edward Kardelj - Djilas' old nemesis, but also Ranković's arch rival for the leadership succession to Tito's position - stressed constitutionalism and legality as the twin principles underlying the Yugoslav model of communism. One of the most novel features of the 1963 Constitution was the establishment of a separate Constitutional Court charged with the protection of citizens' rights.[35] Kardelj viewed the Constitutional Court as a "protection against all forms of arbitrariness and abuses of democratic rights." The Constitutional Court was also empowered to review the constitutionality of laws and to resolve conflicts between the Federation and the Republics. Although judicial in character, the Constitutional Court was viewed essentially as a "political-legal" body, separate from the other courts of "general jurisdiction" and closely tied to the structure of state authority (explicitly the "assembly system," and implicitly the party organization). Kardelj emphasized that the Constitutional Court could not function as a "purely judicial organ" dealing with cases in a solely formal and legal manner, but rather "would assess them according to the objective social and political content of the process from which such problems and phenomena emanate." The intention therefore was not to "depoliticize" justice in this new higher court, but to create a quasi-judicial body that would review potiential abuses of legality by other political forces and "organs of authority." To that end, the Constitutional Court encompassed the powers, at least in a formal sense, of an administrative tribunal, ombudsman, and court of human rights.[36] In the first two years of its existence (February 1964 - February 1966) over 3,000 cases belonging to the category of "human and self-government rights" were filed before the Constitutional Court of Yugoslavia. Genuine constitutionalism and legality did not have any real chance to flourish, however, until after the removal of Alexander Ranković.

The Yugoslav Judiciary, 1966-1988: The Transformation of a Professional Bureaucracy

The Ranković affair marked a fundamental change and an important turning point in Yugoslav communist development. The unmasking and elimination of the worst political abuses in the system was a sharp defeat for the conservative wing of the party which had worked hard to obstruct tendencies toward increased political, economic, and cultural pluralism. Supporters of expanded one-party state pluralization had, of course, been present in Yugoslav communist ranks for some time (the perspectives of Djilas and Ranković simply represented two ends of a complex ideological spectrum), and had already achieved limited success through the Constitution of 1963 and decentralizing economic reforms of 1965. During the twenty years following the fall of Ranković, the fortunes of reformist and conservative tendencies within the party would wax and wane owing to a variety of factors (see Chapter 3). Briefly, at least three rather distinct phases can be identified during the two decades following the purge of the secret police: *Pluralist Socialism (1967-1971)*, characterized by a flowering of reformist institutional innovations together with provincial centrifugal tendencies in the area of ethnic relations; *Pragmatic Consolidation (1972-1980)*, an attempt by Tito and party conservatives to reinstill a more cohesive spirit and greater party unity through a campaign against liberalism and nationalism, and; *The Post-Tito Period (1980-1988)*, a struggle for regime maintenance amidst growing factional struggles, an upsurge of dissidence, and serious economic difficulties.

As in earlier periods, the Yugoslav judiciary essentially remained a dependent variable after 1966, subject to the changing political climate shaped by party personalities and other circumstances. Leaving aside the details of

The Socialist Pyramid: Elites and Power in Yugoslavia

important post-1966 political swings and institutional changes, it is quite clear that by the mid-1980's certain patterns of change and continuity within the judicial elite had become rather well established. Structural innovations and procedural experimentation in the judicial system continued, of course, especially with the adoption of a new Constitution in 1974, but such measures basically represented embellishments and nuances of trends which were initiated in the 1950's and which gained momentum after 1966. The next section of this chapter will examine several major facets of Yugoslav judicial development between 1960 and 1988, as reflected in the composition, political role, and professional outlook of judicial elites.

The Recruitment and Social Composition of the Judiciary

Election as a judge in a regular (i.e., non-military) Yugoslav court is open to any Yugoslav citizen who is a graduate lawyer, has passed the bench examination (only for commune and district courts), and is deemed "morally and politically suitable" for the performance of judicial functions. This latter requirement has been interpreted by one observer to mean the "qualities worthy of the high function to which a judge is to be elected," and "a self-management orientation."[37] Eligibility for election to certain courts also requires some work experience in the legal sector after graduation from law school. Persons seeking election to the supreme courts must further demonstrate that they are "prominent" legal experts who can properly perform the functions they seek. Judges are elected by legislative assemblies at the particular level of the political system - federal, republican/provincial, communal, municipal - constitutionally empowered to elect the judicial officers of the various courts. Most Yugoslav judges are elected for a term of eight years and may be continuously re-elected for terms of a similar length. Thus re-election is not restricted, but nor is it guaranteed.

After judicial vacancies are publically announced, applications for a judgeship are generally sought by the legislative assembly charged with judicial elections. As a rule, the assembly's commission on elections and appointments invites various institutions, socio-political organizations, professional lawyers' associations, and sometimes selected individuals, to propose judicial candidates. The Socialist Alliance of the Working People of Yugoslavia - a mass political organization closely tied to the League of Communists - plays a major role in the judicial nomination process. The Socialist Alliance offers its opinion with respect to the various judicial candidates to the legislative assembly, or in some republics it is legally required to forward a list of appropriate candidates to the representative bodies. Following such consultations, the legislature's commission for elections and appointments (often together with coopted personnel experts from the Socialist Alliance serving as ex-officio members) puts forward a proposal for the election of a judge. The role which legislators (most of whom are party members, especially on the commission for elections and appointments), and socio-political organizations play in the initial selection, periodic re-election, and possible recall of judges, is an important factor influencing judicial independence in Yugoslavia.

The requirement introduced in the 1950's that judges be selected from among the ranks of professionally trained lawyers, who must have passed judicial exams and have had work experience in the legal field, has considerably upgraded the overall educational level of the Yugoslav judiciary. To ensure the judiciary's awareness of legal and constitutional revisions (an especially important factor given the Yugoslav regime's penchant for constant reorganization) increased emphasis has been placed on continuing legal education. The importance of the judicial elite's university background may also help explain 1981 survey data from Serbia which indicates that nearly a third of the lower court judges have social origins above the working class and the peasantry.[38] Such data parallels overall trends in recent years toward the diminished representation of children from proletarian and peasant families in the universities, a pattern which is apparent in the law faculties. The educational and class background of judge-jurors or lay judges in Yugoslavia - over 57,000 in 1979-1980 - not surprisingly, is substantially lower than that of members of the professional judiciary. For example in 1980, 60 percent of the 5,447 lay judges employed in the Courts of Associated Labour had not received a University education[39] (judge-jurors are elected for four-year terms by legislative assemblies and the position is open to any Yugoslav citizen over 18 years of age, without a criminal record).

The laws governing appointments to regular courts do not stipulate any age requirements for judges, but the need for applicants to complete a law degree, pass a judicial bench examination, and serve an apprentice period before directly trying cases, results in most judges in the lower courts beginning work in their mid-20's. Data (Table 6.3) on the age composition of Yugoslav judicial staff (a broad category of judges, prosecutors, specialists, trainees, and other workers) at the end of 1979 indicates a relatively young generational configuration in the lower level of the regular courts and prosecutorial branch, with most personnel at or above the republican provincial level falling in the over-40 or over-50 age cohorts. This pattern reflects an extensive rejuvenation of staff in the lower organs of the judicial structure in recent years, most likely as a result of the death or retirement of many individuals from the Partisan and early postwar generation. Evidence of this generational trend is supported by a recent study of 866 communal and district judges in Serbia which indicates that 32 percent of these judges are under forty years of age and another 36 percent are between forty and fifty. The same study from Serbia reveals that 30 percent of the judges are women compared to about five percent of the judges at the same level in 1948. Data for the whole country indicates that women make up 56.3

Table 6.3
The Age Composition of Yugoslav Judicial Staff, December, 1979 (%)

Age Structure	Regular Courts				Public Prosecutors' Offices			
	Commune	District	Republican/Provincial	Federal	Commune	District	Republican/Provincial	Federal
Up to 30	23.4	1.0	-	-	22.3	5.0	-	-
30 - 40	43.8	24.7	1.1	-	49.0	16.8	2.1	-
40 - 50	24.3	45.8	43.6	-	21.6	48.6	32.3	12.5
Over 50	8.5	28.5	55.3	100.0	7.1	29.6	65.6	87.5
Total	100.0	100.0	100.0	100.0	100.0	100.0	100.0	100.0
(Number)	(14,511)	(3760)	(685)	(80)	(1895)	(1036)	(166)	(33)

Location of Staff

Source: J. Vrhunec, "Judicial Staff," *Yugoslav Survey*, XXII, No. 4 (1981), p. 92.

percent of all types of judicial staff, and 24 percent of judicial officers (i.e., judges, prosecutors and functionaries), however, there are fewer women in the higher ranks of the judiciary. Overall, Yugoslav women appear to have been quite well represented in the legal profession. By the mid-1970's the number of women lawyers had reached 50 percent of the entire profession, and in 1980 the number of women law school graduates slightly exceeded male graduates.[40]

As with the educational, generational, and genderic composition of the Yugoslav judicial elite, data on ethnic representation also reveals certain important changes. For example, the striking overrepresentation of Serbs in the interwar period (Table 6.1), and of Serbs together with Montenegrins in the first half of the postwar period, appears to have significantly diminished (Table 6.4). The Serbian and Montenegrin contingents in the judicial elite are still sizeable and overrrepresented compared to their representation in the total population, but the overall ethnic composition of the judiciary is roughly in line with the country's ethnic diversity. Problems still remain, however, in certain regions of the country. Thus Albanians are underrepresented both in the country-wide figures and in the Kosovo region where they compose over 77 percent of the population, but hold only 66 percent of the judicial positions. In Macedonia, Albanians compose 20 percent of the population, yet they only make up five percent of the judicial officers. Moslems (leaving aside the Albanians who are also Moslems) constitute another very underrepresented group, especially in Montenegro where they constitute 13 percent of the inhabitants but only seven percent of the judges and judicial officers. In view of the upsurge of nationalism among both Albanians (see Chapter 8) and other Moslems in post-Tito Yugoslavia, such disproportions in the judiciary's ethnic arithmetic acquire more than simply academic importance. Serbian overrepresentation in the Republic of Croatia, and especially in the Province of Vojvodina where Serbs hold 14 percent more judicial posts than their proportional demographic situation would warrant, also represent weaknesses in an otherwise improved pattern of ethnic representation.

Judicial Independence: The Norm and the Reality

Official Yugoslav commentators are fond of emphasizing the independence of judges in their country. Moreover, it is alleged that such autonomy derives from constitutional prohibitions against outside interference in judicial decision-making. According to the 1974 Constitution (Article 210) "courts shall be independent in the performance of their judicial functions and shall administer justice in accordance with the Constitution, statutes, and self-management enactments." Further articles (230 and 231) stipulate that judges must be elected and relieved of their functions in a manner which shall "ensure judicial independence" and guarantee that "no one who takes part in the administration

The Socialist Pyramid: Elites and Power in Yugoslavia

Table 6.4
The Yugoslav Judicial Elite by Ethnicity and Region, 1979/1980 (%)

	Republics and Provinces								
Ethnic Groups	Serbia "Proper"	Kosovo	Vojvodina	Montenegro	Croatia	Slovenia	Macedonia	Bosnia-Hercegovina	Total Judges	Total Population (1981)
Serbs	87.5	22.9	68.2	0.8	16.2	1.3	2.8	39.2	42.2	36.3
Montenegrins	6.0	5.8	4.4	89.0	1.3	0.4	0.9	3.1	6.2	2.6
Croats	0.8	0.3	3.6	1.8	75.9	0.8	0.5	17.8	19.6	19.8
Slovenes	-	-	0.3	-	0.8	96.9	0.1	0.2	9.4	7.8
Macedonians	0.5	0.3	0.2	-	0.1	-	89.3	-	7.3	6.0
Albanians	0.3	66.4	0.1	0.4	0.1	-	5.1	-	3.8	7.7
Moslems	1.7	2.0	-	7.2	0.4	-	-	35.5	6.1	8.9
Yugoslavs	1.5	0.3	2.8	-	3.7	0.3	0.5	3.7	2.1	5.4
Hungarians	0.1	-	13.3	-	0.1	0.3	-	-	-	-
Others	1.6	2.0	6.9	0.8	1.4	-	0.8	0.5	1.8	3.6
Total	100	100	100	100	100	100	100	100	100	100
(Number)	(2227)	(393)	(881)	(264)	(1728)	(763)	(646)	(1176)	(8078)	(22.4 M)

Source: J. Vrhunec, "Judicial Staff," *Yugoslav Survey*, XXII, No. 4 (1981), p. 93.

of justice may be called to account for an opinion given in the process of judicial decision-making."

Despite such constitutional provisions, the reality of judicial independence in Yugoslavia certainly cannot be considered, as one Yugoslav specialist points out, "a settled issue."[41] Thus, while the constitutional provisions regarding judicial independence are quite impressive, most Yugoslav legal scholars emphasize that judicial independence in no way implies judges should function without regard to the regime's core political values, or that judicial independence somehow implies judicial supremacy:

> The independence of the courts is functionally institutional and legal, and not socio-political. The court is independent in specific decision-making, in settling disputes within its competence, and no state or self-management body even the highest, may exercise pressure on the court in the expectation of its duties .... However, this independence does not mean, by any means, that the court stands beyond and outside the socio-political system, or above this system .... The independence of the court is inextricable from the court's bonds with constitutionality and legality ... which do not preclude but presume the right and duty also to appraise socio-politically the work of the courts.[42]

Several factors guarantee the politically contingent or politically circumscribed independence of Yugoslav judges described above. First, legislative assemblies in cooperation with the League of Communist's allied political organization, the Socialist Alliance, play the dominant role in judicial recruitment. The moral and political qualities which form part of the established criteria for the election of judges are therefore interpreted by elected political functionaries at the time of the judge's initial election, and at each subsequent re-election. As one Yugoslav legal scholar observes: "proposing of candidates by the socio-political organization in an election effected through public competition, means favouring particular candidates, who may be politically outstanding, but not so in terms of professional and working levels."[43] The general and convenient practice of considering membership in the League of Communists as evidence of a person's "moral-political suitability" - if there are no other circumstances to the contrary - also tends to eliminate well qualified candidates who are not party members. This can violate, it has been observed, the "equality between citizens."[44]

In most cases, membership in the League of Communists is a minimum requirement for election as a full-time judge in the regular courts, and is virtually mandatory in the higher courts. Data reported for 1979-1980 with respect to over 8,000 judges and other judicial officers indicate that 87.2 percent were members of the League of Communists: 84.7 percent in the law courts; 93.2 percent in courts of associated labour; and 93.7 percent in public prosecutors' offices.[45] Data on 866 judges in the lower courts of Serbia reveal that 92 percent were members of the party.[46] To a certain extent, the importance of party membership and a good party record in the judicial recruitment process creates a similarity (or at least a strong affinity) between judicial officers and politicians which obviates the need for cruder forms of political interference in the administration of justice.

Political considerations also become important when a judge is considered for re-election. As one observer remarks, "the electing body (agency) in such a case is motivated also by the political stand of the judge, but the decision is of a discretionary nature and there is not assignment of reasons for the decision."[47] Some judges and legal specialists have argued that provisions for periodic re-election of judges have a "harmful effect" and that such provisions create "insecurity among judicial cadre, which is reflected in the work of judges and in some way undermines their independence and autonomy."[48] Such critics maintain that the judicial profession is not a political leadership group to which the regime formula of rotation and deprofessionalization should apply, but a specialized career which requires stability and security. Moreover, it is alleged that the provisions for periodic re-election keeps many skilled applicants from choosing a judicial vocation. In addition to political criteria for election and re-election, Yugoslav judges may also be relieved of their functions at any time on grounds of "moral-political incapability," as well as other specified reasons. The definition of "moral-political incapability" is extremely vague and does not specify whether such a criterion applies only to actions inside the court or outside as well.

In practice, Yugoslav judges are rarely relieved of their functions on political grounds, and almost always re-elected after the expiration of their first term in office. This suggests two possibilities in the opinion of one specialist on the Yugoslav judicial system: either the threat of being relieved from office has "influenced judges to render decisions which would not make complications for them"; or the provisions for judicial recall and non-election are "used rather cautiously and exceptionally."[49] It may be true, remarks the same author, that judicial independence "is endangered only in an exceptionally small number of cases, but these are rather of an important character."[50] The susceptibility of courts and judges to informal political pressures from party and state functionaries is most extreme with regard to the hundreds of cases involving political dissent (a relatively small percentage of all cases) which are heard in the courts. Such political pressure, as well as violations of court proceedings has been confirmed by many Yugoslav and outside observers of such trials, as well as the defendants themselves.[51] For example, in March 1981 the President of the Federal Court of Yugoslavia noted that judges were still subjected to political pressures, but in his opinion such incidents were not very common:

> ... there is such pressure, even today, particularly in small communities for judges to enforce "communal justice." Where there is an usurpation of power and a monopoly of so called "responsible comrades" there is also pressure on the judges ... there are also attempts to make the judges dependent upon political structures in various ways, such as making their re-elections conditional, or even attempts to prevent their re-election ...[52]

A more extreme and direct case of political intervention in judicial affairs occurred in May 1976, when a district judge in Slovenia was arrested in his courtroom while conducting a trial. The judge was accused of advocating the separation of his native republic from Yugoslavia (based on passages from his personal diary) and, after a four day trial, was sentenced to six years imprisonment. In order to avoid embarrassing the defendant's former associate judges, the trial was conducted in another community. During the course of the trial the former judge defended his position: "I am accused of trying to separate Slovenia from Yugoslavia, but all I have done is exercise freedom of thought in a private diary, as guaranteed by the Constitution."[53] Such a case is very exceptional, all the more so because the judge involved was one of the country's few remaining pre-World War II non-communists still on the bench.

One of the most important political pressures exerted on Yugoslav judges stems from the prosecutorial branch of the judicial system rather than directly from the party or other political organizations. After the Ranković affair the Federal Office of the Public Prosecutor lost its authority to appoint prosecutors at lower levels of the federal structure, but, the prosecutorial branch remains a highly politicized sector of the justice system. The duties of the public prosecutor to detect and prosecute criminals are, in the words of one official discussion: "functions of a socio-political and ideological character." Prosecutors at each level of the federation are appointed (not elected), reappointed and relieved from office by legislative assemblies at the same level. The regular term of office for a public prosecutor is eight years and reappointment is unrestricted. As with the recruitment of judges, political organizations play a major role in the appointment of prosecutors. Moreover, while territorial decentralization in the recruitment and appointment of presecutors has been in effect since 1967, in practice the prosecutorial structure continues to operate in a hierarchical and "monocratic" manner.[54] Thus, public prosecutors' offices are described as "independent" state judicial agencies, but such independence is understood to include a close working relationship with all other state and political organizations. The continued linkage of prosecutors to both the party apparatus and the State Security Police (SDS) creates a significant constellation of pressure upon the other actors in the judical system, especially in legal cases having political overtones. Such pressure is not always appreciated, nor always accepted. Survey data from 1981 interviews with judges in Serbia indicate that judges and public prosecutors are certainly closer to one another in many respects (reciprocal contacts, ideals, etc.) than either group is to regular lawyers.[55] Public prosecutors, however, have a higher estimation of judges, than judges have of prosecutors. For example, a large number of Yugoslav judges share the view of many lawyers that public prosecutors as an occupational group are characterized by a "repressive orientation," "inflexibility in interpreation," and "the use of any means to prove guilt." Judges and prosecutors generally share many common political perspectives, but a latent role-conflict also exists between members of the two professions, with each seeing themselves as the sole true defenders of the state. Prosecutors and judges also tend to blame each others' profession for those weaknesses which are alleged to exist in the country's legal system.

Yugoslavia's constitutional courts are another highly politicized sector of the judicial system. Established in 1963, the constitutional courts on the federal and republican/provincial levels play a special quasi-political role through their powers to review the constitutionality of laws and to resolve conflicts among various territorial and institutional sectors. Composed of prominent "socio-political" workers and legal experts, the constitutional courts are considered more a part of the assembly system than a component of the judiciary. Mandatory time limits imposed on the holding of office, i.e., the rotation principle which is directed at political positions, also apply to the constitutional courts but not to courts of general jurisdiction. For example, the 14 members of the federal level Constitutional Court of Yugoslavia (a president and thirteen judges) are elected for the typical judicial term of eight years, but unlike other judges they may not be re-elected to the same office. Since the adoption of new constitutional amendments in 1981, the President of the Court is elected from among the other judges for a one year term and always from a different republic or province. In a technical sense, judges serving in the constitutional courts cannot easily be removed from office, but their dependence on changing political considerations is ensured by their limited terms and the importance of party and state experience in their recruitment. As one Yugoslav specialist and constitutional court justice has remarked:

> Nobody is allowed to interfere with the decision-making of the constitutional court on concrete matters ... but there is no doubt that the overall action of the political system of socialist self-management must be expressed also in the decisions of the constitutional courts, for they are a part of it ... the character of the overall constitutional institutionalization in the SFRY is indeed that of the reign of law, but is should by no means turn into the reign of the courts.[56]

283

Lenard J. Cohen

Yugoslav Judges in the 1980's: Professionalism and Political Consciousness

In the mid-1980's, after forty years of communist rule, Yugoslav society and its judicial system have undergone a profound transformation. From moderately educated practitioners of "revolutionary justice" in a predominantly peasant and underdeveloped society, the Yugoslav judiciary had become a professionalized bureaucracy, carrying out its tasks in a modern and complex environment. One of the most useful insights into the Yugoslav judicial system is provided by the recent publication in Belgrade of a book-length sociological study concerning the "Profession of Judges."[57] Written by Dr. Uglesa Zvekić, a sociologist at the Institute for Sociological and Criminological Research, the study is quite remarkable for two reasons: first, it is the first systematic analysis of the judicial profession in Yugoslavia, a fact which in itself is quite revealing about the growing importance and evolution of the judiciary in that country; and secondly, it is the first sociological study focusing upon the judiciary in a communist party state. Portions of the Zvekić data have already been referred to in the chapter, but a futher summary of the study's major findings is important to consider in this concluding section.

Based on interviews with 866 judges throughout Serbia (Yugoslavia's largest republic), or 70 percent of the total judges serving in that region's municipal and district courts, the Zvekić study data was gathered using mail questionaires and direct questioning between April and June 1981 (i.e., about one year after Tito's death). The survey results indicate that the Yugoslav judiciary has become a professional bureaucracy whose members have a very strong sense of occupational and organizational identification, as well as common perspectives approximating a professional ideology. Important factors contributing to the judges' sense of professional identification and their "judicial ideology" include: the process of professional identification in the law schools, organizational socialization during professional work, and a common professional "role-set" regarding their professional and overall status in society. For example, the judges interviewed believe that they are the principal actors in the justice system, serving as defenders of moral values, legality, and the social order. Judges also agree with other Yugoslav surveys which rank their profession at or near the top of the country's occupational prestige, income, and educational hierarchies. Judicial professionalization is reinforced by the occupation's "socio-professional" isolation, or social distance from other skill groups and professions in terms of life styles, friendship patterns (more than half of the judges' friends come from the legal sector), and use of leisure time. Such aspects of the judicial profession also tend to distinguish it as an elite group with lifestyles markedly above the "lower strata" and "working class." As Zvekić points out:

> ... the analysis of the social characteristics of the judicial profession reveal it to be an occupation of high social status and power .... Objectively and subjectively it is a profession outside and above the working class: as much by its features as a status group, as by the nature of its basis in knowledge, sources of professional authority, the characteristics of its tasks, and the world in which [judges] live and work. As with other professions, judges act with superiority in relation to occupations of lower standing in the social system of inequalities, and that is a clear conspicuous fact.[58]

Yugoslav judges apparently have progressed significantly in comparison to postwar Partisan activists dispensing "people's justice" to their fellow citizens as a prelude to the abolition of classes and the state.

The findings from the Zvekić study also reveal that relationships between judicial professionals and political professionals are more complex and subtle than commentaries often allege. It is not simply a matter of political forces or party organization dominating the activities of all judicial professionals, nor is it a question of all judges constantly asserting their autonomy against political interference. Rather, judges are subjected to an interplay of professional, bureaucratic, political, and other influences. For example, judges are members of a high status group which is directly within the overall system of state power, and evidence indicates that they support such power from which they derive considerable benefits. At the same time, many judges appear to resent the fact that arbitrary and changing political considerations can sometimes impinge upon their career advancement. One-third of the Serbian judges interviewed believe that the requirement for their periodic re-election is a barrier to the autonomous exercise of the judical function. Moreover, in their evaluation of what facts would *ideally* characterize the judicial role, politics and a person's political standing are accorded very little significance. In practice, however, most Yugoslav judges perceive political factors to be of much more importance than professional factors in a judge's career progress (Table 6.5). As might be expected, professional factors are given the most weight by those at the top of the judicial hierarchy, such as the presidents of courts. In view of such findings, Zvekić maintains that the traditional argument about whether judges are state bureaucrats or professionals is a "forced and false dilemma." The survey of judges in Serbia indicates that Yugoslav judges are "professional bureaucrats" whose recruitment, outlook and behaviour are shaped by a combination of factors, including politics. Such a situation, not unlike that found in so many other countries, may prove to be a source of continual inner tension and ambiguity for members of the Yugoslav judicial elite.[59] As Zvekić emphasizes: "the system tries to take care about which people are to be responsible for serving justice according to the conception of the ruling strata in society."[60]

Table 6.5
*Opinions of Yugoslav Judges Concerning the Five Major Factors
For Advancement in a Judicial Career*

Ranking of Factors	Judges in the Communal Courts (N = 642)	Judges in the District Courts (N = 224)	Presidents of Courts (N = 78)
1	Socio-Political Activity	Socio-Political Activity	Personal and Professional Principles
2	Personal and Professional Principles	Support from the Local Power Structure	Socio-Political Activity
3	Professional Competence	Personal and Professional Principles	Diligence in work
4	Support from the Local Power Structure	Membership in the League of Communists	Professional Competence
5	Diligence in work	Professional Competence	Support of the Local Power Structure

Source: U. Zvekić, *Profesija sudija* (Belgrade: Institut za Kriminološka i Sociološka Istraživanja, 1985), p. 141.

The increased professionalism of Yugoslav judges in recent years has been closely linked to the development of the country's judicial system as a relatively more independent and competent segment of "self-managing socialism." Yugoslav socialism still operates within the context of overall one-party hegemony, but the occupational differentiation and professionalization of the judicial sector is an important facet of the limited pluralization which is embodied in the novel communist regime. Perhaps the next best step forward in judicial development should be the one advocated by a member of Yugoslavia's small band of civil rights lawyers, who quotes the medieval Serbian Emperor Dušan: "The Court should not judge in fear of the ruler, but according to the law."[61]

NOTES: CHAPTER SIX

1. F.J.M. Feldbrugge, "The Untapped Potential in the Study of Soviet and East European Law," *Studies in Comparative Communism*, XV, No. 4 (1982), 384-390.

2. Miodrag Jovičić, "Yugoslav Internal Comparative Law," *Yugoslav Law* (1978), 57-73.

3. Other aspects of the pre-communist political system are discussed in Chapter 2.

4. Charles A. Beard and George Radin, *The Balkan Pivot: Yugoslavia* (New York: Macmillan, 1919), 274-275.

5. The renowned efficiency and legality of the Austo-Hungarian bureaucracy was also generally applicable in Vienna's administration of the Balkan areas within the Empire. See Ivo Banac, *The National Question in Yugoslavia* (Ithaca: Cornell University Press, 1984), 219. As Serbian and Croatian pressure for South Slav unification mounted near the turn of the century, however, Austro-Hungarian justice at times became more highly politicized and corrupt. For example, R. W. Seton-Watson, who attended the Zagreb treason trial of 1909 at which a large group of Serbs were charged with plotting against the state, remarked: "I have spent a good many hours in court, and ... I can honestly say the the judges give me the impression of being collected from a *Verbrecherkolonie* [penal colony]." His pencil jottings include the following: "the President (of the Court) is the best of an exceptionally bad lot." Of one judge he observed: "a voice which can only be described as *slimy*. Shoves head forward and strains eyes in expectancy of favourable answer (from witnesses). Endless *Suggerieren* [prompting of witnesses]." Hugh Seton-Watson and C. Seton-Watson, *The Making of a New Europe: R.W. Seton-Watson and the Last Years of Austria-Hungary* (London: Methuen, 1981), 69.

6. Under the Hapsburg pattern of legal administration from 1878 to 1918, each of Bosnia-Hercegovina's forty-eight subdivisions had district courts (*Bezirksgerichte*) operating on the basis of Austro-Hungarian law (actually a military penal code so as not to discriminate between the different Austrian and Hungarian civil codes), as well as Moslem religious courts (*Scheriatsgerichte*) operating on

the basis of Sharia, the Moslem Canon Law. See Peter Sugar, *Industrialization of Bosnia-Hercegovina* (Seattle: University of Washington Press, 1963), 31-32.

7. Cristopher Boehm, *Montenegrin Social Organization and Values* (New York: AMS Press, 1983). See also by the same author, *Blood Revenge* (Lawrence: University Press of Kansas, 1984).

8. Mary Edith Durham, *Some Tribal Origins Laws and Customs of the Balkans* (London: G. Allen and Unwin Ltd., 1928), 81.

9. Duncan Wilson, *The Life and Times of Vuk Stefanovic Karadzic* (London: Clarendon Press, 1970), 241-242.

10. *Ibid.*, 243.

11. Of the presiding judges in Serbia in 1844, "three were totally illiterate, ten could barely sign their names, only three had any education beyond elementary school, and only one was a lawyer. Among the other judges, twenty-one were illiterate, fourteen were semi-literate, only fifteen had more than an elementry education, and only one was a lawyer." By 1853 matters had improved somewhat. Of the 242 officials in the courts "15 were illiterate, 76 had elementary education, 69 had gymnasium education, 13 had studied theology, 19 had studied philosophy, and 49 had studied the law." Michael B. Petrovich, *A History of Modern Serbia, Volume 2* (New York: Harcourt Brace Jovanovich, 1976), 275.

12. *Ibid.*, 310-311.

13. An interwar study prepared in Belgrade found that in September 1934, Croats (who made up 23 percent of Yugoslavia's population) held 28 percent of all judicial positions in the country, including 40 percent of the appellate court judgeships and 34 percent of those in the administrative courts. See Bogdan Prica, *Hrvatsko pitanje i brojke* (Belgrade: Javnost, 1937). Such data has been cited by Western historians as revealing "fair" or "strong" Croatian representation in the interwar judicial sector. See Ivo Banac, *The National Question in Yugoslavia*, 220 and Alex N. Dragnich, *The First Yugoslavia* (Stanford: Hoover Institution Press, 1983), 141.

14. Vilko Vinterhalter, *In the Path of Tito* (Tunbridge Wells: Abacus Press, 1972), 122-23.

15. Rodoljub Čolaković, *Zapisi iz Oslobodilačkog Rata* (Sarajevo: Svjetlost, 1948), 56.

16. H. Modić, "Pravo v prehodnem razdobju," *Ekonomski Zbornik*, II (1957), 91.

17. M. Šnuderl, *Zgodovina ljudske oblasti* (Ljubljana: Državna Založba Slovenije, 1950), 144.

18. A survey of People's Courts in Croatia published at the end of August, 1946 revealed that 12,226 individuals were working as judicial personnel, including 278 permanent judges with some legal training, 46 permanent judges with no legal training, and 11,902 lay judges (of whom 7,235 were peasants and 1,552 were workers). Only three of the 324 permanent judges were women but there were 1,444 women among the lay judges. Ferdo Čulinović, *Pravosudje u Jugoslaviji* (Zagreb: Nakladni zavod Hrvatske, 1946), 194.

19. Branko Petranović, *Politička i ekonomska osnova narodne vlasti u Jugoslaviji za vreme obnove* (Belgrade: Institut za savremenu istoriju, 1969), 274.

20. Charles Zalar, *Yugoslav Communism, A Critical Study* (Washington: U.S. Government Printing Office, 1961), 220.

21. See Branko Petranović, *Politička i ekonomska osnova narodne vlasti u Jugoslaviji za vreme obnove*, 275. A highly critical account of the judiciary's lack of independence in this period is in Vojislav Kostunica and Kosta Cavoski, *Party Pluralism or Monism: Social Movements and the Political System in Yugoslavia, 1944-1949* (Boulder: East European Monographs, 1985), 133-145.

22. For a fascinating "docu-novel" on the link between elite factionalism and politicized justice in this period, and also its legacy for Yugoslav communism see Ivan Supek, *Crown Witness Against Hebrang* (Chicago: Markanton Press, 1983).

23. Alexander Ranković, "Za dalje jačanje pravosudja i zakonitosti," *Četvrti plenum centralnog Komiteta Komunističke partije Jugoslavije, III* (June 4, 1951), 22.

24. Milan Jovanović, *Porota u pravosudju Jugoslavije* (Belgrade: Savremena administracija, 1958).

25. M.J. "Juror-Judges in the Yugoslav Judicial System," *Yugoslav Survey*, III (1962), 1562.

26. *Ibid.*

27. Charles P. McVicker, *Titoism: Pattern for International Communism* (London: St. Martin's Press, 1957), 217.

28. Jovan Djordjević, "Život s državom", *Nedeljne Informativne Novine, No. 1125*, (1980), 10.

29. Milovan Djilas, *Rise and Fall* (New York: Harcourt Brace Jovanovich, 1985), 242.

30. Milovan Djilas, *Borba* (December 31, 1953), 6-7.

31. Milovan Djilas, *Rise and Fall*, 387.

32. *Ibid.*, 46. After Tito's death in 1980, Djilas bitterly observed that "the Kingdom of Yugoslavia was a corrupt and undemocratic state, but it was a state in which law exacted more respect, and the courts more independence, than they do today in Yugoslavia." *Tito* (New York: Harcourt Brace Jovanovich, 1980), 18-19. Speaking about a recent trial of political dissidents in Belgrade, Djilas has also claimed that current defects in the Yugoslav justice system can be traced to the Marxist-Leninist revolution itself, and that he must shoulder part of the responsibility: "I am ashamed for my country and for my past. I never suspected that forty years after the revolution and the 'affirmation of the Constitution' that justice would be administered in this way. To the extent that my own revolutionary past has contributed to this state of affairs, I ask everyone, and most of all the six men who stand accused, to accept this article as an expression of solidarity and regret." *Le Monde*, (November 15, 1984), 3.

33. Nenad Petrović, "The Fall of Alexandar Ranković," *Review*, VI (1967), 533.

34. *Ibid.*, 46.

35. Edward Kardelj, "On the Principles of the Preliminary Draft of the Constitution for the Federalist Socialist Republic of Yugoslavia," *Socialist Thought and Practice*, VII-VIII (1962), 7-8.

36. Frederik W. Hondius, *The Yugoslav Community of Nations* (The Hague: Mouton, 1968), 300.

37. Jernej Vrhunec, "Judicial Staff," *Yugoslav Survey*, XXII, No. 4 (1981), 86.

38. Ugleša Zvekić, *Profesija sudija* (Belgrade: Institut za kriminoloska i socioloska istrazivanja, 1985), 90-92.

39. Jernej Vrhunec, "Judicial Staff," 92. It was orginally intended that the Courts of Associated Labour established in 1974 would be presided over by workers, but by 1981 nearly two-thirds of the judges heading panels in those courts had professional legal training. The presence of recent law graduates serving as secretaries to the judicial panels in the Courts of Associated Labour also influenced the growing "legalization" of such "self-management courts." In view of the regime's ideological support for worker's self-management, such legal professionalization is regarded as an unfortunate necessity. See Robert Hayden, "Labour Courts and Workers' Rights in Yugoslavia: A Case Study of the Contradictions of Socialist Legal Theory and Practice," (manuscript), 11, 26.

40. Ugleša Zvekić, *Profesija sudija*, 88.

41. T. Vasiljević, "An Essay on the Legality of Administration and on Independence of Judges," *Yugoslav Law*, II (1980), 3.

42. Alexander Fira, "Transformation of Executive and Judicial Functions in Yugoslavia," *Yugoslav Law,* II (1980), 23. "As an institution," writes one specialist, "the judiciary is directly related to other social subjects. In a society such as the Yugoslav society today, the relationship between politics and the judiciary is extremely important. Although not a political office, the judiciary is 'the most political institution,' because it implements and applies the law which is in fact a concentrated expression of politics." Josif Trajković, *The Judicial System of Yugoslavia* (Belgrade: Jugoslovenski pregled, 1984), 19. The Constitutional Commission which drafted the 1974 Constitution rejected a proposal which would have defined the judiciary as an "independent organ of the community" because such a formulation incorrectly viewed the courts as "independent and autonomous in relation to the working class state." *Nedeljne Informativne Novine*, (October 19, 1986), 54.

43. T. Vailjević, "An Essay on the Legality of Administration and on Independence of Judges," 2, 23.

44. *Ibid.*

45. Jernej Vrhunec, "Judicial Staff," 92.

46. Ugleša Zvekić, *Profesija sudija*, 143.

47. T. Vasiljević, "An Essay on the Legality of Administration and on Independence of Judges," 20-21.

48. Ibid., 2, 23. See also I. Vuković, "Diskusija," *Arhiv za pravne i društvene nauke*, III (1972), 325.

49. T. Vasiljević, "An Essay on the Legality of Administration and on Independence of Judges," 26.

50. *Ibid.*, 17.

51. A Yugoslav sociologist has astutely remarked that while his country has made considerable progress in the transition from revolutionary legal consciousness to legal institutionalization, the only "firm yardstick" for evaluating legality in a given socialist state is the "... realisation of international human rights' norms, of which the right to freedom of opinion, freedom of expression, freedom of assembly and association, the right to take part in the government, equal access to public service, and free elections still are prime examples." Peter Jambrek, "The Economic Base of Legality: The Case of Yugoslavia," *International Journal of the Sociology of Law*, XIII (May, 1985), 200-201.

52. *Nedeljne Informativne Novine*, (March 29, 1981), 22. Other Yugoslav judges have also drawn attention to political intervention in the judicial process. For example, the President of the Supreme Court of Serbia pointed out that "some functionaries who acquire sufficient power, consider the courts in their region as basic instruments of their policies, and the judges as personal executors and bureaucrats." He also suggested that there are "demands that the judicial organs inform communal authorities concerning different matters in a way which isn't proper to the constitutional independence of the courts" and that such improper influence is one of the reasons for the "dissatisfaction of the public with the work of

the courts." Another Belgrade judge also claimed that those who "appoint and pay judges demand unreserved obedience from them." *Nedeljne Informativne Novine*, No. 1913, (August 30, 1987), 20-22. There is considerable regional variation in the administration of Yugoslav justice both with respect to judicial independence and the prosecution of political dissidence. See, for example, Kosta Cavoski, "Why There is More Free Speech in Belgrade than in Zagreb," *Index on Censorship*, VIII (1986), 22-24.

53. *New York Times*, (October 16, 1976), 3. In February 1986, three judges in the Serbian town of Cuprija went on a two day public hunger strike to protest party interference in their work. The local party authorities claimed that by imposing "ideological and political measures" on the judges they had acted in accordance with the Serbian party statutes. *Foreign Broadcast Information Service*, (February 20, 1986), I10. The view of the protesting judges was shared by a Serbian social scientist who suggested that political interference in judicial elections and "the financial dependence of the courts also threatens to reduce judges to an appendix of the administrative apparatus and socio-political communities." *Radio Free Europe Research, Situation Report*, No. 11 (March 14, 1986), 19-21.

In early 1988, the Assembly of Kosovo removed a district court judge for participating in Albanian nationalist demonstrations in 1988 and "remaining silent when counterrevolutionary events which took place in Kosovo in 1981 were being assessed." *FBIS-EEU-88-023* (February 4, 1988), 60.

54. Vuko G. Gucetić, "Public Prosecutors," *Yugoslav Survey*, XVIII, No. 4 (1977), 43. A rare exception to the "monocratic" pattern was a 1987 public conflict between the public prosecutor of Slovenia and the federal public prosecutor in Belgrade over how to handle dissent in Slovenia. When the federal prosecutor condemned the failure of his Slovenian counterpart to prosecute certain authors for publishing "hostile propoganda," the Slovene official complained about federal "pressure on the prosecutor and indirectly on the judiciary." *Danas*, No. 278, (July 16, 1987), 22-23.

55. Ugleša Zvekić, *Profesija sudija*, 72-83.

56. Alexander Fira, "Relations between the Constitutional Courts and the Assemblies of Socio-Political Communities," *Socialist Thought and Practice*, IV (1984), 83-84. See also Nikola Srzentić,

Lenard J. Cohen

The Constitutional Judiciary in Yugoslavia (Belgrade: Jugoslovenski pregled, 1984).

57. Ugleša Zvekić, *Profesija sudija.*

58. *Ibid.*, 106.

59. Jovan Djordjević, dean of Yugoslavia's community of legal scholars, has pointed out that law "will not automatically change even under developed conditions of socialism ..." and that there will be a need for gradually changing the mixture of "semi-statist-semi-socialist law" which now exists in Yugoslavia. In his opinion, while the courts need to play a special role in guarding the law and the constitution against party domination, "the courts in particularly, have a contradictory status. Theirs is to eliminate the instances of abuse, violation of law, and subjectivism of all kinds, particularly on the part of those in power, while, in fact they become an arena in which the very statist and positivist conception of the constitution and law is defended." Jovan Djordjević, "The Constitution of the Socialist Federal Republic of Yugoslavia of 1974," *Socialist Thought and Practice*, IV (1984), 42-43.

60. Ugleša Zvekić, *Profesija sudija*, 228.

61. Melanie Anderson, "The Trial of Mihajlo Mihajlov," *Index on Censorship*, V, No. 1 (Spring, 1976), 10.

PART FOUR

ELITES AND ETHNONATIONALISM: REGIONAL AND CULTURAL CONFLICTS

> *... among us who have led the revolution, who have been unanimous in the war, there is no discord. We have identical views. There are others who have emerged from unhealthy intellectual environments, from non-socialist intelligentsia. They are the ones who are opposing us .... What is important for us is to have unity at the summit .... Nationalism and socialism simply cannot go together.*
>
> Josip Broz Tito

> *Tito understood, I believe ... that the danger to him and his system sprang from the top; only if the top is disunited would such danger filter down to its base foundation, the middle ranks and the people .... Tito's favorite slogan was 'Brotherhood and Unity!' - they did not inhibit the affirmation of state or cultural identities on a national basis.*
>
> Milovan Djilas

CHAPTER 7

BALKAN CONSOCIATIONALISM: ETHNIC REPRESENTATION AND ETHNIC DISTANCE IN THE YUGOSLAV ELITE STRUCTURE

The composition, attitudes and behaviour of elite decision-makers are generally regarded as major factors influencing the dynamics and development of political systems. The political significance of elites is assumed to have an even greater influence when the population of a society is deeply divided along ethnic and cultural lines. Thus, numerous studies concerning "multi-ethnic," "plural," or "segmented" societies have suggested that elites can and should play a major role in the moderation or regulation of political conflicts among diverse subcultural groups inhabiting a common state.

The most fully developed argument concerning the importance of elite "accommodation" in culturally plural regimes is Arend Lijphart's theory of "consociational democracy," initially based on his case study of Dutch politics and later developed on a broader comparative basis.[1] Lijphart's work, which is well-known and has been summarized elsewhere,[2] maintains that "overarching elite cooperation" among culturally distinct political elites is a prerequisite for political stability and democracy in countries with deep and persistent subcultural cleavages. Lijphart's detailed exposition of the motivating factors and constraints on ethnic accommodation goes beyond the simple equation of elite bargaining with democratic stability, but the salience of elite level decision-making is central to his theory. Although the theory of consociational democracy is vulnerable to a number of serious criticisms both for its normative

Lenard J. Cohen

implications (e.g., that it is an elitist theory of democracy) and its empirical basis (i.e., that it explains away or underestimates the importance of mass/citizen attitudes and behaviour), Lijphart has succeeded in drawing attention to some of the most important factors influencing the political development of multi-ethnic states.[3] Eric Nordlinger, in a more historical analysis of "divided societies," has also suggested, in an argument similar to Lijphart's, that it is the attitudes and behaviour of diverse subcultural elites that are decisive for the success or failure of conflict-management.[4] The arguments of Lijphart and Nordlinger are most significant as antidotes to earlier unicausal and determinist theories which argued that the likely reduction of ethnic conflict and subcultural differences was an inevitable result of socio-economic modernization and intensified mass social communications among subcultures. These latter views have been disconfirmed both by the mounting tide of nationalism in contemporary regimes,[5] and the salient role of elites in moderating or intensifying ethnic conflict.

This chapter examines the impact of elite structure and elite behaviour on ethnic accommodation in contemporary Yugoslavia. A society with very pronounced ethnic, religious and regional cleavages, Yugoslavia provides an excellent laboratory in which to examine the various factors affecting the political dynamics of multi-national states. As Yugoslavia is an essentially *elite-managed* multi-ethnic society with various confederal features, it also provides a good case study of consociational practices.[6] Indeed, the importance accorded in Yugoslav federal politics to collegial decision-making bodies composed of regionally selected representatives has accentuated the influence of elites in recent years.[7] This chapter will explore the crucial role of both ethnic cleavages and elite activities in Yugoslav politics through an analysis of the following three dimensions: (1) the ethnic composition of major Yugoslav elite sectors; (2) the patterns of ethnic distance and interaction within those elite sectors; (3) the consequences and importance of ethnic relations in different elite sectors with regard to political cohesion in multi-ethnic states.

THE ETHNIC COMPOSITION OF YUGOSLAV ELITES

A Supra-regional or "Yugoslav" Perspective

One of the principle arguments of consociational theory is that the maintenance of stable democracy in ethnically divided societies requires negotiation and agreement among the representatives of different subcultural groups. Such elite-level ethnic accommodation is regarded as a necessary corrective or substitute for mass level divisions and conflicts among segmented subcultural groups. Some level of proportionality in the distribution of elite

The Socialist Pyramid: Elites and Power in Yugoslavia

positions is also viewed as a precondition for the establishment of such elite negotiated accommodation.

The question of equity in the ethnic composition of societal elites has long been a sensitive political issue in Yugoslavia. Inquiries regarding this issue have usually focused upon ethnic representation in the top leadership of the political sphere, or other major organizational and occupational sectors such as the military, the bureaucracy, and the economy. During the 1970's and 1980's, ethnic representation in the Yugoslav elite has reflected a conscious effort by the regime to utilize a nationality formula or "ethnic key" in filling top level positions. Use of this key ensures that representation of ethnic groups in the elite is at least roughly proportional to the distribution of ethnic groups in the general population. The formula has operated to provide parity or equal representation for each of the eight major regions of the country with respect to the most visible and symbolically important political posts at the highest level of the government and party structure. Each region is further given the responsibility of selecting their top leadership delegations in a manner which reflects the ethnic proportionality of that section of the country. For example, in the selection of candidates to the Chamber of Republics and Provinces in Yugoslavia's federal legislature, Croatia with 22 percent of the country's population and Macedonia with only eight percent are awarded the same number of delegates. Each of these republics then *proportionally* adjusts the representation of their various ethnic communities when selecting delegates to the federal legislature. The use of such methods in elite recruitment has provided greater equity in the ethnic composition of political positions than ever before in Yugoslav history. Important areas of ethnic imbalance still exist (e.g., in the military and security services, where traditionally high levels of Serbian and Montenegrin representation persist) but such problems are openly acknowledged by the regime and are not the result of official discrimination.[8]

The results of the 1971 Yugoslav population census offer some very interesting data regarding the ethnic composition of both political elites and the less researched non-political elite sectors. The data was not publically available in Yugoslavia until 1974 when special volumes of the 1971 census were finally published. In contrast to sample surveys of elites or studies based on a limited number of positionally defined top elite offices, the census data provide information on the entire universe of individuals in each elite sector of Yugoslav society. This allows an analyst to study the alleged operation of the ethnic key in elite recruitment, as well as to compare the political and non-political elite sectors of the elite structure. Table 7.1 provides data on the ethnic composition of seven selected elite sectors which collectively include approximately 286,000 individuals. The following sectors were analyzed: (1) professional functionaries in socio-political organizations including the League of Communists and other mass organizations (Socialist Alliance, Trade Unions, etc); (2) professional functionaries in legislative bodies and the governmental bureaucracy; (3) management personnel, a broad category including the directors of economic enterprises and non-economic institutions; (4) the technical intelligentsia including engineers and technical specialists; (5) physical scientists; (6) natural scientists; and (7) the literary and artistic intelligentsia. A more detailed breakdown of the positions and occupations included in each of the seven sub-groups can be found in Appendix 7.1.

Analysis of each of the seven elite sectors reveals a relative level of ethnic group representation that generally corresponds to the distribution of ethnic groups in the total population of the country. For example, when all elite sectors for the entire country are combined, there is no evidence of the exceedingly high Serbian ethnic overrepresentation and Croatian underrepresentation which caused such political difficulties in the interwar and early post-World War II Yugoslav regimes (the data, of course, does not reveal the differential power of each ethnic group represented within a specific elite sector). Such near proportional representation does not alter the fact, however, that Serbs are still proportionately somewhat overrepresented in the two political elite sectors, and that Croats are slightly underrepresented and outnumbered three to one by Serbs in absolute terms. Moreover, Montenegrins, who are ethnically linked to the Serbs, are highly overrepresented in the political elite where their representation is twice as great as in the non-political sectors.

The situation for the Slovenes is the reverse of the Montenegrins. For example, Slovenes make up 15 percent of the physical scientists but only eight percent of the party-mass organization functionaries, the latter figure matching their "correct" proportion based on the total population. Moslems are underrepresented in all elite sectors, although because a large number of the group identified as "Yugoslavs" are actually Moslems (who have not chosen to adopt "Moslem" as an ethnic affinity in reply to the 1971 census), their underrepresentation is not as great as it would first appear. Macedonian representation in the party and mass organization sectors corresponds precisely to that group's share of the total population. Such representation is a striking tribute to the regime-contrived ethnic key, and contrasts sharply with the pre-communist regime's identification of Macedonians as "South Serbians." The Macedonians actually outnumber the Slovenes in the party-mass organization political subsector.

In 1971, Albanians were the most underrepresented of any of the officially designated major "peoples" of the state. This situation, which continues to prevail even in the carefully "keyed" political sectors, is partially explained by the Albanians' political subordination up until mid-1966, together with the sensitive political situation in the predominantly Albanian Kosovo region (see Chapter 8). Despite such imbalance, the representation of the Albanians, Macedonians, Moslems and the country's small nationalities (Hungarians and others) in each of the elite sectors has considerably improved in comparison to the position of these groups in interwar and early socialist Yugoslavia.[9] Not surprisingly, however, the numerically dominant position of

The Socialist Pyramid: Elites and Power in Yugoslavia

Table 7.1
The Ethnic Composition of Elites in Yugoslavia: A Country-Wide Profile, 1971

Ethnic Group	Total Population (1971)	Party and Mass Organization Functionaries	Legislative and Government Personnel	Elite Sectors					
				Managerial Personnel	Technical Intelligentsia	Physical Scientists	Natural Scientists	Literary/Artistic Intelligentsia	Total Elite
Serbs	39.7	44.6	42.9	40.1	43.5	43.8	48.0	42.9	43.0
Montenegrins	2.5	5.8	8.0	4.2	3.4	2.9	3.4	1.6	3.6
Croats	22.1	16.6	15.2	22.5	23.0	22.3	19.5	20.9	22.0
Slovenes	8.2	7.8	10.8	13.0	13.0	14.5	8.7	8.2	12.1
Moslems	8.4	5.6	5.6	4.6	4.2	0.3	2.7	3.1	4.1
Yugoslavs	1.3	3.8	4.7	3.6	3.6	3.5	2.4	4.7	3.6
Macedonians	5.8	8.2	6.7	7.4	5.3	5.8	9.5	5.7	6.4
Albanians	6.4	3.7	3.0	0.9	.05	0.7	0.9	1.4	0.9
Hungarians	2.3	1.7	1.1	1.6	1.4	1.7	2.4	3.7	1.7
Others	2.7	1.6	1.2	1.5	1.3	1.1	1.9	6.9	1.9
Did Not Declare a Nationality	0.3	0.4	0.5	0.4	0.5	0.5	0.4	0.7	0.5
Unknown	0.3	0.2	0.3	0.2	0.3	0.2	0.2	0.3	0.2
Total	100.0	100.0	100.0	100.0	100.0	100.0	100.0	100.0	100.0
(Number)	(20,522.9)	(4518)	(8887)	(98,731)	(129,448)	(11,936)	(28,560)	(23,888)	(285,968)

Source: Popis Stanovništva i stanova 1971. Stanovništvo. Ekonomiske Karakteristike I Deo, (ukupno i aktivno stanovništvo) Rezultati po republikama i pokrajinama. Knjiga III. (Beograd: Savezni Zavod za Statistiku, 1974), pp. 68-112.

the larger ethnic groups (Serbs, Croats, and Slovenes) in almost every elite sector remains very pronounced.

Intra-regional and Cross-regional Perspectives

Due to the high level of intra-regional ethnic heterogeneity in Yugoslavia, the ethnic composition of different elite sectors *within* the various sections of the country is an important subject for inquiry. The four most ethnically heterogeneous regions of the country are analyzed in this chapter: two republics, Croatia and Bosnia-Hercegovina; and the two autonomous provinces within Serbia, Kosovo and Vojvodina.

In Croatia, the most important ethnic conflicts have occurred between the republic's 80 percent Croat majority and the Serbian minority which constituted 14 percent of the population in 1971. The data in Table 7.2 reveal a pattern which was submerged in the above analysis of representation for the entire country, namely, the extent of Serbian proportional overrepresentation in Croatia's political sectors (21 percent), and Serbian underrepresentation in the technical and humanistic intelligentsia (9.8 percent). Many critics of this situation would argue, as they did during the region's sharp Croat-Serbian debates from 1968 to 1972, that such ethnic disproportions result directly from the actions of the groups concerned: i.e., that the political elite situation had been manipulated by the Serbs, and the position of the intelliegentsia manipulated by the Croats. The explanation is, however, somewhat more complex. Serbian overrepresentation in Croatia's political elite can be traced to the wartime suffering of Serbs in the region and the consequent influx of Serbs into the Partisan movement. Indeed, it was Croatian opposition to the sustained presence and influence of local Serbs in the republic's political elite structure, as well as central - perceived as Serbian - interference with the republic's "national interests" which helped to precipitate the Croatian crisis of 1971-1972. This situation eventually led to Tito's harsh purge of nationalists in the Croatian political elite along with other leaders of the so-called nationalist "mass movement." The very small proportion of Serbs in Croatia's literary-artistic elite sector is also quite remarkable. The dominant Croatian presence in the region's intellectual elite is probably closely connected to the significant role of the literary-artisitic elite in Croatian nationalist circles. Although the overt influence of political and intellectual nationalism diminished after the crisis of 1971-1972, tensions concerning regional elite representation remain an important undercurrent in Croatian political life (see Chapter 9).

Ethnic relations are even more delicate in Bosnia-Hercegovina where a large Moslem group (39.6 percent in 1971) resides alongside the Serbian (37.2 percent) and Croatian (20.6 percent) communities. As in Croatia, the data for Bosnia reveal Serbian overrepresentation and Croatian underrepresentation in

The Socialist Pyramid: Elites and Power in Yugoslavia

Table 7.2
The Ethnic Composition of Elite Sectors in Croatia (%)

Ethnic Group	Total Population (1971)	Party and Mass Organization Functionaries	Legislative and Government Personnel	Managerial Personnel	Technical Intelligentsia	Physical Scientists	Natural Scientists	Literary/Artistic Intelligentsia	Total Elite
Serbs	14.2	21.0	21.5	11.7	9.8	11.5	15.3	8.5	11.1
Montenegrins	0.2	0.6	0.6	0.8	0.6	0.8	0.6	0.7	0.7
Croats	79.4	71.9	71.8	79.3	81.7	79.6	77.3	76.4	79.8
Slovenes	0.7	1.0	0.8	1.4	1.4	1.1	0.8	2.2	1.4
Moslems	0.4	0.4	0.3	0.3	0.4	0.5	0.3	0.8	0.4
Yugoslavs	1.9	2.6	3.2	3.6	3.4	3.7	3.5	4.2	3.4
Macedonians	0.1	-	0.2	0.3	0.3	0.3	0.3	0.9	0.4
Albanians	0.1	-	0.1	0.1			-	0.4	0.1
Hungarians	0.8	0.1	-	0.4	0.4	0.8	0.8	1.7	0.6
Others	1.3	0.1	0.6	1.2	1.2	0.8	1.2	3.1	1.3
Did Not Declare a Nationality	0.4	0.1	0.2	0.2	0.2	0.1	0.2	0.2	0.2
Unknown	0.4	0.1	0.2	0.2	0.2	0.1	0.2	0.2	0.2
Total	100.0	100.0	100.0	100.0	100.0	100.0	100.0	100.0	100.0
(Number)	(4.4 M)	(823)	(1259)	(18,345)	(30,440)	(2894)	(5891)	(5377)	(65,026)

Source: Same as Table 7.1.

303

Table 7.3
The Ethnic Composition of Elite Sectors in Bosnia-Hercegovina (%)

Ethnic Group	Total Population (1971)	Party and Mass Organization Functionaries	Legislative and Government Personnel	Elite Sectors Managerial Personnel	Technical Intelligentsia	Physical Scientists	Natural Scientists	Literary/ Artistic Intelligentsia	Total Elite
Serbs	37.3	47.4	43.3	37.5	35.7	37.6	45.3	28.9	37.3
Montenegrins	0.3	1.7	2.5	2.4	1.8	1.1	1.3	1.2	1.9
Croats	20.6	14.1	15.9	19.7	19.9	20.0	22.3	23.3	19.9
Slovenes	0.1	0.4	0.3	0.7	0.7	0.5	0.3	1.8	0.7
Moslems	39.6	29.9	30.4	31.1	32.4	34.0	24.6	29.7	31.1
Yugoslavs	1.2	5.6	6.0	6.7	6.9	5.0	3.5	8.6	6.5
Macedonians	-	0.3	-	0.2	0.3	0.2	0.4	1.0	0.3
Albanians	0.1	-	-	-	-	-	0.1	0.1	0.1
Hungarians	-	-	-	0.1	0.2	0.2	1.0	1.2	0.2
Others	0.3	0.3	0.6	0.5	0.7	0.2	0.1	2.6	0.7
Did Not Declare a Nationality	0.3	0.3	0.6	0.7	1.0	0.9	0.8	1.2	0.9
Unknown	0.3	-	0.4	0.4	0.4	0.3	0.2	0.2	0.3
Total	100.0	100.0	100.0	100.0	100.0	100.0	100.0	100.0	100.0
(Number)	(3.8 M)	(743)	(1408)	(10,378)	(15,393)	(937)	(2739)	(1837)	(33,334)

Source: Same as Table 7.1.

the political elite (Table 7.3), with the two groups having roughly proportional representation in the non-political sectors. In 1971 the Moslem community was significantly underrepresented in both the political and non-political sectors of the elite. The fact that Moslem ethnic and regional consciousness was only officially recognized and encouraged in 1961 is primarily responsible for the pattern of underrepresentation in the 1971 data. The Serbian elite representation is weakest in the literary and artistic elite, the only sector in which Moslems outnumber Serbs and the sector in which the Croats of Bosnia have their highest level of representation.

In Vojvodina where Serbs comprised 55.8 percent of the population in 1971, Serbian elite overrepresentation is manifest across the entire elite structure (Table 7.4). This pattern is understandable when it is recalled that Vojvodina's Serbs have traditionally been the most intellectually and politically active section of the Serbian community in Yugoslavia. This traditional pattern of political activism continued during the war when the persecution of the Serbs at the hands of the Hungarian occupation authorities and their local Hungarian auxiliaries drove thousands of Serbs into the Partisan movement. The postwar expropriation of the region's German farmland as patronage for Partisan soldiers and their families who had originally resided in the more populated and underdeveloped regions of the country (mainly Serbs from Bosnia and Croatia), also contributed to an influx of Serbs into Vojvodina's political elite. Considering such factors, the underrepresentation of Hungarians in the party, mass organizations, and state elite sectors is not unexpected, although the regime's explicit use of ethnic criteria in recruitment might have been anticipated to correct this pattern of representation. The Croats' underrepresentation in the elite structure is less extreme and less difficult to understand in view of the traditional Serbian position in this region (Vojvodina is part of the Serbian republic). Only in the artistic and literary elite are Hungarians and other small nationalities well represented. As in Bosnia and Croatia, it is in the humanistic intelligentsia where the Serbian elite presence is least overwhelming.

The difficulties stemming from the efforts of Kosovo's population to secure greater elite representation has been a significant factor in contemporary Yugoslav politics. Albanian representation in Kosovo's political elite appears somewhat better in 1971 than in previous years (Table 7.5), although it is still far below the group's proportional size in the region's population. This pattern is especially apparent in the legislative-governmental elite where Serbs constituted one-third of the total membership, while only comprising less than one-fifth of the region's population (the Serbian presence in Kosovo's urban centers if far higher). In view of Kosovo's traditionally weak economic and educational infrastructure and also considering past discrimination against local Albanians, it is not surprising that the representation of Albanians was weakest in the scientific and technical intelligentsia. Serbian dominance in this sector as revealed by the 1971 data, was especially striking considering the sizable

Lenard J. Cohen

Table 7.4
The Ethnic Composition of Elite Sectors in Vojvodina (%)

Ethnic Group	Total Population (1971)	Elite Sectors							
		Party and Mass Organization Functionaries	Legislative and Government Personnel	Managerial Personnel	Technical Intelligentsia	Physical Scientists	Natural Scientists	Literary/Artistic Intelligentsia	Total Elite
Serbs	55.8	63.0	63.4	64.4	64.6	62.9	68.5	54.1	64.0
Montenegrins	1.9	5.7	5.2	5.2	3.7	4.6	4.8	0.8	4.1
Croats	7.1	5.1	5.4	5.8	6.0	5.0	4.7	4.8	5.5
Slovenes	0.2	-	0.1	0.5	0.5	0.9	0.2	0.4	0.4
Moslems	0.2	0.2	-	0.1	0.1	0.1	0.1	0.4	0.1
Yugoslavs	2.4	4.0	6.8	4.9	5.0	5.6	3.6	4.8	4.8
Macedonians	0.8	0.6	0.4	0.6	0.7	0.5	1.0	0.4	0.7
Albanians	0.2	-	0.1	-	-	-	0.1	0.1	-
Hungarians	21.7	13.9	12.4	13.3	14.8	15.7	11.6	23.5	14.7
Others	9.0	7.1	5.1	4.4	3.8	4.0	4.9	9.7	4.9
Did Not Declare a Nationality	0.3	0.2	0.1	0.3	0.2	0.3	0.2	0.3	0.2
Unknown	0.3	0.2	0.3	0.2	0.3	0.2	0.2	0.3	0.2
Total	100.0	100.0	100.0	100.0	100.0	100.0	100.0	100.0	100.0
(Number)	(1.9 M)	(495)	(789)	(8286)	(9793)	(1014)	(5332)	(3037)	(28,746)

Source: Same as Table 7.1.

The Socialist Pyramid: Elites and Power in Yugoslavia

migratory outflow of Serbs from Kosovo following their weakened political position in the region after 1966 (see Chapter 8). The large Montenegrin contingent in Kosovo's 1971 elite structure is also noteworthy, particularly since Montengrins can be considered together with Serbs as a single ethnic constellation. Joint Serbo-Montenegrin representation in the important governmental elite is nearly equal in size to the Albanian's representation. Thus, in 1971 only one-third of Kosovo's total elite was composed of Albanians, although that group constituted nearly three-quarters of the provincial population.

The preceding cross-regional survey clearly reveals the prominent position of the Serbs in Yugoslavia's 1971 elite structure. Serbs were overrepresented in the Croatian political elite, enjoyed a numerical majority in all of Vojvodina's elite sectors, had a plurality lead in the Bosnian elite, and were in an exceptionally strong position along with Montenegrins in Kosovo's political, economic and scientific-technical elites. This pattern leaves aside Serbian control of their own republic (the largest in the country) and the important role of Serbs in the affairs of the federal party, mass organizations and governmental apparatus centered in Belgrade. Moreover, considering the close ethnic bond between the Montenegrins and the Serbs, only two republics, Slovenia and Macedonia, are without strong regionally-based Serbian political influence.

A contrasting interpretation of this data would emphasize that by 1971, Serbian proportional overrepresentation in the regional and total elite structures of the country was far less extreme than the role of the Serbs in the interwar state (except perhaps within Croatia) and was set within a far different type of constitutional system and ideological framework. Moreover, statistical dominance in elite sectors cannot be automatically equated with political dominance. Politics in Yugoslavia since the late 1960's, especially at the federal level, has been far more poli-centric and confederal than the data discussed above would suggest, even during the years of resurgent centralization. Thus, a good case can also be made for a gradual erosion of Serbian political influence in the decision-making processes at both the regional and federal levels. One generalization which needs less qualification, however, is that the Serbs because of temperament, historical circumstances, and the size of their community in the total population, remain well ensconced in the elite structure of the Yugoslav state.

The Yugoslav regime's effort to accommodate the aspirations of the different nationality groups for more political and economic influence is also illustrated in data on the graduates of university faculties. Two post-secondary faculties have been selected for analysis: (1) the "Higher Schools" of Political Science which, despite having become regular university faculties in most regions, are essentially feeder channels into the party apparatus, government structure, mass organizations and media (Table 7.6); and (2) the faculties of economics at each of the universities in Yugoslavia (Table 7.7). These latter educational institutions have played an important role in training a new

Table 7.5
The Ethnic Composition of Elite Sectors in Kosovo (%)

Ethnic Group	Total Population (1971)	Party and Mass Organization Functionaries	Legislative and Government Personnel	Managerial Personnel	Technical Intelligentsia	Physical Scientists	Natural Scientists	Literary/Artistic Intelligentsia	Total Elite
Serbs	18.4	23.9	33.5	39.7	54.1	58.1	52.7	24.3	45.2
Montenegrins	2.5	10.7	11.5	12.7	12.1	7.2	16.1	2.7	11.7
Croats	0.7	-	0.2	1.1	1.0	-	0.7	2.0	0.9
Slovenes	-	-	-	0.7	0.4	-	0.1	0.2	0.4
Moslems	2.1	1.0	2.6	2.0	3.2	1.2	1.7	1.8	2.4
Yugoslavs	0.1	-	0.5	0.2	0.3	0.3	0.5	1.6	0.5
Macedonians	0.1	0.5	0.5	1.1	0.5	0.8	0.9	0.7	0.8
Albanians	73.7	62.4	48.8	40.5	26.0	30.3	25.9	43.6	34.5
Hungarians	-	-	-	0.1	-	0.4	-	0.4	0.1
Others	2.3	1.5	2.2	1.8	2.0	0.4	1.1	22.2	3.4
Did Not Declare a Nationality	-	-	-	-	0.2	-	-	0.2	0.2
Unknown	0.1	-	0.2	0.1	0.2	-	0.3	0.2	0.1
Total	100.0	100.0	100.0	100.0	100.0	100.0	100.0	100.0	100.0
(Number)	(1.2 M)	(197)	(418)	(1482)	(2012)	(241)	(750)	(451)	(5551)

Source: Same as Table 7.1.

The Socialist Pyramid: Elites and Power in Yugoslavia

Table 7.6
Graduates from "Higher Schools of Political Science" by Ethnicity and Region (%)

Ethnic Group	Yugoslavia	Serbia	Montenegro	Croatia	Slovenia	Macedonia	Bosnia-Hercegovina	Kosovo	Vojvodina
Serbs	37.2	63.5	3.2	16.3	1.0	3.0	43.5	36.4	56.7
Montenegrins	7.0	11.7	96.8	2.2	0.5	-	2.3	13.6	7.5
Croats	19.5	3.3	-	69.2	1.5	-	13.1	-	4.5
Slovenes	11.6	1.7	-	1.1	95.0	-	0.2	-	-
Moslems	7.5	1.5	-	0.5	-	-	28.0	-	-
Yugoslavs	8.1	12.2	-	6.8	0.5	-	10.2	-	4.5
Macedonians	4.4	2.6	-	0.3	0.5	88.0	0.2	-	-
Albanians	1.0	0.7	-	-	-	6.0	-	40.9	-
Hungarians	1.0	0.6	-	-	-	-	-	-	17.8
Others	1.1	1.0	-	0.8	0.5	3.0	2.0	9.1	6.0
Did Not Declare a Nationality	1.0	0.6	-	2.0	-	-	1.3	-	1.5
Unknown	0.6	0.6	-	0.8	0.5	-	1.0	-	1.5
Total	100.0	100.0	100.0	100.0	100.0	100.0	100.0	100.0	100.0
(Number)	(1709)	(539)	(31)	(367)	(195)	(67)	(421)	(22)	(67)

Source: Popis Stanovištva i stanova 1971. Stanovištvo. Pismenost i Školovanost. Rezultati po republikama i pokrajinama. Knjiga II (Belgrade: Savezni Zavod za Statistiku, 1974), pp. 192-292.

Table 7.7
Graduates from Faculties of Economics by Ethnicity and Region (%)

Ethnic Group	Yugoslavia	Serbia	Montenegro	Croatia	Slovenia	Macedonia	Bosnia-Hercegovina	Kosovo	Vojvodina
Serbs	41.8	83.2	9.0	12.0	2.4	5.1	36.4	41.7	65.1
Montenegrins	5.5	5.2	78.7	0.9	0.6	0.9	2.5	12.7	7.1
Croats	26.7	1.9	1.8	78.7	2.5	0.4	17.0	0.6	6.3
Slovenes	6.2	0.9	0.3	1.3	92.3	-	0.4	0.2	0.4
Moslems	4.4	0.8	3.1	0.7	0.1	-	34.9	2.0	0.1
Yugoslavs	3.9	4.5	4.6	3.3	0.7	0.8	6.6	0.4	5.6
Macedonians	7.0	1.1	0.1	0.4	0.3	87.4	-	0.3	0.4
Albanians	1.2	0.1	0.8	0.1	0.1	1.2	0.1	40.2	-
Hungarians	0.9	0.1	-	0.4	-	-	0.1	-	9.8
Others	1.6	1.5	0.4	1.3	0.6	4.2	0.6	1.5	4.1
Did Not Declare a Nationality	0.5	0.4	0.3	0.7	0.2	-	0.9	0.4	0.8
Unknown	0.6	0.6	-	0.8	0.5	-	1.0	-	1.5
Total	100.0	100.0	100.0	100.0	100.0	100.0	100.0	100.0	100.0
(Number)	(32,998)	(10,862)	(953)	(9836)	(1923)	(2479)	(3605)	(805)	(2535)

Source: Same as Table 7.6, pp. 192-292.

generation of more professionalized managerial personnel to replace the more politicized managers who directed the economy during the early period of Yugoslav socialist development. The data indicates that a considerable number of young Albanians in Kosovo, and Hungarians in Vojvodina have been trained for political and economic work, although hardly in proportions which are representative of their distribution in the total populations of those regions. The disproportionately small number of Albanians in Kosovo with formal political science training is most striking, however, when the rapid demographic and political "Albanianization" of the region after 1966 is considered. The educational progress of the Moslem group in Bosnia is more uneven. Moslems comprise an equitable proportion of all graduates from the economic faculty, but Serbs continued to be overrepresented among graduates from the political faculty (although the inclusion of ethnic Serbs and Moslems in the large group of graduates declaring a "Yugoslav" ethnic identity prevents a clear picture of the two groups).[10] The number of Serbian and Montenegrin political science graduates in Croatia is also disproportionately high, with the Croatians having a ten percent smaller contingent in this field than that group's share in their own republic would ideally justify. It should also be noted, however, that Serbs and Montenegrins are slightly underrepresented among the graduates of the economic faculty of Croatia using the same yardstick of representativeness. Yugoslavia's Serbs might also argue in response to these findings that their ethnic group is underrepresented among the political science graduates in their own republic, i.e., at the Faculty of Political Science in Belgrade. The large Montenegrin political science contingent which graduated from the faculty in Belgrade and lives in Serbia (11.7 percent in a republic where Montenegrins compose only one percent of the population) might be considered to compensate, however, for the Serbian underrepresentation.

Leaving aside the rather skewed cases of Croatia and Kosovo, the data clearly reveals that an explicit ethnic key is being used in student recruitment, a development which will probably have long-term consequences for ethnic relations in Yugoslavia. Thus, in view of trends and policies first adopted in the 1960's, the ethnic makeup of both the political and non-political elite sectors has gradually become more statistically representative. It is unclear, however, how this development will actually affect ethnic conflict in the country. As each elite sector becomes more ethnically heterogeneous, both regionally and in the country as a whole, larger contingents of self-confident and aspiring leaders from the different subcultural groups are very likely to emerge. It is possible that such a trend might intensify intra-elite rivalry and thus offset the symbolic gains of greater group equity or proportionality in the overall composition of societal leadership. It is also possible that various obstacles - ethnic discrimination or lack of room at the top - will create a surplus of highly trained individuals from the emerging intelligentsia of the previously underrepresented ethnic groups. Such ethnically skewed unemployment may create serious tensions, especially if the situation is not alleviated by other opportunities (e.g., the possibility of foreign employment reduced such pressure during the 1970's).[11]

While suffering from certain inherent limitations, the statistical data on ethnic group representation does provide certain useful political insights. For example, although such data cannot predict what actions members of a given group will undertake, it can indicate if members of that group are present in sufficient numbers to initiate meaningful action, to react to events, or to acquire skills and experience. Data on representation is also important in terms of political symbolism; and in a cleavage-ridden society such as Yugoslavia symbols have significant political consequences. Such statistics are thus closely watched and interpreted by both political actors and analysts. Even more important, however, are the behavioural patterns of individuals within the elite groups being examined. Who and what do the so-called ethnic representatives in each elite sector actually represent? What aspect of their identity has the strongest influence on their behaviour? Does the increased presence (passive representation) of individuals from a certain ethnic group in one elite sector or another increase the substantive (active) representation of the ethnic group when the state makes and implements policy?[12] A related issue considered in the next section of this chapter concerns the extent to which members of different ethnic groups interact within the Yugoslav elite structure, and what that pattern of interaction suggests about political cohesion in Yugoslavia and other multi-national states.

The Pattern of Interaction

An important precondition for consociational accommodation is the willingness of different subcultural elites to cooperate in the governance of a regime, as well as in other spheres which require interdependent group action, such as the public bureaucracy, the economy, and the military. In brief, subcultural elites must interact and communicate in order to achieve a stable level of intergroup accommodation. Culturally segmented states contain various incentives for such interaction. Lijphart has remarked, for example, that "elites cooperate in spite of the segmental differences dividing them because to do otherwise would mean to call forth the prophesied consequences of the plural character of the society. An alternative or additional factor predisposing political leaders to be moderate and cooperative is the prior existence of a tradition of elite accommodation."[13] Jurg Steiner, another member of what has been called the "incipient school" of consociational theory, has also suggested that the relatively small size of elites in small segmented states is conducive to cooperative behaviour necessary for the success of consociationalism. "Hence," he maintains, "the probability is greater that the members of the political elite will interact relatively frequently" and "frequent interaction tends to increase mutual goodwill." This goodwill in turn makes political leaders less likely to "perceive politics as a zero sum game, in which a strategy of 'all or nothing' is applied. For the winners in such a game would forfeit the loser's goodwill, and this would entail high costs relative to the rewards to be gained."[14]

Consociational theorists regard interaction among subcultures on the *elite level* as a learning process which can offset the political instability and conflict sometimes found to derive from social communication or routing interaction among members of different cultural groups on the *mass level*. Thus, while consociational theory incorporates the basic assumption of "transaction theorists" such as Karl Deutsch, regarding the importance of personal social contracts and communication as an impetus to inter-cultural harmony, it does so only with regard to the elite level of society.[15]

Important issues which have not yet been fully explored theoretically or empirically in the literature on consociationalism include the patterns and propensities of interaction among different cultural groups (either on the mass or elite levels), and the extent to which different elite sectors vary as contexts for subcultural interaction. There is a small but important body of research on these questions which demonstrates not only that specific political situations (e.g., the issues, desired outcomes, the perceived balance of advantages and disadvantages) affect elite level accommodation, but that such accommodation is also influenced by both the extent of established *ethnic distance* among elite members of diverse subcultural groups, and varies according to the *type* of elite sector in question. Ethnic distance refers to a social-psychological factor reflected in personal attitudes toward other subcultures. Such distance, that is, levels of ethnic closure and openess, tends to be shaped by the history of previous contacts among different groups, as well as by the patterns of socialization within each group and within other spheres of society. The type of elite sector involved also affects the extent of group interaction. An analysis of ethnic distance must therefore consider the influence of different functions, jobs, careers, and elite level socialization on ethnic relations. It may be, as consociational theory maintains, that a high level of inter-subcultural interaction within the *political* elite helps to reduce hostility in culturally segmented societies. Even if this is so, however, what effect does interaction in other elite sectors have on political stability and ethnic conflict or interaction within other elite sectors? For example, high levels of cross-cultural interaction within the economic, military, or media elite sectors, may be essential if the activities of political and governmental leaders are to be genuinely effective. Conversely, high levels of hostility among members of different subcultural groups in some elite sectors, for example among intellectuals, may suggest that expanded cross-cultural contact in a specific sector is undesirable. In such elite sectors it may prove beneficial to reduce direct cross-cultural contact and channel the articulation of "cultural interests" through political spokesmen.

Lenard J. Cohen

Analysis of segmented societies also necessitates the differentiation of elite subsectors within the political realm, e.g., the legislature, the party organization, administration, etc. For example, accommodation among elected ethnic spokesmen in a legislature may be meaningless if subcultural conflicts flourish and "distance" is maintained among ethnic cliques in the leadership of the public bureaucracy. It is also possible that the accommodationist efforts of political and other elites may have little success because of persistent and vitriolic conflicts among intellectuals or other "symbol manipulators" (e.g., the media) who can influence sizable popular audiences. Accordingly, the recognition of different *elites* and not simply *an elite* is important to further research on consociationalism.

In order to explore such issues in the Yugoslav context, it is useful to examine information concerning ethnic interaction within various Yugoslav elite sectors. The data derived from a survey conducted by the Institute of Social Sciences in Belgrade in cooperation with the Bureau of Applied Social Research at Columbia University during 1968 and 1969. A total of 517 Yugoslav leaders were interviewed out of a positional universe list of 1,462 persons. The survey included members of six elite sectors: federal legislators, federal administrators, party (the League of Yugoslav Communists) and mass organization leaders, economic leaders, mass communicators, and intellectuals.[16] Two of the survey questions relate to the issue of elite interaction:

(Question 78): With what three people in the past month have you most often had discussions about problems in your field?

(Question 79): With what three people in the last month have you most often discussed important questions of general significance?

By examining the characteristics of the individuals named as interaction partners by the elite respondents surveyed, it is possible to explore the nature of contacts within and between the elite sectors of Yugoslav society, including the pattern of ethnic interaction (see Chapter 5 on the pattern of organizational interactions). The responses to the interaction questions were unfortunately not as numerous as answers to most other questions in the survey; a situation which can most likely be attributed to both the natural reticence of elite individuals about their personal contacts, and also to the political sensitivity of such questions. Analyzing the responses on interaction is further complicated by the fact that the social background characteristics, including ethnicity of the persons named by elite respondents as their interaction partners could not be determined for those persons named outside the positional elite universe list (i.e., the

The Socialist Pyramid: Elites and Power in Yugoslavia

combined list of 1,462 individuals encompassing six elite sectors). Thus, the analysis of the pattern of interaction is limited to contacts among respondents and their interaction partners within the universe of elite positions drawn up for the survey, that is, individuals for whom information on ethnic identity was known.

For purposes of analysis the answers to the two interaction questions were combined, i.e., individuals nominated as interaction partners on problems in a specific field (Question 78) and on issues of general significance (Question 79) were considered together. Table 7.8 presents a breakdown of the entire sample in terms of ethnic composition and elite sectors, and provides the same information for those individuals who responded to the interaction questions. A total of 271 out of 517 elite members interviewed provided responses concerning their interaction patterns which could be analyzed in terms of the ethnic group characteristics of the persons named.

The ethnic breakdown of respondents who provided interaction data closely parallels the overall distribution of ethnic groups in the sample. Thus, among the respondents on interaction, Macedonians are most overrepresented and Slovenes are most underrepresented when compared to the total population (see Table 7.8). Despite the limitations of the data, the responses on interaction, nevertheless, offer a rare insight into the nature of elite ethnic contacts in Yugoslavia. Table 7.9 illustrates the pattern of inter-ethnic contacts in the elite based on responses available for five of Yugoslavia's major ethnic groups represented in the sample (the other ethnic group subsamples and response rates were too small to yield useful insights). On a general level two very interesting findings are revealed: first, the pattern of interaction varies considerably among ethnic groups; and second, the pattern of elite level contacts is very similar to patterns of mass level ethnic interaction and ethnic distance which have emerged in various Yugoslav studies.

A consideration of different levels of out-group contacts, reveals that Montenegrins manifest the highest level of ethnic interaction, and are the only group in which the number of interactions with other groups exceeds intra-group contacts. It should be noted, however, that Montenegrin interactions occur mainly with Serbs who, as discussed earlier, are of the same broad ethnic grouping as Montenegrins. Such excessively high interaction levels between Monenegrins and Serbs can also be attributed to the fact that Montenegrin respondents hold positions in the federal administrative elite (see Table 7.8), and therfore live in Yugoslavia's capital, the Serbian city of Belgrade. In contrast, the respondents in other sectors are more geographically dispersed. Moreover, the federal administration happens to be the particular sector exhibiting one of the highest levels of cross-ethnic interaction (see below). The small number of Montenegrins in the total population, as well as in the elite universe sample, also suggests that they have a small potential pool of in-group contacts; a factor which

Table 7.8
The Ethnic Composition of the Survey Sample by Elite Sector
and Respondents to Questions on Interaction* (%)

	Federal Legislators		Party and Mass Organization Functionaries		Federal Administrators		Economic Elite		Media Leaders		Intellectuals		Total	
Ethnic Group	Total Sample	Total Respondents	Total Sample	Total Respondents	Total Sample	Total Respondents	Total Sample	Total Respondents	Total Sample	Total Respondents	Total Sample	Total Respondents	Total Sample	Total Respondents
Serbs	41.0	39.0	32.9	36.8	38.9	35.6	69.0	66.7	57.4	61.3	38.5	34.1	45.6	45.0
Croats	15.4	14.6	13.8	7.9	16.7	18.6	13.6	11.1	11.9	6.5	15.4	22.7	14.7	13.7
Slovenes	10.8	14.6	11.9	13.2	7.8	3.4	4.9	3.7	7.9	6.5	5.8	-	7.9	6.6
Macedonians	16.9	22.0	17.1	26.3	6.7	10.2	6.2	14.8	6.9	8.1	11.5	18.2	10.4	15.5
Montenegrins	3.1	2.4	6.6	-	18.9	16.9	3.7	-	4.0	4.9	5.8	6.8	7.2	6.3
Moslems	1.5	-	1.3	-	2.2	3.4	1.2	-	-	-	1.9	2.3	1.4	1.1
Yugoslavs	4.6	-	6.6	5.3	5.6	6.8	4.9	3.7	5.9	4.8	13.5	13.6	7.2	5.9
Hungarians	1.5	2.4	3.9	5.3	1.1	1.7	1.2	-	2.0	1.6	1.0	-	1.7	1.9
Albanians	1.5	2.4	1.3	2.6	2.2	3.4	1.2	-	-	-	1.9	-	1.4	1.5
Others	1.5	2.4	2.6	2.6	-	-	-	-	1.0	1.6	2.0	2.3	1.2	1.5
Unknown	1.5	-	-	-	-	-	-	-	3.0	4.8	2.9	-	1.4	1.1
Total	100.0	100.0	100.0	100.0	100.0	100.0	100.0	100.0	100.0	100.0	100.0	100.0	100.0	100.0
(Number)	(65)	(41)	(76)	(38)	(90)	(59)	(61)	(27)	(101)	(62)	(104)	(44)	(517)	(271)

* Respondents choosing interaction partners whose ethnic identity could be determined.

may also affect the Montenegrin propensity for out-group contact revealed in the analysis.

The total elite subsample of Croatian respondents also exhibits a high level of out-group interaction, but with a higher level of in-group contacts and a more diffuse pattern of cross-group interactions than in the case of the Montenegrins. The second and third largest number of Croatian contacts are with Serbs and Montenegrins (contacts which taken together exceed intra-Croatian choices). Serbian respondents occupy a midway position between the extremes of high intra-group contacts and high out-group contacts, which is understandable considering that the Serbs are the largest ethnic group in both Yugoslavia and in the country's elite. The Serbian elite respondents also have the most diffuse pattern of responses. In fact, they are the only group in the sample who collectively exhibit a pattern of interaction with all of the other major ethnic groups, including the smaller nationalities.

Table 7.9
Internationality Contact in the Yugoslav Elite (%)

Nationality of Persons Chosen	Nationality of Elite Respondents						
	Serbs (n-22)	Croats (n-37)	Slovenes (n-18)	Macedonians (n-42)	Montenegrins (n-17)	Yugoslavs (n-16)	Total (n-252)
Serbs	63.5	26.8	11.1	8.3	38.9	41.7	42.3
Croats	9.9	41.1	11.1	3.6	16.7	25.0	14.0
Slovenes	5.4	8.9	74.1	6.0	8.3	8.3	11.0
Macedonians	2.3	5.4	-	69.0	2.8	-	14.9
Montenegrins	6.8	16.1	3.7	6.0	30.6	20.8	10.2
Yugoslavs	7.7	1.8	-	-	2.8	-	4.2
Albanians	0.5	-	-	3.6	-	-	1.0
Moslems	0.5	-	-	-	-	-	1.0
Others (minorities)	3.6	-	-	3.6	-	4.2	2.7
Total Choices	100.0	100.0	100.0	100.0	100.0	100.0	100.0
(Number)	(222)	(56)	(27)	(84)	(36)	(24)	(449)

At the other extreme from the Montenegrins and Croats are the Macedonian and Slovene respondents who reveal very high levels of intra-subcultural interaction. This pattern is likely the result of each group's very distinct linguistic and cultural position relative to the broad Serbo-Croatian language group. The elite interaction data for the Slovenes and Macedonians is very similar to other data available on patterns of intermarriage and, in the case of the very ethnocentric Slovenes, on attitudes and migration patterns.[17] The Slovene elite respondents choice of Croats as their second most frequent interaction partners (parallelled by their contacts with the Serbs), and their lack

317

Lenard J. Cohen

of interaction with members of Yugoslavia's southeastern and smaller nationalities, also corresponds to other data on Slovenian mass level interaction.

As the above discussion indicates, the total pattern of ethnic interaction in Yugoslavia at the elite level bears a close resemblance to interaction patterns within the general population. Indeed, the striking similarity of elite and mass patterns of ethnic interaction suggests - at least in terms of the sociometry of elite level contacts - that a rather weak basis exists in Yugoslavia for the "overarching" elite accommodation so crucial to consociational theory. A closer examination of the interaction data by elite subsectors indicates, however, that it may also be important to consider other factors and other subpatterns within the overall elite pattern. Table 7.10 offers a breakdown of interaction choices by elite sectors for Serbs, Croats and Macedonians, namely, those groups which provided a sufficient number of survey responses in each elite sector to warrant analysis. Several interesting insights emerge from a consideration of the findings. First, there are significant differences among elite sectors in the level of inter-subcultural contact. It appears that the highest level of cross-ethnic interaction occurs within the federal administrative elite (that is, they have the fewest in-group contacts), while the lowest level is found among the media leaders, i.e., the communications elite. Economic leaders and the intellectual sector also manifested very low levels of intergroup contact. The members of the two political elite subsectors, the party/mass orgranization and the legislative elites, occupy a mid-range position in terms of their interaction, with approximately half of these respondents' total interactions occurring with members of their own ethnic groups.

Table 7.10
Ethnic Interaction in the Yugoslav Elite by Elite Sector and Selected Ethnic Groups (%)

Elite Sectors	Serbian Respondents (N-122) In-Group Choices	Croatian Respondents (N-37) In-Group Choices	Macedonian Respondents (N-42) In-Group Choices	Total Three-Groups (N-201) In-Group Choices
Party and mass organization leaders	57.9	33.3	80.0	53.8
Federal legislators	50.0	50.0	50.0	50.0
Federal administrators	40.0	26.3	27.3	34.3
Economic leaders	65.2	25.0	100.0	66.6
Intellectuals (artistic & scientific intelligentsia)	52.0	66.7	82.4	64.8
Media leaders	82.0	33.0	90.0	80.0
Total Sample	63.5	41.1	69.0	-

The Socialist Pyramid: Elites and Power in Yugoslavia

The different interaction patterns characteristic of the various elite sectors appears to pertain in the case of each ethnic group studied, with some notable exceptions. For example, Serbian, Croatian, and Macedonian legislators all manifest the same combination of in-group and out-group ethnic interaction that was revealed in the legislative sector as a combined category. This finding seems to support other observations concerning the dual pressures stemming from ethnoregional loyalties and non-ethnic (pan-ethnic or supra-regional) values which influenced federal legislators during the late 1960's.[18] Viewed from another perspective the relatively high pattern of cross-ethnic interaction exhibited by all the political elite sectors - administrative, party/mass organization, and legislative - suggests that political service on the federal level may be a very important factor underlying the stability of the Yugoslav regime. Thus, there are numerous and well-known *conflicts* among the different ethnic groups in each political sub-elite, but there are also numerous *contacts* which may provide a basis for consensus formation.[19] The interactions of the party and mass organization leaders from different nationalities is less uniform than the pattern revealed by the legislators. For example, there is a sharp contrast between the very intra-group oriented Macedonians, and the high level of out-group contacts exhibited by Croatian functionaries. The latter finding, which is somewhat surprising in view of the surge of nationalism in the Croatian party leadership during the period of the survey (1968-1969), might be explained by the small number of Croatian respondents in this elite sector (three individuals). Moreover, because all those Croats surveyed in this sector had served for a considerable period of time at the federal level of the party and mass organizations, it is likely that they were more "open" and personally interconnected than most Croatian elite members.[20]

The very high level of cross-ethnic interaction revealed in the federal administrative sector as a whole was also manifest among Serbian and Macedonian administrators analyzed as individual groups, while the Croatian administrators manifested very close to that nationality's highest level of out-group contacts. In contrast, the Serbian and especially the Macedonian economic leaders revealed very high rates of intra-group contact. This situation probably derives from the regional concentration of most economic leaders in various enterprises, and also to the highly autarkic aspects of Yugoslavia's decentralized market economy. Surprisingly, this high rate of intra-group contact was not manifest in the sample of Croatian economic leaders responding to the interaction qustions. Again, however, the sample of Croatian economic leaders was very small (three persons). Of course, the findings may also be representative of a broader pattern of cross-ethnic contacts among Croatian managerial personnel and other Croatian economic leaders. In any case, it is important to caution that even with larger samples, the pattern of contacts discussed here cannot provide definitive answers concerning a particular elite's or ethnic group's commitment to nationalism, or about the ethnic-oriented views of those particular individuals who are interacting. Thus, the interaction data only suggest a *basis* for elite level inter-ethnic accommodation which may have consequences for ethnic relations in Yugoslav society. Viewed from this perspective, findings such as the total lack of interaction by Macedonian managers with other ethnic groups, for example, suggest a very poor basis for either cross-cultural communications or accommodation by economic leaders in that republic. In contrast, within each ethnic group studied the legislative and administrative elite sectors appear to have the highest potential for inter-ethnic contact. This latter finding would seem to lend some very general support to the argument of consociational theorists concerning the importance of political elite sectors for conflict resolution in multi-ethnic societies.

The Croatian group's highest level of intra-ethnic contact occurred within the intellectual sector; two-thirds of the interaction partners chosen by the Croatian artistic and scientific intelligentsia respondents were fellow Croatians. This level of response was well above the average rate of intra-group contact for Croatians in all sectors of the sample combined (41.1 percent), as well as slightly above the average rate for the entire intellectual elite sector in the sample (64.8 percent). Such findings may reflect the prominent role played by the intellectuals in the upsurge of Croatian nationalism during the late 1960's.[21] Thus, one basis for "overarching" elite accommodation, namely, personal cross-ethnic contacts, appears less prevalent among Croatian intellectuals than among the Serbian intellectual sector. The Macedonian intellectual respondents exhibit even fewer inter-ethnic contacts than the Croats. The media leadership sector exhibited the most ethnocentric pattern of elite interaction except in the case of the Croatian respondents (again based on a very small subsample, nearly ten times smaller than that of the Serbian group).[22] In all three of the ethnic groups considered, either the intellectuals or the media sectors manifested the highest levels of intra-ethnic elite contacts.

Elite Sectors and Ethnicity

The analysis of interaction patterns within Yugoslavia's leadership offers a systematic basis for understanding certain trends and patterns in the country's political development. For example, although the strong outburst of nationalism which occurred during the late 1960's can be traced to various sources, the central leadership's strong attack against nationalism was particularly directed at two alleged villains: the media leaders (especially in Serbia), and the intellectuals (particularly in Croatia),[23] that is the same two groups which exhibited a very noticeable ethnocentric interaction pattern in the survey findings analyzed above. Such findings do not suggest, of course, that a high level of intra-group contact within an elite sector *causes* nationalism or ethnic-oriented political commitments, anymore than frequent interaction with members of other ethnic groups causes intergroup harmony. Moreover, the general interaction patterns discussed above do not reveal homogeneous elite behaviour with respect to individuals in any particular sector or ethnic group, but only relative differences in orientation, or tendencies of group interaction. On the other hand, such interaction tendencies do suggest rather important patterns of communication among elite members from different ethnic identities, which together with other factors certainly influence ethnic relations in a society.

Little research has been devoted to how and why aspects of ethnic conflict become deeply associated with (and are more quickly articulated by) certain elites or certain occupational and organizational sectors rather than by others. How, for example, do the "objective" determinants of ethnic divisiveness based in material disparities become linked to social distance among members of various subcultural groups working in different functional elite sectors. Elites are intervening variables in ethnic conflict, but in which direction and to what extent? Answers to these questions vary depending upon the specific elite sectors examined and the specific ethnic groups involved. In order to understand the political dynamics of multi-ethnic societies such as Yugoslavia, it would be useful to have additional information concerning the proclivity of specific elite sectors and organizational settings to encourage the cross-cultural accommodation of particular ethnic groups. For example, one hypothesis suggested by the above findings is that the tasks carried out by higher administrative personnel influence their high levels of inter-ethnic contact and are conducive to inter-ethnic accommodation. In view of the specialized tasks and technical training of the Yugoslav administrative elite, the same "optimistic" hypothesis about ethnic interaction might be applied to the technical intelligentsia (a group not included in this elite survey, but discussed earlier in the analysis of census data). Conversely it might be hypothesized that many members of both the communication elite and the humanistic intelligentsia - whose work often expresses the cultural dimensions and distinct symbols of a society - will be less prone to inter-ethnic contact and accommodation.

The available literature concerning precisely how different occupational and organization roles affect ethnic identity does not provide any clear-cut answers to these questions. There is some evidence from Canada, for example, that high-ranking individuals from minority ethnic groups working in the "creative" areas of highly professionalized and technically specialized fields have a greater tendency than those with non-creative job responsibilities toward assimilation with the society's dominant ethnic group. It is suggested that individuals in such creative roles have invested many years preparing for their specialized employment, are career-minded, seek to develop rapport with their peers irrespective of background, and manifest the kind of intense involvement with their work that tends to spill over into off-work personal contacts. The Canadian findings further suggests that in contrast, minority individuals in lower level and more routine professional and technical posts do not exhibit such characteristics and thus are more likely to maintain their ethnic identity and preserve links with their ethnic communities.[24]

Another study of inter-*Lager* accommodation in politically (but not ethnically) fragmented Austria, found that the technocratic elites and middle level economic elites engage in the highest "cross segmental contact" and defend the system against the "'threat' of centrifugal evolution." In contrast to partisan elites who were ideological, rancorous and accusatory, the technocratic elites were found to have a political style which was "moderate, their rhetoric subdued, and nonrancorous. They generally approach pending public policy issues empirically and pragmatically."[25]

Evidence from a study of the Israeli public service also reveals that bureaucratic recruitment and socialization do not easily overcome the importance of cultural background with respect to bureaucratic attitudes. The study points out, for example, that high-ranking Israeli officals of Asian-African background actually have fewer opportunities than their ethnic counterparts at lower levels of the bureaucracy for social interaction with those Israelis of European cultural backgrounds. The study even suggests that the contacts which high-ranking officials of Asian-African background do have with bureaucrats from other cultural groups are essentially negative, leading the "non-European" Israeli officials to expect inferior treatment and to develop a weaker self-image of their role in the bureaucracy.[26]

Such research is interesting, but only suggests that the professional rasks and role expectations associated with technical and administrative jobs tend to conflict with and diminish the ethnic facets of an individual's identity and behaviour more often than jobs in other fields. Resolution of such conflict depends ultimately upon the particular individual and the situational factors involved. The complex relationship between occupational tasks and ethnic identity is illustrated in the case of the non-technical intelligentsia. Thus, the "humanistic" or "literary-artistic" intellegentsia has alternatively manifested both very low and very high support for nationalism and particular ethnic causes. One of the paradoxical features of this group is that while they are sometimes characterized as maintaining a commitment to universal or transnational ideals, they frequently associate the realization of those ideals with extremely parochial forms of nationalism. Leszek Kolakowski has drawn attention to this ambiguity as it relates to the role and political commitment of the intellectual elite:

> ... the awareness of universality being visible only from a particular perspective makes it difficult to separate the universal and the particular in our own consciousness, since to grasp our participation in universal patterns we are bound, perhaps, to belong to one particular civilization .... This belief in the universality of certain cultural patterns (including

patterns of thinking) runs against the need for total 'commitment' or for 'global belonging' to one particular culture or subculture or militant group .... Total commitment is difficult if we remain aware that we share with our enemies some basic values, even intellectual ones .... Precisely because social functions of intellectuals include the acceptance of universally valid patterns of thinking as obligatory norms, intellectuals are unable to constitute a group giving to its members that feeling of total commitment or the sense of belonging that many religious and political groups are able to supply .... The feeling of belonging may be extremely strong and is produced ... also by all circumstances that make life in contemporary society more and more dependent on rationally organized technological and administrative systems which destroy all remnants of the tribal community and all village-like communication.[27]

The commitment of many Yugoslav intellectuals to nationalist causes, especially those concerning language and artistic expression, as well as their alienation resulting from the pressures of bureaucratic centralism and modernization (particularly in the 1940's and 1950's and again in the 1970's), might partially reveal the operation of factors described by Kolakowski. The high level of intra-ethnic contacts evidenced among Croatian intellectuals and among intellectuals of other ethnic affiliations, certainly provides a basis for segmental or nationalist commitments, or may reflect the development of such commitments. Moreover, in Croatia as in other culturally segmented sections of Yugoslavia, intellectual elite sectors are often concentrated at locations and in jobs (e.g., universities, the editorial boards of cultural magazines, etc.) where the major indigenous ethnic groups (or the titular nationality of a region) have had the strongest representation. There is also some evidence from a 1968-1969 survey - "The Problems of Artistic Creativity in Croatia" - conducted by the Institute for Social Research of Zagreb University, that the supposedly trans-ethnic perspectives of socialist ideology so prominent in the 1950's had diminished as an influence on artistic expression by the 1960's, and had been replaced by a mixture of support for the "universal tendencies of European culture" and national (Croatian) traditions, especially among older intellectuals.[28] Such intellectual attitudes may help explain why, during 1972, that group played such a highly visible role in the nationalist "mass movement" which engulfed Croatia[29] (see Chapter 8 for a discussion of nationalism among Albanian intellectuals in the 1980's). The efforts and difficulties faced by dissident intellectuals in the establishment of a multi-ethnic and cross-regional "common platform" during the late 1970's again highlighted the political importance of the ethnic distance and ethnic bonds generated within different occupational and elite sectors.[30]

Lenard J. Cohen

Conclusion

The above theoretical discussion raises a number of complex and important issues which require further research. The preceding analysis of the available data is, nevertheless, very suggestive and potentially useful. Thus, the similarity of the findings concerning the pattern of ethnic distance in different elite sectors with the results of other studies concerning ethnic distance in the general population provides a sound empirical basis for making generalizations about inter-ethnic dynamics in Yugoslavia. The study's findings with regard to ethnic interaction within different elite sectors also provides a better understanding of why certain sectors in Yugoslavia, such as the intellectuals and media leadership, have become such hotbeds of nationalism and targets of attack by the central political authorities.

Additional research concerning how different elite occupations and organizations influence ethnic conflict would also be very useful for the analysis of multi-ethnic societies. For example, it would be interesting to explore whether individuals coopted into the political elite from other elite sectors retain habits of cross-ethnic interaction shaped by their prior occupational or organizational experiences. Do party and legislative politicians with engineering or administrative experience have a higher liklihood of interacting and compromising with politicians from other ethnic groups than, for example, politicians with other occupational backgrounds? Do intellectuals engaged in political activity tend to be inflexible on cultural questions which involve compromises among different ethnic groups? Such questions are also pertinent with respect to the different occupational groups recruited into higher ranks of the public bureaucracy.[31] Ethnic accommodation within an elite sector may also be influenced by the fact that certain elites, such as intellectuals, have relatively few routine contacts with other elite sectors. High-ranking administrative personnel, on the other hand, may have a more open communication network with other elites, which in turn may affect inter-ethnic relations within the administrative sector. Until such issues are adequately explored, the broad-ranging generalizations of consociational theory concerning the existence or need of "overarching" elite accommodation in multi-ethnic societies will remain very perceptive, but incomplete.

APPENDIX 7.1

ELITE SECTORS BY OCCUPATIONAL SUBGROUPS ACCORDING TO THE OFFICIAL CENSUS CATEGORIES

A. **Party and Mass Organization Functionaries**

1. Functionaries and other leading personnel on permanent duty in socio-political organizations (e.g. The League of Communists, Socialist Alliance, Trade Unions, Youth Organizations, Veterans' Organizations and the official organization for women).

2. Functionaries and other leading personnel on permanent duty in professional organizations and other social organizations.

3. Functionaries and other leading personnel on permanent duty in Chambers of Commerce and business associations.

B. **Legislative and Government Functionaries**

1. Members of representative bodies on permanent duty.

2. Elected functionaries of the executive organs of the assemblies and governments on permanent duty.

3. Leading personnel of the judicial organs.

4. Other functionaries of the exectuve organs of the assemblies and governments.

C. **Managerial Personnel**

1. Directors and other leading personnel of economic ogranizations.

2. Leading personnel of institutions for education and upbringing (except the directors of schools).

3. Leading personnel of cultural centers and cultural institutions.

4. Leading personnel of health institutions.

5. Leading personnel of scientific organizations.

6. Leading personnel of other working organizations (except in representative bodies and their executive organs).

D. Technical Intelligentsia

1. Specialists in the technical areas and technology - engineers.

2. Specialists in technical areas - technicians.

E. Physical Scientists

1. Chemists, physicists and specialists in related sciences.

2. Technicians of the chemical, physical and related sciences.

F. Natural Scientists

1. Specialists in the area of the natural sciences.

2. Technicians in the area of the natural sciences.

G. Literary/Artistic Intelligentsia

1. Writers and literary critics.

2. Set designers and their collaborators.

3. Musicians and their collaborators.

4. Choreographers and dancers.

5. Painters and their collaborators.

6. Artists and actors.

NOTES: CHAPTER SEVEN

1. See Arend Lijphart, *The Politics of Accommodation: Pluralism and Democracy in the Netherlands* (Berkeley: University of California Press, 1975), and also Lijphart's, *Democracy in Plural Societies: A Comparative Explanation* (New Haven: Yale University Press, 1977).

2. See for example, Kenneth McRae (ed.), *Consociational Democracy: Political Accommodation in Segmented Societies* (Toronto: McClelland and Stewart, 1974), as well as the studies cited in note 3.

3. For critical studies see Brian Barry, "Review Article: Political Accommodation and Consociational Democracy," *British Journal of Political Science*, V (1975), 477-505, and also Barry's, "The Consociational Model and Its Dangers," *European Journal of Political Research*, III (1976), 393-412, Hans Daalder, "The Consociational Democracy Theme," *World Politics*, XXVI, No. 4 (1974), 604-621, Jeffrey Obler, Jung Steiner, and Guido Dierickx, *Decision-Making in Smaller Democracies: The Consociational 'Burden'* (Beverly Hills: Sage Publications, 1977).

4. Eric Nordlinger, *Conflict Regulation in Divided Societies*, Occasional Paper in International Affairs, No. 29 (Cambridge: Harvard University Press, 1972). Two other major works employing the consociationalist approach are Jung Steiner, *Amicable Agreement Versus Majority Rule Conflict Resolution in Switzerland* (Chapel Hills: University of North Carolina Press, 1974), and Robert Prethus, *Elite Accommodation in Canadian Politics* (Cambridge: Cambridge University Press, 1973).

5. See for example, Walker Conner, "Nation-Building or Nation-Destroying?" *World Politics*, XXIV, No. 3 (1972), 319-355, Melanie Burgess, "The Resurgence of Ethnicity: Myth or Reality," *Ethnic and Racial Studies*, I, No. 3 (1978), 265-285.

6. In his comparative survey Lijphart only once mentions Yugoslavia as a case of "intermediate pluralism" which, in his opinion, would benefit from some form of "consociational engineering." Arend Lijphart, *Democracy in Plural Societies*, 235. The Yugoslav marxist regime, which abhors liberal democracy, would certainly

Lenard J. Cohen

view Lijphart's elite-centered normative model with distaste. This chapter, however, is concerned with the empirical analysis of political life, not with ideological goals. In this respect the dynamics of the Yugoslav regime are similar to many consociational patterns described in Lijphart's empirical analysis of segmented societies. Features of the Yugoslav case which Lijphart would view as conducive to consociationalism include: the small size of the country, the existence of external threats, and the fact that Yugoslavia's one-party system which is segmented along ethno-regional lines often functions more like a culturally segmented multi-party system. For other consociational facets of the Yugoslav case (e.g., proportionality, mutual veto, segmented autonomy and federalism, etc.), see the author's "Conflict Management and Institution-Building in Socialist Yugoslavia: The Role of the Parliamentary System," *Legislatures in Plural Societies: The Search for Cohesion in National Development*, ed. Albert Eldridge (Durham: Duke University Press, 1977), 122-165.

7. For a balanced account of the achievements and limitations of the Yugoslav system with regard to workers' control and local self-government see M. Broekmeyer, "Self-Management in Yugoslavia," *Annals of the American Academy of Political and Social Sciences*, XXIII (May, 1977), 180-196.

8. For example, an article in a Yugoslav periodical on the background of military officers noted the "infusion of cadres from all our republics and autonomous provinces into our officer corps ... this is one of the important principles and criteria applicable to the military academies. Although more and more favourable ratios are being achieved in this respect, there are still insufficient numbers in particular of Albanians, Hungarians, and Slovenians .... This is largely the result of objective circumstances, yet it is in part the outgrowth of a tradition for people in various regions to opt for the military calling or not ... a graduate of a secondary school in Slovenia can earn the pay of a sub-lieutenant without the further schooling involved in the four-year military academy .... So far as the other regions are concerned (e.g. there is no reason for the dearth of Moslems from Bosnia-Hercegovina among military officers), young people are thought to be uninformed, but other aspects of military life may be involved: discipline, subordination, scale of obligations and responsibilities, physical and mental strains, transfers ..." *Nedeljne Informativne Novine*, (March 14, 1976), 17-18.

Utilizing Yugoslav data, Ross Johnson has shown that in 1970 Serbs composed 46.7 percent of the general officers, and 57.4 percent of the officer corps, Croats 19.3 percent and 14.7 percent respectively, and Montenegrins 19.3 percent of the total population, Croats 22 percent and Serbs, 39.7 percent. Ross Johnson, *The Role of the Military in Communist Yugoslavia* (Santa Monica: The Rand Paper Series, January, 1978), P-6070, 19.

9. The diplomatic elite is one particular sector of previous nationality imbalance which has gradually improved as a result of the ethno-regional "key." See Lenard J. Cohen, "Federalism and Foreign Policy in Yugoslavia: The Politics of Regional Ethnonationalism," *International Journal*, XLI (Summer, 1986), 12-15.

10. The relationship to the two groups is less ambiguous in the "higher administrative schools" of Bosnia (not shown in the tables) which are additional training grounds for government work. Although in 1971 Moslems comprised 40 percent of Bosnia's total population, Serbs represented 54 percent of the students in these schools, Moslems 20.3 percent, Croats 14 percent and Yugoslavs 4.4 percent. It is also interesting to note, however, that in 1930-1931 only 1.3 percent of all students in Yugoslavia were Moslem by religious affiliation (197 individuals of whom six were women) and no university existed in Bosnia. *Statistički godisñjak knjiga I* (Belgrade, 1932), 336-337.

11. It was precisely such intellectual protest which contributed to the outbreak of serious "counter-revolutionary" demonstrations by members of the Albanian population in the province of Kosovo (March-April 1981). Thus, Yugoslav analysts have suggested that a major source of the political instability in Kosovo is due to the overproduction of specialists from the Albanian ethnic group; a situation brought about by the rapid expansion of the university in Pristina. "It is paradoxical, but in our most underdeveloped region we can speak about a certain surplus of highly educated persons. Evidently, the university advanced more quickly than the economy." *Nedeljne Informativne Novine*, (April 12, 1981), 10. See Chapter 8 for a detailed discussion of the Albanian elite in Kosovo.

12. See Lenard J. Cohen, "Conflict Management and Institution-Building in Yugoslavia: The Role of the Parliamentary System," 122-165.

13. Arend Lijphart, *Democracy in Plural Societies*, 100.

14. Jurg Steiner, "The Principles of Majority and Proportionality," *Consociational Democracy*, ed. Kenneth McRae (Toronto: McClelland and Stewart, 1974), 100.

15. Deutsch points out, for example, that transactions are "the first step to salience. The study of quantitative densities of transactions are the first step toward estimating the degree to which people are connected with each other," and that "transaction flows establish mutual relevance of actors. An actor with whom you have very much to do is relevant to you. This does not mean that the transactions are necessarily associated with rewards, that they are felt to be pleasant or beneficial, or that they are free of conflict. The one thing which is unlikely to accompany a high level of transaction is continued high tension and conflict, but it is quite possible to have high levels of transactions in certain fields combined with very elaborate social barriers." See Karl Deutsch, "Communication Theory and Political Integration," *The Integration of Political Communities*, eds. Philip Jacob and James Toscano (New York: J.B. Lippincott, 1964), 51, 67.

16. See note 13 in Chapter 4.

17. See for example, Ruža Petrović, "Etno-biološka homogenizacija Jugoslovenskog društva," *Sociologija*, X, No. 2 (1968), 5-34, Dragomir Pantić, *Etnička distanca u SFRJ* (Belgrade: Institut društvenih nauka, 1967), Oli Hawrylyshyn, "Ethnic Affinity and Migration Flows in Post-war Yugoslavia," *Economic Development and Cultural Change*, XX, No. 1 (1977), 93-116, John Besemeres, "The Demographic Factor in Inter-Ethnic Relations in Yugoslavia," *Southeastern Europe/L'Europe du Sud-Est*, IV, No. 1 (1977), 1-31. For data concerning the lack of ethnic distance between Serbs and Montenegrins see Djordje Djurić, "Ispitavanje etničke distance kod dece," *Zbornik za društvene nauke*, LVI (1971), 126-132.

18. See Lenard J. Cohen, "Conflict Management and Institution-Building in Yugoslavia: The Role of the Parliamentary System."

19. In 1981, Stane Dolanc, a Slovenian representative in the 23 member Party Central Committee Presidium, suggested that persons wishing to serve as functionaries in republican and provincial admini-

strations should complete a four year course in Belgrade as federal administrators. "Only if he is acquainted with common Yugoslav interests and problems could someone honestly and correctly behave in his own republic or province." *Nedeljne Informativne Novine*, (January 18, 1981), 11. He recently repeated the same advice to the Slovenes who "are accustomed to 'firing big cannons' from Ljubljana toward Belgrade, but very reluctantly, or almost never, will ... come to Belgrade ..." *Politika*, (April 29, 1986), 6. Studies of other political systems have shown the importance of elite interaction for political stability. A good theoretical discussion of this point is in John Highly and Gwen Moore, "Elite Integration in the United States and Australia," *American Political Science Review*, LXXV, No. 3 (1981), 581-585.

20. For example, the three Croatian responses in the party/mass organization sector came from: (1) a member of the Central Committee of the party at the federal level who was also a member of the Council of the Federation and vice-president of a federal mass organization; (2) a member of the federal conference of a mass organization; and (3) a member of the presidium of the central chamber of the trade union organization on the federal level.

21. The most comprehensive treatment of social forces and ideas in the Croatian nationalist movement of the 1960's is Ivan Perić, *Ideje "masovnog pokreta" u Hrvatskoj* (Zagreb: Centar za aktualni politicki studij, 1974).

22. Gertrude Robinson has pointed to "the ethnic specificity of Yugoslav media content" and has remarked that "in multi-national Yugoslavia, communications positions are staffed by the ethnic majority living in a particular republic. They write and broadcast in their distinctive languages and script. In addition, communicators and politicians come from the same social background, belong to their own regional League of Communists, and see each other at frequent board meetings." See Gertrude Robinson, *Tito's Maverick Media* (Urbana, Illinois: University of Illinois Press, 1977), 191-197.

23. Speaking to a public meeting in Croatia on May 1, 1971, over six months before he was to take "surgical" measures against nationalism in the country, Tito pointed out that: "many distortions and misinformation, many slanders and irregularities are sometimes carried in some newspapers ... we have resolved to act most

resolutely and energetically against those who introduce trouble among our people, untruths, and misinformation, who slander the leaders elected by the people .... Such a press has caused tremendous harm so far, I tell you: radio or rather television can do tremendous harm, for the whole of Yugoslavia, or an entire republic, watches television. We shall also have to see who appears on television and how. You know you cannot have everybody saying whatever occurs to him ..." *Foreign Broadcast Information Service*, (May 3, 1971), I10. On April 11, 1972, in their secret talks with Serbian leaders, Tito again referred to problems with the media: "my speeches have always met with good support at the base of society ... but only infrequently among certain leaders and ever responsible leaders. I have not encountered good support in some of the republics, including Serbia, where my speeches have been interpreted rather differently and where efforts have been made to present my speeches in a different manner. Or they have been passed over in silence .... The information media, that is, the press, radio, and television, should be in our hands and not in the hands of those who work against our unity and the interests of socialist Yugoslavia. But this is not yet so in Belgrade." *Nedeljne Informativne Novine*, (April 15, 1973), 7, 17.

24. Christopher Beattie, *Minority Men in a Majority Setting* (Toronto: McClelland and Stewart, 1975), 156-183. Other Canadian research suggests that the content of engineering and scientific research "is shaped by interaction with users of technology" in different societies and that such interaction creates "reference boundaries" which tend to cross ethnic and linguistic groups. See Thomas Eisman and Yakov Rabin, "Linguistic Influences of Professional Communication and Recognition: A Study of Chemists and Engineers in Two Québec Universities," *Higher Education*, IX (1980), 277-292.

25. Rodney Stiefbold, "Segmented Pluralism and Consociational Democracy in Austria: Problems of Political Stability and Change," *Politics in Europe*, ed. Martin Heisler (New York: David McKay Co., 1974), 160-162, 172.

26. David Nachmias and David H. Rosenbloom, "Bureaucracy and Ethnicity," *American Journal of Sociology*, LXXXIII, No. 4 (1978), 967-973.

27. Kolakowski also notes the recent enthusiasm of intellectuals "for movments inspired by the ideology of national minorities is an

enthusiasm for that which in these movements is reactionary and hostile to culture - for their contempt of knowledge, for the cult of violence, for the spirit of vengence, for racism. Racism is still racism even when it is the racism of a discriminated minority ..." Leszek Kolakowski, "Intellectuals against Intellect," *Daedalus*, CI, No. 3 (1972), 12-15. Seymour Martin Lipset has also discussed intellectuals who adopt the role of the preserver: "Even though for the most part intellectuals see themselves in a world 'they never made' they have been 'bound' by an 'unexpungible identity' with the nation, since it has been the *raison d'etre* of the literary and scholarly intellectuals." Seymour Matin Lipset, "Intellectual Types and Political Roles," *The Idea of Social Structure*, ed. Lewis Coser (New York: Harcourt Brace Jovanovich, 1975), 457.

28. Maja Minček, "Problemi likovnog stvaralaštva u Hrvatskoj," *Komunistički pokret i inteligencija: istraživanja ideoloskog i političkog djelovanja inteligencije u Hrvatskoj (1918-1945)* (Zagreb, 1980), 225.

29. The Yugoslav economist, Branko Horvat, has emphasized the role of occupational elites in the ethnic problems of his country: "It is of interest to enquire which social groups are the bearers of nationalism in our milieu. It is not surprising that republic, state and political functionaries appear in the forefront here. Their existence in a Balkan state is based on nationalism and justified by it. It is more difficult to explain why the so-called humanistic intelligentsia is so loudly nationalistic .... It seems to me that here we have a case of ideological confusion, ignorance of facts, as well as frustrations, which these groups experience more severely than others. The ignoring of national culture and linguistic particularities on the part of the bureaucratic apparatus hits these groups more directly than others. In addition, a type of frustration that results from mediocrity and lack of talent has for a long time been compensated for by nationalism. On the other hand, that part of the humanistic intelligentsia which we might conditionally call the New Left, i.e., which has a certain developed critical stance toward society, has shown itself resistant to nationalism. This probably follows from the fact that the type of education they receive and the work they perform make them more resistant to ideological psychoses, as well as from the fact that they have a real alternative - going abroad." See Branko Horvat, "Nationalism and Nationality," *Gledišta*, Nos. 5-6 (1971), translated in the *International Journal of Politics*, II, No. 1 (1972), 32-33.

30. See Zdenko Antic, "Yugoslavia's Pluralist Dissent," *Radio Free Europe, RAD Background Report*, (October 12, 1978), 216, and Mihajilo Mihajlov, "The Dissident Movement in Yugoslavia," *The Washington Quarterly*, II, No. 4 (1979), 64-73.

31. Robert Merton has argued that the operational code of technicians in bureaucracies leaves very little room for the incursion of private sentiments and values and that "the state bureaucracy exerts a pressure upon the alienated intellectual to accommodate himself to the policies of those who make the strategic decisions, with the result that, in time, the role of the one-time alienated intellectual may become indistinguishable from that of the technician." See Robert Merton, *Social Theory and Social Structure* (Glencoe, Ill.: The Free Press of Glencoe, 1957), 214.

CHAPTER 8

ELITES IN YUGOSLAVIA'S THIRD WORLD: THE CASE OF KOSOVO

The special impact of elite composition and behaviour on the political stability of societies has frequently been noted by social scientists.[1] As emphasized in the preceding chapter, elites become especially significant to political stability when their members become the spokesmen for the competing interests of various nationality and subcultural communities. In such multi-ethnic societies, elites are poised as an intervening variable between the diverse clusters of subcultural communities and the policy-making agencies of the regime. Located in the centers of societal power and prestige, elite members can act to either dampen or exacerbate the strong passions generated by ethnic loyalties and intergroup rivalry.

The salience of elites to political stability is especially acute in multi-ethnic states experiencing the pressures of rapid development and social mobilization. As Malloy and Beck have pointed out, in "non-crystallized societies" lacking a durable elite structure and established behavioural norms among elites, the favoured techniques for maintaining elite control have become "suppression of opposition elites and manipulation of the constituency through such emotionally filled symbols as nationalism and xenophobia."[2] The same authors add that an important aspect of analysis in such non-crystallized systems is the "discovery of major trends" relating to elite structure and elite behaviour, and particularly "what form the aggregate composition of elites will take in these countries" as development proceeds.[3]

One specific elite group which plays a crucial role in the articulation of ethnic or nationalist perspectives, particularly in societies experiencing the early stage of industrialization, is the intelligentsia. In such newly industrializing societies the intelligentsia is a rather disparate group composed of politically concerned persons who have achieved, or are pursuing, some form of post-secondary educational or specialized training. While generally better educated than most of the population, the intelligentsia may include many individuals of only very modest intellectual attainment and professional skill (for example, part time university students or revolutionary activists in underground party schools, etc.), who are located in very dissimilar occupational and organizational sectors of a society. An important component of the intelligentsia, however, "consists of members of the modern intellectual elite, in a still underdeveloped society, who are above all interested in general political ideas."[4]

Despite their relatively high educational status and distinctive sociopolitical involvement, members of the intelligentsia, or "intelligentsia elites"[5] (including groups of such sub-elites as writers, artists, bureaucratic officials, teachers, students, etc.), are distinguished in most cases by their "marginality" vis-à-vis the rest of the population and usually behave as "a class which is alienated from its own society by the very fact of its education."[6] Such alienation, often intensified by a high rate of intellectual unemployment, may lead members of the intelligentsia to embrace and articulate radical programs of social and national revolutionary change. "Nationalism's primary function," writes Anthony Smith, drawing together the views of many authors on the subject, "is the resolution of the crisis of the intelligentsia ... they are the most relevant group in exploring the *emergence* of nationalism rather than its subsequent diffusion. The ideology of nationalism is born of their situation and problems."[7] Intellectuals in underdeveloped societies are inclined to become nationalists, it has also been asserted, because they seek to modernize their environment according to their own plan or vision. Colonial or non-indigenous elites from more developed regions are viewed as a direct impediment to the modernizing goals of the new or "native" intellectuals. As John Kautsky has observed, "colonialism is regarded as an obstacle in the intellectuals' path to modernization as well as in their path to power .... To the intellectuals in underdeveloped countries nationalism and modernization have become inextricably intertwined as means and ends. Each has become an essential aspect of the other."[8] Thus, how the intelligentsia of a developing society is formed, as well as its internal divisions and role in the expression of nationalist ideas, will have important consequences for political stability, especially in a multi-ethnic setting.

This chapter will examine elite formation and the elite origins of nationalism in the Yugoslav province of Kosovo,[9] a relatively underdeveloped and ethnically heterogeneous area adjacent to Albania which has been a focal point of irredentism and political strife throughout Balkan history. The succession of different regimes since the creation of the Yugoslav state in 1918, the intermingling of Slavic (mainly Serbs and Montenegrins) and non-Slavic (mainly Albanians and Turks) nationality groups in Kosovo, and the rapid socio-

The Socialist Pyramid: Elites and Power in Yugoslavia

economic changes in the provinces over the past four decades of communist rule, offer an excellent context in which to explore the complex relationship between elite behaviour, nationalism and political stability. Particular attention will be devoted to the gradual emergence and political behaviour of the indigenous Albanian and Slavic intelligentsia elites during successive phases of Kosovo's political history.

Internal Colonialism and Elite Formation: 1912-1940

Wipe away Kosovo from the Serb mind and soul and we are no more ... if there had been no battle at Kosovo the Serbs would have invented it for its suffering and its heroism.

Milovan Djilas

Kosovo, as the region where the Turks initiated their domination of the Balkans by defeating a Slavic army in 1389, has been a prime focus of Serbian nationalism throughout modern history. In 1912, during the First Balkan War, the newly independent Serbian state reconquered the Kosovo region from Turkey, thereby achieving a goal that had been kept alive for centuries among the Serbs by means of a rich oral poetry and literature. When Serbian politicians spearheaded the formation of a broader South Slav or "Yugoslav" state at the end of World War I, it seemed only natural that Kosovo would be treated as an integral part of the Serbian component in the new unitary state. The administration of the new tri-national Kingdom of Serbs, Croats, and Slovenes thus included Kosovo (along with Macedonia) as part of what was then called "South Serbia."

The ethnically Serbian dynasty and political clique that dominated interwar Yugoslavia welcomed the opportunity to reassert Belgrade's control over "liberated" Kosovo for the first time since the fourteenth century. Kosovo, after all, had an enormous historical significance for the Serbs and the Montenegrins (the latter usually considered as ethnic Serbs) that went far beyond the region's small size and population (approximately 11,000 square kilometers, with roughly 439,000 people in 1921 and 552,000 in 1931). At the beginning of the interwar period, approximately two-thirds of Kosovo's inhabitants were ethnic Albanians (66 percent) who, together with a small Turkish minority (6.1 percent) were almost all of the Moslem faith (see Table 8.1).[10] Approximately one quarter of the region's population were ethnic Slavs, most belonging to the Orthodox faith. Adopting an official strategy toward cultural diversity which might be termed *charter-group hegemony*, the central government in Belgrade set out to Serbianize Kosovo through demographic engineering and political manipulation. In the same way that the Ottoman authorities up to 1912 had encouraged the colonization of Kosovo by Albanian Moslems from elsewhere in the Balkans, the Yugoslav regime in the 1920's began to sponsor the migration of Serbs and Montenegrins into the region as a means "to correct the national composition of the area."[11] In 1928 the top administrator responsible for the colonization of South Serbia claimed that in some places the central government's policy had significantly changed the "ethnic composition of the entire region," whereas in 1913 there were areas in which "there had been not a single Serbian inhabitant."[12] By 1940 approximately 18,000 Slavic families had been settled in Kosovo, many coming from impoverished areas of Bosnia-Hercegovina and Montenegro, as a reward for their service to Serbia in the World War.

Although labelled as a "national minority" in interwar Yugoslavia, the Albanian population of the country was denied any legitimate political symbols or channels for the expression of their corporate identity as a separate ethnic group. Albanians could risk voting for one or another of the Moslem political parties, as many did during the more liberal period of interwar rule (1918-1928), but any advocacy of union with the neighbouring kingdom of Albania or political autonomy for the Kosovo region and the Albanian population within the Yugoslav state was regarded by the authorities as outright subversion. The fact that Kosovo was of considerable importance to the history and goals of "greater Albanian nationalism" made Serbian politicians only more intransigent in their treatment of minority issues.[13] All leading positions of administrative authority in the region were in the hands of ethnic Serbs appointed by the central government. The intention of the regime in Belgrade was not to agressively assimilate the Albanian population, i.e., by conversion to the Serbian nationality in a cultural or religious sense, but rather to maintain and expand the presence and political hegemony of the Serbs in Kosovo while suppressing any trace of non-Slavic national consciousness. Faced with brutal and heavy-handed treatment, first from the Serbian and Montenegrin armies during the wartime liberation of Kosovo (in 1912 and 1917-1918),[14] and later from the local gendarmerie, many Albanians fled the country while others resorted to traditional forms of Balkan guerrilla resistance against governmental authority. Such Albanian rebel bands were not effectively suppressed until the late 1920's, after the mass detention of family members who could only be ransomed by the surrender of their outlaw relatives. Many other Albanians in this period joined the various irredentist organizations which flourished as underground movements throughout Southern Serbia. The majority of the Albanian population, however, adopted a more passive role toward their new colonial masters, preferring to let their anxiety and hatred seethe below the surface of daily life in the region, waiting for later opportunities to seek revenge and autonomy.[15]

The elite structure of Kosovo during this period reflected both the area's extreme backwardness and political domination. Indeed, it is difficult to even

The Socialist Pyramid: Elites and Power in Yugoslavia

Table 8.1
Ethnic Composition of Kosovo in 1921

	District					Total	Percent
	Zvečane	Kosovo	Metohija	Prizren	Kačanik		
Religion							
Orthodox	19,288	42,935	16,247	14,482	251	93,207	21.2
Roman Catholic	533	3,644	8,227	3,359	2	15,765	3.6
Moslem	50,205	124,336	65,581	78,906	10,474	329,602	75.0
Other	111	350	25	34	2	522	0.1
Total	70,137	171,285	90,080	96,781	10,727	438,910	100.0
Language							
Serbo-Croatian	20,679	47,229	17,761	28,179	247	114,145	26.0
Albanian	42,275	108,541	70,409	57,216	10,466	288,907	65.8
Turkish	5,180	10,619	1,430	10,681	5	27,915	6.4
Total	70,137	171,283	90,080	96,781	10,727	438,910	100.0

Sources: District-by-district data (*okrug* and *srez*) from *Definitivni Rezultati Popisa Stanovnisrva od 31 January 1921 God.* (Sarajevo: Opšta Državna Statistika, 1932), pp. 94-119; *Stanovništvo Narodne Republike Srbije od 1834-1953* (Belgrade: Zavod za Statistiku i Evidenciju N.R. Srbije, 1953); and Vladimir Simeunović, *Stanovništvo Jugoslavije i Socijalističkih Republike 1921-1961* (Belgrade: Savezni Zavod za Statistiku, 1964).

speak of a very sizeable or truly indigenous elite in the region. The end of Ottoman power and wartime chaos witnessed the exodus of Turkish officials from Kosovo, along with many Albanian Moslems from urban areas who had either served in the region's civil administration or had been members of the small mercantile community (skilled artisans, small merchants, etc.). As a result, the population of Kosovo actually decreased by about 60,000 between 1913 and 1920. This vacuum was soon filled by an influx of Serbian civil, military, and police officials along with a contingent of skilled technicians to run the region's minuscule industrial structure. Apart from the sizeable British-controlled Trepca-Mines Ltd. and some smaller mines, only twenty-three industrial plants existed in the area in 1939 (ten sawmills, two brickyards, five lumber mills, three icehouses, and three small electric plants). Small industry composed the major portion of Kosovo's domestic non-agricultural economy. In 1939, Kosovo had approximately 2,300 shops owned by artisans who employed another 1,800 skilled workers and 1,400 apprentices. Prizren, the largest city in interwar Kosovo, had a population of about 19,000 people in 1931 and Priština (the current capital) had only 16,500 citizens (the administrative capital of South Serbia was Skopje, Macedonia). About 25 percent of the population of both cities worked in the agricultural sector (the equivalent figure was less than three percent in Belgrade, Zagreb, and Ljubljana). Many of the largest and choicest tracts of agricultural land previously owned by Turkish and Albanian families were divided by the authorities among the new Serbian and Montenegrin colonists. Nikola Pašić, one of the country's first prime ministers (formerly the prime minister of Serbia), appropriated 3,000 hectares of land for himself near one of the region's most historic sites.

The social background of parliamentary deputies elected from Kosovo to the National Assembly in Belgrade (Table 8.2) provides an interesting illustration of elite development before World War II. As might be expected, the overall occupational composition of the legislators reveals the mixture of skills typical of a traditional elite in an underdeveloped colonial area, namely, merchants, landed gentry, government officials, and a few members from the so-called "free professions."[16] The presence in the early postwar period of a sizeable number of Albanian landowners and small farmers from the traditional elite, together with a small number of dissident professionals and officials elected on the Communist list in 1920, reflected the weak legitimacy which the Serbian-dominated Belgrade regime and the ruling Radical party enjoyed in Kosovo. Although opposition parties had little influence on the governance of the region or the country as a whole, voting in the new state initially offered an outlet for political protest and non-Slavic representation.

In 1920, the Communist Party in its only chance to contest a free national election in interwar Yugoslavia, captured 17 percent of the votes in Kosovo, and 27 percent of the votes throughout South Serbia (their best success in any region and receiving more votes than any other party). Another 16 percent of the vote

The Socialist Pyramid: Elites and Power in Yugoslavia

Table 8.2
Occupational and Ethnic Background of Parliamentary Deputies from the Kosovo Region, 1918-1939

Occupational Group	1920	1923	1927	1935
Small farmers[a]	3	3	1	3
Landowners[a]	3	4	2	-
Merchants	-	4	3	6
Politicians/bureaucrats	7[b]	2	3	4
Lawyers	4[c]	1	2	1
Teachers/educators	5	4	3	3
Technical intelligentsia	-	-	2	-
Doctors	-	-	3	-
Journalists	-	-	-	1
Clergy	1	-	-	-
Total	23	18	19	18
Percentage of non-Slavic deputies[d]	39.1	61.0	23.3	22.2

Sources: *Statistika izbora Narodnih Poslanika Kraljevine Srba, Hrvata, i Slovenaca 1920, 1923, 1927*, (Belgrade: 1921, 1924, 1928); *Statistika izbora Narodnih Poslanika za Narodnu Skupštinu Kraljevine Jugoslavije* izvršenih 5 maj 1935 (Belgrade: 1938).
Note: Includes deputies from Kosovo, Metohija, Prizren, the Sandjak, and Tetovo (in western Macedonia). No data is given for the election of 1925 which included most of the same deputies as in 1923, or the very corrupt and administratively muddled 1931 election.
[a] In 1920 all of the landowners and two small farmers were non-Slavic; in 1923 and 1927, all in both groups were non-Slavic. In 1935 only one of three farmers was not Slavic.
[b] Includes three judges, two from the Communist Party.
[c] Includes one law student and one "peasant-lawyer," both Communist deputies.
[d] Non-Slavic includes mainly Albanians and a few Turks.

went to the National Turkish organization (Džemijet), a party which appealed to South Serbia's Moslem Albanian majority, as well as to the residual Turkish population. A few Albanian legislators were also elected from the dissident Democratic Party, which received 13 percent of the vote in the Kosovo region (at this time the Democrats, although Serbian-based, had a more pluralistic and federal program than the ruling Radical party). Although by the election of 1923 the Communists had been driven underground, an upsurge of support for the Džemijet party and increased support for the Democrats resulted in a considerable increase of formal Albanian representation. By 1927, however, the government policy of Serbianization, political intimidation, and electoral manipulation contributed to the collapse of the Džemijet and a sharp decline in the number of Albanian legislators. The imposition of a highly centralized royal dictatorship in 1929 further undermined the position of the Albanian population. By 1935, the 79 percent Slavic and heavily mercantile-political composition of

Lenard J. Cohen

Kosovo's legislative elite betrayed the weakness of Albanian-Turkish landed interests and the supremacy of the mainly Serbian "police regime." Political and economic power were far more concentrated in the hands of the central and local Serbian elite members, especially top administrators, than the data on a relatively small number of legislators would suggest, but the general tendency is, nevertheless, very clear.

An examination of the only biographical directory published in interwar Yugoslavia, which includes information with respect to over 3,700 eminent persons (in a population of approximately fourteen million), yields less than a dozen names from Kosovo.[17] A few deputies to the National Assembly from the Kosovo area are listed in the 1938 directory, but it is apparent that the traditional and largely non-Slavic leaders from the pre-1912 period had either left the country or lost their influence, and that the newly imposed stratum of Serbian officials and colonists were not yet prominent enough to warrant elite status. The biography of one non-Slavic leader illustrates the difficulty of making the transition from the old to the newly emergent elite, and also the absence of elite cohesion across ethnic lines:

> *Ferad-beg, Draga*, Born 1873 (district Raško-Zvećanski); Schooling, Lower gymnasium (Turkish) in Salonika. Landowner. Former parliamentary deputy and President of the Moslem Political Organization of South Serbia "Djemijet." During the war, under occupation [Austria] he was the central president of the commune of Kosovo-Mitrovica district; 1918 proclaimed a collaborator, 1923 elected a parliamentary deputy, 1924-1927 imprisoned as a result of legal measures.[18]

Another biography from the same directory, but more characteristic of the "new" elite, is of a younger Serbian deputy who was both a war veteran and member of the ruling party. His background further reveals the inadequate formal skills of the regional leadership and the historical absence of local educational facilities which impeded the elite's capability to deal with the area's backwardness:

> *Popović, Toma*; Born 1882. Gnjilane. Schooling, four years of Serbian school and two years of Turkish gymnasium in Salonika and Skopje. Merchant, and parliamentary deputy (Radical Party). Involved in Journalism and literature ... military honours.[19]

The Socialist Pyramid: Elites and Power in Yugoslavia

The most striking characteristic of Kosovo's elite structure between the wars was not so much its small size, but its ethnic composition. A largely imported Serbian intelligentsia, itself undergoing the first stage of elite development, was ruling the region's majority population of Albanian peasants and proletarians. This pattern of a regional ruling class drawn from one ethnic group, and a subordinated class from another ethnic background, closely resembles what has been described as a system of "internal colonialism," and is often found in states with marked regional economic disparities.[20] The most distinctive feature of internal colonialism is the attempt by a more modernized "core" group (i.e., a "charter group") from one culture to establish a persistently discriminatory system of stratification upon less modernized groups from other cultures. In this way a system of objective cultural differences is superimposed upon, or merged with class divisions creating what has been termed a "cultural division of labour."[21] While it is not the explicit aim of this chapter to apply or test the theory of internal colonialism as an explanatory model, it appears that many dimensions of the model are exhibited in the elite structure and ethnic politics of the Kosovo region.[22] Although the internal colonialism model cannot be applied to Eastern Europe without certain difficulties,[23] a good deal of Albanian group consciousness and "reactive politics" up to and beyond 1940, resulted from the prevailing cultural division of labour in Yugoslavia. Indeed, to apply the model further, the status of the Albanians in interwar Yugoslavia was not unlike the colonial position earlier accorded the Serbs by their Ottoman and Austro-Hungarian imperial rulers in different sections of the Balkans. Thus the Serbian "national liberation movement" against Turkish and German predominance in the cultural division of labour could also be considered an example of reactive ethnicity. The success of Serbian arms from 1912 to 1918 had simply established a new pecking order in Southeastern Europe.

The educational system, a key factor in elite development, both reflected and reinforced the colonial status of South Serbia and its predominantly Albanian population. The central authorities in Belgrade were more concerned with the political mission of the few schools in Kosovo, namely, cultivating loyalty to the new government in Belgrade, than with expanding educational opportunities. The language of instruction was Serbian, and every effort was made to obstruct the development of an Albanian national consciousness. It is rather doubtful, however, that the school system played much of a role in the political socialization of students from any nationality, as only about 30 percent of eligible children were actually receiving an education in the region.[24] Over 90 percent of the Albanian population was illiterate and only about two percent of the eligible Albanians were enrolled in secondary schools. During the 1940-1941 school year, which immediately preceded the war, approximately 25,000 Serbian and Montengrin children and 12,000 Albanian students were enrolled in Kosovo's secondary schools. The region had no facilities for higher education, and only a handful of Albanian students attended universities elsewhere in Yugoslavia or abroad. While the interwar regime had a better record with respect to educational development than their Turkish predecessors, such progress had little effect on modernization or elite formation in Kosovo.

Ethnic War and Elite Circulation: 1941-1945

The invasion and dismemberment of the Yugoslav Kingdom in March 1941 was not an unwelcome event to the country's Albanian population. Most of Kosovo was incorporated into Italian-controlled Albania, with smaller portions of the region parcelled out to the new German-run Serbian puppet state (including the Trepca lead and zinc mine) and to Axis Bulgaria's enlarged province of Macedonia.

The "liberation" of Kosovo's Albanians from three decades of Serbian domination and the opportunity to be reunited in a single territorial unit with Albania proper, initially offset the reality of Fascist control from Rome. Offering the inhabitants of the newly coopted territory the vision of a "greater" and "ethnically pure" Albania allied to the Axis, the Italians found enthusiastic collaborators among the Albanians of Kosovo. Reverting to the situation before 1912, the Slavic inhabitants of the region again became second-class citizens, while Albanians assumed a position similar to the one they enjoyed under Ottoman rule. Indeed, some members of the former Turkish and Albanian economic elite were even allowed to reassert their earlier feudal control over agricultural production. The small Albanian intelligentsia was recruited to work in the bureaucratic apparatus of the occupation authorities, and an Albanian gendarmerie was established to police each local district. The new regime also provided Albanians with schools, media facilities, and other outlets for ethnic expression in their own language, opportunities which had been prohibited under the Yugoslav regime. For their part, a large number of Serbian and Montenegrin colonists exposed to an official policy of discrimination, violent harassment, confiscation of their properties, and sometimes deportation simply fled from Kosovo, anxiously looking for new allies who could help them restore their former dominance. Inter-ethnic animosity reached a high pitch as the population chose up sides in an emerging civil war and resistance struggle.[25]

At the outbreak of the war in Yugoslavia, the Communist party had only a very modest foothold in Kosovo.[26] In April 1941, there were 260 members in the region, 240 of whom were Serbs and Montenegrins (many of them children of colonists). The Communists' most serious activity in Kosovo between the wars had been concentrated in the area around the Trepca mine, where they had helped organize a strike in 1936.[27] The party could also claim to have aided in organizing a protest by Belgrade University students in 1938 against a government plan (never carried out because of the war) to expel 150,000 Albanians

The Socialist Pyramid: Elites and Power in Yugoslavia

from South Serbia to Turkey. The Communists were most proud, however, of their multi-national program adopted in the mid-1930's, which offered equality to the Albanian population along with other ethnic groups in a new federalized Yugoslav state. By implication, Kosovo was to receive separate status as a territorial unit in the new federation, although the precise details of this plan were left open. The party resolution adopted in October 1940 simply promised a "struggle for the freedom and equality of the Arnaut [Albanian] minorities in Kosovo and Metohija, and the Sandjak" and "against the colonizing methods of the Serbian bourgeoisie in these regions."[28]

Despite its programmatic intentions, the Communist Party of Yugoslavia had great difficulty attracting Albanians to the Partisan resistance organization. In addition to the rather successful appeal of the occupation authorities to the Albanians, the communists also had to compete with a non-communist resistance movement (Balli Kombetar or "National Front") which advocated an "ethnic Albania" including the population of Kosovo, Western Macedonia, and sections of Montenegro. Perhaps more significantly, and an early indicator of later difficulties, the members of the communist resistance movement were themselves divided about the future status of Albanians in Kosovo. In a speech made at the end of 1943, Mehmet Hoxha, an Albanian communist leader from Kosovo working with the Yugoslav Partisans, suggested that Albanians must join with "the other nations of Yugoslavia and the [communist] National Liberation Army of Albania" to fight against the Fascist forces, though he did acknowledge that "we know that Kosovo and Metohija are inhabited mostly by Albanians who want to unite with Albania.[29] The meeting which he addressed resolved that "Kosovo and Metohija form a region in which Albanian inhabitants preponderate; they as always still wish to be united with Albania." It was only after a reprimand from the Central Committee of the Yugoslav Communist Party in March 1944 that the resolution was amended to remove the section that referred to the desired union of Kosovo's Albanians with their brethren in Albania.

The content of theoretical debates in the party leadership had no effect, however, on the Albanian masses who showed little enthusiasm for the Partisan movement. It was not until late 1943 (after the capitulation of Italy) and 1944 that the communists succeeded in organizing Albanian military detachments on a substantial scale. A 1977 survey of the ethnic composition of Partisan veterans and the families of veterans living in Kosovo, Macedonia and Montenegro (Table 8.4) reveals the underrepresentation of Albanians in the Partisan war effort and the disproportionately high contribution of Serbs and Montenegrins. In 1948, Albanians in Kosovo made up roughly 68 percent of the population and comprised only 51 percent of those who fought in the war (Table 8.3 also provides 1971 census data in order to illustrate population shifts in the Partisan's ethnic representativeness). Serbs and Montenegrins constituted 35 percent and 11 percent of the Partisan forces respectively, while representing only about 24

Table 8.3
The Ethnic Origin of Partisans Who Fought in World War II, as of 31 Dec. 1977 (%)

	Serbs	Montenegrins	Macedonians	Albanians	Other
Yugoslavia					
Population					
1948	41.5	2.7	5.1	4.8	45.9
1971	39.7	2.5	5.8	6.4	45.5
Veterans and families of veterans, 1977	53.0	5.5	2.7	1.7	37.2
Kosovo					
Population					
1948	23.6	3.8	-	68.4	4.2
1971	18.4	2.5	-	73.7	5.4
Veterans and families of veterans, 1977	34.7	11.0	-	50.8	3.4
Macedonia					
Population					
1948	2.6	-	68.5	17.1	10.6
1971	2.8	-	69.3	17.0	10.9
Veterans and families of veterans, 1977	3.0	0.5	82.4	8.7	5.4
Montenegro					
Population					
1948	1.8	90.7	-	5.2	2.3
1971	7.5	67.2	-	6.7	18.6[a]
Veterans and families of veterans, 1977	1.7	88.5	-	2.0	7.8[a]

Source: *Borci, Vojni invalidi i porodice palih boraca Statistički Bilten*, no. 1174 (Belgrade: Savezni Zavod za Statistiku, April 1980). Population figures from the 1948 and 1971 censuses.
Note: Dashes indicate less than half of 1 percent.
[a] Includes mainly Moslems (a category not encouraged in the 1948 census) and a small percentage who choose the supranational designation "Yugoslavs."

percent and four percent of the population. In Macedonia, Albanians comprised 17 percent of the population, yet represented only nine percent of the Partisan war participants; Montenegro's Albanians constituted five percent of the inhabitants and two percent of the Partisan movement.

While Tito and his colleagues had at least some late success in attracting Albanian recruits (most of whom were not party members) to the mass-based Partisan "National Liberation Movement," the communists made very slow progress in either expanding the size or improving the ethnic composition of the party organization in Kosovo. At the end of 1944, the party had only 1,238 members in the region, of whom less than 30 percent were Albanians. Admittedly, this was a five-fold increase in the size of the party since 1941, but party membership was still only miniscule (.16 percent of the population). Controlling the regional party organization, and playing a major role in the Partisan movement of Kosovo (as well as the country as a whole), the Serbs and Montenegrins felt that they should have the greatest influence on political decision-making. The rapid homecoming to Kosovo (from late 1944 to early 1945) of the interwar Serbian and Montenegrin colonists who had been dispossessed by the Italian and Albanian authorities during the occupation period, again brought inter-ethnic tension to a boiling point. Matters were not ameliorated when newly established "poverty committees" for the redistribution of land to the needy began working under the control of Serbian and Montenegrin party officials, who favoured members of their own nationality groups. The more general inter-ethnic tensions were revealed in an internal Communist party communication urging the Kosovo organization to: 1) purge the party of all chauvinists; 2) secure the ideological improvement of the younger party members against the phenomenon of chauvinism; 3) enroll more Albanians in the party and raise their ideological level; 4) "implant the conviction among Serbian and Montenegrin communists that the Albanian masses can quickly achieve a higher cultural and political level having in mind the experience of the backwardness of nationalities in the USSR;" and 5) see that the Montenegrins stop emphasizing their contribution during the war.[30] The last point reflected the existence of a certain intra-ethnic rivalry between the Serbian and Montenegrin minorities in Kosovo which existed alongside the more serious tension between Slavs and non-Slavs.

Having collaborated with the Fascists, and once again displaced from their superior position vis-à-vis the Slavic population, most Albanians naturally expected to become the target of communist persecution and collective retribution. In December 1944, immediately following the conclusion of the war in Yugoslavia and the establishment of the communist government, a "mass counter-revolutionary uprising" broke out among the Albanians of Kosovo. The rebellion was led by members of the Balli Kombetar anti-communist resistance forces, who, having failed to achieve their wartime goals in Kosovo or Albania, now saw a final opportunity to mobilize the Albanian population against the Partisan victors (the "Ballists" had opposed the occupation authorities but often fought the communists more vigorously than the Fascists). The magnitude of the uprising forced the newly installed communist regime to place Kosovo under military administration, and to dispatch armed forces to the region from elsewhere in Yugoslavia, raising communist troop strength in Kosovo to over 30,000. The rebelling Albanian forces initially numbered around 15,000 and were divided into numerous small units, capable of attacking many of Kosovo's major towns. Military administration was lifted only after six months of fighting, and it was not until the end of 1945 that the communist forces had driven the principle Albanian Ballist units through Macedonia and over the borders of Greece and Albania.[31] Years later, Milovan Djilas (a Montenegrin) commented that "[the Albanian rebellion] didn't disturb our top echelon .... For us this was a military problem. Our regime was as foreign to the Albanian peasant masses as that of the Serbian kings .... The public knew hardly anything about this broad uprising."[32] Both the Albanian masses' support of the uprising and the ethnic character of the armed struggle, sharply revealed the tenuous legitimacy and ethnically skewed basis of communist power in Kosovo. These early postwar events presaged and help explain later troubles in this region.

Socialist Modernization and Elite Control: 1946-1966

By 1946 the "pacification" of Kosovo had been accomplished, at least superficially, and the region settled into a more routine pattern of postwar reconstruction and transformation. Kosovo was established as an Autonomous Region (Oblast) *within* the Republic of Serbia - a symbolic recognition of the region's separate position in the federal structure - and the Albanian population was granted the same rights and privileges as other minorities in the country. The creation of Albanian schools was accelerated together with other cultural outlets for the "free use" (mainly *de jure*) of the Albanian language. Other constitutional and statutory laws provided for the equal accessibility of all citizens to public office and made ethnic "hatred and discord" a punishable offense. Most importantly, the regime offered a solemn commitment to the rapid economic modernization of the country's backward areas. "It is clear," remarked the regime's top economic decision-maker, "that we would not be able to speak of a full definite solution of the national question if inequality existed in the economic respect among the republics, or if, on the other hand, our Yugoslav economy were not to develop in the sense and in the direction of a united socialist economic whole."[33]

Despite the well-meaning legal provisions and modernizing policies adopted by the new regime, the most striking aspect of Kosovo's first two decades of "socialist construction" was the continued political weakness and economic backwardness of the Albanian population in the midst of the very rapid political and economic changes overtaking the country as a whole. By 1948 Kosovo had a population of 728,000 people (compared to 439,000 in 1921), of whom 68 percent were Albanians, 24 percent Serbs, and about four percent Montenegrins. An examination of 1948 and 1953 census data indicates some interesting patterns of change and continuity. Information on the generational structure and field of specialization of Kosovo's inhabitants with a higher education in 1948 (Table 8.5) reveals a very small educated elite (449 persons

Table 8.4
Albanians in Yugoslavia, 1948-81 (%)

	Percentage of Total Number of Albanians in Yugoslavia, by Republic or Province					Albanians as a Percentage of the Total Population of Republic or Province				
	1948	1953	1961	1971	1981	1948	1953	1961	1971	1981
Slovenia	0.0	0.0	0.0	0.1	0.1	0.0	0.0	0.0	0.1	0.1
Croatia	0.1	0.1	0.2	0.3	0.3	0.0	0.0	0.1	0.1	0.1
Bosnia-Hercegovina	0.1	0.2	0.4	0.3	0.2	0.0	0.0	0.1	0.1	0.1
Montenegro	2.6	3.1	2.8	2.7	2.1	5.1	5.6	5.5	6.7	6.3
Macedonia	23.9	21.5	20.0	21.4	21.8	17.1	12.4	13.0	17.0	19.8
Serbia										
Serbia proper	4.4	5.3	5.6	5.0	4.2	0.8	1.9	1.1	1.2	1.3
Vojvodina	0.1	0.1	0.2	0.2	0.2	0.1	0.1	0.1	0.2	0.2
Kosovo	66.4	69.5	70.7	70.0	70.9	68.4	64.0	67.1	73.7	77.5

Sources: George W. Hoffman, "The Evolution of the Ethnographic Map of Yugoslavia: A Historical Geographic Interpretation," in *An Historical Geography of the Balkans*, ed. Francis W. Carter (London: Academic Press, 1977), pp. 437-99; Slobodan Stankovic, "Yugoslavia's Census-Final Results," *Radio Free Europe Research, RAD Background Reports* 59 (Yugoslavia), 10 Mar. 1982, p. 5.
Note: There were 750,431 Albanians in Yugoslavia in 1948; 754,245 in 1953; 914,760 in 1961; 1,309,523 in 1971; and 1,730,000 in 1981.

or .06 percent of the population), of whom over three-quarters were under 50 years of age and 27 percent under 35 years of age. Most individuals received training in traditional disciplines such as law and philosophy, although the emergence of a more technically proficient elite group (e.g., degrees in engineering, agronomy, etc.) from the young generation is already visible. Not surprisingly, the majority of persons with a higher education were males, with more women beginning to appear among the younger age cohorts. Roughly 70 percent of the educated elite resided in Kosovo's four largest towns, of whom 29 percent lived in Pristina, the new capital of the region. As the first postwar census captures only the initial traces of modernization, it actually offers a picture of the residual elite from the prewar period, together with those few members of the new administrative and political leadership who had completed a higher education.

An analysis of information on the ethnic composition of the work force in Kosovo indicates remnants of the cultural division of labour so characteristic during the interwar years. In 1948 and 1953 when Albanians constituted over two-thirds of the economically active population, they composed only about one-third of the active white collar employees in the province (the fact that in 1948, 75 percent of all pensioners in the "employee" category were Serbs and Montenegrins is also historically revealing).[34] By 1953 Serbs and Montenegrins, who together made up 31.5 percent of Kosovo's active population, still held 68 percent of the "administrative and leading" positions in the province. Albanians also made up only one-third of the personnel in the important "defense and security" area in 1953, although they composed about one-half of all industrial workers and two-thirds of the agricultural workers. The Montenegrins were especially well placed, having approximately three times as many employees in administrative and security posts as their small relative size in the active population (four percent) would seem to warrant. In 1953 only one-third of the 11,430 Montenegrins actively employed in Kosovo were actually born in the region, compared with 85 percent of the Serbian work force, and 98 percent of both the Albanian and Turkish nationality groups. As far as the latter two groups were concerned, the Montenegrins and Serbs represented a *communist colonial elite* reaping the fruits of wartime success.

In spite of these imbalances in the pattern of ethnic employment and the intergroup tensions they generated, important changes were taking place in postwar Kosovo. Between 1947 and 1965 the province's economy had an average annual growth rate of about 6.1 percent (compared to a national rate of seven percent).[35] During the same period, industrial production's share of the overall income in the region rose from around 20 percent to 37 percent, and the percentage of the actual work force in agriculture dropped from approximately 85 percent in 1948 to 70 percent in 1961. Educational expansion was also impressive. For example, in 1939-1940 only 30 percent of eligible children were enrolled in elementary schools, while by 1958-1959 this percentage had doubled

The Socialist Pyramid: Elites and Power in Yugoslavia

Table 8.5
Kosovo Residents with Higher Education Degrees in 1948, by Age and Specialization (%)

	Age Group					Percent of Total	(N)
	20-34	35-49	50-64	Over 65	Total		
Law	33.6	39.6	23.7	3.0	100.0	22.4	(101)
Philosophy/natural science/mathematics	33.7	56.6	8.4	1.2	100.0	18.4	(83)
Economics	27.2	45.4	27.2	-	100.0	2.4	(11)
Agronomy/forestry	22.8	71.4	5.7	-	100.0	7.7	(35)
Medical/veterinary/pharmacy	24.5	50.0	18.6	6.8	100.0	22.7	(102)
Engineering/technical faculties	20.0	53.0	25.0	1.5	100.0	14.2	(64)
Other	18.8	45.2	16.9	18.8	100.0	11.8	(53)
Total	26.9	50.3	17.8	4.8	100.0	-	(449)
Total women	18.2	15.9	11.3	5.0	13.1	-	(68)

Source: *Konačni Rezultat: Popisa Stanovništva od 15 Marta 1948 godine Knjiga IV, Stanovništvo po Školskoj Spremi* (Belgrade: Savezni Zavod za Statistiku i Evidenciju, 1952).

and by 1963-1964 had reached 85 percent. Albanian children comprised 46 percent of the enrolled elementary schools students in 1945-1946, but 67 percent in 1962-1963. During the same period, Albanian representation in secondary schools rose from 23 percent to 47 percent.[36] In 1962-1963 Albanians still made up only 40 percent of the approximately 1,400 students in Kosovo's few facilities for post-secondary education (no regional university had yet been established), although that represented an enormous increase from the prewar period. In 1961, 59 percent of the population over ten years of age was literate, compared with only 37 percent in 1948. Kosovo was slowly becoming more urbanized. Between 1945 and 1960, Priština, the region's new capital grew from about 16,000 to over 35,000 inhabitants and the share of the urban sector in the total population grew from 15 to 20 percent. Some two decades after the communists took power, the province was beginning to develop a sizeable indigenous Albanian intelligentsia.[37]

The modernization process was not, however, quite as successful or untroubled as the above indicators of growth and change would first suggest. For example, the annual growth rate of the country as a whole, and especially in its more developed regions, considerably outstripped the dynamic progress within Kosovo. By the 1960's, this led to a greater gap between the more advanced and less developed regions of the country than had existed just after the war. From 1946 to 1964, the per capita income of Slovenia, the most developed region of the country, rose from three times the level of Kosovo, to five times greater.[38] A growing resentment also existed in the more developed regions where it was believed that even greater strides could have been made had not the federal government - dominated, as it was usually alleged, by personnel from the less developed southeastern part of the country - transferred resources to Kosovo and the more backward regions. This argument was supported by pointing to many federally subsidized and generally inefficient show projects or so-called "political factories" in the less advanced areas.

Economic difficulties including insufficient or delayed capital investment, capital allocation in the wrong industrial sectors, and poor productivity undoubtedly contributed to Kosovo's persistent lag behind the rest of the country. The most serious problem hampering modernization, however, was the rapid increase in the size of the region's total population. Between 1947 and 1966, the population of Kosovo grew by 54 percent, or at twice the rate for the country as a whole (the equivalent figures were 15 percent for Croatia, 16 percent for Slovenia, and 17 percent for Vojvodina, i.e., the three most prosperous regions). Kosovo's mortality rate dropped slowly in the decades after World War II, mainly as a result of improved hygiene, health care, and nutrition, while the region's overall birth rate remained rather constant and above levels in other parts of the country. The region's unique demographic development can be attributed to the exceptionally high fertility rate of its Albanian population, which at the end of the 1960's was twice that of the Serbs and Montenegrins. About 95 percent of the region's total population growth in the decade after 1961 consisted of Albanians.[39]

Kosovo's spectacular and ethnically skewed population expansion diluted the benefits of economic progress and set the stage for heightened intergroup tensions in the province. For example, the rapid population growth outstripped even a growing economy's capacity to provide jobs, thereby leading to an increase in unemployment, especially among younger Albanians eager to enter the work force.[40] The same problem also undercut other aspects of the modernization process. Thus, while the relative size of the Kosovo work force employed in agriculture declined, the absolute number of persons in farming actually increased, unlike in other regions.[41] Similarily, the relative proportion of illiterates in the province declined in each succeeding postwar census, but because the construction of education facilities could not keep pace with the birth rate, the absolute number of illiterates remained almost constant. The negative impact of demographic factors on modernization in Kosovo seriously offset the overall pattern of advancement in the province and intensified the frustration of the Albanian majority.

Kosovo's relative socio-economic deprivation was not, however, the region's only problem in the two decades after the war. Of even more potential danger was that while the rest of the country had embarked on a hopeful experiment in political liberalization, Kosovo remained locked in a far more rigid pattern of "administrative socialism." Although the province manifested the more symbolic features of Titoist reform - workers' councils, communual self-government, etc. - political control remained tightly concentrated in the hands of state and party functionaries, especially those having links to the security services. That the "leading personnel" in the party and police were also mainly Serbs and Montenegrins created a pattern of ethno-political stratification with disquieting similiarities to the prewar regime. By the mid-1960's about half of the party membership in Kosovo was ethnically Albanian, but that ethnic group enjoyed very little real political influence in the province.

Given the indifference or outright resistance of much of Kosovo's Albanian population to the Partisans and communists during and just after the war, it was not difficult for more conservative Serbian and Montenegrin politicians to make a case for their own tight control over the province. This argument received additional force after the Tito-Stalin break in 1948 and the participation of communist Albania in Cominform pressure on the Yugoslav state.[42] The infiltration of agents and irredentist propaganda from neighbouring Albania, and the undoubted reservoir of support for such advances in Yugoslavia, encouraged the tendency of the authorities to collectively treat the Albanian population (both of Kosovo and other regions) as a subversive element not yet entitled to the fruits of self-managed socialism.[43] In 1955 and 1956, the problem of political control in Kosovo prompted the authorities to forcibly collect firearms from the Albanian population under a "state of emergency." Political subversion and political repression remained a strong undercurrent in the province over the next decade, with frequent arrests and trials for espionage and conspiracy against the government.[44] In this atmosphere, a considerable number of Albanians chose to reclassify themselves as Turks and take advantage of the opportunity for emigration to Turkey in the mid-1950's.

The data also illustrate the dissatisfaction of the Yugoslav Albanians and the vigilance of the regime in dealing with this group.[45] Thus, when the number of convictions for "crimes against the state" between 1953 and 1961 are calculated as a percentage of total crimes for various ethnic groups (Figure 8.1), Albanians generally manifest a political crime rate double or triple that of Serbs and Montenegrins. The relative political dissidence levels of the Albanians even exceed the rate for Croats during this period. Moreover, while the level of Serbian political criminality declines gradually, and remains rather constant in the case of the Montenegrins, the Albanian pattern is far more erratic, reflecting frequent outbursts of dissidence and repression. It was only in 1966 after the dismissal of Alexander Ranković, the Vice-President of the country and head of the internal security service, that the full extent of repression against the Albanians and the nature of political tutelage in Kosovo became known.[46] During the previous twenty years of impressive socio-economic transformation, Kosovo had evidently functioned more as a satrapy of the Serbian-dominated security forces (and their chief in Belgrade) than as an autonomous region in a truly federal system.

Political Reforms and Elite Polarization: 1967-1979

The "democratization" of the party and security forces in the wake of the Ranković dismissal opened a new period in the development of Kosovo and Yugoslavia's Albanian population. A first step was the implementation of the nationality "rights" and the principles of provincial "autonomy" which had been in place since 1948, but had remained mainly decorative or symbolic features of the system. For example, Albanians were now encouraged to study and use their national language freely, and criticism was levelled at the earlier *de facto* position of Serbo-Croatian as a "state language" in Kosovo.[47] Plans were developed for the expansion of local higher educational facilities that would enable Albanians to receive instruction in their own language and surroundings. Members of the Albanian intelligentsia began to re-examine the portrayal of Albanians in historical studies and to offer a more balanced or multicultural picture of the positive factors in the region's ethnic heritage. Cultural exchanges were arranged between Yugoslavia and neighbouring Albania, including visits to Kosovo by professors from the University in Tirana, and the importation of

The Socialist Pyramid: Elites and Power in Yugoslavia

Figure 8.1
Political Crime Convictions as a Percent of All Crime Convictions for Selected Ethnic Groups in Yugoslavia

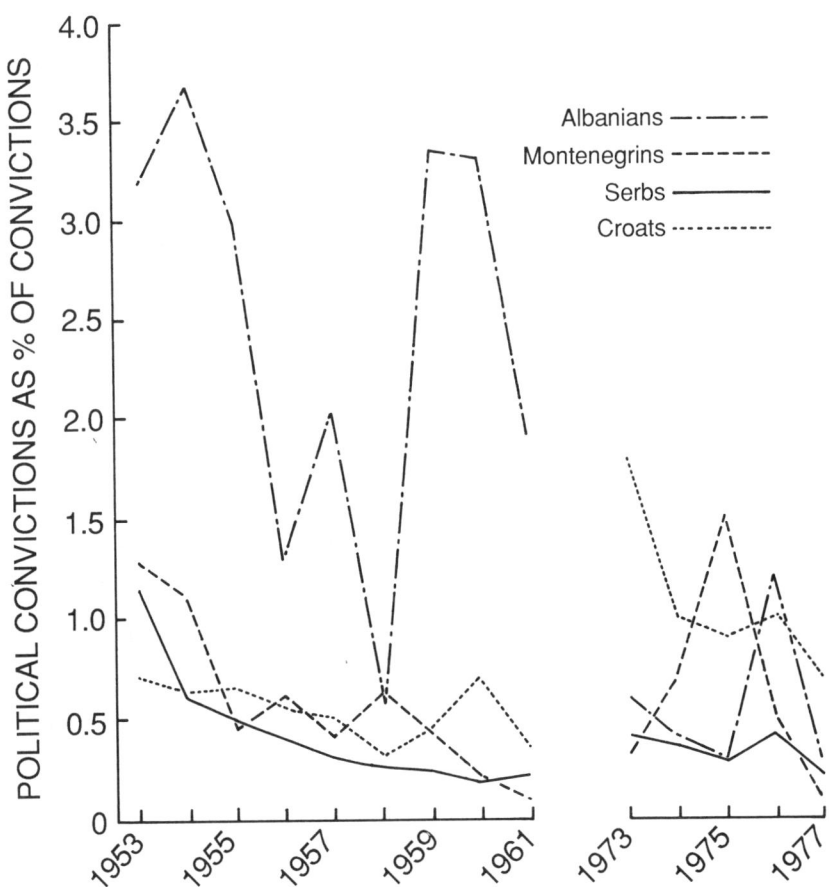

Source: Lenard Cohen, "Political Crime in Yugoslavia: The Ethnic and Regional Basis of Anti-State Dissidence, 1929-1980, presented at the Thirteenth National Convention of the American Association for the Advancement of Slavic Studies, 1981, Monterey, Calif.

Albanian language books and materials printed in Albania. The term *Siptari* was replaced by the name *Albanci* for Yugoslav Albanians, a change designed to avoid the derogatory connotations of the old usage and to eliminate any distinction in reference to Albanians within or outside of Yugoslavia. Kosovars, (*Albanci* who lived in Kosovo) were also permitted to display the Albanian flag, not as a "state" symbol, but as a sign of "national" or ethnic expression.

While the constitutional status of Kosovo had already been changed from an "Autonomous Region" to an "Autonomous Province" in 1963 (thereby placing the area on an equal footing with Vojvodina in the Serbian Republic), it was only after 1966 that the indigenous Albanian ethnic majority of Kosovo (67 percent in 1961) was provided with a real opportunity to assert itself in cultural, economic and political life. In March 1967, Tito, paying his first visit to Kosovo in 16 years, drew attention to the earlier pattern of elite control and the need for a change in recruitment policy. He commented in this respect that one "cannot talk about equal rights when Serbs are given preference in the factories, even when they are disqualified, and Albanians are rejected although they have the same or better qualifications."[48] The new atmosphere encouraged some officials to urge even bolder steps in the new quest for equality. For example, Mehmet Hoxha, the prominent Albanian resistance leader of the Yugoslav Partisans (who was chastized during the war for suggesting that the Kosovars desired to join Albania proper), now raised the question at a political meeting in Serbia: "Why do 370,000 Montenegrins have their own republic, while 1.2 million Albanians don't even have total autonomy?"[49]

As might be anticipated, the sudden improvement in the position of the Kosovo Albanians, who had suffered years of police repression and discrimination, unleashed more disorderly expressions of "ethnic affirmation." The first signs of difficulty which occurred during May through October 1968, were distinguished by a few minor incidents such as student celebration of events and personalities in Albanian history, disruption by Albanian young people of entertainment events performed in the Serbo-Croatian language, and street processions displaying Albanian flags in a few provincial towns. At the end of November 1968, however, a full-scale "organized demonstration" erupted, first at the Humanities Faculty of the University in Priština, and then spreading to other localities in Kosovo and western Macedonia. Some of the demonstrators - mainly university and secondary school students - called for the creation of Kosovo as a separate republic (i.e., outside of Serbia) within Yugoslavia, with its "own constitution" and the "right of self-determination." Other demonstrators also using the Albanian flag as their banner took a more extreme stance, advocating the union of Kosovo with communist Albania, cheering the Albanian chief of state, Enver Hoxha, and denouncing Yugoslav Albanian officials such as Veli Deva, the provincial party committee chairman. The authorities carried out widespread arrests and quickly restored order, but only after one demonstrator was shot to death and about forty others wounded.[50]

The Socialist Pyramid: Elites and Power in Yugoslavia

While the authorities urged much greater vigilance against Albanian chauvanists and irredentists after the demonstrations, the regime moved ahead with the program of Albanianization and local reforms. Criticism of the use of newly achieved rights (e.g., language use and flag display, etc.) did not result in the withdrawal of these rights, and what was viewed as the misguided nationalistic orientation of certain Albanian intellectuals did not halt support for the development of a more broadly based Albanian intelligentsia. Kosovo's party chief, Veli Deva, attributed the large participation of Albanian intellectuals in the demonstrations to their "one-sided structure," i.e., the fact that they are "predominantly representatives of humanist, social and historical linguistics," and suggested that among the intelligentsia "and not only the Albanians ... national romanticism has increasingly gained ground, because there was formerly not an opportunity to live it out."[51] It was also alleged that irredentist propaganda had an "influence on events" in Kosovo, but "the first order of significance were internal movements."[52]

The most ominous consequence of the demonstration, according to leading officials, was the growing sense of mistrust between Slavic and non-Slavic ethnic groups in Kosovo, which resulted in a sizeable exodus of Serbs and Montenegrins from the province after 1968. In a January speech to a Belgrade symposium of academics and politicians convened to assess the state of internationality relations throughout Serbia, Veli Deva discussed the complexity of ethnic relations in Kosovo, as well as the impact of the situation on the role of the party and elite development:

> In the wood processing plant Uroševac ten days ago one worker, a bully, whose father is an immigrant from Albania, hit an engineer with a screwdriver, and inflicted a so-called minor bodily injury. It is certain that such an injury, if it was inflicted by one Albanian on another Albanian would not be recorded anywhere. If the same thing happened in Raška [a mainly Serbian area] between two Serbs, you wouldn't hear about it in the communal party committee. However, the events in Uroševac understandably, set in motion a mass of other processes; the reaction of the Serbs in Uroševac that they are unprotected, that they are attacked by bullies, so that a hundred Serbs will not go to work in the plant. The public prosecutor released the bully from jail, saying it was a minor injury, and jail isn't the place for him. Because he didn't see a serious political offense but only a minor bodily injury. We were obliged to order the arrest of that bully. We asked ourselves this question: How should the League of Communists behave in that situation? It is certain that in a series of such situations the League really doesn't have a place, because communists must demonstrate to the Serbs that things are accounted for in a normal way, and to the Albanians that a bully is

Lenard J. Cohen

convicted, not as a bully, but because of a political act which destroyed brotherhood and unity ... after this event I heard that five engineers sought to leave Uroševac. We must urgently take note of this phenomenon, not only in Uroševac, but all over, because there are more signs of departing specialists, and for more reasons .... The departure from Kosovo of a large group of Serbs, Montenegrins, and specialists of other nationalities would embolden bullies, enemies and other forces in the ranks of the Albanians to increase surly incidents because they would see a chance to drive the Serbs and Montenegrins away from here.[53]

Table 8.6
Higher Education, Generational Change, and Ethnicity in Kosovo, 1961-71 (%)

	Ethnic Group				
	Serbs	Montenegrins	Albanians	Others	(N)
Total Workers[a]					
1961	36.5	8.6	47.6	7.3	(86,913)
1971	32.6	6.4	54.2	6.8	(112,063)
Workers with university or post-secondary education					
1961	54.9	17.2	16.5	11.4	(3,599)
1971	38.6	11.8	41.9	7.7	(11,372)
Kosovo residents with higher education, by age group (1971)[b]					
Under 34	35.0	11.5	46.3	7.2	(2,833)
35-49	48.8	13.2	31.2	6.8	(1,867)
50 and over	53.5	12.0	18.3	16.2	(333)
Unknown	39.4	15.2	24.2	21.2	(33)
Total	41.3	12.2	38.7	7.8	(5,066)

Sources: *Popis Stanovništva 1961, Knjiga IV. Ekonomska Obeležja Stanovništva, II Deo (Radnici-Službenici)* (Belgrade: Savezni Zavod za Statistiku, 1969); *Popis Stanovištva i Stanova 1971, Stanovništvo, Ekonomske Karakteristike II Deo (Zaposleno Osoblje)* (Belgrade: Savezni Zavod za Statistiku, 1974).
[a] Workers in "direct production" and white-collar workers.
[b] Faculties and *visoke skole* (high schools).

By the early 1970's the various reforms adopted by the regime, together with the departure of many Serbian and Montenegrin families from Kosovo, noticeably affected the region's elite structure. As Table 8.6 indicates, considerable changes had occurred in the overall size and ethnic composition of the work force between the censuses of 1961 and 1971. The number of actively employed persons with higher education had more than tripled in the intervening decade, and there was an eight-fold increase in the absolute number of Albanians in this category. By 1971 non-Slavs made up 50 percent of all highly specialized personnel compared to only 20 percent in 1961. The generational structure of persons with a formal higher education in 1971 (a smaller group than those included in the category "highly specialized") revealed the significant changes occurring in Kosovo and the potential difficulties which might unfold. Thus, while Albanians made up less than one fifth of all individuals over 50 years of age with a higher education, and under one third of those in the 35 to 49 year old age range, they composed nearly half of the educated elite under 35 years of age. In short, the data reveal the emergence of a Yugoslav Albanian elite that could begin to challenge the Slavic ethnic groups which had predominated in Kosovo's elite structure since 1912. Such highly qualified Albanians found themselves functioning in a political environment still heavily influenced by Serbs and Montenegrins, as well as by older Albanians from the Partisan generation, who often lacked higher or modern educational credentials. While aggregate census data alone is not an indicator of elite cleavage or behaviour, information concerning the changing number and nationality composition of elite actors by generation illustrates the new context of elite and ethnic relations. For example, evidence of the marked decline in the relative position of Serbs and Montenegrins in Kosovo's elite structure undoubtedly contributed to the great anxiety expressed by members of those groups about their influence and future role in the province.

The changing circulation of the two major ethnic newspapers in the province (Figure 8.2) offers yet another indicator of the diminished Slavic presence in Kosovo and the expanding size and politicization of the emergent Albanian intelligentsia. The gradual increase in the number of educated Albanians concerned with the affairs of the province and the use of their own language is revealed in the steady rise in the readership of the Albanian daily *Rilindja* throughout the mid-1960's. With the increased emigration of Serbs in the aftermath of the 1968 demonstrations, and also the growing Albanianization of Kosovo, readership of the Albanian newspaper finally surpassed and eventually tripled that of the equivalent Serbian publication. The Albanian intelligentsia had clearly become more active spectators and participants in Kosovo's elite structure and in the Yugoslav political system.

Further examination of the 1971 census data reveals that although the Albanian position in the overall elite structure had greatly improved over a relatively short period of time, significant inequities still existed with regard to the ethnic "representativeness" of most elite sectors. For example, the data regarding various occupational groups (Table 8.7) reveal that while Serbs and Montenegrins made up approximately 21 percent of the total population in Kosovo, they still composed over a third of the functionaries working in the party and mass organizations, 45 percent of the legislative and government functionaries, and 52 percent of the province's managerial personnel. The region's

Lenard J. Cohen

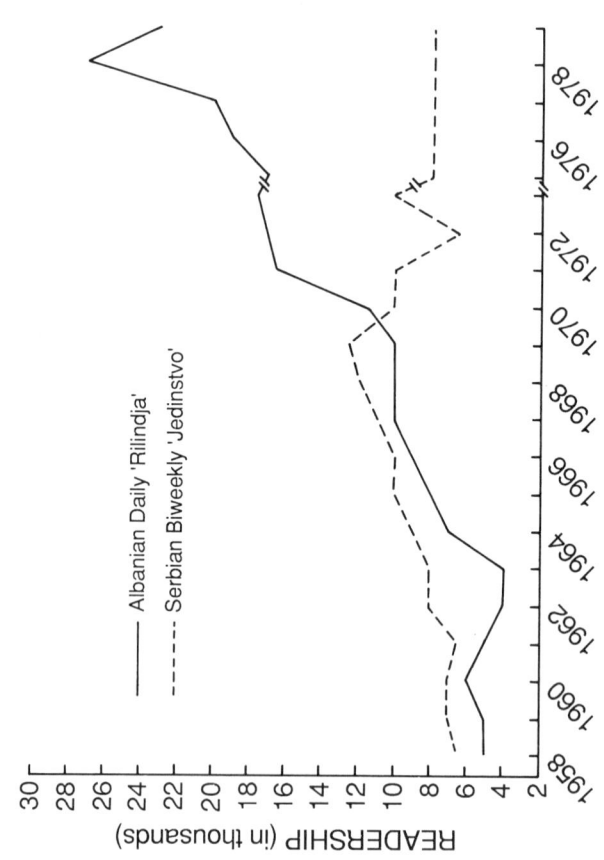

Figure 8.2
Newspaper Readership in Kosovo, by Language

Source: Živorad K. Stojković, Štampa Naroda i Narodnosti u SFRJ, 1945-1973 (Belgrade: Jugoslovenski Institut za Novinarstvo, 1975); Kultura i Umetnost, 1979 (Belgrade: Savezni Zavod za Statistiku, May 1981), Statistički Bilten 1241, p. 44.

The Socialist Pyramid: Elites and Power in Yugoslavia

technical intelligentsia and scientific elite in 1971 were also still overwhelmingly non-Albanian in ethnic composition.

Leaving aside the ethnically more balanced recruitment of political positions after 1966, the increasing Albanian presence was most apparent among teaching personnel and the literary-artistic intelligentsia, that is, the portion of the elite most self-conscious about "ethnic affirmation" and most susceptible to the appeals of "national romanticism." In 1971, approximately 80 percent of the Albanians in Kosovo's elite were teachers. Such "one-sided" Albanian elite development hindered the contribution and influence that Kosovo's ethnic majority could have had on the province's economic growth and created an added basis for inter-ethnic and inter-elite friction. While in earlier years the cultural division of labour in Kosovo had been largely "hierarchical" with Slavs controlling the elite and Albanians making up the non-elite, the division of labour now was more "horizontally segmented," with members of both the Slavic and non-Slavic ethnic groups enjoying higher training and social rank, but predominating in different elite occupational sectors.[54]

As was shown in Chapter 7, the extent of ethnic domination and ethnic distance within an elite or between elites depends on the particular occupational sector or sectors involved. Thus Slavs and non-Slavs in Kosovo appear to have enjoyed rather good relations in the instrumental technical and scientific intelligentsia, with members of both groups resenting the influence of all outside intervention, Albanian or non-Albanian, from the less qualified political sector. On the other hand, cross ethnic intra-elite bonds were probably less close-knit in both the predominantly non-Slavic literary intelligentsia, or mainly Slavic managerial elite, with Albanian members of the latter sector undoubtedly resenting the continued influence and colonial mentality of Serbian and Montenegrin "leading cadre." Throughout the 1970's, in any case, the principle meeting ground for this segmented or polarized elite was in the formal political arena, usually in agencies and organs intentionally and proportionately balanced among representatives of all nationalities.

During the next decade, developments in higher education had the most profound impact on Kosovo's elite structure and ethnic relations. The creation of a separate university in Priština in 1970, based upon a few core faculties formerly associated with the University of Belgrade, opened the way for a very rapid acceleration in the size and expectations of the Albanian intelligentsia. Officially reported data (Table 8.8) with respect to enrollment in Kosovo's higher educational institutions revealed an increase from approximately 8,000 students in 1967-1968 to 47,000 in 1978-1979. Local authorities were later to admit that enrollment figures provided at the end of the 1970's were inflated as a result of bad evidence, boasting, and the need for greater economic aid from the federal budget.[55] The corrected figure offered was approximately 30,000 full-time and part-time students in nine faculties and seven higher schools throughout Kosovo. By 1980, the province's university system also employed

Table 8.7
Elite Sectors in Kosovo: Selected Ethnic Groups, 1971 (%)

	Ethnic Group						
	Serbs	Montenegrins	Albanians	Moslems[a]	Others	Unknown	(N)
Party and mass organization functionaries	23.9	10.7	62.4	1.1	1.9	–	(197)
Legislative and government functionaries	33.5	11.5	48.8	2.6	3.5	–	(418)
Management personnel	39.7	12.7	40.5	2.0	5.1	–	(1,482)
Technical intelligentsia	54.1	12.1	26.0	3.2	4.4	0.2	(3,012)
Physical scientists	58.1	7.2	30.3	1.2	3.2	–	(241)
Natural scientists	52.7	16.1	25.9	1.7	3.6	–	(750)
Teachers and professors[b]	24.7	7.2	64.3	1.0	2.8	0.1	(12,221)
Literary/artistic intelligentsia	24.3	2.7	43.6	1.8	27.4	0.2	(451)
Total	31.2	8.6	54.9[c]	1.4	3.8	0.1	(17,772)

Source: *Popis Stanovništva i Stanova 1971. Stanovništvo, Ekonomske Karakteristike I Deo (ukupno i aktivno stanovništvo) Rezultati po republikama i pokrajinama, Knjiga III* (Belgrade: Savizni Zavod za Statistiku, 1974).
[a] Moslem as ethnic affinity. Most Albanians and many non-Albanians are also Moslem by religion (see note 10).
[b] Includes elementary and secondary teachers and teachers in higher education.
[c] Excluding teachers, this figure would be 34.5.

Table 8.8
Higher Education and Ethnicity in Kosovo, 1966-79 (%)

	Ethnic Group			Albanians as a Percentage of Total for the Country[a]	(N)
	Serbs	Montenegrins	Albanians		
Enrollment in Higher Education					
1967-68	41.6	12.9	38.3	2.2	(8,671)
1969-70	33.7	10.9	48.8	3.2	(12,064)
1973-74	28.1	6.9	56.5	5.1	(25,600)
1978-79	17.4	4.2	71.7	8.5	(47,019)[b]
Graduates with Degrees in Higher Education					
1966	49.1	15.5	26.5	1.3	(798)
1970	36.5	13.7	45.2	2.3	(1,178)
1975	33.6	9.1	50.5	2.5	(1,668)
1978	29.6	8.8	54.2	3.9	(2,987)[c]

Sources: *Statistički Bilten, Visoke škole* (Belgrade: Savezni Zavod za Statistiku, 1969, 1971, 1975, 1980); *Statistički Bilten, Diplomirani Studenti* (Belgrade: Savezni Zavod za Statistiku, 1967, 1971, 1976, 1979).

[a] Includes Albanians in areas outside Kosovo.
[b] Corrected figure for 1979-80 is approx. 30,000.
[c] From 1970 to 1981, about 22,000 students graduated from the University of Kosovo, including 142 with doctoral degrees and 155 with master's degrees (*NIN*, 20 Dec. 1981, p. 22).

about 1,200 instructors, one third of whom had graduated from faculties in Kosovo and were mainly in the 30 to 35 year old age group.[56] Even after the revision of enrollment data, the growth in higher education is still quite striking, especially when keeping in mind that in 1960-1961 Kosovo had only 98 university students and seven university teachers. Moreover, the number of Albanian students increased from approximately 38 percent of total regional university enrollment in 1967-1968 to 72 percent by the end of the decade. By 1978, four times as many students were enrolled in universities in Kosovo than in 1966, and the percentage of Albanians among those who graduated had doubled from 27 percent to 54 percent. The ominous aspect of this impressive educational explosion was the inability of Kosovo's economy to absorb the newly qualified graduates seeking to enter the work force. Indeed, while Yugoslavia had embarked on an ambitious program of economic reform beginning in 1965, this program was actually followed by a period of declining growth rates, and also an increasing disparity between the more advanced and less developed parts of the country.⁵⁷ Another difficulty in this regard was that during the mid-1970's approximately two-thirds of university enrollments and graduations in Kosovo were in nontechnical faculties, a situation which did little to overcome the already one-sided elite structure discussed above.

The spectacular increase in the size of the province's population - an increase of 27 percent from 1971 to 1981, or three times the country-wide rate - further compounded the problem by exerting even more pressure on the authorities to expand school facilities and enrollments and by undermining the overall progress of the modernization program. It is doubtful, in fact, whether even a slightly more successful program of economic growth could have coped any better with the simultaneous pressures of rapid intellectual overproduction and agrarian overpopulation which afflicted Kosovo in the 1970's. Moreover, the concentration of a large number of upwardly mobile and ethnically mobilized Albanian students at Kosovo's urban university centers (mainly in Priština, which virtually became a university town), who were painfully aware of both dismal job prospects in a slow growth economy and the relative underdevelopment of their potentially rich and populous province, created a tinderbox for nationalist unrest. It was only at the beginning of the 1980's that the authorities were to learn about the combustible properties of excessively rapid university growth under conditions of persistent economic backwardness and sharp ethnic rivalry.

The decade following the 1968 student demonstrations in Kosovo was also characterized by a process of Albanianization in the political sphere. Increasingly, Slavic and non-Slavic party professionals from the Partisan generation were retired or transferred to sinecure positions, while younger more highly educated Albanian personnel were recruited to top positions. The replacement in 1971 of Kosovo party chief Veli Deva by Mahmut Bakalli, a younger Albanian *apparatchik*, symbolized the transformation taking place in the regional political elite. Bakalli, only thirty-five years old, had joined the party after the war (in fact, after the break with the USSR), completed some postgraduate university work, and had even served for a time as a university professor. He had attracted special attention with respect to his work first as a youth leader and later as a Priština official struggling against the student demonstrations. Deva not only had the misfortune of being regional party chief during the 1968 demonstrations but also had angered Tito and others because of his old-fashioned "strong-arm" tactics and criticism of Serbian nationalism in Kosovo.

The party membership also became ethnically more Albanian in this period, partially as a result of Serbian and Montenegrin emigration from the province, and also because of the recruitment of larger numbers of non-Slavs (Figure 8.3). Albanians composed only eight percent of the communist membership in Kosovo in 1941 and 30 percent in 1945, but increased to comprise half of the provincial organization in the 1950's, and nearly two-thirds of the

The Socialist Pyramid: Elites and Power in Yugoslavia

Figure 8.3
Changes in the Ethnic Composition of Kosovo's Population and Party Organization, 1953-1981

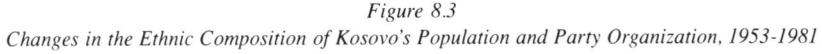

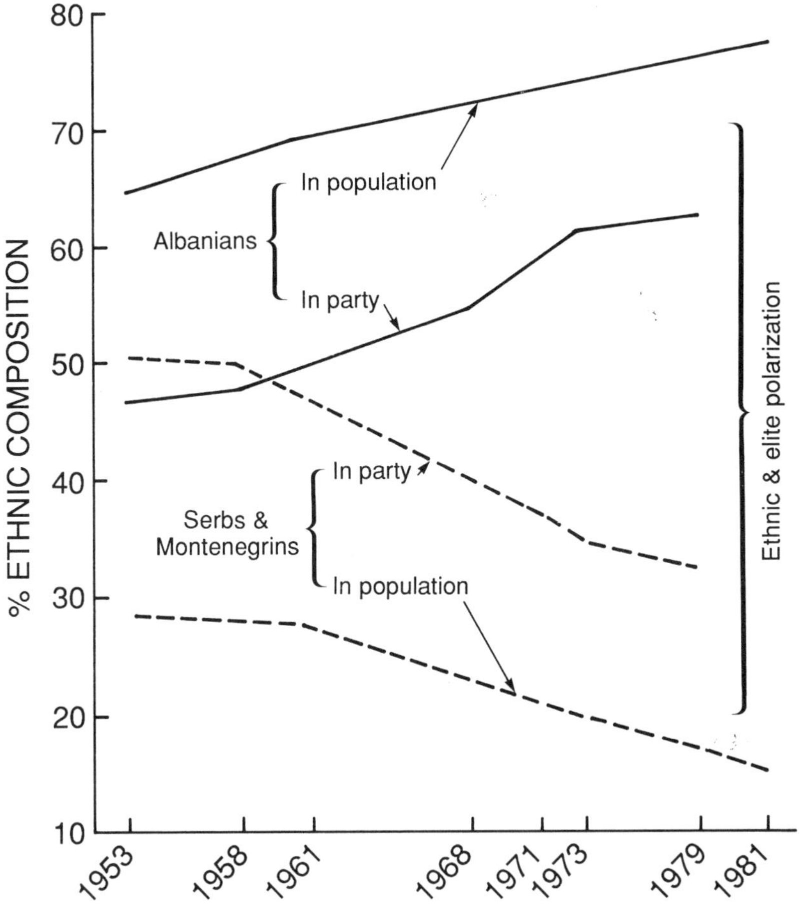

Source: Othmar Nikola Haberl, *Parteiorganisation und Nationale Frage in Jugoslawien* (Wiesbaden: Otto Harrassowitz, 1976); *Statistički Podaci o Savezu Komunista Jugoslavije izmedju desetog i jedanaestog Kongresa SKJ* (Belgrade: Komunist, 1978); Desna Vlačić, *Statistički Podaci o Savezu Komunista Jugoslavije* (Belgrade: Presedništvo Saviza Komunista Jugoslavije-Stručna Služba, 1974).

membership by 1978. Although the political influence of Kosovo's Slavic inhabitants did not drop as precipitously as their relative position in the population and party membership, it was apparent that a fundamental change was taking place. Despite the rapid Albanianization process underway in the province and the clear threat to the hegemony of the previously ruling Slavic elite contingents, the political authorities in the 1970's expressed public confidence that ethnic relations could be kept "stable." Regime spokesmen admitted, however, that "individuals and groups" did exist within the Kosovo party whose "proletarian communist consciousness had been extinguished." Moreover, they suggested, that among these individuals and groups there existed some "false national leaders" who use "bureaucratic, demagogic and careerist methods" and affect to "protect" the national interests by turning toward the past rather than toward the future.[58] Ultra-nationalist groups and agents from Albania were also closely monitored by security forces (who, it was claimed, were 75 percent Albanian by 1981), and numerous arrests were made,[59] but the level of police vigilance and repression was far below the pre-1966 level. In the 1970's the rate of Albanian political crime (Figure 8.1) dropped off markedly, as Croatian nationalism and political dissatisfaction within other ethnic groups (e.g., Montenegrin "Cominformists") assumed more visibility and importance in the country.

    Yugoslav politicians were well aware of persistent nationality difficulties in Kosovo and of sources of dissatisfaction within the Albanian population of the country, but it was generally maintained that constitutional reforms and economic development would gradually resolve any remaining traces of the "national question."[60] Visiting the province in October 1979, Tito commented that Kosovo "is subjected to the increased activities of nationalists, irredentists, a hostile sector of the clergy and other ideological forces," but he suggested that the fuller development of "self-managing relations" could resolve the threats from such "diverse prophets." Speaking to a local audience, Tito claimed to see a "great difference" from his visit four years earlier, "not only in the construction of various projects, but also in the people." He reported: "They look different, more cheerful ... on my way here in the car from Priština I watched to see how people bear themselves. All right, someone may come out because he was asked to do so, but in such a case he is really absent. On his face there would be no smile which is an expression of joy, pleasure. And this is what followed us along the whole route. All of this amounts to a belief in a better future. To me this is a good indication."[61]

The Socialist Pyramid: Elites and Power in Yugoslavia

Counter-Revolution and Elite "Differentiation": 1980-1981

In March and April 1981, just one year after Tito's death, violent nationality conflict once again erupted in Kosovo. As in 1968, the collective dissidence began with demonstrations by Albanian students at the university in Pristina, and quickly mushroomed throughout the province and throughout the Albanian population in neighbouring regions. Demonstrating street crowds sometimes numbering in the thousands and composed largely of students and young people, put forward a wide array of nationalist and separatist demands (including those made a dozen years before), such as the establishment of Kosovo as a separate republic in the Yugoslav federation, and the union of Yugoslvia's predominantly Albanian regions with Enver Hoxha's neighbouring regime in Albania. Violent clashes resulted in nine deaths (eight demonstrators and one policeman), more than 200 injured, as well as a significant loss in property and economic output. Shocked by the scale of violence and resistance, the Yugoslav authorities took strong measures to quash the demonstration which was officially termed a "counter-revolutionary uprising." Declaring a state of emergency, the regime rushed in armed internal security forces and military units from elsewhere in the country and, for a short period, virtually sealed off the province from all outside contact. By July, after carrying out widespread arrests and suppressing most overt opposition, the regime was sufficiently confident to lift the state of emergency, but it was admitted that the situation in Kosovo would remain exceptionally "complex" for some time to come, and only superficially "stable."[62]

Not surprisingly, one of the most immediate consequences of the 1981 Kosovo crisis was the deterioration in relations between Yugoslavia and Albania. Accusing the regime in Tirana of actively encouraging the separatist and irredentist group who spearheaded the demonstrations, the Yugoslav authorities abrogated a formal agreement for the exchange of instructors and cultural material with Albania.[63] A propoganda campaign was also launched in Belgrade and Pristina to illustrate the difficulties of life in Albania, and the comparative advantage enjoyed by Albanians in Yugoslavia. The polemics emenating from Tirana were even more intense, charging the Yugoslav authorities and particularly the Serbs with exploitation and repression of the Kossovars. In a November 1981 speech to the Eighth Congress of the Albanian Worker's Party, Albanian head of state, Enver Hoxha, went so far as to claim that in 1946 Tito had acknowledged that Kosovo and other regions inhabited by Albanians belonged in Albania and should be returned to it, but that the Yugoslav leader had cautioned, "we cannot do this for the time being because the Serbs would not understand us." According to Hoxha, "the official promise of Tito's on this great issue of principle was not accompanied with any further action on the part of Yugoslavia. The whole thing was a fraud on their part."[64]

Based on an eyewitness account of the meeting, one Yugoslav official responded that Hoxha and Tito did not disagree on the matter of Kosovo's status, and that both in 1946 and in 1948 (just before the break with Stalin) Tito had actually resisted requests by Hoxha to have Albania rapidly integrated into the Yugoslav federation.[65] Given the clear reluctance of Yugoslav Communist leaders during the war to endorse any statements about the eventual merger of Kosovo with Albania, Hoxha's account of his meeting with Tito seems very unlikely. At the same time, however, it is not difficult to imagine Tito contemplating an eventual merger of all ethnic Albanians in a new territorial unit that would be part of his plan for a broader Yugoslav or Balkan federation. What appears most certain, is that together with a host of other animosities and current problems in Kosovo, mobilized dissatisfaction about the nonfulfillment of Tito's alleged "promise" became another source of justification for ethnic discord.[66]

While Yugoslav leaders were eager to identify external support behind the violence in Kosovo (including allusions to Soviet meddling in the region), they were frank in admitting that much deeper internal problems were also at work. As Stane Dolanc, a member of the top party leadership, told a press conference soon after the demonstrations, "we should be politically blind and deaf if we reduced all that [trouble] only to a foreign factor."[67] Both Yugoslav commentators and foreign observers tended to treat the problem of relative economic backwardness as basic to Kosovo's difficulties. After the 1981 demonstrations, plans were developed to increase economic aid to Kosovo, and criticisms were levelled against both the inefficiency of earlier economic investments, as well at the poor labour productivity in the province. According to Yugoslavia's medium-term development plan for the 1981-1985 period, approximately $2.5 billion was to be invested in Kosovo, two-thirds of which was to come from the federal fund for assisting the development of insufficiently advanced areas (Kosovo's share was about 42 percent of the total fund allocation). Two-thirds of the overall economic investment program was alloted to industry, with a priority on the development of processing industries. The overall development program envisaged an average annual growth rate of 8.4 percent for industrial production and 5.7 percent for agricultural production, both target rates notably higher than for the country as a whole.[68] Suggestions were even made that some of the region's surplus intellectual cadre be employed elsewhere in Yugoslavia.[69] The sensitive matter of the very high Albanian birth rate in Yugoslavia and its impact on Kosovo's continued economic difficulties also received very candid discussion. Although some experts warned that because of demographic trends in Kosovo the country may face some kind of demographic "catastrophe" in the years ahead, it was also pointed out by the Croatian political sociologist and politician, Stipe Šuvar, that "any reproaches to Albanians that they are multiplying too rapidly in relation to members of other Yugoslav peoples would be akin to racism."[70]

The Socialist Pyramid: Elites and Power in Yugoslavia

Given the long range and complex nature of the economic and demographic issues, the first response of the Yugoslav regime to the events in Kosovo focused on the tractable areas of political control and educational policy. In addition to meting out rather severe sentences to those convicted of participating in the demonstrations,[71] the regime acted to chastize and remove officials and other party members whose policies or indifference allegedly permitted matters in the province to get out of hand. A detailed assessment of the internal counter-revolution issued by the League of Communists at the end of November 1981, placed the major blame for the crisis on Kosovo's political leadership for allowing or encouraging the isolation of the province from the Republic of Serbia and the rest of the country, and failing to resolutely resist "enemy" forces and the Albanianization of the region. "In some cases," the report pointed out, "there was insistence that members of nations and nationalities in Kosovo must know Albanian if they want to obtain employment in specific places of work.... National affirmation is conceived of as being cultural and socio-psychological 'homogenization' of all Albanians at all costs."[72] The implication clearly was that a pattern of elite cleavage and elite direction was behind the mass pattern of ethno-political dissidence which had finally erupted:

> Such events were made possible mostly because of the concessions which the League of Communists and other political factors made to the nationalistic and irredentist forces over quite a long period and because nationalism had penetrated into the ranks of the League of Communists in the leadership .... The Kosovo leadership's policy was oriented first and foremost toward a struggle to gain the greatest possible resources on the basis of special rights arising from Kosovo's underdevelopment .... The leadership of Kosovo submitted the thesis that Kosovo was lagging behind because it was receiving small amounts of money. It sent a letter to the SFRJ [Federal] Presidency in which it expressed its dissatisfaction with the already concluded agreement between the republics and the provinces on the social plan for Yugoslavia for the period 1980-1985. It also threatened to publicize the protest and the dissatisfaction within the rank and file of the League of Communists of Kosovo. In this way dissatisfaction was created among the cadres which provided for its spread in the masses.[73]

Attention was also drawn to the difficulties created by the educational explosion which had occurred over the past decade: "It is no accident that the highest number of participants in the demonstrations and those who carried enemy slogans came from the ranks of the young university students and grade school pupils and from a selection of the intelligentsia, especially as hostile

Lenard J. Cohen

indoctrination has had a broad area opened to it and parts of the leadership itself were affected by nationalism."[74] In an earlier analysis, Vladimir Bakaric, one of the top leaders from Tito's Partisan inner circle, pointed even more emphatically to the crucial role of the educational system in generating rivalry between an established elite, composed in large part of a regional ethnic minority, and a generation of upwardly mobile young people from the majority indigenous population:

> ... the events in Kosovo ... have taught us a whole series of things, to which attention has been repeatedly drawn without success. We warned that a mass of young people were students, that these young people were studying not to become what they should become, but what they should like to become, in other words to become gentlemen, to cease to work with their hands, to sit in offices. And now it has been shown, first that the Kosovo economy cannot support so great a mass of students and pupils, and second, that on completing their studies they have no chance of getting a job. In other parts of Yugoslavia the situation is not the same but it is on the way toward becoming the same. So what happens next? The young man begins to feel that his prospects are poor, that he cannot become a "gentleman," that he can no longer come to "rule" society, and that consequently, in the present structure of the society, he is relatively without any prospect.[75]

In order to deal with these matters, political organizations in Kosovo launched a process of "political differentiation" designed to remove those persons deemed responsible for the escalation of nationalism, or who were unable to support the new hardline against nationalism adopted by the authorities. As one provincial politician put it, "because something has been routed and taken off the streets, it has not necessarily been annihilated ideologically."[76] Between March 11 and November 6, 1981, over one thousand members of the League of Communists (that is, roughly one percent of the regional party) were either formally expelled or simply struck off the membership rolls, and eleven basic party organizations were completely eliminated. Nearly 350 people were expelled from their jobs, approximately one-half of whom were working in the field of education.[77] The leading politicians in Kosovo were not immune to the regional political purge. One of the first steps taken was the removal of Mahmut Bakalli, Kosovo's party president, who had presided over a decade of de facto Albanianization in Kosovo (he was not expelled from the League, however, until two years later). Bakalli was initially succeeded by Veli Deva, the popular Albanian *apparatchki* who had been pushed aside in the reform at the beginning of the 1970's and who had been serving out his political retirement as director-general of the Trepca mining complex. A number of other experienced political leaders were also rotated back into political positions, replacing generally younger and more highly educated officials who had failed to "behave decisively and combatively" in opposing the growth of nationalism. Some younger political functionaries were also advanced in the personnel reshuffle, and it was made clear that future cadre policy would stress the "moral-political suitability" of appointees.[78]

Steps were also taken following the 1981 demonstrations to eliminate nationalist influences in the educational system and to see that the schools "coordinate better with the needs of the economy."[79] Many Albanian instructors were fired, suspended, or reprimanded for taking a "nationalist-oriented" approach to their subjects, and a campaign was launched to purge chauvanistic and separatist perspectives from the curriculum and school materials. Books imported from Albania were discontinued, and a more careful examination of educational materials was undertaken to prevent further "legalized indoctrination of the young" (or more accurately, to allow for correct indoctrination in the future). A limit was placed on the number of new enrollments at the university in the Fall of 1981, in contrast to the open admission policy employed in earlier years, and greater care was taken to screen out potential trouble-makers during registration. An effort was also made to reduce the previously excessive enrollments in the arts faculties and to recruit students for "vocations required by economic development." Despite all these measures, disruptive behaviour (e.g., short demonstrations, nationalistic wall slogans, etc.) continued at Kosovo University throughout the 1981-1982 academic year.[80] In addition to organizing an intense round of meetings at the university to correct matters, the authorities responded by trying to mobilize public opinion against student protesters, and especially the type of student labelled as a "spoiled class opponent":

> Everybody who is an organizer, a participant, or even an accidental protagonist in the latest demonstration, by sitting in his warm room, which does not differ from a room of a Category "A" hotel, is a direct opponent of that contemporary of his, the miner, smelter, agricultural worker, shepherd .... Because let us not forget, that they [the working class] have allocated the resources not only for the residence halls, the university and various social activities, but also for the maintenance of its student's consistent class orientation ... [81]

The intensification of ethnic tension between Slavs and Albanians as a result of the 1981 demonstrations led to a new exodus of Serbs and Montenegrins from Kosovo. It was estimated, for example, that between March and October

1981 approximately 10,000 people left the province, and although the authorities condemned this trend and its causes, reports of continued Serbian and Montenegrin emigration persisted throughout the 1980's.[82] Serbian Communists have been especially critical of commentaries which attribute such emigration to economic reasons, and instead emphasize the need for severe action against the harassment of Slavs by Albanian nationalist and local bullies. Ironically, as was the case after the 1968 events, the process of demographic Albanianization in Kosovo has not been most marked during the period when the momentum of Albanian nationalism and discontent was building up, but directly after the violent climax of ethnic tension, or the point at which officials belatedly reacted to serious difficulties. Thus it was only in the aftermath of the 1981 events, in an atmosphere hardly conducive to inter-ethnic accommodation, that regime spokesmen began emphasizing the importance of bilingual education, and suggesting that the very delinquent efforts to ensure Albanian language rights after 1966 may have sometimes resulted in reverse discrimination against those speaking Slavic languages (e.g., Serbo-Croatian, Macedonian etc.). A public relations campaign was also launched to enhance the "togetherness" (*zajedništvo*) of all nationalities residing in Kosovo and to denigrate the notion that the region can or should ever be made ethnically "pure."[83]

The Yugoslav regime has been less flexible or innovative regarding Kosovo's territorial status as an autonomous province within the Republic of Serbia. The official view is that nationalist agitation to make Kosovo a "seventh republic" in the Yugoslav federation, or even more radical proposals that such a new governmental unit should include predominantly Albanian areas of other republics adjacent to Kosovo (i.e., Montenegro and Macedonia) are simply part of the "first stage" of a broader plot, hatched in Tirana, for the eventual incorporation of Yugoslavia's Albanian population into an enlarged Albanian state. Beyond their natural fear of ethnic secessionism, the Yugoslav authorities are also worried that any concessions to Kosovo's demand for a republic might create a precedent for other territorially concentrated nationalities in Yugoslavia (such as Hungarians in Vojvodina) who might seek a similar political status and eventual association with a neighbouring state. Such official anxiety in the period since the 1981 Kosovo crisis has encouraged an outpouring of comments by political functionaries and constitutional specialists, all trying to support the firm legal basis and continued necessity for Kosovo's position as a province within Serbia.[84]

Leading Serbian officials and "loyal" Yugoslav Albanians have gone to great pains to demonstrate the inextricable link between Kosovo and Serbia, and have strongly criticized the tendency, especially since 1966, to "isolate" the predominantly Albanian province from the rest of the predominantly Slavic republic. Even the habit of referring to Serbia "proper" in order to distinguish that core territorial area from the two autonomous provinces in the republic of Serbia, has been alleged to have encouraged "isolationism" and nationalist feeling in the provinces. It is not surprising, of course, that after five centuries of yearning for the reintegration of Kosovo into a Serbian territorial unit (1389-1912), the Serbs would be reluctant to alter the existing structure of Yugoslavia.[85]

Elites and Politicized Ethnicity: Kosovo in Continuing Crisis

The pattern of political development and conflict in Kosovo, although certainly influenced by many special features endemic to the region, nevertheless vividly illustrates the significance of elite-mobilized nationalism and elite cleavages to political instability in a modernizing multi-ethnic environment. The traditional animosities between Serbs and Albanians have both stimulated and reflected the alternating sequence of political domination and subordination of these major nationalities in the region, with each succeeding nationalist-oriented political elite applying some brand of brutality, discrimination, or exclusion to the cultural group formerly in power. During each historical period up to the most recent decades, the social structure of Kosovo was characterized to some extent by a hierarchical cultural division of labour and other aspects of internal colonialism, favouring the particular ethnic group and political forces who had forcibly occupied the regional authority structure - Turkish and Albanian pashas, Royalist Serbian bureaucrats, Italian and Albanian Fascists, and Serbian and Montenegrin Partisans. For most of the period after 1912, Serbs wielded the greatest influence in Kosovo, first (1912-1941) as a nationalist state-building elite who had liberated the area from Ottoman rule, and then (1945-1966) as a revolutionary Communist vanguard dedicated to economic growth and, at least theoretically, to pan-ethnic equality. During both instances of hegemonic Serbian control, the subordinate Albanian majority of Kosovo regarded the authorities as a colonial elite imposed or directed from Belgrade, either opposed or unsympathetic to genuine ethnic pluralism and equality. When during World War II the Albanian population was allowed to resume the special regional status and power it had enjoyed before 1912, the Serbian population was subjected to a similar pattern of ethnic oppression. It is only against this historical background, i.e., the coercive and often violent circulation of ethnic elites, that an observer can fully understand and appreciate the basis of Kosovo's "national problem" in the last part of the twentieth century.

The liberalization of the Yugoslav political system in the mid-1960's and the subsequent opportunities offered to the country's rapidly growing Albanian population opened the way for important changes in Kosovo's elite structure and ethnic relations. A new generation of Yugoslav Albanians, and particularly members of the emergent intelligentsia created by the enormous expansion of the educational system in the province, became committed to the "affirmation" of their ethnic identity and influence. Moreover, the size of the Albanian majority in the region was growing rapidly, reaching over three-quarters of the population by 1981. Census data also indicate that by the eve of the 1981 demonstrations the proportion of Albanians having a higher education had greatly increased.[86] Adopting a self-conception found among newly educated elites in many countries, and certainly following a pattern found throughout Balkan history,[87] members of Kosovo's modern Albanian intelligentsia have increasingly viewed themselves as the bearers of the "national" destiny, responsible for the progress and future of their ethnic group.

Confronted with this surge of national feeling in the 1970's, the Albanian members of Kosovo's communist leadership, themselves a part of the new intelligentsia, were under tremendous pressure to encourage or acquiesce in the gradual "Albanianization" of the region. Ironically, some of Kosovo's top Albanian communists became a kind of "national" communist leadership fighting against external control from Belgrade in much the same way as Tito and his pan-ethnic elite had opposed Stalin in 1948 (the nationalism of top Croatian communists in 1968 also bore a certain resemblance to the case of the Kosovo communists). More often than not, such elite-guided Albanianization was viewed not simply as a means to ensure ethnic equality after years of Serbian and Montenegrin domination, but as a process of indigenization or "national majorization"[88] which would gradually expunge the minority Slavic influence and presence in Kosovo. By the end of the 1970's, this "wrongly conceived" Albanianization, as it was later termed,[89] resulted in a sharp polarization between Slavs and non-Slavs on both the elite and mass level. Faced with growing Serbian anxiety and resistance to the course of events in Kosovo, and deeply aggrieved over the province's persistent economic backwardness, some members of the region's Albanian elite (mainly but not entirely in non-political positions) became even more strident and ambitious in their plans for ethnic recognition and political autonomy, either within or outside the Yugoslav state. Heavily concentrated in urban university centers and frustrated by the dismal prospects of realizing their nationalist goals or even white collar employment, it did not take much provocation for the aspiring Albanian intelligentsia (including university and secondary school students, or the intelligentsia-in-training) to explode in a collective expression of solidarity and protest.

Although the use of punitive measures against demonstrators and an extensive purge of the Albanian political and cultural intelligentsia has enabled the regime to stifle the most vocal manifestations of nationalism in Kosovo, a fuller and non-coercive solution to the region's difficulties will be a long and arduous task. Moreover, any solution which ignores the goals of Yugoslavia's young and burgeoning Albanian elite is not likely to have much real success. In this regard the suggestion by a top party official in 1983 that Kosovo's considerable economic problems might be alleviated by a "countermigration" of non-Albanian specialists of all nationalities into the province, while perhaps a well intentioned and technically efficacious idea, was naturally viewed by many Albanians (especially educated ones) as simply a means for the reimposition of colonial elite tutelage. In response to the idea, one influential Albanian official remarked that the time had passed when people could be sent "by decree" to settle somewhere else, an obvious allusion to the colonial policies practiced in Kosovo by the Serbian and Yugoslav royalist regimes.[90]

The heritage of ethnically-based elite cleavage and violence in the Balkans, together with the history of the communist movement itself as a vehicle for intellectual protest, and the recent outbreaks of student unrest (Belgrade 1968, Croatia 1971-1972, Kosovo 1968 and 1981), have made Yugoslav leaders keenly aware of the revolutionary potential deriving from a politically and ethnically disenchanted intelligentsia. Indeed, by the early 1980's many Yugoslav politicians began to seriously question the policy of massive and rapid expansion in the country's educational institutions over the previous decade, an achievement earlier touted as one of the symbols of economic and ethnic equality in the underdeveloped areas. In 1980, Yugoslavia had over 500,000 students in 19 universities (seven of which were established between 1970-1979), or roughly one higher-level student per 50 inhabitants, compared to one such student per 1,000 inhabitants in 1940. The relative proportion of the population receiving a university education was higher than in most industrialized European countries, and five to ten times greater than in the developing countries. The rector of Belgrade University admitted that "the faculties have become a refuge for those escaping from productive work."[91] "Higher education," as another Serbian official remarked, "cannot be a parking spot at which the young wait for employment .... Data concerning the number of unemployed already show that there is no deficit of personnel with a faculty diploma."[92]

The growth of higher education can gradually be slowed, but a large, aspiring and potentially surplus intelligentsia is already a part of the Yugoslav educational system. Given the unpopular measures that may be required to deal with educational problems (such as retrenchment in university growth), and the other serious economic, ethnic and political/constitutional problems faced by the regime, it is likely that further episodes of political instability, if not necessarily counter-revolutionary uprisings, lie ahead for the Yugoslav communists, both in Kosovo,[93] and in other regions of the country. Indeed, in the wake of the 1981 Kosovo events, the regime was forced to contend not only with a continuation of Albanian political dissidence but also with a serious upsurge of nationalism by members of the intelligentsia in the Moslem and Serbian ethnic communities. As in so many other states, multi-national harmony remains an elusive goal, easily disturbed by emergent ethnic elites who are eager to mobilize and guide the destiny of their broader cultural communities.[94]

NOTES: CHAPTER EIGHT

1. See, for example, Robert Putnam, *The Comparative Study of Political Elites* (Englewood Cliffs, N.J.: Prentice-Hall, 1976), Thomas Bottomore, *Elites and Society* (New York: Basic Books, 1964), Carl Beck and James Malloy, *Political Elites: A Mode of Analysis* (Pittsburgh: University of Pittsburgh Archives of Political Elites in Eastern Europe, 1966), Seymour Martin Lipset and Aldo Solari (eds.), *Elites in Latin America* (New York: Oxford University Press, 1966), P.C. Lloyd (ed.), *The New Elites of Tropical Africa* (London: Oxford University Press, 1966).

2. Carl Beck and James Malloy, *ibid.*, 31-32.

3. *Ibid.*, 31,33.

4. Hugh Seton-Watson, *Nationalism and Communism, Essays 1946-1963* (New York: Praeger, 1964), 13-14.

5. Harry Benda, "Political Elites in Colonial Southeast Asia: An Historical Analysis," *Comparative Studies in History and Society*, II (1965), 233-251.

6. Ernest Gellner, *Thought and Change* (London: Wiedenfeld and Nicolson, 1964), 169-170.

7. Anthony Smith, *Theories of Nationalism* (New York: Harper and Row, 1971), 33, 36. For further perceptive comments on the elite origins of nationalism see by the same author, *The Ethnic Rival* (Cambridge: Cambridge University Press, 1981), 108-133, Richard Fox, Charlotte Aull, and Louis F. Cimino, "Ethnic Naitonalism and the Welfare State," *Ethnic Change*, ed. Charles Keyes (Seattle: University of Washington Press, 1981), 198-245, Paul Brass, "Ethnic Groups and Nationalities: The Formation, Persistance and Transformation of Ethnic Identities," *Ethnic Diversity and Conflict in Eastern Europe*, ed. Peter Sugar (Santa Barbara: ABC-CL10, 1980), 1-68.

8. John Kautsky, "An Essay in the Politics of Development," *Political Change in Underdeveloped Countries: Nationalism and Communism*, ed. John Kautsky (New York: John Wiley, 1962), 48.

9. The name "Kosovo" is used for convenience throughout this study rather than the formal designation of the area in each period of recent history: part of "South Serbia," 1912-1941; part of "Greater Albania," 1941-1944; the Autonomous Region (Oblast) of Kosovo and Metohija (Kosmet), 1945-1963; the Autonomous Province of Kosovo-Metohija, 1963-1968; the Autonomous Province of Kosovo, 1968-1973; the Socialist Autonomous Province of Kosovo, since 1974 (Metohija, a Serbian term, was dropped from the title in deference to Albanian demands).

10. The Albanian population of Kosovo is almost entirely Sunni Moslem (with few Christian Albanians, as in Albania proper), and the Slavic population, Serbian Orthodox. As nationalist regimes alternated in power, some Albanians became "Serbianized" and accepted the Orthodox faith, while a good number of ethnic Serbs and Montenegrins became "Islamicized" or "Albanianized Serbs." Confessional cleavages and discrimination are thus closely connected to ethno-political conflicts in the Kosovo region.

11. Ramadan Marmullaku, *Albania and the Albanians* (Hamden, Conn.: Archon, 1975), 138.

12. *Ibid.*, 139.

13. In 1878 Albanian tribal leaders, merchants, and intelligentsia met at Prizren in Kosovo to form the League for the Defense of the Albanian nation, usually called the "League of Prizren." Designed initially to oppose the decision by the Congress of Berlin to allocate Turkish areas inhabited by Albanians to Montenegro, the League became the nucleus of the Albanian "national awakening." See Stavro Skendi, "Beginning of Albanian Nationalist and Autonomous Trends: The Albanian League 1878-1881," *American Slavic and East European Review,* XII (1953), 219-232.

14. The Albanian population of Kosovo fought with the Turks against the Serbs in the Serbo-Turkish War of 1876-1877 and during the Balkan Wars.

15. The anthropologist Vera St. Erlich, discussing family relationships in interwar Yugoslavia, comments on the repression of the Albanian population: "Yet, although they had dropped from a high position to a rather low one, the effects on family life were hardly noticeable. The subjective reactions to the objective measures were

surprisingly weak. People in these areas did not appear pauperized, or declassed; alcoholism and prostitution, squandering of property, and crime did not enter. The patriarchical dignity and responsibility remained, the concentrated pressure could not bend or break them." Vera St. Erlich, *Family in Transition: A Study of 300 Yugoslav Villages* (Princeton: Princeton University Press, 1968), 362.

16. In 1931 Kosovo had an economically active population 226,226, 86 percent of whom worked in agriculture (compared to 76 percent for all of Yugoslavia), 4.9 in industry and trade, 1.9 percent in commerce credit and transportation, 3.9 percent in the public service, and 3.1 percent in other occupations. Women made up 29 percent of the active work force, 95 percent of whom were engaged in agricultural activity. This data was generated by combining the 1931 census districts of "South Serbia" which comprise present-day Kosovo. *Definitivni rezultati popisa stanovništva od 31 marta 1931 godine. Knjiga IV prisutno stanovništvo po glavnom zanimanju* (Sarajevo: Opšta državna statisika, 1940).

17. *Ko je ko u Jugoslaviji* (Belgrade and Zagreb: Jugoslovenski godišnjak and Nova Europa, 1928).

18. *Ibid.*, 34.

19. *Ibid.*, 121.

20. Michael Hechter, *Internal Colonialism* (Berkeley and Los Angeles: University of California Press, 1975), Michael Hechter, "Ethnicity and Industrialization: On the Proliferation of the Cultural Division of Labor," *Ethnicity,* III (1976), 219-224.

21. Michael Hechter, *Internal Colonialism, ibid.*, 34-43.

22. Rebecca West's notes of an interview in the late 1930's with "Gospodin Mac," the Serbian manager of Kosovo's large Trepca mine complex, provide a fascinating example of the condescending colonial mentality with which members of the ruling elite tended to gloss over serious intergroup tension: "I've a soft spot for Albanians. We all like them. And it's not just because they knuckle down to us. They've got plenty of spirit. They're good trade unionists. When we had a wages dispute some time ago the Albanians stood firmer than anybody, and I admired them for it. Afterwards the Government sent a commission down to inquire into

the causes of the strike, and they hinted to me they thought it a pity we employed so many Albanians, but I wasn't having any. I said straight out we employed them because we found them decent, hard-working fellows, and we'd go on employing them. But that's something that's getting better. The Serb administrators all get to like the Albanians and less and less make a distinction between them and their own people. *This country's getting over its past nicely.*" West's elite respondent added that: "everybody likes the Albanians. That is, universally said: the enmity the Turks fostered between the Albanians and all the other Slav races is being allayed simply by Albanian charm." Rebecca West, *Black Lamb and Grey Falcon* (New York: Viking, 1942), 923-924, 933, [author's emphasis].

23. Karen Verdery, "Internal Colonialism in Austria-Hungary," *Ethnic and Racial Studies*, II (1979), 378-399.

24. Mark Krasnici, *Savremene društveno-geografske promene na Kosovu i Metohiji* (Priština: Muzej Kosova i Metohije, 1963), 265. A 1938 report prepared by the Ministry of Internal Affairs emphasized the link between educational development and political stability. In view of the events of the 1970's and 1980's, it strikes a rather prophetic note: "Up to two years ago educational activity among the Albanian minority wasn't so dangerous, but then a greater number of Albanian students distributed leaflets in both our and the Albanian language with the aim of stimulating Albanian national consciousness .... The danger of the enlightenment of the Albanians grows stronger each day. This year a larger number of Albanian students registered at the university and that number grows from year to year. The question arises of what the function of these Albanians will be when they return to their ethnic group as educated persons with a knowledge of all established laws." Cited in Pavle Jovičević and Mita Miljković, "Odbrana Albanaca," *Nedeljne Informativne Novine*, (September 17, 1978), 61.

25. *Ibid.*, 32-35, and Ramadan Marmullaku, *Albania and the Albanians*, 139-145.

26. Milutin Folić, "Obnavljanje i konsolidacija KPJ, pojava frakcija na Kosovu i uticaj Titovog delovanja na njihovom prevažailazenju," *Osma konferncija Zagrebačkih Komunista i razoj KPJ-SKJ kao moderne partije radničke klase* (Zagreb: Vjesnikova Pres Agencija, 1978), 129-160.

27. After the strike at Trepca, the membership picked up in the district party organization around the mine. From 1938 to 1941 the local party unit grew from 46 to 75, of whom 29 were Serbs, 25 Montenegrins, 9 Albanians, and 12 others. *Ibid.*, 134.

28. See, "Josip Broz Tito on the National Question," *Yugoslav Survey*, XVIIII (May, 1978), 3-24.

29. Ramadan Marmullaku, *Albania and the Albanians*, 143.

30. Branko Petranović, *Politicka i ekonomska osnova narodne vlasti u Jugoslaviji za vreme obnove* (Belgrade: Institut za savremenu istoriju, 1969), 44-45.

31. *Ibid.*, 177-179.

32. Milovan Djilas, *Wartime* (New York: Harcourt Brace and World, 1977), 430. The uprising of 1944-1945 has received almost no attention from Western scholars of Yugoslav "minority problems."

33. Boris Kidric, *On the Construction of Socialist Economy in the FPRJ* (Belgrade: Office of Information of FPRJ, 1948), 40.

34. *Konačni rezultati popisa stanovništva od 15 marta 1948 knjiga IX stanovništvo po narodnosti* (Belgrade: Savezni zavod za statistiku, 1954), *Popis stanovništva 1953. Knjiga I. Vitalna i etnička obelezja* (Belgrade: Savezni zavod za statistiku, 1959).

35. Ilija Vakić, "Razvoj položaj i perspecktive Autonomne Pokrajine Kosova i Metohije," *Društveno-politicke Zajednice, Tom 11, Socijalističke Republike i Autonomne Pokrajine*, ed. Nine Opačić (Belgrade: Medjunarodna Stampa-Interpres, 1968), 555.

36. Mark Krasnici, *Savremene društveno-geografske promene na Kosova i Metohije*, 299.

37. The "first generation of Shqiptar intellectuals" or "minority professionals," as one official study refers to the few educated Yugoslav Albanians right after the war, were mainly hastily trained primary and secondary school teachers. See Ljubiša Stojković and Miloš Martić, *National Minorities in Yugoslavia* (Belgrade: Jugoslavija, 1952), 112 and 128.

38. M. Bazler-Madzar, "Regional Development," *The Yugoslav Economic System*, ed. Branko Horvat (White Plains, N.Y.: International Arts and Science Press, 1976), 62.

39. H. Islami, "Osvrt na Razvitak Stanovništva Kosovo," *Sociologija*, I (1977), 153-73, and "Problemi društvenog razvitka Kosovskog sela," *Sociologija*, IV (1979), 397-417.

40. One study reported a 25.6 percent level of unemployment in Kosovo in 1973. See Miroslav Rasevic, T. Mulina, and M. Macura, *The Determinants of Labor Force Participation in Yugoslavia* (Geneva: International Labor Organization, 1978). Many unemployed workers obtained jobs in the more developed regions of northwestern Yugoslavia contributing to both an increased cultural division of labour and an increased level of ethnic discrimination in those areas. In some of the most underdeveloped regions of Kosovo the percentage of workers abroad was also higher than for the country as a whole. See S. Mežnarić, "Imigracije radnika iz drugih Jugoslovenskih republika u SR Sloveniju," *Sociologija*, II-III (1978), 293-312, H. Islami, "Osvrt na razvitak stanovništva Kosovo," 412.

41. The Albanian population of Kosovo and Yugoslavia live primarily in rural areas and exhibit characteristics of a "traditional rural social life." In 1961, 16.7 percent of the Kosovo Albanian population lived in cities, and by 1971 this figure had only increased to 23.4 percent. Traditional practices such as a patriarchical authority structure in the family and blood feuds to settle disputes among family members have continued among Kosovo's Albanian rural inhabitants, although to a lesser extent than in the past. The extended family structure (the *zadruga*) in rural Kosovo also persists and often includes members of more "modern" occupations such as employees, teachers, professors, and engineers. See H. Islami, "Problemi društvenog razvitka Kosovskog sela," 415, M. Kavran, "Rugovska povolja-dokument samoupravnog suzbijanja krvne osvete u Kosovskom selu," *Sociologija Sela,* XII (1974), 28-36, Ruža First, "Struktura autoriteta u seoskim domacinstvima," *Sociologija Sela,* VII, (1969), 53-61, and M. Marković, "Relativno duže održavanje porodičnih zadruga u Albanca na Kosovu," *Sociologija Sela*, XII (1974), 95-100.

42. Vladimir Dedijer, *Jugoslovensko - Albanski Odnosi* (Belgrade: Borba, 1949).

43. Prior to 1966, the training handbook of the security forces had emphasized that "national feelings among national minorities are strong; because of this the minorities are very often ready to work for the intelligence agencies of their mother countries." Paul Shoup, *Communism and the National Question in Yugoslavia* (New York: Columbia University Press, 1968), 217.

44. *Ibid.*, 216-218.

45. A fuller elaboration of the data on political criminality is offered in Lenard J. Cohen, "Political Crime in Yugoslavia: The Ethnic and Political Basis of Anti-State Dissidence, 1929-1980," presented at the American Association for the Advancement of Slavic Studies (Monterey, California), 1981.

46. The more dissident position of the Albanians would likely be even more apparent if such data were available for the immediate postwar period, the 1961-1966 period, or for Kosovo separately. At the Sixth Plenary Session of the Serbian League of Communists, Kosovo party chief Veli Deva reported that the state security services kept dossiers on thousands of individuals in the province: "Since 1960 more than 9,000 dossiers on political activists in the villages, or members of the party committee ... and delegates ... have been submitted. Everyone who has concerned himself with politics at all or has any significance in his vicinity was suspected ... special measures were taken against the intelligentsia among the Albanians. Teachers of the Albanian language found themselves in the most difficult position." *Borba*, (September 15, 1966), 6.

47. Speaking to a closed meeting in Serbia shortly after the Ranković dismissal, one specialist on language rights observed: "In Trepca [the mining complex], for example, about 63 percent of those employed are Shiptars [Albanians]. For quite some time ... skilled producers operated only in the Serbo-Croatian language, in the language of 37 percent of those employed. Is that a privilege in socio-economic relations? I think it is. Because a Serbian or Montenegrin worker can conduct his specialty much easier in his own language, and also have a general knowledge concerning the areas of social insurance, the political system, etc., and advance more quickly than a Shiptar who must master Serbo-Croat. But the Shiptars in Trepca contribute twice as much as do others to the general revenue for education." Koca Jončić, *Medjunacionalni*

odnosi i idejno političko delovanje Saveza Komunista-Jugoslavije (Belgrade: Centar za političke studije i obrazovanje, 1967), 18. The traditional language of the Kosovo Albanians is the Gheg dialect of Northern Albania. The Albanian students and intelligentsia of the region, however, have supported the use of the literary language of Tirana (a mixture of Gheg and the Tosk dialect) under the slogan "one nation, one language." Stavro Skendi, *Balkan Cultural Studies* (Boulder, Colo.: East European Monographs, 1980), 38-41.

48. *Vjesnik*, (March 30, 1967), 4.

49. *Borba*, (April 10, 1968), 5.

50. "The Problem of the Albanians in Yugoslavia," *Wissenschaftlicher Dienst Suedosteuropa, XVIII* (1969), 1-9. Translated in *Joint Publication Research Service, Eastern Europe, Political, Sociological, and Military Affairs* (Belgrade: June 5, 1969), 100-119.

51. *Ibid.*, 17.

52. Veli Deva, "Medjunacionalni odnosi i politička situacija na Kosovu," *Politička situacija medjunacionalni odnosi u savremenoj fazi socijalističkog razvitka i zadaci Saveza Komunista Srbije*, ed. Ljubiša Stankov (Belgrade: Institut za političke studije FPN, 1969), 142.

53. *Ibid.*, 140.

54. Erik Allardt, "Changes in the Nature of Ethnicity: From the Primordial to the Organizational," *Directions of Change: Modernization Theory, Research, and Realities*, ed. Mustafa Attir *et. al.* (Boulder, Colo.: Westview Press, 1981), 102. According to one Albanian sociologist at the university in Priština, a pattern of ecological stratification has continued among different nationalities in Kosovo's urban centers: "In the so-called core of the cities and other urban settlements in Kosovo one finds those nationality groups who have the most favourable material and social positions (Serbs, Montenegrins, and even Turks) while the periphery of those settlements are occupied by the most underdeveloped strata in a socio-professional and cultural sense (Albanians, Gypsies, etc.). The Serbs and Montenegrins live in socially [state] owned apartments, while the Albanians live mainly in private homes which

were constructed during the recent years of increasing urbanization." H. Islami, "Problemi društvenog razvitka Kosovskog sela," 415. A 1986 study of Priština found that while Serbs and Montenegrins together made up 29 percent of the city's population, they occupied 49 percent of the state housing. The least developed district of Priština is 89 percent Albanian. The authors of the study suggest that such data "is a mirror in which we see social segregation according to national groups, and even 'ghettos'." *Foreign Broadcast Information Service*, (February 13, 1986), I14.

55. *Politika*, (August 11, 1981), 6.

56. *Komunist*, (August 28, 1981), 9. The pre-collegiate school population and teaching staff of Kosovo has already been an important source of recruits for nationalist groups. In 1979 there were approximately 307,000 students enrolled in elementary schools and some 75,000 in high schools (compared with enrollment figures of 98,000 and 3,300 respectively in 1948), that is, almost every third inhabitant of Kosovo was attending school. It has recently been pointed out that in many places in Kosovo teachers are the "most numerous professional class and that among approximately 20,000 instructors, teachers, and professors, behaviour is dictated above all by a distinct awareness of the national affirmation of the Albanians. *Nedeljne Informativne Novine*, (March 28, 1982), 14-17.

57. A. Sapir, "Economic Growth and Factor Substitution: What Ever Happened to the Yugoslav Economic Miracle?" *Economic Journal*, LXXXX, No. 358 (June, 1980), 294-313.

58. *Jedinstvo*, (February 14, 1974), 5.

59. *Foreign Broadcast Information Service*, (April 13, 1985). The federal secretary for internal affairs has reported that from 1974 to the beginning of 1981 the state security forces had identified 618 persons in Kosovo who were active in irredentist and nationalist activity and that 89 persons had received sentences of from one to 15 years. *Skupština SFRJ, Stenografske beleške, Savezno veće*, (June 9, 1981), 47. The Serbian Secretary for Internal Affairs claimed that a 1977 proposal for greater coordination between the security forces of Serbia and its two autonomous provinces had been rejected by the provincial secretaries. *Foreign Broadcast Information Service*, (December 31, 1981), I24. Such a "united inspectorate" of the three security agencies was established on

January 1, 1982 in the wake of the 1981 Kosovo crisis. *Foreign Broadcast Information Service*, (June 12, 1978), 119-120.

60. In a 1977 secret speech to Kosovo party leaders (officially quoted only in part in 1981), Edward Kardelj warned against the serious danger of both continued Serbian and Albanian nationalism in the province, but added that "today the Albanians in Kosovo bear a particular responsibility because they are the people in the majority here in Kosovo." *Foreign Broadcast Information Service*, (November 27, 1981), 120. According to another top Slovenian official, Kardelj suggested that nationalism in Kosovo could erupt into "direct counter-revolution." *Nedeljne Informativne Novine*, (June 7, 1981), 13. In May 1982, one of Kosovo's top political leaders claimed that during Tito's 1979 visit to the region he had secretly warned officials that Albanian nationalism was underestimated. *Foreign Broadcast Information Service*, (May 13, 1982), 16.

61. *Foreign Broadcast Information Service*, (October 17, 1979), 114, 115.

62. According to an official report, in the two months after the March-April demonstrations, "repressive and preventative measures were taken against 1,700 people of whom 506 were convicted: because of participation in the demonstrations 287, because of offering support to the demonstrators 38, because of attempts to organize demonstrations 31; 46 more were authors of enemy slogans and 104 because of public enemy secessionist acts. Stricter criminal procedures were begun against 154 of these persons, including 39 members of illegal organizations, 29 direct organizers of demonstrations and others involved in destructive behaviour. Among the individuals against whom judicial measures were taken the largest number were intellectuals." *Skupština SFRJ, Stenografske beleške, Savezno veće*, (June 9, 1981), 46. For Western surveys of the 1981 crisis in Kosovo see Pedro Ramet, "Problems of Albanian Nationalism in Yugoslavia," *Orbis*, XXV, (1981), 369-388. Christopher Cviic, "Yugoslavia - Bitter Inheritance," *Washington Quarterly*, IV, No. 4 (1981), 18-23, Patrick Artisien and R. Howells, "Yugoslavia, Albania, and the Kosovo Riots,"*World Today* (November, 1981), 419-427, and Stevan Pavlowitch and E. Biberaj,"The Albanian Problem in Yugoslavia: Two Views," *Conflict Studies*, Nos. 137/138 (1982), 7-43.

63. According to one report, during the 1975-1981 education exchange program with Albania, 237 professors from Tirana taught in Yugoslavia, while only 62 Yugoslav professors travelled to Albania. However, 183 Yugoslav Albanian students from Priština University had been studying in Tirana, and 20 percent of the textbooks at Priština University were printed in Albania. *Foreign Broadcast Information Service*, (November 18, 1981), I20. The rector of Tirana University claimed that "our pedagogues and scientific workers who have gone to Kosovo and elsewhere have behaved with 'exemplary correctness.' Therefore the Great Serb chauvanists, by tring to fling mud on the stand of the representatives of our sciences became ridiculous with their unscrupulous inventions and slanders. They are and will be powerless to deaden or subdue the national and patriotic sentiments of the youth, scientists, and teachers of Kosovo." *Foreign Broadcast Information Service*, (December 7, 1981), I6. Despite negotiations in 1984 between Yugoslavia and Albania, cultural cooperation had not improved by late 1987.

64. *Ibid.*, (November 20, 1981), I6-7.

65. *Ibid.*, (November 18, 1981), I15.

66. It is possible, of course, to interpret Tirana's anti-Yugoslav polemics and solicitations to the Kosovo Albanians as a case of political self-defense and fear of Titoism by the elite in Albania. See John Kosti, "Albanianism: From the Humanists to Hoxha," *The Politics of Ethnicity in Eastern Europe* (Boulder: East European Monographs 1981), 25-28. Yugoslav polemicists made considerable efforts to demonstrate the weak historical and ideological grounds for Albanian irredentism and "bureaucratic nationalism in Kosovo." See Jovan Raičević, "Ideological Grounds for Albanian Irredentism and Bureaucratic Nationalism in Kosovo," *Socialist Thought and Practice* (1981), 23-37. The death of Enver Hoxha in early 1985 seemed to provide an opening for improvement in Albanian-Yugoslav relations, although initial progress was limited to the area of trade. Albania's new leader, Ramiz Alia, has a personal connection to Kosovo (his parents emigrated to Albania from the region to escape Yugoslav rule before World War II) and this is likely to make the province one of his special concerns. See Patrick Artisien, "Albania in the Post-Hoxha Era," *World Today*, No. 41 (June, 1985), 107-111, and Louis Zanga, "Ramiz Alia's

Latest Foreign Policy Speech," *Radio Free Europe*. Background Report, No. 110 (July 6, 1987).

In February, 1988, Yugoslavia and Albania signed an agreement providing for a renewal of cultural exchanges and other forms of cooperation between the two countries, although continued difficulties in Kosovo threatened to delay operationalization of the accord.

67. *Foreign Broadcast Information Service*, (April 13, 1981), 17.

68. *Ibid.*, (November 2, 1981), I6.

69. *Ibid.*, (November 27, 1981), I26.

70. *Nedeljne Informativne Novine*, (November 8, 1981), 17-19, *Foreign Broadcast Information Service*, (September 4, 1981), I6. Kosovo has the highest annual birth rate in Europe: 27 live births per thousand population. It has been officially estimated that the region's population (1.6 million in 1981) will reach 2.6 million by 2001 and 3.5 million by 2021. At this rate Yugoslavia's Albanian population may be greater than that of neighbouring Albania by the middle of the 21st century. *Radio Free Europe Research*, (August 7, 1987), 11.

71. By the end of August 1981, approximately 30 trials had taken place in district courts throughout the province with 245 persons sentenced to serve up to fifteen years. The provincial public prosecutor (a Serb) claimed that the "trials had their effect" but other leading Yugoslav political figures such as the Slovenian ex-prime minister of the country, Mitja Ribičič and the Croatian political sociologist Stipe Šuvar, were critical of such strict sentences. *Foreign Broadcast Information Service*, (September 15, 1981). "I think" commented Ribičič, "that an 18 year old boy there who knows nothing and who thinks that the slogan 'we want a republic' is some kind of radicalism should not be sentenced to a 12 year prison term. It would be better to explain certain things to him, and to influence him by other, mainly educational means. As it is, a wrong picture, in which he appears a hero, will be formed in his young head .... I am not in favor of this judicial-administrative approach; political methods are more effective." *Vjesnik*, (September 19, 1981), 3-4, *Nedeljne Informativne Novine*, (August 30, 1981), 14-17. Data on the nationality of all those accused of political crimes in Yugoslavia

during 1981 revealed that 65 percent (380 people out of 588) were Albanians, a radical change from the previous year. Croats were next highest in political criminality, composing 13.3 percent of the accused. The number of those accused of political crime in Kosovo during 1981 also was 65 percent higher than in 1980. It was estimated that more than 40 percent of the "political criminals" are students and intellectuals." *Politika*, (March 21, 1981), 7. Political criminality by Albanian nationalists and irredentists in Kosovo remained high throughout the 1980's. From 1981 to 1985, 1,652 individuals were convicted of political crimes in Yugoslavia, of whom 1,019 (62 percent) were Albanians charged with separatism and nationalism. *Borba*, (June 8, 1987), 6. In 1986, 55 percent of all persons charged with political crime in Yugoslavia were Albanians. *Borba*, (May 22, 1987), 7.

72. *Foreign Broadcast Information Service*, (November 27, 1981), I19.

73. *Ibid.*, I2-3.

74. *Ibid.*, 13-4.

75. *Foreign Broadcast Information Service*, (July 18, 1981), I16. Bakarić died in January 1983.

76. *Ibid.*, (August 7, 1981), 13.

77. *Ibid.*, (November 18, 1981), I32.

78. By 1986, moral-political suitability was still a necessary, but not an entirely sufficient factor in Yugoslav elite recruitment. A new generation of younger leaders combining political reliability with higher educational specialization and a fresh perspective appeared to be gaining control in the Kosovo party organization. Louis Zanga, "The New Strong Men of Kosovo," *Radio Free Europe RAD Background Report*, No. 77 (May 31, 1986). See Chapter 9 for a more detailed discussion of the same trend in the broader process of selection. It is also worth noting that in May 1986, the first party leader of Albanian origin became President of the nine-member collective state Presidency. His election to this one-year post was a previously scheduled rotation among the republics and provinces, but it undoubtedly helped to assuage, at least symbolically, Albanian grievances about their previous exclusion from top political positions.

79. *Ibid.*, (November 27, 1981), I23. It is now alleged that the policy of Albanianization at the university had resulted in "pushing out the teaching staff of Serbian and Montenegrin nationality leading to absurd situations, such as the one now in which about 170 professors and lecturers of Albanian nationality hold lectureships in Serbo-Croatian, while there are faculties without a single assistant lecturer of Serbian or Montenegrin nationality." *Ibid.*, (May 11, 1981), I22. Nepotism is also alleged to have been rampant with more than 20 instructors in the philosophy faculty related to one another. *Ibid.*, (May 19, 1981), I11.

80. About 1,000 Albanian students demonstrated in Priština and protests were repeated in other towns on the first anniversary of the 1981 "counter-revolution." Demonstrators were dispersed by special riot police. *Borba*, March 15, 1982, 3. Protests on a smaller scale marked the second anniversary. *Foreign Broadcast Information Service*, (March 14, 1983), I10-I11. A professor at the philosophy department of Priština University claimed that the center of the counter-revolution was at the university and that Kosovo's Albanian professors could be divided into three groups: (1) extremists who endorse Albanian irredentism; (2) those who support the League of Communists and work to implement its policies; and (3) "sympathizers," the largest of the three groups, including those who verbally support the League of Communists but privately support the ideas of Albanian nationalism and irredentism. *Foreign Broadcast Information Service*, (April 7, 1982), I7-I8. The number of newly enrolled students in the 1981-1982 academic year at Kosovo University (formerly Pristina University) fell by 24 percent, and two-thirds of the new students were enrolled in the natural sciences, mathematics, and technical sciences. *Ibid.*, (April 27, 1982), I5.

81. *Ibid.*, (November 10, 1981), 19.

82. *Politika*, (October 27, 1981), 7. The Priština Communal Assembly reported that during the six months following the 1981 demonstrations, 4,000 Serbs and Montenegrins had emigrated from Priština. *Ibid.*, (October 5, 1981). This figure suggests that roughly eight percent of the Serbs and Montenegrins living in Priština emigrated directly after the 1981 crisis. Another report from Priština noted that "there is the phenomenon of the departure of highly trained and qualified cadres, cadres who are essential to the economy, and social activities in the municipality." *Ibid.*, (November 12, 1981),

131. From 1981 to February 1987, 22,307 Serbs and Montenegrins were reported to have left Kosovo, lowering their proportion in the province's total population from 14.9 percent to 13.5 percent. Out of 1,445 communities in Kosovo, 650 have no Serbs and Montenegrins. *Nedeljne Informativne Novine*, No. 1904, (June 28, 1987), 12.

83. After the 1981 events, leaders in Kosovo became increasingly outspoken in defense of the local Slav population. Kosovo state president, Ali Šukrija, lectured a youth organization meeting: "What nation and what honorable person can be proud of the fact that the girls of Serbian nationality dare not go to school, that graves are desecrated or that church windows are broken? How would Albanian families feel if their graves were desecrated and their religious objects damaged? These are very serious and crude things." *Foreign Broadcast Information Service*, (December 9, 1981), 16. One Serbian correspondent ironically noted that for several months the mention of such nationalist acts in Kosovo was "the privilege of Serbian and Montenegrin politicians, but that now reports from individual communes show that a greater number of Albanian cadre are repeating the principled arguments." *Nedelnje Informativne Novine*, (January 17, 1982), 10.

84. *Borba*, (June 19, 1981), 7, *Nedeljne Informativne Novine*, (December 27, 1981), 19-21, *ibid.*, (January 3, 1982), 24, 32.

85. There has been a strong Serbian backlash to the events in Kosovo. In early 1986, for example, a petition signed by 212 Serbian intellectuals was sent to both the federal and Serbian legislatures accusing the Albanian leaders in Kosovo of practicing genocide against the Serbs and other nationalities in the region. The petition also criticized Yugoslav politicians for not reacting strongly enough against Albanian nationalism. *Radio Free Europe, Situation Report*, II, No. 11 (March 14, 1986), 13-14. In the fall of 1987, strong differences of opinion concerning the problem of Kosovo led to unprecedented political quarrels between leading party and state officials in Serbia. The President of the Belgrade Party Committee was forced to resign his position and give up his membership in the Presidency of the Serbian Central Committee after he criticized other Serbian officials and newspapers for an excessively anti-Albanian approach to the Kosovo situation.

86. Data on the educational structure of Kosovo in 1981 indicates that Albanians made up 62 percent of the economically active population having a higher education. This was still short of their representation in the total active population (67.1 percent), but an enormous leap forward in their relative position compared to earlier years. *Stanovništvo SR Srbija, osnovna obeležja za aktivnoj stanovništvo u zemlji* (Belgrade: Republički zavod za statistiku, September 1985), 183. In 1980, Albanians made up 64 percent of the students who had graduated from faculties of higher education. "Diplomirani studenti," *Statistički bilten*, No. 1291 (April, 1982), 8.

87. Traian Stoianovich, "The Social Foundations of Balkan Politics," *The Social Foundations of Balkan Politics*, eds. Charles and Barbara Jelavich (Berkely: University of California Press, 1963), and Dimitrije Djordjevic and Stephen Fischer-Galati, *The Balkan Revolutionary Tradition* (New York: Columbia University Press, 1981), 228-230.

88. *Foreign Broadcast Information Service*, (December 29, 1981), 116.

89. *Nedeljne Informativne Novine*, (August 30, 1981), 16.

90. Louis Zanga, "Rise of Tension in Kosovo Due to Migration," *Radio Free Europe*, (June 28, 1983), 2.

91. Miroslav Pečujlić, "The University of the Future," *Socialist Thought and Practice, XX*, No. 9 (1980), 45. Yugoslav officials planned for a 10 percent cut in university enrollment in the 1983-1984 academic year. "This is one of the steps within nationalization of the system of education and bridging the gap between the needs and possibilities. It might seem that these measures clash with freedom of choice of the young. It is quite contrary for it is the worst hypocrisy when one enjoys freedom with which nothing can be started or achieved." "Education Policy: Coordination with Needs of Social Development," *Yugoslav Life*, XXVIII, Nos. 6-7 (1983), 6.

92. *Nedeljne Informativne Novine*, (June 24, 1982), 14.

93. In October, 1987, special federal riot police were sent to Kosovo after thousands of Serbs staged street demonstrations in protest against alleged comments by an ethnic Albanian leader that inci-

Lenard J. Cohen

dents of Albanians raping Serbian women could be reduced if Serbian women worked as prostitutes.

94. As ethnic relations worsened in Yugoslavia during the second half of the 1980's, surveys revealed that young people put more blame on political functionaries than on intellectuals for the rise in nationalism. *Nedeljne Informativne Novine*, No. 1906, (July 12, 1987), 22-23. The capacity of both political and intellectual elites to influence their broader ethnic communities in Yugoslavia is considerable. Sociological research in 1985 showed, for example, that individuals of the same nationality - whether party members or not - tend to be closer in their outlook on socio-political questions than party members of different nationalities. Vladimir Goati, "Remarks," *Gledišta*, XXVII, No. 11-12 (November-December, 1986), 170-171.

PART FIVE

CHOOSING TITO'S COMRADES AND HEIRS: YUGOSLAV ELITES IN FLUX

Every Partisan who distinguishes himself in the struggle can achieve a commanding position.

Partisan Regulation, World War II

Beginning the reconstruction of the economy in society will require educated, creative personnel acquainted with the development of contemporary technology and organization of labour and business .... This will be an opportunity for growth and the affirmation of many new people, capable producers and managers. This will make it possible for those with competence to achieve places where they can give their upmost, a condition for our general and individual progress.

Draft Resolution of the League of Communists (1986)

CHAPTER 9

ELITE RECRUITMENT AND ELITE COMPOSITION: THE PAST AND THE FUTURE

Who governs post-Tito Yugoslavia? Will Tito's successors, having proved successful in maintaining their own authority, also be able to preserve their regime's unique institutions and policies? Finding answers to those questions requires an analysis which goes beyond the relatively small number of personalities who routinely serve short terms of office as chief executives of the collective party and state leadership bodies at the summit of the Yugoslav political hierarchy (e.g. the annually rotating President of the nine-person state Presidency, and the President of the 14-person Presidency of the Central Committee of the Yugoslav League of Communists). Indeed, throughout the 1980's it has been the individuals who occupy important positions of political authority in the middle (republican and provincial) levels of the political system, i.e., the regional political elites, who are the major actors affecting the continuation and vitality of the Yugoslav socialist experiment. The incumbents of most federal level political posts are chosen from the ranks of such regional elite groups and, after a limited term of service at the "center" of the system, federal functionaries generally return to those elites. Moreover, the importance accorded to "harmonizing" divergent ethnic and regional interests prior to the formulation of Yugoslav federal policies - a practice now firmly institutionalized in the constitution and in elite political culture - adds even more significance to the selection, characteristics, and preferences of middle level elites. Thus, information concerning the degree of cleavage and consensus among regional

Lenard J. Cohen

elites, and especially their propensity for intra-elite cooperation and conflict in the decision-making process, is crucial for any overall assessment of political stability in post-Tito Yugoslavia.

This chapter will examine the recruitment and socio-political composition of political elites at the regional level of the Yugoslav system, namely, in the six republics and two provinces. Four organizationally distinct regional elites will be considered: (1) the *party elite*, consisting of members of the presidencies, and the executive secretaries of the regional central committees of the League of Communists (SKJ); (2) the *state administrative elite*, composed of the secretaries and directors of the various secretariats, committees and institutes that constitute the state (public) administration in each republic and province; (3) the *state executive elite*, i.e., members of the state executive councils (the equivalent of the cabinet in each region) responsible to the Assemblies; and (4) the *legislative elite*, consisting of the presidents and vice-presidents of the regional assemblies. It is the individuals who comprise these four regional elites who have the greatest influence on the operation of the Yugoslav political system in the post-Tito era.

In order to systematically examine the political and social characteristics of the various regional elite groups, biographical information was gathered on 423 individuals.[1] Except in cases for which information is unavailable, the study embraces the entire universe of elite members in regional political positions at the beginning of 1980. In order to provide a context for the examination of elite composition, the first part of this chapter surveys changing trends and issues in the recruitment of Yugoslav decision-makers between 1945 and 1981. The second section analyzes those elite characteristics for which information was available: age, political generation (party membership and participation in the Partisan struggle), level and type of education, and ethnic background. Although it is not possible to accurately extrapolate elite attitudes and behaviour from data on socio-political background, such information can provide valuable insights regarding the potential character and magnitude of cleavages within and among different sub-elites. The lack of recent systematic data on Yugoslav political elites, and the difficulty of obtaining such information during the first part of the 1980's, makes such background data especially useful for the analysis of "self-managed socialism."

Patterns of Elite Recruitment: 1945-1981

The institutional methods and criteria for selecting governing elites in Yugoslavia, i.e., the process of elite recruitment, can be divided into a number of patterns which relate to specific stages of the communist regime's political history. Despite the variation among the patterns and stages of elite recruitment, three issues appear to be very significant throughout the entire course of postwar political development: (1) the *scope* of party influence over the selection of non-party elites, i.e., both the extent of party influence over recruitment decisions in other sectors of direct political authority (legislatures, executive organs, the state administration, and mass socio-political organizations) and also over less directly political sectors such as the economy, the arts, the universities, etc; (2) the *centralization* of party influence over its own and other elite personnel, i.e., the extent to which influence over elite recruitment is concentrated in central (federal level) party organs; and (3) the *professionalization* of political elites, i.e., the extent to which political office-holding constitutes a full-time career as opposed to an episodic and avocational form of activity. This section of the chapter offers an examination of the successive phases and patterns of elite recruitment devoting particular attention to the regime's approach to the preceding three issues.

Partisan Ascendancy and Elite Formation: 1945-1949

The first period opens with the political ascendancy of the relatively young, politically cohesive, and ethnically diverse group of Partisan leaders who had triumphed in a bloody civil war and national liberation struggle; the period ends in the wake of the traumatic rift between the "Soviet Bloc" and Yugoslavia. Recruitment throughout this period was characterized by highly centralized and pervasive party control of elite personnel including the preferential allocation of elite level jobs to professional party functionaries and tested political activists who had served in the Partisan movement. The routine supervision of recruitment was carried out by the Personnel Department of the Central Committee's apparatus in Belgrade. The scope of the Personnel Department and also its close resemblance to similar Soviet institutions of the time is best described by an authoritative political history of the period:

> The Personnel Department was headed by an organization secretary of the Central Committee under whose jurisdiction were the leading personnel in the party and the youth organizations. Other members of this department were responsible for personnel questions in non-party institutions, the apparatus of the government and its institutions, the security services, and the selection of specialized personnel. The prerogatives of the department also extended to lower level party committees, the sending of students to party schools and courses, the revision of party penalties, the personnel services of the state organs, questions of personnel in sensitive services (Post, Telephone, and Telegraph, etc.) ....

> The higher leadership was not elected, but entirely chosen by the method of co-optation. For lower leaderships, the proposals for new committee members were compiled by higher committees and their personnel commissions. The criteria for selection included, however, that proposed candidates be authentic fighters both in the war and in the peactime construction of the country, long party seniority and a clean past .... In leaderships communists were elected according to their *'partijnost'* and not according to functions in the state apparatus.[2]

Other factors contributing to the centralized operation of the party and recruitment policy in this early period included the complete absence of regular plenary meetings of the regional central committee memberships, and the extreme secrecy surrounding the activities and meetings of the top leadership in each region of the country.

Despite the rigid hierarchical and conspiratorial procedures, internal criticism was soon raised about the "degradation of specialized skills" in personnel selection to the state apparatus, and its consequences for economic development. As early as September 1946, for example, a government commission proposed "the re-education of older specialists, correct relations towards specialists, and the improvement of their material position." A campaign was also launched to improve the geographical distribution of specialists and to discourage their out-migration from the poorest and most devestated regions of the country.[3] Political expediency as interpreted by central party functionaries remained the primary consideration in elite recruitment, but the imperatives of economic development and economic planning soon led to demands for the increased utilization and expansion of the technical intelligentsia. Indeed, it was even acknowledged that professional revolutionaries (Partisan fighters) did not always make the best (ideologically well-educated and administratively qualified) professional politicians.[4] The education system, which was mobilized to both train a new generation of professionals in political and non-political fields, and also retrain existing cadre to aid in the construction of socialism, became the Yugoslav regime's most significant instrument inovercoming personnel deficiencies.

Elite Consolidation and Resocialization: 1950-1965

After an initial period of disorientation and reflection (1948-1950) the Tito-Stalin break precipitated a major institutional transformation of the Yugoslav political system. Measures such as the creation of workers' councils, the elimination of central planning, the decentralization of the state apparatus, the enhanced position of local governments and legislative bodies, and the reorganization of the Communist Party - to mention only the most important changes - introduced an entirely new basis for Yugoslav socialist development. The actual impact of this new "model" upon elite recruitment was, however, relatively insignificant. For example, although important changes were introduced with respect to the party's name, operational principles,[5] and the relative size of its' bureaucratic apparatus (Table 9.1), these alterations had only a negligible impact on the process of elite recruitment. Despite the innovations in the party organization, the selection of personnel to fill top positions throughout the political sector remained highly centralized and limited largely to individuals with professional political experience.[6] One change in this period which represented an incremental shift in the basis of power and pattern of personnel selection was the increased role of the central state security apparatus and especially its chief, Alexander Ranković. Ranković's continuation as an organizational secretary of the League of Communists, a member of the Politburo, and Minister of State Security, allowed him to dominate political elite recruitment up until 1966, despite the formal reduction in the scope of party control. Moreover, party pronouncements (particularly after the adoption of a new program in 1958) which encouraged greater independence and control by non-party ogranizations and sectors over their own personnel recruitment, do not appear to have been very effective. Even the official party and constitutional endorsements (1963) of new provisions to discourage the professionalization of political activity, such as limitations on the occupancy of governmental positions and prohibitions on simultaneous office-holding in party and state bodies, did not have much influence on the continuity of elite rule above the local level of the political system.

Looking back at the remarks made in 1964 by Alexander Ranković at the Eighth Party Congress (where he gave the major speech concerning personnel questions), it is easier to perceive his lukewarm support for what he then lauded as the "democratization of cadre policy." His comments were undoubtedly a signal to members of the Partisan generation that as far as he was concerned, they had little to fear from the new personnel measures and perhaps even something to gain from them. For example, he pointed out that one of the positive effects of "rotation" would be the increasing availability of individuals to fill the plethora of political and governmental jobs, thereby lessening the pressure on a small number of aging individuals to simultaneously conduct several jobs. Or considered in another way (as it undoubtedly was by his audience), since there were plenty of jobs to go around, rotation could provide less strain and more variety in one's work.[7] It was only at the Fourth Plenum in July 1966, after the removal of Ranković and his allies in the security service, that a more candid appraisal of recruitment policy was provided.

Table 9.1
Size of the Yugoslav League of Communists and the Party Apparatus, 1950-81

Year	Number of Party Members	Central Apparatus			Regional (republican and provincial) Apparatus			Total Party Apparatus (central and regional)			Total Party Apparatus as a Percentage of Total Party Membership
		Function-aries[a]	Workers[b]	Total	Function-aries	Workers	Total	Function-aries	Workers	Total	
1950	607,443	n.a.	n.a.	n.a.	n.a.	n.a.	n.a.	11,930	n.a.	n.a.	n.a.
1952	772,920	n.a.	n.a.	n.a.	n.a.	n.a.	n.a.	n.a.	n.a.	5,156	0.67
1957	755,066	n.a.	n.a.	n.a.	n.a.	n.a.	n.a.	n.a.	n.a.	2,579	0.34
1958	829,953	n.a.	n.a.	n.a.	n.a.	n.a.	n.a.	n.a.	n.a.	2,860	0.34
1963	1,019,013	n.a.	n.a.	n.a.	n.a.	n.a.	n.a.	n.a.	n.a.	3,339	0.32
1965	1,046,262	58	88	146	1,311	2,026	3,337	1,369	2,114	3,482	0.33
1966	1,006,285	19	131	150	1,090	1,990	3,080	1,109	2,121	3,230	0.32
1967	1,013,500	11	137	148	1,112	1,822	2,934	1,123	1,959	3,082	0.30
1968	1,146,084	13	148	161	791	2,099	2,890	804	2,247	3,051	0.27
1969	1,111,682	14	189	203	671	2,244	2,915	685	2,433	3,118	0.28
1970	1,049,184	13	213	216	758	2,346	3,104	771	2,559	3,330	0.32
1971	1,025,476	14	205	219	748	2,284	3,032	762	2,489	3,251	0.31
1972	1,009,947	15	198	213	796	2,364	3,160	811	2,562	3,373	0.33
1973	1,076,711	15	199	214	938	2,468	3,406	953	2,667	3,620	0.34
1974	1,192,466	17	234/10	261	1,127	2,550	3,677	1,114	2,794	3,938	0.33
1975	1,302,843	18/1[c]	240/13	272	1,130	2,861	3,991	1,149	3,114	4,263	0.33
1976	1,460,267	18/1	245/13	277	1,216	3,265	4,481	1,235	3,523	4,758	0.33
1977	1,623735	17/2	267/13	299	1,290	3,514	4,804	1,309	3,794	5,103	0.31
1980	1,950,000	n.a.	n.a.	n.a.	n.a.	n.a.	n.a.	ca1,500	n.a.	n.a.	n.a.
1981	2,117,083	25	n.a.	n.a.	1,489	n.a.	n.a.	1,514	4,358	5,872	0.28

[a] Elected functionaries and 'professional sociopolitical workers' on the payroll of the Central Committee.
[b] Employees in the 'specialized services' of the Central Committee; in the middle of 1971, for example, 22 percent of these employees were 'specialized political workers', and the remaining workers in analytical-statistical, technical and auxiliary affairs.
[c] Individuals working in the Committee of the Conference of the Central Committee in Organizations of the Federation.

Up to the Fourth Plenum conservative forces had a considerable influence on personnel policy in the League of Communists which, in different ways, contradicted proclaimed principles. In personnel policy and in practice, there were many different phenomena, solving personnel questions in closed circles, subjectivism, bureaucratic conservative relations, etc. The characteristics of individual members and leaders of the League of Communists often was based on data from the organs of state security which contained simplistic, manufactured, and subjective interpretations, behind which were concealed a definite political background .... Rotation was applied chiefly on the occasion of electing communal leadership, while the republican leaderships and the organs on the federal level of the League were renewed by broadening the size of their composition.[8]

It is also important to note, however, that alongside the often overlooked continuities in recruitment policy during the Ranković era, a profound societal transformation was taking place, including changes that were beginning to have at least an indirect effect on personnel selection. In fact to a certain extent, these changes may have even contributed to the successful implementation of the Fourth Plenum's anti-bureaucratic resolutions. For example, during the same years that the Ranković forces had monopolized elite recruitment, a massive expansion and transformation of the educational system had produced a large new generation of trained specialists. These university graduates were now seeking advancement and the adoption of policies which responded to their newly acquired occupational perspectives. During this period, the total number of individuals classified as "specialists and artists" grew from 222,000 in 1953 to 490,000 in 1961, or an increase of approximately 120 percent. While from 1919 to 1940, two-thirds of all university graduates were enrolled in law and philosophy, only 27 percent graduated in those fields from 1945 to 1961. The number of students receiving diplomas in economics and in the engineering faculties alone doubled from 1945 to 1961.[9] The goals and expectations of the new intelligentsia were moulded during the more stable and promising years of emergent self-management after 1950, and were not significantly influenced by the sacrifices and solidarity of the earlier revolutionary struggle. Although the removal of Ranković was quite unanticipated, many members of the new generation of specialists undoubtedly regarded the event as a positive signal.[10]

The increasing professionalization of occupations was a second and closely related social change which affected both the political and non-political sectors of society. Both younger and older individuals working in different specialized fields now began to identify more closely with certain standardized modes of behaviour and job performance (enterprise managers were a prime example). Such professionalization also led to a greater differentiation between political subsectors such as legislative work, state administration, journalism, and party affairs (ironically, even affecting the security services because of their great institutional exclusivity and conspiratorial methods). Each political subsector began to see its respective field of work as a professional and distinct branch of "socio-political activity."[11] Elite positions within each political and non-political sector were still within the scope of the central party apparatus and the security organs, but each sphere was becoming relatively more specialized and differentiated both in outlook and interests.

Finally, the successful modernization and industrialization of the country itself made the nature of decision-making far more complex and technical, a change requiring more sophisticated political and economic management skills. Taken together with the growth of the technical intelligentsia and the professionalization of occupations, such complexity and technicality created a climate, a constituency, and a pressure for reform of personnel policy. A demand emerged for less arbitrary, centralized, and personalized forms of elite selection with less deference to ascribed political credentials (i.e., service in the Partisans), and increased opportunities for the influence and advancement of the new generation of specialists. Since many of the advocates and potential beneficiaries of such changes were located in the more economically developed regions of the country (i.e., the northwestern, more dissident, less "Partisan," and more religious areas), their reformist views often were intermingled with demands for greater regional and ethnic autonomy. The ascendancy of a new generation within the elite, and the impact of different reforms would provoke a strong response from the older and more conservative party leaders at the end of the next stage in Yugoslav political development.

Elite Modernization and Elite Succession: 1966-1971

The reorganization of the League of Communists which resulted from the Ranković affair, led to a substantial change in elite recruitment and personnel policy. These changes involved all three aspects of personnel selection discussed above: the scope of party control, centralization, and professionalization. New policy guidelines stipulated that the party organs, and certainly the security organs, would no longer dominate or manipulate the recruitment of leading political and non-political personnel.

The impact of this change was quite significant. For example, the Commission for Elections and Appointments in the Federal Assembly was permitted to assume a greater role over personnel policy within the Assembly System (i.e., leadership posts in the legislature, and in federal executive and administrative organs). Interestingly, a normative and operational shift of control over personnel decisions from the Federal Executive Council to the

Federal Assembly had begun as early as 1963. It was only in 1967, after the removal of Ranković, however, that the Assembly's commission was delegated the authority to formulate the proposals for higher administrative appointments and dismissal "after hearing the opinion" of the Federal Executive Council. This shift completely reversed earlier procedure and practice whereby proposals on personnel were submitted by the executive organs after simply consulting with the Assembly, and represented a significant change with respect to legislative institutionalization and personnel recruitment. Thus, elected members of legislative assemblies increasingly attempted to recruit higher civil servants and legislative staff personnel whose professional credentials were relevant to their performance of specific tasks. An interesting exchange in a plenary session of the Federal Assembly's Economic Chamber (at the time composed mainly of members of the managerial and technical intelligentsia) illustrates the new official outlook toward political recruitment, and the reaction to it. The issue was no longer, as after the war, whether higher civil servants needed to have technical training together with political qualifications, but exactly how technically specialized an official's background had to be in order to qualify for the job. Moreover, the fact that such questions could even be raised by Yugoslav legislators also marked a significant development.

Agenda (4 December 1971):

A Proposal by the President of the Federal Government (Federal Executive Council) to appoint a new Federal Secretary for Transportation.

Question by a federal deputy:

Has the proposed candidate for the job of Federal Secretary of Transportation had any experience in transportation or any connection with it?

Answer by a spokesmen for the Government:

The function of the head of a department calls for: competence, knowledge of things, affinity, and consultations with the republics and provinces. Hence the proposal to appoint as a federal secretary ... an economist, a man versed in economics, as a member of our government. But is he an expert in transportation? This question has not been posed quite correctly. He will have experts in his secretariat.

Lenard J. Cohen

Comment by a second federal deputy in support of the government's position:

Something which we have not had in post-war practice has cropped up: we have to discuss the professional skill of a minister ... this could lead to exclusion; no worker could be a member of the Federal Executive Council. Unfortunately such is the case now ... for many years now we have not had a worker in the highest organs.[12]

The role of the central party organs in the appointment of higher legislative and administrative personnel was not completely eliminated during this period, but the extent and method of party influence changed in a manner which tended to disperse (pluralize) control over elite recruitment. The decline in party interference and the use of political critieria in personnel selection were even more noticeable on the local level of the system, especially in the recruitment of enterprise management. A new generation of more professionalized managerial functionaries and technical intelligentsia began to predominate in both the operation of the economy and as part-time political decision-makers in representative assemblies.[13]

Perhaps the most striking change in recruitment policy which occurred during this period was the decentralization of authority over personnel selection within the League of Communists itself. New policy guidelines made regional party organs responsible for the selection of their own officials. After 1966, the personnel commission of the top party central committee in Belgrade was discontinued, although such commissions were retained in some of the republics and provinces. Beginning in 1968 as part of the effort to increase the influence of regional party organizations over federal party decision-making, republic and provincial congresses of the League of Communists were held before, rather than after the central party congresses. The latter change, although not unlike procedure in other communist countries, represented more than a symbolic gesture. More candid and intense discussions began to occur in the republics and provinces concerning the criteria and methods utilized in elite recruitment. At the December 1968 Sixth Congress of the League of Communists of Croatia, for example, one delegate expressed his criticism of the recruitment process with unusual candor (actual names are replaced by letters in the passage quoted below).

I would like someone to explain why on the list of candidates there are many directors, legislators, and professional functionaries from socio-political organizations who live outside Croatia. I would like someone to explain how the following people got on the list to be permanent

> members of the Conference of the League of Croatian Communists: 'A', director of the Shipbuilding Industry in Split, 'B', a federal legislator and president of a committee in the Federal Assembly who lives in Belgrade. These people were not proposed and not elected by the Communal Conference of the League in Split. Why aren't direct producers, workers and specialists, mainly young people, on the list such as, 'C', a highly skilled worker in the shipbuilding enterprise in Split, 'D', a highly skilled worker in the water works in Split ... 'E', a vice-admiral and commandant of the Split army district, 'F', an engineer .... All these comrades were proposed and elected as candidates for organs of the Yugoslav League of Communists. It is simply unacceptable that the Central Committee discards them and places on the list people who the Conference of the League in Split, and their basic organizations have not proposed. How can we explain this to the membership of the League and Conference?[14]

A new generation of regional political activists also began to make their appearance in this period. For example, approximately 90 percent of the delegates elected to regional congresses in 1968 and 1969 were attending their first congress, and about 69 percent of the individuals elected to the regional central committees were new members.[15] A history of the League of Communists emphasizes the significant impact of these and other changes following the fall of the group around Alexander Ranković.

> Namely, until Brioni (the Fourth Plenum) of the Central Committee of the League of Communists, the nomination, appointment, and replacement of higher and middle range cadre often was exercised by the (federal) Central Committee of the League of Communists. Such practice created bureaucratic obedience to the leading officials who posted and changed them. This meant obedience to the organs of the federation. After the Fourth Plenum of the Central Committee that right completely shifted to organs of the republics. It strengthened the power of the republican factors, turning the organs of the federation to the republics because public leadership functions frequently represented the only source of personal (private) existence of public functionaries .... Now that important decisions were no longer taken on the federal summit, contacts among representatives of the republics were strengthened in the form of bilateral and multilateral visits of state and party delegations. Consequently, a significant role was played by Josip Broz Tito. Increasingly he entered into political conversations with republican delegations and in that way created a basis for political decisions. In

Lenard J. Cohen

daily political life the slogan of unity was replaced by the slogan equality, negotiations, and agreements between republics.[16]

The reduction and devolution of party control over personnel selection after 1966 were also accompanied by important changes concerning the professionalization of political and non-political work. Briefly, a dual process was taking place: first, a reduction in political professionalization, i.e., an increase in party and mass organization office-holding on an amateur or avocational basis, and secondly, the increased occupational differentiation and professionalization of job sectors that were previously included in the broad area of "socio-political activity" (managerial, legislative, higher civil service, journalistic and military positions), as well as jobs in more explicitly non-political sectors (e.g., engineering, teaching, medicine, etc.). The latter development represented an intensification of earlier trends in the country's occupational structure. The increased deprofessionalization of careers in the party and mass organizations comprised, however, the first significant transformation of these employment areas since the war. Although the introduction of measures during the early 1950's had considerably reduced the overall number of political officials and the relative size of the party apparatus (Table 9.1), contradictory developments had also been at work. Thus by the late 1950's, the expansion of special schools for political-administrative education (which included the continuing education and certification of former Partisans) and the multiplication of political jobs at the communal level of the federation, together with the increased differentiation and complexity of all political roles in society, had gradually contributed to a growth in political professionalism.[17] It was only during the two years after the 1967 party re-organization that the relative size of the central and regional party appartuses again began to decline (Table 9.1).

Increasingly, leadership posts in the party and mass organizations were filled on either a part-time or amateur basis, often by individuals who worked mainly in the non-political sectors.[18] Separate higher party schools, the traditional vehicle for elite political education, were discontinued and such institutions became regular university faculties (a change which ostensibly eliminated party training as a distinct field but actually tended to professionalize political training). One interesting result of the above changes during this period was that fewer young people aspired to a career in politics. Lacking its earlier status, security, and influence, political work appeared to have lost most of its glamour and appeal for the brightest members of the younger generation, a development which did not go unnoticed by party conservatives who were already anxious about the course of political development.

Party leaders also worried about the class composition of elite recruitment in this period. Despite pronouncements and token efforts to forestall the steady decline in the number of direct producers in positions of leadership during the 1950's and 1960's, party leaders continued to tacitly encourage and rationalize the overwhelming predominance of professionally trained personnel in political decision-making bodies. For example, during a Commission session at the Sixth Congress of the League of Communists of Croatia in December 1968, a proposal was adopted that three-fourths of the members of the forums and organs to the League of Communists should be made up of "communists from the working collectives of economic and societal spheres of activity" who would continue to remain on their jobs. This motion was defeated by a majority of delegates to a plenary session of the Congress at the insistence of the prominent Croatian leader Vladimir Bakarić.[19] According to Bakarić, it was necessary to defeat the motion for the following reasons: first, in some organizations the working class was actually in the minority so its numerical predominance in party forums would be unjustified; second, a direct producers' majority in the Central Committee would tend to strengthen the influence of the permanent bureaucratic apparatus because of the complexity of the tasks confronting the Central Committee, especially with respect to foreign affairs; third, the preoccupation of workers with their blue collar experience would promote the transformation of the League of Communists into an organization concerned exclusively with instrumental (economic) matters; and fourth, such a large representation of workers in the League of Communists would be tantamount to the introduction of a form of dictatorship not of the proletariat, but of the direct producers, which would signify a slowdown in the rate of growth that Yugoslavia had so far enjoyed. Bakarić's argument was a fascinating commentary not only with respect to the broadened and modernized definition of the "working class" in Yugoslavia and other socialist states, but also with regard to the salient role played by the political and non-political (technical and "humanistic") intelligentsia in that *new class*.

Elite Retrenchment and Anxiety: 1972-1981

Recruitment policy underwent a basic change at the end of 1971 in the wake of Tito's vigorous campaign against the supporters of liberalism, nationalism and technocracy in the regional party organizations. This shift in policy was occasioned by a strong disavowal of the centrifugal and devolutionary trends in party development which had begun at the Sixth Congress in 1952, and considerably accelerated after 1967. More specifically, party organs were again given the task of monitoring and actively influencing the appointment of personnel in all important political and non-political posts. Thus, control of personnel appointments in the assemblies and the state administration once more reverted to the strengthened executive branch of the governmental structure, despite the introduction of the much-heralded "delegate system" in

1974. This growth in executive control allowed the League of Communists to exert greater direct and indirect influence, since the earlier prohibition on simultaneous office-holding in the state and party was now also relaxed and party members were urged to work for the new policies of the party organization wherever they were employed. The "party within the system" became the new slogan, supplementing earlier emphasis on a League of Communists "divorced from power." As one regional party functionary observed, "whenever the executive bodies of the state become stronger, that means that something similar is taking place in the party as well. And conversely: when the government executive is 'weakening' then the party is 'weakening' as well. Sometimes the connection gives strength to centralistic tendencies, and sometimes to particularistic tendencies."[20] The growing influence of party organizations over appointments in the universities (most explicitly in Belgrade and Ljubljana), the media, cultural institutions, and industrial enterprises represented another manifestation of the new recruitment policy.[21] The following exchange which occurred during an interview with Stane Dolanc, a member of the Presidency of the League of Communists, illustrated the official elite perspective regarding the scope of party involvement in personnel decisions.

Interviewer:

A certain high official has told us the following anecdote: Participating in discussion at a session, he asked why the party is interfering in everything and even dismisses and replaces directors. Another participant in the same discussion replied: It is natural that the party is dismissing and replacing people because it appointed them in the first place. That was naturally said in jest but it did point out a serious problem. Do you agree?

Dolanc:

This question is now frequently raised in various ways and in various places. I think that the League of Communists has the right, not to dismiss and replace, but to provide the initiative for replacing a director, a minister or some office-holder. It has that right even under the Constitution, as a socio-political organization ...[22]

After 1971, in addition to the specialized qualifications of candidates for important posts, renewed emphasis was also placed on their "moral-political qualities and suitability." As shown in the detailed elite analysis in Chapter 3, the question was not so much the selection of "reds" instead of "experts," but selecting the proper red-experts. A campaign was also launched to improve the class composition of the League of Communists and striking, if basically token successes, were soon recorded in the number of direct producers enrolled as party members and elected to party organs. At the Tenth Party Congress in 1974, Tito sharply criticized the earlier emphasis on the "renewal of cadres" urging that "everyone who is fit to do so should continue to be active in every way, for communists must work in the interest of the revolution to the very end." The composition of the new party Central Committees elected in 1974 and 1978 reflected this view and included a core group of loyal professional politicians from the Partisan generation, and even some individuals who had retired from active political work as a result of the elite changes introduced during the late 1960's.[23] Beginning in 1972, the absolute number of professional functionaries and workers in the party apparatus also began to increase as did the size of the party membership, a trend which continued unabated into the early 1980's (see Table 9.1). One Yugoslav analysis noted that in mid-1981 the country had more than 10,000 politicians and the "experience up to now shows that the delegate system can't secure an automatic reduction in the force and influence of political professionalism. On the contrary, in everday life we often can see that such influence increases as do the number of professionals."[24] Although elaborate provisions were adopted in the spring of 1981 to accelerate the rotation (or reduce the tenure) of Yugoslav politicians in most elite positions, prior experience suggested that such policies would likely accelerate inter-organizational or inter-apparatus mobility rather than reduce the number of career politicians.[25]

One expression of renewed party interest in recruitment during the 1970's was the re-introduction of personnel commissions in the federal and in all regional party organizations. The personnel commissions were given the task of ensuring that "all those selected for responsible and leading functions in society would give the highest guarantee that they will create the new course of the League of Communists."[26] The Tenth Congress of the League of Communists in 1974, condemned the "earlier dilemma concerning 'non-interference' which in fact had served as a smoke screen for blocking out the League of Communists in the area of personnel policy .... Organs of the League have begun to concretely involve themselves in questions of personnel policy and to directly engage in their solution."[27] In order to combat "party federalism" and the "political disintegration of the League of Communists," measures were also taken to "restore the firm connections and responsibilities in the spirit of democratic centralism between the leadership of the League of Communists of the republics and the leadership of the (federal) organs of the League."[28] The practice of ensuring equitable (usually parity) nationality and regional representation in all federal party organs was continued (the so-called ethnic key in recruitment), but the new policy stressed the responsibility of all party officials to behave as members of a single (pan-ethnic and cross-regional) political organization and not, as earlier, to function as delegated ambassadors of republican and provincial party machines. The effort to restore centralized coordination and consensus in the League of Communists, although temporarily important, had little significant impact on the growing devolution of power to the party's regional elites. Organizationally, the party was able to recussitate some of the prestige and influence that it had lost in the 1960's, and also to assume greater control over personnel matters, but the trend toward a territorially segmented or "federalized" party organization was not abated.

The continued importance of professional experience in the League of Communists as a prerequisite for political recruitment during the 1970's is illustrated by data on the organizational history and circulation of elite members at the regional level of the political system. Specifically, by comparing two personnel directories which list all of the occupants of federal and regional political positions (published in 1972 and 1980 respectively), it is possible to ascertain the organizational background of elite incumbents at the onset of the post-Tito period.[29] Briefly, what positions, if any, were held in 1972 by members of the regional political elites in 1980? This particular time period, that is 1972-1980, was chosen for two reasons. First, the period begins immediately following Tito's purge of Croatian elite officials and thereby opens an entirely new phase of Yugoslav political development (ending with Tito's death in May 1980); and second, it covers a period in which, at least hypothetically, a good deal of inter-organizational rotation and personnel movement should have occurred (a state election and a party congress were both held in 1974 and 1978). As a basis for analysis, information was gathered on the 1972 positions held by more than 600 officials serving in four elite sectors during 1980 (Table 9.2). Although the method of analysis is not ideal (precise data on the career changes and chronology of each person were not available), it does provide some very interesting and important insights concerning the circulation of persons within and among different organizational sectors.

As Table 9.2 indicates, just over two-thirds of the individuals serving in the regional party elites at the outset of the 1980's also held elite positions in 1972 on either the regional or federal level. This finding contrasts sharply with the situation of members in the other three regional sub-elites in the state sectors (top administrators, executives, and legislators) who were either outside or below the political elite in 1972 (working in the economy, finishing their education, in temporary retirement, working on the communal and municipal level, etc.). Moreover, of those members in the regional party elites who already had participated in elite activities in 1972, 58 percent were working in the same or a very closely related elite sector, that is, some position in the League of Communists or other mass socio-political organization. In other words, on the eve of Tito's death the regional party elites were composed largely of individuals with considerable elite level political experience and organizational specialization. The much smaller group of regional state executives and top legislators

The Socialist Pyramid: Elites and Power in Yugoslavia

Table 9.2
Organizational Background and Circulation of Yugoslav Regional Political Elites, 1972-80 (%)

	Sector of Elite Activities in 1980 (%)				
	I	II	II	IV	V
	Party Elite[a]	State Administrative Elite	State Executive Elites	Legislative Elite	Total
(a) Activity in 1972					
Activities outside the political elite[b]	32.6	78.4	74.7	62.2	65.0
Elite activities (regional or federal)	67.4	22.4	25.3	37.8	35.0
Total	100.0	100.0	100.0	100.0	100.0
(Number)	(138)	(250)	(150)	(74)	(614)
(b) Sector of elite activities in 1972					
Party (SKJ) and mass sociopolitical organizations	58.0	33.9	47.3	60.8	50.2
State administration	9.7	53.6	21.1	7.1	27.0
State executive bodies[c]	18.3	1.8	18.4	25.0	10.7
Legislatures	10.8	10.7	13.2	7.1	10.7
Other elite activities[d]	3.2	–	–	–	1.4
Total	100.0	100.0	100.0	100.0	100.0
(Number)	(93)	(56)	(38)	(28)	(215)

[a] This subelite includes the members of the Presidencies of the Central Committes for each of the 8 republics and provinces; in each of those areas it also includes the President of the Executive Council (state) and legislative assembly and thus in 16 cases overlaps with subelites III and IV.
[b] Work on the communal and municipal level, working in the economy, finishing education, in temporary retirement, etc.
[c] Includes members of state executive councils, state presidencies and the Council for the Federation.
[d] Administrators of mass media, etc.

with earlier elite-level political experience also acquired most of their major previous organizational affiliations in the party and mass socio-political organizations, a fact which reflects the heightened party control of the assembly system in the period after 1971.

Perhaps the most interesting sub-elite is composed of the regional administrative functionaries in the state bureaucracy. This group had the highest percentage of fresh recruits to the elite level (78.4 percent), and those civil servants who had earlier elite level experience, were primarily recruited (54 percent) from within the administrative sector. Only the party elite demonstrates a higher level of intra-sectoral recruitment. The regional administrative elite appears to be the subgroup most open to new talent (a trait which also shows up in the data on the state executive elite), and the only political subgroup other than the party elite with a real basis for organizational solidarity. Data not presented here, also indicate that of all of the 1980 regional elite members who served earlier at the federal level, the state administrators tended most frequently to return to their own organizational sector (i.e., going from federal administrative to regional administrative work). These findings tend to support other observations concerning the less "partisan," but still "politicized" and highly techo-bureaucratic outlook in the state administration, a trend which continued even after the resurgence of party influence in the mid-1970's.[30]

The Socio-Political Background of Yugoslav Regional Elites: The End of the Tito Era and Beyond

By the time of Tito's death in May 1980, power in socialist Yugoslavia had significantly devolved to the regional levels of the political system. In each of the six republics and two provinces the political functionaries in top party and state posts operated collectively as the leaders of quasi-sovereign territorial units, periodically "delegating" members from among their own ranks to serve in federal level political offices. Increasingly Yugoslav socialist democracy was described, by both domestic and foreign observers, not as a "self-managing form of pluralism" (conceptualized by Edward Kardelj and his colleagues in 1977), but as a pluralism of competing elites in an essentially confederal regime. What are the socio-political characteristics of the regional elites who have exercised political hegemony in the twilight and aftermath of the Tito period, and what are the features which divide and unite those elites? This section will examine the generational structure, educational background, and ethnic composition of Yugoslavia's current regional elites and also the implications of those characteristics for the political life of the post-Tito regime.

The Socialist Pyramid: Elites and Power in Yugoslavia

Age Structure and Political Generations

Generational cleavage and generational succession to elite positions have been important problems for communist political systems.[31] The generational structure of regional elites in Yugoslavia illustrates the dynamics of continuity and change in a society governed by an aging revolutionary elite. Each regional sub-elite includes a cross-section of different age cohorts within its ranks, but important modal tendencies exist within each elite group and there are interesting contrasts among the different elites.

The diminished representation of the older generation of political leaders, that is those individuals who were at least 21 on the eve of World War II, is one of the most striking tendencies revealed in the data on the age composition of Yugoslav regional elites in 1980 (Table 9.3). Only 17 out of 391 elite members (4.3 percent) in the whole regional sample were over 60 years of age. Most older individuals were concentrated in either the influential party presidencies or the more symbolic top legislative positions. The older character of the party and legislative presidencies is also revealed by the large number of individuals in the 50 to 60 year old age cohort. An equally striking contrast relates to the extreme youth of the party secretaries, a group which increasingly has been entrusted with the routine management of the party apparatus. While the party presidencies exhibit the oldest composition of any sub-elite, the party secretaries comprise the youngest group in the sample.

Perhaps the most important age cohorts in any consideration of Yugoslavia's post-Tito political development, however, are the two subgroups who were between 46 and 55 years of age in 1980. Individuals in these two cohorts, who might be called "children of the revolution," constitute the bulk of the entire elite sample, as well as each sub-elite (with the exception of the very young party secretaries). Indeed, the cohort of individuals between 51 and 55 years of age constitutes the largest subgroup within the administrative and legislative elites. The members of that group were born between 1925 and 1929 and were therefore from 12 to 16 years of age when the war started. Only 50 percent of the group participated in the Partisan movement, and most of those individuals joined the movement in 1943 and 1944, i.e., near the end of the war.

The succession of the late Partisan and post-Partisan generation at the regional level is also revealed in the comparative data on political generations (Table 9.4). Fewer than one-third of all regional elite members served in the Partisan movement, and those who did were mainly concentrated in the party and legislative presidencies. The data on party affiliation suggest a similar tendency. Only two individuals joined the party before Tito became head of the organization in 1937. Except for the party and legislative presidencies, the majority of regional elite members joined the party in the period of emergent self-

Table 9.3
Age Structure of Yugoslav Regional Elites, 1980 (%)

Age in 1980	Years of birth	Regional Elite Groups					
		Party Elites		State Elites			
		Members of Party Presidencies	Party Secretaries	State Administrative Secretaries	Members of State Executive Councils	Legislative Functionaries	Total
-35	since 1945	2.9	8.0	2.3	1.3	1.9	3.1
36-40	1940-4	8.7	12.9	5.5	3.8	5.8	6.9
41-45	1935-9	5.8	50.0	23.4	10.0	11.5	20.2
46-50	1930-4	26.1	19.4	21.9	37.5	13.5	24.3
51-55	1925-9	20.3	8.0	31.3	30.0	30.8	25.3
56-60	1920-4	29.0	-	13.3	13.8	26.9	13.9
61+	1919 and earlier	7.2	1.6	2.3	3.8	9.6	4.3
Total		100.0	100.0	100.0	100.0	100.0	100.0
(Number)		(69)	(62)	(128)	(80)	(52)	(391)

The Socialist Pyramid: Elites and Power in Yugoslavia

Table 9.4
Yugoslav Regional Elites by Political Generation (%)

	Regional Elite Groups					
	Members of Party Presidencies	Party Secretaries	State Administrative Secretaries	State Executive Councils	Legislative Functionaries	Total
(a) Participated in the National Liberation Movement (Partisans)						
Yes	49.3	3.2	24.8	21.3	56.6	29.3
No	50.7	96.8	75.2	78.7	43.4	90.7
Total	100.0	100.0	100.0	100.0	100.0	100.0
(Number)	(69)	(62)	(129)	(80)	(53)	(393)
(b) Year of joining party						
-1936	-	1.8	-	-	-	0.3
1937-40	6.1	1.8	0.9	1.3	6.1	2.8
1941-4	39.4	1.8	18.1	14.5	40.8	21.8
1945-8	16.7	10.7	21.6	28.9	24.5	20.9
1949-58	25.8	50.0	37.9	46.1	20.4	36.9
1959-63	6.1	25.0	14.7	6.6	6.1	11.8
1964	6.1	8.9	6.9	2.6	2.0	5.5
Total	100.0	100.0	100.0	100.0	100.0	100.0
(Number)	(66)	(56)	(116)	(76)	(49)	(363)

Lenard J. Cohen

management after 1950. In a pattern which parallels the diminished influence of Yugoslav representative assemblies in recent years, legislative leadership appears to have become a sinecure or "exit" arena for older politicians. The regional party secretaries, in contrast, stand out as the group whose members have most recently joined the League of Communists.

Educational Background

Overall, Yugoslavia's regional elites tend to be highly educated (Table 9.5). This generalization is even more true of the state administrative secretaries and the members of the state executive councils who have two or three times as many doctorates in their ranks as the party and legislative elites. The data on educational levels reveal, however, that the young, new generation of party secretaries is not that well educated compared to other regional sub-elites, and particularly in contrast to the relatively young state secretaries. This finding may partially be attributed to the youthful age structure of the party secretaries, but also very likely reflects the party's incomplete success in attracting a new generation of functionaries possessing both political commitment and educational achievements. The insecurity and negative perceptions often associated with professional political work, as well as the availability of more secure and prestigious avenues of opportunity outside politics would tend to support the latter explanation.

The party's deficiencies in the area of educational specialization also emerge from the data regarding types of educational background. Not surprisingly, individuals with technical and economic training tend to be concentrated in the state administration and the executive councils, while those individuals with political, administrative, military, and journalistic training are more typically found in the party and legislative presidencies (although a good number of vice-presidents of assemblies have economic and technical education). A large number of the younger group of party secretaries received training in law and philosophy. The very large percentage of unknown higher educations revealed in both party sub-elites further accentuates the contrast in specialization between the party and state sectors. The different attitudes and modes of behaviour which usually result from such diverse training will undoubtedly contribute to other sources of inter-elite conflict during the post-Tito period of Yugoslav development.

Type of education also bears an interesting relationship to age and political generation in a manner which suggests that cleavages derived from training are both inter-elite and intra-elite phenomena. Thus, further analysis of the entire sample reveals that nearly one-third of those individuals who served in the Partisan movement had educational training in politics, administration,

The Socialist Pyramid: Elites and Power in Yugoslavia

Table 9.5
Yugoslav Regional Elites by Level and Type of Education (%)

	Regional Elite Groups					
	Members of Party Presidencies	Party Secretaries	State Administrative Secretaries	Members of State Executive Councils	Legislative Functionaries	Total
Level of Education						
No higher education	4.7	13.6	0.8	-	4.3	3.9
Higher education	92.2	81.4	87.3	91.5	91.5	88.6
Higher education with doctorate	3.1	5.1	11.9	8.5	4.3	7.5
Total	100.0	100.0	100.0	100.0	100.0	100.0
(Number)	(64)	(59)	(118)	(71)	(47)	(359)
Type of Higher Education						
Political science, journalism	19.7	9.8	7.7	7.0	24.4	12.2
Administration and security	-	2.0	7.7	4.2	6.7	4.6
Law	9.8	25.5	24.0	18.3	17.8	19.7
Philosophy	6.6	11.8	7.7	8.5	-	7.2
Economic	18.0	11.8	24.0	33.8	20.0	22.6
Technical	1.6	2.0	23.1	16.9	17.8	14.2
Arts and sciences	3.3	7.8	-	2.8	2.2	2.6
Unknown*	41.0	29.4	5.9	8.5	11.1	16.8
Total	100.0	100.0	100.0	100.0	100.0	100.0
(Number)	(61)	(51)	(117)	(71)	(45)	(345)

* Mainly unfinished higher education, 2-year 'higher schools', and political schooling, etc.

Lenard J. Cohen

and security while this was the case for fewer than one-fifth of the nonparticipants. Close to half of all those individuals who did not belong to the Partisans had higher technical and economic training. Those persons with technical and economic training, who also were Partisans, tended to join the movement rather late (1942-1944), while those with political science, administration and military training joined for the most part during 1941 (although their education may not have been acquired until after the war). The data also indicate that among younger elite members, those individuals with technical and economic education tended to join the party at a slightly older age, that is, after they had completed their education.

Ethnic Background

The official use of ethnic arithmetic in elite recruitment is a well documented feature of Yugoslav political life (see Chapter 7). Indeed, since the mid-1960's responsibility for maintaining an ethnic balance in regional and federal elite contingents has fallen to the republican and provincial organizations. Consequently, political sub-elites in all sections of Yugoslavia reveal considerable superficial representativeness, i.e., when their nationality composition is compared to the makeup of the general population. Despite this policy, however, certain interesting features and trends still require consideration. For example, although the ethnic representativeness of elites is only of rather minimal interest and sensitivity within the more homogeneous regions of the country (Slovenia, Montenegro, Serbia proper, and Macedonia), the issue is of greater importance in regions of substantial ethnic diversity. Secondly, there appears to be significantly different degrees of representativeness depending on the specific sub-elite in question.

Table 9.6 offers data on the nationality composition of sub-elites and party organizations in three of Yugoslavia's most sensitive areas of cultural diversity: Croatia, Bosnia, and Kosovo. These regions contain large Serbian ethnic communities, ranking second in size to the region's principal nationality. Although the ethnic identities of a considerable number of elite members is unknown (particularly in Croatia and Bosnia), some generalizations can still be made. For example, relative to their group size in the general population the Serbs are markedly overrepresented in the party membership of each region considered. The main reasons for this situation relate to the generally high level of political activity manifest by Serbs - particularly in regions outside "Serbia proper" - and the disproportionately high participation of Serbs in the Partisan movement. Although not as extreme as the disproportions in the party membership, Serbian overrepresentation is also apparent in the political elite structure of Croatia and Kosovo (the large number of "unknown" cases in Bosnia

The Socialist Pyramid: Elites and Power in Yugoslavia

incorrectly makes the Serbs appear very underrepresented in that region's elite). Overall, the data on party membership and the political elites in these regions indicate that Serbian overrepresentation, while still marked, has diminished considerably in comparison with the immediate postwar period. Serbian representation in the Bosnian and Kosovo elites and party organizations has continued to decline in the decade after 1978, and in the latter region this trend has engendered a serious political backlash by the Serbs (see Chapter 8).

Table 9.6
Ethnic Composition of Selected Yugoslav Regional Elites (%)

Region and Ethnic Group	Total Population (1971)	Party Membership (1973)	Party Membership (1978)	Party Elite (1980)	State Elites (1980)	Total Regional Elite (1980)
Croatia						
Serbs	14.2	24.7	24.2	26.3	18.2	21.2
Croats	79.4	64.8	64.2	57.9	63.6	61.5
Others	6.0	10.5	11.6	-	6.1	3.8
Unknown	0.4	-	-	15.8	12.1	13.5
Total	100.0	100.0	100.0	100.0	100.0	100.0
(Number)				(19)	(33)	(52)
Bosnia						
Serbs	37.3	52.1	47.0	31.8	30.2	30.8
Croats	20.6	10.9	11.9	13.6	16.2	13.4
Moslems	39.6	31.1	33.9	31.8	41.9	38.5
Others	2.2	5.9	7.2	9.1	-	3.0
Unknown	0.3	-	-	13.6	11.6	12.3
Total	100.0	100.0	100.0	100.0	100.0	100.0
(Number)				(22)	(43)	(65)
Kosovo						
Serbs	18.4	26.2	25.7	20.0	18.5	19.1
Montenegrins	2.5	8.0	7.0	10.0	3.7	6.4
Albanians	73.7	61.7	62.8	65.0	70.4	68.1
Moslems	2.1	1.7	2.3	5.0	3.7	4.2
Others	3.2	2.4	2.2	-	-	-
Unknown	0.1	-	-	-	3.7	2.1
Total	100.0	100.0	100.0	100.0	100.0	100.0
(Number)				(20)	(27)	(47)

A noticeable contrast also exists between the ethnic composition of the party elite and the state elite. In each multi-ethnic region Serbs are more overrepresented in the party elites (Montenegrins should be considered together with Serbs in Kosovo), while the principal, i.e., largest ethnic group of each region is five to ten percent better represented in the state elite. Thus, in the case of the principal ethnic group of each region the level of representation in the party elite bears a much closer resemblance to the group's relative size in the party membership than to its relative demographic position. The source of Serbian overrepresentation in the party elite of multi-ethnic regions including Vojvodina, emerges from another finding: 50 percent (91 individuals) of all those regional elite members in the sample who had backgrounds in the Partisan movement were Serbs and Montenegrins, a figure which increases considerably when Bosnia, Croatia and Kosovo are considered together and compared to the rest of the sample. In contrast, the pattern of ethnic representation among the younger members of the party and state sub-elites corresponds much more closely to the ethnic composition of each region. If past experience is any guide, such generational intra-elite and inter-elite ethnic differences may become a source of political tension in the years ahead.[32] One regional political functionary noted in 1979, for example, that the "complex and delicate subject" of disproportions in the ethnic structure of the League of Communists in Croatia is a very important "ideopolitical question":

> Let us not forget that even today the Croatian nationalists have not abandoned their thesis that the Serbian nationality in Croatia has a dominant influence and that the Croats are in a subordinate position .... It is not a question of the need to reduce the numbers of the representatives of those nationalities that until now have been more strongly represented in the League of Communists of Croatia, but one should concentrate more on the inclusion of the representatives of those nationalities whose participation lags behind their share in the national structure of the population.[33]

Conclusion: Recruitment Imperatives and Elite Cleavages

The skills, values, and behaviour of regional political elites are key factors affecting the political stability of post-Tito Yugoslavia. Such elites not only exert a significant influence on their respective republics and provinces, but must also coordinate and compromise their views in the process of inter-regional decision-making on the federal level of the political system. Regional elites also constitute the primary source from which federal-level officials are selected, i.e., the elite group making the most important systemic decisions in the Yugoslav "self-managed" system.[34]

The survey of elite recruitment in the first section of this chapter reveals important changes and continuities in the selection of political decision-makers and other strategic leaders. After a five year period (1966-1971) in which the pattern of elite recruitment had been more pluralistic, decentralized and depoliticized, the next decade witnessed a return to the greater influence of party agencies over personnel selection, within and outside the party organization. Thus, at both the Tenth and Eleventh Congresses (1974 and 1978) of the League of Communists, the principle of "moral-political fitness" - a concept characteristic of the other socialist states and reminiscent of the very early years of Yugoslav socialism - again assumed prominence as a criterion in elite recruitment.

It would be wrong to conclude from the preceding analysis, however, that recruitment policy in the years after 1971 simply represented a throw-back to the period of "statist" or "administrative" socialism. Although the policy of political deprofessionalization slowed considerably and the absolute number of persons employed in the party apparatus nearly reached the same level as in 1952, it is also significant that the party had more than doubled in size in the intervening period (Table 9.1). Thus, the ratio of professional party functionaries to members had not changed appreciably in the decade after 1971 and there was even a slight decrease in 1981. It is not surprising, therefore, that during the halcyon days of political pluralism and political deprofessionalization in the late 1960's many seasoned and more conservative party officials worried about the capacity of the League of Communists to effectively manage Yugoslav society.

The actual operation of the party apparatus in the political system is, however, far more important than its size. A second distinguishing feature of elite recruitment after 1971 was the new methods by which the party wielded influence over personnel selection in other organizational sectors. In contrast to the comprehensive and centralized nomenklatura-type system described in the early postwar years, the party began to place more emphasis on persuasion and consensus-building when formulating criteria for personnel appointments in various elite sectors. "Cadre policy" was increasingly based on "social accords" worked out by officials of the League together with leaders from other mass socio-political organizations and specialists in personnel selection. Formulated at each level of the federal system, the accords serve as a programatic basis for the screening and final selection of job applicants. The implementation and monitoring of such personnel procedures falls within the jurisdiction of the Socialist Alliance of Working People of Yugoslavia (SSRNJ, a broad mass socio-political organization) rather than the League of Communists, although there is a very close connection between the two organizations. For example, on the central level the implementation of the social accords on cadre policy is controlled by the SSRNJ Federal Conference's Coordination Committee for Cadre Policy in the Federation, a body composed of and headed by experienced professional political functionaries. While the locus of organizational control and personnel policy may have only shifted slightly, i.e., from the League to the Socialist Alliance, federal appointment procedures reveal a genuine pluralism of different specialized interests and regional views.[35] Considerable interregional competition for federal governmental and political positions also exists, a situation which, although not as politically turbulent as during the late 1960's, appears to be firmly institutionalized in the 1980's.[36]

Finally, although the "moral-political suitability" of candidates became a more prominent consideration in political leadership selection after 1971 there was also continued pressure on the regime to recruit highly specialized and technically qualified individuals for elite positions. Both official and unofficial dissatisfaction was expressed, for example, to rigid tests of political suitability that deny positions to professionally competent job applicants whose training does not happen to include sufficient political work. Social accords on cadre policy in the mid-1970's emphasized that it was a person's overall "political and action orientation" towards self-management and "not membership in the League of Communists alone" which constituted a "true gauge for the evaluation of cadres," and also that personnel policy should "strengthen even more the inter-connection and unity of the moral-political, working and vocational qualities."[37] Thus in the late 1970's and 1980's, as in the late 1960's, one encountered frequent attacks on the requirement that applicants for all leading posts should be party members. Party affiliation, this view maintains, is too often based simply on careerism and the pursuit of privileges.[38] One political functionary in Croatia has gone even further in his criticism, suggesting that university faculties for political science may be unnecessary in a society attempting to minimize political office-holding on a professional basis. In his opinion, special "cadres faculties" for political training are superfluous, since all working people and citizens are political "cadre."[39]

The abandonment of the formula "moral-political qualities and suitability" in the federal personnel accords proposed immediately after Tito's death[40] indicated the depth of reservations regarding the overt use and frequent misuse of political criteria in personnel selection.[41] Although Yugoslav research studies conducted in the 1970's and 1980's indicated that "moral-political fitness" and political experience were the most significant criteria in political elite recruitment, even on the local level of the federal system (Table 9.7), such research also revealed the importance of many non-political factors. Moreover, the criterion of moral-political fitness is usually very broadly interpreted and flexibly utilized by participants in the recruitment process.[42] Indeed, well before the onset of the post-Tito era the most successful candidates for leading positions in Yugoslavia were typically individuals demonstrating both political reliability and established professional credentials outside the political sector. As research regarding members of the intelligentsia in other European socialist states has illustrated, such dual qualifications tend to create "pluralists of job-holding" as a new privileged group *within* the party and ruling class. It has been observed that "anyone lucky enough to possess this double seal of approval can be as secure as a person with dual citizenship."[43] The growing challenges to political leadership which emerged during Yugoslavia's economic crisis in the mid-1980's only accentuated the need for such dual qualifications and engendered additional anxiety among those who possessed traditional political backgrounds.

The analysis of elite composition in the second part of this chapter reveals interesting sources of both potential cohesion and dissensus among Yugoslav regional decision-makers. Thus, despite the policy of conservative retrenchment launched by older party professionals during the early 1970's, at the time of Tito's death in 1980 a new *post-Partisan elite generation* appeared well ensconced on the regional level. In terms of their socio-political characteristics the political sub-elites in the republics and provinces were relatively young, highly educated, trained in a variety of skills, and ethnically quite representative of their respective regional populations. The ascendancy of the post-Partisan elite generation to the highest level of the political hierarchy received striking recognition at the 13th Congress of the Yugoslav League of Communists in June 1986. Thus, while 58 percent of the former Central Committee elected in 1982 had participated in the National Liberation War, this was true of only 24 percent of the 1986 Committee (of whom only 19 individuals had joined at the beginning of the struggle in 1941). From the 165 members of the 1986 Central Committee elected for four years, 127, or 77 percent - the highest figure in postwar Yugoslav party history - were newly elected. Moreover, for the first time, a professional politician - Milanko Renovica, born in 1928 - who had joined the party after the war, was elected as party President.[44] Renovica was succeeded in 1987 by another postwar party adherent, Boško Krunić, who was born in 1929. Even more striking, Radisa Gačić, the current Secretary of the Party Presidency (elected for a two year term, 1986-1988) only joined the League of Communists in 1957, and was just three years old at the beginning of the Partisan struggle. From 1982 to 1986, Gačić had served as Secretary of the party organization in Serbia, again revealing the relative youth of the regional party secretaries that emerged in the above analysis. Forty years after founding the communist regime, Tito's "younger" comrades-in-arms were relinquishing the country's highest positions to a new political generation.[45] A self-made political elite was being replaced by the elite of self-managing socialism.

The findings concerning the regional elites also reveal, however, areas of potential conflict which may create difficulties for the regime in the post-Tito period. The juxtaposition of different generational cohorts, with different formative experiences and different levels and types of skills emerges very clearly in the data on particular sub-elites, and also in the contrast among sub-elites. Thus, the 1980 data on the party leadership indicates a clear distinction between a relatively older group of professional revolutionaries having only incomplete higher education or very general political training, and another group of much younger and specialized functionaries. The former group of party officials is concentrated in the Presidencies of the League of Communists within

Lenard J. Cohen

Table 9.7
Perceptions of Communal Legislators in Croatia Concerning the Main Criterion which Determined their Own Nomination (%)

Criteria	Delegates in the Communal Assemblies by Chamber		
	Chamber of Associated Labor	Chamber of Local Communities	Sociopolitical Chambers
Age	2.21	2.16	1.47
Sex	1.47	4.32	2.21
Education	4.41	1.44	-
Position in production	8.09	2.16	0.74
Nationality	1.47	0.72	2.21
Moral-political fitness	20.59	12.95	32.35
Local reputation	5.15	17.27	6.62
Connection with the interests of the locality	7.25	15.83	10.29
Responsibility and independence	7.35	5.04	4.41
Knowledge	5.88	5.76	4.41
Previous success in the delegate system	14.71	22.30	21.32
Involvement in self-management	12.50	5.04	11.03
Other	-	-	-
Don't know or no reponse	8.79	5.04	2.93
Total	100.0	100.0	100.0

Source: Ivan Grdešić, *Neki Aspekti Izbora Delegata u Općinsku Skupštinu* (Zagreb: Institut za Političke Nauke Fakulteta Političkih Nauka, 1980), p. 47; the precise number of delegates interviewed and actual responses was not given.

The Socialist Pyramid: Elites and Power in Yugoslavia

each region and include a disproportionately high number of Serbs and Montenegrins. The latter group, in contrast, consists mainly of the party secretaries, a subgroup more ethnically representative of their regional populations. The party secretaries represent a subgroup which is prominently defined by its almost total non-participation in the Partisan struggle.

The generational and educational contrast between the regional administrative elites composed of officials in the state bureaucracy on the one hand, and the party sub-elites on the other, is another potential source of inter-elite cleavage. Much younger and more technically proficient than the party decision-makers, most of the state administrative functionaries joined the party after the war and at an older age (usually after completing higher education). Even when compared to the party executive secretaries who, taken as a separate party sub-elite, are the most youthful group in the whole sample, the regional state administrative functionaries emerge as the group most qualified to manage a technically complex and modernized economy. While Yugoslav leaders generally recognize that highly specialized expertise is indispensable for the successful management of their society, individuals possessing technical and modern administrative skills are frequently and perhaps conveniently charged with constituting a threat to the continuation of the self-management system, i.e., as that system has been structured and guided by the less technically educated and more "Partisan" (in terms of their generational cohort and ideological commitment) generation of politicians. Less than six months after Tito's death, one top party official predicted that such inter-elite conflict was unavoidable and necessary:

> The power of the technocrats in the administrative and political bureaucracy is very great. For this reason any further postponement of a decisive conflict between the League of Communists and other organized socialist forces with the holders of this [technical and administrative] power is impossible. Without such a conflict even greater difficulties could emerge.[46]

Different elite backgrounds and skills do not, of course, automatically translate into serious political conflicts. Thus, while the "technobureaucracy" continued to be the favourite subject of derision in political circles during the 1980's, Yugoslavia's urgent need for highly skilled personnel to address the country's enormous economic difficulties would seem to preclude any iminent revival of the vigorous anti-technocratic campaign witnessed during the first half of the 1970's. Indeed in 1986, as political leaders in Belgrade came under sharp attack because of the economic deterioration of the country, there was a large influx of individuals with technical and economic expertise into the Federal Assembly.

Political leadership characteristics and recruitment policies will remain a major source of tension in Yugoslavia, particularly in view of the country's prolonged economic difficulties and the pronounced resurgence of ethno-regional conflicts. During the second half of the 1980's, for example, controversy concerning which leaders should assume responsibility for the country's economic crisis, and also the type of leaders necessary to correct the situation, became a prominent feature of Yugoslav political life. Although throughout the history of the communist regime the majority of Yugoslavia's working class acquiesced in the rule of a political elite in return for economic and political stability, the disappearance of such stability in the post-Tito period has considerably eroded popular support for the regime. Not surprisingly, in the fall of 1987 when the country was racked by its biggest postwar financial scandal, some observers discerned the deeper roots of widespread economic corruption in the substitution of political criteria for professionalism and expertise in the management of the economy.[47] The intensification of nationalism and ethnic conflict during the post-Tito period - most demonstrably, but not exclusively in the province of Kosovo - added to the Yugoslav population's increasing pessimism and cynicism about the regime's political leadership and the country's future viability.

Citizen dissatisfaction with the regime has manifest itself in a number of ways during the second half of the 1980's. For example, after a dozen years of steady growth in membership during which the League of Communists more than doubled in size, the party declined from 2.3 million members in 1984 to two million members in the middle of 1987. The reduced size of the party paralleled the aging of its membership. Between 1981 and the end of 1985, the percentage of members under 27 years of age dropped from 31 percent to 23 percent. Moreover, despite constant efforts to establish a "workers' majority" in the League of Communists, the representation of blue collar workers in the party declined from 31 percent in 1982 to 29.5 percent in mid-1987. The unprecedented outbreak of labour unrest which swept the country in 1987 (978 strikes from January to September involving approximately 150,000 workers) presented an even more serious example of popular disenchantment, and directly challenged the political elite's self-proclaimed role as the vanguard of the working class. Strikes by professionals, such as doctors, school teachers, and journalists during 1986 and 1987 also reveal a growing sense of frustration and disapproval among white collar workers, the occupational sector which in recent decades has been the major social base of the League of Communists and the regime.

Considering the overall climate of economic malaise, political uncertainty and dissatisfaction in Yugoslavia at the end of the 1980's, the increasing ascendancy of new skill groups, age cohorts, and ethnic spokesmen in the country seems likely to preview future controversies concerning the proper criteria (e.g. the degree of technical training, generational turnover, ethnic proportionality, etc.) for the selection of political elites.[48] The organization and openess of the political recruitment process is another issue which may evoke political disputes, especially when various imperatives of political and economic management (e.g. "cohesion," "stability," "unity," "efficiency," etc.) in a culturally diverse industrial society such as Yugoslavia confront the strong anti-elitist and participatory impulses of self-management's more ardent supporters. Indeed, the extent of organizational pluralism and decentralization in the selection of political personnel will significantly influence whether or not Tito's heirs can thwart the elitist tendencies which have afflicted the entire history of revolutionary socialism. As one Belgrade political scientist remarked in mid-1986, Rosa Luxembourg's trenchant criticisms of those proletarian movements which concentrate power at the apex of a party hierarchy remain highly pertinent to an assessment of current political life in Yugoslavia.

> I would say that all of the changes which we have enacted in our country have been blunted by such a hierarchical pyramid; its base has been broadened, but it is fundamentally a pyramidal structure, which we wanted to pull down - but which we did not pull down. We wanted to establish two summits, so that the party would be independent, so that the state could be within the circumference of its jurisdiction, we wanted to create a Socialist Alliance that would transcend the League of Communists's monopoly of power, we wanted a trade union that would be an autonomous organization. We wanted all that. Yet in place of several summits, we again have one pyramidal structure, the foundation of which is the monopoly over personnel selection.[49]

NOTES: CHAPTER NINE

1. The biographical information is found in *Politički i poslovni imenik, III Deo, Biografije* (Belgrade: Dokumentacija Tanjuga, October 15, 1978, December 12, 1979), 1-102.

2. Branko Petranović, *Politička i ekonomska osnova narodne vlasti u Jugoslaviji za vreme obnove* (Belgrade: Institut za savremenu istoriju, 1969), 51-52, 57.

3. *Ibid.*, 269.

4. In public statements party leaders suggested that such problems were temporary. At the Fifth Party Congress in 1948, Alexander Ranković remarked that "the workers, peasants, and a large number of intellectuals found themselves doing work they had never done before. This explains a certain rigidity and inflexibility which existed in the very beginning as regards complex economic and administrative problems. But they overcame these difficulties and introduced a new creative elan .... Our enemies said that we knew how to wage war but that we would not know how to organize a state. Practice has shown that is was precisely the cadre that passed through the difficult school of war that was also the best bearer of the building up of the new state." Alexander Ranković, *Report of the Central Committee of the Communist Party of Yugoslavia on the Organizational Work of the CPY* (Belgrade, 1948), 53 and 56.

5. Fred W. Neal, The Communist Party of Yugoslavia," *American Slavic and East European Review*, XVIII, No. 3 (1959), 334-350, and Paul Shoup, "Problems of Party Reform in Yugoslavia," *American Slavic and East European Review*, XVIII, No. 3 (1959), 334-350.

6. R. Radonjić, *Sukob KPJ i Kominform i društveni razvoj Jugoslavije (1948-1950)* (Zagreb: Centar za kulturnu djelatnost, 1979), 146-147, 178-180.

7. Ranković explained that "rotation does not mean demotion or the replacement of the older generation but the normal reconstitution of executive bodies .... Nevertheless there has been some uneasiness among some of the senior cadres who played a part in the

revolution .... Even some of the relatively young people who took part in the People's Liberation War have been somewhat inclined to feel that retirement or pension is the only way out .... It would be neither expedient nor wise to settle the question of the veterans merely by pensioning them off ... it would be extremely difficult for them today to go back to their original occupations .... Although the principle of obligatory rotation has not been officially inserted into the Statute of the League of Communists it has also been carried out to a certain extent. Of course the principle as it is applied to the representative bodies and central government organs cannot be automatically transferred to the League of Communists." "Current Problems in Relation to the Work and Role of the League of Communists of Yugoslavia," *VIII Congress of the League of Communists of Yugoslavia* (Belgrade: Medjunarodna politika, 1965), 148-149, 151-152.

8. *Deveti Kongres Saveza Komunista Jugoslavije* (Belgrade: Komunist, 1970), 151-152.

9. Milosav Janićijević, *Osvrt na strukturalne promene Jugoslovenskog društva* (Belgrade: Jugoslovensko udruženje za sociologiju, 1967), 283-312, and Rade Aleksić, "Inteligencija u Jugoslovenskom društvu," *Sociologija*, VI, Nos. 1-2 (1964), 115-133. Changing occupational demography aside, there was also an increase in the political and social influence of the technical intelligentsia in the decade before 1966. See Milosav Janićijević, "Jedan pogled na karakteristika nastanka i razvitka Jugoslovenska inteligencije," *Gledišta*, I, No. 2 (1959), 31-45, and Ivan Perić, "Neke karakteristika socijalne strukture Saveza Komunista Hrvatske," *Reforma Saveza Komunista Hrvatska* (Zagreb: Centar za aktualni politički studij, 1970), 42-69.

10. For the ideological differentiation of the intelligentsia during this period see Živorad Djordjević, *Za i protiv inteligencije* (Belgrade: SSO Srbije, 1981).

11. See Chapter 5 and Lenard J. Cohen, "Devolutionary Socialism: The Political Institutionalization of the Yugoslav Assembly System, 1963-1973," (Ph.D. Dissertatation, Columbia University, 1978).

12. *Politika*, (Belgrade, 1971), 7.

13. Josip Županov, "Da li se rukovodjenje preduzećem profesionalizira?," *Moderna organizacija*, No. 10 (1968), 803-823, Živan Tanić, "Direktori i predstavinci samoupravnih tela," *Naše teme*, XIII, No. 2 (1969), 186-206. See also Chapter 3. For the significant increase of the technical intelliegentsia in the party membership during this period see Vladimir Milić, *Socijalni portret partije* (Belgrade: Mladost, 1985).

14. *Šesti Kongres Saveza Komunista Hrvatska, Stenografske belješke, Zagreb December 5-7, 1968, Volume III* (Zagreb: Komunist, 1969), 120.

15. Dušan Bilandžić, "SKJ u borbi za transformacija državno-centralistickog sistema u samoupravnu organizaciju društva (1961-1970)," *Istorija Savez Komunista Jugoslavije*, eds. P. Morača, Dušan Bilandžić and Svetozar Stojanović (Belgrade: Rad, 1976), 280.

16. *Ibid.*, 281-282.

17. D. Knežović, "Kadrovska politika: politički profesionalizam u Savezu Komunista," *Socijalizam*, XXII, No. 11 (1977), 138-153.

18. A communal party functionary has explained the change from professional to deprofessionalized political work on the local level in the period just before the removal of Ranković: "When I was elected secretary of the communal committee four years ago, it didn't seem right to me that I had to give up my specialization .... Right from the start I confronted difficult tasks, mainly in the economy. People referred their biggest and smallest problems to the committee, generally to the secretary .... The secretary was asked and expected to give his opinion and judgment about everything, to be everywhere. Others hid themselves behind him and fled from responsibility. In concrete political work, many obligations and tasks were heaped upon the secretary. Since he was a paid official, many people thought he was required to accept the duties of other members of the communal committees and other socio-political activists, to write papers, reports, and analyses, to prepare and organize all meetings of the committee, to attend meetings of primary organizations of the League, etc. .... Whether he wished it or not the secretary became a professional practitioner and administrator and his colleagues hid themselves behind him, as passive spectators .... Two years ago I was again elected as secretary

but this time as a non-professional .... I am performing the duty of secretary while simultaneously working at my profession. I can't say it is easy because it requires great physical and psychological effort .... It allows the secretary to pay more attention to real political work .... Since there isn't a 'principal' personality in the person of the paid secretary, collective leadership (*kolektivnost*) is more apparent in the work of the committee .... That alsô assumes an equitable division of functions and tasks among a greater number of people, each of them assuming responsibility for the implementation. *Komunist*, (June 2, 1966), 4.

19. Šesti Kongres Saveza Komunista Hrvatska, Stenografske belješke, 200-202, 205.

20. *Nedeljne Informativne Novine*, (May 29, 1977), 6-8.

21. A director of a Belgrade enterprise with 25 years experience explained the nature of the political pressure in his job. "The director is located between two social forces whose interests are not the same. On the one side is the enterprise, or the workers employed in it, and on the other, the socio-political organizations - the [party] committee, communal assembly, trade union .... To whom should one look for royal assent when there are sharp differences of opinion ... to the members of the [worker's] collective, at the head of which I sit ... or the president of the commune, the secretary of the committee ...? It is more honourable to respond to my collective, but many directors do the opposite, conscious of the fact that their place, their business career depends more on socio-political workers, or even exclusively depends on them." *Nedeljne Informativne Novine*, August 31, 1980, 16.

22. *Nedeljne Informativne Novine*, (January 18, 1981), 10.

23. The Central Committee elected at the 12th LCY Congress in June 1982 continued this trend. In 1974 only one-third of the members were over 50 years of age, in 1982 over two-thirds of the 163 persons elected were in this mature age group. Continuity and seniority in the initial post-Tito elite was also reflected in political seniority data. Thus, 51 percent of the 1982 Central Committee joined the party before 1945, 58 percent were in the liberation war, and 39 percent served in the Partisan forces beginning in 1941. *Foreign Broadcast Information Service*, (July 7, 1982), I9.

24. *Nedeljne Informativne Novine*, (January 4, 1981), 22.

25. See Chapter 4. A 1982 Yugoslav analysis of cadre policy maintains "no real breakthrough has yet been made in lessening the professionalization of the country's political elite. There are rare examples, particularly on 'higher' levels, of people who after their term of office has expired ... returned to the post from which they came. Not infrequently the functions continue to be performed according to the principle of 'rotation,' from one post to another, from a 'lower' post to a 'higher' one." *Borba*, (June 7, 1982), 7.

26. Dušan Bilandžić, SKJ u borbi za transformacija državno-centralistickog sistema u samoupravnu organizaciju društva (1961-1970)," 315. One analysis noted that in Belgrade alone approximately 2,000 party cadre commissions exist in socio-political organizations, institutions and enterprises. *Nedeljne Informativne Novine*, (April 13, 1980), 9.

27. *Deseti Kongres SKJ: Dokumenti* (Belgrade: Komunist, 1975), 394.

28. Dušan Bilandžić, "SKJ u borbi za transformacija državno-centralističkog sistema u samoupravnu organizaciju društva (1961-1970)," 313-314.

29. The two directories used in the analysis were *Politički i Poslovni Imenik SFR Jugoslavije 1972* (Belgrade: Tanjug, February 18, 1972) and *Politički i Poslovni Imenik* (Belgrade: Tanjung, October 15, 1978 and supplements for 1979 and 1980).

30. See Chapter 5, and Radomir Lukić, "Rotation Among Top Government Officials in Yugoslavia," *The Mandarins of Western Europe*, ed. Mattei Dogan (New York: Halstead Press, 1975), 293-304.

31. There is little consensus in the literature about the urgency or consequences of generational and skill differentiation in communist elites. For example, William Griffith has argued that "Yugoslavia has not had genuine generational change although there has been a rejuvenation that Tito has in a way, artificially prevented from coming to fruition, I would suspect that there is in Yugoslavia, a great deal of built-up generational resentment." "Generational Change and Political Leadership in Eastern Europe and the Soviet

Union," *Political Generations and Political Development*, ed. Richard J. Samuels (Lexington: Lexington Books, 1977), 127.

32. A more detailed analysis of the problem is offered in Chapter 7.

33. *Politika,* (Belgrade, November 16, 1979), 8. Variation in the degree of ethnic commitment to the party by different ethnic groups continued to be politically significant in the second half of the 1980's. In 1986, for example, party membership was held in Yugoslavia by every fifth Montenegrin, every eighth Serb, 10th Macedonian, 11th Moslem, 16th Slovene, Croat and Hungarian, and every 19th Albanian. *Foreign Broadcast Information Service* (May 15, 1986), 14. The extent to which the League of Communists has been able to appeal to different ethnic groups varies considerably by region. As a rule, members of ethnic groups living outside their "native" region are better represented in the party than are members of that ethnic group living within their native region. The only exceptions are the Albanians who have a lower representation in the party outside Kosovo than within that province, and the Moslems, who show no difference in representation inside and outside Bosnia. *Danas,* (December 10, 1985), 5-9.

34. The head of the Federal Government's Personnel Commission observed in 1980 that there were still some functionaries serving in federal organs who manage to remain on the federal level in new jobs after the mandatory termination of their terms of office, although the problem of such so-called "federal cadre" is decreasing in importance from year to year. He also mentioned that care is taken so that in individual organs there is no concentration of cadre from the same republic or province. *Nedeljne Informativne Novine,* (September 21, 1980), 26-27.

35. Recent accords, however, stress the need for regional recruits to maintain a cross-national perspective during their term of service in federal agencies.

36. See for example, Lenard J. Cohen, "Federalism and Foreign Policy in Yugoslavia: The Politics of Regional Ethnonationalism," *International Journal*, XLI (Summer, 1986), 12-15. Vučina Vasović describes the Yugoslav political recruitment process as a subtle system of "personnel alchemy" and claims that control over personnel policy is not located at the summit of the "state-party complex" but rather "in the depths ... of personal-clientelistic,

Lenard J. Cohen

    predominantly authoritarian complexes of power which emit a system of teleguided suggestions and recommendations which a very broad sub-political stratum receive as messages and a task to be implemented in a definite period and in the framework of the official electoral process." *Nedeljne Informativne Novine*, (October 25, 1987), 25.

37. *Foreign Broadcast Information Service*, (December 15, 1975), I7-I16, and (May 20, 1976), I4-I10.

38. See for example, *Borba*, (June 29, 1972), 5. A Montenegrin party functionary remarks: "What does it mean to inquire into the background of a young man who is just starting out? What can a check tell us about a student who has just graduated or a technician who has just reached age 20? Who are we to ask and what are we to check? I agree that we should make certain that his is suitable for the job, but we should not go looking for any trumped up elements .... There are, I repeat, places in the government and the economy where every society wants people of a certain background. But to take this to the extreme where points are even given in the competition for jobs to those who are members of the party could be dangerous." *Nedeljne Informativne Novine*, (May 29, 1977), 8.

39. *Nedeljne Informativne Novine*, (July 27, 1980), 10-12. The Yugoslav author did not expand his argument to include the Josip Broz Tito Political School, established in Croatia during the mid-1970's, which had already graduated hundred of professional "socio-political workers."

40. *Foreign Broadcast Information Service*, (June 16, 1980), I30.

41. A Belgrade political scientist has observed that "it isn't rare that the narrow and closed administrative structures on the lower levels of organizations often have greater possibilities for communication with higher personnel and political decision-makers and services, and are the main sources of information about personnel opportunities and the capabilities of people in their area. It isn't impossible that relying on such information specific personnel authorities carry out not only personnel sorting, or the selection of specific people, but also ideological differentiations .... It is perhaps one of the most sensitive and most vulnerable points or weaknesses in our political and party fabric today. Such personnel policy and political

involvement broadens the space for 'politics as the sleight of hand,' or Machiavellianism and reduces the room for creative activity especially in the sphere of associated labour." *Nedeljne Informativne Novine*, (April 20, 1980), 9.

42. The surveys also indicate that "moral-political fitness" is a less important recruitment criterion at the lower levels of the delegate structure, for example, among voters at meetings to select members of delegations. I. Perko-Šeparović, *Analiza zborova birača u izbornim procesima* (Zagreb: Institut za politička nauka FPN, 1979), 111-119. Moreover, whatever criteria are used the League of Communists and other socio-political organizations play the dominant role in the recruitment process. Ivan Grdešić, *Neki aspekti izbora delegata u općinsku skupštinu*, 45-60.

43. Gyorgy Konrad and Ivan Szelenyi, *The Intellectuals on the Road to Class Power* (New York: Harcourt, Brace, Jovanovich, 1979), 191. When Yugoslavia's Prime Minister, Milka Planinc, was asked in April 1983 whether she had considered recruiting "more young blood" into her cabinet, she answered that she "needed people with experience who could enter the government and make decisions the next day .... I do not think that all these individuals must necessarily have grey hair, but the problem is that today ... there are not many of these 30-year old individuals whom I would like to have in the Federal Executive Council .... Anyone who joins the Federal Executive Council either to head a department or on the basis of the parity distribution of positions must have political experience and must be an expert in his field." *Nedeljne Informativne Novine*, No. 1685, (April 17, 1983), 11. Yugoslav sociologists have shown that the combined emphasis on political loyalty and technical expertise in elite selection has meant that technical specialists, managers, and other highly educated members of the "middle classes" have replaced the blue collar working class as the "recruitment reservoir" for political elites. See Danilo Mrkšić, "Podela rada i stratifikacija Jugoslovenskog društva" and Mladen Lazić, "Mobilnost i homogenizacija vladajuće klase u Hrvatskoj," *Revija za sociologiju*, XVI, Nos. 1-4 (Winter, 1986), 3-17 and 57-66, and Duško Selulić, "Regrutacija na elitne položaje," *Sociologija*, XXIX, No. 3 (1987), 411-425.

44. Ten members of the 1986 Committee are under 27 years of age. Less important, except symbolically, 16.3 percent of the Committee are from "material production," i.e., workers and farmers,

compared to six percent in 1982. *Politika*, (June 28, 1986), 1 and (June 29, 1986), 2.

45. One analysis of the activities leading up to the recent changes in the party leadership observed that the "long-heralded process of cadre renovation with new, younger, and professional people is not exactly easy and painless. There are many who believe that their pensioning and falling out is the 'end of the revolution' and therefore they tenaciously struggle to 'save' it by postponing their departure from the political scene at least for another four years." *Borba*, (April 3, 1982), 2.

46. *Borba*, (September 22, 1980), 6.

47. The major 1987 financial scandal centered around mismanagement by the directors of the Bosnian economic enterprise Agrokomerc, and was dubbed by some Yugoslav observors as "Agrogate." The scandal not only involved enormous sums of money and touched 63 Yugoslav banks but also led to the resignation of the Bosnian representative in the nine-member collective state Presidency who was scheduled to become the head of that body in 1988. Todor Kuljic has argued that difficulties which arise from trying to reconcile a market economy with a decentralized state administration and a one-party political leadership contribute to considerable confusion in the criteria and methods used in Yugoslav personnel recruitment as well as for the country's economic "irrationality" and political crisis in the 1980's. "Modeli birokratije i kadrovska uprava razvijenog socijalizma," *Gledišta*, XXVII, Nos. 9-10 (September-October, 1986), 3-47.

48. Yugoslavia's Constitutional Court recently annulled a "social compact" on personnel policy adopted by socio-political organizations in Kosovo which would have required representation in socio-political bodies to be directly proportional to the ethnic structure of the population. *Foreign Broadcast Information Service*, (April 11, 1986), I6. The Croatian sociologist, Vjeran Katunarić, has argued that the ideological principle of social equality has been superceded by the norm of ethno-regional equality in Yugoslav elite recruitment and that this has contributed to an "equality of oligarchies which operates on the standards of the division and allocation of resources, based upon the parity or quota system .... Such a situation produces the closure of federal units, whose political elites solidify their linkages to local economic and cultural elites. This results in

a system of power which always has three parts: political authority, economic power, and cultural intelligence as sources for the legitmation of power." "Sistem moći, socijalna struktura i nacionalno pitanju," *Revija za sociologiju*, XVI, Nos. 1-4 (Winter, 1986), 75-89.

49.   *Nedeljne Informativne Novine*, No. 1851 (June 22, 1986), 38. Some Yugoslav social scientists maintain that direct competitive legislative elections - albeit one-party contests - are essential for democratization of the recruitment process: "The indirect elections conducted in our country," argues Vladimir Goati, "result among other things, in the strengthening of narrow informal groups (characteristic of 'personnel commissions,' 'personnel bodies,' 'narrow personnel organs') which far from public view decide on the delegates who will serve at the highest levels of the political pyramid and that inevitably leads to a negative selection of personnel. The key criteria for such selection isn't capability, but subject-like loyalty toward the real stage managers of the 'electoral dance' in which Yugoslav voters are only unimportant scenery. Perhaps this is the greatest societal evil, because the formation of a capable leading stratum which enjoys the confidence of citizens is one of the essential preconditions for getting out of the societal crisis." *Nedeljne Informativne Novine*, No. 1920, (October 18, 1987), 22-23. Multi-candidate direct elections for Yugoslav legislative assemblies will probably be reintroduced through constitutional amendments in 1988.

EPILOGUE
THE PYRAMID IMPERILED

All of us in this country are faced with a choice - either we all resolve this together or we all head to destruction.
  Stipe Šuvar, President of the
  League of Yugoslav Communists (1988)

... there is no way out under this system .... We will go deeper into the crisis and the party will continue to disintegrate.
  Milovan Djilas (1988)

Political instability in Yugoslavia increased sharply during 1988, as ethnic relations and the economic situation of the country continued to deteriorate. Despite a plethora of institutionalized channels for citizen self-management, strikes and public demonstrations became the preferred mode of participation for groups expressing strong dissatisfaction with the management of the economy and political system. Unpopular government-sponsored economic controls proved unable to reverse sky-rocketing inflation, mounting unemployment, food shortages, and a huge foreign debt. According to official figures, salaries in Yugoslavia dropped by 24 percent in 1988 and living conditions plunged to the level of the mid-1960's.[1]

Throughout Yugoslavia, but especially within the Serbian and Albanian ethnic groups, economic discontent became closely intermingled with growing ethno-regional nationalism. The Serbs (and their close ethnic cousins, the Montenegrins) were particularly outraged at the serious problems faced by their ethnic brethern in the predominantly Albanian province of Kosovo, a region which has been a volatile zone of inter-nationality conflict throughout the post-Tito era (see Chapter 8).² Ethnic tensions in Serbia reached an especially high pitch during 1988, after seven years of constant media emphasis on alleged acts of Albanian "terrorism" against Serbs and Mongenegrins. The approaching 600th anniversary of the legendary 1389 Serbian defeat by a Moslem army in Kosovo — which seared the goal of recovering the region (a feat not achieved until 1912) deeply into the Serbian collective psyche — promised to add even more fuel to the already heated relations between Albanians and Serbs.

From the perspective of the major themes and theoretical issues discussed in this book, two related aspects of the 1988 Yugoslav crisis are most significant: 1) the rapid erosion of popular support for the country's ruling party and political elite, and; 2) the growing appeal to nationalist sentiments by regional and ethnic leaders seeking a new basis for career advancement and political legitimacy.

Delegitimation of an Elite: The New Class in Crisis

Since the early 1950's, Yugoslav communism has been reknowned for its ideological commitment to the democratization of socialism and the reduction of centralized bureaucratic methods. Vocal criticism of class inequalities, elite privileges, and the foibles of state and party bureaucrats has also been a conventional feature of Yugoslav political discourse. Typically, the expression of anti-elitist and anti-bureaucratic sentiments was an intramural matter for the political elite, as well as a subject of discussion among a relatively small number of establishment academics and dissident intellectuals. Periodic media and political campaigns criticizing communist officialdom's more conspicuous consumption (e.g., the size and number of "weekend houses," hunting preserves, automobiles, etc.), were relatively tame affairs, and had little effect on the structure of power and privilege. It was only in the second half of the 1980's, primarily as a result of the deepening economic crisis, that populist or extra-institutional protests against political elitism and bureaucratic authority spilled into the streets and seriously destabilized the political system. By 1988, shrill anti-elitist chants and slogans ("thieves," "down with the arm-chair officials," "you betrayed the people," "how much do you earn?" etc.) had become a prominent element in mass rallies which sought changes in the leadership of the League of Communists.

The rapid delegitimation of the Yugoslav political leadership during the 1980's, was rather surprising to most domestic and foreign observers. The wartime communist struggle, Tito's bold declaration of independence from the Soviet camp, and the formulation of a unique socialist model, had all provided the Yugoslav elite with a level of political legitimacy and cohesion rarely found

The Socialist Pyramid: Elites and Power in Yugoslavia

in communist regimes (Chapters 2 and 3). The heterogeneity of the Yugoslav elite was considerable in terms of its diverse ethno-regional identities and interests, but the many socio-political bonds and shared values uniting the elite were also quite impressive. The preservation of elite cohesion from the early 1950's to the late 1970's, can be traced to the astute mixture of authoritarian and quasi-democratic methods employed by Tito and his chief lieutenants. When serious inter-regional conflicts resurfaced and progressively deepened following the regime's liberalization in the mid-1960's, Tito periodically intervened to quell the most nationalistic party voices and manufacture temporary elite harmony. Yugoslavia's elaboration of novel socialist institutions for citizen participation in political and economic affairs also gave the regime an unusual veneer of vitality and democratic commitment that was frequently heralded both internally and abroad.

Tito's death not only removed the principal symbol of the regime's legitimacy, but also the only public figure able to forge — or, if necessary force — a working consensus among the increasingly divided political elite. Although long accustomed to lively factional struggles and sharp polemical exchanges among its leading cadre, the regime found itself facing a deep-seated crisis of legitimacy. A younger and quite highly educated generation of the political elite did manage to acquire influential positions in the mid-1980's, but this new group proved no more successful than earlier leaders at resolving the country's serious problems. Moreover, the routine oligarchical methods which were used in selecting the new elite generation, as well as that elite's generally conservative commitment to traditional policy perspectives, inspired little public confidence that a solution to the country's crisis was forthcoming. Revelations of widespread corruption in leading political circles (e.g., the Bosnian "Agrokomerc affair" of 1987 which led to the removal of several prominent regional and federal officials), also weakened public support for the political elite and the regime which they directed. Thus, when public protests regarding economic conditions moved from the workplace (there were approximately 1,500 strikes in 1987) into the streets during 1988, it was not surprising that the entire stratum or elite of professional politicians, and the very organization of Yugoslav socialism, became targets of popular dirision. As the spiral of economic decline continued, together with heightened anxiety throughout the country about the regime's management of ethnic and regional issues, the already tenuous legitimacy of Tito's heirs rapidly evaporated. Citizens, who in good economic times had cynically tolerated elite privileges and the routine use of political cronyism in elite selection, were unwilling to accept such practices when their own standard of living was clearly at stake. Despite the comprehensive 'restructuring' of the communist regime on a more democratic basis over the previous four decades, even loyal party members found it difficult to justify the glaring gap between the rhetoric and the reality of self-management socialism.

Lenard J. Cohen

Although reeling from the serious mass protests against their managerial record, the political elite, quite naturally, remained committed to both its "vanguard" role and the regime's single-party structure. As one of Yugoslavia's most prominent political scientists recently observed about his country's ruling stratum:

> From the standpoint of the special interest of the stratum of party and state professional functionaries the ideology of self-management is, in terms of its consequences, an ideology of self-destruction .... Thus, all radical demands, and even measures of a more modest scope, aimed at reducing and finally eliminating bureaucratic paternalism over self-management-based relations and institutions have met inevitably with spontaneous or deliberate resistance within the powerful stratum of professional rulers, including part of the party leadership ....
> Despite all the genuine democratic changes that have taken place in Yugoslav society during the past decades, one thing that has actually remained untouched is the monopoly of the "narrow political circle 'over' personnel policy" i.e., over the recruitment of political personnel and distribution of political and other executive functions. This monopoly is the main source of arbitrary bureaucratic power in Yugoslavia.³

Temporarily at least, the large and angry public demonstrations of 1988 introduced a new and unprogramed element into the recruitment of Yugoslav political leaders. Thus, mass demonstrations in October by thousands of Serbs protesting economic trends and the plight of their ethnic group in Kosovo, forced the resignation of the entire party leadership in one province, the "retirement" of several top leaders, and prompted calls for significant "cadre renewal" throughout the political struture.⁴

Nationalism as an Elite Resource: The Milošević Phenomenon

Throughout Yugoslav communist history some party leaders have regarded ethnic tension not as a danger, but as an opportunity. In the late 1960's and early 1970's, for example, several leading Croatian party leaders tapped the nationalism that was sweeping their republic in order to build a popular base of support. A similar development occurred in the province of Kosovo between 1968 to 1981, when the regime's unprecedented tolerance for ethno-regional autonomy in that area allowed local Albanian leaders to politically mobilize the long-supressed aspirations of their ethnic group. The elite use of nationalism for building regional political machines in Croatia and Kosovo was eventually terminated by the intervention of central political authorities, but only after local

The Socialist Pyramid: Elites and Power in Yugoslavia

expressions of nationalism exceeded the boundaries of acceptable dissent and challenged the fundamental authority of the socialist regime.

Although reacting strongly against any "anti-socialist" manifestations of nationalism, the Yugoslav regime's commitment (from the mid-1960's onward) to a pluralist brand of socialism permitted a considerable devolution of central authority to the republics and provinces. The Constitution of 1974 significantly advanced such centrifugal tendencies in the Yugoslav federal system, and resulted — particularly after Tito's departure in 1980 — in a very significant growth in the power of regional political elites (see Chapter 9). The territorial and ethnic "pluralism of elites" which became the hallmark of the post-Tito period, together with the delegitimation of the incumbent party leadership during the crisis of the 1980's, dramatically expanded opportunities for the use of nationalism as a political resource.

The most successful Yugoslav communist functionary to exploit ethnic nationalism as a political tool in recent years has been Slobodan Milošević, the President of the Serbian republic's party organization since 1986.[5] Associating himself with growing Serbian outrage about both the Kosovo issue and economic conditions in the country, Milošević deftly engineered the removal of regional Serbian political and media leaders who were considered to be "soft" on the issue of Albanian nationalism. Milošević also endorsed new constitutional provisions which would reassert the firm control of Serbian republican authorities over the autonomous provinces of Kosovo and Vojvodina (the latter, although predominantly Serbian in ethnic composition, has tended to protest the hegemony of officials in Belgrade).[6] In effect, Milošević exploited a backlash of Serbian nationalism in order to build a cross-regional alliance of ethnic Serbs unprecedented in Yugoslavia since the formation of Tito's World War II Partisan movement (which also, although having a multi-ethnic leadership, heavily exploited reactive Serbian nationalism in attracting recruits). When mass protest demonstrations of Serbs and Montenegrins took place in Kosovo, Serbia, Vojvodina and Montenegro in 1987 and 1988, "Sloba" Milošević emerged as a hero to the crowds. After years of reporting on the relatively faceless and uninspiring post-Tito elite, Yugoslav commentators recognized the new and unconventional personality in their midst.

He has become the most popular Serbian politician. A well known Kosovo poet has written a poem about 'the sun gliding through his rough hair' and most prominent heads of Kosovo households have stated that '200,000 Kosovo Serbs are behind Sloba' .... He solved the problem of credibility and legitimacy through plebicite-type support. He was the first party leader to be inaugurated as the people's leader and not as head of the 'workers class vanguard,' and he defined his program as being one of an 'energetic approach and unity' contrary to the other school which advocated 'dialogue and democratization.' Mass support strengthened Milosevic's position at the top of the

Lenard J. Cohen

federal party .... It is an irrefutable fact, however, that he has pawned his 'political head,' promising to his people results and changes![7]

While both the explosive Albanian issue and economic problems were certainly important catalysts for the outbreak of Serbian nationalism, a large number of Serbs also harboured a more general dissatisfaction with recent trends in political development. For example, the regime's decentralizing policies and constitutional initiatives during the two decades after 1967 were viewed by many Serbs as having seriously weakened the influence of both their republic and their ethnic group (the largest in the country) in the Yugoslav federation. As the core nationality in the 1918 creation of the original Yugoslav state, and also the group which predominated in the ranks of the wartime communist movement (mainly Serbs outside central Serbia), Milošević's ethnic brethren feel that they have a very strong basis for voicing their dissatisfaction with recent constitutional development.

The pluralizing tendencies of Yugoslavia's "confederal" constitutional system are also blamed for the country's recent economic decline. Thus, from the Serbian vantage point, constitutional imperatives requiring the representation and lengthy coordination of the country's many ethnic and regional interests, including the accommodation of smaller but ethnically aggressive nationalities such as the Albanians, prevent the central government from decisively responding to the economic crisis. Excessive concern with "ethnic arithmetic" in elite selection is also viewed in many quarters as having prevented the selection of a technically qualified and influential team of central officials. Thus, even many Serbian intellectuals and dissidents (including Milovan Djilas) who have reservations about Milošević's demagogic methods and his support for the policy of the "hard hand" are, nevertheless, impressed with his commitment to "Serbian rights" and disdain for elite mismanagement and corruption. Indeed, the Milošević program might be termed *ethno-technocratic populism*, a simultaneous appeal to both mass ethnically-based sentiments and the widespread conviction that economic competence should replace political and ideological credentials in elite recruitment.

For many Yugoslav leaders, Milošević is seen as a dangerous political opportunist who has imperiled the communist regime. His appeals to Serbian nationalism in 1988 have not only inflamed relations between the nationalities in his own republic, but have the potential of provoking similar behaviour by ambitious leaders of other groups and regions. Such encouragement to intra-elite fragmentation flies directly in the face of Titoism's approach to the nationality question: i.e., maintaining the broad "class" ties of the party leadership across Yugoslavia in order to transcend the limited autonomy permitted to each regional and ethnic group.[8] In the eyes of his critics, however, Milošević's most grievous error may have been to exacerbate virulent Serbian nationalism, namely, the very force that obstructed ethnic peace in pre-communist Yugoslavia and foreshadowed the bloody inter-nationality struggles during World War II. Indeed, by the Fall of 1988, Milošević had come under sharp attack from his colleagues for having fanned ethnic unrest and party disunity. Janez Stanovnik, Slovenia's top state official, was perhaps the most blunt in describing the Milošević brand of charismatic nationalist leadership: "When you start worshipping a leader you no longer have a population that is able to act democratically ... Earlier I advocated the view that we should talk to Milošević .... I'm sorry I don't see any more the point of talking. I saw him yesterday but turned to another circle of people. I knew we had nothing to talk about."[9] Stanovnik's comments came only two weeks after the resignation of Slovenia's representative on the party Politburo who claimed that he was "afraid of people who manipulate the grievances and emotions of Serbs and Montenegrins in Kosovo."[10]

Considering Yugoslav communism's strong antipathy to overt nationalist tactics, and particularly the historic opposition to Serbian nationalism on the part of leaders from the other major nationalities, it is very doubtful that an ethnic spokesman such as Milošević can capitalize on his sectarian success and emerge as a "second Tito." Although his technocratic support for market-oriented economic reforms is very attractive in liberal circles throughout Yugoslavia, Milošević's crowd-oriented ethnic rhetoric has won him few friends among the non-Serbian members of the communist elite.[11] At a time of diminished elite legitimacy, the mobilization of mass fervour is a disquieting experience even for those who desire radical improvements in the existing regime. Whether the powerful emotional force unleashed by Milošević would catapult the young Serbian leader further up the socialist pyramid, sacrifice him to the outraged justice of his less ethnically sectarian comrades, or radically alter the very shape of the Yugoslav communist state, remained very open questions near the close of 1988.

NOTES: EPILOGUE

1. At the end of October, 1988, the government eased an austerity program of wage cuts introduced in May, but only for workers in profitable companies and in hard-pressed social services such as health and education. It is estimated that approximately half of Yugoslavia's firms, employing more than two million workers are unprofitable and will not be able to increase wages. At the same time, prices for meat and bread rose sharply.

2. The proportional size of Kosovo's Albanian population rose from approximately 78 percent in 1981 to nearly 90 percent in 1988, due to the group's record high birthrate (5 and 1/2 times the rate in the developed part of the country), and the outmigration of Serbs and Montenegrins. According to estimates, early in the first part of the 21st century, Kosovo's population will exceed that of neighbouring Albania.

3. Najdan Pašić, "From Party-State Monolithism to Pluralism of Self-Management Interests," *Socialist Thought and Practice*, XXVIII, No. 3-4, 79-80, 83. Pašić's preceding article is a translation of his earlier article in *Socijalizam*, XXX, No. 9 (1987), 3-16.

4. Among those resigning from the 23-member party Politburo in October, 1988 as a result of mass demonstrations and the growing crisis were two recent Presidents of the League of Communists (Bosnia's Milanko Renovica and Vojvodina's Boško Krunić) who had seemed to represent the advent to power of a new elite generation when they had assumed top posts only a few years earlier. A meeting of the party Central Committee in mid-October failed to produce major changes in the country's political leadership as expected, but did recommend that at least one-third of their membership be rotated by the end of the year.

5. Slobodan Milošević is a literal "child of the revolution." He was born on August 29, 1941, four months after Yugoslavia's dismemberment by Nazi Germany and its allies, and two months after Tito and the Yugoslav Communist Party began a guerrilla struggle against both the fascist occupation and those supporting the interwar power structure. Thus, Milošević was only seven years old at the time of the Tito-Stalin rift and just ten when "workers' self-management" became the ideological platform of the communist

state. It is worth considering that the most formative stage of Milošević's education and career development from 1961 to 1986, coincides with the reemergence and official recognition of internationality conflicts in Yugoslav political life.

The son of a Serbian orthodox clergyman of Montenegrin ethnic background, Milošević received a law degree from Belgrade University before entering a managerial career in manufacturing and banking. After rising to become the President of a major bank in Belgrade, Milošević entered Belgrade urban politics in the early 1980's, and in 1986 was selected to head the Serbian republic's party organization.

6. On October 22, 1988, the Yugoslav federal legistature adopted a package of amendments giving Serbia more control over its autonomous provinces, but strong opposition to the constitutional proposals is expected when they are considered for approval by the legislatures of Yugoslavia's individual republics and provinces.

7. *FBIS-EEU-88-004* (January 7, 1988), 49-50. In speeches, Milošević makes no apologies for his mass support, and differentiates it from the "mass-movement" in Croatia at the beginning of the 1970's. As he told Serbian republic officials: "Of course masses can be the carrier of conservative ideas, intolerance, and hate toward other nations and peoples ... but, in this case evidently it isn't so. Because in Serbia, as everyone knows today, there isn't one place nor one locale where someone is discriminated against because he isn't a Serb. *Nedeljne Informative Novine* (September 11, 1988), No. 1967, 9.

8 The absence of a unified elite strategy to deal with the management of ethnic conflict has been an important factor in the prolonged Yugoslav crisis of the 1980's. A prominent party theoretician on nationality affairs observed, for example, that while the "leading social forces" of the country were very "allergic to all manifestations of nationalism ... one can perceive — even in the ranks of the league of Communists of Yugoslavia — phenomena of some incomplete research, wandering, and certain differences in approaches and options." Kiro Hadži-Vasilev, "Relations Between the Nationalities in the Conditions of Socialist Self-Management," *Socialist Thought and Practice*, XXVIII, No. 3-4 (1988), 64-65.

9. *New York Times* (October 15, 1988), 4

10. *Globe and Mail* (September 27, 1988), 6. While Slovenian politicians have been in the forefront of attacks on Milošević, he also has been opposed by Croatian leaders and a minority of leading Serbian political figures opposed to his exploitation of nationalist passions. In September, 1988, a journalist of the Zagreb weekly *Danas*, described Milošević as "Serbia's Tripalo," a reference to Mika Tripalo, the top ranking Croatian party leader who Tito purged in December, 1971, for having been overly tolerant of nationalism in Croatia. *Radio Free Europe Report* (September 9, 1988), 15.

11. At a meeting in mid-October, Central Committee members voted against renewing a key Milošević ally on the party Politburo, but the move only intensified nationalist emotions among the Serbian population and its leadership.

BIBLIOGRAPHY

Books (In the Languages of Yugoslavia)

Almanah Kraljevine Jugoslavije: IV. Jubilarni svezak 1929-1931. Zagreb, 1932.

Berković, Eva, *Socijalne Nejednakosti u Jugoslaviji.* Belgrade: Ekonomika, 1986.

Bićanić, Rudolf. *Ekonomska podloga Hrvatskog pitanja.* Zagreb: Stjepan Vidović, 1938.

Bilandžić, Dušan. *Jugoslavija poslije Tita 1980-1985.* Zagreb. Globus, 1986.

Blagojević, Borislav. *Položaj i uloga društveno-političkih organizacija u us tavnim i političkim sistemu SFRJ.* Belgrade: Savremena administracja, 1977.

Bolčić, Silvan. *Razvoj i kriza Jugoslovenskog društva u sociološkoj perspek tivi.* Belgrade: Studentski izdavački centar univerzitetske konferencije SSO Belgrade, 1983.

Borba za oslobodjenje Jugoslavije 1941-1944, Second Edition. Belgrade: Državni izdavački zavod Jugoslavije, 1945.

Bottomore, Thomas, *Elite i društvu.* Belgrade: Sedma sila, 1967.

Čemerlić, Hamdija. *Mesto i uloga odbora i komisija predstavnickih tela.* Ed. Borislav Blagojević, Belgrade: Saveza udruženja pravnika Jugoslavija, 1969.

Čolaković, Rodoljub. *Kazivanje o jednom pokoljenju, Volume 2.* Zagreb: Naprijed, 1968.

—. *Zapisi iz oslobodilačkog rata.* Sarajevo: Svjetlost, 1948.

Lenard J. Cohen

Čulinović, Ferdo. *Pravosudje u Jugoslaviji*. Zagreb: Nakladni zavod Hrvatske, 1946.

Damjanović, Milica. *Napredni studentski pokret na Beogradskom Univerzitetu, 1929-1941*. Volume II. Belgrade: Nolit, 1974.

Dedijer, Vladimir. *Jugoslovensko - Albanski odnosi*. Belgrade: Borba, 1949.

Dedijer, Vladimir. Rudolf Rizman, Momčilo Stefanović, and Mirjana Stojanović (eds.). *Svedočanstva o drugom svetskom ratu*. Belgrade: Narodna knjiga/Partizanska knjiga, 1980.

Definitivni rezultati popisa stanovništva od 31 marta 1931 godine. Knjiga IV prisutno stanovništvo po glavnom zanimanju. Sarajevo: Opšta Državna Statistika, 1940.

Deveti Kongres Saveza komunista Jugoslavije. Belgrade: Komunist, 1970.

Djordjević, Jovan. *Ogled o birokratiji i birokratizmu*. Belgrade: Kultura, 1962.

Djordjević, Živorad. *Za i protiv inteligencije*. Belgrade: SSO Srbije, 1981.

Dragosavac, Dušan. *Aktualni aspekti nacionalnog pitanja i Jugoslavija*. Zagreb: Globus, 1985.

Gersković, Leon. *Državna uprava*. Belgrade: Savez udruženja pravnika Jugoslavije, 1956.

Grdešić, Ivan. *Neki aspekti izbora delegata u općinsku skupstinu*. Zagreb: Institut za političke nauke Fakulteta političkih nauka, 1980.

Guzina, Ružica. *Opština u Kneževini i Kraljevini Srbiji 1804-1839*. Belgrade: Institut za pravnu istoriju, 1966.

—. *Opština u Srbiji 1839-1918*. Belgrade: Rad, 1976.

Janićijević, Milosav. *Stvaralačka inteligencija medjuratne Jugoslavije*. Belgrade: Institut društvenih nauka, 1984.

Jončić, Koča. *Medjunacionalni odnosi i idejno politicko delovanje Saveza Komunista-Jugoslavije.* Belgrade: Centar za političke studije i obrazovanje, 1967.

Jovanov, Neca. *Dijagnoza samoupravljanja 1974-1981.* Zagreb: Sveučilišta naklada liber, 1983.

Jovanović, Milan. *Porota u pravosudju Jugoslavije.* Belgrade: Savremena administracija, 1958.

Jovanović, Žarko. *KPJ prema seljastvu, 1919-1941.* Belgrade Narodna knjiga, 1984.

Jugoslovenski savremenici, Ko je ko u Jugoslaviji. Belgrade: Hronometer, 1969.

Kardelj, Edward. *Neka pitanja daljeg razvoja skupštinskog i političkog sistem.* Belgrade: Sekretarijat za informativnu službu Savezne Skupština, 1967.

—. *Pravci i razvoja političkog sistem socijalističkog samoupravljanja.* Belgrade: Komunist, 1978.

Klisinski, Angel. *Uloga organa uprave odnoso stručnih službi radnih organizacija u normativnoj delatnosti skupštine društveno-političkih zajednica odnoso organa upravljanja radnih organizacija.* Belgrade: Jugoslovenski savez udruženja za upravne nauke i praksu, 1969.

Ko je ko u Jugosaviji: Biografski podaci o Jugoslovenskim savremenicima. Belgrade: Sedma sila, 1957.

Ko je ko u Jugoslaviji. Belgrade and Zagreb: Jugoslovenski godišnjak and Nova Eruopa, 1928.

Konačni rezultati popisa stanovništva od 15 marta 1948 godine knjiga IX stanovništvo po narodnosti. Belgrade: Savezni zavod za statisiku, 1954.

Konferencija Saveza Komunista Jugoslavije održana od 29 do 31, oktobra 1970. Belgrade: Komunist, 1971.

Kongresi Saveza Komunist Republika, 1965. Belgrade: Sedma sila, 1965.

Krasnici, Mark. *Savremene društveno-geografske promene na Kosovu i Metohiji*. Priština: Muzej Kosova i Metohije, 1963.

Kulundžić, Zvonimir. *Politika korupcija u Kraljevskoj Jugoslaviji*. Zagreb: Stvarnost, 1968.

Kumulativni statistički pregled rada skupstinških tela u periodu od 15.05 1974 do 15.05 1978 godine. Belgrade: Skupština SFRJ, Služba za informativno-dokumentalističke poslove, 1978.

Leko, Ivan. *Velike revolucije i obrazovanje*. Belgrade: Zavod za izdavanje udžbenika Socijalističke Republike Srbije, 1968.

Marinković, Radovoje. *Delegatski sistem: funkcionisanje i ostvarivanje*. Belgrade: Institut za političke studije Fakulteta političkih nauka, 1979.

Marjanović, Jovan. *Delegatski sistem i političke studije*. Belgrade: Fakultet političkih nauka, 1978.

Matić, Milan. *Politička misao Rajta Milsa*. Belgrade: Institut društvenih nauka, 1966.

—. *Skupštinski i delegatski sistem*. Belgrade: Delta Press, 1975.

Milić, Vladimir. *Revolucija i socijalna struktura*. Belgrade: Mladost, 1978.

Miljanić, Gojko. *Kadrovi revolucije, 1941-1945*. Cetinje: Obod, 1975.

—. *Rukovodjenje komandovanje u oslobodilačkom ratu, 1941-1945*. Belgrade: Vojnoistorijski institut, 1980.

Mills, C. Wright. *Elita vlasti*. Belgrade: kultura, 1964.

Miloslaveski, Slavko and Milan Nedkov. *Uloga i položaj državne uprave u našem samoupravnom društvu*. Belgrade: Jugoslavenski savez udruženja za upravne nauke i praksu, 1970.

Mirić, Jovan. *Sistema i kriza*. Zagreb: Cekade, 1984.

Mitrović, Milovan. *Jugoslovenska predratna sociologija*. Belgrade: SSO Srbije, 1982.

Neka iskustava iz dosadašnjeg rada saveznog vijeća i njegovih radnih tijela. Belgrade: Skupština SFRJ, Savezno vijeće, 1975.

Neka zapažanja iz dosadašnjeg rada veća Republika i Pokrajina period od 14. maja 1974 do kraja 1975 godine. Belgrade: Skupština SFRJ Veće Republika i pokrajina, 1976.

Nikolić, Pavle. *Skupstinški sistem.* Belgrade: Savremena administracjia, 1973.

Normativna delatnost društveno-političkih zajednica: priručnik za kadrove u državnim organima i stručnim služba posebno opštinskim. Belgrade: Republicki zavod za javnu upravu, 1967.

Novosel, Pavle. *Delegatško informiranje.* Zagreb: Centar za informicije i publicitet, 1977.

Obradović, Sava *et. al. Stanovnistva Narodne Republika Srbije od 1834-1953.* Belgrade: Zavod za statistiku i evidencija, 1953.

Osmi Kongres SKJ: Stenografska beleška. Belgrade: Kultura, 1965.

Pantić, Dragomir. *Etnička distanca u SFRJ.* Belgrade: Institut društvenih nauka, 1967.

Pečujlić, Miroslav. *Društvene grupe i politički zivot.* Belgrade: Komunist, 1969.

—. *Klase i savremeno društvo.* Belgrade: Savremena administracjia, 1967.

—. *Promene u socijalnoj strukturi Jugoslavije.* Belgrade: Visoka škola političkih nauka, 1963.

—. *Studija za političke sociologije.* Belgrade: Visoka škola političkih nauka, 1965.

Pegan, Sergije. *Skupstinški izbori, 1965.* Belgrade: Institut društvenih nauka, 1966.

Perić, Ivan. *Ideje "masovnog pokreta" u Hrvatskoj.* Zagreb: Centar za aktualni politički studij, 1974.

Lenard J. Cohen

Perko-Šeparović, I. *Analiza zborova birača u izbornim procesima*. Zagreb: Institut za političke nauke FPN, 1979.

Petranović, Branko. *AVNOJ-Revolucionarna smena vlasti: 1942-1945*. Belgrade: Nolit, 1976.

—. *Politička i ekonomska osnova narodne vlasti u Jugoslaviji za vreme obnove*. Belgrade: Institut za savremenu istoriju, 1969.

—. *Revolucija i kontrarevolucija u Jugoslaviji (1941-1945). Volume II*. Belgrade: Rad, 1983.

Pleterski, Janko et. al. *Istorija Saveza Komunista Jugoslavije*. Belgrade: Komunist, 1985.

Politički i poslovni imenik SFR Jugoslavije 1972. Belgrade: Tanjug, February 18, 1972.

Politički i poslovni imenik. Belgrade: Tanjug, October 15, 1978; 1979, 1980 supplements.

Politički i poslovni imenik, III Deo, Biografije. Belgrade: Dokumentacija Tanjuga, October 15, 1978, December 12, 1979.

Popis stanovništva 1953. Knjiga I. Vitalna i etnička obeležja. Belgrade: Savezni zavod za statistiku, 1959.

Popović, Mihailo et. al. *Društveni slojevi i društvena svest*. Belgrade: Centar za sociološka istraživanja, Institut društvenih nauka, 1977.

Prica, Bogdan. *Hrvatsko pitanje i brojke*. Belgrade: Javnost, 1937.

Pusić, Eugun. *Samoupravljanje: Prilozi teoriji i praktični problemi*. Zagreb: Narodne novine, 1968.

Radonjić, R. *Sukob KPJ i Kominform i društveni razvoj Jugoslavije (1948-1950)*. Zagreb: Centar za kulturnu djelatnost, 1979.

Ribičič, Ciril. *Razvoj skupščinskega sistema v Jugoslaviji*. Ljubljana: Pravna Fakulteta v Ljubljana, 1978.

Savezna narodna skupština izabran 22 i 23 novembra 1953 godine. Belgrade: Sedma sila, 1955.

Sekulić, Duško. "Regrutacija no elitne položaje," *Sociologia*, XXIX, No. 3 (1987): 411-425.

Šesti Kongres Saveza Komunista Hrvatska, Stenografske belješke, Zagreb December 5-7, 1968, Volume III. Zagreb: Komunist, 1969.

Seton-Watson, R.W. *R.W. Seton-Watson i Jugoslaveni: Korespondencija 1906-1941, Volume II*. Zagreb, London: Sveučilište u Zagrebu/British Academy, 1976.

Šiber Ivan. *Delegatski sistem i izbori procesi*. Zagreb: Institut za političke studije Fakulteta političkih nauka, 1979.

Simovska, Lidija et. al. *Funkcioniranjeto i ostvarivanjeto delegatskiot sistem vo opštinite vo SRM*. Skopje: Institut za sociološki i političko-pravnia istrauvania, Fakultet za pravni i politički nauki, 1979.

Šnuderl, M. *Zgodovina ljudske oblasti*. Ljubljana: Državna založba Slovenije, 1950.

Stanojević, Stanoje (ed.). *Narodna enciklopedija srpsko-hrvatsko-slov enačka*. Belgrade: Bibliografski zavod, 1929.

Stanovništvo SR Srbija, Osnovna obeležja za aktivnoj stanovništvo u zemlji. Belgrade: Republicki zavod za statistiku, September, 1985.

Statistički godišnjak, knjiga I. Belgrade, 1932.

Statistički godišnjak Kraljevine Hrvatske Slavonije, Volume I (1905). Zagreb, 1913.

Statistika izbora narodnih poslanika Kraljevine Srba, Hrvata, i Slovenaca. Belgrade: Narodna Skupština, 1924, 1926, 1928.

Statistika izbora narodnih poslanika za Narodnu Skupštinu Kraljevine Jugoslavije. Belgrade: Narodna Skupština, 1932, 1938.

Statistika Kraljevine Srbije, XIII. Belgrade, 1899.

Statistički pregled izbora narodnih poslanika za Ustavatvornu Skupštinu Kraljevine Srba, Hrvata i Slovenaca. Belgrade: Narodna Skupština, 1921.

Stipetić, Zorica. *Komunistički pokret i inteligencija: Istraživanja ideološkog i političkog djelovanja inteligencije u Hrvatskoj (1918-1945)*. Zagreb: Centar za Kulturnu djelatnost, 1980.

Stojanović, Alexander. *Uloga funkcionera i upravnih stručnjaka u razovju javne uprave*. Belgrade: Savez udruženja pravnika Jugoslavija, 1965.

Supek, Rudi and Maja Minček. *Likovni Stvaraoci i kultura sredina*. Zagreb: Institut za društvena iztraživanja sveučilišta u Zagrebu, 1970.

Supek, Rudi. *Humanistička inteligencija i politika*. Zagreb: Razlog, 1971.

Šuvar, Stipe. *Samoupravljanje i alternative*. Zagreb: Centar za kulturnu djelatnost Saveza Socijalističke Omladine Zagreba, 1978.

—. *Sociološki presjek Jugoslovenskog društva*. Zagreb: Školska knjiga, 1970.

Tomić, Stojan. *Politički profesionalizam*. Sarajevo: Institut za društvena istraživanja Fakulteta političkih nauka, 1972.

—. *Profesionalizam u politici*. Belgrade: Radnička stampa, 1975.

Toš, Niko. *Pregled skupnih podatkov iz raziskave poslanska aktivnost*. Ljubljana: Visoka šola za sociologijo politične vede in novinarstvo- Centar za raziskovanje javnog menja, 1968.

V. Kongres Komunistične Partije Jugoslavije. Ljubljana: Cankarjeva založba, 1948.

Vreg, France. *Delegatski sistem v SR Sloveniji*. Ljubljana: Centar za samoupravno normativno dejavnost, 1979.

—. *Komuniciranje in odločanje v delegatskem sistemu*. Ljubljana: Centar za samoupravno normativno dejavnost, 1978.

Zbornik narodnih heroja Jugoslavije. Belgrade: Omladina, 1975.

Zečević, Miodrag. *Skupština SR Srbije u periodu 1963-1969, godine*. Belgrade: Institut za političke studije Fakulteta političkih nauka, 1972.

Žena: odbornika i zastupnika. Zagreb: Konferencija za društvena aktivnost žena Hrvatska, 1969.

Zubrinić, Dušan. *Marksizam i teorije elite.* Zagreb: Školska knjiga, 1975.

Županov, Josip. *Marginalije o društvenoj krizi.* Zagreb: Globus, 1983.

Zvekić, Ugleša. *Profesija sudija.* Belgrade: Institut za kriminološka i sociološka istraživanja, 1985.

Articles (In the Languages of Yugoslavia)

Aleksić, Rade. "Inteligencija u Jugoslovenskom društvu," *Sociologija,* VI, Nos. 1-2 (1964): 115-133.

Babić, Milan. "Statistika pismenosti u Jugoslavije," *Statisticka revija,* Nos. 1-2 (July, 1959): 209-229.

Bilandžic, Dušan. "SKJ u borbi za transformacija državno-centralističkog sistema u samoupravnu organizaciju društva (1961-1971)," *Istorija Savez Komunista Jugoslavije.* Eds. P. Moraca, *et. al.* Belgrade: Rad, 1976: 261-294.

Bernik, Ivan. "Klasna i slojevna struktura Jugoslovenskog društva i plurali zam samoupravnih interesa," *Sociologija,* XXIV, Nos. 2-3 (1983): 348-353.

Caratan, B. "Društveno-političke organizacije u delegatskom sistemu," *Teorija i praksa delegatskog sistema.* Eds. Ivan Šiber and Zdravko Tomac. Zagreb: Fakultet političkih nauka, 1979: 225-242.

Cetinić, Marin. "Uvid i kontrola koristenja i raspolaganja društvenim sredstvima," *Simpozijum savezne skupštine: sistem finansiranja i poreski sistem, referati.* Belgrade: Kultura, 1970: 81-96.

Damjanović, Mijat. "Rezultati izbora u 1967 godini: Načelo smenjivosti i promene u sastavu skupština," *Skupštinski izbori 1967.* Eds. Milan Matić *et. al.* Belgrade: Institut društvenih nauka, 1968: 149-185.

Deva, Veli. "Medjunacionalni odnosi i politička situacija na Kosovu," *Politička situacija medjunacionalni odnosi u savremenoj fazi socijalističkog razvitka i zadaci Saveza Komunista Srbije.* Ed. Ljubiša Stankov. Belgrade: Institut za političke studije: 131-146.

"Diplomirani studenti: 1970," *Statistički Bilten, No. 714.* Belgrade: Savezni zavod za statistiku, 1972.

Divjak, Pero. "Sastav delegacija osnovnih samoupravnih organizacijia i zajednica i delegata u skupštinama društveno-političkih zajednica u 1978," *Jugoslovenski pregled* (March, 1979): 91-100.

Djordjević, Jovan. "Prilog teoriji avangarde," *Pregled*, No. 4 (1975): 405-429.

Djurić, Djordje. "Ispitavanje etničke distance kod dece," *Zbornik za društvene nauke*, LVI (1971): 126-132.

First, Ruža. "Struktura autoriteta u seoskim domaćinstvima," *Sociologija sela*, VII (1969): 53-61.

Folić, Milutin. "Obnavljanje i konsolidacija KPJ, pojava frakcija na Kosovu i uticaj Titovog delovanja na njihovom prevazailaženju," *Osmakonferencija Zagrebačkih komunista i razvoj KPJ-SKJ kao moderne partije radničke klase.* Zagreb: Vjesnikova Pres Agencija, 1978: 129-160.

Goati, Vladimir. "Sistem moći, socijalna struktura i nacionalno pitanje," *Revija za sociologiju*, XVI, Nos. 1-4 (Winter, 1986): 75-89.

Golubović, Zagorka, Djordjije Uskoković, Miša Stojanović, Aljoša Mimica, "Analiza studija u strukturi Jugoslovenskog društva," *Klase i slojevi.* Ed. Rudi Supek. Zagreb: Čovjek i sistem, 1977: 7-52.

Graovac, Igor. "O proučavanju struktura sudionika NOB-e i socijalističke revolucije u Hrvatskoj 1941-1945," *Časopis za suvremenu povijest*, VI, No. 2 (1974): 7-64.

Grbić, Čedo. "Udruženi rad i skupštinski sistem," *Skupštinski sistem u ustavnim promjenama.* Zagreb: Centar za aktualni politički studij, 1972: 47-66.

Horvat, Branko. "Integriranost Jugoslovenske privrede i samoupravne dogovoranje," *Ekonomist*, XXII, No. 2 (1969): 287-312.

Islami, H. "Osvrt na razvitak stanovnistva Kosovo," *Sociologija*, I (1977): 153-173.

—. "Struktura uticaja u opštini," *Sociologija*, II (1979): 397-417.

Janićijević, Milosav. "Osvrt na strukturalne promene Jugoslovenskog društva," *Promene Klasne strukture savremenog Jugoslovenskog društva*. Belgrade: Jugoslovensko udruženje za sociologiju, 1967: 283-312.

Kangrga, Milan. "Fenomenologija ideološko-političkog nastupanja Jugo slavenske srednje klase," *Praxis*, VIII, Nos. 3-4 (May-August, 1971): 425-446.

Kardelj, Edward. "Da li je samoupravljanje u Jugoslaviji gradilište ili fasada jednog empirijskog socijalizma," *Socijalizam*, Nos. 7-8 (1969): 891-911.

Katunarić, Vjeran. "Kriza i revizija društvene strukture," *Naše teme*, VII, No. 9 (1983): 1378-1392.

Kavran, M. "Rugovska povolja-dokument samoupravnog suzbijanja krvne osvete u Kosovskom selu," *Sociologija sela*, XII (1974): 28-36.

Kilibarda, Risto. "O socijalnoj hijerarhiji u Jugoslovenskom društvu," *Sociologija*, XXV, Nos. 2-3 (1983): 221-245.

Knežović, D. "Kadrovska politika: politički profesionalizam u savezu komunista," *Socijalizam*, XXII, No. 11 (1977): 138-153.

Lukić, Radomir. "O pojmu kaste i klase," *Pregled*, No. 9 (1955): 101-108.

—. "O sukobima interesa u socijalističkom društvu," *Arhiv za pravne i društvene nauke*, XLVI, No. 1 (January-March, 1959): 10-23.

—. "Teorije elite u Pareta i Marksa," *Sociologija*, VII, No. 1 (1965): 19-28.

—. "Uticaj radničkog samoupravljana na klasni sastav Jugoslovenskog društva," *Sociologija*, (1961): 10-28.

Marinkovic, Radovoje. "Polozaj, moc i uticaj osnovnih subjekata delegat

Marinković, Radovoje. "Polozaj, moć i uticaj osnovnih subjekata delegat skog sistem," *Delegatski sistem: funkionisanje i ostvarivanje.* Ed. Radovoje Marinković. Belgrade: Institut za političke studije Fakulteta političkih nauka, 1979: 261-322.

Marjanović, Jovan. "Delegacije i delegati društveno-politickih organizacija," *Funkcionisanje delegatskog sistema: Iskustva Aktuelni problemi*, Ed. R. Marinković. Belgrade: Institut za političke studije Fakulteta političkih nauka, 1976: 161-177.

Marković, Branislav. "Uprava i zakonodavni proces federacija," *Karakter i funkcije federacije u procesu konstituisanja samoupravnog društva.* Ed. Ljubiša Stankov. Belgrade: Institut za političke studije, VŠPN, 1968: 323-330.

Marković, M. "Relativno duže održavanje porodičnih zadruga u Albanca na Kosovu," *Sociologija sela*, XII (1974): 95-100.

Marković, Mihajlo. "Struktura moći u Jugoslovenskom društvu i dilema revolucionare inteligencije," *Praxis,* VIII, No. 6 (1971): 811-826.

Matić, Milan. "Skupštinski izbori 1967: Dalja evolucija društveno-političkog sistema," *Skupština izbori 1967.* Eds. Milan Matić et. al. Belgrade: Institut društvenih nauka, 1968: 35-36.

Mesić, Milan. "'Nova klasa' ili novo društvo i nova klasa," *Naše teme*, XXVIII, No. 9 (1984): 1670-1682.

—. "Politička kultura samoupravljanja radničke klase Zagreba," *Naše teme*, II (February, 1978): 354-376.

Mežnarić, S. "Imigracije radnika iz drugih Jugoslovenskih republika u SR Sloveniju," *Sociologija*, II-III (1978): 293-312.

Miljević, Milan. "Jedinstvo vlasti i samoupravljanje," *Arhiv za pravna i društvena nauka*, No. 1 (January-March, 1985): 27-36.

Minček, Maja. "Problemi likovnog stvaralaštva u Hrvatskoj," *Likovni stvaraoci i kulturna sredina.* Eds. Rudi Supek and Maja Minček. Zagreb: Institut za društvena istraživanja sveučilista u Zagrebu, 1970: 63-228.

Modić, H. "Pravo v prehodnem razdobju," *Ekonomski zbornik*, II (1957): 91-109.

Mratović, Veljko. "Uloga organa državne uprave u ostvarivanju funkcija skupština društveno-političkih zajednica," *Naša zakonitost*, XXV, No. 1 (January, 1971): 7-15.

Mujačić, Mahmut. "Značaj informisanja delegatske baze za proces dogovaranja republika i pokrajina," *Novinarstvo*, I-II (1978): 129-135.

Nasakanda, Pero. "Razvoj promjena klase strukture KP Hrvatske u NOB-u i socijalističkoj revoluciji," *Časopis za suvremunu povijest*, XIV, No. 2 (1982): 95-128.

—. "'Sredniji slojevi' u Jugoslovenskom društvu," *Naše teme*, XXVIII, Nos. 4-5 (1984), 633-652: 117-123.

Pašić, Najdan. "Profesija protiv profesionalizma," *Politika* (May, 1978): 6.

Pečujlić, Miroslav. "Promene u socijalnom sastavu Jugoslovenskog socijalističkog društva," *Društveno-politički sistem, SFRJ*. Belgrade: Radnicka Stampa, 1979: 127-169.

—. "Sastav predstavničkih tela i izborni sistem," *Izborni sistem u uslovima samoupravljanja*. Ed. F. Džinić. Belgrade: Institut društvenih nauka, 1967: 100-105.

Pečujlić, Miroslav and Dusan Ničić. "Skica strukture društvene svesti," *Gledišta*, VII, No. 12 (December, 1966): 68-89.

Perić, Ivan. "Neke karakteristika socijalne strukture Saveza Komunista Hrvatske," *Reforma Saveza Komunista Hrvatska*. Zagreb: Centar za aktualni politički studij, 1970: 42-69.

—. "Nosioci stručno-rukovodjenih funkcija i društveno političke organi zacije i poduzećima," *Direktor u samoupravnim odnosima*. Eds. Drago Goropić and Jovo Brekić. Zagreb: Informator, 1967: 103-109.

Perović, Milun. "Proces političkog odlučivanja u Skupstini SFRJ." Ph.D. Dissertation, Faculty of Political Science, Belgrade University, 1979.

Petrović, Ruža. "Etno-biološka homogenizacija Jugoslovenskog društva," *Sociologija*, X, No. 2 (1968): 5-34.

Polić, Zoran. "Učvršćivanje i razvijanje skupštinskog sistema," *Socijalizam*, XXII (1979): 15-31.

Popović, Mihailo. "Administracija, birokratija, birokratizam," *Sociologija*, XXV, No. 4 (1983): 383-395.

—. "Klasno-slojne nejednakosti u Jugoslovenskom društvu," *Pogledi*, XV, No. 1 (1985): 18-41.

Prelević, Milŏs. "Neki podaci o oružanim formacijama NOR-a 1941-1944 godine," *Zbornik Radova: Politička Škola JNA, Volume III*. Belgrade: Politička Škola JNA, 1970.

Radenović, Predrag. "Sve veći broj pravih directora," *Direktor*, No. 2 (1969): 54-56.

Ranković, Alexander. "Za dalje jačanje pravosudja i zakonitosti," *Četvrti plenum centralnog komiteta komunističke partije Jugoslavije*, III (June 4, 1951).

Sekulić, Duško. "O pristupima izučavanju stratifikancione strukture Jugo slovenskog društva," *Sociologija*, XXV, No. 2 (1983): 1-20.

Šiber, Ivan. "Empirijski pristupi istraživanju socijalne strukture," *Naše teme*, XXVIII, No. 11 (1984): 2248-2268.

—. "Nekoliko napomena o istraživanju delegatskog sistema," *Politička miaso*, III (1978): 325-330.

Stambuk, Vladimir. "Teorijski model socijalne stratifikacije C.W. Milsa," *Sociologija*, Nos. 1-2 (1968): 32-43.

Stanovćić, Vojislav. "Elita," *Mala politička enciklopedija*. Belgrade: Savremena administracija, 1966: 285-286.

Stojanović, Svetozar. "Rajt Mils o marksizmu," *Gledišta*, No. 2 (1966): 301-307.

—. "Socijalistička demokratija i SKJ", *Marks i savremenost*. Eds. Dragutin Leković *et. al.* Belgrade: Institut za izučavanje radničkog pokreta i Institut društvenih nauka, 1964: 26-37.

Stojanov, Mladen. "Nekoliko podatka o uticaju u praksi delegatskog odlučivanja," *Savremenost*, I-II (January-February, 1978): 99-111.

Sultanović, Vladimir. "Elita i avangarda," *Zbornik radova ekonomski Fakultet-Univerzitet Sarajevo*, VI, No. 6 (1971): 35-46.

Šuvar, Stipe. "Srednije slojevi ili srednja klasa u Jugoslovenskom društvu," *Marksističke sveske*, Nos. 1-2 (1972): 77-96.

Tadić, Ljubomir. "Moć, elite, i demokratija," *Praxis*, VII, Nos. 1-2 (January-April, 1970): 64-77.

Tanić, Živan. "Direktori i predstavnici samoupravnih tela," *Naše teme*, XIII, No. 2 (February, 1969): 186-206.

Tomić, Stojan. "Sociološke dijagnoze i prognoze savremenog sela," *Sociologija*, XXI, No. 3 (1979): 317-318.

Tozi, D. and D. Petrović. "Politički odnosi i sastav skupština društveno-političkih zajednica," *Socijalizam*, XI (1969): 1581-1599.

Vakić, I. "Razvoj položaj i perspektive autonomne pokrajine Kosova i Metohije," *Društveno-političke zajednice, tom 11, socijalističke republike i autonomne pokrajine.* Ed. Nine Opačić. Belgrade: Medju narodna stampa-interpres, 1968: 553-559.

Vlahović, Veljko. "Samo u akciji mogu se prepoznati i ljudi i odnosi," *Klasa i avangarda: Jugoslovensko iskustvo (prvi svezak).* Eds. Jovan Mirić, *et. al.* Zagreb: Globus, 1983: 577-586.

Vucetić, Slobodan. "Delegatski sistem u organizacijama udruženog rada," *Gledišta*, XVI (January, 1975): 23-37.

Vujović, Stevan. "Socijalna diferencijacija i socijalne segregacija u našim gradovima," *Lica*, No. 5 (May, 1972): 52-67.

Vuković, I. "Diskusija," *Arhiv za pravne i društvene nauke*, III (1972): 321-325.

Živković, Miroslav. "Jedan primer segregacije u razvoju naših gradova," *Sociologija*, X, No. 3 (1968): 37-58.

Lenard J. Cohen

—. "Mit i dogma u Jugoslovenskoj ideologiji," *Sociologija*, XXVII, Nos. 1-2 (1985): 159-172.

Županov, Josip. "Da li se rukovodjenje preduzećem profesionalizira?" *Moderna organizacija*, No. 10 (1968): 803-823.

—. "Egalitarizam i industrializam," *Naše teme*, XIV, No. 2 (February, 1970): 271-276.

—. "Samoupravljanje i društvena moć u radnoj organizaciji," *Moderna organizacija*, Nos. 6-7 (1971): 447-471.

Other Books

Aron, Raymond. *Main Currents in Sociological Thought, Volume II*. Garden City: Doubleday, 1970.

Bahro, Rudolf. *The Alternative in Eastern Europe*. London: New Left Books, 1978.

Balfour, Neil and Salley MacKay. *Paul of Yugoslavia*. London: Hamish Hamilton, 1982.

Banac, Ivo. *The National Question in Yugoslavia*. Ithaca: Cornell University Press, 1984.

Barton, Allen H. *et. al.* (eds.) *Opinion-Making Elites in Yugoslavia*. New York: Praeger, 1973.

Baylis, Thomas A. *The Technical Intelligentsia and the East German Elite*. Berkeley: University of California, 1974.

Beard, Charles A. and George Radin. *The Balkan Pivot: Yugoslavia, A Study in Government and Administration*. New York: Macmillan, 1929.

Beattie, Christopher. *Minority Men in a Majority Setting*. Toronto: McClelland and Stewart, 1975.

Beck, Carl *et. al.* (eds). *Comparative Communist Political Leadership*. New York: David McKay Co., 1973.

Bendix, Reinhard and Guenther Roth. *Scholarship and Partisanship: Essays on Max Weber*. Berkeley: University of California Press, 1971.

Bensman, Joseph, Arthur Vidich, and Nobuko Gerth (eds.). *Politics, Character, and Culture: Perspectives from Hans Gerth*. Westport, Conn.: Greenwood Press, 1983.

Bienkowski, Wladyslaw. *Theory and Reality*. London: Allison and Busby, 1981.

Boehm, Christopher. *Blood Revenge*. Lawrence: University Press of Kansas, 1984.

—. *Montenegrin Social Organization and Values*. New York: AMS Press, 1983.

Bottomore, Thomas. *Elites and Society*. New York: Basic Books, 1964.

Bukharin, Nikolai. *Historical Materialism: A System of Sociology*. Ann Arbor: University of Michigan Press, 1969.

—. *Selected Writings on the State and the Transition to Socialism*. Ed. Richard B. Day. Armont, New York: M.E. Sharpe, 1982.

Bukharin, Nikolai and E. Preobrazhensky. *The ABC of Communism*. London: Penguin Books, 1970.

Burks, R.V. *The Dynamics of Communism in Eastern Europe*. Princeton: Princeton University Press, 1961.

Charlton, Michael (ed.). *The Eagle and the Small Birds*. Chicago: The University of Chicago Press, 1984.

Ciliga, Ante. *La Yugoslavie Sous la Menace Intérieure et Extérieure*. Paris: Les Isles d'Or, 1951.

—. *The Russian Enigma*. London: George Routledge and Sons, 1940.

Clissold, Stephen. *Yugoslavia and the Soviet Union, 1939-1973*. London: Institute for the Study of Conflict, 1975.

Cohen, Lenard J. and Paul Warwick. *Political Cohesion in a Fragile Mosaic: The Yugoslav Experience*. Boulder: Westview Press, 1983.

Cohen, Stephen. *Bukharin and the Bolshevik Revolution.* Oxford: Oxford University Press, 1980.

Conner, James E. (ed.). *Lenin on Politics and Revolution: Selected Writings.* New York: Pegasus, 1968.

Crocker, David A. *Praxis and Democratic Socialism.* Atlantic Highlands, N.J.: Humanistic Press, Inc., 1983.

Czudnowski, Moshe M. (ed.). *Does Who Governs Matter?: Elite Circulation in Contemporary Societies.* Dekalb, Illinois: Northern Illinois University Press, 1982.

Daniels, Robert (ed.). *A Documentary History of Communism.* New York: Vintage Books, 1962.

Dedijer, Vladimir *et. al.* (eds.). *History of Yugoslavia.* New York: McGraw Hill, 1974.

Dedijer, Vladimir. *The Beloved Land.* New York: Simon and Schuster, 1960.

—. *Tito.* New York: Simon and Schuster, 1953.

Denitch, Bogdan (ed.). *Working Papers of the International Study of Opinion-Makers, Volume I.* New York: Columbia University, 1968.

Dick, Howard (ed.). *Selected Political Writings of Rosa Luxembourg.* New York: Monthly Review Press, 1971.

Djilas, Milovan. *Memoir of a Revolutionary.* New York: Harcourt Brace Jovanovich, 1973.

—. *Montenegro.* New York: Harcourt Brace and World, 1963.

—. *The New Class.* New York: Praeger, 1969.

—. *Of Prisons and Ideas.* San Diego: Harcourt Brace Jovanovich, 1986.

—. *Rise and Fall.* New York: Harcourt Brace Jovanovich, 1985.

—. *The Unperfect Society: Beyond the New Class.* New York: Harcourt Brace and World, 1969.

—. *Wartime*. New York: Harcourt Brace and World, 1977.

Djordjevic, Dimitrije and Stephen Fisher-Galati. *The Balkan Revolutionary Tradition*. New York: Columbia University Press, 1981.

Djordjevic, Dimitrije (ed.). *The Creation of Yugoslavia 1914-1918*. Santa Barbara: CLIO Books, 1983.

Dolgoff, Sam (ed.). *Bakunin On Anarchy*. New York: Alfred A. Knopf, 1972.

Donaldson, Robert H. and Derek Waller. *Stasis and Change in Revolution ary Elites: A Comparative Analysis of the 1956 Party Central Committees in China and the USSR*. Beverly Hills: Sage, 1970.

Dragnich, Alex N. *The First Yugoslavia*. Stanford: Hoover Institution Press, 1983.

Durham, M. *Some Tribal Origins Laws and Customs of the Balkans*. London: G. Allen & Unwin, Ltd., 1928.

Eldridge, Albert F. (ed.). *Legislatures in Plural Societies: The Search for Cohesion in National Development*. Durham, N.C.: Duke University Press, 1977.

Eulau, Heinz and Moshe Czudnowski (eds.). *Elite Recruitment in Democratic Politics: Comparative Studies Across Nations*. New York: Halstead Press, 1976.

Eulau, Heinz and Kenneth Prewitt. *Labyrinths of Democracy: Adaptations, Linkages, Representation and Policies in Urban Politics*. Indianapolis: Bobbs-Merrill Co., 1973.

Farrell, Robert Barry (ed.). *Jugoslavia and the Soviet Union, 1948-1956*. Hamden, Conn.: The Shoestring Press, 1956.

— (ed.). *Political Leadership in Eastern Europe and the Soviet Union*. Chicago: Aldine Publishing Co., 1970.

Feher, Ferrenc, Agnes Heller and Gyorgy Markus. *Dictatorship Over Needs*. Oxford: Basil Blackwell, 1983.

Gellner, Ernest. *Thought and Change*. London: Wiedenfield and Nicolson, 1964.

Gerth, Hans and C. Wright Mills. *From Max Weber: Essays in Sociology*. New York: Oxford University Press, 1958.

Giddens, Anthony and David Held (eds.). *Classes, Power, and Conflict: Classical and Contemporary Debates*. Berkeley: University of California Press, 1982.

—. *A Contemporary Critique of Historical Materialism*. London: Macmillan, 1981.

—. *Politics and Sociology in the Thought of Max Weber*. New York: Macmillan, 1972.

Gouldner, Alvin. *Against Fragmentation: The Origins of Marxism and the Sociology of Intellectuals*. New York: Oxford University Press, 1985.

—. *The Future of Intellectuals and the Rise of the New Class*. New York: Oxford University Press, 1979.

Graham, Stephen. *Alexander of Yugoslavia*. New Haven: Yale University Press, 1936.

—. *Peter II King of Yugoslavia, A King's Heritage*. London: Cassell, 1955.

Greene, Thomas. *Comparative Revolutionary Movements*. Englewood Cliffs: Prentice-Hall, 1984.

Gregor, James. *Italian Fascism and Developmental Dictatorship*. Princeton: Princeton University Press, 1979.

Gruenwald, Oskar. *The Yugoslav Search for Man: Marxist Humanism in Contemporary Yugoslavia*. South Hadley, Mass.: J. F. Bergin, 1983.

Haberl, Othmar. *Parteiorganisation and Nationale Frage in Jugoslavien*. Berlin: Otto Harrassowitz, 1976.

Hammel, Eugene. *The Pink Yo-Yo: Occupational Mobility in Belgrade, 1915-1965*. Berkeley: University of California, Institute of International Studies, 1969.

Harris, Lawrence, V.G. Kiernin, and Ralph Milibrand (eds.). *A Dictionary of Marxist Thought.* Cambridge: Harvard University Press, 1983.

Haynes, Michael. *Nikolai Bukharin and the Transition from Capitalism to Socialism.* London: Croon Helm, 1985.

Heady, Ferrel. *Public Administration: A Comparative Perspective.* Englewood Cliffs, N.J.: Prentice-Hall, 1966.

Hechter, Michael. *Internal Colonialism.* Berkeley: University of California Press, 1975.

Highly, John *et. al. Elite Structure and Ideology.* New York: Columbia University Press, 1976.

Hirszowicz, Maria. *The Bureaucratic Leviathan: A Study in the Sociology of Communism.* Oxford: Martin Robertson, 1980.

Hoare, Quentin and Geoffrey Nowell Smith (eds. and trans.). *Selections from the Prison Notebooks of Antonio Gramsci.* New York: International Publisher, 1971.

Hodges, Donald C. *The Bureaucratization of Socialism.* Amherst: The University of Massachusetts Press, 1981.

Hoffman, G.W. and Fred W. Neal. *Tito's Yugoslavia.* Berkeley: University of California Press, 1960.

Hondius, Frederik W. *The Yugoslav Community of Nations.* The Hague: Mouton, 1968.

Hopkins, Raymond. *Political Roles in a New State: Tanzania's First Decade.* New Haven: Yale University Press, 1971.

Hoptner, Jacob B. *Yugoslavia in Crisis 1934-1941.* New York: Columbia University Press, 1962.

Horowitz, Irving Louis. *C. Wright Mills: An American Utopian.* New York: The Free Press, 1983.

Horvat, Branko. *The Political Economy of Socialism.* Armonk, New York: M.E. Sharpe, 1982.

Hunt, Richard N. *The Political Ideas of Marx and Engels*. Pittsburgh: University of Pittsburgh Press, 1984.

Janos, Andrew. *Politics and Paradigms: Changing Theories of Change in Social Science*. Stanford: Stanford University Press, 1986.

— (ed.). *Authoritarian Politics in Communist Europe: Uniformity and Diversity in One-Party States*. Berkeley: University of California Press, 1976.

Jelavich, Barbara. *History of the Balkans, 2 Volumes*. Cambridge Mass.: Cambridge University Press, 1983.

Johnson, A. Ross. *The Role of the Military in Communist Yugoslavia: An Historical Sketch*. Santa Monica: The Rand Paper Series, (January 1978), P-6070.

—. *The Transformation of Communist Ideology: The Yugoslav Case, 1945-1953*. Cambridge, Mass.: MIT Press, 1972.

—. *Yugoslavia in the Twilight of Tito*. Beverly Hills: Sage Publications, 1974.

Kardelj, Edward. *Reminiscences*. London: Blond and Briggs, 1982.

Kautsky, John. *Communism and the Politics of Development*. New York: John Wiley and Sons Inc., 1968.

—. *The Political Consequences of Modernization*. New York: John Wiley and Sons Inc., 1972.

Kidrić, Boris. *On the Construction of Socialist Economy in the FPRJ*. Belgrade: Office of Information of FPRJ, 1948.

Kolakowski, Leszek. *Main Currents of Marxism, Volume 1*. Oxford: Clarendon Press, 1978.

Konrad, Gyorgy and Ivan Szelenyi. *The Intellectuals on the Road to Class Power*. New York: Harcourt Brace Jovanovich, 1979.

Kornberg, Allan and William Mishler. *Influence in Parliament: Canada*. Durham, North Carolina: Duke University Press, 1976.

Kornhauser, Lloyd, P. (ed.). *The New Elites of Tropical Africa*. London: Oxford University Press, 1966.

Lovell, David. *Trotsky's Analysis of Soviet Bureaucratization*. London: Croom Helm, 1985.

Ludz, Peter C. *The Changing Party Elite in East Germany*. Cambridge: MIT Press, 1972.

Luxembourg, Rosa. *The Russian Revolution and Lenin or Marxism?* Ann Arbor: University of Michigan Press, 1961.

Macek, Vladko. *In the Struggle to Freedom*. New York: Robert Spellner and Sons, 1957.

Marković, Mihajlo. *The Contemporary Marx: Essays on Humanist Communism*. Nottingham: Spokesman Books, 1974.

—. *Democratic Socialism, Theory and Practice*. New York: St. Martin's Press, 1982.

Marković, Mihajlo and Robert S. Cohen. *The Rise and Fall of Socialist Humanism: A History of the Praxis Group*. Nottingham: Spokesman Books, 1975.

Marmullaku, Ramadan. *Albania and the Albanians*. Hamden, Conn.: Archon, 1975.

Marx, Karl and Frederick Engels. *Writing on the Paris Commune*. Ed. Hal Draper. New York: Monthly Review Press, 1971.

Marx, Karl, Frederick Engels and V.I. Lenin, *Anarchism and Anarcho-Syndicalism*. New York: International Publishers, 1972.

McCauley, Martin and Stephen Carter (eds.). *Leadership and Succession in the Soviet Union, Eastern Europe, and China*. Basingstoke: Macmillan, 1986.

McClellan, Woodford D. *Svetozar Markovic and the Origins of Balkan Socialism*. Princeton: Princeton University Press, 1964.

McRae, Kenneth (ed.). *Consociational Democracy: Political Accommodation in Segmented Societies*. Toronto: McClelland and Stewart, 1974.

McVicker, Charles P. Titoism: *Pattern for International Communism*. New York: St. Martin's Press, 1957.

Meisel, James Hans. *The Myth of the Ruling Class: Gaetano Mosca and the 'Elite'*. Ann Arbor: The University of Michigan Press, 1958.

—. *Pareto and Mosca*. Englewood Cliffs, N.J.: Prentice Hall, 1965.

Merton, Robert. *Social Theory and Social Structure*. Glencoe, Ill.: The Free Press of Glencoe, 1957.

Michels, Robert. *First Lectures in Sociology*. Trans. Alfred de Grazia. New York: Harper and Row, 1965.

—. *Political Parties*. New York: Dover Publications, 1959.

Mićunović, Veljko. *Moscow Diary*. Garden City, New York: Doubleday, 1980.

Milenkovitch, Michael and Deborah (eds.). *Milovan Djilas: Parts of a Lifetime*. New York: Harcourt Brace Jovanovich, 1975.

—. *Class Power and State Power*. London: Oxford University Press, 1977.

Moore, Gwen (ed.). *Research in Politics and Society, A Research Annual: Studies of the Structure of National Elite Groups*. Greenwich, Conn.: JAI Press, 1985.

Mosca, Gaetano. *The Ruling Class: Elementi di Scienza Politica*. Ed. Arthur Livingston. New York: McGraw Hill, 1939.

Moses, Joel. *Regional Party Leadership and Policy-Making in the USSR*. New York: Praeger Publishers, 1974.

Nagle, John. *System and Succession: The Social Basis of Elite Recruitment*. Austin: University of Texas Press, 1977.

Nomad, Max. *Apostles of Revolution*. New York: Collier Books, 1961.

—. *Aspects of Revolt*. New York: The Noonday Press, 1959.

Nordlinger, Eric. *Conflict Regulation in Divided Societies. Occasional Paper in International Affairs, No. 29.* Cambridge: Harvard University Press, 1972.

Obler, Jeffrey, Jurg Steiner, and Guido Dierickx. *Decision-Making in Smaller Democracies: The Consociational 'Burden'.* Beverly Hills: Sage Publications, 1977.

Pareto, Vilfredo. *The Rise and Fall of Elites: An Application of Theoretical Sociology.* Totwa, N.J.: Bedminister Press, 1968.

Parkin, Frank. *Marxism and Class Theory: A Bourgeois Critique.* New York: Columbia University Press, 1979.

—. *Max Weber.* London: Tavistock Publications, 1982.

Parsons, Talcott and Edward Shils (eds.). *Toward a General Theory of Action.* New York: Harper and Row, 1962.

Petrovich, Michael B. *A History of Modern Serbia, 2 Volumes.* New York: Harcourt Brace Jovanovich, 1976.

Popović, Nenad. *Yugoslavia: The New Class in Crisis.* Syracuse: Syracuse University Press, 1961.

Prethus, Robert. *Elite Accommodation in Canadian Politics.* Cambridge: Cambridge University Press, 1973.

Prewitt, Kenneth. *The Recruitment of Political Leaders: A Study of Citizen Politicians.* Indianapolis: Bobbs-Merrill Co., 1970.

Putnam, Robert. *The Comparative Study of Political Elites.* Englewood Cliffs, N.J.: Prentice-Hall, 1976.

Quandt, William B. *The Comparative Study of Political Elites.* Beverly Hills: Sage Publications, 1970.

Raikovitch, Bogomir. *L'Avancement et le traitement des fonctionaires publics du Royaume des Serbes, Croates et Slovenes.* Paris: Labour, n.d.

Rakovski, Marx. *Toward an East European Marxism.* London: Allison and Busby, 1978.

Ranković, Alexander. *Report of the Central Committee of the Communist Party of Yugoslavia on the Organizational Work of the CPY*. Belgrade, 1948.

Rasevic, Miroslav, T. Mulina, and M. Macura. *The Determinants of Labor Force Participation in Yugoslavia*. Geneva: International Labor Organization, 1978.

Rayner, Louisa. *Women in a Village*. London: William Heinemann, Ltd., 1957.

Reinhartz, Dennis. *Milovan Djilas: A Revolutionary as a Writer*. Boulder: East European Monographs, 1981.

Rejai, Mostafa. *Leaders of Revolution*. Beverly Hills: Sage Publications, 1979.

Riggs, Fred (ed.). *Frontiers of Development Administration*. Durham, N.C.: Duke University Press, 1980.

Ristić, Dragiša. *Yugoslavia's Revolution of 1941*. University Park: Pennsylvania State University Press, 1966.

Robinson, Gertrude. *Tito's Maverick Media*. Urbana: University of Illinois Press, 1977.

Rothberg, Abraham. *Anatomy of a Moral: The Political Essays of Milovan Djilas*. London: Thames and Hudson, 1959.

Rothschild, Joseph. *East Central Europe Between the Wars*. Seattle: University of Washington Press, 1974.

Runciman, Walter Garrison. *Max Weber, Selections in Translation*. London: Cambridge University Press, 1978.

Rusinow, Dennison. *The Yugoslav Experiment, 1948-1974*. Berkeley: University of California Press, 1977.

Schlesinger, Joseph. *Ambition and Politics: Political Careers in the United States*. Chicago: Rand McNally, 1966.

Seton-Watson, Hugh and C. Seton-Watson. *The Making of a New Europe: R.W. Seton-Watson and the Last Years of Austria-Hungary.* London: Methuen, 1981.

Seton-Watson, Hugh. *Nationalism and Communism, Essays 1946-1963.* New York: Praeger, 1964.

Sher, Gerson S. *Praxis: Marxist Criticism and Dissent in Socialist Yugoslavia.* Bloomington, Indiana: Indiana University Press, 1977.

Shoup, Paul. *Communism and the National Question in Yugoslavia.* New York: Columbia University Press, 1968.

Siberman, Bernard. *Ministers of Modernization.* Tuscon, Arizona: University of Arizona Press, 1964.

Singleton, Fred. *Twentieth-Century Yugoslavia.* New York: Columbia University Press, 1976.

Skendi, Stavro. *Balkan Cultural Studies.* Boulder: East European Monographs, 1980.

Smith, Anthony. *The Ethnic Rival.* Cambridge: Cambridge University Press, 1981.

—. *Theories of Nationalism.* New York: Harper and Row, 1971.

Spriano, Paolo. *Stalin and the European Communists.* London: Verso, 1985.

Srzentić, Nikola. *The Constitutional Judiciary in Yugoslavia.* Belgrade: Jugoslovenski Pregled, 1984.

St. Erlich, Vera. *Family in Transition: A Study of 300 Yugoslav Villages.* Princeton: Princeton University Press, 1966.

Steiner, Jurg. *Amicable Agreement Versus Majority Rule: Conflict Resolution in Switzerland.* Chapel Hill: University of North Carolina Press, 1974.

Stojanović, Svetozar. *Between Ideals and Reality.* New York: Oxford University Press, 1973.

Lenard J. Cohen

—. *In Search of Democracy in Socialism.* Buffalo: Prometheus Books, 1981.

Stojković, Ljubiša and Miloš Martić. *National Minorities in Yugoslavia.* Belgrade: Jugoslavija, 1952.

Stokes, Gale. *Legitimacy Through Liberalism, Vladimir Jovanovic and the Transformation of Serbian Politics.* Seattle: University of Washington Press, 1975.

Sugar, Peter. *Industrialization of Bosnia-Hercegovina.* Seattle: University of Washington Press, 1963.

Supek, Ivan. *Crown Witness Against Hebrang.* Chicago: Markanton Press, 1983.

Tomasevich, Jozo. *Peasants, Politics, and Economic Change in Yugoslavia.* Stanford: Stanford University Press, 1955.

Tomasic, Dinko. *Personality and Culture in Eastern European Politics.* New York: George W. Stewart, 1948.

Trajković, Josif. *The Judicial System of Yugoslavia.* Belgrade: Jugoslovenski Pregled, 1984.

Trotsky, Leon. *My Life.* New York: Universal Library, 1930.

—. *Our Political Tasks.* London: New Park Publications, n.d.

—. *The Revolution Betrayed.* New York: Merit Publishers, 1965.

Trouton, Ruth. *Peasant Renaissance in Yugoslavia, 1900-1950.* London: Routledge and Kegan Paul, 1952.

Tucker, Robert C. (ed.). *The Lenin Anthology.* New York: Norton and Company, 1975.

Turoslenski, Severin K. *Education in Yugoslavia.* Washington: Government Printing Office, 1939.

Vinterhalter, Vilko. *In the Path of Tito.* Tunbridge Wells, Abacus Press, 1972.

Weber, Max. *The Theory of Social and Economic Organization.* Trans. Talcott Parsons and A.M. Hnderson. New York: The Free Press, 1964.

Welsh, William A. *Leaders and Elites.* New York: Holt Rinehart and Winston, 1979.

Wesolowski, Wodzimierz. *Classes, Strata, and Power.* London: Routledge and Kegan Paul, 1979.

West, Rebecca. *Black Lamb and Grey Falcon.* New York: Viking, 1942.

Who's Who in Central and East Europe. Zurich: Central European Times Ltd., 1935-1937.

Wilson, Duncan. *The Life and Times of Vuk Stefanovic Karadzic.* London: Oxford Clarendon Press, 1970.

Wong, Paul. *China's Higher Leadership in the Socialist Transition.* New York: The Free Press, 1976.

Wright, Eric Olin. *Class, Crisis and the State.* London: NLB, 1978.

Yugoslavia: The Mediterranean Regional Project, Country Reports, Education and Development. Paris: OECD, 1965.

Zalar, Charles. *Yugoslav Communism, A Critical Study.* Washington: US Government Printing Office, 1961.

Other Articles

Allardt, Erik. "Changes in the Nature of Ethnicity: From the Primordial to the Organizational," *Directions of Change: Modernization Theory, Research, and Realities.* Eds. Mustafa Attir, *et. al.* Boulder: Westview Press, 1981: 75-120.

Anderson, Melanie. "The Trial of Mihajlo Mihajlov," *Index on Censorship,* V, No. 1 (Spring, 1976): 3-12.

Artisien, P. "Albania in the Post-Hoxha Era," *World Today,* No. 41 (June, 1985): 107-111.

Artisien, P. and R. Howells. "Yugoslavia, Albania, and the Kosovo Riots," *World Today,* (November, 1981): 419-427.

"Association of Yugoslav Volunteers in the Spanish Republican Army," *Yugoslav Survey,* (October-December, 1961): 957-959.

Auty, Phyllis. "The Ninth Congress of the League of Communists," *The World Today,* XXV, No. 6 (June, 1969): 264-276.

Avakumovic, Ivan. "Yugoslavia's Fascist Movements," *Native Fascism in the Successor State, 1918-1945.* Ed. Peter Sugar. Santa Barbara: ABC-CLIO, 1971: 135-144.

Avrich, Paul. "What is Machaevism?" *Soviet Studies,* XVII (1965): 66-73.

Babic, Ivan. "Military History," *Croatia: Land, People, Culture,* Volume I. Eds. Francis Eterovich and Christopher Apalatin. Toronto: University of Toronto Press, 1964: 163.

Banac, Ivo. "The Communist Party of Yugoslavia during the Period of Legality, 1919-1921," *War and Society in Eastern Europe.* Ed. Bela K. Kiraly. New York: Atlantic Research and Publications, 1983: 188-230.

Barry, Brian. "The Consociational Model and Its Dangers," *European Journal of Political Research,* III (1976): 393-412.

—. "Review Article: Political Accommodation and Consocational Democracy," *British Journal of Political Science,* V (1975): 477-505.

Barton, Allen. "Determinants of Leadership Attitudes in a Socialist Society," *Opinion-Making Elites in Yugoslavia.* Eds. Allen Barton, *et. al.* New York: Praeger, 1973: 220-262.

Bazler-Madzar, M. "Regional Development, "*The Yugoslav Economic System.* Ed. Branko Horvat. White Plains, N.Y: International Arts and Science Press, 1976: 60-75.Beck, Carl *et. al.* "Bureaucracy and Political Development in Eastern Europe," *Bureaucracy and Political Development.* Ed. Joseph LaPalombara. Princeton: Princeton University Press, 1963: 268-300.

—. "Bureaucratic Conservatism and Innovation in Eastern Europe," *Comparative Political Studies,* I, No. 2 (July, 1968): 275-294.

—. "The Career Characteristics of East European Leadership," *Political Leadership in Eastern Europe and the Soviet Union.* Ed. Barry Farrell. Chicago: Aldine Publishing Co., 1970: 157-194.

—. "Political Succession in Eastern Europe," *Studies in Comparative Communism,* IX, Nos. 1-2 (Spring-Summer, 1976): 35-61.

Been-Lee, Hahn. "The Role of the Higher Civil Service Under Rapid Social and Political Change," *Development Administration in Asia.* Ed. Edward Weidner. Durham, N.C.: Duke University Press, 1970: 107-132.

Beetham, David. "From Socialism to Fascism: The Relation Between Theory and Practice in the Work of Robert Michels," *Political Studies,* XXV, No. 1 (1977): 3-24.

Begović, Vlajko. "The Communist Party of Yugoslavia and the Spanish Civil War (1930 to 1939)," *Socialist Thought and Practice,* No. 4 (April, 1975): 71-86.

Benda, Harry. "Political Elites in Colonial Southeast Asia: An Historical Analysis," *Comparative Studies in History and Society,* II (1965): 233-251.

Bennett, R.J. "The Elite Theory as Fascist Ideology - A Reply to Beetham's Critique of Robert Michels," *Political Studies,* XXVI, No. 4 (1977): 474-488.

Besemeresm, John. "The Demographic Factor in Inter-Ethnic Relations in Yugoslavia," *Southeastern Europe/L'Europe du Sud-Est,* IV, No. 1 (1977): 1-31.

Bialer, Seweryn. "The Soviet Political Elite and Internal Developments in the USSR," *The Soviet Empire: Expansion and Detente.* Ed. William Griffith. Lexington: Lexington Books, 1976: 25-55.

Bielasiak, Jack. "Lateral and Vertical Elite Differentiation in European Communist States," *Studies in Comparative Communism,* XI, Nos. 1-2 (Spring-Summer, 1978): 121-141.

Black, Gordon. "A Theory of Professionalization in Politics," *American Political Science Review,* LXIV, No. 3 (September, 1970): 865-878.

Brass, Paul. "Ethnic Groups and Nationalities: The Formation, Persistence and Transformation of Ethnic Identities," *Ethnic Diversity and Conflict in Eastern Europe.* Ed. Peter Sugar. Santa Barbara: ABC-CLEO, 1980: 1-68.

Broekmeyer, M. "Self-Management in Yugoslavia," *Annals of the American Academy of Political and Social Sciences,* XXIII (May, 1977): 180-196.

Brown, Archie. "Political Power and the Soviet State: Western and Soviet Perspectives," *The State in Socialist Society.* Ed. Neil Harding. London: Macmillan Press, 1984: 51-103.

Bruce-Briggs, B. "An Introduction to the Ideas of the New Class," *The New Class?* New Brunswick, N.J.: Transaction Books, 1979: 1-18.

Burgess, Melanie. "The Resurgence of Ethnicity: Myth or Reality," *Ethnic and Racial Studies,* I, No. 3 (1978): 265-285.

Castellan, Georges. "Les villes serbs au milieu du XIX siècle: Structures sociales et modèles cultures," *Southeastern Europe/L'Europe de Sud-Est, Part II,* (1979): 121-133.

Cavoski, Kosta. "Why There is More Free Speech in Belgrade than in Zagreb," *Index on Censorship,* XV, No. 8 (1986): 22-23.

Cengle, Franc. "Toward a Marxist Interpretation of Political History," *Survey,* II, No. 1 (1975): 56-57.

Cohen, Lenard J. "Conflict Management and Institution-Building in Socialist Yugoslavia: The Role of the Parliamentary System," *Legislatures in Plural Societies*. Ed. Albert F. Eldridge. Durham, N.C.: Duke University Press, 1977: 121-165.

—. "Devolutionary Socialism: The Political Institutionalization of the Yugoslav Assembly System, 1963-1973." Ph.D Dissertation, Columbia University, 1978.

—. "Federalism and Foreign-Policy in Yugoslavia: The Politics of Regional Ethnonationalism," *International Journal*, XLI, (Summer, 1986): 627-654.

—. "Political Crime in Yugoslavia: The Ethnic and Political Basis of Anti-State Dissidence, 1929-1980," Paper Presented at the American Association for the Advancement of Slavic Studies. Monterey, California, 1981.

—. "Political Science in Socialist Yugoslavia: The Regime Management and Self-Management of a Discipline," *The Soviet Union and East Europe Into the 1980's: Multi-disciplinary Perspectives*. (eds.) Simon McInnes, William McGrath, and Peter Potichnyj. Oakville, Ontario: Mosaic Press, 1978: 59-98.

Conner, Walker. "Nation-Building or Nation-Destroying?" *World Politics*, XXIV, No. 3 (1972): 319-355.

Cviic, Cristopher. "Yugoslavia - Bitter Inheritance," *Washington Quarterly*, IV, No. 4 (1981): 18-23.

Daalder, Hans. "The Consociational Democracy Theme," *World Politics*, XXVI, No. 4 (1974): 604-621.

Denich, Bette S. "Sources of Leadership in the Yugoslav Revolution: A Local-Level Study," *Comparative Studies in Society and History*, XVIII, No. 1 (January, 1976): 64-83.

Denitch, Bogdan. "Elite Interviewing and Social Structure: An Example from Yugoslavia," *Opinion-Making Elites in Yugoslavia*. Eds. Allen Barton, et. al. New York: Praeger, 1973: 3-23.

Deroc, M. "The Former Yugoslav Army," *East European Quarterly*, XIX, No. 3 (September, 1985): 364-365.

Deutsch, Karl. "Communication Theory and Political Integration," *The Integration of Political Communities*. Eds. Phillip Jacob and James Toscano. New York: J.B. Lippincott, 1964: 46-74.

Djilas, Milovan. "The Storm in Eastern Europe," *The New Leader* (November 19, 1956): 3-6.

Djordjevic, Dimitrije. "Historians in Politics: Slobodan Jovanovic," *Journal of Contemporary History*, VIII, No. 1 (1973): 21-40.

Djordjević, Jovan. "The Constitution of the Socialist Federal Republic of Yugoslavia of 1974," *Socialist Thought and Practice*, IV (1984): 11-45.

Donaldson, Robert H. and Derek J. Waller. "A Comparison of the Current Chinese and Soviet Central Committees," *Studies in Comparative Communism*, VI, Nos. 1-2 (Spring-Summer, 1973): 51-65.

Dukić-Veljović, Zlatija. "The Assembly of the Socialist Federal Republic of Yugoslavia," *Yugoslav Survey*, XVIII (February, 1977): 3-21.

"Education Policy: Coordination with Needs of Social Development," *Yugoslav Life*, XXVIII, Nos. 6-7 (1983): 6.

Eisman, Thomas and Yakov Rabin. "Linguistic Influences of Professional Communication and Recognition: A Study of Chemists and Engineers in Two Québec Universities," *Higher Education*, IX (1980): 277-292.

Fainsod, Merle. "Bureaucracy and Modernization: The Russian and Soviet Case," *Bureaucracy and Political Development*. Ed. Joseph LaPalombara. Princeton: Princeton University Press, 1963: 233-267.

Feldbrugge, F.J.M. "The Untapped Potential in the Study of Soviet and East European Law," *Studies in Comparative Communism*, XV, No. 4 (1982): 384-390.

Fira, Alexander. "Relations Between the Constitutional Courts and the Assemblies of Socio-Political Communities," *Socialist Thought and Practice*, IV (1984): 79-90.

—. "Transformation of Executive and Judicial Functions in Yugoslavia," *Yugoslav Law*, II (1980): 11-30.

Fisk, Winston. "The Constitutional Movement in Yugoslavia: A Preliminary Survey," *Slavic Review* (June, 1971): 277-297.

Fleron, Frederick J. Jr. "System Attributes and Career Attributes: The Soviet Political Leadership, 1952 to 1965," *Comparative Communist Political Leadership*. Eds. Carl Beck, *et. al.* New York: David McKay Co., 1975: 43-85.

Fox, Richard, Charlotte Aull, and Louis F. Cimino. "Ethnic Nationalism and the Welfare State," *Ethnic Change*. Ed. Charles Keyes. Seattle: University of Washington Press, 1981: 198-245.

Galli, Giorgio. "Gramsci e le teorie delle 'elites'," *Gramsci e la Cultura Contemporanea, Volume II*. Rome: Editori Riuniti-Instituto, 1975: 201-217.

Gouldner, Alvin. "Prologue to a Theory of Revolutionary Intellectuals," *Telos*, No. 26 (Winter, 1975-1976): 3-36.

Griffith, William. "Generational Change and Political Leadership in Eastern Europe and the Soviet Union," *Political Generation and Political Development*. Ed. R.J. Samuels. Lexington: Lexington Books, 1977: 125-134.

Gross, Mirjana. "Social Structure and National Movements Among the Yugoslav Peoples on the Eve of the First World War," *Slavic Review*, XXXVI No. 4 (December, 1977): 628-643.

—. "The Positions of the Nobility in the Organization of the Elite in Northern Croatia at the End of the Nineteenth and the Beginning of the Twentieth Century." *The Nobility in Russia and Eastern Europe*. Eds. Ivo Banac and Paul Bushkovitiz. New Haven: The Concilium on International and Area Studies, 1983: 137-176.

Gucetic, Vuko G. "Public Prosecutors," *Yugoslav Survey*, XXIII, No. 4 (1977): 43-56.

Haberkern, Ernst. "Machajsky: A Rightfully Forgotten Prophet," *Telos*, No. 71 (Spring, 1987): 111-128.

Harris, Richard. "The Effects of Political Change on the Role Set of the Senior Bureaucrats in Ghana and Nigeria," *Administrative Science Quarterly*, XIII, No. 3 (December, 1968): 386-401.

Hawrylyshyn, Oli. "Ethnic Affinity and Migration Flows in Post-war Yugoslavia," *Economic Development and Cultural Change*, XX, No. 1 (1977): 93-116.

Hayden, Robert. "Labour Courts and Workers' Rights in Yugoslavia: A Case Study of the Contradictions of Socialist Legal Theory and Practice," (manuscript).

Hechter, Michael. "Ethnicity and Industrialization: On theProliferation of the Cultural Division of Labor," *Ethnicity*, III (1976): 219-224.

Highly, John and Gwen Moore, "Elite Integration in the United States and Australia," *American Political Science Review*, LXXV, No. 3 (1981): 581-597.

Hollander, Paul. "Politicized Bureaucracy: The Soviet Case," *Newsletter on Comparative Studies Review*, LX (September, 1961): 12-22.

Ibrahimpashich, Mensor. "The Military Profession in a Self-Managed Society." Paper Presented at the Seventh World Congress of Sociology, Varna, Bulgaria, 1970.

Jackson, Marvin and John R. Lampe. "The Evidence of Industrial Growth in Southeastern Europe Before the Second World War," *East European Quarterly*, XVI, No. 4 (January, 1983): 385-415.

Jambrek, Peter. "The Economic Base of Legality: The Case of Yugoslavia," *International Journal of the Sociology of Law*, XIII (May, 1985): 191-202.

Johnstone, Monty. "Marx, Blanqui and Majority Rule," *The Socialist Register, 1983*. Eds. Ralph Milibrand and Jack Saville. London: The Merlin Press, 1983: 296-318.

Jovanović, Milan. "Elections for the Assemblies of Socio-Political Communities Held in 1982," *Yugoslav Survey*, XXIV, (November, 1983): 39-54.

Jovičić, Miodrag. "Yugoslav Internal Comparative Law," *Yugoslav Law* (1978): 57-73.

Kadushin, Charles and Peter Abrams. "Social Structure of Yugoslav Opinion-Makers," *Opinion-Making Elites in Yugoslavia*. Eds. Allen Barton. New York: Praeger, 1973: 155-219.

Karaman, Igor. "The Socio-Economic Structure of the Urban Population in Northern Croatia During the Early Industrial Period (Before World War I)," *Southeastern Europe/L'Europe du Sud-Est, Part II*, (1979): 134-147.

Kardelj, Edward. "On the Principles of the Preliminary Draft of the Constitution for the Federalist Socialist Republic of Yugoslavia," *Socialist Thought and Practice*, VII-VIII, (1962).

Kautsky, John. "An Essay in the Politics of Development," *Political Change in Underdeveloped Countries: Nationalism and Communism*. Ed. John Kautsky. New York: John Wiley, 1962: 3-119.

—. "Patterns of Elite Succession in the Process of Development," *Journal of Politics*, XXXI, No. 2 (May, 1969): 359-396.

—. "Revolutionary and Managerial Elites in Modernizing Regimes," *Comparative Politics*, I, No. 4 (July, 1969): 441-467.

Kerr, Clark, et. al. "Postscript to 'Industrialism and Industrial Man'," *International Labour Review*, CIII, No. 6 (June, 1971): 519-540.

Kilibarda, Krsto. "Changes in Public Office," *Socialist Thought and Practice*, IX (January, 1963): 105-115.

Kolakowski, Leszek. "Intellectuals Against Intellect," *Daedalus*, CI, No. 3 (1972): 1-16.

Kolsti, John. "Albanianism: From the Humanists to Hoxha," *The Politics of Ethnicity in Eastern Europe*. Boulder: East European Monographs, 1981: 25-28.

Kornberg, Allan, Samuel Hines, Jr., and Joel Smith. "Legislatures and the Modernization of Societies," *Comparative Political Studies*, V, No. 4 (January, 1973): 471-491.

Krygier, Martin. "Bureaucracy in Trotsky's Analysis of Stalinism," *Socialism and the New Class: Towards the Analysis of Structural Equality within Socialist Systems*. Ed. Martin Sawer. Adelaide: Australian Political Studies Association, Monograph No. 19, 1978: 46-67.

Kuvačić, Ivan. "Middle Class Ideology," *Praxis, International Edition*, IX, No. 4 (1973): 335-356.

Lane, David. "The Structure of Soviet Socialism: Recent Western Theoretical Approaches," *The Insurgent Sociologist.* (Winter-Spring, 1984): 101-112.

Lasswell, Harold D. "Introduction: The Study of Political Elites," *World Revolutionary Elites.* Eds. Harold D. Lasswell and Daniel Lerner. Cambridge: MIT Press, 1965: 3-28.

—. "The World Revolution of Our Time: A Frame-work for Basic Policy Research," *World Revolutionary Elites.* Ed. Harold D. Lasswell and Daniel Lerner. Cambridge: MIT Press, 1965: 29-96.

Lipset, Seymour Martin. "Intellectual Types and Political Roles," *The Idea of Social Structure.* Ed. Lewis Coser. New York: Harcourt Brace Jovanovich, 1975: 433-470.

Lowenthal, Richard. "Development vs. Utopia in Communist Policy," *Change in Communist Systems.* Ed. Chalmers Johnson. Stanford: Stanford University Press, 1970: 33-117.

Lukić, Radomir. "Rotation Among Top Government Officials in Yugoslavia," *The Mandarins of Western Europe.* Ed. Mattei Dogan. New York: John Wiley and Sons Inc., 1975: 293-304.

Marinković, Radovoje. "The Organization and Work of the Commune Assemblies," *Yugoslav Survey*, XVIII (May, 1977): 3-21.

Marković, Mihajlo. "Decentralization: A Precondition for More Rational Societies," *The Future of Politics: Governance Movements and World Order.* Ed. William Page. London: France Pinter, 1983: 112-123.

—. "The Power Structure in Yugoslav Society," *Student,* (November 2, 1971): 6-7.

—. "Praxis: Critical Social Philosophy in Yugoslavia," *Praxis: Yugoslav Essays in the Philosophy and Methodology of the Social Sciences.* Eds. Mihajlo Marković and Gajo Petrović. Dordrecht, Holland: D. Reidel Publishing Co., 1979: xi-xxxvi.

—. "The Purpose of Social Research," *Social Science - For What?* Eds. Hans Henrik Hom and Erik Rudeng. Oslo: Universtetsforlag, 1980: 46-52.

—. "Socialism and Self-Management," *Praxis, International Edition*, I, Nos. 2-3 (1965): 178-195.

Marx, Karl. "Conspectus of Bakunin's State and Anarchy," *Marx-Engels Werke, Volume XVIII*. Berlin: Dietz Verlag, 1964: 634-636.

Matić, Milan. "Conditions for the Realization of Collective Decision-making and Responsibility," *Yugoslav Law*, II, No. 1 (January-March, 1984).

McDonald, John Jr. "Political Themes in the Thought of Milovan Djilas," Ph.D. Dissertation, Columbia University, 1971.

McRae, Donald. "Notes on Elites," *Comparative Goverment and Politics*, Eds. Dennis Kavanagh and Gillian Peele. Boulder: Westview Press, 1984: 144-158.

Meyer, Alfred. "Authority in Communist Political Systems," *Political Leadership in Industrialized Societies*. Ed. Lewis Edinger. New York: John Wiley and Sons Inc., 1967: 84-107.

Mihajlov, Mihajlo. "The Dissident Movement in Yugoslavia," *The Washington Quarterly*, II, No. 4 (1979): 64-73.

Mills, C. Wright. "Comment on Criticism," *C. Wright Mills and the Power Elite*. Eds. G. William Domhoff and Hoyt B. Ballard. Boston: Beacon Press, 1968: 229-250.

Mommson, Wolfgang J. "Capitalism and Socialism: Weber's Dialogue with Marx," *A Weber-Marx Dialogue*. Eds. Robert Anteio and Ronald M. Glassman. Lawrence: University of Kansas, 1985: 234-261.

Moorstein-Marx, Fritz. "The Higher Civil Service as an Action Group in Western Political Development," *Bureaucracy and Political Development*. Ed. Joseph LaPalombara. Princeton: Princeton University Press, 1963: 77-85.

Nachmias, David and David H. Rosenbloom. "Bureaucracy and Ethnicity," *American Journal of Sociology*, LXXXIII, No. 4 (1978): 967-973.

Nadel, Mark and Frances Rourke. "Bureaucracies," *Governmental Institutions and Processes Handbook of Political Science, Vol. 5*. Eds. Fred I. Greenstein and Nelson Polsby. Menlo Park, Calif.: Addison-Wesley Publishing Co., 1975: 411-429.

Nagel, John D. "A New Look at the Soviet Elite: A Generational Model of the Soviet System," *Journal of Political and Military Sociology,* III, No. 1 (Spring, 1975): 1-13.

Neal, Fred. "The Communist Party of Yugoslavia," *American Slavic and East European Review,* XVIII, No. 3 (1959): 88-111.

Nedimovic, Uroš. "A Comparison of the Actions of Young Bosnia (1914) and Red Justice (1921)," *Survey,* II, No. 1 (1975): 27-32.

Obradović, Josip. "Participation in Enterprise Decision-Making." *Workers' Self-Management and Organizational Power in Yugoslavia.* Eds. Josip Obradović and W.N. Dunn. Pittsburgh: University Center for International Studies, 1978: 232-261.

Olorunsola, Victor A. "Patterns of Interaction Between Bureaucratic and Political Leaders: A Case Study," *Journal of Developing Areas,* III (October, 1968): 51-68.

P. M. "Juror-Judges in the Yugoslav Judicial System," *Yugoslav Survey,* III (1962): 1557-1562.

Pantić, Dragomir. "Some Practical Problems of Compiling the Universe and Its Characteristics," *Working Papers of the International Study of Opinion-Makers, Vol. 1.* Ed. Bogdan Denitch. New York: Columbia University, 1968.

Pašić, Nadjan. "How the Manner of Nominating Candidates Affects the Character and Role of the Assembly," *Review of International Affairs,* XII (September 1966): 26-27.

—. "Pluralism of Interests within the Political System of Socialist Self-Management." Paper Presented at the Canadian Association of Slavists, 1967.

—. "Self-Management as an Integral Political System," *Yugoslav Workers' Self-Management.* Ed. M.J. Broekmeyer. Dordrecht, Holland: D. Reidel Publishing Co., 1970: 1-29.

Pavlowitch, Stevan and E. Biberaj. "The Albanian Problem in Yugoslavia: Two Views," *Conflict Studies,* Nos. 137/138 (1982): 7-43.

Pavlowitch, Stevan. "How Many Non-Serbian Generals in 1941?" *East European Quarterly*, XVI, No. 4 (January, 1983): 447-452.

Pečujilić, Miroslav. "The University of the Future," *Socialist Thought and Practice*, XX, No. 9 (1980): 26-53.

Perucci, Robert and Marc Pilisuk. "Leaders and Ruling Elites," *American Sociological Review*, XXXV (December, 1970): 1040-1056.

Petrović, Nenad. "The Fall of Alexandar Ranković," *Review*, VI (1967): 533-551.

Pryor, Federick L. "The 'New Class': Analysis of the Concept, the Hypothesis and the Idea as a Research Tool," *American Journal of Economics and Sociology*, XXXX, No. 4 (October, 1981): 366-379.

Putnam, Robert D. "Elite Transformation in Advanced Industrial Societies: An Empirical Assessment of the Theory of Technocracy," *Comparative Political Studies*, X, No. 3 (October, 1977): 383-411.

—. "The Political Attitudes of Senior Civil Servants in Western Europe: A Preliminary Report," *British Journal of Political Science*, III, Part 3 (July, 1973): 257-290.

Radich, Stephan. "The Autobiography of Stephen Radich," *Current History* (October, 1981): 106.

Raičević, Jovan. "Ideological Grounds for Albanian Irredentism and Bureaucratic Nationalism in Kosovo," *Socialist Thought and Practice* (1981): 23-37.

Rakovsky, Christian. "Bureaucracy and the Soviet State," *Essential Works of Socialism*. Ed. Irving Howe. New York: Bantam Books, 1971: 370-382.

Ramet, Pedro. "Problems of Albanian Nationalism in Yugoslavia," *Orbis*, XXV (1981): 369-388.

Ranković, Alexander. "Current Problems in Relation to the Work and Role of the League of Communists of Yugoslavia," *VIII Congress of the League of Communists of Yugoslavia*. Belgrade: Medjunarodna Politika, 1965: 148-152.

Rawin, Solomon. "Social Values and the Managerial Structure: The Case of Yugoslavia and Poland," *Journal of Comparative Administration*, II, No. 2 (August, 1970): 131-195.

Reinhartz, Dennis. "Milovan Djilas: The Transcendence of a Revolutionary," *The Walter Prescott Webb Memorial Lectures on Modern Revolutionary History*. Eds. Bede Lackner and Kenneth Roy Philip. Austin: University of Texas Press, 1977: 69-88.

Remington, Robin Alison. "Armed Forces and Society," *Political Military Systems: Comparative Perspectives*. Ed. C. Kelleher. Beverly Hills: Sage Publications, 1974: 163-189.

Riggs, Fred. "Bureaucratic Politics in Comparative Perspective," *Journal of Comparative Administration*, I, No. 1 (May, 1969): 5-38.

Rizzi, Bruno. "Introduction," *The Bureaucratization of the World, The USSR: Bureaucratic Collectivism*. Ed. Adam Westoby. London: Tavistock Publications, 1985: 1-33.

Robinson, Gertrude. "The New Yugoslav Writer: A Socio-Political Portrait," *Mosaic*, VI, No. 4 (Summer 1973): 185-198.

Roucek, Joseph S. "The Social Character of Yugoslav Politics," *Social Science*, IX (1934): 293-305.

—. "Yugoslavia's History of Education Before 1918," *Paedagocica Historica*, XIII (1973): 66-84.

Rus, Vekjko. "Institutionalization of the Revolutionary Movement," *Praxis, International Edition*, III, No. 2 (1967): 201-213.

Sapir, A. "Economic Growth and Factor Substitution: What Ever Happened to the Yugoslav Economic Miracle?" *Economic Journal*, LXXXX, No. 358 (June, 1980): 294-313.

Sayre, Wallace. "Bureaucracies: Some Contrasts in Systems," *Readings In Comparative Public Administration*. Ed. Nimrod Raphaeli. Boston: Allyn and Bacon, 1967: 341-353.

Scalapino, Robert A. "Political Modernization and the Intellectual," *Comparative/International Series*. Berkeley: University of California Press, n.d.

—. "The Transition in Chinese Party Leadership: A Comparison of the Eighth and Ninth Central Committees," *Elites in the People's Republic of China.* Ed. R. Scalapino. Seattle: University of Washington Press, 1972: 67-148.

"Selected Documents on the National Liberation War and Revolution," *Yugoslav Survey*, XXXI, No. 2 (May, 1985): 3-52.

Shatz, Marshall. "Jan Waclaw Machajski: The Conspiracy of Intellectuals," *Survey*, No. 62 (January, 1967): 45-57.

Shoup, Paul. "The Limits of Party Control: The Yugoslav Case," *Authoritarian Politics in Communist Europe: Uniformity and Diversity in One-Party States.* Ed. Andrew Janos. Berkeley: University of California, 1976: 176-196.

—. "Problems of Party Reform in Yugoslavia," *American Slavic and East European Review*, XVIII, No. 3 (1959): 334-350.

—. "The Yugoslav Revolution: The First of a New Type," *The Anatomy of Communist Takeovers.* Ed. Thomas T. Hammond. New Haven: Yale University Press, 1975: 244-272.

Skarića, Dubravka. "The Attitude of Progressive Youth of Bosnia-Hercegovina Between the Two World Wars Toward the Young Bosnian Movement," *Survey*, II, No. 1 (1975): 44-46.

Skendi, Stavro. "Beginning of Albanian Nationalist and Autonomous Trends: The Albanian League, 1878-1881," *American Slavic and East European Review*, XII (1953): 219-232.

St. Erlich, Vera. "Historical Awareness and the Peasant," *The Peasant and the City in Eastern Europe.* Eds. Irene Portis Winner and Thomas G. Winner. Cambridge: Schenkman, 1984: 99-110.

Steiner, Jurg. "The Principles of Majority and Proportionality," *Consociational Democracy.* Ed. Kenneth McRae. Toronto: McClelland and Stewart, 1974: 98-106.

Stiefbold, Rodney. "Segmented Pluralism and Consociational Democracy in Austria: Problems of Political Stability and Change," *Politics in Europe.* Ed. Martin Heisler. New York: David McKay Co., 1974: 117-177.

Stoianovich, Traian. "The Conquering Balkan Orthodox Merchant," *The Journal of Economic History*, XX, No. 2 (1960): 234-313.

—. "The Pattern of Serbian Intellectual Evolution: 1830-1880," *Comparative Studies in Society and History*, I, No. 3 (March, 1959): 242-272.

—. "The Social Foundations of Balkan Politics, 1750-1941," *Balkans in Transition*. Eds. Charles Jelavich and Barbara Jelavich. Berkeley: University of California Press, 1963: 297-345.

Stojanovic, Svetozar. "From Post-revolutionary Dictatorship to Socialist Democracy," *Praxis, International Edition*, IX, No. 4 (1973): 311-334.

—. "Marxism and Democracy: The Ruling Class or the Dominant Class," *Praxis, International Edition*, I, No. 2 (July, 1981): 160-170.

—. "The Morality of the Revolutionary Avant-Garde as the Historical Presupposition of Socialism," *Praxis*, II, Nos. 1-2 (1966): 151-158.

—. "The Social Theory and Ideology of Marxism," *Alternatives*, IX, No. 3 (Winter, 1983-1984): 397-406.

Suh, Dae-Sook. "Communist Party Leadership," *Political Leadership in Korea*. Eds. Dae-Sook Suh and Chae-Jin Lee. Seattle: University of Washington Press, 1977: 159-191.

Tadić, Ljubomir. "Order and Freedom," *Self-governing Socialism*. Eds. Branko Horvat, Mihajlo Marković, and Rudi Supek. White Plains, New York: International Arts and Science Press, 1975: 405-415.

Thomas, Norman. "Bureaucratic-Congressional Interaction and the Politics of Education," *Journal of Comparative Administration*, II, No. 1 (1970): 52-80.

Tito, Josip Broz. "Josip Broz Tito on the National Question," *Yugoslav Survey*, XVIII (May, 1978): 3-24.

—. "Report of Comrade Tito on the Previous Work and the Tasks of the Party," *Komunist* (October, 1946): 73.

Todorović, Mijalko. "Reorganization of the Leading Bodies of the League of Communists of Yugoslavia," *Socialist Thought and Practice*, No. 24 (October-December, 1966): 30-59.

Tomasevich, Jozo. "Foreign Economic Relations, 1918-1941," *Yugoslavia*. Ed. Robert J. Lerner. Berkeley: University of California Press, 1949: 185-197.

Vasiljević, T. "An Essay on the Legality of Administration and on Independence of Judges," *Yugoslav Law*, II (1980): 3-28.

Verdery, K. "Internal Colonialism in Austria-Hungary," *Ethnic and Racial Studies*, II (1979): 378-399.

Vrhunec, Jernej. "Judicial Staff," *Yugoslav Survey*, XXII, No. 4 (1981): 85-94.

Vucinich, Wayne. "The Yugoslav Revolutionary Movement 1908-1914," *Slavia*, XVI, No. 4 (August, 1941): 103-117.

Waller, Derek J. "Elite Analysis and Communist Systems." Paper Presented at the Southern Political Science Association, 1973.

Weaver, Jerry. "Role Expectations of Latin American Bureaucrats," *Journal of Comparative Administration*, IV, No. 2 (August, 1972): 133-166.

Welsh, William A. "Elites and Leadership in Communist Systems: Some New Perspectives," *Studies in Comparative Communism*, IX, Nos. 1-2 (Spring-Summer, 1976): 168-186.

Wiatr, Jerzy. "Political Elites and Political Leadership: Conceptual Problems and Selected Hypotheses for Comparative Research," *Indian Journal of Politics*, No. 7 (1973): 137-149.

Wright, Eric Olin. "To Control or to Smash Bureaucracy: Weber and Lenin on Politics, the State, and Bureaucracy," *Berkeley Journal of Sociology*, XIX (1974-1975): 69-108.

Yovanovitch, Dragoljub. "Les Classes Moyennes Chez les Slaves du Sud," *Inventaires III. Classes Moyennes*. Paris: Felix Alcan, 1939: 217-250.

Zaninovich, George. "Yugoslav Party Evolution: Moving Beyond Institutionalization," *Politics in Modern Society: The Dynamics of Established One-Party Systems*. Eds. S. Huntingdon and C. Moore. New York: Basic Books, 1970: 484-508.

Zannoni, Paolo. "The Concept of Elites," *European Journal of Political Research*, VI, No. 1 (March, 1978): 1-30.

Zimmerman, William. "The Tito Succession and the Evolution of Yugoslav Politics," *Studies in Comparative Communism*, IX, Nos. 1-2 (Spring-Summer, 1976): 62-79.

Other Sources

Borba. Belgrade.

Danas. Zagreb.

Foreign Broadcast Information Service, Daily Bulletin, Eastern Europe. Washington.

Jedinstvo. Priština.

Joint Publications Research Service, Eastern Europe, Political, Sociological, and Military Affairs. Springfield, Virginia.

Komunist. Belgrade.

Le Monde. Paris.

Nedeljne Informative Novine. Belgrade.

New York Times. New York.

Politika. Belgrade.

Radio Free Europe. Munich.

Vjesnik. Zagreb.

INDEX

Administrative Elite
    and legislative system, 227-8
    and technical expertise, 242-47
    influence of, 238-41
    interaction of (with other elites), 233-37
    role of, 229-33, 247-8
Albanians, 98, 129,
    and Albanianization, 311, 364, 374
    see also, Chapter 8; Ethnic Representation; Kosovo
Assembly System
    structure of, 187-9
    see also, Legislative Elite

Bakalli, Mahmut, 364, 370
Bakarić, Vladimir, 61, 63, 123, 407
Bakunin, Mikhail, 23-4, 32
Balli Kombetar, 347-8
Blanqui, Louis, 24
Bosnia-Hercegovina, 107
    see also, Ethnic Representation
Bottomore, Thomas, 22, 50
Bukharin, Nikolai, 34-5, 47
Bureaucracy
    and Administrative Elite, see Chapter 5
    and socialist elites, see Chapter 1, passim
    in communist systems, 225-6
    see also, Judicial Elite
Burnham, James, 39, 61

Ciliga, Ante, 38-40, 45, 47
Class Composition, see Elites (occupational background of), see also, Social Stratification
Class Structure, see Social Stratification

Communist Party of Yugoslavia (CPY), 37, 103-4, 131, 148, 340, 344-5
    and judicial organs, 266
Communist Youth Movement (SKOJ), 120
Consociationalism, 312-13
    and ethnic distance, 313-14
    see also, Nationalism
Croatia, 98-9, 106, 114-15, 127 and nationalism, 323
    see also, Ethnic Representation
Croats
    and interaction of, 315-20
    see also, Ethnic Representation

Dedijer, Vladimir, 151, 271-2
Deutsch, Karl, 313
Deva, Veli, 357, 364, 370
Djilas, Milovan, 40, 42-8, 55, 61-2, 68, 157, 271-3, 337, 348, 439

Educational Background, see Elites; Kosovo
Elitist Socialism, see Socialist Elites
Elite Recruitment, see Chapter 9
    and moral-political suitability, 422-3
    and Partisan ascendancy (1945-49), 397-8
    and resocialization (1950-65), 398-402
    patterns of (1945-81), 396-412
    see also, Administrative Elite; Legislative Elite; Judicial Elite
Elites
    and "Belgrade Study," 52-7
    and internal colonialism, 337-44
    and interwar period, 95-132

495

Elites-contd.
   and leadership of League of Yugoslav Communists, see Chapter 3 and Chapter 9
   and middle sectors, 101, 122
   and "Milošević phenomenon," 442-5
   and Partisan movement, 119-21
   and politicized professionals, 156-7, 161, 203-6
   and revolution, 97-8
   circulation of, 30
   consolidation of, 149-51, 398-402
   delegitimation of, 440-2
   educational background of, 106-16, 150, 152, 3, 157, 159, 416-18
   ethnic origins of, see Ethnic Representation
   genderic background of, 126-7
   generational background of, 125-6, 150, 152, 159, 413-16, 423-5
   in Kosovo, see Chapter 8
   interaction of, 312-24
   military representation in, 159
   occupational background of, 116-23, 150, 153-4, 157-8
   political deprofessionalization of, 161-189
   regional, see Chapter 9
   retrenchment of, 155-60, 407-12
   rotation of, 212-14, see also, Elite Recruitment
   succession of, 151-4, 202-7
   transformation of, 95, 132, 160-3
   urban and rural backgrounds of, 123-5
   Yugoslav perspectives on, 37-68
   see also, Administrative Elite; Judicial Elite; Legislative Elite

Engels, Frederick
   and elites, 23-4

Ethnic Distance, see Consociationalism

Ethnic Representation, 128-30, 150, 154, 160, 299-300, 311-12, 418-20
   and composition of Yugoslav elites, 298-312
   and university faculties, 307-11
   in Bosnia-Hercegovina, 302, 305, 418-20
   in Croatia, 302, 311, 418-20
   in Kosovo, 305, 307, 311, 418-20
   in Macedonia, 307, 418
   in Serbia, 311, 418-20
   in Slovenia, 307
   in Vojvodina, 305
   of Albanians, 300-1
   of Croatians, 300-2, 311
   of Hungarians, 311
   of Macedonians, 300
   of Montenegrins, 300-1, 307, 311, 419-20
   of Moslems, 300, 305, 311
   of Serbs, 300, 7, 311, 418-19
   of Slovenes, 300-1
   of "Yugoslavs," 300-1
   see also, Ethnicity

Ethnicity
   and elite interaction, 312-20
   and elite sectors, 320-4
   and ethno-technocratic populism, 444
   see also, Nationalism; Ethnic Representation

Federalism
   legal, 261

Filipović, Filip, 38

Genderic Background (of elites),
　　see Elites
Generational Background (of elites),
　　see Elites
Gouldner, Alvin, 36
Gramsci, Antonio, 35-6

Has, Zdenko, 195-6
Hoxha, Enver, 356, 367-8
Hoxha, Mehmet, 345
Hungarians, 98, 129
　　see also, Ethnic Representation

Inequalities (in Yugoslavia),
　　see Social Stratification

Judicial Elite
　　and educational background
　　　　of, 269
　　and constitutional courts, 283
　　and depoliticization of, 270-4
　　and interviews with, 284-86
　　and judicial reforms (1950-
　　　　1966), 268-74, 276
　　and genderic background of,
　　　　269, 276, 278
　　and lawyers, 270
　　and occupational background
　　　　of, 269
　　and party membership of, 280-1
　　and public prosecutors, 267,
　　　　270-1, 281-3
　　and removal for political
　　　　grounds, 281-3
　　and secret police, 267
　　as a professional bureaucracy,
　　　　284-6
　　criteria for election of, 275-6
　　ethnic origins of, 262-4, 278
　　generational background of,
　　　　276-8

historical context for, 258-9
in early communist period
　　(1945-50), 265-8
in pre-communist period, 259-
　　65
judicial independence, 278-83
professionalization of, see
　　Chapter 6
recruitment and social compo-
　　sition of, 275-8
transformation of, 274-86

Karadžić, Vuk, 260-1
Kardelj, Edward, 40-2, 62-3, 115,
　　162, 201, 273-4, 412
Kautsky, John, 160-336
Kidrić, Boris, 123, 151
Kosić, Mirko, 37-8
Kolakowski, Leszek, 322
Kosovo, 99, see also, Chapter 8
　　and Albanians, 245, 353-5, 366-
　　　　8
　　and elite control (1945-66), 348-
　　　　54
　　and elite differentiation (1980-
　　　　81), 367-73
　　and elite polarization (1967-79),
　　　　354-66
　　and ethnic newspapers, 359
　　and Moslems, see Chapter 8,
　　　　passim
　　and party membership, 364-6
　　and political crime, 354
　　and politicized ethnicity, 373-5
　　and Serbs, 443-5, see also,
　　　　Chapter 8, passim
　　demographic development in,
　　　　352-3, 368
　　economy in, 340, 352-3, 368-9
　　education in, 343-4, 348-52,
　　　　354, 356, 358-9, 361-4,
　　　　369-71, 375

497

Kosovo-contd.
  elite circulation in (1912-40), 337-44
  elite formation in (1912-40), 344-8
  see also, Albanians; Ethnic Representation
Kus-Nikolayev, Mirko, 38

Lawyers, see Judicial Elite
League of Yugoslav Communists, 51, 409-10
  leadership of, Chapter 3 and Chapter 9
  and Central Committee, 148-9
  and control of legislature, 206-9
  and judicial elite, 280-1
  and state administration, 226-7
  of Croatia, 204-5, 407
  see also, Communist Party of Yugoslavia
Legislative Elite
  deprofessionalization of, 189
  Has, Zdenko, 195-6
  influence on administrative elite, 238-41
  interaction with administrative elite, 233-7
  participation and influence of, 196-200
  professionalization and participation of, 194-6
  professionalization of, see Chapter 4
  recruitment of (before 1974), 190-4; (1974-78), 200-8; (1978-88), 209-11
Legitimacy (of elites)
  see Elites, delegitimation of
Lenin, V.I., 25-7
Lijphart, Arend, 297-8, 312
Lowenthal, Richard, 166

Lukić, Radomir, 49-50, 63
Luxembourg, Rosa, 32-3, 427

Macedonia, 99, 107, 127
  see also, Ethnic Representation
Macedonians, 98, 128-9
  and elite interaction, 315-20
  see also, Ethnic Representation
Maček, Vladko, 114
Machajski, Waclaw, 31-2, 47
Marković, Mihailjo, 61
Marković, Svetozar, 25
Marxism
  and elites, 22-3
Metohija, see Kosovo
Michels, Robert, 31, 35, 47
Middle class, 54, 58-60
Mills, C. Wright, 50, 131
Milošević, Slobodan, 442-5
Montengrins, 98, 112, 128-30, 154
  and elite interaction, 315-20
  see also, Ethnic Representation
Montenegro, 99, 107, 127
  see also, Ethnic Representation
Mosca, Gateano, 29-31, 35
Moslems, 129
  see also, Ethnic Representation; Kosovo

National Liberation War
  see Elites, Partisan movement
Nationalism
  and consociationalism, 297-8
  and ethno-technocratic populism, 444
  and intelligentsia, see Chapter 8, passim
  as an elite resource, 442-5
  Serbian, 443-5
  see also, Ethnicity; Chapter 7 and Chapter 8
New class, 39-40, 43-48, 104
  see also, Djilas

New Class (The), 46-48
Nordlinger, Eric, 298

Obrenović, Miloš, 260-1
Occupational background (of elites), see Elites

Pareto, Vilfrado, 29-30, 35, 160
parliamentary deputies, 118
    see also, Legislative Professionalization
Party Elite, see Elites, and leadership of League of Yugoslav Communists
Pašić, Najdan, 50-1, 64
Pašić, Nikola, 24-5, 340
Pečujlić, Miroslav, 61
Political recruitment, see Elites, recruitment of
Pijade, Moša, 151
Post-Tito era, 412-427, passim
Praxis group, 48, 57, 65
Public Prosecutors, see Judicial Elite

Radić, Stjepan, 128-9
Rakovsky, Christian, 33-4
Ranković, Alexander, 120, 273-4, 354, 399, 401-3, 405
Regional Elites, see Elites
Ribičič, Mitija, 67-8
Revolution, see Elites
Rizzi, Bruno, 39

Schactman, Max, 39
Serbia, 24-5, 38, 98-9, 106, 122
    and Serbianization, 341
    see also, Ethnic Representation
Serbo-Croatian conflict, 99
Serbs, 112, 128-30, 154
    and elite interaction, 315-20
    see also, Ethnic Representation; Kosovo; Nationalism

Slovenes, 98, 112, 128-30
    and elite interaction, 315-20
    see also, Ethnic Representation
Slovenia, 38, 98, 106, 127
    see also, Ethnic Representation
Smith, Anthony, 336
Social stratification, 52-4, 102-3
Socialist Alliance of the Working People of Yugoslavia, 421
Socialist Elites, 22-36
Stalin, Joseph 33, 42, 374
Stanovnik, Janez, 445
State bureaucracy, see Administrative Elite
Steiner, Jurg, 312
Stojanović, Svetozar, 57-8, 61-66
Supek, Rudi, 65
Šuvar, Stipe, 66-7, 368, 439

Tito, Josip Broz, 49, 63, 104, 131, 265, 273, 346, 356, 368, 374, 410, 412-13
Titoism, 40
Trotsky, Leon, 33-5, 41-7, 160

Unperfect Society (The), 48
Urban-rural backgrounds (of elites), see Elites

Vesna, David, 1-2
Vojvodina, 99
    see also, Ethnic Representation

Weber, Max, 27-30

Yugoslavia
    and the interwar period, 95-132
    as elite-managed society, 21-2, 148, 298

Živković, Miroslav, 65
Županov, Josip, 64